Elijah H. Pilcher

Protestantism in Michigan

Being a Special History of the Methodist Episcopal Church and Incidentally of Other Denominations

Elijah H. Pilcher

Protestantism in Michigan
Being a Special History of the Methodist Episcopal Church and Incidentally of Other Denominations

ISBN/EAN: 9783337161644

Printed in Europe, USA, Canada, Australia, Japan

Cover: Foto ©ninafisch / pixelio.de

More available books at **www.hansebooks.com**

Yours Elijah H. Pilcher

PROTESTANTISM IN MICHIGAN:

BEING A

SPECIAL HISTORY

OF THE

METHODIST EPISCOPAL CHURCH

AND INCIDENTALLY OF

OTHER DENOMINATIONS.

NOTICES OF THE ORIGIN AND GROWTH OF THE PRINCIPAL TOWNS AND CITIES OF THE STATE; BIOGRAPHICAL SKETCHES OF MANY PROMINENT PASTORS AND LAYMEN CONNECTED WITH THE BIRTH AND GROWTH OF PROTESTANTISM IN MICHIGAN.

ILLUSTRATED.

BY ELIJAH H. PILCHER, D. D.

DETROIT:
R. D. S. TYLER & CO., PUBLISHERS,
66 Griswold Street.

Entered, according to Act of Congress, in the year Eighteen Hundred and Seventy-eight, by
ELIJAH H. PILCHER,
In the office of the Librarian of Congress, at Washington, D. C.

COMPOSITION BY
W. H. SWAIL, 66 Griswold St., Detroit.

RAND & WHITTLESEY, Griswold St.,
Electrotypers.

EMIL SCHOBER, 7 Fort St. West,
Bookbinder.

Engravings by
THE WESTERN ENGRAVING Co., Detroit.

Press-work by
WM. GRAHAM, 52 Bates St.

TO THE

PEOPLE OF THE STATE OF MICHIGAN,

AMONG WHOM I HAVE LIVED SO PLEASANTLY AND LABORED

FOR SO MANY YEARS, THIS VOLUME

IS AFFECTIONATELY

DEDICATED.

THE AUTHOR.

PREFACE.

It is now over twenty years since the idea was entertained by me of writing a History of the introduction and growth of Methodism in this State, and I began to make preparations to do so. I thought I had rare opportunities for such a work, being personally acquainted with the first five persons who made a profession of a Christian experience, and who, with two others, constituted the first Christian Protestant Church in Michigan; and, also, being personally and well acquainted with the minister who was sent here in 1815—the first after the War of 1812. From these persons the lack of documentary statement was supplied. These persons are all deceased now. Having come into Michigan in 1830, and having been extensively connected with the work at an early day, added to my means of presenting facts, I have continued this work, with various interruptions, to the present day.

No one who has never undertaken such a task can form any conception of the difficulty of obtaining accurate information. I might have had this work ready years ago had it not been for a desire to be accurate. I myself have, from time to time, published short sketches, some of which contained errors. This work contains the latest and most accurate information that I have been able to obtain; and if there should, in any case, be found a discrepancy between any of those sketches and this work, this is to be the authority.

I should explain, also, why such prominence is given to the

Methodist Church over others in a work entitled "Protestantism." The fact is this: the first purpose was simply that of Methodism, but I had obtained so much information as to others, as to enable me to give an outline of them, which I have done. I have desired, also, to furnish more in regard to other Churches, but have found it impossible to obtain the information, as those who had it, or the means of obtaining it, either neglected or declined to furnish it. But they will find here embodied, in regard to their own Churches, what they will not find elsewhere without a great deal of time and labor.

This work has cost me a vast amount of toil, as well as a considerable amount of money. Some will be disappointed in one way and some in another. I cannot hope to satisfy everybody. But such as it is I now commit it to the public. Whatever may be thought of its style, the statement of facts are reliable and valuable for all.

ELIJAH H. PILCHER.

DETROIT, MICH., March 12th, 1878.

ENGRAVINGS.

Albion College, ...
Central Methodist Church, Detroit, . .
Council Held at Saginaw, .
Desolation, ...
First Protestant Church in Michigan,
First M. E. Church, Jackson, .
First M. E. Church, Kalamazoo, .
Grand Rapids in 1830, ...

PORTRAITS.

Rev. J. M. Arnold, . . .
" W. H. Brockway, . .
" B. F. Cocker, . .
" W. H. Collins, ...
" Arthur Edwards, . .
" L. R. Fiske, . . .
" E. O. Haven, . .
" D. C. Jacokes, . . .
" Luther Lee, . . .
" E. H. Pilcher, ...
" J. H. Potts, ...
" H. F. Spencer, ...
" J. T. Robe, ...
L. R. Atwater, . . .
H. Fish, ...
John Owen, ...
Mary A. Palmer, ...
David Preston, ...
William Phelps, . . .

HISTORY OF PROTESTANTISM IN MICHIGAN.

CHAPTER I.

Introductory—Jesuits—Their Course Accounted for—The Case with Protestants—Tenderest Ties Sundered—Detroit Isolated—English-Speaking Population—First Settlers—Settled 1701—State of Society—First Methodist Preacher, 1804—Freeman—Rev. David Bacon—N. Bangs—Detroit Burned—Bangs' Second Visit—W. Case—Territory Organized—Efforts to Save Detroit—New City—Richard Preaches 1807—Case Appointed—Prospect—Society Organized—Members—First Quarterly Meeting—Roads and Accommodations—Case's Difficulties—Mrs. Abbott—Conversion of Mr. Abbott—First Camp-Meeting—N. Holmes—Wm. Mitchell—Retrospect.

AN examination of the circumstances and facts connected with the introduction of the Christian religion and church into a new country, or incident thereto, always forms an interesting subject of contemplation; and especially if that new country, in its settlement, is isolated or far removed from the rest of the world. Such a subject we have before us at this time. The work of planting the gospel in such a country is always attended with much sacrifice of ease and comfort, and accompanied with severe labor upon the part of those ministers who have consented to be its messengers. The self-sacrifices of the Roman Catholic missionaries, who have left their country to carry their religion to distant lands, and sometimes to barbarous tribes, have been made the theme of many a panegyric, and have been held up as a proof of their love of religion. But their course of life may be accounted for on other principles than a love for religion or the souls of the people; for they were set apart for the work of the priesthood without any reference to a divine call to that office, or even without any profession of spiritual regeneration, and they had chosen that as a mere occupation rather than something else. They could—as they did—easily become associates of Indians, or any savage tribes, which contributed largely to their success among them. Taking this view, we may readily account for the course adopted by them independently of any love for the interests of humanity. We, however, are disposed to give them full credit for sincerity and an honest purpose to diffuse what they believed to be the true religion.

The case is far different with Protestant ministers—with those who came forth into the wilderness to proclaim the everlasting gospel to the scattered dwellers in the wilderness, or to uncivilized tribes. These have been taught that their religion, so far from destroying their natural relationships, only tends to refine and exalt them—it makes the endearments of home only more dear—father, mother, brother, sister, wife or children are the more dear to them, while their love for these is only subordinated by their love for their divine Saviour. With these, then, there must be a sundering of the tenderest cords that exist in the human heart; and nothing but a thorough conviction of a divine call to the work could have impelled them to go out as laborers in such a field. This was particularly the case with the men who first established Protestantism in the city of Detroit. No hope of glory among men or pecuniary emoluments offered them any inducements to make the sacrifice of the endearments of home and to endure the labors and privations, and brave the perils, necessarily connected with travel as ministers in this new, and then distant country; for it is to be remembered that the settlement at Detroit was, during its early history, and until a comparatively recent date, almost entirely separated from all other settlements of any importance. The route across Canada from Montreal or Buffalo was beset with many difficulties and perils, and attended with almost incredible labors and hardships; and it was nearly impossible to reach it from any other direction.

A few English and American adventurers had braved the difficulties of settlement here. Stimulated either by the hope of repairing dilapidated fortunes, or carving out new ones, or perhaps by a disrelish for more refined society, or perhaps from a spirit of adventure without any very definite object in view, they had intermingled themselves with the old French population and the Indians. There were also a few soldiers in the garrison. This was the English-speaking population with which the first Protestant missionaries had to associate and labor. Surely not a very promising prospect of success.

Another thing, also, is to be called to mind—that is, that the first settlers at Detroit were French Roman Catholics; that the first company who came out to make the settlement, with *La Motte de*

Cadillac, had a Catholic priest sent out with them as a necessary appendage; that, therefore, from the first settlement in 1701, until the place came into the possession of the English Government in 1760, the entire population was French and Indians. They were all Roman Catholics, for even the Indians had substituted the ceremonies of Romanism for their old rites. From the time it came into the hands of the British, until it passed into the hands of the United States in 1796, the entire English-speaking population, with a few exceptions, consisted of the soldiers in the garrison. After the city and country had passed into the possession of the United States until after the war of 1812, but few English or Americans had turned their attention in this direction, so that the whole population became largely imbued with the French spirit and frivolity; and, of course, they were but little inclined to true piety. From the newness of the country, and from its isolation, there was scarcely any commerce except the fur trade, and that was carried on by means of Indian canoes coasting along the bays and shores of the lake. The long winters were passed without any serious or valuable employment, as nothing to which they could turn their attention could be remunerative, for the want of commerce. The consequence was, their time was spent in idle frivolity, which is adverse to mental or spiritual culture.

The wants of the people were few and easily supplied, and no necessity was felt for any considerable mental culture. As the natural result of this state of things, the people gave themselves up, especially during the winter months, to pleasure, particularly to music and dancing, which tended to weaken the mind, vitiate the moral sensibilities, and to disincline them to religion. The mere ceremonies of Romanism did not lay any restraint on the people in these respects.

We have now given a general view of the country and society up to 1804. While the people were so given up to pleasure they were not a little startled, in the spring of 1804, by the announcement that a Methodist minister, or preacher, had come to the place and would preach on the next Sabbath afternoon. The very announcement had astonished them greatly, and their astonishment was unabated when they heard him. He preached the gospel in a very plain and earnest manner, accompanied by the unction and power of the Holy Spirit. This was the first *Methodist* sermon ever preached in Michigan. The preacher was a venerable-looking man. His name was *Freeman*. He was a local preacher from Canada, and remained but a few days. Whence he came and whither he went the people did not concern themselves to know. No very permanent good was accomplished, except that Mrs. Maria C. McCarty received such convictions for sin as never left her till she was converted some years afterwards.

This was generally supposed, for a long time, to have been the first Protestant sermon ever delivered in Detroit. But this is found to be a mistake; for Rev. David Bacon had been sent out by a society in Connecticut to establish a mission among the Indians at Mackinaw and in the Northwest. He was a Congregational minister. He, finding no opening among the Indians, stopped in Detroit, and had preached a few times before Mr. Freeman came. He came to Detroit in 1801. What success he had will hereafter be related. He had no converts and was quickly forgotten by the people. Moravian ministers had spent a winter in Michigan—about 1780—with their Indian flocks who had been driven from Ohio by persecution, but they did not make any attempt at preaching among the white people.

The astonishment and wonder of the people caused by the meteor-like visit of Mr. Freeman had but just died away, and he had been nearly forgotten, when another, a youthful and energetic man, made his appearance at Detroit, as if he had dropped down from heaven, and announced that he was a Methodist preacher. This was in July or August, probably the latter, 1804. He opened his mission among them for a few times and then disappeared. This was the active, talented and laborious Nathan Bangs, who afterwards shone so conspicuously in the affairs of the Methodist Episcopal Church, and stood so deservedly high in its councils, and became its historian.

At the session of the New York Conference, held in the city of New York, beginning July 12th, 1804, Nathan Bangs was appointed to the *River Le French*—that is, the Thames—Circuit in Upper Canada District, and came to Detroit with the intention of making it a regular appointment of his Circuit. For a long time it was supposed that this was the first Protestant preaching that had ever been had here. But Mr. Freeman had been here before him and Mr. Bacon had preached and was still here. Dr. Bangs, in his history, says he met here a Congregational preacher, who had been preaching for a while, until nobody would come to hear him except a few children. He said to the young and zealous itinerant, "If you can do the people any good, I shall be glad of it, for I cannot." This was Mr. Bacon of whom we have before spoken. Mr. Bangs made three visits—the first two on a week day evening and the third and last on a Sabbath. At the first, he states "the light-hearted people flocked to hear" him, but at the third, which was on the Sabbath, only a few children came out to hear him. So he left them, wiping off the dust from his feet as a testimony against them. This last visit was in the month of October, 1804, or early in November of that year.

A few months after this the whole town was consumed by fire except one house. Detroit, at the time, contained about *one hundred and fifty* houses. Dr. Bangs, in his history of the Methodist Episcopal Church, says that the town was consumed by fire a few weeks after his last visit; and this statement is repeated by Dr. Stevens in his life and times of Dr. Bangs. But this statement is incorrect as to time, as Mr. Bangs left in the last of October or early in November, 1804, and the fire did not occur until *the eleventh day* of June, 1805. The error, however, refers only to the date and not the fact. Whether this destruction had any relation to their rejection of the gospel, every one must judge for himself.

Dr. Bangs furnished us with the following note respecting his second visit to Detroit. He says: "I preached in the old council house on a week-day evening The house was pretty well filled with hearers. While preaching there arose a terrible thunder storm; the lightning flashed, the thunder rolled through the heavens with awful noise. But I kept on preaching. I was afterwards informed that two young men sat trembling, fearing that God was about to strike them dead for what they had done, as they had put powder into the candles in the expectation that they would burn down to the powder and explode during the sermon. They were disappointed, as I concluded my sermon and closed the meeting without any accident, though they said when I took up the candle to see to read my hymn, they feared the explosion would take place and burn my face and eyes." Mr. Bangs, though not the first Protestant minister who preached here, was nevertheless the first who came with the design of supplying them with the word of life. That his predecessors had preached here was only accidental, and incidental to something else. But the sole business of Mr. Bangs was to preach to the people. What an amount of zeal it must have required to undertake this work! His nearest appointment was on the River Thames, about forty miles distant, and an almost impassable road to be passed over to reach it; yet he came, and would have continued to do so had there been any hope of doing good. Detroit was thus abandoned by Protestant ministers and the people left to themselves to pursue their follies unrestrained.

Five years now roll over this dark city before any other effort is made to Protestantize the place or to afford services for those who were already Protestants. We have no records or information that any minister of any Protestant denomination ever visited or preached an occasional sermon after November, 1804, till in the summer of 1809. According to the general minutes of the Methodist Episcopal Church, at a session of the New York Conference which embraced all this country, held in May, 1809, Rev. William Case, a talented, active, energetic and persevering young man, a member of that Conference, was appointed to Detroit. This is the first time the place appears on the records of the Church, or among the lists of appointments. What the circumstances were which led to the appointment at this time, it is impossible now to determine with certainty. The Conference session, which was held in the City of New York, commenced May 10th. There was no Society, and no particular prospect of organizing one, as there were no Protestant professors of religion, as far as known, in this city or even in the Territory. The fact that the Territorial Government of Michigan had been organized for four years, and that Detroit was the residence of the Territorial officers, and the importance of the locality itself, certainly indicated that this field ought to be occupied. It is further probable that Mr. Robert Abbott, who was a fur-trader, in some of his visits to Montreal had taken occasion to solicit Methodist preaching, as he, doubtless, retained some recollection of the visits of Mr. Freeman and Mr. Bangs. This supposition is strengthened by the fact that when Mr. Case came to Detroit he found a home with Mr. Abbott. It is now surprising that a Territorial Government should have existed for four years before any denomination of Protestant Christians should have made any vigorous and persistent effort to establish true Christianity among the people; but such is the fact. It is very true there were but few people in the Territory except the French, and they were Romanists.

The Territory of Michigan was organized in 1804—that is, the law was passed providing for it—and the officers were appointed so as to put the Government into operation the following year; and General Hull, who had been appointed Governor, arrived at Detroit on June 12th, 1805, to enter upon the duties of his office. He found the city in ashes, the whole town having been consumed by fire, except one house, on the preceding day. No special effort was made by the panic-stricken people to save the town or to extinguish the flames, except that the Catholic priest fell down on his knees and said low mass. The following is the account given of this sad event, by Mr. Dilhett, one of the resident Catholic priests: "I was occupied with Mr. Richard, when a messenger came to inform us that three houses had been already consumed, and there was no hope of saving the rest. I exhorted the faithful who were present to help each other, and immediately commenced the celebration of low mass, after which we had barely time to remove the vestments and furniture of the church, with the effects of the adjoining presbytery, when both buildings were enveloped in the flames. In the course of three hours, from 9 o'clock A. M. till noon, nothing was to be seen of the city except a mass of burning coals and chimney tops stretching like pyramids into the air. Fortunately there was no wind during the conflagration, which allowed the flames and smoke to ascend to a prodigious height, giving the city the appearance of an immense funeral pile. It was the most majestic, and at the same time the most frightful spectacle I ever witnessed. The city contained at least one hundred and fifty houses, mostly frame, which caused the fire to spread with the utmost rapidity. The number of people in the town being unusually large, there was ample force for removing the merchandise and furniture of the inhabitants, which were in great measure saved. No personal injury was sustained during the fire." *

This was the condition of affairs when Governor Hull arrived to enter upon the duties of his office. The General Government rendered important assistance to the inhabitants in this time of their calamity. They also granted to the city a large tract of land—*ten thousand acres.* A new city was laid out under the supervision of Judge Woodward, who was a man of some eccentricity and who had some peculiar ideas of taste; after whom one of the great avenues was named. He desired to give the new city the form of a spider's web, which he did in part —a form which, though fine on paper, has been found to be very inconvenient in practice; and it has been very much broken in upon in more modern utilitarian days. After such a calamity and with so little connection with the commercial world, as might have been expected, the growth of the city was very slow for many years.

In 1807, there being no Protestant minister in Detroit or in the Territory of Michigan, the Governor of the Territory, General Hull, and other Protestant gentlemen, invited Mr. Richard, the Roman Catholic priest, to preach to them in the Council House, in the English language. He consented to do so, though he spoke the language very indifferently. On one occasion he tried to quote the expression, "Ye are my sheep." He said, "Ye are my muttons." But this showed that these officers and gentry wanted some religious service and thought that an indifferent one was better than none. In writing to his bishop in regard to this matter, Mr. Richard uses the following language; "Although I was

*Metropolitan Almanac, 1855.

sensible of my incapacity, as there was no English minister here of any denomination, I thought it might be of some utility to take possession of the ground." In accordance with this invitation, he held meetings at noon every Sunday in the Council House, in the English language, for some time, and delivered instructions "on the general principles of the Christian religion, the principles to be adopted in the investigation of truth, the causes of errors, the spirituality and immortality of the soul, and the evidenes of Christianity in general," intending at a later period to present the peculiar doctrines of the Romish Church. But he never reached the latter topic. Thus things continued for two years longer. This was the condition of affairs when Rev. William Case received his appointment to this field. He was appointed as a missionary, without any Missionary Society to support him. Here was an open field—at least there was no Protestant competition. But sin was rife and folly predominant.

This field would have presented a very dark and forbidding prospect, had it not been that the Circuit extended into Canada and embraced a few societies there. Yet they were so distant and small that the dark horizon was not relieved by them. But our missionary came in the name of his Master, and opened his mission in the strength of Divine grace. He labored and prayed—sowed the seed and watered it with his tears, and though the year closed and no Society was organized in the city or on this side of the river, it was not in vain, as we shall see; for, before he finally left for the Conference, he had the satisfaction of knowing that he had not labored altogether for naught, as one man had been converted, of whom a more particular account will be given hereafter. In a few months after he left, a Society was organized by a successor sent from the Western Conference, which increased to about thirty members in the next two years, and was prospering, when the War of 1812 broke out and scattered most of them.

The first Protestant religious Society, or Church, which was a Methodist one, in Michigan, was organized in Detroit in the autumn of 1810, by *Rev. William Mitchell.* We have seen that Mr. Case left without effecting this object. But the good work had been begun by the conversion of Robert Abbott, which was quickly followed by that of Mrs. Abbott, of her sister Mrs. McCarty and her husband, and three or more of their neighbors. Nearly three months intervened between the time that Mr. Case left and the coming of his successor, William Mitchell, from the Western Conference, which included Ohio, West Virginia and a part of Kentucky.

Ninian Holmes was also sent from the Genesee Conference. The former gathered the converts into a Church. This first Church was composed of *seven* members, viz: *Robert Abbott, Betsey Abbott his wife, Wm. McCarty, Maria C. McCarty his wife, William Stacy, Betsey Stacy his wife,* and *Sarah Macomb*   Wm. McCarty was appointed class-leader. These have all died in the faith and have gone to receive their reward. This was the beginning of Protestant Christianity in this peninsula.

According to the Minutes of the New York Conference for 1809, *Joseph Sawyer* was the Presiding Elder of Upper Canada District, which included Detroit Circuit, but there are no recollections of his having visited Michigan. It is probable he did not, as there was no Society formed till after the next Conference. The first quarterly meeting ever held in Michigan, with love feast, baptism and the sacrament of the Lord's Supper, was held by Wm. Mitchell, in the spring of 1811, in the house of William Weaver, a Roman Catholic, on the River Rouge. The next year, 1812, *Rev. Henry Ryan* was Presiding Elder, and attended the second quarterly meeting in this peninsula. It was held in the house of Robert Abbott, in Detroit. The time is not definitely settled, though it is probable it was late in the autumn of 1811. We think that this was the fact from two considerations or circumstances: All the old members agreed that it was in the autumn and within a year of the time the Church was organized; and, in the next place, the interest created by the conversion of Mr. Abbott and his friends, and the consequent organization of a Methodist Church or Society, would have induced the preacher in charge to have a quarterly meeting and a visit from the Presiding Elder as soon as possible. We may safely say, then, that the second occasion of the administration of baptism and of the sacrament of the Lord's Supper, by Protestant hands in Michigan, was in the autumn of 1811, under the direction of Rev. Henry Ryan, Presiding Elder, assisted by Rev. Ninian Holmes, the preacher in charge.

We may well pause a moment and admire the Christian heroism connected with the introduction of Protestant Christianity into this peninsula. We say Protestant Christianity because, although we do not recognize the Romish Church as a true Christian Church, yet she has some semblance to Christianity, and claims to be *the* Christian Church. Taunts, sneers, cold neglect and petty persecutions had to be encountered, as well as the toil, labor and dangers of travel, in these distant parts. Amidst all these the young itinerants persevered, with no worldly emoluments promised them. They were allowed to receive *one hundred dollars* per annum, provided the people would give it to them, with the privilege of "boarding 'round." This part of the country, at this time, was so completely isolated from the rest of the world, except a few scattering settlements along the Canada shore, that it was a vast undertaking to reach it. We will here give the state of the case as *Nathan Bangs* found it when he was appointed to the River Thames Circuit, which included Detroit. This was in 1804, as we have before stated. There was not much improvement for many years after, as the reader will learn when he comes to hear *Joseph Hickox* speak of the same matter in 1815.

Mr. Bangs left the City of New York on horseback, in the latter part of the month of June, "went into Canada by the way of Kingston, thence up the country along the northwestern shore of Lake Ontario to the Long Point Circuit, and thence on through Oxford to the town of Delaware, on the River Thames. Here he lodged for the night in the last log hut in the settlement. The next morning, just as the day began to dawn, he arose and took his departure, and after traveling through a wilderness of forty-five miles, guided only by marked trees, he arrived at a solitary log house about sunset, weary, hungry and thirsty. Here he was entertained with the best the house could afford, which consisted of some Indian pudding and milk for his supper and a bundle of straw for his bed. The next day, about 12 o'clock, he arrived at an Indian village on the north bank of the River Thames, the inhabitants of which were under the instruction of two Moravian missionaries.

"About 3 o'clock P. M. of the same day he arrived at the first house of the settlememt, when the following conversation took place between the missionary and a man he saw in the yard before the door of the house. After the introductory salutation the misionary inquired:

"'Do you want the Gospel preached here?' After some deliberation it was answered, 'Yes, that we do. Do you preach the Gospel?' 'That is my occupation.' 'Alight, then, from your horse and come in, will you?' 'I have come a great distance to preach the Gospel to the people here; and it is Saturday afternoon, to-morrow is the Sabbath, and I must have a house to preach in before I get off my horse.' After a few moments consideration, he replied: 'I have a house for you to preach in, provender for your horse, and food and lodging for yourself, and you shall be welcome to them if you will dismount and come in.' Thanking him for his kind offer, the missionary dismounted and entered the hospitable mansion in the name of the

Lord, saying, '*Peace be to this house.*' A young man mounted his horse and rode ten miles down the river, inviting the people to attend meeting in that house the next day at 10 o'clock A. M."

Here he commenced his labors on this Circuit. He then sent appointments down the river, along through the settlements, which he filled; and was everywhere cordially received by the people. "He proceeded down the shore of the lake, crossed over to Detroit, and preached in the Council House; thence to Fort Malden, and down the shore of Lake Erie, into a settlement made up of American, English, Scotch, Irish and Dutch immigrants. The people everywhere flocked to hear the word." Of the condition of the people he thus speaks: "A more destitute place I had never found. Young people had arrived at the age of sixteen who had never heard a Gospel sermon, and he found a Methodist family who had lived in that country for seven years without hearing a sermon preached. But although the people generally were extremely ignorant of spiritual things, and very loose in their morals, they seemed ripe for the Gospel, and hence received and treated God's messenger with great attention and kindness. He continued among them about three months, when he left them for the Niagara Circuit, intending to return again soon, but was prevented. He was succeeded the next year by William Case, who was instrumental of great good to the souls of the people. Societies and regular circuits were formed, which have continued to flourish and increase to the present time."

The foregoing quotations are made from the "History of the Methodist Episcopal Church," by Dr. Bangs. He writes of scenes in which he participated. In regard to his successor he made a mistake in the date. He says he (that is himself) "was succeeded the next year by William Case." This is an error as to the time, and not as to the man. It was from some time in July, probably the last of the month, till some time in October or November, 1804, that Mr. Bangs was here. According to the General Minutes for 1805, William Case was appointed, as junior preacher, with Henry Ryan, on the Bay Quinte Circuit, and the Thames Circuit was left off the Minutes entirely, and no appointment was made that could include this region until 1809, when William Case was appointed to Detroit. So William Case was his successor, but not till five years had passed, during which time the people had been left without the preaching of the Gospel. Dr. Bangs doubtless wrote from memory, without referring to the Minutes, and so missed the date. The fact is stated correctly, but not the time, as shown by the official Minutes, confirmed by the testimony of Robert Abbott, Wm. McCarty, and others.

In his history, Dr. Bangs furnishes the following account of things in Detroit during the time of his stay on the Circuit: "Detroit, at that time, seemed to be a most abandoned place. On his second visit the missionary was introduced to a Congregational minister,* who told him that he had preached in Detroit until none but a few children would come to hear; 'and,' said he, 'if you can succeed, which I very much doubt, I shall rejoice.' On the third visit, which was on the Sabbath, sure enough, only a few children came to the place of worship, and no one appearing to take any interest in hearing the Gospel preached there, our missionary shook the dust off his feet as a testimony against them, and took his departure from them." From the foregoing statements of the difficulties of travel and the condition of the people, it will be readily seen that it required some courage and perseverance to fulfill the duties of a preacher here.

When William Case came, five years later than Mr. Bangs, he found no special improvement in the people, in the country, in the accommodations, or in the facilities for traveling. At the time he came to Detroit, which was in the month of July or August, 1809; for, although the appointment was made in the latter part of May, for some reason he did not reach Detroit until some time after—there were no Methodists here, or any Protestant professors of religion, so far as known. He had to shift for himself as best he could. As a single man, he was only allowed to receive *one hundred dollars* a year, and no provision for board. He could not afford to hire his board out of this sum. Besides, it was altogether uncertain whether he would receive even that small sum. However, the Lord soon raised him up a friend in the person of Robert Abbott, Esq., who, although not a professor of religion or a Christian, kindly invited him to the hospitalities of his house. But here he met with an unexpected difficulty; that was, Mrs. Abbott was very strongly prejudiced against the Methodists, of whom she had heard something unfavorable from her mother. This prejudice was so strong, that she took occasion to annoy Mr. Case as much as she dared to. At this time Mr. Abbott was Auditor General of the Territory, and much of his time at his office. On one occasion, he called at Mr. Abbott's office in the city and found him very busy, so that he could not go with him to his house at that time, but he directed Mr. Case to go down and said he would follow as soon as he could. Mr. Abbott then resided about a mile out of the city, down the river. The weather was now cold, and Mr. Case had been very much chilled and fatigued with his traveling. Mrs. Abbott saw him coming and determined he should find no entertainment there. Though she knew who he was and that

*Rev. David Bacon, before mentioned.

he must be both cold and hungry, she refused him admittance to the house; she kept him standing in the cold until he became satisfied that he would not be admitted, when he turned away and sought for entertainment at a hotel. When Mr. Abbott came home he inquired for the minister, but she said he had not been there—she had not seen him. Mr. Abbott immediately searched him out, and finally brought him back to his house. Mrs. Abbott had contracted this prejudice mostly from her mother, and partly from the fact that her father was a Roman Catholic. Her mother had told her that the object of these Methodist preachers was to separate husbands from their wives—to break up families, and the like. This prejudice was afterwards strengthened by the fact that when Mr. Case was there, they had spent much time in private conversation. Mr. Abbott was seeking for religious light and instruction. On one of these occasions she determined to ascertain what they were about, so she came silently to the door, and placing her eye and ear alternately to the key-hole, she was much astonished to find them engaged in prayer together. She studiously avoided his society, and neglected to minister to his comfort when there, leaving him to occupy a cold room alone, and not furnishing him with needful food if her husband was not present. These facts were obtained from her own lips by the writer, with the expectation that they would be given in this history.

Some time early in the month of June, 1810, a Camp-Meeting was held on the River Thames, in Canada, which Mr. Abbott was induced to attend. He had not been converted as yet, but was deeply anxious for his salvation. He took his family with him and had his own tent. We once asked Mrs. Abbott how she happened to go to the Camp-Meeting while she had such a bitter prejudice against the Methodists. She replied, "I was obliged to go; Mr. Abbott governed his own house." As to the general results of the meeting we have taken no pains to inquire, as we were interested only in one particular, that is, the effect it had on the work in Michigan. As the meeting progressd in its services, Mr. Abbott became more and more anxious about himself—using the means to secure what he desired, "Peace with God through our Lord Jesus Christ." In his case, as well as in many others, all his notions and plans for obtaining this manifestation of grace were set aside, and the Lord led him by a way that he knew not, and that he had not conceived of before. Yet it was the very way taught in the Bible—the way of simple faith in Jesus Christ as a present Saviour. One night, after he had retired to bed and the encampment had become still and all was quiet, as he lay meditating and looking to Jesus, he was enabled to put his whole trust in Him; in a moment the darkness passed from his mind, and the true light shone into his heart. He bounded from his bed and ran out in his night clothes, as he was, shouting "Hallelujah to the Lamb." So overwhelming was the sense of Divine love to him, that he neither knew nor cared for anything else than to praise God for it. There was joy in the encampment that night, as well as among the angels of God, over a sinner saved by grace through faith. This was the first Camp-Meeting held in this region, and Mr. Abbott was the first inhabitant of Michigan who was converted. This was the first fruit of the seed sown by Mr. Case in this unpromising field, though it did not appear until after he had left. Mr. Abbott holds so important a relation to the Protestant cause in Michigan, that it will be interesting to have a somewhat extended sketch of his life and character, which will be found in the next chapter. Mr. Case's labors had been very successful on the Canada side and along the Thames, so that he reported *seventy-eight* members for Detroit Circuit, but they were all in Canada. He left for Conference in May, and visited his parents before the session.

The Genesee Conference had been created by the authority of the General Conference, embracing this country, and held its first session in Lyons, New York, commencing on the 20th of July, 1810. At this Conference Mr. Case was appointed Presiding Elder of Cayuga District, which separated him from Michigan for the present, but he returns to it again in the capacity of Presiding Elder.

Mr. Case was succeeded on the Circuit by *Rev. Ninian Holmes* in July, 1810—that is, at the session of the Genesee Conference, commencing July 20th. Mr. Holmes was appointed. Precisely at what time he arrived at Detroit we have no means of ascertaining; probably however, it was from six to eight weeks after the session. When he did arrive he found Rev. William Mitchell, from the Western Conference, who had been appointed also. Mr. Holmes labored principally in Canada, and Mr. Mitchell on this side, and they returned *one hundred and thirty-four* members for the Circuit, mostly in Canada. The Society in Detroit and on the Rouge had grown to about thirty members.

At the next session of the Genesee Conference, which commenced on the 20th of July, 1811, Mr. Holmes was returned to Detroit Circuit, with a young man named Silas Hopkins for a colleague. He continued his Circuit as far as Monroe on the south, where Mr. Mitchell had organized a Society of over *twenty* members. At the next Conference, in 1812, the Minutes show *one hundred and thirty-*

four members. About *fifty* of them were in Michigan. The returns this year do not afford an accurate statement of the membership, as Mr. Holmes did not attend the Conference, and the report of last year was adopted for this year. Probably there was no material change in the numbers. The Conference was to meet, or did meet at Niagara, Canada, on the 23d day of July of this year—1812—and *George W. Densmore* was appointed to Detroit, but never came; the reason being that hostilities between the United States and Great Britian had commenced, war having been declared by the United States on the 18th of June. With the Conference of July 23d, 1812, closes the period of peace and begins a time of darkness and desolation; and here we must pause in the line of our narrative for a time, to be resumed after the storm has passed. Henry Ryan has been the Presiding Elder for the last two years.

We will now take a hasty retrospect of this first period of the history of Protestantism in this peninsula, before closing this chapter. The first conversion to experimental Christianity occurred in June, 1810, and the first Methodist Church was organized at Detroit, in the late autumn of the same year, which was the first Protestant Church organized in Michigan. After the organization, this Society steadily increased in numbers and moral strength until the summer of 1812, at which time they numbered about thirty in Detroit and on the Rouge. The last two years had been years of religious prosperity, and gave promise of large and glorious triumphs to the cause of vital Christianity. But alas! a dark cloud is gathering thick around, which is to lay waste these bright prospects and darken these fair hopes. The ravages of war are to lay waste the heritage of the Lord, and brethren in Christ are to be arranged in hostile ranks against each other. The brethren on each side of the river, which divides the two countries, had pledged themselves to each other not to take up arms in the war which was threatening. But they knew not what they would be called upon to do. When once they were required to enter the ranks they could not choose to spare their brethren, when brought into conflict. The effect on the Societies was just such as might have been expected. They were scattered, being deprived of pastors for three years. Yet there were a few who kept the faith—kept up their organization, and were found to constitute a Christian Church when the storm of war had passed away. To these we shall have occasion to refer in our next chapter.

The following is the list of ministers who were appointed to serve here prior and up to the time of the war, viz:

1804.—*Nathan Bangs*, to the Thames Circuit, called River Le French, which included Detroit.

1809.—Upper Canada District, Joseph Sawyer, Presiding Elder. Detroit Mission, William Case.

1810.—Upper Canada District, *Henry Ryan*, Presiding Elder. Detroit—William Mitchell, from the Western Conference; Ninian Holmes, from the Genesee Conference.

Henry Ryan was continued on the District until the war interrupted the appointments.

1811.—Detroit, Ninian Holmes, Silas Hopkins.

1812.—Detroit, George W. Densmore.

The last of these rendered no service, as the war commenced before he could reach his appointment, and he never came on to it.

DESOLATION.

CHAPTER II.

Biographical Sketches—D. Freeman—Nathan Bangs—William Case—Ninian Holmes—Silas Hopkins—Henry Ryan—William Mitchell—Robert Abbott—William McCarty—Betsey Abbott—Maria C. McCarty—William Stacy—Betsey Stacy—Sarah Macomb—Amy Witherell.

SO little is known of Rev. Mr. Freeman, the first Methodist preacher that ever visited Detroit, that not much can be said of him. Mrs. McCarty, who was then quite a young lady, and was very much impressed by his preaching, said he was a very venerable-looking man, that he was a local preacher, and that he appeared to be deeply pious. His preaching was characterized by much earnest sympathy. What brought him to Detroit they knew not, and where his home was they could not tell. We have ascertained that his name was *Daniel Freeman*, and that his home was in Canada. Of all the other early characters we have fuller information, and it will, doubtless, be very interesting to trace their career to some extent in connection with, and as forming a part of this history. We here introduce them.

NATHAN BANGS, D. D. What can be more sublime and grand than to see a man devoting the vigor and sprightliness of early manhood to elevate and ennoble humanity! What more God-like than for such an one to forsake father, mother, home and friends, and to renounce all prospects of worldly gain, honor or preferment, and to consecrate his talents, energies and life to the work of preaching the Everlasting Gospel to lost sinners; to brave dangers, encounter perils, endure hardships, suffer hunger, experience fatigue and weariness, in order to carry peace to the wretched, hope to the disconsolate, and light to those who sit in darkness. It is above all else—it is heavenly. All this is what Nathan Bangs did. He had as fair a prospect for this world as young men of his day had, of honor and gain. He had talents, energy and industry, to succeed in anything he might undertake, as well as others. But all these he laid on the altar of sacrifice to God, and laid himself at the feet of the blessed Saviour, to be used as would best promote His glory and the salvation of men lost in sin. At the time he made the devotion he could not have had the remotest conception of the honor which came to him in after years; for the denomination—the Methodist— to which he attached himself, was small, poor, and generally despised by the worldly-wise. He could have seen before him nothing but hard labor, great suffering and anxiety, so far as this world was concerned, only as he relied on the Divine promise, "In Me ye shall have peace." After his conversion, which occurred in 1800, in Upper Canada, and which was sound and clear, he soon entered the work of the itinerant ministry in the Methodist Episcopal Church. He united with the Church on trial before he had any satisfactory assurance of adoption into the Divine family, a very proper act for any one. He gives the following very interesting account of the exercises of his mind at this period: " Having thus united myself with the children of God, it was now my principal concern to make sure work of my salvation. Though I had frequent manifestations of the grace of God, and could occasionally rejoice in Him, I had not yet attained to a clear witness of my acceptance with Him. The subject of religion engrossed my attention, and I sought every opportunity to converse with devout people on my state and prospects. Some said they believed me to be already justified, while others exhorted me to be thankful for what I had received, and to persevere until I should find a satisfactory evidence of my acceptance with God. My prayer was for some miraculous, some physical manifestation of Divine grace. It pleased the Lord to disappoint me in this respect, as in so many others. After struggling hard, praying much, reading the Holy Scriptures, fasting, and conversing with religious friends for some days, He showed to my mind a scene such as I had never fully seen before. All my past sins seemed pictured upon my memory; the righteous law of God, so often broken by me, shone in overwhelming splendor before me. I saw and acknowledged the justice of my condemnation. Christ was then exhibited to my mind as having 'fulfilled the law and made it honorable,' 'bearing my sins in His own body on the tree,' so that I, receiving Him by faith, need not bear them any longer myself. This view humbled me in the dust. At the same time, I felt a gracious power to rely upon his atoning merits by simple faith. Instantly I felt my sins were cancelled for Christ's sake, and the Spirit of God bore witness with mine that I was adopted into the family of His people. My mind was filled with awe and reverence. The wisdom, power and goodness of God in devising such a scheme for the recovery of fallen man, struck me with astonishment. And with ecstasy of holy joy did I lay hold upon the cross of the Lord Jesus as my Saviour. All boasting was excluded, except the matchless love of God, who sent His Son to die for the world, 'that whosoever believeth in Him should not perish, but have everlasting life.' This view of the plan of redemption and salvation was as clear to me then as it has been at any time since, though not by any means so comprehensively defined as in later experience and studies. It has since been enlarged, and made to appear more exact, symmetrical and beautiful in all its parts. Here let me record my grateful, adoring sense of the lovingkindness of my God in watching so providentially over my infant days, in leading me through the intricacies of youth up to manhood, bearing with my sinfulness, conducting me to a strange land, where He directed my steps among His people, opening the path of life and peace to my troubled soul, receiving me at last, by adoption, into the household of His saints. It was now August, 1800, in the twenty-second year of my age, I having been twenty-one on the 2nd of May preceding."*

Having now fully identified himself with the people of God, he moved forward in his work without faltering, for more than three score years,—abundant in labors and crowned with glorious success. He united with the New York Annual Conference on trial, in 1802, and passed through the various grades of the ministry. His first appointment was on Bay Quinte Circuit, in Canada West, as the third preacher, with Joseph Sawyer and Peter Vannest. These were noble associates for a young man. Next year he was returned to the same Circuit, as the second preacher. The following year, 1804, he was appointed alone to the *River le French* Circuit, which brought him to Detroit. The name of the Circuit was thus called through mistake. It should have been the *River Thames* Circuit. It is this appointment which brings him into the range of our history. He continued on this Circuit only about three or four months. He left his Circuit to make a visit to his friends in the bounds of the Niagara Circuit, with the expectation of returning soon, but did not, for some reason not now ascertainable, as he has left us no information on the subject. But if he had returned to the Circuit it would have made no difference with Detroit, as he had left it for good, having "shaken the dust off his feet for a testimony against them," because they were so given up to folly and wickedness that they would not come to hear him preach the word of life. The circumstances were cer-

---
*Life and Times of Nathan Bangs, D. D.—Stevens'—pp. 47, 48, 49.

tainly very discouraging, and perhaps any one would have done the same thing in the same circumstances, that is, to leave them. But the probability is, if he could have devoted some time to the place, and called among the people, they would not have forgotten the meeting and some good might have been accomplished. In those days of vast circuits, but very little time could be given to any one place for calls on the people at their homes. What could we expect to accomplish now, to come around and preach one sermon only once in three or four weeks? Certainly, nothing. The people of Detroit, then, had no appreciation of the value of the Gospel to them. They knew but very little about it and cared less, and considered the preaching only an interference with their pleasures. There are vast multitudes in the same city now, as in all large cities, who have the same opinion of the preaching of the Gospel, and it requires patient, continuous labor to gain their attention to the things of religion.

Mr. Bangs was full of energy and characterized by an active zeal for the cause of God, and desired, very naturally, to see the fruit of his labor. How trying the situation! Here he was, a lone laborer in a vast region of country, with few or no Christian hearts to sympathize with him. He had no place of entertainment in the city, except at the hotel, and that was poor enough. Who could blame him for leaving the people to themselves, or for devoting his labors to a more promising field? Surely, none. There were no members returned for the Circuit at the next Conference, from which we infer there were no societies formed in it and he was sent to it simply with the hope of making a Circuit and organizing societies. We suppose the reason he did not return to it, after his visit to his friends, to be that his Presiding Elder thought he could be better employed elsewhere. The importance of Detroit was not then realized. This Circuit, by that name, never again appears in the list of appointments. That Mr. Bangs had talents and perseverance enough to have succeeded, if any one could, is evident from his subsequent successes. We have but a few more words in regard to this Circuit.

Dr. Stevens says: "We have witnessed the severity of his trials in these new countries. He had endured them 'as a good soldier of the Lord Jesus;' and he would have appeared justified had he, in retracing his steps to his paternal home and to the Conference in New York City, asked for an appointment nearer his kindred and in a more genial climate, especially as he went to the session almost wrecked in health. But he went thither for the express purpose of soliciting permission to throw himself into a still more westward and more desolate region, a region noted, at that time, for pestilential disease and religious destitution—the recent settlements on the River Thames, a stream which enters the St. Clair, opposite Detroit, beyond the northwestern shore of Lake Erie."* This was noble in him, to desire to enter this perilous but destitute field. In this quotation there is a geographical mistake, which it may be well to correct —"*The River Thames, a stream which enters the St. Clair, opposite Detroit.*" The Thames "enters the St. Clair," not "opposite Detroit," but about *thirty* miles a little north of east from Detroit. Detroit is situated on the north bank of Detroit River, several miles below Lake St. Clair. The field of labor, however, is the same and he desired to cultivate it, and with what success we have already seen. It is much to be regetted that there should have seemed to be any necessity for abandoning Detroit at that time.

In due course of time Mr. Bangs rose to the highest position a man can occupy in the Methodist Episcopal Church, unless it be the Episcopacy. He was editor of the church organ, *The Christian Advocate*, for a long time, and wielded a controlling influence in the councils of the Church for many years. He originated the Missionary Society, an organization now doing a vast amount of good and extending its benign influences into all parts of the globe; and when the office of Missionary Secretary was created, the General Conference instinctively turned to him as the man for the place—a place which he successfully filled for many years. He was the founder of American Methodist periodical literature, and in due time was deservedly titled "*Doctor of Divinity.*" Dr. Bangs is so widely and favorably known in his writings, both controversial and historical, that it is not necessary to say much more concerning him here. The reader is also referred to the "Life and Times of Nathan Bangs, D. D.," by Dr. Stevens, a work of great merit, from which we have already quoted.

In the latter part of his life, Dr. Bangs was a very earnest advocate of Christian holiness as a distinct experience, and maintained the blessing of perfect love in his own heart and experience for many years. He devoted a long life actively to the cause of Christ, and was finally gathered to his fathers in peace, like a shock of corn fully ripe. There is something so noble, so God-like, in such a life, so devoted to the interests of humanity, that we should expect its termination to be like the sun setting in a sea of glory. Such was the demise of this great and good man, for he was good in greatness and

---
*Life and Times of Nathan Bangs, D. D., p. 131.

great in goodness. That he had his trials and discouragements, is undoubtedly true, for these are common to all men, but he realized the truth of the promise of Divine help, " My grace is sufficient for thee." His entire hope was in the atonement of the Lord and Saviour Jesus Christ. He was a noble specimen of a Christian gentleman—of a sanctified human nature. He died in the City of New York, "on the 3d day of May, 1862, one day after his eighty-fourth birthday," having been in the ministry of the Methodist Episcopal Church for sixty years.

We shall now take leave of Dr. Bangs in the language of Dr. Stevens: "Singularly effective, definitive and symmetrical in his life—in the struggles and self-dicipline of his youth, the activity and success of his manhood, the sanctity and peace of his old age, we take our leave of him at the grave, assured that it has been good for the world that he lived, and for us that we have traced the lessons of his life."

REV. WILLIAM CASE. Five years have passed since Mr. Bangs left Detroit, before a successor has appeared. How many of "the light-hearted people," and wicked inhabitants, have floated down the stream of time to eternal despair! But the spell which has bound the people is to be broken, in a measure. Who will do it? Who will be sent to this dark and dreary region, and who will consent to come to it? Well may we ask these questions, for at the time of which we write, it was more of a task to reach Detroit from the seat of an Annual Conference, than it is now to go to India or China, and a minister was more separated from his brethren than now in the distant missionary fields. The fatigues and difficulties of travel were certainly as great. Yet there are here perishing sinners to be looked after, and to be saved if possible. Ministers must not, and will not count their lives dear unto themselves, so that they may but win Christ Jesus, and secure the salvation of souls—souls bought by the precious blood of Christ.

At the session of the New York Conference, held in the City of New York, commencing May 10th, 1809, it was determined to send a *missionary* to Detroit. He is so designated in the Minutes, although there was no Missionary Society to aid in his support. In accordance with this determination, Rev. William Case, who had been four years in the ministry, having joined the Conference in 1805, was appointed to Detroit. This chapter, and indeed our whole History, would be very defective did we not furnish a somewhat detailed biography of this early and active missionary, for, although he was not the first who attempted to plant the standard of the Gospel and Protestantism on Michigan soil, he was the first who made any persevering effort for that purpose, and continued in it until fruit appeared, and with his name Detroit first appears on the records of the Church—in the Minutes of the Conference, as an appointment. Mr. Case, by giving time and devoting attention, succeeded in leading one man to embrace the cause of Christ. Others had received the spirit of conviction, which subsequently resulted in sound conversion, but of this fact he was not advised at the time. So he labored in hope. If no other good had resulted from the labors of this year, than the conversion of Robert Abbott, it would have been abundant compensation for the labor put forth and the toil endured; for Mr. Abbott became a nucleus around which a Church soon clustered, so that the work assumed form and permanency.

William Case was born in the town of Swansea, Massachusetts, August 27th, 1780; so he was twenty-nine years old when he came to Detroit. He made profession of religion and joined the Church—the Methodist Episcopal Church—in 1803, when he was twenty-three years of age. He was admitted on trial in the New York Conference in 1805, at its session held in Ashgrove, beginning June 12th. Having volunteered for the work in Canada, he was appointed to the Bay Quinte Circuit, in the Upper Canada District, as junior preacher. The next year he was appointed to the Oswegotchie Circuit, in the same District. The first year Henry Ryan, and the second Gershom Pearse was in charge, and Joseph Sawyer was the Presiding Elder. The next year, 1807, he was appointed to Ulster Circuit, in Albany District, as junior preacher, under *Elias Vanderlip*, with Henry Stead as Presiding Elder. According to the Minutes of the New York Conference, Mr. Case was ordained an Elder at its session held at Amenia, beginning April 6th, 1808. At this Conference he was appointed in charge of Ancaster Circuit, in Upper Canada District, alone, Joseph Sawyer still being Presiding Elder. We now find him intrusted with the responsibility of being in charge of a Circuit, and never after do we find him in any inferior position. In these appointments is shown the changes to which men were subjected, and to which they were called to submit in those early days. At the session of the New York Conference, held in the City of New York, beginning May 10th, 1809, he was appointed to Detroit as a missionary, but his labors were not by any means to be confined to that place, for he extended his work up the Thames, and down the lake shore in Canada. Look at the undertaking! A missionary sent, having to travel from New York City to Detroit on horseback, to form a Circuit, gather up members wherever he might find them, and then depend on them for a support; for, though he was appointed and called a missionary, there was no Society—no funds to fall back on for his support, as our Missionary Society had not then been organized. With all this labor and these dark prospects before him, he went into the work in the name of his Divine Master.

In regard to his having gone to Canada, Mr. Case, in his semi-centennial sermon, makes the following remarks; "I have much reason to believe that my appointment to this country was in the order of providence, and divinely directed. A field thus distant was the more suitable to wean one from a numerous circle of friends, and a new country was best adapted to my youth and inexperience. I have every cause to be satisfied with my choice, and abundant reason to be grateful to my Christian brethren, and to the inhabitants of Canada generally, for their generous and kind treatment, and the marked *hospitality* which has everywhere been shown me in every part of the Province. In connection with this subject, I beg to relate an incident which occurred in my journey to this country. It was while traveling through the forest of Black River. As I was drawing near to the field of my future labor, I felt more and more deeply impressed with the importance of my mission, and my insufficiency for preaching to a people already well instructed. As yet but a boy—only about two years since my conversion—devoid of ministerial talent as I was of beard—I feared, on account of my incompetency, that I should not be received in a strange land. So strong were the emotions of my heart that I dismounted from my horse and sat down, and wept and prayed. While thus weeping, these words were spoken to me in a voice that I could not misunderstand: 'I will go before thee,—will prepare the hearts of the people to receive thee; and thou shalt have fathers, and mothers, and children in that land.' This promise I have seen fulfilled to the letter, and hereby give glory to God for this and a hundred promises more, which have by his blessed word and his Holy Spirit been impressed on my heart."

We must furnish one more incident. It will be remembered that Canada was embraced in the New York Conference until 1810; so he had to come over into the States to attend the sessions. In 1808 he had attended the session, and on his return found difficulty in getting back. But hear his own words: "In 1808, on my arrival at Black Rock, the *embargo* prohibited the transportation of property across the river. At first I was perplexed, and knew not what to do. So I went to the hay loft, and fell on my face in prayer. I asked the Lord, as I was engaged in *His* work, to open my way to fulfill my mission in Canada. Having committed all to God, I returned to my lodgings at the inn, when a stranger smilingly said: 'I should not wonder if the missionary should jump into the boat, take his horse by the bridle, and *swim around the embargo.*' I did so, swam across the Niagara River, and landed safely in Canada."

It is now time to return to his relation to the work in Michigan. He is to be regarded as the founder, under God, of Protestantism in Michigan, although he did not organize the Church, for he cleared the way for those who entered into his labors. In the midst of many discouragements he persevered, trusting in God. His way was not always smooth. Although he found a friend in Robert Abbott, Esq., who did all he could to make him feel at home and to render him comfortable, it was otherwise with Mrs. Abbott. Her mother, who had been educated an Irish Presbyterian, had become a Roman Catholic, and for some reason had acquired a most bitter enmity toward the Methodists, having resided in Philadelphia for a time and heard something of them. Mrs. Abbott's father was a French Catholic, and inherited all the Roman Catholic virulence against all Protestants. With this education the idea of having a Methodist preacher in the house was most abhorent to her. She, therefore, sought every opportunity and resorted to all the means she dared to make his stay there as uncomfortable as possible.

Mr. Case was a plain, earnest and faithful preacher, and did not spare the follies and wickedness of the people. This, of course, was not always palatable to those who were described. On one occasion some of the baser sort about the town, wishing to vent their spleen—to show their contempt for religion and the minister—and being too cowardly to do it openly, stole into the stable at night and trimmed the hair from the tail and mane of his unoffending horse. In the morning Mr. Case found his horse in that sad plight; but nothing daunted, he mounted his Pegassus and rode through the principal streets of the town, making full show of what had been done. Some of the principal citizens were much chagrined at this circumstance and offered him a high price for the animal, but he refused to sell him at any price and rode him away. In this way he defeated the purpose they had in view, and turned the shame on themselves.

By permission of the General Conference of 1808, as they understood it, the bishops organized the Genesee Conference, embracing the Susquehannah, Cayuga, Upper and Lower Canada districts, in 1810, and the first session thereof was held at the village of Lyons, New York, in a corn-house belonging to Judge Dorsey. This session commenced July 20th, 1810. It may be that from the place— a corn house—in which the Conference sessions were held this year, originated the remark of an enemy of Methodism, that "a *corn crib* would now hold all the Methodists, and in a short time a *corn basket* will hold them." Mr. Case, from his appointment at Detroit, became a member of this Conference and continued so until the Canada Conference was created, the first session of which was held at Hallowell, in Upper Canada, beginning August 25th, 1824. At this first session of the Genesee Conference, Mr. Case was appointed to the Cayuga District, as Presiding Elder, on which he remained four years. Upon the expiration of this period, at the session of the Genesee Conference held in Genoa, Cayuga County, New York, he was appointed in charge of Chenango District, on which he remained only one year, and was, at the session of the Conference commencing June 29th, 1815, appointed Presiding Elder of Upper Canada District, which brought him once more to Detroit, as this was included in his district. He remained on this district one year only, and was transferred to the Lower Canada District. Why these frequent changes from district to district occurred, we have no means of determining. One thing, however, is certain, that is, it was not for want of ability to sustain himself for a longer period. Very probably it arose from the fact that the districts were so difficult to travel and so laborious, that it was thought advisable to afford relief by change.

Mr. Case remained in the Lower Canada District for four years, viz: from July, 1816, to July 20th, 1820. From the time of his appointment to the Upper Canada District, in 1815, he became fully and entirely identified with the interests of Methodism in Canada—that became his home. In July, 1820, he was re-appointed to the Upper Canada District, in charge of which he remained four years, but was not officially connected with Michigan Methodism, as Michigan, (that is, Detroit,) was transferred to the Ohio Conference, by act of the General Conference, in 1820. Mr. Case, however, was at the first Camp-Meeting held in Michigan, on the River Rouge. It was held by Rev. John P. Kent, in 1822. His labors at this Camp-Meeting were highly appreciated and were very useful. At the expiration of his term of four years on the Upper Canada District, he was appointed to the Bay Quinte District, and from thence forward he became identified with the Indian Missions of that region, although he supplied this district for four years—that is, from 1824 to 1828. By permission of the General Conference of 1828, the Canada Conference erected itself into an independent Church, entitled the Methodist Episcopal Church in Canada. In this new body Mr. Case held a very conspicuous place and rendered very important services. His whole soul became wrapped up in the interests of the Indian

Missions in Canada, of which he might be said to be the father. He was once elected Bishop of the Methodist Episcopal Church in Canada, before the union of a part of the body with the Wesleyans of Great Britain,—that is, while the Methodists of Canada were all one body,—but he declined to be ordained, and continued his labors among the Indians. In the good providence of God he was permitted to visit Detroit in 1853, and to attend the session of the Michigan Conference, which met in that city for the third time this year. He preached on the Sabbath, and reviewed the past with great interest and much pleasure, contrasting the past with the present. It was a great pleasure to the Conference to be favored with his presence at this time.

Mr. Case was a man of athletic frame, dignified and commanding in his personal appearance, of indomitable perseverance, of a strong and vigorous mind, of close observation, of a kind and sweet spirit. He was a devoted Christian, and was a very earnest and successful laborer. God gave him many souls as seals to his ministry. He died in 1855, honored and respected by all who knew him. Indeed, so transparent and pure was his character, that to know him was to love him. We in Michigan love and honor him, and even venerate him, because he was honored of God as the instrument of laying the foundation of Methodism in our Peninsular State. But he has gone to his peaceful and glorious rest in heaven.

REV. NINIAN HOLMES was admitted on trial in the New York Conference in 1807, and was appointed as the third preacher, with Nathan Bangs and Thomas Whitehead, on Niagara Circuit. In 1808 he was appointed in charge of Bay Quinte Circuit. In 1809 he was admitted into full connection in the Conference, and ordained both as Deacon and Elder, as a missionary. Why he was so designated does not appear. He was appointed to Augusta Circuit. These appointments were all in Canada West, now Ontario; or as it was then called, Upper Canada. In 1810 he was appointed to Detroit, alone, but found Mitchell here from the Western Conference, as before stated. The next year, 1811, he was returned to Detroit, with Silas Hopkins as his colleague and junior. This has the appearance of a determination to prosecute the work here with vigor. Some success attended their labors. This is the last appointment that Mr. Holmes ever supplied, for although at the Conference of 1812 he was appointed to Niagara Circuit, in Canada, the breaking out of the war prevented his going to it. He continued in Detroit until after the surrender of the place by General Hull, for on that day he was in the city and baptized a child for Wm. McCarty.

In consequence of the war, all communication with his Conference—the Genesee—was broken off; and when the smoke of battle and the clouds of war were cleared away, and peace was declared in 1815, and the scattered members were to be gathered up and reorganized, Mr. Holmes did not report himself at headquarters for duty in the itinerant field. His name disappears, in this way, from the records of the workmen. Though he had assisted "at the introduction of strangers among the workmen," he himself now declined "to assist in the work of rebuilding the temple" of our God. He settled down on the Thames, engaged in business, and so has passed from our view. It is sad to think of a man capable of doing much good, as he was, settling down to mere secular employments while there was so much need of his help, " to restore and build the waste places of Zion." While on this Circuit, he and his colleague seemed disposed to take in all the places they could, for they continued to extend their labors to Monroe, and made that journey of forty miles and back to preach to a small congregation. They had some success there. A small Society had been organized the year before, all of whom were scattered by the war. We have not been able to obtain any information in regard to Mr. Holmes' religious experience or the finale of his existence. He is said to have been a very good preacher and faithful to his work while here.

REV. SILAS HOPKINS. We can say but very little in regard to this young man. He was admitted on trial in the Genesee Conference, at the session, July 11th, 1811, and appointed to Detroit, as above stated. The next year, 1812, he was appointed to Augusta, in Canada, but as everything was in confusion, by the war, he could not attend to it, and so disappears. We have no further mention of him in the records of the Church.

JOSEPH SAWYER appears on the Minutes for 1809, as the Presiding Elder, but as he does not appear to have visited Michigan at all, we make no further mention of him.

HENRY RYAN stands at the head of Upper Canada District for the years 1810, 1811 and 1812. He appears again in 1816, 1817, 1818 and 1819, in the same office, making seven years in all that he was connected with Michigan Methodism, in this relation. It is proper, therefore, to furnish some sketch of his life and character. Mr. Ryan was a very large man, of Herculean strength; of a vigorous mind and a determined will. This last trait in his character finally led him astray, and induced him to abandon the Church in which he had labored very successfully for many years and to set up a small party for himself. His party, from a common disposition to designate a people by the name of the leading spirit among them, was called Ryanites. He had done much hard service, and had seen much rough fare. He was emphatically a pioneer. He could preach with great power and effect. The largeness of his frame was sometimes of service to him. The following anecdote has been related of him: On one occasion he had preached with great plainness and effect, so much so that a certain son of Vulcan became very much exasperated and swore he would whip the first Methodist preacher who should pass his shop. He lived on the road Mr. Ryan had to pass to reach his next appointment. Some one who had heard the threatening informed the preacher of it, and advised him to seek some other road, as the blacksmith was a very desperate and determined man and would be likely to execute his threat. Mr. Ryan thought it not advisable to be driven from his course by any such apprehension, so when the time came he started on his way. The blacksmith had seen him coming and was prepared for him. When the preacher came up to where he was by the side of the road, the fellow accosted him, asking him if he was not a Methodist preacher, to which inquiry the preacher responded that his name was Ryan, and that he was a Methodist preacher. "Well, then," said the fellow, "you must dismount, as I have sworn I would whip the first Methodist priest that comes this way." Mr. Ryan very coolly told him he thought he had taken a very foolish oath, and that he had better let him pass. This only increased the fury of the man, as he thought the preacher was afraid of him; so he told him he could not pass without a flogging. On this Mr. Ryan alighted from his horse, saying, "If I must, then, I must." Mr. Ryan then deliberately laid aside his coat, rolled up his sleeves, exhibiting an arm something like a hand-spike and a fist resembling a sledgehammer. Having made these preparations, he approached the blacksmith with his arm uplifted, exclaiming, "The Lord have mercy on your poor soul, as I shall have none on your body." The poor fellow was not prepared for this kind of exhibition, and quailed before the preacher. But the preacher did not let him escape without a wholesome exhortation, and exacting from him a pledge never to insult another minister. There are several editions of this story, but something of the kind occurred and we give it as we received it. A large body was of good service at that time. He was the last Presiding Elder sent out from the Genesee Conference, whose district included Detroit. He has gone to his long account; we trust in peace, for we think him sincere, though in error in his last years. We will honor him for the hard, beneficial service which he rendered in this field, and draw the veil of charity over the foibles and errors of his separation from the Church.

Henry Ryan was admitted into the traveling connection in 1800, and was appointed in charge of Vergennes Circuit, in the New York District, with Robert Dyer as his colleague and Freeborn Garretson as his Presiding Elder. This was before the connection was properly divided into Annual Conferences, or rather so distinguished in the Minutes of the appointments, as is now the case. The bishops called certain districts together, as was convenient, and made the appointments for the year. The Conference met in New York City, June 19th, 1800. The next year it met in the same place, June 16th, and Mr. Ryan was returned to Vergennes Circuit, alone, and the district was now called Pittsfield, with *Shadrach Bostwick* as the Presiding Elder. In 1802, June 1st, he was admitted into full connection and ordained Deacon, and was appointed in charge of Fletcher Circuit, with Elijah Hedding as his colleague. The District and Presiding Elder are the same. The conferences are distinguished in the Minutes this year, for the first time, and Pittsfield District is included in the New York Conference. At the session of the New York Conference, held in New York, beginning June 12th, 1804, he was ordained an Elder and appointed in charge of Plattsburg Circuit, of which he had charge the year before. It is not necessary to follow him through all his appointments. The next year he was appointed in charge of Bay Quinte Circuit, in the Upper Canada District, and from this time he becomes identified with Canada, and in 1810 he was appointed to the Upper Canada District as Presiding Elder, which brought him into the range of our History, as before related. In the Minutes of the Canada Conference, for the year 1827, we find Henry Ryan's name returned as having withdrawn from the connection this year. This was a great mistake in him. We find this one peculiarity in his case—that is, he was appointed in charge of a Circuit his first year, and always after continued in charge of circuits or districts as long as he was effective; while such men as Bangs, Case and Hedding had to serve for a time as juniors. Mr. Ryan had been on the list of superannuates for the last two years preceding his severance of his connection with the Methodist Episcopal Church.

Mr. Ryan had superior executive abilities, as was acknowledged in the appointments he received. It will be remembered that, for three years during the war, the Church in Canada being connected with the Genesee Conference, could not be supplied with ministers. During this time Mr. Ryan called the ministers in Canada together, and as a kind of self-constituted bishop, assigned them to their fields of labor. This, of course, was without any legal authority; but such was their confidence in his executive ability that they acquiesced in it. He having an inexorable will, by the exercise of this power became, as was thought by many, a little too arbitrary; and when the fitting occasion appeared, they repudiated him. He was deserving of great praise for his skill and supervision over the work during the war, and that was freely accorded to him; but when they thought he had demanded too much they refused, and that refusal he could not well brook. So he withdrew, and led in the organization of a new body which has been known as the "Methodist New Connection," but has now united with the Wesleyan body in Canada, and become absorbed in "The Methodist Church of Canada."

REV. WILLIAM MITCHELL, who acted so conspicuous and important a part in the history of Methodism at its organization in Michigan, must not be confounded with *Joseph Mitchell* who spent the winter of 1816-17 in Detroit, and of whom we speak elsewhere. Our materials for making up a memorial sketch of William Mitchell are very few. He was regarded by those who knew him here as a very good man and a fine preacher. We gather the following facts from our General Minutes, concerning him: He was admitted on trial by the Western Conference in 1807, and expelled in 1812; for what cause is not stated. In the meantime he had been appointed as follows, viz: 1807, Mad River Circuit, in Ohio, as junior preacher; 1808 and 1809 (two years), Little Kanawha, in Virginia; 1810, he was ordained Elder and stationed on Detroit Circuit, on which he remained only one year; 1811, Tuscarawas, in the Muskingum District, in Ohio; 1812, the sad announcement is made that he was expelled from the connection. Here he is lost to our view. Why Mr. Mitchell should have been sent from the Western Conference, when Mr. Holmes was sent from the Genesee, we cannot tell. But the fact is, so little was known of Detroit that the mistake might easily occur. How they settled the matter of jurisdiction we are not informed, but we infer that Mr. Holmes attended to so much of the Circuit as was in Canada, and Mr. Mitchell to Michigan; so Mr. Mitchell organized the Church in Detroit and on the Rouge, as before stated.

This closes our ministerial list for the first period of our History. There were but a few men, but they were men of ability. They laid a good foundation and commenced to rear a goodly structure, and were only interrupted by the breaking out of the war. But we have reason to be very thankful that the fruit of their labor was not all destroyed—that a few were found steadfast at the end of the conflict. We will now proceed to give some account of the laymen, and of some of the women of this period, which will be interesting and valuable.

ROBERT ABBOTT, Esq., holds such a relation to the work of Protestantism in Michigan, that our History would be quite incomplete without a pretty full notice of his life and experience. Some time in the month of June, 1810, there was a Camp-Meeting held on the River Thames, which Mr. Abbott attended. He had not yet experienced renewing grace, but was deeply anxious for his own salvation. The circumstances of his conversion have before been fully related.

Robert Abbott was born in Detroit, in 1771, and was probably the first American born here. We use the term American, in distinction from Indian and French; for although both these were American by their residence, they are usually distinguished as Indian or French, as the case may be. He was Anglican in his origin. His mother is said to have been the first American woman speaking the English language who settled at Detroit. She was born at Albany, N. Y., of Dutch parentage. His father, James Abbott, was a merchant from Dublin, Ireland, and is said to have been the first English-speaking person who opened business in this city. He was here some time before he was married.

Mr. Abbott was born in the midst of wild savagism; for it would seem that his family was the only English-speaking family here at the time. Indians were numerous, and the few French settlers had conformed themselves almost entirely to the Indian costumes and habits of life, and instead of elevating the former they had been reduced to their level. This grew partly out of the French adaptability to their surroundings. The circumstances were such that it was with the utmost difficulty they could obtain a supply of the conveniences, or even the necessaries of civilized life. It is a universal principle of human nature to avoid much exertion, unless there is a very strong stimulus to it. The free and easy kind of indolent life of the savage, relieved only by the excitement of the chase, suited the French settlers better than the labors and restraints of civilization. Agriculture was of no value beyond the supply of their immediate wants—it furnished no remuneration. The materials for civilized costumes were costly, while they had little or nothing to pay. Hunting, fishing and trapping formed their chief occupation, and furnished them with what means they had to obtain money or goods. Up to this time, the nearest settlement of any account was at Montreal, in Canada, one that was too far off to exercise any civilizing influence on the inhabitants of Detroit and its vicinity. The British Government had had a garrison of soldiers here for eleven years, at the time of Mr. Abbott's birth; they having wrested Fort Ponchartrain from the French, November 29th, 1760. But we know a garrison of soldiers never promotes civilization. Indeed, there were none here over whom to exert any civilizing influence, except the Indians and French. These had made common cause against the English, and were alike uninfluenced by them. So complete was the identification of the French and Indians, that at the time of Pontiac's siege of Detroit the persons and property of the French settlers were unharmed. The Indians called them *brothers*, and treated them as such. Pontiac, the great Chief of the Northwest, was not pleased with the occupancy of the country by the English, and in 1761 commenced a plan for the destruction of the garrison and all English persons who might chance to be in the country. He collected his allies from all parts of the country, and made to them the most incendiary speeches and aroused all the blood-thirsty dispositions of their savage natures. He besieged the garrison at Detroit. He cruelly murdered all soldiers, officers, and others whom he could by any means get into his possession. One poor old woman who lived outside the fort was cruelly murdered, and an unoffending old man, who resided on what is now called Belle Isle, was likewise slain. He laid a deep plot to get into the fort and take it by treachery, but this was revealed to the commanding officer, General Gladwin, and so failed. He finally abandoned his project, and in 1764 raised the siege of Detroit and returned to the Maumee River. The population at this time, for the whole of Michigan, was said to be about 2,500; but a census taken in 1768 reports only 572. It is quite probable that the former number is an exaggeration; but a reason is given for the decrease; that is, that many of the inhabitants, fearing the consequences of having taken a part with Pontiac, fled to Illinois. But this is hardly sufficient to account for the difference. The place now being under the British Government, and having become comparatively safe for English people, Mr. James Abbott, a merchant from Dublin, Ireland, and father of our subject, settled here for trade. He was born here as before stated, in the midst of exciting and savage scenes, for society had not much improved in the last ten years. Detroit was a great point of concentration for the natives to dispose of their peltries and to receive annuities from the British Government.

When Mr. Robert Abbott came to maturity he entered into the

fur trade with the Indians and succeeded in acquiring a good property for the times. He also acquired a respectable business education, so that he was in a condition to fill the Government offices of the times with credit and satisfaction, he having been Auditor General of the Territory for several years. Under the circumstances with which he was surrounded and brought up, he was utterly destitute of religious knowledge until after he had attained his majority, or manhood. He probably heard Mr. Freeman and Mr. Bangs preach when they were here in 1804. He married into a Roman Catholic family, and it is rather a matter of wonder that, under the circumstances, he did not drink in that faith; but he seemed not to have done so. When Mr. Case came to Detroit, in 1809, as a Methodist Missionary, he found a home with Mr. Abbott, and after many conferences on the subject, he made up his mind to enlist under the banner of Christ as presented by Mr. Case, and was happily converted in June, 1810. The fact that he made a profession of experimental religion indicates a decision of character which is very commendable. None of his family or friends were quite ready to join with him then, though some did soon after. He had to take his stand alone. Even his wife and her friends were strongly against him, and he had every reason to expect he would meet with scorn and contempt, if not open persecution. It was only after long and very earnest thought that he decided the question of becoming a Christian; but having once decided he ought to do so, he entered upon it with alacrity. It is not to be wondered at that, after so severe and long-continued a mental struggle, the change should be marked and that his Christian joy should rise very high, as it did when he received the evidence of pardoning grace. Having put his hand to the plow, he never looked back nor turned aside from his profession of faith in Christ.

When Rev. Mr. Case came to Detroit, in 1809, there were no Protestant professors of religion in the Territory, so far as then known, and consequently there were no Christians to greet him on his coming or to give him welcome. He came to Detroit as a Christian adventurer, seeking to save the lost in sin. Mr. Abbott, by some means not now ascertainable, found out that such a man was in the city, and was at once strongly drawn to him, and invited him to his house. He proved to be an angel of love and mercy. Mrs. Abbott and her relatives were very bitterly opposed to this procedure. It will at once be apparent that, under the circumstances, it required a great amount of firm decision on the part of Mr. Abbott to take a Methodist preacher into his house and furnish him a resting place. But he did it. How the preacher was received by the wife, and what fears she entertained, have been before narrated. When the Church was to be organized here he united with it, helping to constitute it. For many years he took as active a part in the affairs of the Church as his health and the duties of his office would permit, and contributed liberally of his money for the maintenance of the Gospel. The latter he continued to do to the end of his life.

When it was decided to build a church on the River Rouge, about five miles out of the city, which was done in 1818, he took a very active interest in obtaining and collecting subscriptions for that purpose. Indeed, he had to manage the business mainly himself, because he had more means and time at command than any other member. All the members did what they could, but he necessarily had to be very active in it. About the time of the building of this church, for a few years he resided on a farm in its immediate vicinity, surrounded by French Roman Catholics mainly, who had little or no regard for the Sabbath. Mr. Abbott having been appointed a Justice of the Peace, fined many of them for working on the Sabbath. He met with much opposition in this, and some threats of violence to his property for it, but he persevered and effected quite a reformation in this respect for the time being.

He was firm and decided in his attachment to the Christian cause and the Church of his choice, and his end was peace. A few days before his death one of his sons asked him how he felt in his mind. He said, "There is not a cloud, betwixt me and heaven, as big as a hand." As he came to the valley of the shadow of death he feared no evil. He died very easy and peacefully, for God was with him.

There are a few incidents occurring in his life worthy of note. He was the first Anglo-American born in Detroit. He was the first person who experienced the forgiveness of sins, through faith in the blood of Christ, of the residents here. He was one to help form the first Protestant Church in Michigan—at Detroit—and to take an active part toward the erection of the first Protestant meeting-house in Michigan. These are events which do not often occur in the history of one man. The late Bishop Thomson, who was once stationed in Detroit for two years, and knew Mr. Abbott well, writes of him; " Mr. Abbott was what Pope calls the noblest work of God, 'an honest man.' He was much of his time in political life, and was one of those rare men who can sacrifice office to principle, and expose corruption even in those who have power to displace them."

Many of Mr. Abbott's later years were spent in much suffering, but these physical sufferings were endured patiently, "as seeing Him that is invisible." He died at Coldwater, 1853, aged eighty-two years. He had temporarily removed his residence from Detroit to Coldwater, Michigan, and made his home with a married daughter, Mrs. Chandler. Here he waited patiently for his release from the labors and sufferings of earth, and met death with a smile.

WILLIAM McCARTY, who was the first class-leader ever appointed in Michigan, and who held the office for many years, comes next to our notice and is worthy of a memorial sketch. He was born on Grosse Isle, in 1798. His father was an Irishman and had been pressed into the British Army, but as soon as he could get released from the army he came to Michigan and settled on Grosse Isle, having married, and where William was born. The educational advantages were very few in Michigan at that time, and William received but very little help in that direction in his youth. Our subject possessed all the lively sympathy and warm-heartedness for which the Irish are so proverbial. He was led to a consecration of his heart to God and a Christian experience, under the labors of Rev. William Mitchell, of whom mention has already been made. The precise time is not given, but it must have been within a few months after the conversion of Robert Abbott, who was his brother-in-law, as he was one of the seven to form the first Society or Church, when it was organized in late autumn of 1810, and he was appointed the class-leader and continued to perform the duties of that office while the preachers remained, before the war. When the occurrence of the war took the ministers away, he kept the flock together as well as he could, holding religious services with them, so that when they were permitted to come again, which was after three years of privation, *seven* were found to be recognized as a Church. His care and supervision over them during this interval of ministerial service had great influence, at this critical period, to keep them alive in the cause —" steadfast in the faith." When Rev. *Joseph Hickox* came to Detroit Circuit, in 1815, he found *seven*, that is the seven named as constituting the original Society, still standing fast in the faith. These he immediately recognized as members of the Church—and continued William McCarty as the class-leader. Mr. McCarty was well adapted to that office. He possessed a warm and lively temperament, ready utterance, very respectable talents, and a sound Christian experience. These are very important qualifications for a successful class-leader. He held this office most of the time until his death. He was licensed as an exhorter, April 20th, 1822, by Rev. John P. Kent. This was while Mr. Kent was supplying Detroit Circuit, after the death of Rev. Platt B. Morey, as noticed in its proper place hereafter. He continued to hold license as an exhorter as long as he lived. In this department of Church labor he had few equals.

Mr. McCarty continued to reside in the County of Wayne and in the vicinity of Detroit until the summer of 1831, at which time he removed to the County of Branch and settled on a small prairie in the township of Girard. In this locality he was one to help constitute the second Christian Church organized in Branch County. The first Society was organized by Rev. E. H. Pilcher, on the 19th of June, 1832, at Coldwater, consisting of Allen Tibbitts, Caroline M. Tibbitts, Joseph Hanchett and Nancy Hanchett. This second Society was organized a few weeks later, by Rev. E. S. Gavit, the junior preacher on the Circuit. When the county of Branch was organized, in 1833, he was elected the first sheriff and removed his residence to Coldwater, where he finally ended his career. At this place he entered into trade in the days of wild speculation—in 1836 and 1837, but failed in business, as many others did. Now there came a hard struggle for him and a test of his Christian character. If he attempted to pay his debts, it would strip him of everything, and he and his wife, with part of his family who were still dependent on him for support and education, would be thrown upon the world with nothing—to begin the world anew. He had it in his power now to keep a sufficient amount of property under cover to make himself and family very comfortable during his life. The temptation was very strong to do so, and the reasoning very specious. He struggled with this temptation for some time; but, as might have been expected, he was without religious life or consolation. Finally, he saw clearly what would be the result to his soul, and grace triumphed. He immediately determined to do right—to make a clean sweep of the matter, and expose all his property to meet his debts, as far as possible. No sooner had he made this determination than he became exceedingly happy, and ever after thanked God that he had been able to resist the temptation and do right. He died very happy in 1844, aged fifty-five years, having been a member of the Methodist Episcopal Church for thirty-four years. It had been a very common remark with him that he expected "to go straight from Coldwater to heaven." While on his death-bed he said to his children, "*Live religion.*" To a Christian brother who called to see him a few days before his departure he said: "Brother Fisk, if I could get loose from this old body, how quick I would be there—in heaven."

Thus he died, in the faith for which he had contended for so many years, and has gone to receive that "crown of righteousness which the Lord the righteous Judge" had prepared for him. He was the second man who professed conversion in Michigan. We are indebted to him for much valuable information in regard to the organization of the Methodist Church in this peninsula.

BETSEY ABBOTT. How soon will all means of obtaining information of the early history of Protestantism in Michigan be gone! All the members of the first Protestant Church in Michigan are now laid in the grave. Betsey Abbott was the wife of Robert Abbott, and was brought to the knowledge of salvation soon after he was, and she was ready to join the Methodist Church as soon as there was one to be organized. She was sister to Mrs. Maria C. McCarty. We have already given sufficient notice of her early religious training and prejudices. These prejudices yielded to the power of grace and she became decidedly attached to the Church she had so violently opposed. After her conversion she always retained her relation to the Church as a member. She was not at her own home at the time of her death, as she had resided, ever after the death of her husband, with her daughter at Coldwater. She had been visiting her daughter, Mrs. E. V. Cicott in Detroit, for a short time previous to her death. The following brief notice of her, written by her pastor, was published at the time: "Died, in Detroit, Michigan, March 24th, [1858], Betsey Abbott, of this place, aged seventy-three years and four months. The deceased had been a useful member of the Methodist Episcopal Church for forty-eight years. Herself, her companion and her sister, were three of the first class of seven organized in Detroit—the first Methodist class formed in the State. The sister of the deceased, who also is a resident of this place, is the only one now living.

"Sister Abbott was an amiable and faithful Christian, highly esteemed and loved while she lived, and her death has caused deep sorrow among acquaintances and friends. She died in peace, trusting in the merits of the Saviour.

"COLDWATER, MICH., April 5th, 1858, N. ABBOTT."

In relation to Mrs. Abbott, the late Bishop Thomson, in an article in the *Western Christian Advocate*, dated Oct. 6th, 1858, thus speaks: "She had a strong attachment to the Church, and opened her house with grace to its ministers. It was amusing to hear her tales of early days, and particularly her anecdotes of the eccentric Mitchell, who said on one occasion, while preaching in Detroit: 'You, General Macomb, and you, General Cass, will burn in hell like common sinners, if you do not repent!' and on another occasion cried out, at the commencement of religious services, 'Stop that ungodly big fiddle till we get done worship!'

"It was no less amusing to hear her account of the reproofs she administered on such occasions, when she got the offending minister seated at her hospitable table."

Thus are the relics of the early days of Methodism in Michigan passing away; for when the preparation for this History was commenced Mrs. Abbott and Mrs. McCarty, with their husbands, were both living and were freely consulted; but they are now both gone, thus severing the last living links of this period of our Methodistic History, because all the ministers who officiated here then are also gone.

MARIA C. MCCARTY was the last survivor of the seven who constituted the first Protestant Church organization in Detroit, and was the first to feel the true conviction for sin, though not the first one converted in the city. She resided in the City of Detroit in 1804, and always retained a lively recollection of the visit and preaching of Rev. Mr. Freeman, in that year, of whom we have before spoken. His bold, earnest preaching impressed her heart deeply, so that she never was satisfied with her condition till she found peace in Christ, some years afterwards. The conversion of her brother-in-law, Robert Abbott, took such hold upon her already awakened heart that she soon gave herself up to Christ and found peace in His name. As soon as there was a minister to organize a Church, she was ready to unite with it. She had been educated, as her sister Mrs. Abbott, in abhorence of the Methodists, but did not appear to have partaken of the spirit of opposition in the same measure. But whatever her prejudices might have been, they all finally yielded to the power of truth, when she gave her heart to the Saviour. Her life was consistent with her profession, and she always remained firm in her attachment to the Church of her choice. Her last days were cheerful and happy.

We avail ourselves of the following obituary notice, written by Hon. Albert Chandler and published in one of the papers of the City of Coldwater, at the time of her death:

"Died, in the City of Coldwater, on the morning of the 10th ult., Mrs. Maria C. McCarty, widow of the whilom Wm. McCarty, at the advanced age of seventy-six years, after an illness of three months. The deceased was born in the City of Philadelphia. At an early age her parents with their children moved to Pittsburgh, Pa., where she received her education, and at the age of twelve years she with her parents removed to Detroit, where she resided for a number of years, and especially during the war of 1812; she passing through all the trials incident to that war on the frontier. She witnessed the disgraceful surrender of Detroit. In 1831, she with her husband emigrated to Branch County. When she arrived where now stands the flourishing City of Coldwater she was sheltered by her son-in-law, Mr. Allen Tibbitts, in the only house then standing on the ground of the present city. After spending just time enough to visit her children, she and her husband started for their contemplated farm home in the township of Girard, Branch County. At this time Girard was an Indian village, and the whole region round about was in almost the undisturbed possession of the Indians, of whom there were hundreds, while of the whites there were but few. After spending a few years in Girard, more white people having come to join the white population, a Methodist quarterly meeting was announced to be held in Coldwater. The Methodists from far and near were notified, and at the appointed time the Presiding Elder, Rev. James Gilruth, riding one horse and leading another, as was his custom, appeared to fill the appointment he had made. The services were conducted in the aforesaid house of Mr. Tibbitts, which was a house of but one room, and this answered the purpose of church, class room, parlor, sitting room, dining room, kitchen and bed room. Thirty-one worshipped in that house, the deceased among the number, and tarried there during the quarterly meeting. It was a joyous meeting of Christians. The communicants came to worship God— no conventional nonsense prevented the full enjoyment of the occasion. Soon after this memorable quarterly meeting, the first held in the county, the deceased with her husband moved to Coldwater, where she remained uninterruptedly until her death. She was a firm and uncompromising Christian woman. Her religion was a garment worn every day. She was the life and soul of every circle in which she moved. With a wonderful memory of particulars, she always interested and enlivened by her conversation. She was the first to rise when opportunity was given for those who wished to join in the first class of Methodists of the State of Michigan, and is the last to fall in death and go to her reward in heaven, of that class. Her husband, and other members of that first class of *seven* organized in Detroit in 1810, are gone. Her husband was the first class-leader and the first licensed exhorter in the State, and continued to hold these offices, and also that of Sabbath-School Superintendent, until his death, which occurred about eighteen years since. The deceased was punctual to all her engagements as a mother, citizen and Christian. For years, if any of her family or sisters in the Church were sick, the first person sent for was 'Aunty McCarty,' as she was affectionately called. She never made excuses, but night and day, rain or shine, she would promptly repair to the sick couch and intelligently administer to the wants of the sufferer.

"She was a true friend to the Union. She knew what it had cost of sacrifice and blood; and when the rebels struck at the life of the nation she yielded her full share of children and grandchildren for its maintenance. To show her attachment to the Union, it may be proper to give an incident. She had a sister living South during the Rebellion. That sister, in the last letter she wrote the deceased, undertook the defense of the right of secession. She replied warmly, denying the right of the South to go away, maintaining the cause of the Union of our fathers. This closed the correspondence. She has lived to see the State take the place of the Territory, and the city grow up around that one house. In all her stay she was the universal favorite. She was a remarkably healthy and active woman, and industrious to a fault. She was known only to be loved. Her end was such as might have been expected from her life. She had stood up for Jesus for over half a century. Not long before her death she said to the writer: 'I know in whom I trust.' She quietly fell asleep in Jesus—'blessed sleep.'"

Thus far, Mr. Chandler. Her decease occurred June 10th, 1863. In her death we lose the last link connecting us with the Methodist Episcopal Church in Detroit before the war.

WILLIAM STACY was converted soon after Robert Abbott, and joined the Church at the same time with him and others to form the first Christian Church, other than Roman Catholic, in this peninsula. He was not large of stature nor very active in religious meetings, but he was firm, quiet and steady in his religious life. He settled in the vicinity of Detroit some time prior to 1810, though the exact time cannot be ascertained now. At the time of his death, which occurred in 1827, he resided on a farm on the River Rouge, about seven miles out of the City of Detroit. He left a fragrant memorial behind. He was the first of the original seven who entered into the heavenly rest. In his religious devotions he was very devout and earnest, but not boisterous. He attended the prayer and class meetings very constantly, and always took part in the exercises. He was a very devoted Christian, and died in full hope of a glorious immortality.

BETSEY STACY was the wife of the above, and survived him for a number of years. Her maiden name was Thomas. She was born in Newtown, New York, and was converted to God about the same time with her husband, so that she joined the Methodist Episcopal Church on the same day and was one of the noted seven. She was large of stature, commanding and noble in her appearance, and of an ardent temperament. Her early advantages for religious and intellectual culture were very limited, but her conversion was sound and clear. Her religious life was steady and consistent. She was more active in Church work and religious meetings than her husband, and could exhort with great power, sympathy and effect. She lived a widow for a number of years after the death of Mr. Stacy, and then married for her second husband, Philip Warren, a very devoted and excellent Christian man, with whom she lived happily for several years. Her faith and religious activity continued to the last. She died in a good old age, in 1853. Her funeral sermon was preached by Rev. C. C. Olds, who was stationed in the Congress Street Church, Detroit, of which she was a member at the time of her death. In all her life and devotions she demonstrated the power of Divine grace to purify and sustain; and when she came to the Jordan of death she feared no evil, but passed peacefully away.

SARAH MACOMB is the least known of all these seven. We are able at this distance of time, in the absence of records, to obtain but very little information in regard to this Christian lady. She resided on the Rouge; was the wife of Major Macomb, a major in the militia, and who did not live very long after the war. After his death she married a Mr. Corbus, and some time about 1830 she removed to the eastern edge of Branch County, where she lived for a number of years, and has finally gone to her heavenly home, we have no doubt. Of her last years we have not been able to gather much information, especially as it regards her religious life. She was one of the early converts, and joined the Church as soon as it was proposed to organize one here. During the dark days of the war she stood firm in the cause, and was one of the members recognized by the minister who came first after the war. We have no doubt of her peaceful end from the devotion she made in early life and in the beginning of the work here. We have not been able to ascertain the precise time or the circumstances of her death.

Thus have we given a brief biographical or memorial sketch of the original *seven* who constituted the first Protestant Church organized in Detroit—in Michigan. They embraced four families—that is, there were three men and their wives, and one lady whose husband did not join. There are a few particulars, very interesting, worthy of notice. The first of these is, that these original seven should alone have remained faithful and adhered together to the cause of Christ during the struggle of the war, while all the others who joined afterwards were scattered—though they did not all give up the cause of religion, as was the case with Mrs. Witherell, of whom we shall give a notice a little farther along. Another singular and interesting fact is, that not one of these seven ever became an apostate from the faith, but all retained their membership uninterruptedly through life, and died in the faith and peace of the Gospel. A third particular is, that these seven alone, five years later, at the close of the war, should have been recognized as the Methodist Episcopal Church in Detroit, by Rev. Mr. Hickox, while all the others—for the Church had increased to thirty before the war—should have been scattered. This last fact is so singular that we would have been very slow to believe it had we not had the united testimony of four of these same persons. As we have been personally acquainted with five of these original seven, we have received the statement from their own lips. We record these things to the praise and glory of Him who had called them out of darkness into "His marvelous light."

AMY WITHERELL. One very pious lady has generally been overlooked, in speaking of the early Methodists of this State, probably for the reason that she left Detroit on a visit to Vermont sometime in 1811, in a little less than a year from the time she first came here, she being afraid of the Indians, and did not return until 1817—till the country became thoroughly quiet after the war. This lady was Mrs. Amy Witherell, wife of Judge James Witherell, one of the Territorial Judges, and mother of the late Judge B. F. H. Witherell of Detroit. This lady came to Detroit to reside, in the autumn of 1810, soon after the Methodist Society was organized, and had been a member of the Methodist Episcopal Church in Vermont. She was born in 1778, and died in Detroit in 1848, aged 70 years. It was our good fortune to have been somewhat acquainted with her. She possessed a very vigorous and independent mind; had an amiable disposition, and always shed a radiance of delight around her. She was converted to an experience of Christian grace and love in early youth, and joined the Methodist Episcopal Church in Vermont, at a time when it required no little independence of mind to do so, as well as courage to be associated with them. One little incident will serve to show how the Methodist Church was regarded at that time. Her husband had come to Detroit—having been appointed one of the Judges of the Territory—to prepare to bring his family here to reside. Mrs. Witherell wished to attend a Methodist meeting a few miles from her home, and went to a neighbor to procure a horse to ride, as it was rather too long a walk for her. The neighbor said he was willing to lend her the horse, but he wished she would hitch the animal out of hearing of the preaching. He was afraid the Methodist preaching would contaminate even his horse. Mrs. Witherell was a very pious, consistent Christian, an ornament to the Church for many years, and died in great peace. She became a Methodist at a time when it was far from being fashionable to become one. Christianity, as believed and presented by the Methodists, she looked upon as being the religion of the heart, and as such, she gave to it her unqualified assent. Though born in Rhode Island, about 1786 she removed to Vermont, and there first heard the early pioneer Methodist preachers, of whom, in after life, she frequently spoke as earnest men of God. Through a long life there was "no variableness or shadow of turning" with her. She well understood the principles of Methodism, having made herself familiar with Fletcher's Checks, Wesley's Sermons, and other works on the subject. She was always ready to give a reason for the hope that was in her. She was not fond of controversy, but when sought by "the orthodox," as the Calvinists called themselves, she was ready, and they seldom retired with many laurels. Her son, Hon. B. F. H. Witherell, said to us once, "I recollect many years ago in Vermont, she attended a Calvinist Conference meeting. The clergyman, who was a friend of our family, came up to her and said, in his peculiar, friendly way, 'Well, Mrs. Witherell, when shall we have you with us?' She promptly replied, 'Never while I have my senses,'—which at once settled the question."

We take pleasure in introducing the following sketch from the pen of the late Bishop Thomson, when he was editor of the *Western Christian Advocate*, under date of Oct. 6th, 1858: "Of Mrs. Amy Witherell I must be allowed to say something, as, through some oversight, no notice of her death has been taken, I believe. in any of our Church papers. She was descended from Roger Williams, and was born in Smithfield, Rhode Island, on June 17th, 1778. While but a child she was removed to Vermont, where she enjoyed the ministry of Bishop Hedding and some of his worthy associates. Under the first Methodist sermon she ever heard, she became convinced of the truth of Methodist doctrines, and she never changed her opinion. Early a subject of grace and a member of the Church, she remained faithful unto death. In 1810, when Detroit was a mere village and military post, she removed to it. As the Indians here received their annuities, Mrs. Witherell found her home unpleasant, for from early life she had entertained a great fear of the savages. Her husband, therefore, proposed that his wife should take the three youngest children East, and spend the winter there. As the prospect of war soon arose, they did not return in the spring, but were followed by the rest of the family—two daughters—who returned by land.

"In 1813 Judge Witherell purchased the property where the Troy Conference Academy now stands, and where his family remained till 1817. In this year they returned to Detroit. It was before the whistle of the steamboat had been heard upon the Western lakes, and their conveyance from Buffalo was by a small sailing vessel. During the voyage a sudden storm arose, drenching all the passengers on deck. Mrs. Witherell escaped to the hold, where, being fastened down, she remained without food or light for thirty hours. At length the vessel arrived off Cleveland, where the people, surveying her from the shore, were expecting to see it go down. Providentially, through an opening in the bar of driftwood of the river just large enough to admit its passage, it escaped.

"Mrs. Witherell was a lady of a remarkably sweet spirit. Her life was one of trial, affliction, bereavement and persecution; yet she passed it patiently in faith, joyful through hope, and rooted in charity. She was called to lay in the grave several of her children under the most painful circumstances; one shortly after his graduation, another while midshipman in the navy—all of them of great promise; yet she murmured not. The ten last years of her life she spent in widowhood; but cheerful and happy, a pleasant companion either for youth or age.

"During her residence in New England the Methodists were few, feeble, and much misrepresented. Mrs. Witherell was often assailed by sarcasm, raillery and abuse, as well as argument and remonstrance; but having a ready memory and a ready utterance, she always had a reason for her hope, and so happy and so triumphant in her replies that she received from her neighbors the title conferred by the Pope upon King Henry the Eighth, 'Defender of the Faith.'

"She was not so bigoted as to prevent her from attending sister churches when her own was closed, and sometimes catholicity was mistaken for wavering. While in attendance at a hyper-Calvinistic Church, on an examination of candidates for admission, a reverend gentleman approaching her, inquired with a pompous air, 'When, Mrs. Witherell, shall we have you among us?' 'Not while I have my senses,' was the reply. The prejudice against Methodism at that time can now scarcely be conceived. A lady, known as an exemplary Christian, applied to the Church to which she belonged for a letter to unite with the Methodists; but she was turned out to the buffetings of Satan. The pastor of that Church, however, on his dying bed sent for Methodist ministers, to pray and talk with him.

"In Fairhaven the pastor of a Calvinistic Church forbade his son's attendance on the ministry of the Methodists, and when he disobeyed, he followed him, and taking him by the collar, led him out.

"Mrs. Witherell's house was a hospitable home for the preachers, among whom she used often to speak of Byington, White, Draper, Lewis and Dunbar. She died August 7th, 1848. She was one of the excellent of the earth. After her visits to our parsonage, my good wife was accustomed to find some pieces of silver or gold dropped into a vase or concealed beneath a cloth. Of her it might be said, 'She stretcheth out her hand to the poor; yea, she stretcheth out her hands to the needy. She openeth her mouth with wisdom, and in her hand is the law of kindness. Her children rise up and call her blessed; yea, her husband also praiseth her.'

"She served her generation and fell asleep in Jesus, in full prospect of the resurrection morning. I find one daughter of hers still in the Detroit Church, as an ornamental pillar."*

At this point we must close our first period of History, because there is now a chasm in ministerial services for the space of three years. The horrors of war were experienced by the inhabitants of Detroit and vicinity—Eastern Michigan—and, as we have seen, the ministers of the Gospel were prevented from ministering to the Church here. During the past period there was but one year in which there was, designedly, more than one minister on the Detroit Circuit; that was the last year before the war commenced, when Mr. Holmes was assisted by Silas Hopkins. It is probable they so arranged the Circuit that there was preaching regularly at each appointment once in two weeks. But there were a few very earnest men and women, as we have seen, who during their deprivation of ministerial service, kept up their regular services, and maintained the work of God. It is very difficult, if not impossible, for us at this period of the growth of the city and country, and of the Church, to realize the difficulties they had to encounter. But God was with them, and though most of them were dispersed—some going to other parts, and some going back to sin—a few stood fast in the faith, and kept the Church alive, the fortunes of which will be recorded in our further History.

*This was Mrs. Mary A. Palmer, who has since died, viz : March 19th, 1874, after a very brief illness. A memoir of her will be given in the proper place.

CHAPTER III.

Close of the War—First Appointment—Other Denominations—Monteith—Hickox in Canada—
Col. James' Order—Success—Reflections—Presbyterian Ministers—Friendship Interrupted
—Mitchell—Evangelistic Society—Grant of Land—Presbyterian Church Organized—
Laning Appointed—Harmon—Numbers—Davis—Conclusion.

WE had to close our last period just at the opening of the war between Great Britain and the United States. War was declared on the part of the United States against Great Britain in June, 1812, and Michigan being directly on the border, had to be much involved. Detroit and Monroe were the only points where anything of importance could be transacted. The bloody massacre at Monroe or French Town has passed into history. Our business is not so much with the State as the Church, still we must take sufficient notice of the affairs of the State, as to enable the reader to appreciate the difficulties with which the Church had to struggle.

This chapter properly opens a new period in our History, but with no very flattering prospects. The storms and tempests which had raged in this region, from the time the United States declared war against Great Britain until peace was declared in 1815, laid waste every fair prospect and scattered almost entirely the little flock of Christians who lived in and about Detroit.

We may here remark that no other denomination of Christians had as yet made any effort to establish a Church in this place or in this peninsula. Nor had any other ministers ventured to brave the difficulties and dangers and to endure the privations necessary to come here to preach the Gospel, with the one exception before named, and he preached but a few times and gave up the field in despair. All that had been done for the moral and religious improvement of the people, except so far as Romanism does that, had been done by the Methodists alone.

As soon as the clouds of war began to disappear, so that it was practicable to keep open the intercourse between the two nations, ministers were sent to this field; and Detroit appears again on our Minutes in 1815. The Genesee Conference met at Lyons, in the State of New York, June 29th, 1815, when the condition of the people of Detroit and the adjacent country was duly considered. It was determined at this session to send them a minister. According to this determination, *Rev. Joseph Hickox* was appointed to Detroit, which was included in the Upper Canada District, with *Wm. Case* as Presiding Elder. The Circuit at the time was in chaos, and he was expected to include a wide range of country, requiring a vast amount of labor and self-sacrifice to make its rounds. What an undertaking! But where was there ever a field of labor coming within the range of possibilities, that was neglected or abandoned by the Methodist itinerants! They have always been noted for persevering labors.

Mr. Hickox was a young, unmarried man, full of life and energy, having been but three years in the ministry. He was ordained Elder this year, which was a year in advance of the regular time, in view of his being appointed to this distant and isolated field. What more noble spirit could be exhibited than was here displayed! Here he was, a lone man assigned to this distant field of labor, to gain his support as best he could among the people. There was then no Missionary Society upon which he could rely for a support. He had to go out in the name of his Master, hardly knowing whither he went. He was a young man of talent, whose words dropped from his lips with a peculiar unction; he was of the Saint Chrysostom cast. He possessed an earnest piety and zeal that carried him through all the difficulties and embarrassments which presented themselves in his path. Mr. Hickox continued on this Circuit for two years.

This chapter will embrace what we may denominate the second period of Protestantism in Michigan. This period will run through a term of five years and will take in a little wider range than the former, because the country having become a little more settled, the Circuit embraced a wider extent of Michigan soil. We make this period extend to the time when Michigan was transferred from the Genesee to the Ohio Conference, which was done by the General Conference of 1820. This period extends from June 29th, 1815, to July, 1820. The first appointment from the Ohio Conference was made in August, 1820. *Joseph Hickox* was the first minister appointed, and *Truman Dixon* was the last. We shall soon see what changes shall have occurred in these five years.

As was to be expected, the ravages of war had made their impression on the feeble Christian Church which had been organized in Detroit. They had now been three years without a pastor, and in the midst of war scenes. In consequence of this interruption of pastoral and ministerial labor, and the demoralizing influences of war, when Mr. Hickox arrived he only found *seven* who "had not defiled their garments," and who wished to be regarded as members of a Christian Church. It was emphatically a little Church in the wilderness. How their hearts must have leaped for joy when a minister was sent to them again! It was like the dawning of the morning after a long and dreary night. This was the number of Protestant Christians in Michigan in 1815.

They were at once recognized by Mr. Hickox as a Christian Church, and were cheered and animated in their Christian course by the regular visits and ministrations of this young and active minister of Jesus Christ. There were several of the Corbuses, Thomases and Hanchetts residing on the River Rouge, from three to eight miles out of the city, who soon became members, so that the Society increased with considerable rapidity; nevertheless, it was subject to considerable fluctuations. The increase of population was slow, as yet, and the labors of the minister in Michigan was confined to Detroit and its vicinity. The precise numbers in Society for each year cannot be ascertained, as the old class-books are not to be found and the Conference Minutes include the members on the Canada side also. It is much to be regretted that the early records were so loosely kept. Indeed, no book of records was used except the class book, and that often consisted of a single sheet of paper folded so as to make several pages. When this little book was filled, or perhaps when the list of members was revised, the names were transferred to a new one of similar capacity, leaving out all who had died, removed, withdrawn or been expelled; then this was usually thrown aside as a matter of no more consequence. The thought was not entertained that these old books would ever be of any service or interest as historical references. Mr. McCarty, however, who was the first class leader in Michigan and continued in that capacity for many years, took the precaution to preserve nearly all his books—had them all stitched together and neatly preserved until his death. When he died, the minister who preached his funeral sermon called on the widow and obtained these books, with the pledge that he would return them—a pledge that he failed to redeem. As this minister shortly after left the place and the ministry, and died, it has been impossible to reclaim them. We can now only arrive approximately at the numbers in Society in Michigan, from the General Minutes, because the Detroit Circuit extended into Canada, and the majority of the members resided on that side of the river. In this state of facts we have had to rely very much on the recollections of the few relics of those days with whom we have been able to converse. These recollections conflict in some instances. But we have to make the best we can of their statements; for what we have lost in regard to these things is irreclaimably lost.

As before stated, Mr. Hickox was appointed to this field, and after a tedious and perilous journey, he reached Detroit and commenced his labors. An account of his journey will be found in the next chapter. Mr. Hickox gives the following statement of affairs here on his arrival: "In that portion of the work situated on the Canada side I found the remnants of a few societies which had been formed by the Rev. William Case and his successors; but the tumults of war had destroyed every vestige of organization. In Michigan, some itinerants had labored here, partially before the war."

Mr. Hickox continues his narrative: "Among the Methodists I found in Detroit was Robert Abbott, Esq. He was an upright and useful man, and of essential service in building up the Church there. He introduced me to the Governor, General Cass, who received me kindly, expressing his pleasure at finding I was to labor in that field; said that the Council House should always be at my service when I came, and himself and family would be constant attendants. He afterwards showed every favor that could be desired.

"At that time the work placed before the missionary was such as to appall the heart, and such did he feel to be his own inadequacy for it that nothing short of his confidence in the power and abounding grace of God could have emboldened him to undertake it or to persevere in it. Detroit was a sink of iniquity The original inhabitants were Canadian French, characterized by all the loose morals of secluded Catholicism. Besides, it had been under martial law for three years, alternately under the British and American dominancy. The pandemonium created by rum-drinking British soldiers, Indians and French may more easily be imagined than described. It was awful.

"Though the morals of our troops were of a higher grade than the others, yet war in its mildest form is an enemy to righteousness and temperance. The only Americans in the city (Detroit) were a few traders, whose antipathy to religion was proverbial. When I arrived, Generals Harrison, Brown and Cass were holding conferences with the Indians, preparatory to a general treaty of peace.

The garrison consisted of a large number of soldiers. In this state of society but little impression could be made by a sermon once in three weeks. True, the Council House, a large and commodious building, was always filled with attentive auditors—the superior officers setting a decorous example by their uniform presence and respectful attention. But in my hurried rounds on a three weeks' circuit, traveling some *three hundred miles*, my stay in Detroit was necessarily so short that I could not follow up to any extent, by pastoral visitation, any impression that might have been made by the labor of the pulpit."

It will be seen, hereafter, that it was a great mistake and a sad misfortune to our cause—the cause of religion—that more concentrated labor was not bestowed on the City of Detroit at that time. But Methodists have not even yet learned much wisdom, in this respect, from the losses of the past. The fact is, a Metdodist preacher's heart is so overflowing with benevolence and so burdened with desire for the immediate salvation of sinners, that he finds it exceedingly difficult to turn away from the call of any destitute place. The circuits had to be so constituted as to supply as many of these places as possible. In this way they have pioneered most of the new country, and have, too often, left many of the growing towns to be occupied by others. Such was the case with Detroit. Either the ultimate importance of the place was not perceived or it was not regarded. Perhaps this is not much to be wondered at, after all.

The souls of the people scattered through the country were valuable, to be sure; but, then, it is right to have an eye to the greatest amount of good ultimately, and to concentrate labor at the centers of influence. Every one knows that important towns exert a wide influence over a large extent of country ; and that the power of a religious denomination for good is, to a considerable extent, dependent on its position in such towns. The reason of this is so patent that it is not necessary to say anything more about it. Many have thought that the Methodist economy was not adapted to large towns and cities. They have confounded policy with polity, that is all. And herein lies their mistake : for the doctrines of Methodism can be just as well appreciated in cities as in the country, and its earnest ministry is just as valuable for the one as the other. But by this disregard for the ultimate good they have so failed, in many instances, to meet the wishes of the people as to the frequency of services, that they have turned their attention in some other direction for a supply, and when they have waked up to the matter the people have become so bound to others that, though they would have preferred their ministry, they have not been able to call them back, and the Methodists have had to occupy a secondary position. People in towns and cities will not be satisfied with only occasional services; and if they cannot be supplied by the denomination which they would have preferred, they will take up with such as they can get.

We know it may be said, in palliation of this blunder, that they had but few members upon whom a minister might depend for a support. But cannot a Methodist minister live where any other minister can? Take this very case: Mr. Hickox might have secured, at once, the whole of the people that would have given any support to any one—we mean the Protestant portion—because General Cass, who was the Territorial Governor, and others in authority gave him a cordial welcome and attended his ministry whenever he came, and of course, would not then have thought of looking for any other if he could have supplied them every Sabbath; and would have supported him too, at least as well as he was supported on the whole Circuit, as he had the entire ground for one year. But the desire "to possess all the land that joins," led him to give them services only once in *three weeks*, and as he said, not following up the labors of the Sabbath by mingling with the people during the week, all or nearly all the labor was lost; and when another came and offered to supply them more frequently, he gathered them around him. We do not intend to censure Mr. Hickox, because he was only carrying out what was then the policy of the Church. If he had adopted a different line of policy he would have been censured by his superiors in office, as wishing to escape from the hard service of visiting the sparse settlements. The same line of policy is still pursued, to a certain extent. The Rev. Alfred Brunson, who was appointed to Detroit Circuit in 1822, was the first who ventured to change the policy in regard to the City of Detroit. He concentrated his labor here and left the care of the Circuit chiefly to his colleague. This was the beginning of a new era for Methodism in this city, and if it had only been properly carried out afterwards it would have been better for their cause.

The next summer after Mr. Hickox came—that is, in Jnne, 1816, —a Presbyterian minister came and settled himself down among the people and proposed supplying them every Sabbath, and even wished and attempted to crowd Mr. Hickox out from the third Sabbath in the evening, as we shall see after a little. He was sent out under the auspices of the Board of the General Assembly of the Presbyterian Church. The result of his coming, with the proposition

HISTORY OF PROTESTANTISM IN MICHIGAN. 61

to supply them constantly was that the people, not sympathizing with the policy of leaving them two-thirds of the time, in order to supply other places, gave their support to the new comer, and he organized a Society—not a Church—composed of persons of all the different Protestant creeds in the place. This they did, notwithstanding they would have much preferred Mr. Hickox if they could have had his services. Had the Methodist Missionary adopted the same course the first year he was here he might have secured all this, which would have given the Methodists such a position that nothing but the veriest recreancy to their trust could ever have placed them in a secondary position in this community. Another error in policy prevailed in the Methodist Church at that day, which at a subsequent period nearly destroyed what interest they had gained in this city; that is, the location of their churches. It was thought they must be located out of the town, or at least on the outskirts, so as to be out of the noise and bustle of business. But it is useless to speculate about these things now, as that cannot retrieve their losses, and we have introduced these thoughts here simply for the purpose of leaving on record our views of such a policy, and with the faint hope that they may contribute a little to encourage a different course of operation in new places that are yet to spring up. We should concentrate efforts at the centers of influence, and locate our churches in the midst of the people and not hide them away as if we were ashamed to have the people find them.

We have now fully introduced our missionary to the notice of the reader in connection with the field of his operations, and must resume the chain of history. Having gone up and inspected the walls, he set himself at work to rebuild. What a prospect! A lone workman, and such a vast work before him! But he knew in whom he trusted. He was able in a short time to gather in the few who had been members prior to the war, and a few joined anew. The work accomplished this year was that the stakes were stuck, the work was marked out, and the few lay-helpers to be found were arranged so as to operate in concert for the advancement of the great cause. Some of the members of the Church having their residence on the Rouge, they had a place of meeting there, about six miles out of the city; yet not to the abandonment of the city, for Mr. Hickox preached in the city on Sabbath evenings, once in three weeks. He ought to have concentrated all the time for Sabbath services in the city. In like manner, when it was determined to build a church it was located on the River Rouge, instead of in the city. This was another great error.

Mr. Hickox at the close of this year reported one hundred and forty members for Detroit Circuit, at the Conference which met at Paris, Canada, July 17th, 1816; but most of these were in Canada. At this Conference he was returned to Detroit Circuit, and labored faithfully for another year, and with encouraging success; so much so that he reported *thirty* members for Detroit—that is, for Michigan— the members on the Canada side having been attached to the Thames Circuit. This is the first report which gives us the definite numbers in Michigan. The preaching places in Michigan, for the two years in which Mr. Hickox traveled the Circuit, were Detroit City, River Rouge, and French Town, now Monroe. This latter place, he says, was a field ripe for the harvest but it was forty miles distant from the other appointments, and a horrible road must be passed over twice through a lonely wilderness to supply it; and the missionary being obliged generally to leave his horse on the Canada side, on account of the difficulty of ferriage, he could only visit it occasionally. Hence the harvest could not be gathered. Mr. Hickox states that in 1822, after his location, he went there to attend a quarterly meeting with Rev. John P. Kent, at which time a gracious revival occurred and a large class was formed—large for the times. This class met principally a little above the present site of the town. As these were the only points at which the Americans had made settlements, the work could not extend further in Michigan. Happy would it have been for the Methodist cause if he and his successors had confined their labors to these points. This, however, would have been so much in contravention of the spirit of the times that it would not have been tolerated at all.

Although not in the direct line of Michigan Protestantism, we shall be pardoned for giving some notice of the trials and successes of our missionary on the other side of the Detroit River, especially as these were passed through and accomplished in connection with his efforts to establish and advance the cause on this side. The account is given in his own words:

"As I passed through the adjacent parts of Canada, it pleased the Lord to follow the Word with such power that the people were strongly aroused to a consideration of their spiritual interests, and flocked to the places of meeting, on week days as well as on Sundays. This provoked some of the more respectable British sinners, and they accused me of being a disturber of the peace. This was so soon after the war that civil government was not yet reestablished, and the country was under martial law. Col. James was then in command near Sandwich, and seemed to have jurisdiction along the lines. To him the gentry complained of me as a sort of spy, and he issued orders to have me arrested and brought before him. Having obtained information of this movement, it seemed to me to be most prudent to anticipate an arrest; so, mounting my horse, I rode in haste to his quarters before my whereabouts could be discovered. By the advice of friends, I had worn the sash of a British officer, which gave me immunity when among the crowds of Indians that beset my way. When the attendants of the Colonel saw this, they supposed me to be somebody of importance. They held my horse and stirrups, and helped me to dismount. The Colonel himself, misled by this, came to the piazza, received me with the utmost courtesy, and showed me into his best room.

"I opened the matter by saying, 'Col. James, I suppose I am the man you want to see.'

"'What is your name?' he asked.

"'Joseph Hickox,' I replied. 'I am a Methodist preacher doing the work of a missionary through this country, trying to promote peace among men. I have been told you are opposed to this, and I have called to find out the reason.'

"He was taken all aback by the announcement, and looked blank. But soon rallying, he said politely that he had no objections to anything of that nature that I could do, but wished me all success and promised me the freedom of the country."

This incident was only characteristic of the tact and shrewdness of the man. This element of character fitted him well for the times, and demonstrated the sagacity of Bishop McKendree, who made the appointment. He succeeded in forming several new Societies in Canada, but as these are not in the line of our History, no further mention will be made of them. As we have already suggested, the rides and labors of the missionary to fulfill the duties connected with Detroit Circuit for these two years were very fatiguing and excessive. The reader will understand this better by a reference to some facts. Three times every three weeks he had to pass through a wilderness of *fifty-seven miles* without human habitation, and to swim his horse *five times* each trip. In the winter, when the clumsy ferry boats were stopped, he had to leave his horse on the Canada side and to walk up and down the Detroit River, seeking the strongest ice. Sometimes he was obliged to jump from cake to cake of broken ice, and to leap over wide fissures, in order to get to and from Detroit. But God gave him grace to meet all these difficulties and preserved him in the midst of these dangers, and made him happy as he passed through and triumphed over them. We have these statements from his own pen.

At the end of his first year Mr. Hickox makes the following very appropriate reflections: "When the chaotic state of the country, and the multitudes who are perishing for lack of knowledge, are considered, the privilege of preaching the world-wide Gospel and a free salvation is so great that the labor and danger of doing so sink into insignificance, and the remembrance of that work is full of sweetness to me." He adds, "It was no small thing to ride a thousand miles to and from conference." That is very true; besides, the journey had to be made on horseback.

During the second year that Mr. Hickox remained on this Circuit the difficulties of traveling were somewhat removed, as the country was slowly recovering from the disasters of the war—immigration had begun to set in, in this direction, and some improvements were made, as also some other advantages were secured. All the while of his first year he had been a solitary watchman—beyond the hail of any other—and had all the labor and responsibility to himself. During the time of his absence from Detroit attending the Conference, a Presbyterian minister appeared at Detroit, whom Mr. Hickox found on his return, as he hoped, to share the responsibility of holding forth the word of life to an ungodly city, and to be a fellow-laborer—a helper in the Christian work.

This was the first introduction of Presbyterian preaching into Detroit. This was in June, 1816. He was a well educated young man, and gentlemanly in his manners. These two young men soon formed a very pleasant acquaintance, which, however, was interrupted in a short time, very unexpectedly to the Methodist Missionary. The circumstances of the interruption were these, as related to the writer by Mr. Hickox himself: Henry Ryan, the Presiding Elder of the District, had preached to a large congregation in the Council House. Rev. John Monteith, the Presbyterian minister was present. After the sermon he was introduced to the Presiding Elder, whereupon the usual social greetings were exchanged; after which Mr. Hickox remarked: "Mr. Monteith, after you preach, a week from next Sabbath, will you be good enough to give out my appointment for evening worship, to refresh the minds of the people?" "I don't know how that will be," said he, stiffly. "I have an appointment at that hour, myself; and I want you to change your time of preaching to some week-day evening."

Mr. Ryan said, "Brother Hickox, probably you had better

remove your appointment to some week evening, to make all things smooth."

To this proposition Mr. Hickox very justly responded: "Brother Ryan, I have been preaching here for a year past, every three weeks, before any other preacher came here. I think it ungenerous to ask me to change, when Mr. Monteith has all the time to himself except one Sabbath night in three weeks. I cannot consent to change." He ought to have changed so as to have preached in Detroit every Sabbath.

"Act your pleasure," said Brother Ryan. "I don't wish to dictate." He ought to have stood up for his preacher. Instead of advising him to yield, he ought to have encouraged him to hold on, and to have rebuked the other sharply for his assumption.

This occurrence was so public that the difficulty became generally known—the feelings of the people became interested to see how the thing would terminate. The consequence of this interest was, that the house was unusually crowded when Mr Hickox arrived. Mr. Monteith had reached the house before him and occupied the desk. When Mr. Hickox came in the following colloquy occurred:

Mr. Hickox—"Mr. Monteith, do you expect to preach to-night?"

Mr. M. (very short and pettishly)—"*I do. I do.*"

Mr. H.—"Very well. I shall preach after you have done."

Mr. M. preached. After the sermon and prayer the conversation was resumed.

Mr. H.—"I wish you would omit singing and I will preach."

Mr. M.—"I don't think the people will be willing to hear you."

M. H.—"I will ask them."

He immediately stepped into the desk and told the congregation the reason of his being prevented from preaching, and said if they would remain in their seats he would then give them a sermon.

Mr. M.—"I will leave the desk, then."

Mr. H.—"Act your pleasure. The desk is large enough for us both."

The congregation having signified their desire to hear him by remaining quiet, Mr. Hickox gave them a sermon, during the delivery of which they preserved perfect quiet and gave undivided attention to him. When he had finished, he announced that in three weeks from that time he would preach there again, according to his established custom. "I occupy this house by the permission of the Governor. When that permission is withdrawn I shall leave, and not before."

Mr. Monteith, who had remained, replied: "The Governor will not have the impoliteness to *tell* you to withdraw your appointments." To which Mr. Hickox responded: "If the Governor will tolerate you in making appointments in opposition to mine and in refusing me the pulpit when mine become due, it is all I ask. The same authority that admitted me here is necessary to exclude me from the place."

Mr. M., in a somewhat subdued tone, and as if he wished to drop the matter and had laid aside his assumption, said: "Your manner of preaching is so different from mine. You can preach *extempore*; I cannot. You can get a congregation at any time, at three hours' notice. So I thought you might change your time to a week evening, and give me the advantage of all the Sabbath services."

Mr. Hickox then told him that he could not comply with his wishes without deranging the whole plan of his Circuit labor; and the Circuit being very extensive, this would be very difficult to do. The congregation waited very patiently until the parley was over, and, as might have been expected, much prejudice was created against the mistaken man, in consequence of his course, and sympathy was raised in favor of Mr. Hickox. No further attempt was made to drive the missionary from this part of the field. The above circumstances occurred during the early part of the second year that Mr. Hickox was appointed to the Detroit Circuit.

In late autumn or early winter of the second year the Methodist Missionary was much comforted, not exactly "by the coming of Titus," but by the coming of Rev. *Joseph Mitchell*, a venerable local preacher of very popular talents. This Mr. Mitchell must not be confounded with William Mitchell who was here in 1810, and organized the first Society, or Church. Joseph Mitchell was a great and useful pioneer of Methodism in different parts of the Western country. The crossing of Detroit River in the winter being attended with great difficulty and danger, Mr. Hickox confined his labors principally to the Canada side, and gave up the city work mainly to Mr. Mitchell. The latter soon became very popular among the people, and it seemed as if he would carry everything before him. He ought to have remained much longer than he did, and to have gathered in the fruits of his labors and concentrated the Methodistic strength in the city; for although he dealt very plainly with the people, they loved him. His great popularity aroused the jealous indignation of the Rev. Mr. M., the opponent of Mr. Hickox, so that he thought he must be put down, and thought he would try it, not having learned wisdom from his former defeat.

Mr. M. called to see the venerable Mr. Mitchell, when the following conversation took place. The conversation is given as narrated by Mr. Mitchell himself:

Mr. M. asked Mr. Mitchell, "Have you ever been to college?"

Mr. Mitchell responded, "I have been past a college."

Again Mr. M. said, "I wish to make an agreement with you not to preach doctrines."

Mr. Mitchell replied, "What! Not to preach the doctrines of Methodism! I am bound to preach them, for I believe every tittle of them to be true. Not to preach against Calvinism! That I am under the necessity of doing, for I believe it to be an erroneous system of doctrines."

Mr. Mitchell was a great opposer of Calvinism. This ended the colloquy, and the divine went away discomfited and unsatisfied. He had set his trap, but it would not spring as he wanted it to do. We are sorry to say that this same spirit characterized this same gentleman for many years after. He never succeeded in acquiring much love for Methodism.

We are indebted to Mr. Hickox for the following incident illustrative of Father Mitchell's manner and influence in the pulpit. On a certain occasion, the Council House was crowded, as indeed it generally was on Sunday. The Governor, and all the civil and military officers and men of note were present. The preacher's theme was, the necessity of the new birth. In the warmth of his application, with finger pointing with significant force, and eyes fixed upon the persons addressed, he cried out, "You, Governor! you, lawyers! you, judges! you, doctors! you must be converted and born again, or God will damn you as soon as the beggar on the dung hill." Deep silence prevailed, and a lasting impression was made. Some of the timid ones feared they would be offended.

The next morning Governor Cass sent him a complimentary note, containing *five dollars*, saying it was the best sermon he ever heard. Such was the position of Protestantism in Michigan, in the spring of 1817. It is unaccountable to us that this was not followed up, so as absolutely to have taken the City of Detroit for Christ. It is true, they had to contend against great immorality, but the wicked were held in awe. The people would have given the ministers a good support; and if these heavy blows, dealt out by such hands as Father Mitchell's, had been repeated a little longer, and the ends tied up well, by gathering the people into the Church, there might have been raised up such a Society as would, always afterwards, have held the commanding position in the place. Indeed, it is probable the people would have become so thoroughly Methodized, that they would not have thought of looking for any other Church for many years. Not only did the interests of Methodism demand this attention, but the cause of God as well; for the whole people were then so moved that a little more would have led them to a happy experience of divine grace.

Rev. Mr. Monteith commenced his labors in Detroit, as before stated, on the 6th of June, 1816, and the next year he succeeded in the organization of a Society, not a Church, entitled "The First Evangelistic Society," made up of persons of the Protestant faith, without reference to their Church predilections, for the support of the Gospel. They would have given their support to a Methodist preacher just as soon as to any other, if they could have had his services. Subsequently a petition was presented to the Governor and judges for a lot to be granted for a Protestant Church, which grant was not perfected till in 1825. It will, perhaps, be recollected that when the city was destroyed by fire, in 1805, Congress donated about ten thousand acres of land to the city as a relief fund, which included the city location, and that this land, upon a portion of which the city was laid out, was at the disposal of the Legislative Council of the Territory, which at that time consisted of the Governor and judges. Hence the application to them for a church lot. Their petition was not immediately granted, but in 1819, in accordance with said petition, land was granted on the east side of Woodward Avenue, extending from Larned street to within about sixty feet of Congress street. The deed for this was not granted till in December, 1825. Not long after the grant, and before the deed was executed, a small house of worship was built on the lot, by the contributions of all, and it was intended as common property. In a few years, however, the Presbyterians having obtained a controlling influence in the Society, now called "The First Protestant Society," this house and all the lands were voted to their exclusive use, and the Methodists, who had contributed their full proportion towards the erection of the house, were left to find a place of worship where they could. "The First Protestant Society," now become Presbyterian, finally relinquished a narrow strip of this land, on the north side, to the Protestant Episcopal Church, on which they erected a small church, which remained till the spring of 1844.

A Presbyterian Church was not organized in Detroit till 1825, but Mr. Monteith continued his labors among the people until 1822, when his relation was dissolved. The Presbyterians seem not to have had any regular pastor until the Church was organized, in 1825, when Rev. Noah M. Wells came and served for several years.

HISTORY OF PROTESTANTISM IN MICHIGAN. 69

After this little digression, we return to the regular line of our History. Such was the position and influence of Messrs. Hickox and Mitchell that, if they had followed up the labors they had bestowed and the impressions they had made, by devoting their time to the place and by mingling freely with the people, they might have possessed the entire ground for many years. Mr. Mitchell left in the spring. Why he did not remain longer cannot now be ascertained. Probably his business demanded his attention elsewhere. Mr. Hickox felt himself in duty bound to travel his large Circuit, and so let the advantage slip away.

The Genesee Conference held its session in Elizabethtown, Canada, commencing June 21st, 1817, at which time Gideon Laning, a young and active minister, though married, was appointed to Detroit Circuit. Mr. Laning's labors were somewhat interrupted by sickness, but he did what he could and was assisted by Thomas Harmon, a local preacher, who took the principal charge of the erection of the log church on the Rouge, which was built this year. At the end of the year, when he numbered the hosts of Israel under his charge, he found he had gained *ten*, and returned *forty* members of Society.

There was nothing out of the ordinary course of events that occurred this year to be worthy of special record, except the building of the church, noticed elsewhere. The usual labor, toil and suffering accompanied the pathway of the lonely itinerant. God gave him some success, for which all devout hearts will praise Him.

Mr. Harmon, above referred to, was a Canadian, and had been an active and efficient soldier in the then late war. He had fought hard against the Americans. Mr. Ryan, the Presiding Elder, employed him contrary to the advice of William Case. He was not very well liked as a preacher, yet he was active in building that log church. As the whole Circuit was among Americans, it did not seem exactly right or well to employ one who had fought against them to preach to them; yet he did well, on the whole. He was a rough, bold, fearless kind of a man. He returned to Canada, and disappears from our sight.

Alpheus Davis, a young man, succeeded Mr. Laning, and faithfully performed the work assigned him, for one year. He received his appointment to this lonely Circuit at the session of the Genesee Conference, which met at Lansing, Cayuga County, New York, July 16th, 1818. At the close of the year, he returned only *thirty members*, having lost just the number that Mr. Laning had gained the year previous. We are to judge of the progress of the work, ordinarily, by the numbers returned; and yet, this is often fallacious:

for there may be such a condition of things that a decrease of numbers would really give strength to the cause. Again, without any increase in numbers, there may be a deepening and growing spirituality in the existing membership, which is of the greatest value to the cause.

Next in the order of laborers was *Truman Dixon*. The Genesee Conference held its session at Vienna, Ontario County, New York, July 1st, 1819. It was here he received his commission to this isolated field. He came, labored, suffered, triumphed and returned to his Conference, making a report of *sixty-six members* in Church fellowship. This was a great apparent increase of the work. He must have included some Societies in Canada. However this might be, it was cause of devout thanksgiving to the great Head of the Church. We rejoice in the conversion of sinners in any place, but as we are chronicling the progress of Protestantism in Michigan we cannot set down the number as much exceeding *thirty*—perhaps it may have been *forty*, for Michigan. This will close the narrative for our second period. Mr. Dixon was the last minister who was appointed from the Genesee Conference; for by act of the General Conference, held in May, 1820, Michigan was attached to the Ohio Conference, and henceforth is to be supplied from that direction. We must now bid adieu to Genesee, and make our respectful salutation to Ohio.

From the close of the war, in 1815, until July 20th, 1820, this field had been cultivated by laborers from the Genesee Conference. They found the work in a chaotic state, but through their labor it had been arranged into a good degree of order, and some ripe fruit had been already gathered. But now a change of relation is to take place, for in May of this year Michigan was attached to the Ohio Conference. The change produced a slight shock, as will be seen, because the next report gives a decrease of members, as will appear in the next period. William Case was the Presiding Elder for the first year of this period, and Henry Ryan for the other four. We may seem to have blamed the men appointed to this field, for not bestowing more labor on Detroit; but perhaps there is no blame, for at this period there was no appreciation of the value of Michigan. The country had been reported to the General Government as being not worth surveying, and Detroit was nearly all there was of Michigan of any value, and that was but a small town.

CHAPTER IV.

Joseph Hickox—Gideon Laning—Alpheus Davis—Truman Dixon—The Log Meeting-House—
Joseph Hanchett—Note.

HERE seems to be the most appropriate place to furnish a short account of Rev. JOSEPH HICKOX, whose name stands at the head of this period. He was born near Hartford, Connecticut, August 20th, 1788, so that at the time of his death, in 1867, he was seventy-nine years old. His parents were of "the standing order," that is, they were Congregationalists of the old school. As a consequence, he was thoroughly instructed in the doctrines of the Church—that is, Calvinism of the old stamp—and in the external duties of a Christian life. During his early youth he was often the subject of gracious impressions. These impressions were as often set aside by rebellion, and the Spirit was grieved away. When about fifteen years of age, he heard the first Methodist preacher, who visited the neighborhood where he resided—at least he was the first of whom he had any knowledge. His name was Richard Lyon, as he stated. This Mr. Lyon was admitted into the traveling connection in 1797, and located in 1808. It was, probably, during the year 1804 that he preached there. He was appointed to Bristol Circuit in 1797. Mr. Hickox's mother was very unwilling to let him go to hear this Methodist preacher, fearing lest he should imbibe pernicious doctrines, according to the belief of that day. He, however, did go, and his mother finally went with him. Having always heard sermons read, it seemed to him very remarkable that a man could preach such a discourse without his manuscript. The preacher set forth very impressively the universality of the atonement, and very touchingly exhibited the guilt of the sinner in not accepting its provisions at once. The people assembled were fairly electrified with the doctrines they heard, and our lad among the rest. The preacher followed up the impressions he had made by visiting from house to house, exhorting, and praying with the people. As is usual in connection with such labors, there was a very gracious revival in the place, and very soon a large Society was raised up. Young Hickox's mother was one of them. Her fears in regard to the perniciousness of Methodist doctrines had all subsided. Under the advice of Mr. Lyon, young Hickox was induced to begin a religious life in earnest, and sought reconciliation with God. He continued to seek, with varying constancy, for some time, without obtaining any evidence of pardon. At length he was led to forsake all for Christ, and obtained in the following year the peace of reconciliation. We will now give his own language, as descriptive of his state, resulting from his full devotion to Christ. He says: "My peace was unruffled, and the exercises of my mind were as clear as human consciousness could be. Jesus was 'my joy and my song,' not only by day, but in the night watches." His experience was very clear and glorious. He knew that his Redeemer lived. By faith the blood of atonement had been applied to his conscience. His "peace was like a river."

While but a youth, the Church saw fit to lay upon him the responsibiliy of leading a class, and gave him license to exhort. Soon an inward conviction of duty to preach came to him, and this was followed by the urgent request of the brethren. This is usually the order. When a man is called of God to the work of the ministry, the Church, or at least some of the Church, feel the conviction of his call nearly simultaneously with himself. As is common, he now had a struggle. On the one hand was his own inward consciousness of duty, and the convictions of the Church; on the other, was the sense of his inability. The latter produced a hesitancy which occasioned much anxiety, accompanied with great loss to his peace of mind. His life was much troubled on account of this struggle, but his conviction of duty did not abate in its force. At last, with many fears and much reluctance, he consented to receive license as a local preacher, which was signed by Rev. William Case, the Presiding Elder, with the understanding that he was to enter the itinerancy. After a brief service with what he calls "the militia,"—that is, as a local preacher —he was received into the Genesee Conference as a traveling preacher, at the session held at Niagara, in Canada, beginning July 23d, 1812. He was appointed as junior preacher, with James H. Baker, on the Shamokin Circuit, in Pennsylvania.

The next year he was appointed in charge of Canaan Circuit, in Pennsylvania, and the year following he was appointed in charge of St. Lawrence Circuit, in New York. On Canaan Circuit he had a glorious revival at every appointment—many were converted and added to the Church. On St. Lawrence he had but little success, as the people along the border were in such an unsettled state, on account of the war, that they gave but little attention to the preaching of the word of life. These last two years he had the same colleague. His name was Robert Manshall.

This brings us down to the period when he becomes identified with the fortunes and interests of Protestantism in Michigan; for, at a session of the Genesee Conference held at Lyons, New York, beginning June 29th, 1815, he was appointed to Detroit—a place which had been uncared for and unsupplied ever since the beginning of the war. Detroit and its vicinity had been the great focus of operations during the war of 1812, and was, therefore, the theater of much strife and carnage. Although the city itself was ingloriously surrendered by General Hull, without firing a single gun, the honor of American arms had been amply retrieved by Commodore Perry on the lake below, and by General Harrison on the Thames. The strife and smoke of the battlefield had scarcely cleared away when the missionary of peace comes in the name of the Prince of Peace, to bring to the people the gospel of their salvation. It is an adventurous enterprise, to be attended with much toil and suffering but to be crowned with success.

How delightful it is to turn away from the scenes of strife, confusion and blood, which have so recently been enacted on this ground, to a contemplation of the fruits of righteousness brought in by the introduction of the gospel of peace among them. One would have supposed that the people would have received the glad message of love, which was now to be offered to them, with one general acclaim of joy; but, alas! for them, some were so wedded to the superstitions of Romanism, and others were so attached to their worldly pleasures, that little heed was given to his message. Still he found "a few names even in Detroit, who had not defiled their garments." Of these few we have before given some account.

After this digression we must return to Mr. Hickox. At the expiration of his two years of probation—that is, in 1814—he was admitted into full connection with the Conference, and ordained a deacon ; and now, because he was to be sent as a missionary to this frontier work, he was ordained an Elder, one year in advance of the regular time—that is, in 1815—at the end of three years. What an undertaking! All pleasing associations were to be left behind, and he was to go among strangers, far from his Christian and ministerial brethren, to encounter various dangers and sufferings. He was, in fact, to plunge into the wilderness, not knowing among whom his lot should be cast. He, however, faltered not. What were the worldly inducements to the adoption of this course? He was allowed to receive *one hundred dollars per annum*, provided the people saw fit to give it to him. This was all. What a salary for such a service! Who, not moved by the Holy Ghost to the work of the ministry, would undertake it? Long and fatiguing rides were to be performed on horseback; storms were to be breasted; rivers and smaller streams were to be forded and swum; lodgings were to be found in rude log cabins, and sometimes with ruder people; the chilling blasts of winter were to be encountered; various and appalling dangers were to be met and passed; and all for *one hundred dollars* per year, and that by no means certain. Could that be any inducement for a man to adopt that course of life! Certainly not. But he was moved by the Holy Ghost to preach the Gospel to these people, living in these remote regions, secluded from religious services, and he cheerfully obeyed, "not counting his life dear to himself," if he could win them to Christ.

The Conference, as we have already said, held its session at Lyons, New York. This was the second time it met at this place. Bishop McKendree, of precious memory, presided.

Inasmuch as Mr. Hickox was going to a distant and wild portion of the country, it was thought necessary to give him a certificate explanatory of his mission. He received the following, in the handwriting of Joshua Soule, who was then General Book Steward, and signed by Bishop McKendree:

"TO ALL WHOM IT MAY CONCERN:

"This is to certify that I, William McKendree, one of the bishops of the Methodist Episcopal Church in the United States, have appointed Rev. Joseph Hickox to the station of Detroit and the contiguous parts of the country. Done at the Genesee Annual Conference, held at Lyons, in the State of New York, July 24th, 1815.

"WILLIAM McKENDREE."

This paper, which was well worn and brown with age, he retained and preserved while he lived, as a relic of past days. Of the ordination parchments which he received, he makes the following quaint remarks: "My ordination parchments were types of the times. Itinerants were then obliged to live much in the saddle, and wardrobe, books and papers must take the smallest possible dimensions for portability. Hence my parchments were somewhat smaller than a modern funeral note, being two and three-quarters by five inches, with an old-fashioned border like love-feast tickets. In our long rides we could have made no more use of the larger and more elegant ones now in use than of a Byronic shirt collar."

Mr. Hickox was directed to take into his Circuit, Detroit and the few settlements contiguous to it. The two on the rivers Rouge and Raisin, were the principal in Michigan. On the Canada side of the river it was to include Malden, Sandwich, the new settlement down the lake about sixty miles below Detroit, and the River Thames. We have now given an outline of this Circuit of olden times. If, however, one wishes to get an accurate view of it, let him take a map, note the distances of the localities from each other, and then let him call to mind the fact that the country was all new, and that there were none of the facilities for travel which are now so common, but that the roads were unwrought, the streams unbridged —that the roads were, in fact, only trails, having none of the characteristics of a road made by the hand of civilization. Having now introduced Mr. Hickox to the country, we will finish our running sketch of his character, leaving the filling up to be made from his relation to the work in its more minute details. He occupied this wild, uncultivated field for two years, performing faithfully his rounds, and gathering into the fold the few Christians he could find. In Michigan, when he first arrived, he only found seven who professed to be pious, having the Bible, and not the dogmas of the priests for their guide. There doubtless were some others, of other denominations in the City of Detroit, who professed to be Christians. The number was increased during his stay, so that at the end of the first year, including those in Canada—which, by the way, were more than those on this side—he returned *one hundred and forty* members; and at the end of the next year he returned *thirty* members for Michigan. This was in July, 1817.

Having completed his disciplinary term on this Circuit, he was sent, in 1817, to Litchfield Circuit, on the Mowhawk River, among the Dutch. Here his labors were abundantly blest in turning many from sin to holiness. The following year—that is, in 1818—he was sent to Ancaster Circuit, Canada. This was, also, a year of prosperity. Many were added to the Church. Perhaps the value of the work this year did not depend so much on the number of persons converted, as in their character and relations. Among the converts this year was *Peter Jones*, an Indian, who subsequently became so much noted for his successful labors among the Grand River Indians in Canada—whose name stands so deservedly high in the annals of Canadian Methodism. Mr. Hickox was, probably, the first Methodist preacher he ever heard, and "the sword of the Spirit," wielded by him, pierced the heart of the barbarian, transforming him after the image of Christ. He became a Christian minister, and was the instrument of saving many others. We have this statement from the pen of Mr. Hickox, although Dr. Webster in his "History of the Methodist Episcopal Church in Canada," places his conversion in June, 1824. We cannot decide between them.

At the Conference of 1819, Mr. Hickox was sent to the Thames Circuit. This was a part of his old field—that is, it formed a part of Detroit Circuit, when he traveled that. Here, in 1816, he had married a wife. During this year his wife was very sick for most of the time, so that he could not bestow more than half work on his Circuit. His wife continuing very feeble, and as it was feared she was in a consumptive decline, after having considered the matter, and having consulted his Presiding Elder, it seemed to him to be his duty to locate—to settle down. So at the session of the Genesee Conference, for 1820, he asked for and obtained a location.

When he was first in Michigan he entered a tract of land on the River Rouge, about sixteen miles from Detroit. He now removed his family to this new farm, and became fully identified with Michigan and Protestantism in it. Here he resided until 1836, when he removed to Illinois and settled not far from Rockford, where he resided till 1866, living in hope of the rest of the saints in light.

We have now run rapidly through his itinerant life, but cannot close without a further estimate of his abilities and character. He possessed a high order of talent, connected with indomitable perseverance and an ardent zeal for the cause of God. Bishop McKendree re-appointed him to Detroit Mission, in 1816, remarking at the same time that no other man could be found who would endure so much hard service. It has always been the policy of the Methodist Episcopal Church to assign the hardest and severest labors to those who were the most cheerful to perform them. Whether this policy is correct or just, we do not stop now to consider. But as the ministry is a voluntary thing—that is, we cannot compel men to enter and remain in it, it could not very well be avoided. Mr. Hickox was a man of great tact and shrewdness, as some of the incidents heretofore related will show. It is much to be regretted that in his case, as in many others, when men have located, his piety and usefulness were not uniform. Still, he at all times retained his relation to the Church and continued to have an unabated interest in its welfare. The inference from this is that a man whom God has so much honored in "turning many to righteousness," runs a fearful risk when he consents to locate and to cease the active work of the ministry. Mr. Hickox was a very smooth, easy and eloquent speaker—never at a loss for thoughts or words in which to express them, and always attracted large congregations.

We will now add a few reflections from his own pen, furnished at our request: "For about twenty years (1858) I have resided near Rockford, Winnebago County, Illinois. My life here has been as it was in Michigan, save that of late years sickness and advancing age have so enfeebled me that I can seldom preach. Occasionally I am called on to preach a funeral sermon, or to marry a couple, or to baptise a child. But even these duties I begin to avoid, for the reason that the time when the grasshopper becomes a burden is upon me. Formerly all my thoughts were of labor, now they are of rest; and the time draws nigh for my release, and I begin to look to the end of the journey. My animal pleasures fail, my mind flags, and even religious joys move me less than formerly. But he that led me out to vigorous activity, will lead me to the home of the blest if I do not make shipwreck of my faith at this late stage."

Referring to the state of things at Detroit when he first arrived, he says: "And truly, when the corner stones of society were thus to be laid in the Northwest, the workmen stood armed with Gospel weapons, and 'fighting against principalities and powers.' Though so silent, the conflict was more severe, the victory more glorious than those of the Thames, the Raisin and Lundy's Lane. But the glory belongs to the Captain of our salvation, whose two-edged sword shall yet slay the enemies of his kingdom and raise the Lord's house to the top of the mountains, 'and bring in everlasting righteousness.'

'O, long expected day, begin—
Dawn on these realms of woe and sin;
Fain would we leave this weary load,
And sleep in death, to rest with God.'"

It is time now to return to the direct line of our sketch. The reader was left with the appointment of our missionary to Detroit, first after the war-cry had died away, and he has been furnished with some account of his labors and successes, but he has had no account of his journey thither or of his reception when he arrived.

The hiatus would be too great if these particulars should be passed over in silence. We will avail ourselves of free extracts from the diary of Mr. Hickox touching these points, and we cannot do better than to give them in his own words. Having received his appointment, he proceeded with all convenient despatch to Buffalo, with the expectation of getting a passage by water. In this he was disappointed. Hear his own words:

"After waiting two weeks at Buffalo for a vessel to take me up the lake, without avail, I crossed over to Canada, mounted my horse, and commenced a tedious and dangerous journey through the forests, swamps, and savages. About half way I stopped with a friend, who constrained me to stop over the Sabbath with him, and allow an appointment for preaching to be circulated. Sunday morning, however, news came that travelers and emigrants were collecting some thirty miles in advance, preparing to move in a body through a deep forest forty miles wide, and infested with hostile Indians. As it was said to be dangerous to pass through that forest without a formidable company, and as such companies were only occasionally formed, I felt it to be my duty to push on that day, and join the company for Monday's journey. It was the most trying Sabbath day's journey I ever made. Several miles from the settlement I fell in with two or three thousand Indians, painted in the highest style of savage life and yelling like demons. I was alone and knew not what to expect. But they offered me no real injury. Towards the close of the day, I seemed to have passed the host and to be comparatively free from danger. Alighting from my horse, I breathed more freely than I had done during the day, very thankful for a whole skin. In the midst of this reverie of thankfulness, the crack of a rifle near by suddenly put an end to my congratulations of myself. My heart beat quickly, and the hair rose instantly on my head, as a huge Indian stepped from behind a tree, as I feared, to my peril. But summoning up all the coolness I could, I asked, 'Kill 'em?' 'No,' was the laconic reply. He had shot at game and had not aimed at the itinerant. I reached the company in safety.

"Perhaps a worse road than we traveled the next day, was never passed over. We were impeded by sloughs through which a horse could pass only by successive lunges, rendered doubly annoying by the clouds of flies and musquitoes that assailed us. About midway of the forest, a mournful spectacle presented itself. It was the field where Holmes overtook General Proctor, who was retreating from Moravian Town, when a great slaughter took place. The British had buried their dead so slightly that the wolves had dragged their bodies from the loose earth that had been thrown upon them. There lay the skeletons, strewn over the ground. They were yet entire—the hair yet upon the head, and the teeth all perfect, denoting the youth and strength of the slain. Such are some of the desolations of sin which the minister of the Gospel is sent to counteract.

"The next day after having passed this forest a man hailed me, asking:

"'Are you a Methodist preacher?'
"'Yes,' I replied.
"'Well, wont you preach for us?' continued he.
"'Yes, if you will gather a congregation,' said I.

"Lying down to rest, after my toilsome journey, I slept soundly until he awoke me, saying that the people had assembled. Springing up, I was enabled to preach with freedom to this long forsaken people; and the God of all grace blest the word to the conversion of one man at the time. He was the head of a family, and lived and died in the faith. Much encouraged by this incident, at the very threshold of my work, I began the task assigned me with confidence in the power of God to make even this 'wilderness to bud and blossom as the rose.'"

Through such perils and sufferings did Mr. Hickox proceed, until he reached Detroit, where he was kindly received by Robert Abbott, Esq., and the few faithful ones of whom we have before spoken. As before noted, he located in 1820, and settled on his farm on the Rouge. Here he performed much valuable service as a local preacher, and there are many in and around Detroit who kindly remember him, although almost an entire generation has come onto the active stage since he left Michigan.

He removed from Illinois to Beloit, Wisconsin, where he died in the faith and peace of the Gospel, January 16th, 1867. His expressions of personal confidence in the Divine Redeemer were very satisfactory.

GIDEON LANING, who succeeded Mr. Hickox on Detroit Circuit in 1817, was admitted into the Genesee Conference on trial in 1812; received his regular appointments; passed through the grades of the ministry, and labored usefully in the cause. He remained on this charge but one year; and, indeed, he rendered but little more than a half year's service on the Detroit Circuit, because of sickness, and his place was supplied by Thomas Harmon, as has been before stated. The people would have been much better pleased, if they could have had his ministry, than they were with the supply they had. Mr. Laning still lives—1877—so it does not become us to say much concerning him at this time. When appointed to Detroit, it was intended he should devote himself exclusively to Michigan, and he received the following paper, signed by the Bishop making the appointment:

"TO WHOM IT MAY CONCERN:

"The Rev. Gideon Laning is employed on a mission to Detroit to preach the Gospel, under the auspices of the Methodist Episcopal Church, and he is

hereby recommended to the hospitality of all, wherever Providence may call him in the performance of his mission.
Elizabethtown, 25th June, 1816.   (Signed)   ENOCH GEORGE."

Mr. Laning was born in New Jersey, March 23d, 1792. His parents were members of the Methodist Episcopal Church. In 1800 they removed to Western New York, where, when he was thirteen years of age, he was converted and joined the Methodist Episcopal Church. When seventeen years old he began to call sinners to repentance, and officiated as an exhorter and local preacher until twenty years old, when he was admitted on trial in the Genesee Conference. His youthful appearance drew crowds to hear him, and his word was attended with much success—how much, eternity alone will unfold. He had traveled five very extensive circuits in Central and Western New York, before he was appointed to the Detroit Mission in 1817. Detroit had stood on the General Minutes for several years previous, but the preachers appointed had bestowed their labor principally on the adjacent parts of Canada. This year—1817—it was resolved for the first time to have the missionary devote his time exclusively to Michigan, as the above paper, signed by Bishop George, will show. Mr. Laning preached in William McCarty's private dwelling on the Rouge on Sabbath morning, and in the Council House in Detroit at night. He had to leave the mission on account of failure of health. As soon as able after leaving the mission he journeyed South, and his health so much improved that he took an appointment at the next Conference.

For five years ensuing he occupied fields of labor in Pennsylvania, Maryland and Virginia. In 1823 he returned to the Genesee Conference in Western New York, where he has retained his standing ever since. Although he has been on the superannuated list for several years past, he has done effective service nearly *forty years*, including four years of chaplaincy in an alms-house.

In 1857, after an absence of nearly *forty years*, he visited Michigan. He makes the following remarks in regard to this visit: "I was astonished in witnessing the contrast. Where there was but one class of Methodists of less than thirty names, in 1817, there was now, according to the Minutes, a membership of about *twenty-five thousand*. And where I was the only Protestant minister, except a licentiate (John Monteith), in Detroit, there were now two annual conferences, besides a great number of ministers and churches of other evangelical denominations. Then, there was not a building called a church in all Michigan; now, they were numerous. 'What hath God wrought?' Where I had to follow an Indian trail to get to the settlement, and ford rivers, or have the horse swim by the side of a canoe while holding him by the bridle, or if no one was present to paddle it, to lie down and be drawn to the opposite shore, there were railroads now, and every facility for travel. Cities and villages had sprung up as if by magic, where there was only a dense forest forty years before."

In regard to his work, he says: "In respect to my mission field, in 1817, I found the English and Yankee people ready to listen to the preached word. They were quite friendly and hospitable. As to the French, they were under Catholic domination. I saw but one Indian with whom I could converse. He had been educated for an interpreter to a Presbyterian mission, and had served in that capacity for some few years. He told me the missionary wanted him to return with him, but his people would not suffer it. So he had remained and become as wicked as ever. I invited him to attend my preaching at the Rouge, it being only ten miles distant, which he promised to do. I never saw any people more hungry for the preached word, than at a settlement about fifty miles in a northwesterly direction from Detroit. They had never been visited by a preacher before. The whole community would turn out on a week-day, and drink in every word. One man told me he had left his harvestfield and walked eight miles to hear me. At the Raisin (now Monroe) I had a large congregation. At the Rapids of the Maumee, Ohio, I entered an open door. It was affecting in Detroit City, on a bright moonlight evening, to have the Council House yard and adjacent street filled with attentive hearers. O that my health had been such that I could have continued on the mission! But God does all things well."

It is a pity he did not confine his labors to Detroit and the Rouge. His eloquence charmed the people, and his gentlemanly manners gave him access to all classes. At the Raisin, and in a few other places, he found a few persons who had been Methodists previous to their removing to Michigan. So, with what his successor may have received, a grand total of *forty* members was returned at the next Conference, for Michigan. He was a very worthy laborer in this field.

ALPHEUS DAVIS was admitted on trial in the Genesee Conference in 1816, and died in 1820. He was born in Paris, Oneida County, New York, December 11th, 1793. He was, consequently, twenty-three years old when he entered the itinerant work. He experienced religion when about thirteen years of age, and for some time performed faithfully the duties and professed the enjoyments of a Christian life. Unfortunately, then he fell into the snare of the

Devil, and for a short time lived in a careless, backslidden state. In this condition he found no rest to his soul. At length, with deep and earnest penitence, he returned to the fold of Christ—to the fellowship of the saints—"the household of faith." Severe was the struggle when he came back to the Lord. Very soon after his restoration to the life of a Christian he began to exercise himself in religious meetings, exhibiting such talents as to satisfy the Church that he was called of God to the work of the ministry. Having received license as a local preacher, he sustained that relation for one year, and then was employed by the Presiding Elder to supply a Circuit for one year. In these relations he gave such satisfaction that he was recommended to the Conference, and admitted into the itinerant connection. The first two years he traveled in the Eastern portion of the Conference. In 1818 he was sent to these ends of the earth—as Detroit was then regarded—to the care of these sheep in the wilderness. There seems not to have been much success attending his labors here, as he only returned *thirty* members at the close of his term, or year. He continued in connection with this work only one year, as we find by the Minutes he was appointed to Herkimer Circuit, New York, for the next year. He labored faithfully, with declining health.

At the Conference held in August, 1820, he was placed on the superannuated list; but he continued to waste away so rapidly with pulmonary consumption that he fell asleep in Jesus, October 8th, 1820. He had not married. We find the following estimate of his worth in the Official Minutes for 1821 : " Our departed brother and fellow-laborer in the Gospel has left a vacancy in the Church of God which few will be able to supply. To say he had no faults would be to raise him above human beings; but to say few have had less, would be believed by all who knew him. In the private circles of social life he was highly esteemed, as well by the aged as the youth. An assemblage of agreeable and useful qualities, which were the ornament of his mind and the savor of his life, could not fail to interest society. But when we follow our dearly beloved brother through the more retired and obscure scenes of life into the field of his public ministry, we find him no less the faithful pastor of his flock than the agreeable and profitable associate of his friends, and the dutiful child. His private studies, his pastoral visits and his public exercises were happily directed to the great object which the Gospel is designed to promote; and it may be said of him in every station which he filled, that 'his labor was not in vain in the Lord.' Though he sustained every relation in life he held with reputation and usefulness, at no period did he shine with more lustre or appear to greater advantage than in his last illness. The patience which distinguished the last sufferings of Brother Davis, as well as the fortitude and cheerfulness with which he met the King of Terrors, gave evidence of that true piety which is peculiar to the Christian. He was held in such high estimation by the friends among whom he died, that several families contended for the privilege of nursing him in his sickness. But notwithstanding his youth, his rare and promising abilities, and the hopes and solicitudes of his friends, he fell a victim to death! He sleeps to wake no more in time! This promising youth, after having 'fought the good fight, and kept the faith,' finished his course October 8th, 1820. That he *died in the Lord*, and that *he rests from his labors*, we can have no doubt." Thus God lays by his workmen, but yet carries on His work.

We have been able to gather but scanty materials for a memorial sketch of the life and labors of REV. TRUMAN DIXON. He was admitted on trial in the Genesee Conference in 1818; consequently, this was his second appointment, as he was sent to Detroit in 1819, where he labored for one year only. He had good success on this charge, as he returned *sixty-six* members, a little more than double the last year's report. He is said to have been a man of good abilities as a preacher, and attended faithfully to his work here. The Genesee Conference held its session July 20th, 1820, at Niagara, in Canada, at which time the connection of Michigan with that Conference ceased. Mr. Dixon located in 1825, having devoted seven years to the itinerant ministry. We now lose sight of him. He seems to have been a man of considerable mental power, and to have been capable of accomplishing much good. It is a pity that such men, for any cause, should cease the active ministerial work. The world is so much in need of the labors of such men that they ought, unless released by Divine Providence disabling them, to continue their active labors for its reformation.

THE OLD LOG CHURCH. We have before spoken of the fact that the first Protestant Christian Church in Michigan was built by the Methodists in the vicinity of Detroit. It is not to be supposed that this was done without much effort; for, though it was a humble building, the people were poor and few, especially those who felt any interest in such an enterprise. In regard to this old church, Rev. John A. Baughman, now deceased, and who was the last minister who preached in it, remarked to us: "The old log church stood on the north side of the road running from Detroit up the River Rouge, some five or six miles from the city, a short distance from the river. The size, as nearly as I can recollect, was about twenty-four by thirty feet, standing lengthwise east and west, fronting south towards the road and river. The pulpit was on the north side, oppsite the door, built of plain, common boards, dressed, standing directly against the wall. The pulpit was entered by steps at the east end. It had no altar. The floor consisted of plain, rough boards nailed upon sleepers. The seats consisted of plain, rough benches, made by boring auger holes and inserting round sticks of wood into them. These were placed so as to leave an aisle in front of the pulpit, to the door. There were four windows to the house—one in each end and one on each side of the door in the front side of the house. The ceiling was from eleven to twelve feet high from the floor, consisting of round logs from which the bark was peeled, for joists. These were covered with rough boards laid loosely over them. The house was warmed by a large stove which stood in the center, with the pipe running into a chimney, and thus passing out of the roof. The body of the building consisted of quite large, hewed logs, put up somewhat after the old French style."

Our recollection of the position of this building—for it was still standing, though not used for a church, when we came into the country in 1830—is that it stood with the end towards the road, and if we had been about to have a drawing made of it we should have had it in that way. But this is of no consequence, and we are as likely to be mistaken as Mr. Baughman. Though the church was abandoned as a place of worship when we came into the country, and we preached in a private house a little above it, we used to pass it often and have gone into it to look at it with feelings of reverence, as its having been a place where much good had been done; for one who used to worship in it once said to us, "There was much of Divine power in their meetings, and prayer and praise there ascended to Heaven. Peace and joy filled their hearts, while they walked in fellowship and love."

Mr. Hickox said of this old church: "In the spring of 1818 they put up a comfortable hewed-log chapel, for the worship of Almighty God. While they stood in the forest, those trees from which the logs were taken had echoed to the shouts of savages, rendered wild by the spirit of darkness; but now, by the exceeding greatness of the Lord's power in them that believe, they resounded with praise to the Prince of Peace. This was the first house of worship erected in the Territory of Michigan." He means Protestant place of worship.

We may as well finish the history of this house in this place as

to postpone it. From the changes occurring in society by the growth of the country, and from difficulties and disaffections in the Church, the location became very inconvenient, and this house was abandoned as a place of worship in 1828, after having been used in that way for about *ten* years.

When we first came to Michigan, in 1830, having been appointed to Ann Arbor Circuit, which included the ground where this church was located, this house was still standing, but in a dilapidated condition. Being abandoned it soon fell into decay, and a few years later, some one conceiving the idea that it was rather unsightly, and not having any fear of the Methodists before his eyes, set fire to it, which consumed most of the materials of which it was made. Thus passes the glory of the world—of all terrestrial things. It had its day of usefulness, and now, like many other things, when it can no longer be used it is first abandoned and then destroyed.

The remains of this first house, built for the worship of the true and living God, in Michigan, lay undisturbed in their ashes and ruins until in the month of June, 1851. At this time the ministers of the Methodist Episcopal Church residing in the City of Detroit, and officiating in the churches, to wit: *James Shaw*, Presiding Elder of Detroit District, *Elijah H. Pilcher*, of the Woodward Avenue Church, *George Taylor*, of Congress street, and *Lorenzo D. Price*, of Lafayette street—instigated by some kind of a spirit, laudable or otherwise, as any one may please to consider it, at the suggestion of Rev. George Taylor aforesaid—made a sally out of the city, and with force and arms carried off all the remains of the timber that was sufficiently sound, and had it manufactured into canes. These amounted to about thirty in number. Most of these were sold at the succeeding session of the Annual Conference, and the avails were given to the Missionary Society. They reserved one each for themselves. A few were donated as follows, viz: to Bishop Morris, Bishop Scott, after he was elected to the Episcopal office; Rev. Judson D. Collins, who had just returned from the China Mission in very poor health, after having been absent for several years. Robert Abbott, Esq., took one for himself, and donated one to Rev. William Case as a token of remembrance of the good that he had received through his labors.

As the Bible did not prohibit wearing silver, these canes—that is, the reserved and donated ones—were mounted with heavy silver heads, and these words were engraved on the sides: "Relic of the first Methodist, being the first Protestant Church in Michigan, built 1818." Thus has this first church, erected to the glory of God in

Michigan, and which was honored of God by the manifestations of His Spirit in the conversion of precious souls, passed away. We now say, *Requiescat in pace*—rest in peace—but your record is on high and your memorial is not to perish from among men! Thus it is with this world; men and things have their day in which they may be useful, and then to pass away—some to be forgotten and some to be immortalized.

It would be curious and interesting if we could present the original subscription, showing that some subscribed fractions of a dollar, and others so many days of labor or a certain amount of materials, and so on. Rev. Thomas Harmon, the supply in the absence of Rev. Gideon Laning, and Robert Abbott, Esq., were the most active agents in securing the erection of this house; and in its latter years, Joseph Hanchett was the most prominent member of the Society in it.

It is proper here to note that the breaking up of the Society and the abandonment of the church at so early a period was not entirely dependent on the changes in the settlement, although that had a good deal to do with it. Dissensions had sprung up among them, and had run so high that some had been expelled from the Church who had considerable influence in the community. This, as a matter of course, set them in opposition to the Church. They therefore, did all they could to break it down. This dissension grew partly out of a jealousy towards Robert Abbott, Esq., who at this time owned a farm on the Rouge and resided on it. Mr. Abbott, as has before been shown, was a man of considerable influence in the Church, and of high standing in the community. Before the abandonment of the Church he had moved back to the city, and was fully identified with the Church there. We may form a little idea of the spirit of evil which had sprung up by noting a fact or two. Mr. Abbott had taken a very active part in raising subscriptions for building the church, and he acted as collector and treasurer. He was in poor health, suffering very much from dyspepsia, and Mr. Harmon, the preacher, had persuaded him to go with him into Canada and spend a few weeks during the spring. This was before the building was completed. During his absence, one of the members put into circulation the report that Mr. Abbott had run off with the funds of the Church, and managed in some irregular way to have him declared expelled from the Church. When Mr. Abbott returned from his visit he was restored to his standing, as what was done was illegally done. Mr. Abbott had charges preferred against this brother now, for slander, and he was formally expelled. This man, who showed that his expulsion was just by his violence and profane cursing, ever after became an enemy of the Church. With such a spirit as now began to spring up, it required but a few removals to make it impracticable to keep it up. Mr. Abbott removed to the city; William McCarty had settled on a farm several miles farther up the river, and could not attend here—so Mr. Hanchett was nearly left alone to maintain the Church. William Stacy had died, and several of the Corbuses had moved away. The meetings were withdrawn and the church abandoned. It is always to be deplored, when discords and divisions spring up in a Church, for they can only result in evil. Why will members of a feeble Church, especially, ever allow themselves to pursue such a suicidal course?

We must now say a few words more in regard to JOSEPH HANCHETT. We knew him personally. He was a man of sound mind, and seemed to have a genuine religious experience. He removed to Branch County, and his was one of the two families who settled at Coldwater in 1831, and he and his wife, with Allen Tibbits and his wife, formed the first Methodist Society organized there, in 1832. The Society at Coldwater was organized by Rev. E. H. Pilcher, preacher in charge of Tecumseh Circuit, June 19th, 1832, consisting of Allen Tibbits, local preacher, Caroline M. Tibbits his wife, Joseph Hanchett, and Nancy Hanchett his wife. This was the first religious Society, or Church, organized in Branch County. Allen Tibbitts, the local preacher just named, preached the first sermon ever delivered at what is now the City of Coldwater, on the fourth Sabbath of July, 1831, in a little log house in which he resided, and in which Rev. E. H. Pilcher preached the first funeral discourse ever delivered in Branch County, in October, 1831. It was a daughter of Mr. Tibbitts that had died.

Joseph Hanchett died in Natchez, Mississippi, of yellow fever, in September, 1849. He had gone there to visit a son. He was buried by the Order of Odd Fellows. Allen Tibbitts was there on the day of his burial, and attended his funeral. He had removed from Coldwater to Beloit, Wisconsin, several years previous to this, where his wife had died a few years before. He remained faithful to the Church while he lived, and doubtless has gone to receive the reward of the righteous in heaven.

We subjoin the following paper, taken from the *Michigan Christian Advocate*, dated in April, 1877:

THE FIRST PROTESTANT CHURCH IN THE STATE OF MICHIGAN.— Rev. Dr. Pilcher, in his researches in the preparation of a work entitled, "The Introduction and Progress of Protestantism in Michigan," obtained the following statement through Mr. Silas Farmer, accompanied with a note, which we also subjoin. It seems there was a disposition at that time to ignore the existence of a Methodist Church in Michigan. Mr. Abbott speaks of the Society or Church on the River Rouge, simply because they had come to have more members there than in the City of Detroit, and had built a church there. The Society or Church, as originally organized, had a majority of its members in the city, and they held their meetings in both places. This advertisement settles definitely and authoritatively the fact, as so often stated by Dr. Pilcher, that a Methodist Church had been organized here in 1810, and had never become extinct. The place on the Rouge referred to was only a little beyond Woodmere Cemetery. Mr. Abbott himself joined this Church in 1810, he then residing in the City of Detroit. Brother Farmer says:

DEAR BROTHER PILCHER :—The enclosed copy of advertisement from the Detroit *Weekly Gazette* of April 3d, 1818, was only discovered by a careful search through over 20,000 old newspapers, occupying over four months of time, and I judge it is probably the *most definite* information possible to obtain, and the information was sought *specially* for my " Illustrated History of Detroit."

The advertisement reads as follows:

FIRST PROTESTANT CHURCH IN THE STATE OF MICHIGAN, was erected at the River Rouge, on the 31st ultimo, by a Society of Methodists, a body corporate, belonging to the Methodist Episcopal Church in the United States. The said Society was established at the River Rouge in the year 1810, and through the mercies of God has remained inflexible through the storms of war and other trials; and by the Divine blessing is still in a prosperous way.

ROBERT ABBOTT,
April 2, 1818.   One of the Trustees of the River Rouge Methodist Episcopal Church.

CHAPTER V.

Changes — Numbers—Kent, from Ohio Conference — Decrease — Settlements Increase — Morey Appointed—Morey's Death—Supply—First Camp Meeting—Catholic Woman—Society Permanently in Detroit—Ohio Conference, 1822—Two Ministers—Baker is Married, and Dies —Pattee and Plimpton—Hunter—Extending the Work—Reflections—Review—Corporation Formed—Corporators—Meeting in May, 1820—Erection of a Church—Simmons—Pattee Goes East—Offer of Help—New Church—Isaac C. Hunter—Anecdote—Numbers—Incidents of Hickox and Richard—Richard.

E now enter upon the third period of our History, which extends from August, 1820, to September, 1836, a term of sixteen years. More rapid changes will have been made during this time than during all the years of our past History. This period includes the time from the transfer of Michigan to the Ohio Conference, until the Michigan Conference was organized. But what have we to start with? The last report made to the Genesee Conference by Mr. Dixon, July 20th, 1820, gives *sixty-six* members for Detroit Circuit; but we cannot reckon more than *thirty* of these as belonging to Michigan, or else there must have been a very considerable scattering in the few weeks which intervened between the appointments of this year.

At the session of the Ohio Conference held at Chillicothe, Ohio, commencing August 20th, 1820, Detroit is made to appear on its list of appointments. It is found in the Lebanon District, *James B. Finley*, Presiding Elder. *John P. Kent* was appointed in charge of the Circuit, alone. Mr. Kent was an able preacher and labored faithfully; but in numbering up the hosts at the end of the year, we find a return of only *twenty* members for Detroit Circuit at the Conference, September 6th, 1821. Here is a decrease of ten or more. We are not fully prepared to account for this decrease. It probably occurred, in part, in consequence of the transfer of the country from one

Conference to another, which occasioned the severance of all appointments and members which were on the Canada side of the river.

We have now reached a period in our History when all the numbers of the membership returned at the conferences belong in Michigan, so that we can state the numbers with greater exactness than heretofore. Mr. Kent was a young, unmarried man, though an ordained Elder, but his health was not very rugged. Notwithstanding his delicate health, he remained faithfully in charge of his work to the close of the year. By his excessive labors and exposures in this region of country, he became so prostrated that it was necessary for him to take a superannuated relation at the Conference in 1821. Mr. Finley, the Presiding Elder, visited the country in the spring of 1821. A full account of his labors and visits will be found in another chapter, under the memorial notice of James B. Finley.

The settlements in Michigan began now to increase with considerable rapidity, so that the Itinerant could find places enough to employ his whole time and tax his energies to their utmost. Mr. Kent visited as many of these new settlements as he could, and arranged them into a plan for a Circuit for his successor for the next year. We will now state our position at the end of this first year of our third period—that is, September 6th, 1821. *We have one charge (Detroit Circuit), one preacher, twenty members, and one log meeting-house.* Not a very encouraging state of things; and yet, these were nearly all the Protestant professors in the Territory. There had been a Presbyterian Church organized in Monroe in 1820, but that was very feeble; and there were a few professors, besides Methodists, in the City of Detroit. The cause, however, is of God; and we are to look to Him for the success.

At the Conference held at Lebanon, Ohio, beginning September 6th, 1821, Platt B. Morey, a young man of rather feeble health, who had just been admitted on trial, was appointed to Detroit, and it was still included in the Lebanon District. *John Strange* was appointed Presiding Elder. Mr. Strange made one visit to Detroit and preached with great power. His visit was of much advantage to the cause in Detroit.

Mr. Morey reached the work some time in October, but he had not completed a single round on his charge before he was taken sick. He died at Mount Clemens, in December, 1821. His remains were taken to Detroit for interment and were deposited in the graveyard in the midst of the city. Rev. Joseph Hickox preached his funeral sermon. In the spring of 1851, it having been determined to erect a block for stores on this ground, the grave was taken up and the remains transferred to Elmwood Cemetery, where the same plain stone that marked his grave before still marks the spot where lies his dust till the last, loud trumpet shall sound to awake the sleeping dust to life. Mr. Morey was born at Trumansburg, New York, but he had gone into Ohio. He was a very pious, good man, but not a great preacher. He was young, and promised usefulness had he lived. During his sickness his mind was clear, and he was very happy. He died in great triumph. He was the first Methodist preacher who was buried in Michigan soil.

Rev. John P. Kent, who had taken a superannuated relation, was employed by the Presiding Elder to fill out the year. He returned *one hundred and thirty* members at the end of the year. This was an increase of *one hundred and ten*, as it will be recollected that there were but *twenty* returned at the preceding Conference. New settlements had been included, and societies formed among immigrants; many had also been converted and added to the existing Societies. The work was now widening in its circle, and assumed a more permanent form, never again to recede.

Mr. Kent, assisted by Rev. William Case, Presiding Elder on Upper Canada District, held a Camp-Meeting on the farm of William Stacy, on the River Rouge, in the month of June, 1822—the first meeting of the kind ever held in Michigan. It was a very good and profitable time. The whole country turnd out to see the novel spectacle of a meeting in the woods. Among many others who were brought to a knowledge of the love of God for the first time, was a French Catholic woman. While she was penitently asking for a new heart, a relative of hers, a leading Romanist in these parts, came into the altar. Looking on for a few minutes, with a mixture of surprise and alarm; then, in response to the suggestion of some one that she wanted religion, he cried out, "She has got religion! She need not seek religion! She has got religion, *for I have it now in my pocket!*" He probably referred to some note of indulgence, or of confirmation, which had been given to him for her. But she did not think that that was what she needed. She still sought it by faith in Christ. She found peace in His name, and went away much more comforted by the "love of God shed abroad in her heart by the Holy Ghost given unto her" than by the religion in the pocket of her relative. This was a very valuable meeting, and much lasting good was accomplished. The Church was much benefited by it.

Some time during the year 1821 the Society became more fully installed in the City of Detroit, and their meetings were constantly held in the city. Previous to this time, although the preaching was constant in the city—that is, once in three or four weeks—and although the Society had been organized in the city, as before stated, the Society met sometimes in Detroit, and sometimes on the River Rouge in the log meeting-house. As yet, no vigorous effort had been made to build a Methodist church in the city. Our people had been content to occupy, occasionally, the house which had been built by Protestants in common, under the name of "The First Protestant Church or Society." By the way, the Methodists might at this time have possessed themselves entirely of this house and property, if they had adopted the advice given to a young lawyer, who had then recently been converted and had joined the Methodist Church, by an old gentleman who was not a professor of religion but was friendly to the Methodists. He advised this young lawyer to induce a sufficient number of Methodists and their particular friends to become members of that Society, to control it, and then to vote the property to their exclusive use and benefit. "But," said the young man, "that would not be honorable." "No matter," said the old gentleman, "if you do not do so, somebody else will, and you will lose it." "Oh, I think not," said the confiding young man. It was not long after this, however, before he found his confidence was misplaced, and the statement of the old man was fully realized. The Methodists had to find a place of worship as they could, this common house having been voted to the exclusive use of another denomination.

After the death of Mr. Morey, of whom we have nearly lost sight, but whose appointment to this charge, in 1821, is now recalled to mind, Mr. Kent filled out the year until the session of the Ohio Conference, which met in Marietta, Ohio, beginning September 5th, 1822. Marietta is a small town situated on the Ohio River at the confluence of the Muskingum River; so that our Itinerant had to travel on horseback to the southeast part of the State of Ohio to reach the seat of his Conference. Mr. Kent returned *one hundred and thirty* members for Detroit Circuit. The Circuit, however, extended to the Maumee Rapids, in Ohio; and he had reorganized the Society at Monroe. (For a fuller account of this latter Society we refer to Monroe, when it appears on our records.)

The work had so enlarged that at this Conference it was thought advisable to increase the ministerial force—to send two ministers to Detroit Circuit. This begins to seem a little as though we were coming up out of the wilderness. A brighter day begins to dawn, both for the country and for Michigan Protestantism, though a dark cloud still hangs over our heavens in the city. This is mainly the result of previous miscalculation. In September, 1822, *Alfred Brunson* and *Samuel Baker* were appointed to Detroit Circuit, which was still included in the Lebanon District—James B. Finley, Presiding Elder. Mr. Brunson confined his labors mostly to the city. He was the first man who ventured to make a concentration of labor in the city. Mr. Baker attended to the country work. Mr. Brunson still lives—1877—in the enjoyment of a green old age. Mr. Baker, during the year, formed a matrimonial alliance with Miss Sarah Harvey, of Monroe—late Mrs. Rev. John A. Baughman; went to Conference, which met at Urbana, Ohio, September 4th, 1823; was taken sick, and died in a few days. At the Conference of 1823 they returned *one hundred and sixty-one* members, being a net increase of *thirty-one* over last year. Taking all the circumstances into the account, this was doing well. As nigh as we can now ascertain, there were about sixty members in the City of Detroit.

The next year's appointments did not embrace as much strength as the last. In September, 1823, *Elias Pattee* and *Billings O. Plympton* were stationed on this one Circuit. Mr. Pattee was a man of moderate talents and limited education, but of great zeal. Mr. Plympton was a noble-spirited and zealous Christian, but young—just beginning, this being only his second year in the ministry. This Circuit was now included in the Miami District—*John Strange*, Presiding Elder—a District that extended from Cincinnati to Detroit. Why it was severed from Lebanon District cannot be ascertained. It certainly did not make it any more convenient for the Presiding Elder to visit it. As might have been expected from the dimensions of the District, the Presiding Elder does not appear to have visited Michigan at all that year. Indeed, for the two years that Mr. Strange presided, he does not appear to have made more than one visit to the Territory. This is not to be wondered at, from its distance and the difficulties of travel to reach it. The appointment this year was not in every respect such as the character of the work demanded, especially so far as the City of Detroit was concerned. The cause gained no special strength in the city this year, though in the country settlements large accessions were made, so that at the Conference in 1824—at the end of the year—they reported *two hundred and forty-two* members for the Circuit. This was a net increase of *eighty-one*. They have also lopped off the Maumee Rapids, and confined their labors to Michigan. It will be recollected that immigration had now turned its course considerably toward Michigan, and, as the settlements were formed, our ministers were ready to supply them, and new appointments had been made in various localities.

Elias Pattee was reappointed to this Circuit in September, 1824, and *Isaac C. Hunter* was associated with him as his colleague. The Circuit was now included in the Sandusky District—a new District which was organized at this Conference—and *James B. Finley* was Presiding Elder again. It is most probable that Mr. Finley did not visit Detroit more than once this year, as there are no memorials of his having done so. As both preachers were ordained Elders, it was not as essential that he should come, as it otherwise would have been, because the ordinances could be administered without him; and yet the visits of the Presiding Elder were looked for with great interest in those days.

With the increasing population these brethren found increasing demands for labor; and the work was much extended as the new settlements increased, or came into existence, and these itinerants were ready to follow them up and administer to them the Word of Life. Mr. Pattee extended his labors as far west as Ypsilanti, and organized a small Society at Woodruff's Grove, as Ypsilanti was then called, in the summer of 1825. This was the first Christian Church organized in Washtenaw County, or at any point in Michigan west of Wayne County. Of the fortunes and successes of this Society a full account will be given when Ypsilanti comes into notice as a distinct charge, so we dismiss it for the present.

While these brethren were extending their labors to the increasing settlements in the country—to the outposts—the citadel was neglected—the city interests were not much promoted. Upon the whole, there was no increase of membership in the Territory this year, as the number returned was the same as last year—that is, *two hundred and forty-two*. No advance, upon the whole, was made either in the City of Detroit or the County of Wayne.

The real condition of a Church cannot always be determined by the number of members at any given time. This may be stationary, or may even have diminished, while the real moral power has been accumulating and gathering strength, ready to develop itself on some future occasion with the greater success. The Church may be constituted of such fickle and unstable people as that, in a few months, after a flood-tide of prosperity, few of them only may be found walking in the way of righteousness; or it may be constituted of persons of a firm, decided character, whose decision and constancy will make a deep and abiding impression on a community. A Church of the latter description will certainly work its way into the esteem and affections of the people, and will ultimately triumph. Heretofore we have considered our work mostly in respect to its numerical increase. It is now time to take a little review of it in other respects.

"The First Protestant Society of Detroit," having voted to appropriate the small house of worship which had been erected in the City of Detroit, by the common contributions of the people, under the auspices of the "First Evangelistic Society"—a Society which was made up of all Protestants, without reference to their Church relations—to the exclusive use of the Presbyterians, and the Methodists being left to find a place of worship where they could, they thought of providing a house for themselves. They had a few persons among them of sterling fidelity, who had become Methodists from principle and who were disposed to rise or fall, as the case might be, with this Church, and who felt deeply the need of a church of their own. Of some of these men we shall hereafter give some account.

As early as May, 1820, some effort had been made to obtain from the Governor and Judges, who had the coutrol of the matter, a lot on which to build a church, by calling together those citizens who were friendly to the object to petition them for that purpose. No corporation, however, was created until 1822. At this time, in order to constitute a religious corporation, it was necessary to adopt articles of association setting forth the object of the corporation, which must be submitted to the Governor and Judges, and, if approved by them, the signers and their successors were constituted a corporation in law. Such articles of association were drawn up on the 21st day of March, 1822, and signed by the persons whose names are attached thereto.

The names attached to the articles of association did not comprise all who were connected with the Church in the city at that time. They, however, were enough to meet the demands of the law in such cases. As this is the first organization of the kind in the line of our History, it may be interesting to insert these articles here:

CONSTITUTION OF THE METHODIST EPISCOPAL CHURCH OF THE CITY OF DETROIT.

To all whom these presents may come:

Know ye, that we, whose names are hereunto subscribed, being desirous of establishing a Methodist Episcopal Society in the City of Detroit, for the purpose of acquiring and enjoying the powers and immunities of a corporation or body politic in law, according to an act of the Governor and Judges of the Territory of Michigan, entitled "an act to confer on certain associations the power and immunities of corporations or bodies politic in law," do therefore, by these presents, associate ourselves together for the said purpose by the name, style and title of " The First Methodist Episcopal Society of the City of Detroit," under the articles and conditions following, to wit:

SECTION 1. The said subscribers and their successors shall, according to the above-recited act, become and be a corporation or body corporate in law and in fact, to have continuance by the name, style and title of "The First Methodist Episcopal Society of the City of Detroit," and as such shall have full power and authority to make, have and use one common seal with such device and inscription as they shall deem proper, and the same to break, alter or renew at their pleasure, and by the name, style and title aforesaid, be able and capable in law to sue and be sued, plead and be impleaded, in any court or courts, before any judge or judges, justice or justices, in all manner of suits, complaints, pleas, causes, matters and demands whatsoever; and all and every matter or thing to do, in as full and as effectual a manner as any other person or persons, bodies politic or corporate within the Territory of Michigan, may or can do, and shall be authorized and empowered to make rules, by-laws and ordinances, and to do everything needful for the good government and support of said Society. Provided that the said by-laws, rules and ordinances, or any of them, be not repugnant to the Constitution of the United States, or to the laws of this Territory, or to the present instrument upon which said Society is founded and established; and, provided also, that the said by-laws, rules and ordinances shall not extend to the dissolution of said Society, without the consent of all the members thereof.

SECTION 2. The said Society and their successors, by the name, style and title aforesaid, shall be able and capable in law, according to the terms and conditions of these presents, to take and hold all manner of lands, tenements, rents annuities, franchises and hereditaments, and any sum or sums of money, and any manner and portion of goods and chattels, given and bequeathed unto them to be employed and disposed of according to the object, articles and conditions of this instrument, the by-laws of the said Society, or of the will and intention of the donor; provided that the clear yearly value or income of the messuages, houses, lands and tenements and real estate, and the interest of the money by them lent shall not exceed the sum of $2,500.

SECTION 3. There shall be elected annually nine Trustees, on the third Monday in May (a majority of whom shall constitute a quorum for the transaction of business), a Treasurer and a Secretary, who shall be governed in their duties by this instrument and the by-laws and ordinances of the Society.

SECTION 4. The Society shall have authority to make by-laws and ordinances for regulating the admission of new members to this Society; but no member shall be eligible to the office of Trustee, Treasurer, of Secretary unless he be a member in regular standing and communion with the Methodist Episcopal Church.

SECTION 5. All officers who may be appointed by virtue of this constitution shall hold their offices until the third Monday in May in each year and until others shall be appointed in their places.

SECTION 6. All deeds, titles, conveyances of all lands, tenements and hereditaments, and of all goods and chattels made to this Society shall be given to the Trustees (in trust for the Society), and all deeds, titles and conveyances of the like property from this Society shall be given by the Trustees, but no property of the Society shall be sold without their consent.

SECTION 7. The first election of officers for this Society shall be held on the 21st day of March, 1822; and elections may be held at any time to supply vacancies, on public notice being given by the Trustees, and a majority of members present at any such meeting, or at any other meeting of the Society held pursuant to notice given as aforesaid, or at the annual election, shall constitute a quorum for the transaction of business.

SECTION 8. It shall be competent for the Society, at any meeting held pursuant to notice given by the trustees as aforesaid, to levy such amount of tax or taxes as they may deem expedient, upon each and every member of this Society.

SECTION 9. The Society shall have power to elect such other officers as may be deemed necessary for the transaction of business.

(Signed,) Robert Abbott, Joseph Hickox, William Hickox, Joseph C. Corbus, Israel Noble, James Kapple, Nathaniel Champ, James L. Reed, John Ramsey, Joseph Donald, James Abbott, H. W. Johns, Edwin H. Goodwin, P. Warren, Jerry Dean, Joseph Hanchett, Robert P. Lewis, John Farmer.

To this instrument the following approvals were appended:

DETROIT, March 21st, 1822.

Michigan, to wit:

I should greatly prefer the union of all Protestants under the name of Evangelical Churches, as adopted in Germany and Prussia at the third centennial anniversary, October 31st, 1817, to the retention of the existing sectarian distinctions. The objects, however, and the articles and conditions set forth and contained in this instrument are, in my opinion, lawful.

(Signed,) A. B. WOODWARD,

One of the Judges in and over the Territory of Michigan, and Presiding Judge of the Supreme Court thereof.

Tuesday, May 14th, 1822.

I have examined the foregoing instrument and consider it to be within the provisions of the act of the Governor and Judges of this Territory, entitled "An act to confer on certain associations the powers and immunities of corporations or bodies politic in law."
(Signed,) J. WITHERELL.
Territory of Michigan.

I have perused and examined the foregoing instrument, and entertain no doubt of the lawfulness of the objects, articles and conditions therein set forth and contained; and do hereby certify the same pursuant to the statute.
(Signed,) CHAS. LARNED,
Attorney General, Michigan Territory.

The preceding articles of association will be recorded by the Secretary of the Territory at the expense of the applicants.
DETROIT, May 17th, 1822. (Signed,) LEW. CASS,
Governor of the Territory.

Thus the Society has assumed a legal form and existence. This, however, was not the creation of the Church, as that had taken place long before, but it was only giving it a legal organization, so that they might hold property in law. It is both interesting and sad to mark, as we can in this case, the changes that take place in society in the space of a few years. At this present writing, (1877), all the Territorial officers who signed the approval of these articles of association, are dead. Of those who signed the articles of corporation none now reside in Detroit. William Hickox resides in Washtenaw County; Joseph Hickox, Robert Abbott, William McCarty, Joseph C. Corbus, Philip Warren, Jerry Dean, Joseph Hanchett, Israel Noble and Nathaniel Champ, we know to have died in the faith and peace of the Gospel. John Farmer is deceased. Of the rest we can obtain no information, and cannot determine whether they are living or dead; probably they are dead.

At the meeting called May 20th, 1820, to petition for a lot, Samuel Davenport presided, and B. F. H. Witherell acted as Secretary. These seem not to have been present at the meeting in 1822. At this meeting a committee was appointed to make application to the Governor and Judges for a lot and also to circulate a subscription to raise funds to build a house. That committee consisted of Robert Abbott, William W. Pettit and Samuel T. Davenport. Nothing was accomplished at this time, perhaps because they had not as yet been entirely shut out from other places. At the expiration of two years they seemed to have waked up in good earnest, as out of a deep sleep, and to have commenced active operations. A subscription was circulated, and such an amount obtained as that they felt warranted in commencing the work of building. A lot was obtained from the authorities who had the disposal of them, on the corner of Gratiot Avenue and Farrar Street, which at the time was entirely out of the city. This was another of the great mistakes in regard to Methodism in this city. At this date in the history of this denomination, it seemed to be the general policy to keep Methodism at such a distance from the people as to make it cost search and labor to find it. In accordance with this policy, Methodist churches of that day were generally located on the outskirts of towns, or a mile or two in the country. In the present instance, they might just as well have had a lot in the midst of the city as to have taken the one they did. But they were so modest as to wish to get away from the public gaze as much as possible. This lot was taken greatly to the damage of their cause in the city. They saw this mistake when it was too late to correct the whole of the mischief, and yet in time to recover in part. When they saw their mistake and applied to the city authorities for another location, they were told that that was one of their own choosing, and that they must be content with it or pay the full price for another. The authorities were not to blame for that. In the summer of 1823 they commenced the erection of a building, but the subscription was exhausted before the walls were completed. It was of brick. It is said that the prospect was that it would stand during the winter without a roof, which would nearly ruin the walls, as it was now late in the fall, and there were no means of completing them. In this state of facts, the legend is that the mechanics of the city combined and completed this work on a Sabbath day, without having consulted the Society. They chose the Sabbath because they thought they could not afford to give the time on any other day. If the Society had been consulted, of course they would have refused to have the work done on the Sabbath. The building being secured in this way it remained unfinished and unused for several years—indeed, it was never finished. This was the second Methodist Church in Michigan. Alfred Brunson was the minister here when this work of building was begun. Precisely how long the building stood thus unused is not material, only it was not usable except in warm weather, as late as 1825 and 1826; for in the autumn of 1825, *William Simmons* was appointed to the Detroit *station*, and also in charge of Detroit District. He states that the Methodists held their meetings in "the old Academy," while he was the minister, and that they were very much annoyed in the evenings by the choir of another Church holding a singing school in the upper room of the building. Yet, occasionally, the Master of Assemblies manifested himself in the conversion of some soul, when they made noise sufficient to overcome the singing above. Having been deprived of the occupancy of the common church, as before stated, and now annoyed in this manner, one would have supposed that they might be left to themselves to get along as well as they could, but this was not the fact; for when any one who could afford them any influence or pecuniary aid was converted among them, every possible effort was made to proselyte them away. Still they struggled on and finally succeeded, as will hereafter appear. Mr. Simmons remained only one year. In the spring of 1826 he made a trip as far west as Ann Arbor and preached, also at Ypsilanti. He found a desperate road, but had the pleasure of marrying two daughters of Deacon Maynard, at Mallet's Creek, between Ann Arbor and Ypsilanti. But he made no successful effort to fit the church for use. The above we have obtained from Mr. Simmons himself.

This church was partially finished in 1826 and 1827, so that it could be occupied. It was occasionally occupied in warm weather from the time it was enclosed. It continued to be occupied in an unfinished state until Methodism had nearly died out in its influence. It became known, finally, as "the old brick church on the common." During the spring of 1825 Elias Pattee, who was preacher in charge, was permitted to travel as far east as New York City, to raise funds to finish this house. He was absent about three months, and was so successful in his mission, that when the Trustees came to settle with him, they found that after applying all collections and donations, towards defraying his traveling expenses, which they had agreed to pay, *they owed him two dollars and a half.*

The circumstances were now very discouraging indeed. It is a wonder they did not give up in despair. Nothing but a love for the principles of the Church could have induced men to continue in this organization under these circumstances. But they loved the cause, and were determined to hold to it, let what would come. Such noble adherance deserves success, and will finally have it. It is said that an offer of a subscription of *five hundred dollars* was made by one man, besides some other large ones, if they would build in an eligible position and with pews to rent. This would have furnished them with a good house, free from debt. But these offers, on such conditions, were spurned, as being such a departure from "old-fashioned Methodism," as not to be tolerated for a single moment. We admire their firm attachment to what they regarded as principle, but not their judgment; for Methodism has ever been the child of Providence, and in certain externals, not affecting vital principles, has adapted itself to the times and places. Had this offer been accepted, we cannot tell what would have been the effect upon the Church in this community. As it was, under the combined influence of an unfortunate location—"on the commons"—and an unfinished church, they made no progress, but became "beautifully less," until they became nearly extinct in their influence on the community. No improvement of any importance was made until they sold out and built a new church at the corner of Woodward Avenue and Congress Street. "The old brick church on the common" was used, as much and as well as they could, for one decade, as they began to use it in 1824, and left it in 1834, for the new frame one. Their new church was commenced in 1833, and dedicated to the worship of Almighty God, in 1834, and served them well until 1849, when, having purchased a lot, at the corner of Woodward Avenue and State Street, and having erected a larger and more elegant church, they left this and occupied the new. The new one, by the way, was built with pews to rent. At the same time, having sold their lot at the corner of Woodward Avenue and Congress Street, they removed the old frame building to the corner of Lafayette Avenue and Fourth Street, where they had procured a lot, and fitted it up for a new congregation, which was organized in the autumn of 1849, and they continued to worship in the same "old house" until 1873, when they built a new one.

"That old brick church on the common" has had quite an eventful history. Having been sold, it was for a time converted into a Universalist Church. But that society did not succeed, and it was soon disposed of again. It is rather a singular fact that, Universalism has never been able to maintain an organized existence in this city. After a little time, "the old brick church" was converted into a theater, and was so used for a little while. But a theater cannot flourish "on the common," much better than a church, and it was abandoned. "The old brick church" had now to pass into other hands, and was converted into a dwelling house, and is now used as such. Thus ends the history of the second Methodist church erected in Michigan.

It is a singular and significant fact that, in the space of seventeen or eighteen years from the time this locality was abandoned, as being too far out of town, the same Society should get back to within a few rods of it; and that the First Presbyterian Church should have removed onto Gratiot Avenue, still nearer to it. This only shows what mutations may take place in this changing world.

After this long digression, it is time to return to the direct line of our narrative. It has before been stated that, at the Conference held in 1824, Elias Pattee and Isaac C. Hunter were appointed to Detroit Circuit. As yet, there was but one charge in Michigan. We have before said a few things in regard to the senior preacher, so we pass that over now. But we may be permitted to make a few observations, in this connection, in relation to the junior, *Isaac C. Hunter.* He was a man of considerable talent, a little eccentric in his manners, and at this time was not very pious. The preceding year he and his colleague, on a Circuit in Ohio, became involved in a newspaper controversy which, though it began with fictitious names, without one knowing who the other was, became very personal and acrimonious; and when they ascertained who the parties were they did not abate in their acrimony In consequence of this fact, Mr. Hunter supposed he was sent to Michigan as a kind of punishment for his course the previous year. We said, therefore, he was not very pious. He was much chafed in his feelings and made no special effort to please the people. The result was, his labors were not very satisfactory to the people, nor very successful. He was just in that frame of mind which would be likely to make the people dislike him.

On one occasion some of the lower sort of people concluded they would show their spite at him by inflicting an insult upon his unoffending horse. This occured in the vicinity of Mount Clemens. They went into the stable at night and cut the hair from the mane and tail of the animal. Next morning, when the young preacher went into the stable to look after his horse, he found the innocent animal in that sad plight. He was in no frame of mind to pass off such a matter with apparent good humor; but he blustered a good deal about it, which was a source of much gratification to those who had committed the outrage. Such an affair, if passed off with good humor, unless one can bring the offenders to punishment, always brings shame upon those who commit the act and credit to those toward whom it was directed.

A case of an attempt to play off some fun at the expense of two ministers in a small town in Ohio, some years ago, will serve to illustrate. The wags of the town determined to elect the two resident ministers to a menial office. They succeeded in electing one of them as path-master and the other as fence-viewer. The former said a good deal about the matter, and said he regarded it as an intended insult. This was rare satisfaction for them, for it was what they wanted, to make him feel bad. The other coolly took the law, ascertained what were the duties of his office, quietly had a measuring rod made, and immediately set about measuring all the fences in town. Wherever he found a fence too low or otherwise defective, according to law, he made them repair it, so that by this means almost all the fences in town were renovated. In this way he made them heartily ashamed of what they had done. Had Mr. Hunter adopted this independent course he would have made them ashamed of themselves. He had to go to Detroit. When he came near the city he sought a way around to reach the residence of Robert Abbott, which then was some distance below the city. For fear that some one would see the condition of his horse, he took his large cloak and spread it all over the hind part of the animal so as to hide the artificial deformity. Mr. Hunter is dead, now, but he became more pious in after years. We refer to a future chapter for a fuller notice of Mr. Hunter's life and labors.

Nothing of special interest was accomplished in the city this year. At the end of the year—that is, in September, 1825—they reported *two hundred and forty-two* members for this Circuit. This was just the number reported the previous year. They had no increase. How could they have? These were all the members there were in the Territory of Michigan; but not all the Christians, as other Churches were being organized, and growing.

It will not be amiss, nor will it be displeasing to any, to introduce an incident or two which occured about these days, just here, by way of relieving the tedium of the narrative of the fortunes of the Church. The name of *Joseph Hickox* has already become very familiar to the reader, but still we must say a few things more about him, or rather introduce him to notice again. The fact is, he is so intimately interwoven with our early History that he must have frequent notices. Although he had settled his family on a farm on the River Rouge, about sixteen miles from Detroit, his familiarity with the frontier work and his itinerant spirit and habits kept him almost constantly on the move to visit destitute places. He raised up a Society in his own neighborhood, and penetrating the woods to the northeast of his residence, he succeeded in producing a blessed revival, which resulted in the formation of a large Society which afterwards became an important one in the Circuit.

Mr. Hickox visited Detroit frequently. During these visits a rather strange intimacy sprang up between himself and the Roman Catholic priest at Detroit, Mr. Richard. This priest was a perfect gentleman and a fine scholar, very shrewd and diligent in making proselytes to his Church. It was this last feature in his character that laid the foundation of their acquaintance, as he very much desired to gain Mr. Hickox to his faith. He left word, at a certain time, with one of Mr. Hickox's friends that he would be glad to receive a visit from him on his next visit to Detroit. On learning the fact he rather avoided the meeting, knowing that the priest was a thoroughly educated man and he, himself, had only such knowledge as could be picked up in a few years of toil as an itinerant preacher. One Sabbath afternoon, however, he stepped into his church and heard him preach, upon which all his fears of meeting him were dissipated. The next day Mr. Hickox called to see him, and was received with all the politeness of which a Frenchman is capable of exhibiting—which, by the way, cannot be exceeded by any other people. The following conversation then ensued:

Mr. Hickox—"I was to hear you preach yesterday."

Priest—"Ah! I did not know you were present."

H.—"Mr. Richard, you stated yesterday that Protestants say that Catholics were once right, but are not what they were once. But when we ask them in what and when we have changed, they are dumb. Now, I am not dumb, but I can tell you both in what and when you have deviated."

Priest—"In what have we changed?"

H.—"In the doctrine of transubstantiation. That was not known in your Church for three hundred years after Christ, and was not an article of faith until the sixth century. It was contested for three hundred years by the most learned of the Fathers."

Priest—"I acknowledge this to be so, but it was always an article of faith in reality though not in form."

H.—"Do you believe it?"

Priest—"I do."

H.—"What is soul? Is it not the intelligent part of man?"

Priest—"It is."

H.—"Does, then, the lifeless lump of matter become, by your consecration, an intelligent being? If so, it is capable of being taught. Go and teach it. But do you not consecrate more wafers than are received by communicants, Mr. Richard?"

Priest—"I do."

H.—"And each one is a perfect God?"

Priest—"Yes."

H.—"Cannot cats and mice, and such animals, feed on them?"

Priest—"They can."

H.—"Then, if the cat has swallowed the Deity she must have eternal life in her. What an absurd idea!"

Here Mr Richard colored as if displeased, but made no reply. The subject was still pursued but he would only say, with a bland smile, "Mr. Hickox, you are the first Protestant preacher I ever conversed with. I must say, it is a mystery."

After this they had frequent and friendly interviews, he urging Mr. Hickox to call every time he came to town. On one or two occasions he tried, very politely, to bow Mr. Hickox into the Romish Church and priesthood, telling him that his fortune would be made; that he could live like a gentleman, and never soil his hands again. To which Mr. Hickox responded that he would gladly join him if he could remove his objections to his Church. To which Mr. Richard replied, " I have not tried yet." "Well," said Mr. Hickox, " try now. If you believe me to be on the road to damnation—certain to be lost, out of your Church—it is your duty to convince me and save me now, if you can. I may not live to see you again." He only gave his shoulders a peculiar shrug and remained silent.

On another occasion Mr. Hickox was passing his house and felt suddenly moved to call, not knowing what topic to introduce. Mr. Richard met him very cordially, at the door, when Mr. Hickox remarked, " Mr. Richard, I did not intend to call but felt suddenly impressed to ask you a question."

Mr. Richard (quickly,)—"What is it! Ask it, do."

H.—" Were you ever born again! Did you ever see the time when you were in a justified relation in the sight of Heaven?"

R.—"Never! Never!"

H.—"Then I must tell you what the Scriptures say of you."

R.—" What do they say?"

H.—"That you are a blind leader of the blind, and that both will fall into the ditch. You say you are leading a number of people in the way to heaven, and yet you do not know the way yourself. Now get converted yourself, in the name of God, sir, and then you will be a safe guide to your people. That is all I have to say. Good bye, sir." So he left him.

At another time, when the same topic had been under discussion between them, as he left the room a young man who was studying theology with the priest followed Mr. Hickox out and said he knew that his (Mr. Hickox's) doctrine was true—that we must be born again ; and that he was resolved to seek the salvation of his soul by coming to the Saviour alone. He gave every evidence of sincerity, but his death occurred shortly after and nothing could be learned of his state of mind after that conversation.

These incidents are characteristic of the tact and talent of Mr. Hickox. His friend, Mr. Richard, was a talented and well educated Jesuit, but Mr. Hickox was too much for him in argument and could vanquish him every time. These doctrinal discussions do not seem to have produced any beneficial results on the mind of the priest, but they probably were the means of the conversion of the young man mentioned above. As the name of Mr. Richard, the Catholic priest, has occurred several times in our narrative, it may not be amiss to furnish, just here, a somewhat extended account of his life and labors. This we shall produce mainly from the official memoir: " Among the distinguished names that adorn the annals of Catholicity in the United States of America is that of the Very Rev. GABRIEL RICHARD, pastor of St. Ann's Church, Detroit, Michigan. He was born at Saintes, in France, on the 15th of October, 1764, of highly respectable parents. His mother, it is said, was a kinswoman of the illustrious Bossuet. Having finished his classical education, and feeling called to the ecclesiastical state, he entered the Seminary of Angers, where he prosecuted his theological studies." He was admitted to the priesthood in 1791, and shortly afterwards came to America. He arrived in Baltimore, Md., June 24th, 1792. He expected to have been employed as a teacher in a seminary in Baltimore; but that not being well enough established to need his services, he went to Illinois and the Northwest, where he found much need of labor, as, according to his account, there was a very low state of morals. The population was made up, principally, of Canadian French. Of the congregation at Kaskaskia, he gives the following description: " The people of this post are the worst in all Illinois. There is no religion among them—scarcely any one attending mass, even on Sunday. Intemperance, debauchery and idleness reign supreme." In 1798 he was invited by Bishop Carroll to be the assistant of Rev. Mr. Levadoux, at Detroit. He, therefore, left Illinois and arrived at Detroit in June, 1798, "and entered at once upon his duties as assistant pastor of that place, and soon won the confidence of those under his spiritual charge. At that time the jurisdiction of the pastor of Detroit extended over various places now embraced within the limits of Michigan and Wisconsin. The entire Catholic population of these districts did not amount to more than five or six thousand souls. The Catholics of Detroit and its vicinity consisted, almost exclusively, of Canadian French. Mr. Richard had but little opportunity of exercising himself in the English language, the study of which he had undertaken with great zeal in order to increase his usefulness. The inhabitants of the city were mostly persons whose vernacular tongue was English, but there were not more than a dozen among them who were Catholics. About a year after his arrival in Michigan, Mr. Richard visited the Catholics on the Island of Michilimackinac, about twenty miles from the former Michilimackinac, or Point St. Ignatius, where the Jesuit fathers had established a mission more than a hundred years before.

" Mr. Richard's zeal for the welfare of his flock inspired him with the idea of establishing a printing press at Detroit, and publishing a newspaper. This project he undertook in 1809, and for a time he issued a periodical in French, entitled '*Essai du Michigain;*' but the great distances which separated the people of the Territory, and the irregularity of the mails led to the discontinuance of his journal. His press, however, which was the first one introduced into the northwestern part of the United States, and was for several years the only printing apparatus in Michigan, did useful service under his direction."

Mr. Richard continued his relation to the Church in Detroit until his death, which took place in 1832. He died of cholera, on its first visitation at Detroit.

He had served for one term as Delegate in Congress from the Territory of Michigan, having been elected to that office in 1823. He did good service for his constituents while there.

CHAPTER VI.

Population—Difficulties of Settlement—Detroit District—Appointments—The Men—Numbers —Extent of Circuit—Abel Warren—Appointments for 1826—Numbers—Baughman is Married—Society in Ann Arbor—Supply, 1827—Coston—John Janes is Married—Geography of Circuits—The District--Coston Visits Southwestern Michigan—St. Joseph Mission—Goddard—Names of Circuits—Ministers from Ohio--People from the East—Ministers—Circuits —Results—Mary Keeler—Eli Hubbard—An Infidel—A Neglecter Comes to a Bad End— Curious Case—Incidents of Rowdies—"The Power"—Major Maxwell—One Visit—Appointments for 1831—Tecumseh Circuit—Kalamazoo—Increase—Black Hawk War—Love Feast and Sacrament in Jackson and Marshall—Cholera—Camp Meeting—Charges in 1832—First Ministers Raised Up—L. Davis—Indian Settlement—Numbers—Charges, 1834— Increase of the Work—Sunday Schools—Temperance—Literary Institution—Retrospect.

THUS far in our narrative we have had only one charge to look after, and that one charge attached to a distant District, so that it could receive very little assistance or encouragement from a Presiding Elder. This fact, however much to be regretted, cannot be charged to any fault of the Church authorities. The simple fact was, the population of the Territory had increased so slowly that it had not demanded much more ministerial labor. The census of 1810 showed only 4,762 inhabitants, and in 1820 only 8,896, a very slow increase. A very large proportion of these were French Roman Catholics, and could not be reached by our ministry, however many we might have had in the field. If we had had missionary money, so that a man might have confined his labors to the city, it is very likely that much more might have been gained. But that we had not. Indeed, if we had had the Missionary Society, and if the treasury thereof had been well supplied, it is not likely that much of it would have been appropriated to Michigan, because the future importance of the country, and of the City of Detroit was not recognized. This is not much to be wondered at, as so little was known of either its topography or geology that it was supposed the country could never bear a dense population, and consequently the city would be merely a trading post. Up to the period at which this chapter begins, but very few had penetrated beyond the timbered belt which lies along the coast on the east, and they knew nothing of the capabilities and resources of the country. The very few who had gone beyond had very erroneous ideas of the soil. The timber was so different from what they had found elsewhere, and the characteristics of the soil, too, that they thought it would not be productive for any length of time. It was understood to be a swampy, marshy, barren country, fit for little else than hunting grounds for the Indians. Indeed, the Indians were so numerous that it seemed discouraging to the whites to think of settling here. Again, the means of reaching the country was such that it required a great deal of courage or spirit of adventure to come. There had been no steam craft on the lakes earlier than 1819; and then for many years they were of such an inferior kind that, still, the means of access was very poor. In order to come in from the south with teams, a dismal swamp had to be passed through, and it looked fearful to undertake it. One other circumstance operated to retard settlement and tended to depreciate the importance of Detroit and the whole of Michigan, that was, in its first settlement there was a great deal of the ague and fever—it was regarded a sickly country. With all these facts in view, it is not much a matter of wonder that a greater interest in the religious supply of the country was not taken. We, however, have arrived at a period when the population is more rapidly increasing, as, according to the census for 1830, we had increased to 31,639, and this demanded more ministerial labor; still we had not learned the importance of concentration, and our men undertook to "grasp in all the shore," and to meet every call. They showed great zeal and perseverance, and had as good success as could reasonably be expected from such diffusive labors. From this time forward our charges are to increase in numbers.

At the session of the Ohio Conference which was held at Columbus, Ohio, beginning October 12th, 1825, Detroit District was created, embracing Detroit City Station and Detroit Circuit, in Michigan, and Fort Defiance, and Wyandotte Missions, in Ohio. We now have to do only with the two former appointments, as the other two lie out of our limits. *William Simmons* was appointed in charge of the District, and also of the City Station. We suppose he was not expected to visit the two missions in Ohio. *John A. Baughman* and Solomon Manier were appointed to Detroit Circuit. There had been

HISTORY OF PROTESTANTISM IN MICHIGAN. 109

a Presbyterian Church organized in Detroit this year,* and one in Monroe some time previous to this; also a Protestant Episcopal Church in Detroit, and a Baptist Church in Oakland County. A Presbyterian Church had been organized at Mackinaw; so the ministerial force, on the whole, has been considerably augmented. From this time onward we have a gradual expansion of our work for a few years, after which it enlarges much more rapidly, as the tide of immigration had set in more strongly in this direction.

Mr. Simmons was a young man, vigorous and active, and did good service. He remained here only one year. Mr. Baughman was well known in after years, and was remembered in all this country for his earnest and zealous labors. Mr. Manier was also a young man—was of pleasing address and possessed good abilities. He did not, however, have as much activity and energy as his colleague. He remained on the Circuit but one year and then returned to Ohio, where he continued to labor in connection with the Ohio Conference until 1834, when he located—dissolved his connection with the itinerancy. The results of the labors of this year are summed up in the following returns of members as made to the Conference in 1826, viz:

Detroit City, 70; Detroit Circuit, 290—a total of 360, which was a net increase of *one hundred and thirty-eight* members.

The work had been extended, by the indefatigable labors of these active, persevering young men, into all the settlements which had sprung into existence in the growing country. Why the Circuit was called Detroit we are not able to determine. In the report of the membership at the Conference for 1826, is the first time we have a distinct and separate report of the members belonging in the City of Detroit. The Circuit included all of Michigan except the city. A Society had been formed at Ypsilanti; in the Township of Troy, in Oakland County; in the town of Washington, in Macomb County; and Blissfield, in Lenawee County, was also visited. Mr. Baughman went as far west as Ann Arbor, which was just coming into existence, and preached a few times.

The most important Society in the Circuit was at the log meeting-house on the Rouge. Here "the joyful sound of the preaching of the Gospel, of prayer and hymns of praise, had been heard, sometimes mingled with the doleful howl of the wolf." But the glory of this Society had already begun to wane, from internal dissensions and from the changes in inhabitants, and soon after, this Society was discontinued. Another green spot on this Circuit was on the Rouge,

*Noah M. Wells.

a little farther west, where Mr. Hickox resided. To perform the rounds on this Circuit required a great deal of toilsome, lonesome labor, and to accomplish them was attended with much exposure to storms, and occasional lodgings in the woods.

In October, 1826, *Zarah H. Coston* was appointed Presiding Elder of Detroit District and also in charge of Detroit Station. The other appointments for the year were as follows, viz : Detroit Circuit, *John Janes*; Monroe, *John A. Baughman*; St. Clair, *James T. Donahoo*. We now have four charges—a greater division of the work, but only an increase of one to the working force. These four men had an extensive work on their hands, attended with many privations and much toil; for with the increase of charges there was no diminution of labor and suffering to each, as they had to extend their labors to the new settlements which had been made in the wilderness. But they addressed themselves to their work with warm hearts and strong wills, and when they went up to the Conference in September, 1827, and numbered up the hosts of our Israel, they reported members as follows, viz: Detroit City, seventy; Detroit Circuit, two hundred and twenty-six; Monroe, one hundred and fifty-seven; and St. Clair, thirty. Here we have an aggregate of *four hundred and eighty-three*, being a net increase of *one hundred and twenty-three* on the whole ; but no increase in the City Station. We have already seen that the cause in the city labored under great disadvantages on account of the location of the church.

It will be allowed, to state that one of our precious jewels was captured and carried off to Ohio this year. John A. Baughman had married Mrs. Sarah H. Baker, at Monroe, a very capable and efficient Christian laborer—a lady of much intelligence and activity in the cause of Christ. But what we lose in Michigan the cause somewhere else gains ; so we must be content. At the earnest solicitation of two young ladies who had recently settled there, a Society had been organized at Ann Arbor, this year, by Mr. Baughman, under the direction of the Presiding Elder.

Who shall next cultivate this enlarging and important field? Indeed, it was difficult to estimate its importance, or to impress it upon the authorities of the Church, who were to assign the supply; for, although the people in their destitution received with kind attentions any one who was sent to them in the name of the Lord, the foundations of society were to be laid; and men of sound minds and of discretion, as well as of Christian zeal and piety, were needed. The work for the next year was well supplied, as will appear from the list of appointments. The Conference met in September, 1827, at which time the work was supplied as follows, viz:

Detroit District, *Zarah H. Coston*, Presiding Elder, who also had charge of the City Station as before. Detroit Circuit, *William Runnels*, John Janes; Monroe, *George W. Walker*, James Armstrong. St. Clair seems to have been given up this year as a separate charge, probably because the promise of doing good did not bear any proportion to the sacrifice necessary to keep it up. These were all men of fine preaching abilities.

The settlements were now rapidly increasing, as before shown from the census for 1830, and consequently the work was much extended. At the close of this year, it appears we had lost *five* in the City of Detroit, and had on the aggregate gained only *sixty-two* members.

Mr. Coston was a faithful, good man, and an excellent preacher. If he had had a fair chance he would have advanced the cause greatly; but the disadvantages were more than a match for him. There were, however, a few faithful men and women who would not yield to the discouragements that were existing around them. They had identified themselves with the fortunes of this Church, because they believed that it was right, and, therefore, would not forsake it in the days of its trial. Among these we may name Amy Witherell, Sally Noble, Jerry Dean, Nancy Howard, John Owen, Philip Warren, Nathaniel Champ, B. F. H. Witherell, and others of whom we have spoken elsewhere.

This year another of our interesting and valuable ladies was married and taken away from us. *Rev. John Janes* married Miss Hannah B. Brown, of Ann Arbor. She was a very talented and well educated lady, and was the chief agent in securing the organization of the Society there the year before. She was a young lady of deep, thorough Christian experience, and could illy be spared from the feeble Society in Ann Arbor, but her sphere of usefulness was to be enlarged and she joined the itinerant ranks. We will furnish a fuller notice of this lady in connection with Ann Arbor.

We have been quite minute in our details thus far, because the work was confined to so few charges. Probably it will not be displeasing to continue this minuteness a little longer. At the session of the Conference which met at Chillicothe, Ohio, September 18th, 1828, the following appointments were made for Michigan, viz:

Detroit District—*Zarah H. Coston*, Presiding Elder.
Detroit City—*Arza Brown*.
Oakland—William T. Snow.

Huron—Benjamin Cooper.
Monroe—George W. Walker.
St. Clair—*Elias Pattee.*

It will be seen that the work had been extended to such a degree as to render it important that the Presiding Elder should devote his whole time to the interests of the District, and not divide his labors between that and the city. The men were all young, except Mr. Pattee, and unaccustomed to the administration of discipline, and only two of them were authorized to administer the sacrament of the Lord's Supper. In view of these two facts, it was necessary that the Presidihg Elder should visit each quarterly meeting, a thing he could not do and attend to the interests of the City Station. Though he had but five charges, his time was well filled up and thoroughly occupied.

It is proper here to furnish the geography of these charges, as they now appear in our list. The City of Detroit is well enough known not to need any further notice at this time, but not so with the others. Oakland was so named from Oakland County, and included all the settlements in Wayne County north of Detroit, all of Oakland and Macomb Counties. There were considerable settlements at Troy, Bloomfield, Perrin's, Farmington, Pontiac, Auburn, and some other places in this county, and a log meeting house a little northeast of Pontiac, known as Donation Chapel. In Macomb County, Mount Clemens, Romeo, Washington or Shelby, where Abel Warren lived, and Utica were the most noteworthy places. The topography of this Circuit was quite interesting in contemplation, but not so much so in the actual survey by the itinerant ministers; for they had to plod through deep mud and explore the swamps to meet their appointments. Much of this Circuit was in heavy timbered land, and the roads were not made, only blazed out.

Huron Circuit was so named from the Huron River along which it lay, and included that part of Wayne County lying west of the city and watered by the River Rouge. The principal appointments in this county were the old log meeting house, Hickox's, Nankin and Plymouth at Paul Hazen's. It also included Washtenaw County. As yet there was nothing beyond that. The principal settlements were Ypsilanti, Ann Arbor, Boyden's Plains, Dixboro, Superior, and Lodi Plains. There were many smaller settlements intermediate to these, which were faithfully visited and supplied with the word of life, furnishing labor for nearly every day in the week. This name rightly disappears from our records after the next year, and Ann Arbor takes its place, and covering more territory as the settlements were pushed farther into the woods. This year the appointments were visited once in three weeks, by hard travel and much toil and weariness. But the people, at least many of them, were hungry for the bread of life.

Monroe Circuit included the south part of the County of Wayne and all of Monroe and Lenawee Counties. Flat Rock, Monroe, Raisinville, Ten Mile Creek, Maumee Rapids in Ohio, Kedzie's Grove, and Tecumseh, were the chief points of interest at this time. Much of this Circuit was very difficult of travel on account of the swamps and marshes. It was no holiday sport to make the rounds on it.

The most isolated and desolate charge of the whole was St. Clair. This lay along the St. Clair River, embracing Algonac, Marine City, St. Clair and Port Huron, with some small settlements back from the river. The people were few, and most of them had no respect for religion or ministers, and it was then separated almost entirely from the rest of the world. A Society had been formed, some time before, at what is now Algonac, and this was the chief point of interest in the Circuit. The Society had been organized by a preacher from Canada. (*See St. Clair.*)

Thus we have given an outline of the settlements in Michigan at the time of which we write. Everything was new and uninviting, and offered to these ministers little besides toil and suffering. The unbridged streams had to be forded or swum, and they had to wallow through the marshes and swales. Occasionally, as they passed around, as was the case with Walker on Monroe Circuit, when the water was high, slightly frozen, and bridges gone, they would be obliged to plunge in at the peril of life and limb. All this from a love of souls. Of course this kind of labor and of peril was not peculiar to this country, but they are incidental to all new countries. Some of the incidents of travel and suffering we shall notice hereafter.

Detroit District embraced all the settlements there were in Michigan, and so continued until the autumn of 1835, except a little of the southwest corner, which in 1832 was attached to the Indiana Conference. In 1835 the work had so much enlarged that Ann Arbor District was created, embracing all the Territory west of Ypsilanti.

For the last few years there had been settlements springing up in the southwest part of the Territory, the people coming in from Virginia, Ohio and Indiana. They had now become sufficiently numerous for the organization of a county, and to send a Representative to the Legislative Council of the Territory. But they were destitute of Gospel privileges. The Representative called on Mr. Coston, in Detroit, and set forth their condition and requested him to assist them, and, if possible, to make arrangements for supplying them in future. In accordance with this solicitation, in the summer of 1829 he went, spending about three weeks among them. He went as far as Niles. He made arrangements to send them a missionary, which was done, as will appear from the list of appointments for the next year.

The brethren toiled hard and faithfully, and when the next Conference met in September, 1829, and they numbered up the membership, it stood as follows: Detroit, 78; Oakland. 246; Huron, 161; Monroe, 86; St. Clair, 49—total, 620. This shows an increase of *thirteen* for the city and *seventy-five* for the whole work over last year. This is the last time we purpose to give the statistics in detail. Neither do we purpose to introduce the list of appointments in the same manner again but once in the body of the work. We purpose to take occasion, at some appropriate time and place, to furnish minute and interesting accounts of the principal places, and the rise and progress of the cause of religion in them.

It will not be necessary to refer again to the work in the City of Detroit until after the close of this period, and it is sufficient now to say that the work has been regularly supplied, and our cause has gradually advanced in the city and assumed a permanency, and increased in interest, so that in 1836 we find *one hundred and fifty-nine* members returned for the city. They had, also, as before stated, changed the location of their church, and had erected a very neat, even elegant church for the times ; so that, in this respect, they were nearly on an equal footing with any other church in the city. The Sabbath school was large and flourishing.

At the Conference in 1829 St. Joseph Mission was added to the list of appointments. This Mission embraced all the settlements in the southwest part of the Territory. The principal point of interest at this time was White Pigeon. Erastus Felton, who was appointed to this Mission, labored faithfully and visited all the scattered settlements he could, and formed a number of small Societies, and returned *seventy-six* members at the next Conference as the result. Some had been converted, and many of them had been members elsewhere and had their certificates with them. How many of these new homes were made glad by the visits of this indefatigable missionary! He was a man of zeal and respectable preaching talents.

There was also a change in Presiding Elders this year—1829.

Mr. Coston was transferred to the Pittsburgh Conference, and *Curtis Goddard*, a most excellent and worthy man, was appointed in charge of the District. He continued in charge for three years. Mr. Goddard joined the itinerant connection in 1814, and located in 1834, having labored in connection with the Conference just twenty years. He was a very devout, holy and exemplary man and excellent preacher, and did much good in this District.

This year there was an increase of *two hundred and five* in the membership—so their labors " were not in vain in the Lord." This, however, was not any more than keeping pace with the population. As the Circuits were named for the counties or rivers, there will be a change in their names from time to time, and some of the names of this date will be entirely forgotten in this relation; as Huron does not appear again and Oakland will be lost in a few years more; St. Joseph, though now so important, will lose its identity in a little while. We cannot complain of this, for it is right.

In the following year—1830—there was a general change of the ministers. The ministers appointed to this Territory did not, any of them, feel themselves identified with the interests of the Territory, and were here simply because they were appointed by the authorities of the Church. This was a little unfavorable to the interests of religion. They all came from Ohio, too, while a very large proportion of the settlers were from the East, making some difference in manners and customs between the ministers and the people. It was a very common thing in these early days—and, indeed, for a number of years later—in love-feasts and class-meetings, to speak of the time when they were converted "down in Old York State." Many of these Eastern people sighed for their old preachers, and some efforts were made to induce some of them to emigrate to this country, with but little success. As yet, none had been raised up here.

For the year beginning in September, 1830, the appointments stood as follows, viz:

Detroit District—*Curtis Goddard, Presiding Elder.*
Detroit City—Alvan Billings.
Oakland—*Arza Brown,* William Sprague.
Ann Arbor—Henry Colclazer, Elijah H. Pilcher.
Monroe—James W. Finley.
St. Clair—*Benjamin Cooper.*
St. Joseph—Leonard B. Gurley, Erastus Felton.

By this list there appears to be no increase in the number of charges, but there was an increase of three in the number of men to supply them. There had been, also, within a few years last passed, an increase of the force of local preachers, who were rendering very efficient service, among whom were Marcus Swift, in the Town of Nankin, a man of ability and deep piety, Laban Smith and John J. Young of Bloomfield, and Allen Tibbitts of Plymouth. These men rendered very effective service by their activity and devotion to the work. There is one other name too precious and valuable to be overlooked in this connection, although we shall speak of him more fully hereafter, that is, *Joseph Bangs*, of Tecumseh, a brother of the venerated Nathan Bangs, D. D., and father of Francis B. Bangs of the Michigan Conference. He was a man of great power as a preacher, and his piety was so undoubted that all who knew him respected him.

The Circuits this year were enlarged in every direction in which it was possible; as, the Ann Arbor Circuit, which takes the place of the Huron of the last two years, was extended west to Jackson, where a settlement had been commenced in the spring of 1830. In order to do this the preachers had to go from Ann Arbor to Jackson and return on the same route, to preach at Jackson and at Grass Lake, making a journey of *eighty miles* to preach twice. There was no regular road, and they had to follow the Indian trail much of the way. Monroe Circuit was made to include Tecumseh and Adrian; Oakland extended itself towards the northwest. It included Farmington, where, the year before, there had been a very powerful revival, so that almost the entire population had been converted. This was under the labors of William T. Snow. Many of the young people became very active members of the Church. Among these were the Meads and Thayers, whose parents were Presbyterians, but the young people became very active and earnest Methodists. Some of them still remain. The St. Joseph Circuit included all of the southwest part of the Territory, and the two excellent and talented young men found all they could do to meet the calls of the new and growing settlements. They included Kalamazoo, where a Society was organized, of which we shall speak hereafter, Niles, and many minor places. At the end of the year they reported *eleven hundred and eighty-three* members for Michigan, making an increase of *three hundred and fifty-eight* over last year.

It is to be understood that these results were attained by much labor, toil and suffering—also with some opposition. About this time Mary Keeler, a very fine young lady, residing at Ten Mile Creek, in Monroe Circuit, who had been thoughtless and gay, was converted and united with the Church. Her father was bitterly opposed to religion and very determined in his way. So, when Mary came home, being much enraged, he gave her the alternative, to abandon her religion or be banished from her home forever. She chose the latter; but the Lord raised her up friends and supplied her with homes. She became a very devoted, zealous and useful member of the Church. Eli Hubbard, too, of the same neighborhood, was a wonder of Divine grace, being raised up to serve God in the midst of great opposition, and from a low degree of sin; but he served his day and generation faithfully, and has gone home to his reward.

In the neighborhood of Ann Arbor a Mrs. How was converted in the spring of 1830. Her husband was very bitter in his opposition, and persecuted her very much. On one occasion he collected several of his same sort—freethinkers they wished to be considered, but really tyrants, not willing that others should think freely—and supplied the whisky. They drank and caroused, and, finally, to show his contempt for religion, he took his wife's Bible, baptized it in whisky—in the name of the Father, Son and Holy Ghost—and then put it in the fire and burned it up. As might be expected, he lived a wretched life, and finally died a miserable death. It is surprising that others will not take warning from such examples, but, yet, each one seems to think that it will not be so with him. Still, if they would only take counsel of their own feelings as well as these circumstances, they would know that it could not be otherwise; for they would find a wretched, fiendish feeling in them which is opposed to peace.

During the summer of 1831 there were three Camp Meetings held in this country. One in the town of Superior, which was a time of great interest, and many were converted. The writer will never forget one family, in which there were two children, a son and a daughter, coming to maturity. The mother was a Christian, and very anxious for the salvation of her children. They were both very deeply affected with a sense of their guilt at this meeting. The daughter yielded so far as to make a profession of faith in Christ; but the son was very stubborn, and finally declared he would not attend to it now, and turned away from the Saviour—to the great grief of his parents and other friends. It seemed very sad at the time, and we feared he would come to some bad end. We lost sight of that young man for a few years, but the next place we found him was in the State Prison for crime. A few months after we first saw him in prison there was a break among the prisoners, and several of them got out, and were determined to fight their way through the country. Young Norton acted as leader of the gang. When surrounded by those who had been called out to arrest them, he was required to surrender; but he refused, and was making a movement to disable some one, so that he might get on. He was now fired at and mortally wounded, and died in a few hours. We were at his funeral in the prison. How dangerous it is to resist the strivings of the Divine Spirit!

Two of these meetings were held in the town of Bloomfield, in Oakland County, near Birmingham. They were both occasions of great power. Many were converted, and many were physically prostrated, or had what is vulgarly called "the power"—not simply Methodists, but Presbyterians and Baptists. During the time of the second of these latter meetings, there was a pious lady in the immediate neighborhood who was very sick and not expected to live. For some days she had been helpless and in a rather comatose state. She revived a little and seemed to be engaged in prayer for a little while, when she arose from her bed, walked across the room and back to her bed, to the amazement of her attendants, and said she should recover. She did recover. She said she had received the assurance of it in answer to prayer. We knew her well in after years when we traveled the Farmington Circuit. We simply state the facts, and leave every one to draw his own conclusions in regard to the power of prayer.

At the first meeting in Bloomfield. which was in June, the following incident occurred: One of the young preachers from an adjoining Circuit observed, on Saturday evening, that there were several young men who seemed disposed to make disturbance. He determined, if possible, to defeat them. For this purpose he disguised himself, saying nothing to any one, and found a way to drop in among them, so as not to be observed but to be recognized as one of them. Thus he heard their plans and knew their purposes. They did not propose anything very bad, only such as would disturb and annoy. They had gathered around a fire on the outside of the encampment, and were engaged in conversation, and waiting till some opportunity should turn up. Now, to his surprise, he found another young minister, partly disguised, but not so but that they had a little suspicion of him—but by the help of the first this suspicion was quieted. While sitting here, a shout broke out in a tent on the opposite side of the ground. The public meetings had been closed, and most of the tent-holders had retired; but in this tent there was so much interest they could not give up to sleep, but continued their devotions. The power of the Lord came down upon them and some of them shouted. When this shout was heard all must needs go

to see what was up. The young preacher left his comrades a few
moments to reconnoiter. When he returned he found most of them
together, some swearing and some doing other unsuitable things.
He thought his time had now come to make a strike among them.
So he, in a kind of swaggering way, proposed to them to go across
the ground and have a meeting, too, as they in the tent seemed to be
enjoying themselves so well. This, however, they did not like to do.
"Well," said he, "lets us have meeting right here. If you will hear
I'll preach." "Very well," said they; "we'll be glad of that." "Well,
now," said he, "you must all agree to stand by me and hear all I've
got to say." "Yes, we will," said they, and took their seats on a
bench which stood there in front of a tent. There was about a dozen
of them. He took off his hat, took for his text, "Prepare to meet
thy God," and preached for an hour or more. Soon after he began
two of them suspected they had got into a trap, and began to
whisper; probably they were saying, "Guess he's a preacher."
"Your attention," said he; "you promised to hear all I had to
say." They stopped and he went on. He preached, setting forth
the necessity of a preparation, and the awful consequences if they
did not prepare. He had spoken but a few moments before he
and they were surrounded by the people coming from their tents.
When he closed his sermon he called on *Arza Brown*, the preacher
in charge of the Circuit, to pray. After prayer, "Now," said he, to
the people around him, "if you will pray I will hold class-meeting
with them. "He then spoke to them individually, and urged the
necessity and excellency of religion. The most of them were very
much affected. When he closed class-meeting, *James W. Finley*,
from Monroe, struck up and sung the hymn:

"Ye simple souls, that stray
Far from the paths of peace," &c.

When he was done singing he dismissed them, It was now near
the dawn of day. When dismissed, the most of them resorted to
their former place at the fire on the outside of the tents opposite.
The aforesaid disguised preacher was then among them—of course
not the one who had preached, but the other one, who, by the way,
was James W. Finley. "Well," said one, "this is a new thing. I
have heard of a wolf in sheep's clothing, but I never before heard of
a sheep in wolf's clothing." "Well," said another, "we must be very
careful what we say; for, just as likely as not, before we are aware of
it, one of these preachers will be right here among us."

Just as it was getting light, one of the number, an Irishman—a
school-teacher, who intended, as a rule, to be a very decent man—

came to the young preacher and said he wished to speak with him. "Well, now," said the Irishman, "you rather got us into this." "Oh, no," replied the preacher; "you got yourselves into it." "Well, but you took the advantage of us," quoth the first. "Oh, well," said the latter; "it is my business to take all the advantage of the Devil I can." "But," persisted the Irishman, "if you saw me doing wrong it was your place to come and tell me of it." "Oh, no," replied the preacher; "it is my business to preach and yours to hear." "But," continued the other, "it is not the best way. It has a tendency to harden me." "That is a pretty story, for you are now crying like a whipped baby and cannot help it," retorted the preacher. Here ended the interview. There was no more disposition to disturb that meeting, and some six or seven of the young men were converted before the meeting closed.

The next year following there was a Camp Meeting held in this same vicinity, at which there was a wonderful display of the Divine power. Some of the strongest and least nervously excitable men in all the country lay for hours entirely helpless, but yet as happy as they could be. One described the sensation as that of being separated from his body, and looking down upon it as it lay there in that helpless condition, and knew that it was his own body. We are not prepared to say much about this kind of manifestation; only that it seems to be a manifestation of the Divine Spirit, which has been experienced in almost all countries and more or less among all religious denominations. It is a manifestation not to be sought after.

In 1830 we became acquainted with *Major Thompson Maxwell*, who died in 1831, aged ninety-six years, and whose funeral we attended. He had resided on the River Rouge, about sixteen miles from Detroit, for a number of years. He was step-father to Joseph Hickox. He was a very pious, good man; had been, in New England, a member of the Congregational Church, but had united with the Methodist Episcopal Church some time before his death. He was one of the men selected by John Hancock to throw the tea overboard in Boston Harbor. He was in twenty-three battles of the Revolution. In the War of 1812 he was promoted to the rank of Major in the Regular Army of the United States, and served faithfully during the war. He died in the faith and peace of the Gospel of Christ.

The circumstances alluded to above, of throwing the tea overboard in 1773 are thus described in Bancroft's History of the United States: "Every endeavor had been exhausted to induce the consignees of the tea to return it to England and not offer it for sale:

"It had been dark for more than an hour. The church in which they met was dimly lighted; when, at a quarter before six, Rotch appeared, and satisfied the people by relating that the Governor had refused him a pass, because his ship was not properly cleared. As soon as he had finished his report, Samuel Adams arose and gave the word: 'This meeting can do nothing more to save the country.' On the instant a shout was heard at the porch; the war-whoop resounded; a body of men, forty or fifty in number, disguised as Indians, passed by the door; and, encouraged by Samuel Adams, Hancock and others, repaired to Griffin's wharf, posted guards to prevent the intrusion of spies, took possession of the three tea ships, and in about three hours three hundred and forty chests of tea, being about the whole quantity that had been imported, were emptied into the bay, without the least injury to other property. 'All things were conducted with great order, decency, and perfect submission to the government.' The people around, as they looked on, were so still that the noise of the breaking open of the tea chests was plainly heard. A delay of a few hours would have placed the tea under the protection of the Admiral at the castle. After the work was done the town became as still and calm as if it had been holy time. The men from the country carried back the great news to their villages."

Major Maxwell was a very quiet, unobtrusive man, but fearless and courageous, and well fitted for an enterprise of that kind. His last days were spent in quiet retirement in Wayne County, and his dust sleeps in the country graveyard, and in an unmarked grave, awaiting a glorious resurrection.

A little incident, illustrative of the occasional inconveniences of itinerant life, occurred to us on this same Circuit. Belonging to one of the country classes was Brother B., whose home was some three miles distant from the place of meeting, and directly off from the route we had to travel to perform our rounds on the Circuit. This brother became very urgent that we should visit him and stay over night with him. We finally agreed that if he would be present at the next meeting, so as to conduct us into the woods, we would go with him. The meeting was on a week day. We confess we rather hoped he would not be there, as the indications were not very inviting or promising. But when the day came he was on hand and claimed our company. We went. Our way was through thick woods, occasionally deep mud, and not much road. When we reached the habitation we found it to be a very rude log house, standing in the forest with but a small patch cleared around it. There was a partial fence inclosing it, but it did not exclude small animals, so there were young hogs around the house, which occasionally intruded themselves inside, notwithstanding there were two or three dogs lying around the fire-place, though there was not much fire, as it was warm weather. We found there was but one room to the house, and two beds in it. All the appurtenances were such as might have been supposed from the pigs and dogs. There were, also, several small children. It was near night when we reached the habitation, and the good lady was in expectation of our coming, and seemed to be pleased to think the minister was coming to visit them. She made us as welcome as she knew how to do. Our meal was provided, and we sat down to it. But such a meal! Well—we'll not attempt to describe it. We made the best we could of it. As the hour of retiring to sleep approached we kept wondering where we were to sleep. After prayers the brother told us we were to occupy one of the two beds in the same room. There were no curtains around them, and we had to snatch the moments when the lady's face was turned the other way to get into bed, as we were a very modest young man then. When we were about to lie down to slumber, the good brother told us he would be under the necessity of putting two or three of the little fellows into the same bed, as they were not very well supplied. When we looked at the bedding we concluded it had been washed some time, but it must have been so long ago that it had forgotten it. But there was no backing out now, so we turned in. The little ones were turned in with us. But, before we had time to become locked up in sleep, we found we had other companions besides children. These were so pertinacious as to make such attacks on us as to prevent our sleeping. We waited very wistfully for the morning, and as soon as practicable we left the woods, and never found it convenient to visit them again. Every itinerant can relate incidents of this kind—and some much worse, perhaps. But the people are good and kind, in their way, and seem to think they are all right.

We will now look for a few moments at the appointments made in 1831 and to the results. The flood-tide of immigration seemed now to have set in in this direction very strongly, calling for an increase of laborers, and also for enlarging the aggregate of suffering and toil to carry the Gospel to the new settlements. Still there were only three new names of charges introduced to our notice—to wit, Ypsilanti, Tecumseh and Kalamazoo Circuits. Ypsilanti embraced all of Ann Arbor Circuit lying east of Ann Arbor. This is all we need to say of the geography of this Circuit. Tecumseh is introduced to the exclusion of Ann Arbor, so that we only have an increase of two charges. But, as this is new in its boundaries, it will not be uninteresting to furnish its geography and a description of the first round made on it by the preacher in charge. Starting at Ann Arbor, it went west to Marshall, thence south to Coldwater, thence east to Clinton, thence south to Tecumseh and Adrian, thence north, through Manchester and Saline, to Ann Arbor, making nearly *four hundred* miles of travel to be performed every four weeks and to preach *twenty-seven* times regularly in the same time.

It is to be premised that the autumn of 1831 was very rainy; that all the swamps and marshes were full of water and the streams were very high and many bridges were carried away. It is further to be understood that the settlements were mostly made in parallel lines, so that from Ann Arbor westward there were no north and south roads. It will be seen that this Circuit embraced two of these parallels; so, in order to get around, we must find or make some cross road.

We will furnish a few extracts from the journal of the preacher in charge, descriptive of his first round:

"*September 1st, 1831.* I was appointed to Tecumseh Circuit with Ezekiel S. Gavit. Arrived at Ann Arbor on September 21st, and commenced my labors on this Circuit, and had to fix its bounds. I reached Jackson without any special difficulty, but this was as far west as any itinerant had ever gone. Spent Sabbath, October 2d, in Jackson. Monday, October 3d, rode nine miles to Brother Fassett's, and preached at night. The Sandstone Creek was very high and without bridge, so I got into the water pretty badly.

"*October 4th.* Rode twenty-three miles to Marshall—a new place. To-day, in crossing marshes, my horse got mired down twice, so that I had to get off into the mud and water to help him out. I had to cross one creek which was so narrow that a man could step across in most any place where it was not worn by teams crossing it, but when I rode into it my horse sank into the mire and water, so that the water came over the top of my saddle. Reached Marshall late in the afternoon, wet, cold and tired.

"*Sunday, October 9th.* Preached twice in the private residence of Sidney Ketchum. This was the first visit they had had from an itinerant; though Randall Hobart, a local preacher, had been here for a few weeks, and had preached a few times. He has come to settle here. A Presbyterian minister had purchased and was keeping public house, and to-day preached in his own house in the afternoon.

"*Monday, 10th.* Having hired a man to go with me to find the way to Coldwater, we set out. Left my clothes and books at Marshall, and filled my saddle-bags with oats for the horses and bread and raw pork for ourselves. We supplied ourselves with an axe, a gun, a pocket compass and a map, and so started to find our way to Coldwater. We wallowed through marshes and creeks as we came to them; we marked the trees on the south side, so that we could follow the same way back. When we came to the St. Joseph River we found it very high, and did not like to venture in; so we cut a tree, which reached nearly across, and one went over on that and the other drove the horses through and then followed on the tree. Thus we continued until night overtook us. Wet and tired, we kindled a fire, made a hut of brush, roasted our meat, and ate supper and went to bed, after family prayer. My great-coat made my bed, my saddle and saddle-bags my pillow. Slept some. The wolves howled most hideously most of the night.

"*Tuesday, October 11th.* Resumed our journey, but made no progress in the right direction. Becoming satisfied that I could not find my way through from this direction, and reach my appointment at Clinton and Tecumseh on the Sabbath, we returned to Marshall, so as to go back by way of Ann Arbor.

"*Wednesday, 12th.* Rode to Jackson, with about the same difficulties I found on my way out.

"*Thursday, 13th.* Rode to Ann Arbor, forty miles, over the worst road I ever met with. The Grand River at Jackson was very high, so that the log-way on each side of the bridge was all afloat. My horse soon went down across the logs. Had to dismount, help him off, and lead him across by the end of the bridge. All the bridges across the marshes and little streams were either afloat or were carried away. Occasionally I would make my horse leap across the creek, but sometimes I had to strip him and drive him through, and get myself and my baggage over the best I could. Near sundown I reached Mill Creek, at Lima Center, where I found the bridge entirely gone, except the stringers. There was no time to parley. I stripped my horse and drove him into the creek. He went to the opposite bank, but would not leap up, and he came back. Drove him in again with the same result. This time I put the saddle on and mounted, having left my saddle-bags, overcoat and under coat on the bank. The water came over the top of the saddle—made him leap up the bank, and we pressed on, but when we had got about half way over the wide marsh, he mired down and could not help himself. Dismounting, I rolled up my sleeves, plunged my hands down into the mud, pulled out his feet, and got them onto fresh turf, and assisted him up. Went back after my things, mounted, and rode eleven miles to Ann Arbor. Reached there about nine o'clock P. M., wet, cold, tired and hungry."

From Ann Arbor he went southwest, and spent the Sabbath at Clinton and Tecumseh. On Monday he started towards Coldwater. When he stopped for the night at Moscow—it is now—he found a Frenchman who claimed to have been a trader among the Indians and knew the country well. He employed him to go as his guide, but he proved to be a drunken, worthless fellow, and he discharged him at Coldwater. He found there were a few families about five miles north of Coldwater. He went on to that place, but was detained till Friday. On that day and the next we find the following entries in his journal:

"*Friday, October 21st.* Took an early start. Provided myself with an axe and blazed the trees on the south side. A few miles after crossing the St. Joseph River I came to my old blazes. Thus I blazed my way for twenty miles through the woods alone. Reached Marshall about sundown, tired, wet and hungry. Found my colleague, Brother Gavit, here, quite despondent because I had been delayed by a funeral.

"*Saturday, October 22d.* Returned to Coldwater. Brother Gavit came half way with me. We labored hard, and made the way plain, and parted after prayer here, in the wild woods. Thus I have spent four days, carrying an axe and blazing the trees to make a way to get around our Circuit. My right shoulder is so sore and lame that I can scarcely lift my hand to my head. But I am resolved to persevere."

On this Circuit there was one place of ten miles without any house, and in another part a place of twenty miles. On one part of it there were sixty miles between appointments. They had to stop at a tavern and pay their bills.

Kalamazoo Circuit took in all of Kalamazoo County, and whatever there was west and northwest, to the Lake, furnishing a wide and open range for the missionary. We have not been able to obtain anything from the journal of the missionary for this year.

The results of the labors of this year are indicated in part by the figures. Still, mere figures do not give a full view of what has been accomplished by these self-denying labors. The foundations are laid for the growth of Society. The figures show a net increase of *four hundred and ninety-five* in the membership.

The Black Hawk War occurred during this year, and created much excitement in Michigan for a few weeks. It was feared that the Indians of Michigan would be induced to join Black Hawk's party, and occasion a great deal of mischief among us. But the war was soon ended, and the people settled down again to their peaceful pursuits. The tendency of all such excitements is to divert the attention of the people, for a time, from the great interests of the soul; but, through the mercy of our God, this was of short duration. A greater obstacle was found in the eagerness of the people to secure the best locations for farms, mills and villages.

The first love-feasts and sacramental seasons held in the Counties of Jackson and Calhoun were held this year. The one in Jackson was in March, and that in Calhoun—Marshall—in June, 1832.

This, too, was the year of the first visit of that terrible scourge, the cholera, to this part of the country. Ann Arbor and Marshall were specially afflicted. Many died with it in both places.

There was but one Camp Meeting held in our Territory this year. This was near Northville, and was an occasion of great spiritual power. Many were converted, and witnesses of perfect love were raised up, and the cause was much benefited by this meeting. The ministers in attendance were generally young, but they were men of power, for God was with them. The meeting occurred early in June, 1832.

With the opening of another year there is a change in the superintendency of the District and a little change in the boundaries. By act of the General Conference, which met in the City of Philadelphia, in May, 1832, the southwest portion of Michigan was attached to the Indiana Conference, because it was more convenient to supply it from that direction. It continued in that relation till 1840. *James Gilruth* was appointed Presiding Elder of Detroit District, and continued in that office until 1836.

For the year 1832-33 we have some new charges—viz., Ann Arbor is restored; Farmington and Mount Clemens in place of Oakland; Saginaw and Calhoun Missions. The geography of these charges has been before described, as this was mainly the division of the work as the intervals of the great points were filled up, as Tecumseh Circuit of last year was divided into three parts—viz., Tecumseh, Ann Arbor and Calhoun—but the area was not extended, and five preachers occupy the same territorial limits occupied by two last year. The Saginaw Mission was an exception to this remark, as the whole of its appointments were beyond where any other had penetrated. This was rather an experiment, and it was given up at the next Conference, because there were so few people to be reached by it.

It seems a little strange that as yet no one has been raised up as a minister from this field. We have had occupation of Michigan soil and have had Societies for about twenty-three years, and, of late years, a rapidly increasing membership, and yet not one convert has been called into the ministry. The supply has all come from abroad. Perhaps one reason for this is the very dependence we have had on Ohio, which has always been prolific in preachers. The Minutes of 1833 furnish the first instance of a minister from among Michigan converts—to wit, Duncan McGregor. A few others, as L. D. Whitney, Marcus Swift, Richard Lawrence, and William H. Brockway, were recommended to the Conference from the Detroit District; but they were members of the Church before they came to Michigan, and only one of them, Mr. Brockway, was licensed to preach here. The next name of a Michigan convert entering the itinerant work was Lorenzo Davis, who was converted in Ypsilanti, and joined the Conference in 1834. Neither of these two brethren—converts—is now in the itinerant ranks. Messrs. Whitney, Swift and Lawrence located, and have since died. They died in the faith.

At the Conference of 1833 there was no increase of the number of charges, although there had been an increase of *nine hundred* in the membership. Saginaw Mission was left off the Minutes, but Huron Mission was introduced. This Mission lay along the Huron River below Ypsilanti, and extended out to Dearborn. The chief point of interest in this Mission was an Indian settlement a little above Flat Rock. They were Wyandottes, and there was a number of members of the Church among them. Old Blue Jacket was a very important character among them, and a man of considerable mental power. Old Honness was an interesting patriarch among them. He was supposed, at this time, to be something over one hundred years old. He was a white man, but had been taken by the Indians when a little boy—so small that he had only a confused idea of his parents—was of German origin. He was now rejoicing in the consolations of religion, having been converted about two years before. He died shortly after this in the peace of the Gospel. The last year before this Monroe Circuit included this Indian settlement, and we employed William H. Brockway to teach the Mission school. While engaged in this work he was licensed to preach and recommended to the Conference. We shall never forget one visit we made to this Mission. We stayed over night among them, sleeping on the soft side of a bench in the school-house, in company with Mr. Brockway and the boys who attended the school. The next day we visited around among them. About noon we were very weary and hungry, and called at a cabin and had a dinner of hominy and Indian sugar. We did not stop to think how the sugar had been made, or how much filth there might be in the sugar or the hominy. It was one of the most delicious meals we ever ate, according to the princples of the German proverb, "Hunger is the best sauce." It was a hard day, but we have never regretted having devoted it to them. These Indians left their small reservation in a few years after this and went west of the Mississippi.

The year closes up with an increase of *seven hundred and fifty* members. We now have an entire membership of *three thousand three hundred and eighteen*, and *twenty ministers*.

For the next year—1834—we have only one increase in the number of charges—that is Cassopolis—taking the west half of St. Joseph Circuit. In the eastern part of the Territory the Huron Mission is extinguished and Plymouth is introduced, to continue as a permanent charge, though it will, from time to time, be pared down to become a Station. The work went on prosperously this year.

We have but one more year in this third period to complete our annals. This year—1835—shows a considerable increase of the work. Detroit District is divided and Ann Arbor District is created, and there are six new charges. Only one of these, however, is in entirely new ground—that is, Grand River Mission.

We find an increase of *one thousand six hundred* members for this year.

We have, then, at the close of this third period of our History, *two Districts, with three charges belonging to a District, in Indiana, making nineteen charges; twenty-nine itinerant, and a much larger number of local preachers, and four thousand nine hundred and twenty members.*

This, however, does not exhibit the whole work which has been done; for the Sabbath School has secured much attention, as, in every place where it was practicable, Sabbath Schools have been organized and conducted through the joint labors of ministers and laymen and women of God.

The Sabbath School work has all originated within this period of our History, as distinctive Methodist Sabbath Schools, or even any at all. A mission Sabbath School was started in Detroit probably about 1820, and the Methodists were content to co-operate with that school until some time in 1827, when they started a school of their own. We have not been able to ascertain the precise date of the origin of either of these schools, though we have made diligent inquiry. The same thing holds in regard to these schools that does in regard to the Churches here—their early records are not to be found, and we have to depend on the memory of individuals mainly. This union school originated and was maintained by Presbyterian influence, and the records were not preserved. Hon. Alanson Sheley has the first records to be found. This first Methodist Sabbath School in Michigan had to struggle with great difficulties, such as the location of the unfinished "church on the commons," the prestige of the union, and the want of teachers. Mr. Jerry Dean was the prime mover in this enterprise, and was the first superintendent. Hon. John Owen, then quite a young man and a member of the Methodist Church, was secretary of the union school, and did not, at first, join in this Methodist movement. After a time—that is, in 1830—however, he was induced to give up the position which he held as secretary and take the superintendency of the Methodist School, a position which he held for many years after. He procured a small room down on Woodward Avenue, near Congress Street, which had been used as a lawyer's office, to which he removed the school, and kept it there until the new church was erected at the corner of Woodward Avenue and Congress Street. This was, indeed, the day of small things. Down to the date to which this period comes the Sunday School work had not been so systematized as that any statistical reports were made, so we have to content ourselves with the general statement that this work was attended to by the Churches in those days, perhaps not with the same degree of thoroughness as at this day; but, yet, the work was begun and carried forward with a commendable degree of zeal, and with considerable success. Then we had not the appliances for instruction, nor the attractions of the present day. But a noble work was done, and these pioneers in this department of Church work are worthy of all praise. They sowed and we have entered into their labors, and we are gathering a grand fruitage.

The Temperance reform was entered into very heartily and actively. Ministers became earnest lecturers, and in 1832 the membership in this Peninsula almost unanimously signed memorials to the General Conference, asking for a more stringent rule on the subject of the sale and use of intoxicating liquors. Although the Church was considered a Temperance Society, our ministers and people generally united in Temperance organizations and efforts with those who did not belong to the Church but were willing to operate in this cause, and work in this way for the good of humanity.

We copy the following resolutions from the records of the

Quarterly Conference for Ann Arbor Circuit, dated April 5th, 1834, as characteristic of the feelings and action of the Methodists at that date on the subject of Temperance:

"*Resolved* (1), That such is the light that is now cast upon the subject of total abstinence from the use of ardent spirits that no persons can be considered as members in good standing in our Societies who continue to use such articles, except as a medicine in cases of necessity.

"*Resolved* (2), That we highly disapprove of the practice of selling ardent spirits, except in accordance with the last clause of the preceding resolution, and that we will use our influence to dissuade our members from engaging in the traffic.

"*Resolved* (3), That we recommend to all our members to unite in forming and supporting Temperance societies."

Already had the idea of building up a literary institution, under the patronage and fostering care of Methodism been entertained, and a charter had been obtained from the Legislative Council of of the Territory for this purpose. The location was unfortunate, and it became necessary to change the location afterwards; but, yet, the charter obtained in 1835 was the foundation of the Albion College. The ball was put in motion in 1833, by the agreement of Dr. B. H. Packard, of Ann Arbor, Rev. Henry Colclazer and Rev. E. H. Pilcher to undertake it, and at the Conference in 1834 a committee was appointed to fix on a location and to apply to the Legislative Council for a charter. This committee decided to locate the institution at Spring Arbor, in Jackson County, and secured a charter accordingly. We now look upon the movement made at that time as a wild scheme—as it was located in the woods in fact —but, still, it shows the purpose to do a noble work for posterity. As wild as the scheme may now be regarded, it was no more so than the one adopted by the Baptists, Presbyterians and Protestant Episcopalians, about the same time. The Baptists and we have persevered while the other two have failed. Kalamazoo and Albion Colleges are monuments of perseverance and successful battling with great difficulties. We shall have occasion to speak of Albion College more specifically in our next period. (*See Albion.*)

Let us now take a general retrospect of this third period of our History. What has been the gain in these sixteen years? We began with *one charge, one minister and twenty members*. Now we have *twenty-nine charges, twenty-nine ministers, and four thousand nine hundred and twenty members.* Then we had no Sabbath Schools, and now we have them in all our growing villages. Then we had one log meeting-house, and now we have one very neat and pleasant one in the City of Detroit, and one frame one in the town of Plymouth, at Cooper's Corners. In several other places, as in Monroe, Ann Arbor and Ypsilanti, the incipient steps were taken towards buildings, but there were no other churches built during this period, except a log one in the vicinity of Pontiac, which was known as "Donation Chapel," and another small one at Algonac, on the St. Clair River. The age of church building had not yet arrived. Indeed, the country was too new to give much thought in that direction. Most of the people who had come in here to settle were in but moderate circumstances, and they were not in a condition to build churches. The Presbyterians had built a church in Detroit, in Ann Arbor, Monroe, and in the towns of Webster, Farmington and Pontiac, and, perhaps, in a few other places. The Protestant Episcopalians had built in Detroit, Monroe and Troy. The Baptists had erected a small church in Detroit and Troy. These were all the church accommodations furnished in this country at this period, so far as we have been able to ascertain. The people were content to worship in school-houses and in private houses. This, however, is a state of things not to continue, for, as the conveniences of the people are increased at home, they will demand a corresponding increase in church conveniences.

In our extensive Circuits we were in the habit of preaching wherever we could find an open door, whether it was in a private residence, a school-house or a tavern. The first Temperance lecture ever delivered in the County of Jackson was in a bar-room, which was used also as a chapel. We stepped behind the bar and delivered a formal lecture to a crowded audience. This was in 1832. The keeper had just determined to keep a Temperance house, and this was the most commodious room for a public Temperance meeting. And the first quarterly meeting, with love-feast and sacrament, was held in the same tavern in the village of Jackson in March, 1832. The occasion was one of deep and thrilling interest, notwithstanding the surroundings. One young man was converted who proved to be a very firm and devoted Christian.

Thus did the itinerants keep pace with the people in their settlements, and keep them under the civilizing and elevating influences of the Gospel of the Lord and Saviour. No other system but such a one as the Methodist could have met the necessities of this or any other new country. The natural tendency of man in a new and wild country is to barbarism ; and, unless he is constantly reminded of his higher, nobler destiny, he will certainly retrograde. Under the excitement of a new settlement—a struggle with rugged, wild nature —he would soon conform to these circumstances were he left to himself. To the minister, too, there was something interesting, exciting, and even thrilling in his labors and associations. The wild forests have often been made to ring with their songs of praise. The courageous, and even daring perseverance exhibited by them is above all praise. It was not worldly gain or worldly honor that stimulated them onwards, for they had no prospect of either; but "the love of Christ constrained them," and impelled them onward, and they were content to share the inconveniences of the people, if they could do them good; and they did them good, for they preserved them and their children from retrograding, and influenced many of them to become devoted and earnest Christians. It is only an itinerant system of ministerial supply that could have met the exigencies of this country thus far. Some of the towns have been supplied by others, but the country, generally, has been left to our care and labor.

In this encomium on the itinerant system of ministerial supply for a new country, we are not to be understood as entering into the mooted question as to whether it is the best system for a settled state of society. Neither do we intend to say that the Methodists have done all of the pioneer work; for we well remember the persevering labors of Rev. Calvin Clark, of the Presbyterian Home Mission, in this country. His zeal was very commendable and successful in founding Churches. Among the Free Will Baptists, too, Rev. Mr. Limbocker was a very active pioneer, having come into the country as early as 1830. Although the ministers of this denomination were so early in the field, they have never become very numerous. They now have a flourishing college at Hillsdale under their care, and are doing a good educational work, but they are not numerous.

Regular, or Close Communion Baptists, have done much early work, and were among the very first in educational enterprise. They were the first to undertake the publication of a religious newspaper.

All denominations have contributed to the maintenance of Christianity and Christian civilization in this country, though some have done more of the real pioneer work than others during the formative period of our country.

CHAPTER VII.

Prefatory—John P. Kent—Alfred Brunson—Samuel Baker—John Strange—Jerry Dean—John Owen—Sally Noble—Philip Warren—Mary A. Palmer—Isaac C. Hunter—Sarah H. Baughman—Jonathan E. Chaplin—G. Smith.

IT will be both interesting and profitable to devote a chapter to some of the men and women of this period. Some of them have gone to their great reward, while some we shall name still live to honor the cause of our God and to glorify His grace. The first we introduce is the minister who was appointed here at the beginning of this period of our History:

REV. JOHN P. KENT was the first minister sent to the Detroit Circuit from the Ohio Conference, if we except William Mitchell, who was sent here through mistake from what was then called the Western Conference, which included Ohio and much more of what was called the West in 1810. Mr. Kent was appointed to the Detroit Circuit at the session of the Ohio Conference held at Chillicothe, Ohio, beginning August 8th, 1820. Detroit was included in Lebanon District, which extended from the Ohio River on the south to and including Michigan. James B. Finley was the Presiding Elder. Since 1810 Detroit had stood connected with the Genesee Conference, and was included in the Upper Canada District. The transfer of it to another Conference seems to have produced a little confusion. The presumption is that the last preacher from the Genesee Conference did not send to the Ohio Conference any plan of the appointments or any list of the Societies, and the new preacher had to find out the preaching places and the Societies as well as he could. The Presiding Elder, James B. Finley, in his auto-biography, written many years after—that is, in 1854—says: "This year the people of Detroit desired me to send them a preacher;" that he "found a young man by the name of Morey, who went there, carved out a Circuit, and returned to Conference with a plan." He must have written this from memory, and was mistaken, we think, because the Genesee Conference met on the 20th of July, and the Ohio Conference met on the 8th of August, making less than three weeks between them. Mr. Dixon, the last preacher from the Genesee Conference, it is to be presumed, remained till some time in June; for he made his report of members to his Conference. Still, it is possible that, as soon as Mr. Dixon left, some of the people wrote him, fearing they might be overlooked; but it was not possible for him to send Mr. Morey, or any other man, to seek out a plan before Conference. At all events, Mr. Kent was appointed to Detroit Circuit in August, 1820, and came here and worked the Circuit, supplying all the places in Michigan where he could find an open door, and extended his Circuit as far south as the Maumee Rapids. He was a young man, single, and not very robust in health, but performed his work faithfully and well. His health became so much impaired by his long and fatiguing rides and great exposure, that it seemed necessary for him to take a superannuated relation to the Conference at its next session. He, however, was not permitted to remain long inactive; for his successor, Mr. Morey, having died early in the year, he was employed by the Presiding Elder to fill out the year. It was during this year he held a Camp Meeting on the Rouge, which resulted in much good to the cause. These two years constituted his whole service in Michigan.

Mr. Kent was admitted into the itinerant connection by the Ohio Conference in 1815, and regularly admitted into full membership, and ordained Deacon and Elder. The latter took place in 1819, so that he was an Elder of one year's standing when appointed to Detroit, and, being unmarried, he seemed to be well suited to such work. He was of an excellent spirit, possessed very good abilities, and rendered very valuable service to the cause of God. Mr. Kent made the same mistake which had been made by his predecessors and many of his successors—that was, undertaking to do too much; so much that he could not take care of the city as it deserved; and so much as to break down his health. He was a truly pious man, an earnest preacher, who was much respected by the people. He afterwards married, and was transferred to the Genesee Conference, to which he still belongs, and now lives in quiet retirement, in the enjoyment of the consolations of that religion which he labored to promote under such great difficulties in this new country, and in the dignity of a venerable and green old age.

REV. ALFRED BRUNSON, D. D., who was appointed to Detroit in 1822 as the successor of Mr. Kent, was born in Danbury, Connecticut, February 9th, 1793, so that at this present writing—1877—he is eighty-four years old. He was converted to God in Carlisle, Pennsylvynia, February 3d, 1809, and united with the Methodist Episcopal Church in that place April 2d, 1809, "when a runaway 'prentice." He returned to Connecticut, and experienced the blessing of perfect love October 9th, 1809; and was licensed to exhort on March 10th, 1812. In 1812 he removed to Ohio, and settled in Fowler, Trumbull County. In 1813–14 he spent one year in the army; was at the Thames and in the battle in which Tecumseh was killed, under General Harrison, and spent the winter in Detroit. In 1815, April 15th, he was licensed to preach in Hartford, Ohio. In 1818 he was sent by Rev. James B. Finley, Presiding Elder, to organize Huron Circuit, Ohio, including Sandusky City, in which he preached the first sermon ever preached there. In 1819 he was ordained Deacon, as a local preacher, in Cincinnati, Ohio, and was sent to the old Erie Circuit, Pennsylvania, by the Presiding Elder, William Swayzee. He was received on trial in the Ohio Conference in 1820, and was admitted into full connection in 1822, and ordained an Elder. From this Conference he was sent to Detroit, with Samuel Baker for a colleague. The following is his description of Detroit Circuit at that time: "The Circuit then extended over the entire settled part of Michigan, except Sault Ste. Marie. I went from Detroit to Pontiac; thence to Mount Clemens, and back to Detroit; thence to the River Rouge, where was the only Methodist Church in the Territory, a log one, near Robert Abbott's; thence up that river to a point fifteen miles from Detroit; thence back to the Maumee road and to Monroe on the River Raisin, and up that river nine miles to the upper settlement, the road being only an Indian trail; thence back to the Maumee road and to the Maumee at the foot of the Rapids; thence right back on the lake and river road to Detroit. There were returned to us about one hundred and thirty members.

"We arranged so as to preach every Sabbath in Detroit, in the old Council House. After Brother Baker had been once around the Detroit end, he proposed to take the south end of the Circuit, and leave me at Detroit. So we spent the year. We held our quarterly meetings together, but had no Presiding Elder during the year.

"A subscription had been raised, and, in 1823, the foundation of the first Methodist Church in the city was laid—since turned into a dwelling; but it was not made ready to occupy until after I left. I was sick in Detroit; had inflammation of the lungs and then of the liver; was blistered, and then preached with blisters on my breast *six by eight inches*, which burst and discharged a half a pint of water while in the pulpit. This occurred three times."

He left Detroit in the autumn of 1823, and returned to Ohio. While in Detroit he kept a boarding-house in order to get subsistence for his family, and yet he left the Circuit one hundred dollars in debt, which he paid the next year out of private funds. In regard to the traveling he has furnished us with the following sketch: "Our mode of travel was on horseback, except in the winter, when we used 'carry-alls,' or jumpers. In going home from Mount Clemens on the ice, I took a straight *shute* across Lake St. Clair. When about half way, and a mile from shore, with cakes of ice piled ten feet high outside of me, my horse's foot broke through. My heart was in my mouth as quick as thought. In a step or two more he went through again—but this time relieved me, for I found it was only a thin shell over the main ice. On this same trip, just before leaving the land for the lake, I passed a house with *fish* hung out for sale. The man that was with me inquired the price, telling the Frenchman that I was a priest for whom he wanted the fish. "Oh!" said the Frenchman, "I'll give him all the fish I've got if he'll pardon my sins." My friend informed him that I didn't pretend to forgive sins, paid him for the fish, and left. Let the Catholic priests say what they will about referring their people to Christ, their people expect *them* to absolve them."

Mr. Brunson has always continued in the itinerant work, and has been connected for many years with the Wisconsin Conference. He has recently issued a book, entitled, "Incidents of My Life and Times," and we are not at liberty to say more in this work, though he has much more to say in regard to his labors in Michigan. Dr. Brunson—for he is a D. D.—is a noble and great man, and has done much for the cause of true piety.

It seems eminently appropriate that REV. SAMUEL BAKER should be named in this connection, especially as this was the last work he ever supplied, and as he was the colleague of Mr. Brunson. Mr. Baker was born in the City of Baltimore, Maryland, September 13th, 1793, and was only a few months younger than his colleague. He was converted to God through faith in Jesus Christ when about eighteen years of age, and united himself to the Methodist Episcopal Church at once. He commenced the work of the itinerant ministry in the year 1816. In this work he continued to discharge his duties with fidelity and success until his Master called him from the labors of earth to the glorious refreshments of Heaven. His whole energies, physical, intellectual and moral, were devoted to his work. He went to the Conference, from Detroit Circuit, about the first of September, 1823, with his bride, in the possession of ordinary health. He had just been united in marriage to Miss Sarah Harvey, of Monroe, a young lady of talent and piety. She accompanied him to Conference to return a widow; for, while at the Conference, the hand of disease was laid upon him fatally. He probably had contracted the disease from his excessive labors in this new country. An appointment was assigned him, but he never reached it. After the attack of the disease he succeeded in reaching the residence of his brother, Dr. Baker, which was not many miles distant from the seat of the Conference, where he ended his race. His sufferings were great; but when he saw his end drawing nigh, he exclaimed in holy triumph, "Glory, glory to God and the Lamb! There is victory in death." Thus he fell asleep in Jesus, September 26th, 1823, in the thirty-first year of his age, and at the end of his seventh year in the itinerant ministry. Mr. Baker was a good and useful man, and his name is worthy to be recorded in the annals of the Church.

We now introduce a name not very familiar to the religious annals of Michigan, and his name comes into this connection simply from the fact that he was Presiding Elder over this country for two years in the early history. REV. JOHN STRANGE, who was appointed to the Lebanon District, Ohio Conference, which included Detroit, in 1821, "was a native of Virginia, and was born November 15th, 1789. When quite young he emigrated to Ohio, embraced religion in youth, and united himself to the Methodist Episcopal Church. He commenced his itinerant labors in 1810, under the direction of the Rev. James Quin, Presiding Elder. In 1811 he was admitted on trial in the Ohio Conference, where he labored thirteen years with great fidelity, acceptance and usefulness. The balance of his useful life was spent in Indiana. He was zealous and faithful; an eloquent and beloved minister of Jesus Christ. He has left abundant proof, both in Ohio and Indiana, of his success in the great work of winning souls to Christ—'epistles known and read of all men.' He died in peace, December 2d, 1832, but will long live in the memory of endeared thousands." This is the record of him found in the official Minutes of the Indiana Conference for 1833.

Mr. Strange was a man of much more than ordinary talents, a fine speaker, and was very useful in the Church. He was a little eccentric at times—a matter to which some object; but, perhaps, in his case, as it was perfectly natural—this was one means of his usefulness among the masses of the people. On one occasion, as he was preaching at a quarterly meeting in Detroit, he stopped suddenly, and then said: "Some say they shout because they cannot help it; but I think God will not thank them for such shouting. I shout because I love to do so." On another occasion, stopping suddenly as before, he remarked: "Some will say, that is a strange preacher; another, he is eloquent; and another, he preaches too loud; but there is a man—pointing to a lawyer—who for five dollars will labor much more zealously than I do." The manner of saying this was peculiar, and produced a profound sensation. He was a man of deep and earnest piety, and was a zealous and faithful laborer.

Thus far in this chapter we have confined ourselves to sketches of ministers who have labored in this field, but we do not purpose to continue to do so; for there are laymen, and there are holy women, too, who deserve to be remembered by the Church and the world. Several of these we now purpose to introduce to notice, giving a brief sketch of their lives. One of these was JERRY DEAN, who has already appeared by name in our narrative. Rev. James B. Finley, in his account of his first visit to Detroit, in 1821, speaks of him as his "old friend," having known him in Ohio. He has passed to his heavenly rest, but, as he stood by the Church here in the days of its darkness and feebleness, it is proper to make some grateful mention of him in this History. He was an intelligent mechanic—a saddler by trade—a very devoted Christian, and was, for many years, an active and very faithful member of the Methodist Church. He was converted and joined the Church in Ohio when but a young man, and had not been long married when he came to Detroit to reside. He came to Detroit to settle in business early in 1820. Being a member of the Church at the time, his house became one of the resting-places for the weary itinerants. He was industrious and prudent in the management of his affairs, succeeded well in his business, and accumulated a handsome property, which he was always willing to use liberally and freely for the support of religion. He was the first superintendent of the first Methodist Sabbath School in Michigan, established in Detroit in 1827. His end was peace. He died April 22d, 1839, in the forty-fourth year of his age, having been born December 25th, 1796. He was a man of a sound Christian experience, and, though always mild and gentle, he was earnest in his piety. He emphatically possessed "the ornament of a meek and quiet spirit, which in the sight of God is of great price." He was a noble, generous-hearted man. The Church sustained a real loss when he was called to his rest. Of him the late Bishop Thomson once wrote: "Among the lost and loved of my Detroit flock that are still fresh in my memory are Jerry Dean and father Abbott.

Few men that I have ever met with have breathed more of the spirit of Christ than the first. He was gentle as a lamb, loving as a mother, and conscientious as a child." His whole life-study seemed to be to ascertain how he could best promote the cause of the blessed Redeemer.

We shall next introduce one, who, though living, is too far advanced to be inflated by anything we may have to say, and we introduce him here because of his intimate association with the last-named, and because that association was mutually profitable in a religious way, though he was the junior of the other by several years. Some time during the year 1818, a poor boy, who was born in or near Toronto, Canada West, March 20th, 1809, came to Detroit with a widowed mother. He was cast upon the world to shift for himself at the age of nine years. This lad, though attracting no special attention at that time from the Church or the community, was destined to act a very conspicuous part in the interests of the Church in Detroit, as well as in political and financial circles. Being thrown upon his own resources, and having a strong desire to acquire a sufficient education to be able to transact ordinary business, at least, he found a friend in a gentleman who had charge of the only academy in the city. This gentleman, in consideration of his taking care of the school building and waiting on him, gave him his tuition free. This pedagogue was a man of very strict habits, and kept a very close surveillance over the habits of his protege, not allowing him to spend his evenings in the streets with other boys. This restraint seemed hard to him at the time, but it was of great service to him afterwards ; for, by this means, many hours were occupied in acquiring useful knowledge, which otherwise would have been worse than lost; besides, he acquired a habit of close application, which, subsequently, proved to be of incalculable value to him. In consequence of the removal of this gentleman from the city, he had to leave school in 1821. When his friend and patron was about to leave, he gave the lad a recommendation, by means of which he obtained a situation as clerk in the drug store of Dr. Chapin, with whom he remained as clerk until the autumn of 1829, at which time, being twenty years old, he was taken in as partner in the business, in which relation he continued until the death of the Doctor. He was taken into partnership without money, as he had very little ; but he had capacity and application, and these he offset against capital. Both in his relation as clerk and joint partner he had the principal labor to perform.

By close application to business, and ready attention to those who came to trade, there resulted a large increase of business. After the death of the senior of the firm, he continued the same business for a time alone, so that he had to attend to customers during the day, and then post and write up his books at night, so that many a time he has worked all night. Such labor and attention deserved success. Such success attended him in his business that he concluded to retire from trade in the spring of 1853. It is proper to be named here that, when he first entered into business, he devoted himself assiduously to it, so that the employer, first, and then the partner, might not suffer from his neglect. Never did he suffer himself to be called off by the various amusements and recreations usually indulged in by young men. This course was adopted not from penuriousness, or a miserly spirit, because his liberal contributions to benevolent enterprises show that he has no narrow spirit, but he did it from a principle of moral obligation to his employer and partner. Since 1853 he has relaxed a little from the severities of business life, and, yet, he has not abandoned business entirely, as he is the president of a bank and associated in some other financial operations. He is now a man of wealth—of wealth secured in regular trade; for it is to be noted, that notwithstanding the many temptations to withdraw money from regular trade to enter into speculations, he never allowed himself to run the hazard, so that the name of HON. JOHN OWEN is almost a synonym for sound business integrity. We have given this sketch of his business life and its results thus far as a tribute to the mercy of God. He was converted to God in his youth, and united himself with the Methodist Episcopal Church in Detroit, Nov. 2d, 1823, which laid the foundation for his success in after years.

When we call to mind the moral condition of Detroit at that time—the almost entire absence of religious influence—the gayety which prevailed—and that Methodism was "a hissing and a byword;" that the Methodists were a neglected people; that they worshiped in the old Council House, and then in the unfinished and unfurnished "brick church on the common," we find great reason to magnify the grace of God, which led him to identify himself and his spiritual interests with them, and which kept him in the way while in his youth. In conversation with him once he remarked to us: "To this step"—that is, his union with the Church—"I owe my success in business and my present position in society. The influence of the Church kept my feet from those snares which surrounded young men at that time, and dragged them to a dishonorable grave." No doubt the remark is a true one, and happy would it be for every young man if he would follow his example.

The condition of the Church was such that it became necessary he should become active in its operations while he was yet young —an activity, especially, in regard to its finances—an activity which he has never ceased to exercise. The time was, however, when *one dollar and a half per year* was thought to be a large sum for him to pay towards the support of the Gospel. With increasing wealth, he increased in his contributions for the cause of piety. He was early made treasurer of the Church, and has continued to hold that office for many years. After paying such amount as he was expected to pay, if, after the Society had done what they could to raise the salary of the minister, there remained a deficiency, he footed the bill. This he did for many years. During the lifetime of *Jerry Dean* these two men stood shoulder to shoulder in all the financial interests and improvements of the Church, the former—that is, Owen—devising and the latter co-operating, usually making equal subscriptions. If what Solomon says be true, as it is, that "A good name is rather to be chosen than great riches, and loving favor rather than silver and gold," Mr. Owen must be regarded as exceedingly wealthy. Yet we do not mean to say that he has been without fault, or that no one has ever spoken against him; but the blessing of some that were ready to perish is upon him.

Mr. Owen is disposed to hold a low estimate of himself—and it is right to exalt the grace of God. In a communication to us he uses this language in regard to himself: "When I remember the opportunities I have had for doing good and glorifying God, and, yet, how little I have done, I feel I have been a very unprofitable servant. I cannot, therefore, look back with satisfaction on the long term of years which has passed since I gave myself to God and His Church; but feel I have great reason to ask forgiveness for my shortcomings, and need to pray for the influence of the Spirit, that I may be quickened with new zeal in the service of our Lord and Saviour Jesus Christ." He has always been true to the principles of the Church, and an unvarying friend to the ministers who have been appointed to the charge.

No one could have predicted, when he saw that boy blacking the boots of that teacher and rendering other services for him as an equivalent for the care and instruction which he gave him, that he was looking on a future wealthy banker. How much the world— and, even, the Church—is disposed to look upon this as a mere fortuitous circumstance, and not to consider that God's providence is in it. But he never would have stood where he now stands had it not been for his having become a Christian during the formative stage of his life. At a later period of his life he was called, contrary to his own wish, to serve his State in a financial capacity, and held the office of State Treasurer, and administered it admirably well for three terms, or six years.

There are two points in this case worthy of note, and to which we would call special attention, as forming the foundation of his present position, both as regards his wealth and high standing in the public estimation. The first is that he became decidedly pious in his youth, and determined to honor God with his substance, and he faithfully executed the determination. That widowed mother was never forgotten or neglected, and God honored him for it. The other point is that he always transacted his business on Christian principles. He did not "make haste to be rich." Men may become rich by fraud and evil practices, but they forfeit the public esteem. He never allowed himself to venture where there was any probability of his transactions having the appearance of fraud, never undertaking any projects where there was not a clear way before him, and where he could not show a clean sheet. Patient, honest perseverance in honest business, associated with Christian piety and liberality, has been crowned with great success. It is his greatest pleasure, now, to think that he has contributed something towards the advancement of Christianity under the Methodistic form, as he believes that is better calculated than any other—though he is no bigot—to advance true Christian piety. His case is presented as worthy of imitation in the items last named, and as worthy of being considered by all young men, and for the glory of God's grace.

There is one more item of value to be considered in his history, that is, his connection with the Sabbath School cause. About 1820, a little before the time of his conversion, a union Sabbath School was organized in Detroit—the first Sabbath School in Michigan—into which he entered as a pupil, and, after a few years, though but a lad, he was appointed the secretary. In this relation he continued until the summer of 1830. Notwithstanding his necessarily close application to business, he was always faithful to his post, both as pupil and officer. In 1827 the Methodist people concluded it was best for them to organize a Sabbath School of their own, which they did, with very indifferent success for the time being, for it was difficult to get the children to go out to the "brick church on the common." Our subject, though a member of the Church, did not enter into this movement at the beginning, as he found it difficult to break away from his former associations. But, at length, in 1830, by the urgent persuasion of his brethren, he consented to take charge of the school as superintendent. When he was appointed to the superintendency he immediately rented a room on Woodward Avenue, down in the midst of the people, and removed his school to it. This was a small room, but answerd a pretty good purpose until the new church was built, in 1834, at the corner of Woodward Avenue and Congress street. Now, in his new responsibility, notwithstanding his close application to business, he always found time to attend to the interests of his Sabbath School, for his heart was in it, and it was a pleasure to him to attend to it. He feels and says that his relation to the Sabbath School work has been one great means of keeping him so firmly attached to the interests of Christianity. There is no doubt of the correctness of this opinion; for there is nothing so well calculated to bind us to Christianity as Christian work. He superintended this school, with a short interruption, for many years; and, when he finally resigned the superintendency, he took charge of the infant class for several years. It is a most interesting scene to look upon, to see one who, though immersed in business and trade, has been so constant and cheerful in labors of this kind. This matter has been introduced here not for the purpose of lauding him, but to furnish an example for others, by showing what can be done. He still feels a deep interest in all departments of Church work. As the Church prospers he rejoices, and is ever ready, of the ability that God gives him, to assist in its enterprises. As Mr. Owen still lives, it is not permitted us to say anything more than to express the confidence that the grace of God in Jesus Christ, which he experienced in his youth, may abide in him to the end of life.

There was one active and earnest Christian lady who is interwoven with our first recollections of Detroit; one whose zeal was proverbial; who was a member of the Church at Mount Clemens as early as 1820–21, and came to Detroit to reside in 1822. She became a member of the Methodist Episcopal Church in the days of its feebleness in this peninsula, and did not forsake it in its darkest days of trial. It was at her house, at Mount Clemens, that Rev. Platt B. Morey died, after a short illness, in 1821. Her husband was also a member of the Church, but was not so active and earnest as she was, and is not so prominent in our recollection, though a very good man. For many years she sustained an unblemished Christian character, and died in peace. She had an ardent temperament, which showed itself in the earnestness of her religious labors and exercises. A more than ordinary amount of talent had been committed to her trust. Had she lived in these days, she, doubtless, would have been a successful evangelist; as it was, she was always active in religious meetings, praying and exhorting with much feeling and often with great power and effect. She embraced religion in early life, and lived in the enjoyment of its consolations under some very adverse and discouraging circumstances. Early in her Christian life she made a full consecration of herself to God, and felt that "the blood of Jesus Christ cleanseth from all sin;" that "perfect love casteth out all fear." Her profession of such a deep experience of the things of God, was well sustained by a consistent, cheerful Christian life. Her eyes were always weak and defective, but for about nine years before her death she was deprived of her sight, so that the light of this world was entirely shut out, though she enjoyed the light of the spirit very brilliantly. We had the privilege of visiting her occasionally in her blindness, and always found her full of light in the Lord. It was indeed a rich feast to spend an hour in her society.

MRS. SALLY NOBLE died at Monroe, whither she had removed from Detroit, some ten or more years before her demise, which occurred in the spring of 1857, in the fifty-second year of her age. When she came to lie on her bed of death she repeated the following lines of one of our hymns as expressive of her state of mind:

"Jesus can make a dying bed
Feel soft as downy pillows are,
While on his breast I lean my head,
And breathe my life out sweetly there."

What a happy state of mind—a state of mind which no philosophy can produce. Nothing but the religion of the Lord Jesus has ever yet produced triumph in death. Thus in the ripeness of grace she rests in the bosom of her loving Saviour.

"The toils of life are o'er,
Its suffering and its care."

Her husband survived until 1875, when he passed away, in peace, in the city of Monroe, in fulness of years and ripeness of Christian love, and they have joined hands on the blest shore.

Another who was cotemporary with Mrs. Noble in the interests and affairs of the Church in Detroit, and who always stood firm at his post, deserves a few lines of notice. *Philip Warren* was a quiet man, but an active and earnest Christian. All who saw him felt, at once, that they were in the presence of a deeply pious man. He was quite useful in the Church; and he, too, has been called from

the labors of earth to the refreshments of heaven. He died in the ripeness of age and in the maturity of a Christian life.

MRS. MARY A. PALMER was the daughter of Hon. James and Mrs. Amy Witherell, and came to Detroit with her parents, in 1810, but returned East with her mother a short time after. There were two reasons for this return to the East, to wit: the mother was always in fear and dread of the Indians, many of whom were in and about Detroit at that time; the other reason was to have better advantages for educating the children. The mother and family returned to Michigan in 1817. The daughter Mary, in 1821, was married to Mr. Thomas Palmer, who was engaged in the mercantile business in Detroit. Their wedding trip East and return was an adventurous one. At the time there was but one steamboat on the lake, to wit: the Walk-in-the-water, which was a small craft. On the return they, with a few others, went on board at evening, at Buffalo, with fair hopes for a safe voyage. During the night, after having put out, a fearful storm arose, which drove the vessel back, and just at dawn of day it was driven on the rocks at Black Rock, and became a perfect wreck. The winds howled a terrible requiem for the Walk-in-the-water. The passengers were all saved. Mrs. Palmer was the first to leap ashore after the vessel struck. She retained a very vivid remembrance of the awful night, and of the shock, even to her death. There seemed to be very little hope of soon getting to Detroit by sail, and the only other thing which remained to them was to hire a team and drive across Canada, which was both perilous and tedious. Mr. Palmer had been so long absent from his business, he thought he must secure the most speedy return possible. So he and another man engaged a team to take them through with their wives. It required two weeks of hard toil to get through. About half way of their journey, after nightfall one day, the wagon broke down in the midst of a wood, about a mile and a half from any house. It was raining, dark and muddy. They could not stay where they were. One of the men went and procured some kind of a light, by means of which the ladies were enabled to make the distance, being wet and thoroughly bespattered with mud. It was near midnight when they reached the cabin in the woods. They found the poor people very hospitable, and having made a large fire they managed to dry their garments against morning, so that they were enabled to go on their way, when the wagon was repaired. This was a very trying journey for Mrs. Palmer, in the month of November, as it was. Her sufferings did not end when she reached the Detroit River, for that had to be passed over which was more terrible to her than anything she had passed on the way. There were no steam ferries then, nor even row boats, but they had to secure a canoe, and that to be propelled and guided by a drunken Frenchman. Notwithstanding her great suffering in her fears, the river was crossed in safety, and she found herself once more in the association of her family. Mrs. Palmer, some years before her marriage, had connected herself with the Methodist Church, which she adorned by a consistent life, for nearly sixty years. In one respect there was a marked contrast between her and Mrs. Noble, just above mentioned, for although she was quite regular and constant in her attendance on the regular services of the Church, she never took any active part in religious meetings. Although she was a very intelligent woman, well educated, and could converse intelligently on religion or any other subject in private, her natural timidity prevented her from saying anything in public. She was large and commanding in person and of noble presence. She was always strongly attached to the Church and supported it liberally during her life, and had always expressed a purpose to make some kind of a bequest to the Church, but like too many others, not anticipating death so near, she was carried off without having made any such provision. Her husband had died some years before—in 1868. Fortunately she had a son who was the principal heir, who had so much love and veneration for his mother that he afterwards voluntarily carried out what he thought to be, substantially, his mother's design. He gave, in her name, *five thousand dollars* to the "Superannuated Preachers' Aid Society" of the Detroit Annual Conference," for a permanent fund, which, by the action of that Society, is to be known as the Mary A. Palmer Fund, with two conditions—that the interest only shall be used, and, that whenever Manasseh Hickey, Elijah H. Pilcher, and Seth Reed, or either of them become superannuated, one-third of the interest shall be appropriated to each of them, annually, during life, and to their widows after them, in like manner. In the meantime, and after their death the interest goes into the general funds of the Society. These are ministers who had been her pastors in her earlier years, and for whom she had a great friendship; and, further, he annually appropriates *twenty-five dollars* to the Jefferson Avenue Methodist Church in the name of his mother. Thus Hon. Thomas W. Palmer, of Detroit, endeavors to carry out what he thinks would be the will of that mother.

Mrs. Palmer was born in Fairhaven, Vermont, in 1795, and first came to Detroit with her parents in 1810. She died, after a very brief illness, on March 19th, 1874, having the respect and good will of all who knew her. She was a sincere, quiet Christian and charitable woman, and "endured as seeing Him that is invisible." She left a son (Thomas W. Palmer), a daughter (Mrs. Julia E. Hubbard), a grand-daughter (Miss Mary E. Roby), and a host of friends to mourn her absence. She was one of the originators of the Protestant Orphan Asylum in Detroit, and for many years was connected with it in an official capacity, and was deeply interested in the workings of the institution. She had very quick and active sympathies for the sufferings of the needy and distressed.

Thus one of the old, benevolent, Christian women of Detroit has been enrolled with the dead, and, yet, she lives in the agencies put in operation for the benefit of the needy; and we have good confidence that she lives with her Saviour.

There is one point in this narrative on which it is proper to comment—that is, her failure to make the bequest contemplated. In her case it came out well simply because of the honorable veneration of her son for her memory; but there are few such sons and heirs. Men and women of means, who contemplate doing anything for the cause of God and humanity, had better do it themselves, and during their life-time. Time is short and life is uncertain, and wills and bequests are often set aside when made, and this kind of work had better be done at once. There is, also, great carelessness in the preparation of wills, so that very few bequests are ever realized by the objects for which they were designed by the testator. If people depend on wills for benevolence, let them have them carefully drawn, and executed in good time.

REV. ISAAC C. HUNTER was sent to Detroit Circuit in 1824, which brings him within the line of our History. As he is dead, it is very fitting that we should give some special notice of him in this place. He united with the Conference, as an itinerant preacher, in 1819, and labored with a good degree of success and usefulness, upon the whole, until his death. He remained upon the Detroit Circuit only one year, which was rather a barren year for good. The reason for this we have before mentioned when giving an account of the work in Detroit Circuit, in which, also, we gave some account of Mr. Hunter; but we propose now a fuller memoir. After leaving Michigan he became more pious and more useful than he had been before. He was the Presiding Elder in the Kanawha District in Virginia, in 1829-30, which included Nicholas Circuit, when the writer labored on that Circuit—the first year he traveled as a preacher. In those mountain regions we formed a very pleasant acquaintance with him, or rather renewed it, for he had traveled the Circuit in which our father resided, and often stopped there the first year after he left Detroit. We give a short extract from the official memoir, as furnished in the Minutes of the Ohio Conference for the year 1842:

"*Rev. Isaac C. Hunter* was a native of Pennsylvania, born in Bellefonte, Centre County, August 30th, 1793. He received twenty-three appointments to different stations, and for years was a successful Presiding Elder, and had the confidence and esteem of the ministry and membership with whom he labored and to which he belonged. He had a strong and vigorous mind, which he cultivated assiduously by applying himself to the Bible and such other studies as tended to increase his knowledge of the Bible. God honored him in life with success in his labors and with triumph in his death. But he is no more—for the Lord has taken him, and has left the Church shrouded in mourning and his widow and orphan children bathed in tears. In May, 1842, he was seized with a violent cold, which produced inflammation of the lungs, and on the 27th of June terminated in death. During his illness he was patient and happy. Although his afflictions were great, yet grace sustained him; and when the closing scene was nigh, and the lamp of life was flickering in its socket, and his weeping friends stood and gazed on the dissolution of the earthly house, he beheld "a house not made with hands, eternal in the heavens." His face was illuminated with a heavenly smile, and his eyes, even in death, sparkled with joy; and with the triumphant shout he bid adieu to all below, and now, with all the sanctified, enjoys an endless rest."

We here introduce a name which has been incidentally mentioned before, but it is worthy of a further notice. The circumstances of her conversion and the activity of her labor are worthy of note. Her residence was at Monroe, as heretofore mentioned. Her mother was a widow, and, although not a Methodist, she invited Rev. J. P. Kent, when he first went to Monroe to preach, in 1820, to make his home at her house, whenever he came around. He did frequently stop there during the two years he supplied the Circuit. The daughter was handsome and gay—fond of society and worldly amusements; and the circumstances indicated that she was utterly thoughtless on the subject of religion. But Divine truth, under the ministration of Mr. Kent, took effect, and, to the astonishment and chagrin of her gay companions, *Miss Sarah Harvey* made a profession of religion, and joined the Methodist Episcopal Church, which was then very feeble in the place. Being talented and well educated, she at once became active and useful in the cause. She attended the Camp Meeting, which Mr. Kent held on the Rouge in the summer of 1822, and was a very useful laborer. It is not at all surprising, under these circumstances, that the junior preacher, who succeeded Mr. Kent the next year, was so captivated and taken that he sought to make her his companion in his ministerial work; nor is it surprising that, with the ardent desire she then had to do good, she should consent to be identified with the itinerant ministry; and she became *Mrs. Rev. Samuel Baker.* But he soon died, and, in due time, she became *Mrs. Rev. John A. Baughman,* and with him shared the labors and responsibilities of an itinerant minister's life for many years. After she came to have the responsibility of a family, as was very natural, she relaxed somewhat in the activity of her Christian labor. Many of her later years were accompanied with much suffering, and she had to give up Church work entirely; and, yet, she always found great delight in attending the class-meetings whenever it was practicable. After the death of her husband, which preceded hers by five years, she made her home with her son-in-law, Bela Hubbard, Esq. We here subjoin a brief memoir of her:

MRS. SARAH H. BAUGHMAN was born near Rochester, New York, January 22d, 1799, of English parentage. She removed to Monroe, Michigan, with her widowed mother, in May, 1816. She was converted to God and joined the Methodist Episcopal Church at Monroe, under the labors of *Rev. John P. Kent,* in 1821. At the time of her conversion she was very decided in her convictions of the correctness of Methodist doctrines, and identified herself fully with the Church, although it was very feeble in that locality at that time. She was married to Rev. Samuel Baker at Monroe in August, 1823, and went with him to Conference at Urbana, Ohio, on horseback. Mr. Baker was taken sick at Conference, and died in a few days, and she was left alone among strangers and to return to Michigan, which she did. On her return, she was, for some time, lost in the woods, and had to endure all the painful sensations of being hopelessly lost in a forest. She finally succeeded in finding a way out. She remained at Monroe, and did what she could to advance the interests of the feeble Church —for she was an active Christian then—till she was married to Rev. John A. Baughman, which took place in Monroe in May, 1826, when she removed with him to Ohio, where she remained till he was transferred to the Michigan Conference in 1838. After her marriage with Mr. Baughman, her life became merged with his, and she fully shared with him the labors and inconveniences of an itinerant life for many years. She died in Detroit, where she had resided for many of her latter years, March 19th, 1873. She fell asleep in Jesus, and lives with Him in His glorious kingdom.

It is said that, during her girlhood's days at Monroe, she was known as a person of unusually attractive manners, and full of life and frolic. At that time there was much social intercourse between the French and the settlers from the Eastern States, and she was often a visitant with them in gay circles at Detroit. Her conversion and connection with the Methodist Episcopal Church must have cost her a great struggle, and must have made a very marked change in her feelings and life; for she became a decided and active Christian. From the time of her marriage with Mr. Baughman, she devoted herself cheerfully and actively to the duties and hardships, which were inseparable from the position of a Methodist minister's wife, itinerating throughout the large and sparsely populated Circuits of Ohio and Michigan, as they were then.

Mrs. Baughman was a lady of more than ordinary intellectual ability, refined in manners and tastes, and she always moved with grace and elegance in the most refined circles of society in the places where her husband was stationed. For a good many of her last years her health was quite delicate, and she lived in quiet retirement, and in the enjoyment of the sweet consolations of that religion which she had professed for so many years.

We had reserved a space here for a memorial notice of an able and excellent Presbyterian minister, but, failing to receive the items from his family, we now fill it with another, whose memoir will be read with great satisfaction and profit by many.

REV. JONATHAN EDWARDS CHAPLIN, a great-grandson of the much-esteemed and eminent Jonathan Edwards, was born in Chaplin, Windham County, Connecticut, in the year 1789. His parents were respectable, religious, and liberal supporters of religious institutions. He removed, when young, to the State of New York, where he commenced and completed the study of law, after having graduated at Yale College. He was an able logician, and when, in his senior year in college, President Dwight gave the class an opportunity to question his doctrines, he entered the lists, and controverted the doctrines of Calvinism, and, in his own estimation and that of the class, he triumphed over the Doctor. This gave him great self-complacency and consequence in his own eyes. Having no evangelical—Arminian —instruction, he wandered into Unitarianism, then into Universalism, and, finally and naturally, into downright infidelity.

Some time during the War of 1812 he was appointed aid-de-camp to General Porter, on the north frontier, where he acquired the habit of intemperance, from which he was subsequently delivered by converting grace. Soon after the close of the war he came to the

West, and settled at Urbana, Champaign County, Ohio, where he entered on the practice of law, in which he continued until the time of his entrance upon the work of the ministry,

In connection with his law practice he continued the practice of intoxication until he reached the lowest point of degradation. Being a man of great versatility of talent, quick of wit and repartee, and having an almost exhaustless fund of anecdote, after he became a sot landlords and hotel-keepers would board him for days, to collect and hold company for them by his wit and humorous stories. He had proceeded so far in his drunkenness and infidelity that he had been known to administer baptism and the sacrament to a dog. He had become utterly abandoned, and reduced to the lowest state of poverty. In reflecting on his state, he came to the conclusion that there was only one way by which he could be saved from a drunkard's grave and a drunkard's hell, that was, to become a Christian, if possible for him. Having come to this conclusion, his breath still steaming with liquor, he attended a watch-night meeting on the last night of the year 1829, held by Rev. John F. Wright, at which it pleased God to awaken him thoroughly to a sense of his lost condition. He came forward to the altar as a penitent, and, about the time the clock struck twelve, he gave Mr. Wright his hand as an applicant for Church membership. Some of the brethren thought he was now only mocking, but he was sincere. These ministers encouraged him, and, in a few days afterwards, at his own fireside, he received the knowledge of salvation by the remission of sins through faith in Jesus Christ, and never after drank a drop of spirituous liquors. He was saved from the appetite.

In 1833, when Rev. H. O. Sheldon, who had the matter in charge, was looking for a man to take the charge of the Norwalk Seminary, Ohio, which was then under Methodist patronage, Mr. Chaplin was recommended to him as suitable for the place. He went to Urbana and engaged him. He continued in that institution until 1837, and succeeded very well.

In the year 1834 a Camp Meeting was held near what is now Clyde, in Northern Ohio. Mr. Chaplin was present. A missionary sermon was preached. A preacher was carrying a hat to take the collection, still exhorting as he went. Mr. Chaplin and the other ministers were on the stand. Mr. Chaplin arose, and holding out an iron tobacco-box, called to the preacher, who was near the centre of the congregation: " Brother Sheldon ! I have been a slave to tobacco. I was formerly a poor drunkard. When I quit my cups, I thought some stimulant *necessary*, and retained my tobacco. I do not say, I *will* do without it, but I say, by God's grace I will do without it. I here give my tobacco-box to the Missionary Society, and, if I am enabled to do without, I will give, annually, what I now expend for tobacco, which is a shilling a week, or six dollars and a quarter a year. The box was taken and sold to the highest bidder, who kept it a few minutes and returned it, saying: "There, I don't want this. I give it to the Missionary Society." It was sold again to the highest bidder, who was the preacher himself, who has kept it ever since, making use of it, sometimes, when taking missionary collections. At the next Annual Conference Mr. Chaplin came to the preacher, having his countenance much improved, and presented him the *six dollars and a quarter* for the Missionary Society. "Well," said the preacher, "how did you get along without tobacco?" He replied: "The first day I was lost; the second, sick; the third, liked to have died; the fourth, got better; the fifth, still better; in a week was hearty as a bear; and have never enjoyed such health as I have since." Happy would it be for some others if they would adopt the same course and adhere to it firmly.

In August, 1834, he was received on trial in the Ohio Conference, and was appointed Principal of the Norwalk Seminary, in which he had now been for one year. In due time he was admitted into full connection, and ordained Deacon and Elder at the proper periods. After he left the Seminary he served in the following stations successively, viz., Elyria, Detroit, Tiffin and Maumee City.

In 1842 he was transferred from the North Ohio Conference to Michigan, and appointed Principal of the branch of the University located at White Pigeon, a post which he held until death put a period to all his labors. In this truly responsible position, such was his catholic spirit, such the judicious management of his school, that, while he was beloved by his pupils, he acquired the confidence of the entire community in which he lived, and gave satisfaction to all parties.

His last illness was a painful one—his sufferings, indeed, were most intense—yet, grace so sustained him that "patience had its perfect work." For the most part, his mind seemed to be absorbed in the contemplation of God; his continual theme was holiness. He said to a friend that it was "not enough to perform the external duties of religion, we must be holy. O that I could see Brother Steward, and hear him pronounce that word *holiness* with his wonted emphasis! Brother Fuller, we must live holiness." He would sometimes say to his beloved wife: "If God should see fit to raise me up to preach again the Everlasting Gospel, my God assisting me, I will preach it from the *heart.*"

A few hours before he expired, being asked how it as with him, he replied: "All is well; all is peace; all is glory! I shall soon be with the dear Redeemer." That "God would convert poor, perishing sinners," formed his last prayer.

Soon after his conversion, Mr. Chaplin became a successful Temperance lecturer. Rev. William H. Raper, late of the Ohio Conference, in alluding to this fact, says: "In that work he did great good. His Temperance lectures were, sometimes, like a tempest, and scores in the Judicial District where he practiced law were reclaimed."

He took a deep and abiding interest in the cause of education. From the very moment he became identified with the Methodist itinerancy, he did all in his power to elevate the character of our Western ministry, and promote a love of literature among the people generally.

"As a preacher, he was eloquent, impressive, energetic. His eloquence was, emphatically, Ciceronian, strong and terse in style and clear in logic, with little redundancy of language. When a lawyer he was successful, and when he became a preacher and teacher he maintained his success. As a member of Conference, his brethren often had occasion to avail themselves of his legal knowledge; and it is not too much to say that, in matters of common life, as well as in Church polity, he was a safe counselor. He was cheerful under all the vicissitudes of life—indeed, this was a most striking characteristic of his character. He was open-hearted, confiding, and generous, to a fault, ardent in temperament, lively in conversation, agreeable in manners, a warm friend, a social and interesting companion, a gentleman, a scholar, and a Christian. With these qualities, it would have been passing strange if he had not been esteemed and loved by all who knew him. His dying words ought to be imprinted on every minister's heart, so that they should remember and profit by them—' Live *holiness,* and preach it from the heart.'"

As has already been said, Mr. Chaplin possessed a large amount of humor and wit, and, when he was converted, these elements of his nature were not destroyed, but sanctified. His sallies of wit and his anecdotes, instead of being designed to excite the laughter of the silly, gaping crowd, partook of the intellectual and moral.

He died September 15th, 1846, aged fifty-seven years. When such a man was to be laid in the grave, the whole community felt the shock, for he was a man for all. But he is taken from the toils and sufferings of this present world to the enjoyments of the heavenly.

In the foregoing sketch we have mainly copied the official memoir, as found in the Minutes for 1847.

One more minister was brought into connection with the work in Michigan by being appointed Presiding Elder of the Detroit District in 1838. He had previously labored in Ohio, but now he became fully identified with Michigan. His first appointment was to Detroit District, and his last was to Flint District, for a second term, which he was serving at the time of his death. He did a great deal of active work for the Church, and had a good capacity for getting other people to work. He had served more years in the Presiding Eldership than any other man in Michigan, except Dr. Pilcher. We will here record the official memoir, as found in the Minutes for 1868:

"REV. GEORGE SMITH died at his residence in Ann Arbor, May 4th, 1868, aged fifty-nine years. He was born in Hampshire County, Virginia, but in early life was taken by his parents to Ohio, where he was converted and joined the Methodist Episcopal Church. In 1830, at the age of twenty-one, he was licensed as a local preacher, and joined the Ohio Conference in 1832, and was appointed to Mount Gilead Circuit. The next year he traveled Dover Circuit. In 1834 he was ordained Deacon and appointed to Medina Circuit. In 1835 he was appointed in charge of Mansfield Circuit. During this year the Michigan Conference was organized, and Brother Smith, at its first session, was ordained Elder, and stationed at Richfield for 1836-7. In 1838 he was married to Mrs. Elizabeth Smur, of Holmes County, Ohio, and the next September, at the third session of the Michigan Conference, was appointed Presiding Elder of Detroit District. After filling this appointment four years, he was Presiding Elder of Marshall District for four years. In 1846-7 he had charge of South Albion Circuit; in 1848 of Adrian, and in 1849 of Ann Arbor, and in 1851 of Plymouth Circuit. From 1852 to 1856 he was Presiding Elder of Flint District, and, from 1856 to to 1860, Presiding Elder of Ann Arbor District. In 1860 he was appointed to Wayne Circuit, but, from 1861 to 1865, he was again Presiding Elder of Adrian District. In 1865 he was stationed at Chelsea, and in 1866 he was again appointed Presiding Elder of Flint District, which position he held at the time of his death. Thus, it will be seen that twenty-two out of the thirty-five years of his ministry, after he was admitted to the Conference, he held the office of Presiding Elder. His sound judgment, his comprehensive views, and his impartial kindness, and the confidence which others reposed in him, eminently fitted him for the responsible position. In all his appointments he was successful and useful, and many have been converted under his ministry. He was a hearty friend of the educational cause and of all the institutions of the Church. Careful, and rather inclined to be conservative in his views, and charitable towards all, he devoted himself to execute the ordinances of the Church, leaving it to others to change or modify its regulations. He was a member of the General Conference of 1844, and was one of the very few members of the Northern Conferences who voted against the action which led the Southern Conferences to secede from the Church. As a preacher, Brother Smith was eminently earnest and practical, and thousands of people from all parts of our State will cherish his memory with deep affection. His last illness was sudden and protracted, and caused him great suffering, but, though reluctant, at first, to give up his work, he bore his afflictions patiently, and, with unfaltering confidence, resigned his spirit into the arms of his Saviour. He deserves ever to be remembered as one of the pioneers of civilization and Christianity in the State of Michigan."

Mr. Smith was a safe and good counselor in the affairs of the Church, and was very much respected by the people wherever he had labored. He had acquired a good property, and left his family in very comfortable circumstances.

CHAPTER VIII.

Detroit — Origin — Growth — Casualties — Periodicals — Commerce — Religious Societies — Schools — Men.

THIS city holds so important a place in our annals that it would be expected that something more than a mere passing notice should be given; for, for a long time, this was all there was of Michigan, so far as settlement was concerned. We purpose, therefore, to devote this chapter to its history, but we can only furnish a summary.

Until one hundred and seventy-six years ago—1877—none but savages inhabited all of this beautiful Peninsula of Michigan. No foot of civilized man had planted itself, permanently, on this soil. Only a few adventurous travelers had coasted along its lake shores, and had camped for a night among its beautiful groves. Its glades and prairies were unmarked by the plowshare, and its forests were untouched by the axe of civilization. The deer, the wolf, the bear, the elk, roamed its forests freely, or were chased only by the savage, with the rude implements of death. The beaver made his dams without fear, and played sportively in the accumulated waters. But the day has come when a change is to be inaugurated. The adventurers had discovered that there were desirable points for trade with the savages—the aborigines of this country. These adventurers were from France, and were incited by a desire for gain, or for fame as discoverers, and not to find a home for liberty and religious toleration. They were all Romanists, and had no desire for either civil or religious freedom. Neither had they any desire to plant the standard of a high and noble civilization; for they readily conformed to the habits and customs of the wild men of the forest, and were at once received as their brothers. Among the most desirable of these points of trade was Detroit, or the strait connecting Lakes St. Clair and Erie. The banks along the border of this river, or strait, presented a most enchanting appearance, dressed in their native green and gemmed with beautiful wild flowers. In their primeval state they were most gorgeously adorned. So beautiful were they that it seemed almost like a sacrilege to think of disturbing them, and making them the home of restless, civilized man, or to break their quiet by the hum of business or the excitements of pleasure.

Mr. Bancroft says: "The country on the Detroit River and Lake St. Clair was esteemed the loveliest in Canada. Nature had lavished all her charms—slopes and prairies, plains and noble forests, fountains and rivers; the lands, though of different degrees of fertility, were all productive; the isles seemed as if scattered by art to delight the eye; the lake and river abounded with fish; the water was pure as crystal; the air serene; the genial climate, temperate and giving health, charmed the emigrant from Lower Canada."*

Charlevoix, who traveled through this country in 1720, as quoted by Mr. Lanman, says of Detroit: "It is pretended that this is the finest part of all Canada; and, really, if we can judge by appearances, nature seems to deny it nothing which can contribute to make a country delightful; hills, meadows, fields, lofty forests, rivulets, fountains, rivers, and all of them so excellent in their kind, and so happily blended as to equal the most romantic wishes."†

So much for the appearance of the country as it presented itself to the travelers of that early day. At that time all this region was called Canada.

The present site of the city was considered the most favorable spot for establishing the trading-post. There had been a small settlement at "Old Mackinaw" for some time before any was made at Detroit. Jean Marquette, a Jesuit priest, made a settlement there in 1670, and built a chapel for the instruction of the Indians. A few French adventurers had gone to Mackinaw Island. With this exception, no one had attempted to settle in Michigan until Detroit was fixed upon as a place for a fort and trading-post. Indeed, this is to be regarded as the first permanent settlement in the Northwest. It seemed to be admirably situated for such a purpose. The indications have proved true, as we shall hereafter see.

A few more general remarks on the country may be allowed before we proceed directly to the consideration of the city. "The history of this region," in the language of one, "exhibits three distinct and strongly marked epochs. The first may be properly

* History United States, Vol. 3, pp. 194, 195. † History of Michigan.

denominated the romantic, which extends to the year 1760, when its dominion passed from the hands of the French to the English. This was the period when the first beams of civilization had scarcely penetrated its forests, and the paddles of the French fur-traders swept the lakes, and the boat-songs of the *voyageurs* awakened the tribes on their wild and romantic shores.

"The second epoch is the military, which commenced with the Pontiac War, running down through the successive struggles of the British, the Indians, and the Americans, to obtain dominion of the country, and ending with the victory of Commodore Perry, the defeat of Proctor, the victory of General Harrison and the death of Tecumseh, the leader of the Anglo-savage conspiracy, on the banks of the Thames.

"The third may be denominated the enterprising, the hardy, the mechanical and working period, commencing with the opening of the country to emigrant settlers, the age of agriculture, commerce, and manufactures, of harbors, cities, canals, and railroads; when the landscapes of the forests were meted out by the compass and chain of the surveyor; when its lakes and rivers were sounded, and their capacity to turn the wheel of a mill, or to float a ship, was demonstrated, thus opening up avenues of commerce and industry. Its wild and savage character has passed away, and given place to civilization, religion, and commerce, inviting the denizens of overcrowded cities to its broad lakes and beautiful rivers, to its rich mines and fertile prairies, and promising a rapid and abundant remuneration for toil."*

The condition and development of the country has a very important bearing on the condition and growth of the city; for, in all liberal or free governments, commerce and trade will seek their natural channels; and towns and cities will spring up at the most convenient points for that commerce and trade. Good harbors on the lakes, rivers, and ocean shore are regarded as indispensable to the establishment of a city. It is a marvel to us now how the cities of antiquity were ever made to thrive, situated, as many of them were, in the interior of the country, and surrounded by rock-bound hills and towering mountains. But our city, as we shall see, is most favorably situated on the eastern border of a most rich and fertile State, and possessing a harbor, the superior of which does not exist. From its situation, it only requires time, and the appliances of the arts of civilization, to rear up a magnificent city, as enduring as time itself.

---
* Old Mackinaw, by Strickland, pp. 143, 144.

HISTORY OF PROTESTANTISM IN MICHIGAN. 159

This leads us now directly to the historical sketch of the City of Detroit. Where is it? All know that it is the chief city of the State of Michigan and located on its eastern border. Yet this does not exactly answer our question. "The City of Detroit is situated on the north shore of the Detroit River, or strait, connecting Lakes Erie and St. Clair. The river is the boundary line between Michigan and Canada West. The city is eighteen miles north and east of the head of Lake Erie, and seven miles west of Lake St. Clair, three hundred miles west of Buffalo, and five hundred and forty-five from Washington, in latitude 42°, 19', 53", north, and longitude west 82°, 58" or from Washington west 5°, 56', 12". Difference in time from Washington, 33', 44"; New York City, 34', 48".

"The history of Detroit is most intimately connected with the history of the whole Northwest, as its settlement dates among the first on the American continent. Founded in the strife for sovereignty between the English and French Governments, it became, at an early day, a point of central influence, importance and action. No place in the United States, it has been observed, presents such a series of events, interesting in themselves, and permanently affecting, as they occurred, its progress and prosperity. Five times its flag has been changed. First the Lily of France floated over its fortress, then the Red Cross of England, and next the Stripes and Stars of the United States, and then, again, the Red Cross, and, lastly, the Stripes and Stars.

"Three different sovereigns have claimed its allegiance, and, since it has been held by the United States, its Government has been thrice transferred; twice it has been besieged by the Indians; once captured in war, and once burned to the ground. Fire has scattered it—the tomahawk, scalping-knife and war-club have been let loose upon it, in the hands of an unrelenting, savage foe. It has been the scene of one surrender, of more than fifty pitched battles, and twelve horrid massacres.

"The present site of the city was occupied by Indian villages at the period of the discovery of the country. In 1610 it was first visited by the French. The whole lake region, from the period of discovery until 1762, was under the dominion of France, The legitimate settlement of the city was in 1701, at which time a fort called 'Ponchartrain' was erected."*

On the old French maps the River Savoyard is represented as running through the city, and discharging its waters into the Detroit River a little east of the Michigan Central Railroad Depot.

* City of Detroit, 1855, p. 3.

It has long since disappeared. It was formed from the water in the swampy land—heavily timbered, extending back from the Detroit River ; it was, simply, the drainage from this timber-belt. As strange as it may now seem, "it was sometimes a large stream ; and I have known it necessary to take people living on its margin out of their windows into a canoe and carry them *ashore*. This was after long-continued rains. But our modern subterranean rivers have done the work for the Savoyard—its glory has departed—it is among the things that were but are not. It obtained its name from old Peter Berthelet—the grandfather of those yet among us. He kept a pottery on the west side of its mouth, near the outlet of the present grand sewer. He bore the nickname of 'Savoyard' probably because himself or his ancestors were from Savoy. He always went by that name. Mrs. Shelden has, in some way, transformed it to 'Xavier,' which it never bore." We are indebted to the late Hon. B. F. H. Witherell for this quotation. The course of this river was from the woods in the rear of the town, along by the east line of Michigan Grand Avenue into Congress Street, and thence along that street, for some distance, till it made a curve toward the Detroit River. The bank of Detroit River gradually rose to a ridge, where Jefferson Avenue is located, and then declined a little, giving direction to the Savoyard. The subsoil, being a stiff clay, occasioned a great deal of stagnant water in the summer season and a vast amount of mud in the spring and fall. It is still in the memory of many yet living that teams were mired on Woodward Avenue. But, since a thorough system of sewerage has been adopted and carried out, these evils have been removed, and "The Savoyard" is no more. We have given so much space to this river because it has been so completely obliterated that the coming generations would have entirely forgotten it, if its existence were not fully stated. The location of this city is considered to be one of the most delightful in the United States. It is one of the most healthy, too, that can anywhere be found. It is well situated for trade and commerce. The harbor is all that could be desired. The manufactures and mercantile establishments are equal to the demands of the country.

Detroit has been a place of resort for the Indians of the Northwest for so long a time that "the memory of man runneth not" back to the beginning ; and it was selected by its founders for its advantages for trade among the aborigines. *Precisely* at what time it was first visited by any white man we have no means of determining, as the early traders and adventurous hunters made no records of their wanderings amid these far-off wilds. It had been visited as early as

1668—but how much earlier we *know* not, though it is said to have been as early as 1610.

When was the city founded? *M. de la Motte Cadillac*, a French adventurer, made application to the French Government for authority and means, in 1700, to establish a fort and settlement at this point. Through the intervention of M. Ponchartrain, he obtained what he required, so that, in July, 1701, he arrived here, having with him about one hundred French adventurers, some fur-traders and a Catholic priest. He laid out a town, and enclosed it and a fort with pickets, giving it the name of Fort Ponchartrain, in honor of his patron, Count Ponchartrain. They addressed themselves, mainly, to traffic among the Indians. No special effort was made to cultivate the soil to any considerable extent, though a few pear trees were planted and some other fruits.

So far separated from other settlements, on the frontier for many years, Detroit has been the theater of as many perils, stirring scenes, and disasters, in its progress, as any other city on this continent, and perhaps more. While it was under the undisputed dominion of the French, with a single exception all was peace. Why was this? The facility with which the French could adapt themselves to the habits and customs of the Indians gave them perfect immunity among them. They could eat, sleep, sing, dance and hunt with them—in short, be Indians in everything except color. No efforts were made, except by a party of strangers, to disturb this new settlement while it continued under the French dominion; but, as soon as it passed from their hands to the English, annoyances began. This refers to those whose residences were in this region. It seemed at once to become a troubled city.

In 1712 the town of Detroit was attacked by a "party of Ottogamies, or Foxes—a nation, passionate and untamable, springing up into new life from every defeat, and, though reduced in the number of their warriors, yet present everywhere by their ferocious enterprise and savage daring"—the town almost fell before the valor of the party. "Resolving to burn Detroit, they pitched their lodges near the fort, which Du Buisson, with but twenty Frenchmen, defended. Aware of their intentions, he summoned his Indian allies from the chase; and, about the middle of May, Ottawas, Hurons, Potawatamies, with one band of the Sacs, Illinois, Menomenies, and even Osages and Missouris, each nation with its ensign, came to his relief. 'Father,' said they, 'behold! thy children compass thee around. We will, if need be, die for our Father—only take care of our wives and children, and spread a little grass over our bodies to protect them from the flies.'

The warriors of the Fox nation, so far from destroying Detroit, were themselves besieged, and, at last, compelled to surrender at discretion. Those who bore arms were ruthlessly murdered; the rest were distributed as slaves among the confederates, to be saved or massacred at the will of their masters."*

Detroit was given up to the English at the close of the "Old French War," in 1760, by the terms of the treaty of peace between the two powers, though the English did not take possession till 1762. The stiff and uncompliant disposition of the English did not please the savages; and, smarting under the recollection of the conflicts in New England, they were ready to embrace any measure that offered any hope of ridding the country of them. The encroachments of the English on the wild hunting-grounds of the Indians were very displeasing to them; and it is not to be wondered at, as they saw they would have to retire from familiar scenes and the graves of their ancestors, that they should struggle against it. When they came into the possession of the Fort and City of Detroit, the natives were very much chagrined and vexed. They had at this time among them a man of remarkable ability and daring, who wished to destroy the English garrison here; but, like Haman of old, he scorned to lay hands on it alone, and he entered into—or, rather, originated—a scheme to destroy all the forts in the West. Pontiac's conspiracy for the destruction of Detroit, in 1763, is now well known. His object was not so much the destruction of the town as to destroy the English; for, all the time during his siege, the French settlers could circulate freely, without molestation; their property was safe. His general plan was to attack all the chain of forts simultaneously, and he reserved Detroit for himself. Finding he could not succeed by a direct attack, he resorted to stratagem, and so well was his plan laid that it would most certainly have succeeded had he not been betrayed.

There were some of the most tragic scenes enacted in connection with Pontiac's siege that are recorded of any town on this continent. His plot was deep-laid, and would have accomplished his purpose had no one informed the British commander of his intentions. He, with a number of his principal men went to the fort under the pretense of a friendly parley, all armed with short guns, made for the purpose, concealed under their blankets, while many of his men were gathered around, engaged, professedly, in play, who were to rush into the fort at a given signal. But the signal was not given, because he found the commander prepared for him. When he found

* Bancroft's United States, III., pp. 224, 225.

himself betrayed, with great reluctance he raised the siege and retired.

In connection with Pontiac's conspiracy, a most desperate and bloody battle was fought on the banks of a small creek above the city, which winds through Elmwood Cemetery, and gives to it the beauty of its scenery—which battle is said to have given the creek the significant name of " Bloody Run."

Pontiac, having been foiled in his purposes, and having retired with his warriors from the neighborhood of the city, the little garrison and the few English settlers breathed freely, and business resumed its usual course.

Detroit remained in the occupancy and possession of the British until 1796, although, when the peace of the Revolution was concluded, in 1783, it was recognized as belonging to the United States. Why it was so held it is difficult to determine. Probably, if the United States Government had sent soldiers to occupy the fort and protect the inhabitants, the British soldiers would have left. Things were allowed to move slowly along in this locality, without anything, in particular, to break the even current of events, until the Territorial Government of Michigan was provided for by Congress in 1804. General William Hull was appointed Governor, and a Judiciary, composed of Augustus B. Woodward, James Griffin and Francis Bates, who organized a Government at Detroit in July of 1805. The Governor and Judges constituted the Legislative Council. Detroit was made the seat of Government, as a matter of course. "In 1807 Judge Bates resigned, and James Witherell was appointed in his place."

Governor Hull arrived here on the twelfth day of June, 1805, to find the city a mass of charred ruins; for the whole town, excepting one house, was consumed by fire the day before. There were about one hundred and fifty houses in the town at the time of the fire. No special effort was made to extinguish the fire, except that the Catholic priest, Mr. Dilhet, fell upon his knees and said low mass. The distress must have been very great, as there were, at least, a hundred families thus deprived of shelter. Shortly after this catastrophe, an act of Congress was passed, directing the Governor and Judges to lay out a new town, including the site of the one destroyed, and ten thousand acres of adjacent lands were granted. This quantity of land was granted by the General Government for the city, to assist in relieving the calamity.

The plan of the new town was drafted by Judge Woodward, and is very peculiar. The idea seems to have been suggested by a spider's web. The original plan has been somewhat disturbed by more modern utilitarianism; still, some of the old marks are left. The idea of several wide and airy streets or avenues as the main ribs in the web, as, also, several parks, was a very good one, and contributes both to the beauty and healthfulness of the city. The growth of the city in these early years was very slow, as there was nothing, in particular, to stimulate immigration, because of its isolated position. When this new town was laid out it was at once incorporated as a city—that is, in 1805. Detroit continued to be the seat of Government for the Territory, and for the State till 1847, when by act of the Legislature the capital was removed to Lansing.

War having been declared by the United States against Great Britain in 1812, as was to have been expected, Detroit, being situated on the border, was to become the theater of stirring events. Governor Hull had made preparations for defence, and the army had been increased until it was supposed it was prepared for any force that could be brought against it. The British army was concentrated on the opposite side of the Detroit River, at Windsor and Sandwich. It was confidently believed that General Hull could successfully cope with any force that could be brought to bear against him. On the 16th day of August, 1812, the battle opened—or, rather, the army of the British was put in array against Detroit; but, before a single gun was fired from the fort, a demand was made for the surrender, which was ignobly acceded to by the commanding General—Hull— and, to the surprise and astonishment of all, the British flag was hoisted on the ramparts. Various conjectures have been indulged in in regard to the motives which induced him to do so. Some have charged him with cowardice and others with treachery. It certainly looks very much like one or the other. We will not attempt to solve the mystery—for it was mysterious—but will give what light we can. It was our good fortune, a few years since, to make the acquaintance of an old lady of intelligence, who was in the city at the time, then a young lady, and whose father's house was made the headquarters of the British commander, and the family had to retire to a small apartment. This lady subsequently married a British officer, and often heard them speak of General Hull. She said they always spoke of him as not being a coward, but that his surrender had its origin in some other cause. Of course, they did not openly say what the other cause was. On the day of the surrender, after the British officers had become settled in her father's house, she overheard one of the officers say, in relation to the surrender, that "British gold had done its work." Hull was tried for treason and cowardice; was acquitted on the former and convicted on the latter, and sentenced to be shot, but was pardoned by the President. The probability is that vacillation and the want of real courage was the true solution.

The British possession of Detroit was of short duration; for the naval battle on Lake Erie, in which Commodore Perry gained a grand and memorable victory on the 10th of September, and the victory of General Harrison at the Thames, restored the city to the possession of the United States. "When the American flag was hauled down by General Hull, in 1812, at the time of the surrender, James May, Esq., a Colonel of Militia, got possession of it, and kept it until General Harrison arrived." Though the city passed into the hands of the British, the flag did not, and the very same flag waved over it after it was recovered that did so before the surrender. "Colonel Cass, with a brigade of soldiers, was left for the protection of the Territory, which they effectually accomplished until the treaty of peace, concluded at Ghent on the 17th of February, 1815, put an end to all further hostilities." This introduces a new name to our notice, one that is, hereafter, to be identified with the interests of Detroit and to become dear to the people of Michigan—it is that of Lewis Cass.

According to the census taken by the United States, in 1820, the whole population of the Territory was found to be only *eight thousand eight hundred and ninety-six.* "Detroit contained two hundred and fifty houses, and fourteen hundred and fifteen inhabitants independent of the garrison." An event had occurred, the year before, which tended to give new life to commerce on the lakes, and to stimulate immigration; an event which was but the introduction to a series which have given character to the whole West, and, indeed, the influence of the same thing is now felt in every part of the civilized world—that was, the introduction of steam navigation. The Walk-in-the-water, the first steamboat that ever floated on Lake Erie, made its first appearance in Detroit in the spring or summer of 1819. She was a vessel of small tonnage, but was regarded at the time as a magnificent affair, and as one of the wonders of the world. She was so named for an Indian chief, who was associated with Tecumseh in the War of 1812 on the side of the British against us. The name seemed to be appropriate, too, as the vessel seemed to be walking in the water.

Another circumstance, occurring at a little later period, exerted, perhaps, a still greater influence upon the settlement of Michigan and the entire Northwest, as, also, on the interests and growth of Detroit—that was, the opening of the New York and Erie Canal, or, "Clinton's Big Ditch," as some of the people at that time called it. This greatly increased the facilities and comforts of travel and the transportation of goods and merchandise.

The present population of the city is about 120,000. According to the census taken in 1864, the population numbered *fifty-three thousand one hundred and seventy*. It has a little more than doubled its population in the last thirteen years. With the increase of population and wealth, there has been a great advance in the architecture and elegance of buildings, as places of business and residences. There are some very costly and beautiful residences, and there is a constant advance in this respect.

Detroit is abundantly supplied with periodical literature. There are two large daily papers, and one smaller, having an extensive circulation. The *Michigan Farmer* is a weekly, devoted to the interests of agriculture. The *Michigan Christian Advocate* and the *Herald and Torchlight* are weeklies, devoted to religion and literature. There are numerous small papers devoted to specialties, and papers in the German language. The *Michigan Christian Advocate* was established January 1st, 1875, and the *Herald and Torchlight*, the Baptist organ, at a much earlier date. Both are well sustained.

The first attempt at publishing a newspaper here was in 1809. Rev. Gabriel Richard, the Roman Catholic priest, published a paper for a short time, entitled, *Michigan Essay or Impartial Observer*. It did not succeed. It was published in French, and, as the old French inhabitants were not much readers, he could not obtain sufficient patronage. In 1817, John P. Sheldon commenced the publication of the Detroit *Gazette*, which proved a success, though that small weekly sheet has been succeeded by the much larger weeklies and dailies, and the *Gazette* is known only in history.

Detroit, of course, is the principal point from which the daily news is distributed throughout the State, and, as such, the periodicals of the city will flourish and grow. The periodicals will increase in number and importance as the population increases.

In regard to the commerce of Detroit, we quote liberally from one writer:

"Detroit, from its first settlement in 1701, has ranked first as a commercial point on the Western lakes. A company, styled the 'Company of the Colony of Canada,' was incorporated by the Colony of Canada at a convention held at Quebec, October 31st, 1701, which conferred upon them the right 'to trade at Detroit in beaver and peltries, to the entire exclusion of all private individuals.'

"M. de la Motte Cadillac, the first commandant at Detroit, who was commissioned by Louis XIV., in a letter to Count Ponchartrain in 1703, says that his design, in projecting a trading-post here in 1701, was to afford protection to commerce; since from this point we can go by canoe to all the nations that are around the lakes; it is a *door* by which we can go in and out to trade with all our allies. And we find that Charlevoix, a French Jesuit missionary, who visited this city as early as 1720, speaks of a complaint that the English merchants sell merchandise to the savages cheaper than the French do, thereby drawing all the trade to New York.

"In 1787, that patriarch native citizen among us, who was born just after the close of the Pontiac War, Joseph Campau, Esq., actively engaged in mercantile business here, and continued in it for about forty years. In early times, he annually visited the City of Montreal, conveying, in birch-bark canoes, cargoes of furs, etc., and returning with them freighted with goods."

How changed is everything now! Long streets, lined with stores filled with goods; railroads and steamers to bring and carry away the goods and products. Instead of the export of furs, merely, we now export almost everything that can be thought of—lumber, timber, staves, copper and iron ore, wheat, corn, potatoes, apples, pork, beef, fish, and the like, in vast quantities. One, in walking the busy streets now, could hardly imagine that all the exports and imports at this port had once been conveyed in birch-bark canoes, propelled by hand, and, of course, coasting along the lake shore. But so it was.

Various manufactures are carried on here on a liberal scale, and they are constantly increasing.

As to religious Societies, or Churches, it is not necessary to say much in this chapter, as that subject has been thoroughly treated in the early chapters of this work. Still, a few words may be allowed here. The Roman Catholic Church was established at the very origin of the settlement, and has now in its fold a considerable proportion of the present population. There are churches for the French, Irish, Germans, Poles, and English, with various nunneries, sisterhoods, and asylums. They have an immense property in the city. They are making great efforts to retain all their members, including immigrants and native-born. Occasionally, they make a convert from among the Protestants; but these do not begin to equal the number they lose by conversion to Protestantism.

Of Protestant Churches, the first in order was the Methodist Episcopal Church, established in the autumn of 1810, and at the present time—1877—having eight churches, with regular pastors, and two separate Sunday School chapels; with all the necessary appliances for Church work, and with valuable property. The next in order, nearly contemporaneous in organization, are the Protestant Episcopal and Presbyterian Churches. The former was organized November 22d, in 1824, and the latter was instituted as a Church, January 23d, 1825, though they had had preaching, most of the time, since June, 1816. The latter now have six churches and some mission Sabbath Schools. The former—the Protestant Episcopal Church —was fully organized in 1824, and now has five churches, with several mission chapels. The Baptists range next in order, having been fully organized in 1827, and now having two principal churches, one mission among the French, one among the Germans, and some other mission work. There are two Congregational Churches, doing good work. The first was organized in 1844. There are some Churches among the colored people, bearing the name of Methodists, Baptists, and Episcopalians. There are several other Protestant denominations, as Lutherans, having several churches; United Presbyterians, having one church; Scotch Presbyterians, having one church, who have recently changed their name to that of Central Presbyterian Church, and some others. There is, also, a Unitarian Church and a Swedenborgian Church.

Among the religious societies doing Christian work may be mentioned the Young Men's Christian Association, which has become a permanent fixture in the city, having a good property well fitted up for religious and benevolent work. Their rooms have become a great center of attraction. They seem to be doing a noble work.

It may be observed that there was no earnest effort made for the establishment of Protestantism in this city earlier than 1809. All visits of Protestant ministers, prior to that time, were only incidental, and not from any fixed purpose to establish the cause in the city. But, in 1809, Detroit was placed on the list of appointments of the New York Annual Conference of the Methodist Episcopal Church, and a minister was appointed to it; and it has remained in the list of appointments, and ministers assigned to it ever since, except for the years 1813 and 1814, during the prevalence of the war, when ministers could not get here.

The history of education in connection with the City of Detroit is full of interest, and must not be passed by in silence. In the organization of the Territorial Government of Michigan, Congress set apart, or appropriated some valuable lands for the establishment and maintenance of a university or seminary of learning. The organization of this university was provided for by a law passed by the Governor and Judges, who constituted the law-making body at that time. Numerous professorships were provided for under the title of *Didaxia*, and the institution was opened in 1817. Rev. John Monteith, who was sent out here as a missionary, the year before, under commission from "The Board of Missions of the General Assembly of the Presbyterian Church of the United States," was appointed the president, and professor in several *Didaxia*, and Gabriel Richard, a Roman Catholic priest, was associated with him in charge of the remaining *Didaxia*.

As might have been expected from the circumstances of the times, the institution proved a failure, and the university, in its relation to Detroit, died out in a short time, for, when the State Government was organized, in 1837, the original location and organization of the university were entirely ignored, a new law for its organization was passed, and its location was changed to Ann Arbor. Yet Detroit was not without schools in which the classics were taught. "The old Academy" still lives in the recollections of some of the inhabitants of Detroit to the present day, although its obsequies were attended years ago, and its material remains have long since disappeared.

Detroit was left, for a number of years, to the ordinary, or common school system, supplemented by various private enterprises, which did good service, until the present school system of the city was adopted. The present very efficient system embraces a central high school, with ward branches as the exigencies may demand, supported by tax to supplement the moneys from the public school fund from the State; so that the schools are all free to residents of the city. They are graded to meet all degrees of intellectual culture, leaving everyone without excuse. The whole is under the management of one superintendent, under the control of a school board elected by the public in each ward of the city. The Central High School is intended to advance students in the classics and sciences, so that they may enter the State University, if they choose, on graduation.

It is not to be supposed that this system of education for the city has attained to its present gigantic proportions without opposition. It has had to struggle, and, indeed, it is not yet entirely free from struggling. This opposition has arisen from two causes— penuriousness and religious fanaticism. The penurious were unwilling to pay the necessary taxes for buildings with suitable furniture and apparatus, and pay qualified teachers. The religious fanaticism is confined, almost entirely, to the Romish Church, they characterizing them as "Godless schools," because the priests cannot be permitted to teach their peculiar religious dogmas in them. If the priests were permitted to visit the schools, and catechise the children, and take a part of each day to indoctrinate them in their dogmas, all would be well. Their great object is to break down our school system and secure a distribution of the school fund, so that they may be assisted to maintain their sectarian schools. They oppose the use of the Bible—not that they care so much about the Bible, but to secure the co-operation of all classes of skeptics to break down the system. Notwithstanding these oppositions to the system, it has grown strong, and is destined to go on and prosper in its legitimate work of intellectual culture. Notwithstanding the opposition of the Romanists to the system, they manage to secure a large proportion of the teachers to be of their "faith and order."

We shall occupy only a small space in the presentation of sketches of a few men connected with the early history of this city— of those who gave shaping to its interests and its society. All we can do is little more than to record their names.

HON. A. B. WOODWARD, one of the first Judges appointed by the President, was said to be a man of ability and integrity. He had a peculiarly constituted mind, which was shown in several things. He was charged with the work of laying out and platting the new city, after the disastrous fire in 1805, and did that work in a very peculiar manner. What that plan was, every one who knows anything of the city knows. It may look fine for a spider's web, but is very inconvenient for a city. The next particular in which that peculiarity was shown was in the law providing for the organization of the University of Michigan. He was responsible for the peculiar form of that law. The professorships were called *Didaxia*, and many other peculiarities entered into it. That law was so peculiar that no notice was taken of it when the State Legislature provided for the reorganization of the University. We are indebted to a correspondent in *Harper's Magazine* for the following statement: "He was a bachelor—never married. It was often the case that he would buy a dozen shirts at a time, and, as one of them would become soiled, he would put on another one over it, and so keep doing until he would have the whole dozen on at once." This seems hardly credible, but it is given in that Magazine as a veritable fact. When he gave his approval to the articles of association for the incorporation of the Methodist Society of Detroit, he stated that his preference was that there should be but one denomination, according to some plan which had been adopted in Prussia; but, as there was nothing contrary to the statute in their articles, he signed his approval. He is said to have been a very good man.

GENERAL LEWIS CASS succeeded General Hull in the Governorship of the Territory of Michigan, and in that office did much for Detroit and for Michigan in general. He was in General Hull's army, but on the day of the surrender was absent on detached duty, and was very angry when informed of the surrender. He never made an open profession of religion, but always gave his support to the cause. He was one of the signers of the constitution, or articles of association for the incorporation of "The First Protestant Society of Detroit," in December, 1821. His wife became a member of the first Presbyterian Church of Detroit when that Church was instituted in 1825, and her name appears among the first members of it. The Governor gave his support to that Church, mainly. He served as Secretary of War of the United States one term, as Senator of the United States, and as a Minister to a foreign court. In all these positions he did honor to the city, State and nation. He was a very temperate man in his habits, never having used any ardent spirits in all his life, though he sometimes made a very moderate use of wine. He was in the United States Senate at the time of the repeal of the Missouri Compromise line, so as to allow slavery to be extended into any of the territory of the United States. He consented to it reluctantly, but he could not avoid it without breaking away from the Democratic party, which he was not prepared to do. He knew it would, finally, be fatal to his party; but the slaveocracy demanded it, and it must be done. The result is what we have seen—the final abolition of slavery and the displacement of his party from power. From correspondence we had with him while the matter was pending in Congress, we know his convictions were right; but he could not make up his mind to act according to them. It is always a sad thing to see a man of such abilities hesitating to stand up for the oppressed, and stifling his own convictions of the right. He was a great and noble man, and ought to have consecrated himself to the Divine service, which he felt and acknowledged to be his duty. He is deceased.

EUROSTAS P. HASTINGS came to Detroit from the State of New York in 1824 or 1825, and for the most part, if not the entire of his life was connected with one of the banks of the city, and stood high as an accommodating, honest business man. He was a very devoted, earnest Christian man, a member of the Presbyterian Church before he came here. He was one of the forty-nine persons who composed the first Presbyterian Church of Detroit, when that Church was instituted on the 23d day of January, 1825. He was elected and ordained one of the ruling elders at that time. He labored very actively in the cause of religion, and has gone to receive his reward.

HON. B. F. H. WITHERELL was the son of Judge James Witherell, who was appointed one of the Territorial Judges, by President Jefferson, in 1810. The Judge brought his family here in 1810, but they did not remain because his wife was afraid of so many Indians. They returned to the East and remained till after the war. In the meantime B. F. H. had studied law, and had returned here to reside. He had also made a profession of religion and was a member of the Methodist Church here as early as 1820. Mr. Witherell grew to occupy a very important place in the affairs of the city and State. He was called to occupy the bench of the Circuit Court for this Judicial Circuit, which position he well filled. He was a Democrat in politics, and was honored by his party. He died in 1867. The younger Judge was a man of good education, an excellent jurist, and a worthy son of a worthy sire.

HON. WILLIAM WOODBRIDGE was long identified with the interests of the city and of the State. He was a very early settler, of New England origin. He was a lawyer by profession, and a Whig in politics, and in this respect was the constant antagonist of General Cass. He was once elected and served as Governor of the State; and filled other and important offices. He met and fulfilled the responsibilities of his official positions to the entire satisfaction of those who agreed with him in politics. He was a supporter of the Christian religion, and an adherent of the Presbyterian Church; but, like too many men in public life, neglected the vital experience of that religion in which he believed and which he supported. It does seem strange that such men do not more thoroughly realize their responsibility to God and humanity, to submit their hearts and lives to the Divine service. Certainly, their official and public positions do not lessen, but they do increase their responsibility. Position is a source of power, and that power is to be exerted for the purity and elevation of humanity. Christianity, in its experience and practice, is the purifying and elevating agency. They, then, are obligated to do what they can to promote it to the greatest possible extent. Mr. Woodbridge had accumulated quite a fortune—very largely from the increase in the value of his lands by the growth of the city. He owned a large farm just adjoining the city, which has now all become included in it, and furnished many desirable building places. His name is perpetuated in the name of one of the streets of the city.

HON. JAMES WITHERELL. The following sketch of the life of the elder Judge Witherell, written by the late Bishop Edward Thomson, D. D., will be read with interest, and is worthy of a place in our History: "One of the earliest contributions to the Detroit Methodist Church was the family of Judge Witherell, and one of my first pastoral visits was made at his house. Of Puritan stock, a native of Mansfield, Massachusetts, he commenced life, in 1775, by entering the army at the age of sixteen; and, having obtained a commission in the Massachusetts line, he continued in the service till the army was disbanded. He subsequently studied and practiced successfully the professions of medicine and law; and, in 1808, while filling a seat in Congress as a Representative from Vermont, he was appointed by Mr. Jefferson a United States Judge in Michigan. Being in the Territory during the War of 1812, he entered the field again as colonel of a regiment. On the capitulation of Hull, he disbanded his soldiers, but was himself made a prisoner of war. He was, however, exchanged, and permitted to resume his seat on the Bench. * * * He had a kind heart and a strong mind, a fine vein of humor and a vast store of anecdotes.

"Although not a member of the Church, he was a believer in its creed, an admirer of its discipline, and a reader of its literature, particularly of the writings of Adam Clarke. He read the Scriptures daily, and devoted some time to silent, but, we trust, fervent devotion. He often dwelt with delight upon the fifty-fifth chapter of Isaiah. With him, as with most men, the appetite for Divine truth increased as he drew near the grave. On one occasion, while his companion was reading to him an interesting item of intelligence, she complained that her eyes were failing. 'Save them, then, to read the Bible,' said he. He renounced all other refuge but the Cross. What a pity that men who take evangelical views do not profess them publicly, and before they come to die, and especially when their position in society gives them commanding influence! A clause in a will, a dying or public confession made at the last, cannot atone for a life spent out of the Church. At Judge Witherell's death—January 9th, 1838—the Michigan Legislature, as well as the Bar of the Supreme Court, passed resolutions of respect to his memory, and attended his funeral.

"It was my duty to preach on the occasion, and it will afford an insight into the Judge's character to remark that, when I called on his family for materials for a sketch of his life and character, the only docu--

ment that they could find was the following, which was his whole autobiography: 'At the age of sixteen, I joined the Revolutionary army, and stood sentry at Boston Neck. On the evacuation of Boston by the British army, I marched to New York. I was wounded severely at White Plains; marched to Rhode Island; thence to Saratoga; thence to Valley Forge, in Pennsylvania, where I kept a four days' fast; thence to Monmouth, and subsequently to Fishkill, Newburg, and West Point, where, on the 19th of April, 1873, the Revolutionary army was disbanded.'" This ends the Bishop's account of the Judge; but we wish to add our concurrence in his sentiments in regard to the neglect of such men to identify themselves openly with the cause of Christ. It is a mystery to us how such men can hope to find acceptance at the last, or how they can reconcile it with their obligations to poor, fallen, suffering humanity, all around them, calling for the help of their example to enable them to rise.

CHAPTER IX.

Preliminary—Michigan Conference—Protestant Episcopal Diocese—Indian Missions—Detroit—J. B. Finley—J. A. Baughman—Curtis Goddard—James Gilruth—Bishop Thomson—Arza Brown—Progress of the Churches—Congress Street Church—Dr. Duffield—Phelps—Noah M. Wells—W. H. Collins.

WE now enter upon the fourth period of our History—the organization of the Michigan Conference—and the last that we shall designate as such. In this we shall have to take a little more extended and free range. The period properly begins with 1836; but we have to retrospect some, and we shall, also, anticipate some things, so as not to break the connection. There can be no reasonable objection to either of these.

It, perhaps, will be remembered that by act of the General Conference, in May, 1836, the Michigan Conference was created—but it also embraced the northern part of Ohio. In 1840, the Ohio part was taken off, and Michigan alone constituted a Conference. In 1856, the Michigan Conference was divided, and the Detroit Conference was created, so that, at this present writing, we have two Annual Conferences in this State, besides the Michigan District of the Central German Conference.

It may be considered a singular fact that the creation of the Michigan Annual Conference of the Methodist Episcopal Church was contemporaneous with the organization of the State Government—for it was in 1836 that the State Constitution was framed, and ratified by the people, and Michigan was released from its pupilage, and admitted as one of the States of the Union. The ratification by Congress was not completed till 1837, on account of a little difficulty about the boundary with Ohio. So, while we have shown a great increase of Protestantism, there has, also, been a great increase of the population as well.

There are three circumstances, or facts, that have contributed to the growth of the country, worthy of notice: These are the use of steamboats on the lakes; the opening of the New York and Erie Canal; and a better knowledge of the topography of the country furnished by surveyors and other explorers.

The opening of the great New York and Erie Canal, perhaps, had a more direct influence on the settlement of this part of the West than even the steamboating, as it furnished a better and easier mode of travel to the lake, and furnished the prospect of the easy transportation of merchandise westward. The idea that the West was to be the granary of the East had not yet been conceived—but what would the steamboats and canal have amounted to if there had not been a country to sustain a large population? The experiments of the adventurers, in regard to the salubrity of the climate and the fertility of the soil—a soil that had been thought to be barren—showed that large yields, in proportion to expenditure, rewarded the husbandman, and the climate agreeable. These plains and prairies were found to be very fertile; and even the marshes, or wet meadows, were very important to furnish hay for stock. We do not well to separate these facts, and attempt to attach importance to either of them separately. Consider them jointly, and then we may be able to comprehend the rapid increase of the population of this Peninsular State. This rapid increase of population threw a vast responsibility on the Church and ministry, to see that they were supplied with religious instruction—the means of grace. How this responsibility has been met, we shall endeavor to develop in the following pages.

The Protestant Episcopal Diocese of Michigan was organized this same year—1836—and Rev. Samuel A. McCoskrey was elected, and ordained Bishop, and, at the same time, was to serve as Rector of St. Paul's Church, in the City of Detroit. St. Paul's at that time, and until 1852, was located on Woodward Avenue, between Larned and Congress Streets, but, at this time, they erected a large stone church at the corner of Congress and Shelby Streets. The Bishop was a graduate of West Point; large, straight, and very commanding in presence, and has labored much to advance the interests of his Church. The origin and progress of that Church, in different localities, will be noticed in their appropriate places.

We begin this period with two Districts and part of another; for it is to be remembered that the southwest part of the State was connected with the Indiana Conference, and remained so till 1840. We have *thirty-five* intinerant ministers and *five thousand* members. The State had a population of about one hundred thousand, and rapidly increasing, so that, in 1840, there was a population of two hundred and twelve thousand. The Circuits were generally large, though, in a few instances, there had been formed what were called half stations—that is, the Circuits were so constructed that one minister could be in the principal village every Sabbath. It is much to be regretted, however, that we were not more attentive to the centers of influence. In most of the villages, we were there to supply them for a long time before any others made any attempt; but, by our not supplying them with as much service as we ought to have done, others entered, and many who were friendly to Methodism, and would have given their influence to it permanently, were drawn away, because they wanted more ministerial service than we afforded, and so they were lost to us. In some of these places we have since nearly recovered what we had lost, but in most of them it is not so, and we have to occupy a position below that which we might have had, and ought to have had.

The Michigan Conference having been created, held its first session in Mansfield, Ohio, in September, 1836, and was presided over by the venerable and majestic Bishop Soule. He was then in the vigor of his noble manhood, and preached with wonderful eloquence and power. The next session was held in Detroit in September, 1837. The good, sweet-spirited, noble-minded Bishop Roberts presided over this session. The sessions were held in the session room of the Presbyterian Church, on Woodward Avenue, between Larned and Congress Streets. The Conference was well entertained, for all denominations opened their houses for the purpose, and Methodism received much advantage from it. Other denominations were forced, however reluctantly, to cultivate a higher respect for them. Some of them had looked on Rev. Edward Thomson, a man of culture and superior intellect, who had been stationed here the year before, and was still in the station—since Bishop Thomson—with great pity, because of his connection with that ignorant, ranting people, as they regarded the Methodists to be; but now they found that he was not alone in his culture and greatness; and they were very favorably impressed with the ability and dignity of the body. Though the Conference was composed very largely of young men, they were young men of ability and great promise. The sessions of the Conferences alternated between Ohio and Michigan, the fourth session, in September, 1839, being held in Ann Arbor—Bishop Soule presiding—until 1840, when, by act of the General Conference, Michigan, alone, was made to constitute a Conference. According to the Minutes of 1840, there were four Districts—viz., Detroit, Ann Arbor, Marshall, and Kalamazoo—and a Mission District in the Lake Superior country, containing *seventy-seven* ministers and preachers and 11,523 members, as reported to the Conference, which met in Marshall on August 19th, Bishop Hedding presiding.

In the Minutes of 1840, we have a Mission District, with William H. Brockway as superintendent, containing three charges in the Lake Superior region—viz., Sault Ste. Marie, Kewawenon, and Mackinaw —supplied with six ministers and preachers. Two of these preachers were Indians, as will be judged by their names—viz., Peter Marksman and John Kahbage. The Sault Ste. Marie and Kewawenon Mission appears in our Minutes in 1837 as one charge, and it is attached to the Detroit District, and, the next year, the same Mission was attached to the Ann Arbor District, and W. H. Brockway was the missionary; but, in 1839, the Mission District was created, and W. H. Brockway was made the superintendent, and was the preacher in charge of Sault Ste. Marie Mission, with George King as his assistant. Kewawenon was made a separate Mission, and left to be supplied, with the expectation of engaging an Indian preacher. At the next Conference they reported *seventy-seven* members and *seventy-six* of these were Indians, which was an increase of only one Indian over last year. The first report of members among the Indians of this region was made in 1838, which was *forty-two* members. Though in 1837 was the first appearance of this Indian mission work on our Minutes of appointments, the work had been going on for some time. Some two or three years before this time, John Sunday, an Indian preacher from Canada, had visited the Indians of this region, and preached so effectively that a revival originated among them, and they desired a missionary to be sent to them, which was done, with the results named above. Two ministers, or preachers, were raised up among themselves, to preach the Gospel without the tedious process of an interpreter. This seemed to be a call of Providence on the Church for contributions of men and means to carry forward the work among the aborigines. God so prospered the work among them that, in three years, *seventy-six* native members were reported among them. This was, certainly, a very encouraging result for the amount of labor and money expended; especially so when we consider the depths of ignorance and vicious degradation to which they had become subjected. These Missions have been continued ever since. While on this subject of Indian Missions, we would say that the Presbyterian Church had established a Mission among them, at Mackinaw, as early as 1821, and, perhaps, a little earlier, and conducted it with zeal. The Baptists, also, had one in the west part of the Territory in 1830, and, perhaps, earlier, which was carried forward with a good degree of success. Notwithstanding the great expenditure of means, men and labor by the different denominations of Christians, while a few, or, even a good many of them, have become true Christian converts, and have been saved by grace, the mass of them are Indians still—have not been much civilized or elevated. This fact gives coloring to a remark, made by Hugh Miller, that, when a tribe or nation has reached a certain point of degradation, it is impossible to restore it. Millions of money have been expended for the Christianization and civilization of the aborigines of the American continent, with very little to show for it. Something has been done in the former object, but they have to be wards of the Church still, and very little progress has been made in the latter. Sad as it may seem, the indications are that they are to become extinct. In the meantime, it is well for the Christian Church to do all that can be done to save as many of them as possible from the pains of "the second death."

The Christian work in the Lake Superior District is now devoted, mainly, to the white population, which has become numerous, as the mining interests have become developed. Although the Methodists were the first to carry the Gospel into this region, they are not alone in this noble work, as will be seen from the religious statistics as here presented: Methodists, 1,356; Protestant Episcopal, 137, and two parishes not reported; Congregational, 200.

According to our plan, DETROIT must now occupy our attention for a little while longer. For an account of the origin and growth of the city, and some of the men connected with it, we refer to the preceding chapter. It is in its religious, Protestant aspect we must consider it. Except the record of the original Society, as given in our first and second periods, the first *record* we have been able to find, is an old class-book, prepared by Rev. Alfred Brunson, for an evening class, bearing date July 5th, 1823. This old book contained, at the time, twenty-five names, leaving us to infer that there must have been, at least, fifty or sixty members in the city, as the noon class was always larger than an evening one. Levi Brown, who was a Protestant Episcopalian in his predilections and withdrew some time later than the 4th of July, 1824, as he was present, on that day, at class, was the leader. He withdrew to assist in the organization of a Church of his own choice, which took place on November 22d, 1824. Although Mr. Brown stood as the class-leader, Jerry Dean, who was a member of the same class, was the leader in fact. The same book, at a later date, probably for 1825, contains a list of names of members, for the purpose of collecting for ministerial support. This list contains *sixty* names, which is, probably, the number then in Church fellowship. It is much to be regretted that our Church records were so loosely kept. There was no permanent book in which all the names were recorded, but those composing each class were entered in a small book, called a class-book. These class-books, when they were filled, were thrown aside as matters of no consequence, and new ones were prepared, in which only the names of those who were members at the time were entered. They did not, then, think they were making history, or else the ministers and class-leaders would have carefully preserved these books. In that same old book, under date of November 2d, is this entry: "John Owen joined." We have, already, spoken fully in regard to Mr. Owen. In the days of this book, the members, generally, attended class-meeting very constantly; as, for instance, in twenty-four successive weeks, in which class-meetings were held, William Brooks is marked absent only twice. Indeed, the members then believed what was true, that they could not prosper well in spiritual things without this social means of grace.

We must, now, call attention to a sketch of the life and character of some of the men not before noticed, as connected with the work in this city. In these sketches, we cannot confine ourselves to events which have occurred, simply, within this period. We must both retrospect and anticipate, because we must complete what we have to say of them at this time.

REV. JAMES B. FINLEY had but a short connection with the work in Detroit, but it was so important that it is eminently proper that he should find a place in this record. He was a man of mark in the Church; full of labors and good fruits. His life was very thoroughly devoted to the work of the Christian ministry, in which he was very successful. His father was a Presbyterian minister for many years, but, finally, joined the Methodists.

James B. Finley was born in North Carolina, in the month of July, 1781. His father had removed from Pennsylvania to the South to labor as a Christian minister, so that he was not a Southerner by blood, but by the accident of birth. About two or three years after the birth of our subject, his father, Robert Finley, removed to Kentucky, and was an active worker in the great revivals which prevailed in that country at an early day. School advantages were very limited, but the elder Finley had had a collegiate education, being a graduate of Princeton College, New Jersey. He, therefore, supplied, as well as he could. the lack of schools by superintending the education of his sons; so our subject acquired a considerable knowledge of the classics, and, at the same time, had the free-and-easy manners of the backwoods. He was not tied up with the etiquette of the present time. In spirit he was bold, fearless, intrepid, and prepared for any emergency.

Mr. Finley was admitted into the Conference, then called the Western Conference, in 1809, the very year that William Case was sent to Detroit. At the time he was appointed to the Lebanon District, in 1819, he had been in the ministry ten years, and was in the prime of his manhood. His District extended from the Ohio River, on the south, to Detroit. On such an extensive District, he must have encountered very great difficulties in making his visits to the different charges. Michigan was almost entirely cut off from communication with Ohio. The Black Swamp, as the flat country from the Sandusky River to the Maumee, or Miami of the Lakes, was called, was without any roads, and the only way of getting through was to follow Indian trails. The following is his account of his first visit to Detroit Circuit. The meeting was held on the Maumee River, and he started from Upper Sandusky. Hear his own words: "It was late in the fall when I left the white settlements to attend my first Quarterly Meeting at the Maumee Rapids. There was not a single habitation of a white man from the old Indian boundary, on the Scioto, till we reached the Rapids. In this route there were three Indian settlements—Upper Sandusky, Big Spring, and Sawawatown, on a branch of the Carrion River. Through this wilderness I urged my way. I had a dismal journey through the Black Swamp. Two nights I lay out in the woods, during which time I did not see the face of a human being. By the help of God, I at length reached my appointment." * * * * "I was hailed, by preacher and people, with gladness, as one that bringeth glad tidings to the ends of the earth. I had the honor of being the first Presiding Elder that set his foot on the Miami of the Lakes, and had the privilege of holding the first Quarterly Meeting, love-feast, or sacramental meeting ever held in this, now, densely populated country." Thus he actively and courageously pressed through the very trying circumstances in which he was placed, and showed that he was a man of courage and pious zeal.

We here transcribe from his auto-biography a full account of his visit to Detroit and his labors in connection with it, in the spring of 1821, and his return to Ohio. He says: "In the spring I started for the purpose of more thoroughly visiting my Detroit charge. The trip was a very adventurous one. When I arrived at Lower Sandusky, the summer freshet was at its highest. I traveled alone to Muscalunge Creek, and the water covered the entire valley, from hill to hill. Unable to proceed any further, I went back to the town at Lower Sandusky, and hired a Frenchman to pilot me through to the rapids of the Maumee. When he came to the creek, he said it was impossible for us to get through; so we returned, and I directed my course up the river to Fort Ball. Leaving my horse with a friend, I hired two young Indians to take me to the mouth of the river in a bark canoe, so that I might, at this point, get on board the steamer Walk-in-the-water on Friday morning.

"Setting sail in our frail canoe, we darted down the rapid river, and, when we came to the Sandusky Falls, we sped over them like a bird. Night overtaking us before we reached the mouth of the river, we concluded to tarry all night with an old Frenchman by the name of Poscile, who occupied a miserable shanty on the bank, and lived principally on muskrats. The place was dreadfully infested with fleas and mosquitos. My comrades joined in partaking of our host's hospitalities; but I was not sufficiently hunger-bitten to eat muskrats. To protect myself from the foes which swarmed around me I sat all night on a box. When daylight came we pushed off our canoe and paddled on. As we reached the bay we found the wind blowing fresh from land and the waves rolling too high for our little bark. The bay was five miles wide, and, notwithstandisg the boisterous weather, the Indians were for going directly across. To this I objected; and we finally agreed to take the east side and coast around. Several times our canoe filled with water, and we had to run ashore, pull it out, and turn it over—then relaunching, put to sea again. A more serious disaster befell us when we got within two hundred yards of the shore at Goat Island. A sudden squall upset our bark, plunging us all in the deep. Being unable to right up our vessel without something more substantial than water on which to rest our leverage, we swam with our boat to the shore. Here we took our canoe on our shoulders, and carrying it about a mile, we launched again and re-embarked. We paddled on, battling with the waves, and finally arrived within four miles of Portland. Taking my saddle-bags on my shoulder, I walked to town, almost exhausted for want of something to eat. Here I stopped at a tavern, and, ordering a room with a fire, I emptied my saddle-bags, and, spreading their contents, with my clothes, before it, went to bed and slept till the sun arose next morning. Getting up, I found my things tolerably well dried, except my books, and, after taking my breakfast, I got on board the boat, and arrived at Detroit on Saturday morning, where

I put up with my old friend Mr. Jeremiah Dean. At this place I received a letter from brother Kent, informing me of his sickness at the Rapids, and his inability to be with me. In that letter he informed me that he had given out appointments for me every day during the week, except Saturday and Monday. Thus you see, dear reader, I had work enough. The weather was excessively hot; but, notwithstanding, we commenced our meetings. Having no church, we worshipped in the Council House, and the Lord was with us of a truth. Governor Cass, my old friend, treated me with great respect and hospitality, and also his estimable lady. Indeed, God seemed to give me favor in the eyes of all the people. The soldiers who were stationed here treated me with much respect, and many of them were awakened under the preaching. Of all places in the world, a military station is the most unfavorable to religion; and hence there was but little fruit manifested. Several came forward for prayers and were converted to God. Had not appointments been given out for me, the meeting could have been kept up all the week to good advantage. Brother Abbott furnished me a horse, and I started on Tuesday to fill the appointments that had been made. That day I preached twice, and swam the River Rouge three times. I then went to two or three places out north and preached as far as Pontiac. Returning to Detroit, I spent another Sabbath of great interest and profit to myself and many others. My soul was much united to the dear people; for they seemed to be as sheep without a shepherd. On Monday I left for Upper Sandusky. When I arrived at Portland there was no conveyance for me to Lower Sandusky. After considerable search I found an Indian, whose horse I hired. The plan was for me to ride and the Indian to walk or run, as the case might be. Accordingly we started. The Indian would run on ahead in a long trot, and then, stopping, he would say, 'Good horse; how much you give for him?' I would tell him I did not want to buy. He would then run on again a mile or two, and, stopping, would ask the same question. This he continued till, becoming tired of his questions, I told him I had no money. 'You lie!' said he, pointing to my saddle-bags. Then said he, 'How much you give?' I said 'May be ten dollars.' Becoming incensed at this, he exclaimed, 'You rascal! you Kaintuck! you rascal! You cheat Indian!' Shortly after this we came within hearing of several camps of Indians. As we advanced we found them in a drunken spree, singing, dancing and hallooing as if all bedlam had broke loose. He asked me to turn in here and get some 'lum.' 'No,' said I, 'you come on.' 'No; me go, and quick come.' As soon as he was gone I cut a stout hickory stick and put the Indian pony to his best. Soon I heard the Indian yelling behind me; but he was not able to overtake me till I reached Lower Sandusky. When he came up he commenced abusing me and charging me with a disposition to run off with his horse. I told him he must stop his abuse, as I would have no more of it. 'Did I not give one dollar for the use of your horse?' 'Yes.' 'Well,' said I, 'here is a half-dollar besides, to get your dinner with.' At this he turned his tune, and said, 'You good man; you no Kaintuck; you my friend.'"

After some unimportant matter he says: " This was one of the best years of my itinerant life. A petition was sent this year to the bishops for me to be stationed at Detroit. This petition was signed by Governor Cass, the Messrs. Hunt, and principal citizens, In the petition they pledged themselves to pay all expenses, and support me, besides building a church. It was confidently believed by them, that their prayer would be heard; but Bishop McKendree thought the Indian mission of more consequence than Detroit, or any other place that might want me. Bishop Roberts was in favor of sending me to Detroit, and the matter continued in suspense till late in the Conference. My own judgment and feelings led me to Detroit, because I believed that at that time all the English inhabitants of the place would have joined the Church. But the senior bishop prevailed, and I was sent among the Indians." This shows that his visit to Detroit and the adjacent country was very highly appreciated, especially so by the city. As stated above, he was sent to the Indian mission at Upper Sandusky, instead of being sent to Detroit. This was certainly a great mistake, so far as the interests of religion, and of Methodism in this city were concerned. It is true that all he anticipated might not have been realized, but no doubt he would have been a great blessing to the city.

Mr. Finley was appointed to the Lebanon District again in 1822, which still included Detroit. The Sandusky District was created in 1824, and made to include Detroit, and Mr. Finley was appointed to it. He and Mr. Strange had alternated in charge of Lebanon District, and in charge of Detroit. We have no account of Mr. Stange having ever visited Detroit more than once. Mr. Finley was, then, the appointed Presiding Elder over Detroit for 1820, 1822, 1824, three years, but not consecutively; but we have no account of his having visited Detroit, except for the first year. It is to be remembered that the appointment was made in August or September of the year named.

It is not necessary for us to follow Mr. Finley through his long, eventful, laborious, and very useful ministerial life. He was honored by his Conference by being elected a delegate to the General Conference for many terms. He was a grand good man, impelled by the love of Christ to very arduous labors for the salvation of men. He died full of days, in Christian triumph, and was greatly lamented by multitudes in the Church who had been greatly benefited by his ministerial labors. He stood deservedly high in the councils of the Church, as of sound judgment and loyalty to the interests of the Church. The memorial of his name is "like ointment poured forth."

The first relation of REV. JOHN A. BAUGHMAN to Detroit and to Michigan Methodism, and Protestantism, was when he was appointed to Detroit Circuit in 1825. This, however, only brought him into connection with the city in name, for if he preached in Detroit at all it was only incidentally. His Circuit embraced all the accessible settlements in Michigan, outside of the city. It was a very laborious Circuit, for he went up as far as Mount Clemens and Pontiac, and as far out as Ypsilanti and Ann Arbor, and south to Monroe, and west of that as far as to Blissfield and Tecumseh; there was no Adrian then. This general outline will give some idea of the labor and travel required of him in his Circuit. The Circuit was called Detroit simply because there was no other place which had assumed sufficient importance to be recognized as forming the head of a Circuit.

Mr. Baughman's real connection with Detroit commenced when he was stationed here in 1845. He remained in the station for two years. He then became Agent of the American Bible Society for four years, and in 1852 was appointed Presiding Elder of Detroit District, which position he filled for two years. He never removed his residence from Detroit, after he was stationed here in 1845.

Mr. Baughman died in Detroit, March 1st., 1868, aged 65 years and *seven* months. He was born in Hereford County, Md., but removed to Ohio in his boyhood. He was converted at the age of nineteen years and joined the Methodist Episcopal Church. He was admitted, on trial, by the Ohio Conference in 1823, and from that time to the year of his death was an active, energetic, and successful preacher of the Gospel. The only partial interruption being that he sustained a supernumerary relation in 1839. The following is the historical and appreciative memoir found in the Minutes for 1868:

Mr. Baughman "labored *twelve* years in Ohio, and *thirty-two* years in Michigan. He was emphatically a pioneer preacher in both States, being in many places the first man to preach the Gospel to the people. His first two years in the ministry—1823 and 1824—

were spent successively at Piqua and Oxford, Ohio. He then visited the far-off wilderness of Michigan, and traveled the Detroit Circuit in 1825-6, and, the next year, Monroe Circuit. These two Circuits, at that time, embraced whole counties, almost entirely without roads, and a few scattered settlements at great distances from each other, and many of the places he could visit but once or twice during the whole year. The next year—1827-8—he was stationed at Cincinnati, and, subsequently, at Hamilton, Greenville, Eaton, Milford, Union, White Oak, and Lebanon. In 1838, he was transferred to the Michigan Conference, and stationed at Monroe. His appointments in that Conference have been as follows: Tecumseh, Ann Arbor, Adrian, Dexter, First Church at Detroit, Agent of the American Bible Society, four years, Presiding Elder of Detroit District, two years, Agent of the Conference Tract Society, one year, Walnut Street, Detroit, Mount Clemens and Lee Chapel, Birmingham, Walnut Street again, and French Mission, Flint, Hudson, Adrian again, Clifton, Hancock, Houghton, and Lexington. He received forty-three appointments from the Bishop, and never failed heartily to do the work assigned him.

"He was a man of extraordinary physical strength; with a loud voice, a cheerful temper, and untiring industry. He was a warm-hearted Methodist minister, of strong faith, and greatly beloved by all, both children and adults. He was at home in the city or in the country, in family worship and pastoral visiting, or in the great Camp Meeting. He attended every session of the Conference, and, though he spoke but seldom, he was always listened to with attention, and his counsel had great weight. He was a member of the General Conference of 1844, and correctly represented the sentiments of his Conference in that great struggle.

"Brother Baughman labored in many revivals of religion during his long ministry, both on his own charges, and with his brother ministers. He was an earnest evangelist. In the prime of his strength, no man, perhaps, surpassed him in efficiency. For a short time during his ministry, he was embarrassed with business difficulties, in which he was involved by others, but nothing could divert him from the great work of his life.

"At the last session of this Conference, though, seemingly, in good health, he asked for a superannuated relation, stating that the fatigues of regular work wearied him, but expressing his intention still to labor for his Master, and hoping, after a year or two, to resume an efficient relation. He resided in Detroit, and, with his accustomed energy, aided the Presiding Elder and others, and was ready to respond to every call for assistance, within his power. His last sermon was on February 16th, 1868, in the Jefferson Avenue church, Detroit, on 'Faith, Hope and Charity.' He preached with even unusual fervor, and the power of the Holy Spirit was with him. Unable to preach in the evening of the same day, he was feeble afterwards, but not alarmingly so, till in the night of March 1st, without warning, he fell asleep in Jesus. He left no dying testimony, save that noblest and best—the history of his long life spent in the service of his Redeemer.

"Brother Baughman needs from us no eulogy. His labors will never be forgotten. As an advocate of abstinence from intoxicating drink, as an agent of the Bible Society, and as a preacher of the Gospel, he was known all over the State, and no man in it, perhaps, has contributed more to its genuine and solid prosperity. His exclamation, like ours, would be, 'To God, alone, be all the glory.'"

REV. CURTIS GODDARD was appointed Presiding Elder of Detroit District in 1829, and remained in charge of it for three years. He was a very sweet-spirited man, a devout Christian, and a very good preacher. His sermons were plain, and addressed to the heart, as well as to the intellect. He was a very kind and diligent superintendent of the work committed to his charge. He was elected by the Ohio Conference as a delegate to the General Conference of 1832, which met at Philadelphia. Mr. Goddard was admitted on trial in the Ohio Conference in 1814, and located in 1834, having been just twenty years in the ministry. He was born in Connecticut, but emigrated to Ohio in early youth. He had not married up to the time he desisted from the active ministry, and he located from a sense of duty to his parents, who were very aged, and needed his care. Having located, or dissolved his connection with the Conference, he is lost to our sight, and we have very few materials from which to construct an appreciative notice of his life and character. The most we know of him is from having been two years under him as Presiding Elder. The remembrance of these years is very precious. He was useful as a minister. We have learned the fact of his decease, but have not been able to ascertain the date or any of the circumstances.

One of the largest, and, yet, one of the most supple men we ever knew, was REV. JAMES GILRUTH, who was appointed Presiding Elder of Detroit District at the session of the Ohio Conference which met in Dayton, Ohio, September 19th, 1832. The District had been diminished a little in its limits by attaching the southwest corner of Michigan to the Indiana Conference; but the number of charges to be looked after was increased. In consequence of his great weight, Mr. Gilruth found it necessary, on his long routes and bad roads, to have two horses. He would ride one for a time, and allow the other to follow, and then he would change. There was but a very small portion of his route where he could go with a wagon or carriage, and so, to travel it, it was necessary for him to have his two large horses. He had the appearance of being a very stern and ungenial man—but whoever would so judge of him would be mistaken. We were in his District for three years, and were much in his company, and always found him to be one of the most sociable and genial men we ever knew. He was a very conscientious man in all he did. As a preacher, he was plain in language, but, often, deep in thought and energetic in manner. He never shunned to declare what he conceived to be the whole Gospel of Christ. He was a faithful but kind disciplinarian. He continued on the Detroit District for four years. The last year of his service on it, the District was still more reduced by the creation of the Ann Arbor District, so that he was confined to the territory east of Ann Arbor. His services on the District, and in Michigan, terminated with the Conference of September, 1836. At this Conference, he located for the purpose of establishing a community with all things in common; but, finding that human nature was still selfish, he became disgusted with the enterprise, and returned to the ministry after one year. He joined the Ohio Conference, in which he labored for a few years, and then went west, being transferred to the Iowa Conference, and settled his family not far from Davenport. Here he spent his last years in great tranquillity, preaching occasionally, and always to the satisfaction of the people. He deceased in 1873.

Mr. Gilruth was admitted into the traveling connection by the Ohio Conference in 1819, so he had been in the ministry thirteen years when he was appointed to Detroit District. He was born and brought up in the valley of the Ohio River, and had but few scholastic advantages; but, such was his ability to acquire knowledge, and such his diligence in seeking it, that very few errors could be detected in his use of language. He was very plain in his dress, and, possibly, went to an extreme in this respect. His coming to the Detroit District was not his first visit to Michigan, although it was the first in the character of a Christian and minister of the Gospel; for he was here as a soldier in the War of 1812. As a soldier, he was true, and ever ready to obey orders. The same principle of trueness he carried into his Christian and ministerial life. He was one of God's noblemen. There is no doubt of his having gone to receive a crown of life; it will not be a starless crown, for, by his diligence and Christian labor, continued for so many years, he was the means of turning many from darkness to light—from sin to holiness. He has gone; but he lives in those who have been saved from sin through his efforts. So, it may be said of him as of Abel, in his faith and labor, "by it he being dead yet speaketh." He had a deep religious experience, and preached holiness with great effect, and lived according to the doctrines he taught.

There is no name connected with our History which carries with it a sweeter fragrance than that of EDWARD THOMSON, who, according to the Official Minutes, was stationed in Detroit, in the distribution of ministerial labors, in September, 1836. He remained in this station for two years. He had then been in the ministry for three years, having been received into the Ohio Conference in 1833. He was born in Portsea, England, October 12th, 1810. In 1818 his parents came to America, stopping in Pennsylvania for two years; and they settled in Ohio in 1820. He was converted, and joined the Methodist Episcopal Church in December, 1831. In the meantime, he had studied and graduated in medicine, and had settled down for what he considered his life-work—the practice of medicine. How often God changes our life-plans! So here, when he was converted, he soon felt the conviction of duty to give himself up to the ministry. His career was a brilliant and useful one. He was six years a pastor, five years in charge of Norwalk Seminary, in Ohio, where many young men were educated, who became ministers. He was two years editor of the *Ladies' Repository*, fourteen years President of the Ohio Wesleyan University, and four years editor of the *Christian Advocate*, at New York. In May, 1864, he was elected and ordained Bishop, which office he filled to the entire satisfaction of the Church. He died at Wheeling, West Virginia, March 22d, 1870, while away from home, in the discharge of his episcopal work. He was small in stature, but large in intellect, and was a manly man. He was mainly self-educated, not having had the advantages of a college graduation, and, yet, he was a *very* successful college president. He had thoroughly disciplined his own mind, and was well qualified to assist others. As a Christian, he knew the virtue of the blood of Jesus Christ to cleanse from all sin, having devoted all his powers to God and His service through faith in the atonement. We take the following estimate of his character and his work, as given in the memorial services of the General Conference of 1872, and found in the journal of that Conference:

"Bishop Thomson was a man of decided convictions and of deep piety; tender and gentle as a woman, but firm and unwavering as a hero. His reading was extensive and varied; as a speaker he was eloquent; as a writer, he had few equals for aptness of expression and simplicity and beauty of style. In every position—as pastor, teacher, editor and Bishop—he worked successfully, and more than met the expectations of the Church. He lived as he died—in calm and peaceful trust and confidence in God. Living, he was honored and beloved by all who knew him, dying, he is embalmed in the memory and affections of the Church"

REV. ARZA BROWN is a name which must not be overlooked in connection with Detroit. He was appointed to Detroit station in 1828, and continued in it for two years; and was then appointed to Oakland Circuit, which he supplied for one year only. These three years constituted his term of service in Michigan, but yet it will be both pleasing and profitable to trace his life and labors through, as is done in the official memoir, which we shall insert in full. We have been favored with extracts from his journal, which he kept covering the time of his labor in Michigan These extracts will be found to be both profitable and interesting. He says:—

"At the Conference which sat in Chillicothe, Ohio, September 18th, 1828, I was appointed to Detroit station. Rev. Zarah H. Coston was Presiding Elder. With the exception of the last two years of the war with England, the city had been quite regularly supplied with Methodist preaching since 1809. Rev. William Case, of the New York Conference, was the minister in 1809.

"Notwithstanding the city had been so ably and faithfully supplied for so many years with Methodist preaching, yet when I entered upon this charge there were but about sixty members in the Methodist Episcopal Church. This want of success was doubtless owing, in part, to opposition from the Catholic, Calvinistic and Universalist churches, the world and the Devil, and partly for the want of an inviting and commodious house of worship properly located. For several years the Methodist society had no house of their own in which to worship God. They generally occupied what was called the 'Old Council House,' a building used for too great a variety of purposes, to render it a suitable place in which to worship a God of purity.

"In choosing a location for the church, the quite too common error of those days was repeated here. Instead of locating the house of worship where the greater number of citizens, without much labor or inconvenience, could regularly attend divine service, they placed their new church far out on the commons, with no pavements or sidewalks, the streets often during autumn, winter and spring, wet and muddy. At the same time the Catholic, Presbyterian and Baptist churches were properly located in the most compactly settled portions of the city.

"To remedy the evil, in part, I succeeded in laying down a plank walk, after which, as 'free seats,'and the doctrines and usages of the Methodist Episcopal Church, were popular with the masses, our congregations were increasingly large and attentive. The most prominent members were Jerry Dean and wife. His name was as 'ointment poured forth.' He was leader, steward, trustee and superintendent of the Sabbath School. Religion was the first business of his life. His piety was deep, the cause of Christ lay near his heart, hence he was always ready for every good word and work, and his house, like that of Bethany, was a pleasent home for the servants of Christ. Robert Abbott and wife—he was a 'defender of the faith,' a firm friend and supporter of Methodism, a leader, steward and trustee. He and his kind wife furnished the first home for the first Methodist ministers who visited Detroit. Revs. Case, Morey, Joseph Mitchell, J. B. Finley, and others, of precious memory, often found a resting-place with this kind family. Henry Dean and wife —active Christians. Sister Dean was a sweet singer, and delighted in the cross of Christ. Nathaniel Champ and wife—both pious and pursuing the even tenor of their way. Philip Warren and wife— Methodists of the good old stamp. Israel Noble and wife—he was leader, steward, and trustee; she was remarkably gifted in prayer and exhortation. Father and Mother Garrison—old-fashioned Methodists. Father and Mother Cook—consistent and persevering Christians; Methodists of sterling stamp. Brother and Sister Knapp— he was superintendent of the turnpike running·from Detroit to Ohio; was a fast friend and supporter of the Church; she was pious, amiable, and an ornament to society. Mother Witherell, wife of Hon. Dr. Witherell, Secretary of the Territory of Michigan—she was a holy woman, fervently praying daily for many years for the conversion of husband and children. Hon. B. F. H. Witherell and wife—he was a popular lawyer. Sister Witherell was a faithful, devoted Christian woman, attending, as far as within her power, all the means of grace.

"During the year we were favored with some religious prosperity. Near its close I was employed as Chaplain for the Legislative Council, and, with the advice of my Presiding Elder, did not attend Conference, which met in Urbana, September 3d, 1829.* At

* His daughter, Mrs. Isaac Hitt, of Evanston, in a note, says: "This was the only time my dear father was absent from his Annual Conference from 1824 to 1861."

this session of Conference, I was re-appointed to Detroit. The charge continued. A number were awaked, and converted, and united with the Methodist Episcopal Church during the year. God poured out His Holy Spirit, and in copious showers, upon us.

"At one of a series of meetings I was holding, as I was inviting penitents to the altar for prayer, a young and beautiful French-Catholic lady came forward, weeping and penitent. As she knelt at the altar, Mrs. Abbott asked her 'why she had presented herself there?' 'I wish to confess to your priest,' she replied, 'and receive absolution.' So Mrs. Abbott repeated to me this request. I felt humbled and abashed. Painful, indeed, were the emotions of my heart. I would fain have hid my face in the dust. A poor sinner confessing to a sinful man—looking to a frail, erring mortal for absolution! I told her she must confess to God, and look to him, through Christ alone, for pardon and salvation. I exhorted her to give her heart to God, and to pray with all her heart to the blessed Jesus.

"Lifting her streaming eyes towards Heaven, she prayed, 'Lord Jesus, have mercy on my poor soul!' The whole assembly was moved to tears. The altar was crowded, and some precious souls were added to the Church. The good work continued to prosper, and my second year in Detroit wound up pleasantly. I received, as my salary, *one hundred dollars* each year.

"I left the city August 1st, 1830, and, on the 12th of August, was united in marriage to Miss Mary Hyde, at the residence of her father, Joel Hyde, Esq., Farmington, Trumbull County, Ohio. Rev. J. Scott was the officiating minister."

This proved to be a very happy marriage, and Mrs. Brown was and is a very intelligent and educated lady; and has been very useful in the work of God in the Church, in connection with her husband while he lived, and now survives him. We continue the extracts:

"*OAKLAND CIRCUIT.*

"September 8th, 1830, Conference met at Lancaster, Ohio. I was appointed to Oakland Circuit, Detroit District; Curtis Goddard, Presiding Elder, and William Sprague, my colleague. From this Conference we went directly to Farmington, packed our goods, shipped them, at Fairport, for Detroit; then, taking leave of beloved parents and friends, we left in our carriage for our distant field of labor. A toilsome journey it was, through mud and storm. After ten days we reached our Circuit. The territory embraced within its limits was new; accommodations for man and beast were limited; no parsonage—not even a room to be rented.

"Dr. Parke and wife, of precious memory, when we were thus without shelter, invited us to their hospitable home. They were everyday Christians, ready for every good word and work. May they be eternally rewarded for their kindness! After a few weeks, I succeeded in obtaining a room in a house in Auburn. This house was weather-boarded, but not ceiled. A partition of rough boards divided the rooms. It was a cold house in a cold climate; and in this small, cold room we spent the cold winter of 1830-31. But we were, in this manner of living, sharing the privations incident to this new country with our dear friends, who were ever ready to extend to us acts of kindness, which will never be forgotten.

"Now and then I borrowed a team, and, axe in hand, would go to the forest, chop, load, and draw home my own firewood, and, then, prepare it for our use. Early in the spring, I was so fortunate as to obtain a larger and more comfortable room in Bloomfield, and thither we removed. Here our daughter Mary was born, and here we resided until the close of the year.

"This Circuit embraced the villages of Mount Clemens, Utica, Romeo, Troy, Auburn, Bloomfield, Farmington, &c., and a large number of sparsely settled neighborhoods. The following were some of the most prominent and active members of the charge, viz:

"Rev. Abel Warren and wife—he was a popular local preacher, universally beloved and respected; she was a truly pious woman, and active in the cause of Christ. Rev. Laban Smith and wife. They were living in a village called Sodom, settled principally by Universalians, two or three of whom were preachers, and they all seemed to vie with each other in persecuting the Methodist Church; and Brother and Sister Smith, like Lot of old, were vexed by their ungodly conversation, doctrine and practice. But they continued steadfast in the faith, daily witnessing a good profession.

"Once, while preaching in this neighborhood upon the certainty of the doctrine of eternal punishment, as I concluded my discourse, a Scotchman in the congregation arose, and, addressing a Universalist preacher present, said, in his broad accent: 'You musn't try, any more, to put out the lake of eternal fire; for, if you do, Mr. *Brun* will drop a *cowl* in it, and set it on fire again!'

"On this Circuit there were Brother and Sister Beach, Brother and Sister Parker, Brother and Sister Gould, Brother and Sister Holland, Brother and Sister Downer, and, besides these, there were others, faithful, official members—consistent professors, waymarks to Heaven, whose names are written in the Book of Life.

"We held two Camp Meetings this year, and, notwithstanding we were opposed by rowdies of the baser sort, the power of God was gloriously displayed in the awakening and conversion of very many precious souls.

"At one of these meetings, on a dark night, a number of very wicked young men were congregated together near the encampment, and, by their profanity and noisy revelry, were disturbing the meeting. Brother Elijah H. Pilcher, who was there, young and sprightly, borrowed a hat and coat of a farmer—completely disguising himself in this suit, and assuming a swaggering manner, he joined the rowdy crowd, and, while they were concocting their fiendish plans, he seemed to acquiesce. After a short time, he proposed that one of their number should preach a sermon and meet class, 'as the Methodists do,' to which they all agreed. But, who was to preach? One after another refused. At length he consented, provided that each and all of them would pledge their sacred honor that they would sit quietly, and make no disturbance during sermon and class, to which they all consented. After binding them as with the solemnity of an oath, he read his text, and, from the commencement of his discourse, he waxed warmer and warmer until its close. Soon after the opening of the sermon, one of the young men straightened up and said, 'Now, it is not fair to deceive us in that way.' 'Hush! hush!' said Pilcher. 'Remember, you promised, on the honor of a man, you would make no disturbance till I close my sermon and class.' After this appeal to their honor, and, realizing that they were 'sold,' they remained quiet, and, before the close of the class-meeting, nearly all of the company were on their knees, praying for pardon, and, before the next morning several of them were happily converted to God.

"There was in attendance at one of these Camp Meetings, a Baptist gentleman, who, for many years, had delighted in criticising his Methodist neighbors on account of their noisy meetings, their shouting, and their sometimes falling, like men slain in battle, under the influence of the presence and power of God. Under a searching sermon, preached at 11 o'clock A. M., Sabbath, this brother was smitten by the Holy Spirit, and fell prostrate upon the ground. His Baptist friends gathered around him, overwhelmed with grief and fear, while the hearts of his Methodist friends were thrilled with holy delight. After he had lain upon the ground for some time, I pressed through the crowd, and was standing by his side as he opened his eyes. Seeing me, he said, 'Brother Brown, what shall I do? I feel as though I wanted to shout, Glory!' I replied, 'If Joshua says shout, you may shout as loud as you please.' And he did shout, with all his heart and strength. But, at his first shout of 'Glory!' his Baptist friends forsook him and fled.

"Another Conference year closed. The Lord had been with us to bless. My salary, this year, was *one hundred and eighty dollars.*"

Thus far his journal goes. We have given these long extracts simply because they are interesting and valuable; but we must now content ourself by introducing the memoir found in the Minutes of the Conference for 1869.

"REV. ARZA BROWN was born in Hampton, Massachusetts, August 13th, 1792. His religious impressions began at a very early period of his life, and, so thorough were the operations of the Spirit on his heart that he ever cherished the belief that he had experienced the renewing power of Divine grace. In 1805, his father and family moved to Plattsburg, New York, where, amidst the absence of moral and religious privileges, and the temptations of a comparatively new country, young Arza relapsed into the neglect of duty, and wandered from God. Subsequently, in 1816, the Holy Spirit revisited his heart, and, at a prayer-meeting, January 19th, 1817, he was re-assured of pardon and Divine acceptance. This work was so thorough, pervading his entire nature, and developing in the actions of his life, that a glorious revival ensued, resulting in the conversion of a number of souls, who were formed into a class, of which Arza was appointed leader. Such was his growth in grace, and so clearly was the indication of the great Head of the Church of his call to a higher and wider field of usefulness, that he was soon licensed, first, as an exhorter, and, subsequently, as a local preacher. In the meantime, in 1819, he moved to Sandusky City, Ohio, and then to Licking County, Ohio.

"In 1822, convinced that it was the privilege of the believer to enjoy a richer baptism of the Spirit, even to 'know the love of Christ, which passeth knowledge, and be filled with the fullness of God,' he earnestly sought the attainment of that blessing, and became the happy recipient of a living witness of the truth, 'The blood of Jesus Christ, His Son, cleanseth from all sin.' Under this Divine influence he entered his life-work, first, as a local preacher, and, subsequently, September 2d, 1824, he was received on trial in the Ohio Conference. During the early part of his ministry, he enjoyed the society of Jacob Young and Russel Bigelow, as Presiding Elders, by whose wise counsels and holy lives he profited greatly. His itinerant ministry began on Zanesville Circuit, and his subsequent fields of labor were the following: 1825, Straight Creek Circuit; 1826–7, Sandusky Circuit; 1828–9, Detroit Station, Michigan, then in the bounds of the Ohio Conference. Of the high estimate in which Brother Brown was held while stationed in Detroit, it is sufficient to remark that, unsought on his part, he was elected Chaplain of the Territorial Legislature, then in session in that city. August 12th, 1830, he was married, by Rev. J. Scott, to Miss Mary, daughter of Joel Hyde, of Farmington, Trumbull County, Ohio, a lady eminently qualified, by mental culture and grace, for the position of minister's wife. For nearly thirty-nine years, the now bereaved wife contributed, by her wise counsels, faithfulness, and purity of life, to the successful ministerial efforts of her husband.

"Brother Brown's itinerant career covered a large extent of territory, as will be manifest, not only from a survey of the appointments mentioned above, but more particularly from those which follow, namely: 1830, Oakland Circuit, Detroit district; 1831, Columbus Circuit, Ohio; 1832, Dayton station; 1833–4, Piqua; 1835, Xenia; 1836–7, Marietta; 1838–9, Athens; 1840, Chillicothe; 1841, West Union Circuit; 1842, Greenfield; 1843, Frankfort Circuit; 1844, Parkersburg, Va.; 1845, Barlow Circuit, Ohio; 1846–7, Hamilton; 1848–9, Christie Chapel, Cincinnati; 1850–1, South Charleston; 1852, North Bend Circuit; 1853–4, Lockland Circuit; 1855, Raper Chapel, Cincinnati. He was elected a member of the delegation of the Cincinnati Conference to the General Conference which sat in Indianapolis, May, 1856. For thirty-one consecutive years he sustained an effective relation in the ministry, but, prostrated by protracted illness and infirmity, he was finally compelled to request the Conference, at its session in Ripley, Ohio, October 1st, 1856, to grant him a superannuated relation, which he sustained the balance of his life. From this period (1856) the pen of an intimate and long-tried friend has faithfully sketched the remainder of his labors with a thrillingly joyful narrative of the closing scene of his earthly pilgrimage: 'In 1858, he removed to Chicago, and settled in the West Division, on West Indiana Street. He served by appointment of the Presiding Elder, West Indiana Street for three years with great usefulness. In 1863 he and his wife were appointed as delegates, by the Christian Commission, to labor among the soldiers in the army. They went first to Nashville, Tennessee. In 1864, he was authorized to open a branch of the Christian Commission in Natchez, and for two years and a half labored among the soldiers in

the camps and hospitals, and then among the freedmen in Natchez, Vicksburg and Baton Rouge. In the spring of 1868, he greatly enjoyed the company of many of his old companions whom he met during the session of the General Conference in Chicago, Illinois. In the fall of 1868, he went South again, and spent some time in labor in New Orleans. In January last he and his wife left New Orleans and went to the St. Mary's Parish, on the Teche, and labored in the Orphans' Home. Here he was able to do but little. He had a settled conviction, from the first attack, that he would never recover, and greatly desired to return to his home in Chicago to die. He was conveyed on his bed from the Orphans' Home to the boat by four colored men who loved him dearly. Carried by strangers from the boat to the cars, he found his way home. Shortly after his arrival home, he, feeling that his time was short, asked to have a number of the ministers invited, that he might with them once more celebrate the sacrament of the Lord's Supper. Bishop Thomson conducted this service. For eight months he was not able to help himself in the least, and yet from his lips escaped no complaint. He rejoiced continually in the Lord, even in the midst of the greatest agony. He had asked an old friend, whom he had known since 1825, to be with him in his last hour, to close his eyes and comfort his family. This friend watched with him during the last night, and whenever the name of Jesus or heaven was mentioned his face would light up, and he would exclaim, 'Precious Jesus! Glorious heaven!' Towards morning his daughter said, 'Father, do you feel you are going?' He answered, 'Not now, but I shall go very soon;' and then continued: 'The Blessed Savour said, If I go away, I will come again and receive you to myself; that where I am there ye may be also. O how blessed it will be to be with Christ! to see him as he is, and more blessed to be like him!' He then added, 'I am all ready, waiting the descent of the chariot of the Lord, to go home to heaven.' He lingered until noon. He and his wife had often talked about the possibility of seeing Jesus before the soul left the body, and she asked him in some way, when first he saw the Saviour, if he did so before he left the body, to let her know. Just before the last, as he was reclining upon his pillow, with eyes closed, he exclaimed, with a full voice, 'Life! Life!' and his spirit departed. May it not be that this was the signal given when first he saw, with unveiled vision, the blessed Jesus? Thus died Rev. Arza Brown, in the seventy-seventh year of his age, the fifty-third of his Christian life, and the forty-fifth of his ministry. As a preacher, he was eminently practical and useful. He was loving and gentle in his life, kind and affectionate in his family. His whole life was a pure commentary upon the Gospel he so loved to preach.' Appropriate funeral services were observed at the Indiana Street Church, Chicago, Illinois, Monday, August 2d, 1869, and thence he was borne to his final resting-place, his body sleeping in Jesus, and awaiting the resurrection morn. Precious is the memory of the departed who sleep in Jesus." Thus closed the life and labors of a very good and useful minister of the Gospel of the blessed Saviour.

After this long digression, we will return to the line of our History, and further trace the progress of the Protestant Churches in the city. We closed our account of the Methodist Church with the session of the Conference in 1837. Nothing special occurred, calling for any particular notice, till 1843. At the session of the Conference this year, it was determined to appoint two ministers, with the view of organizing a second Church. The second Society was organized shortly after the Conference, in which William Phelps, a local preacher, and L. L. Farnsworth, both still residing in Detroit, and William Scott, now of St. Clair, were leading spirits, and made the sacrifice of their pleasant Church associations to promote the enterprise, and were active laborers.

By the way, William Phelps became the first superintendent of the Sabbath School of this new organization, and continued to act successfully in that capacity for several years. He came to this work with some experience, as he had been superintendent of the First, or Woodward Avenue Methodist Episcopal Sabbath School, for a period of time in which Mr. Owen had resigned. Mr. Phelps commenced business in the City of Detroit, when but a young man, on a small capital, in groceries and confectioneries; but, for a number of years past, he has been engaged in a wholesale, or jobbing business in groceries, and has attained to a good degree of wealth. He professed faith in Christ, and united with the Methodist Church in Detroit, in 1836, under the labors of the late Bishop Thomson.

When the War of the Rebellion broke out, he entered the army in connection with the Paymaster's department, with the rank of Major. In that department he did good service to his country and credit to himself, and was promoted to the rank of Colonel. He has, also, mingled somewhat in politics, having served as Alderman in his ward for two terms; been a member of the State Legislature, and an active member of State and other conventions. In all these positions, he has endeavored to carry his religion with him. He was licensed as a local preacher in 1843, and, in due time was ordained Deacon, and Elder, and has ever been ready, wherever he

CENTRAL M. E. CHURCH, DETROIT.

has been, to supply any lack of ministerial service. He is an active man, and has carried his activity into religious work.

There were some noble women, also, who identified themselves with the new branch. It was difficult to find a suitable and inviting place in which to worship. But they struggled on. The next year— that is, in 1844—the second Church appears among the appointments in the Minutes, with Ransom R. Richards as preacher in charge. The growth of this Society was slow, at first, for the want of a proper place to hold services. The United States Court room was secured for a time, then the State House. Mr. Richards was not content with such accommodations; but, assisted by the brethren, he secured a lot on the corner of Congress and Randolph Streets, on which a brick church, of respectable dimensions, was erected and dedicated in 1846. This new church prospered well for years, but, in 1863, the building was consumed by fire, and, instead of rebuilding on the same ground, they determined to sell and build elsewhere; and, in casting about, they secured lots on the corner of Woodward and Adams Avenues, which led to the consolidation of the Woodward Avenue and Congress Street Societies, under the ecclesiastical name of the Central Methodist Episcopal Church, and to the erection of that magnificent building known by that name. This church was completed and dedicated in 1868.

The church building erected in 1834 by the First Church, having become too small, they erected a new church on the corner of Woodward Avenue and State Street, in 1848-9, which they occupied until the Central was erected, as above. In the spring of 1849, the wooden building on the corner of Woodward Avenue and Congress Street was removed to the corner of Lafayette Avenue and Fourth Street, and a new Society was organized, so that, in 1849, three charges appear in the Minutes. This Lafayette Avenue Church, having become too small, the Society erected a fine brick church on the corner of Howard and Fourth Streets, dedicated in 1875, the name of which was changed to that of the Tabernacle Methodist Episcopal Church. Other Societies, both English and German, were organized, and churches built; so that, in 1876, there were *eight* churches, with ministers stationed in charge of them, besides some Sunday School chapels. Concerning the work among the Germans, we purpose to speak in the concluding chapter.

A Methodist Mission for the benefit of the French population was established in 1851, and continued for about fifteen or sixteen years, and then was discontinued. Good had been done—some had been converted, and added to the Church, who were steadfast in the faith—but the success did not seem to warrant the continuance of the Mission.

The Protestant Episcopal Church has, in the meantime, so increased, that they have ten parishes supplied with services, and they are making large efforts to advance in their influence in the city. They have four costly edifices and several smaller ones.

The Presbyterian Church, from the one church on Woodward Avenue, has increased to five congregations, with large and elegant houses of worship, and are ably supplied with ministers, and two Mission Churches. These churches are well distributed for exerting an influence in the city. In addition to these, a United Presbyterian Church was organized in 1853, which has prospered well, and, probably, in time, will be united with the others.

We here introduce to notice one whose name has been familiar to the Michigan public for many years—for who has not heard of Rev. NOAH M. WELLS, who is now ninety-five years old, in the enjoyment of health and the comforts of the religion of the Lord and Saviour? We take great pleasure in inserting here a brief biographical sketch of him. We regret that we cannot furnish a more extended one, as there must have been many interesting incidents connected with so long a ministerial career. We are indebted to Rev. Dr. Mattoon, of Monroe, for furnishing for our use a skeleton auto-biography deposited with him, in manuscript, and from which we gather the following items: He was born at Bemish Heights, Saratoga County, New York, July 8th, 1772. His parents were not professors of religion, still, they had him baptized in the Protestant Episcopal Church, in the fourteenth year of his age, in New Lebanon, New York, whither they had removed. Here he fell among some Universalists, and, for a time, professed that faith. But, when he was about twenty-one years of age, there was a very gracious revival of religion in the place, through the influence of which he was brought to the Saviour. Shortly after his conversion, he felt deeply impressed with a sense of obligation to preach the Gospel. Against this impression he revolted for a time, but, finally, concluded that it was best to obey God. He, however, found a great difficulty in his way, that was, he had but a limited education, and felt himself too poor to go to college. His parents, in the meantime, had become Christians, and encouraged him to carry out his convictions of duty, though they were too poor to assist him in it, having lost their property, through the dishonesty of others. But, when he resolved to do his duty, the Lord seemed to raise up friends for him, so that he was enabled to graduate, in due time, from Union College. He then prosecuted his theological studies, and graduated, and entered on the pastorate. In the first year of his ministry, he had a very gracious revival, and added seventy-seven persons to the Church on one communion day. He remained in this Church about two years, and went away, much to the regret of the congregation.

He next went to Brownsville, New York. Here he found an irreligious people, without any kind of religious organization. A place of worship was provided. In the midst of his first sermon, some ladies came in, when all the gentlemen arose and bowed to them. At the close of his sermon he told them that a place of worship was not a drawing-room, and that the etiquette of the latter was not appropriate to the solemnities of Divine worship. After a few Sabbaths, he determined to leave them, in discouragement. When he informed them of it, the men pressed him to stay, and the women gathered around him, and, with tears, begged him not to leave them. Being so pressed, he consented to remain for some time longer. Soon after a small Church was organized, which was increased to one hundred and seventy-five members before he left, and they erected a commodious and tasty house of worship. This was a very wonderful work for such a place and time.

Mr. Wells came to Detroit in June, 1825. He says he found Presbyterian members, but no Church or organization. There was what was called the "First Presbyterian Church of Detroit. But, he says, "it was neither Congregational nor Presbyterian." So, after consultation, they concluded to begin *de novo*, and organized a Presbyterian Church with thirty-six members, which, he says, "was the first Presbyterian Church in Michigan." This statement of Mr. Wells does not exactly agree with the published Manual of the "First Presbyterian Church," which claims that the Church was organized in January, 1825, and that there were forty-nine members constituting it. We conclude that Mr. Wells is right—that January was mistaken for June by the copyist for the Manual, and that the excess of persons were members, the exact time of whose joining was not recorded, and they were supposed to have been original members by the compiler, as was the case with some of the persons whose names are attached to the articles of association of the "First Protestant Society of Detroit," for some of them were not residents of Detroit at the time of the organization, but attached their names subsequently. It was also claimed that there was a Presbyterian Church organized at Monroe, in 1820, and Mackinaw, in 1823. But we are not concerned to reconcile these claims. He became the pastor of the new Church, and continued as such for about eleven years. He was succeeded by Rev. John P. Cleveland, for a few years, and he, again, by Rev. George Duffield, D. D. His health having failed, Mr. Wells went into secular business for a time. He taught in the branch of the Michigan University at Niles for a few years. After this, he was appointed a chaplain in the army, and was stationed at Prairie du Chien. He labored for nearly two years at Galena, Illinois, with much success, and then returned East, and supplied the Church at Maumee City, Ohio, for a short season.

We next find him employed by the "Western Seaman's Friend Society," and taking charge of the Bethel work and interests at Detroit. He continued in this work, with success, for six years. Now, being far advanced in years, and feeling the weight of those years pressing upon him, he determined to give up any further active work in the ministry, and retired to the township of Erie, in Monroe County, Michigan, and resides with a son. He has not been without his afflictions and bereavements; for he has buried three wives—most estimable women they were, too—and one daughter. But, in all these things, he has always found the Lord and Saviour a present help.

Father Wells has been rather a remarkable man. Few attain to his present age—ninety-five years. He is cheerful and happy, waiting patiently for the coming of his Lord. He has done a great amount of work for the Christian cause in connection with the Presbyterian Church. He was decided in his attachment to his own Church, without bigotry. He was not brilliant, but sound in intellect. He was laborious in study. He commenced his ministry by writing and memorizing two sermons every week, which he found to be too heavy for him, as any man will who undertakes it. He is worthy of commendation for his efforts to secure a thorough education. He was not converted until he was twenty-one years of age, and then, for a time, he struggled against his convictions of duty, so that he must have been, at least, twenty-two before he began to make his preparations for college, but yet he did so, and took a regular course in college, and in the Theological Seminary, and so fitted himself for his work.

Mr. Wells was succeeded, in the First Presbyterian Church in Detroit, by Rev. John P. Cleveland, who continued as pastor until 1838, when he resigned. He was succeeded by Rev. GEORGE DUFFIELD, who, having received the unanimous call of the Church, resigned his position in the City of New York, and came to Detroit. He commenced his labors in this city on the first of October, 1838, and, on the 11th day of December, in the same year, he was installed pastor by the Presbytery of Detroit. Dr. Duffield continued his relation to this Church until 1868, making a pastorate of the same Church for *thirty* years, and was much beloved by his people.

In 1865, Dr. Duffield's health becoming somewhat impaired he desired to have some relief in his arduous labors, and, at his request, an associate was called. "He, however, continued in the full exercise of his pastorate, preaching half a day, each Sabbath, until his death, which occurred on the 26th day of June, 1868."

Dr. Duffield was a man of untiring industry and perseverance in study, and made very thorough preparation for the pulpit. He, also, was a great friend to educational institutions, and filled the office of Regent of the University of Michigan for many years, he having been one of the original Board appointed under the law of the State for the organization of that institution, in 1837.

In the latter part of his life, especially, he became very deeply devoted to the cause of Christ, and very catholic in spirit. He was much interested in the work of the Young Men's Christian Association. The last work that he did was in connection with that body. We quote from the Manual of the Church:

"He died with his harness on. While addressing the Young Men's Christian International Convention, just then assembled in Detroit, in words of welcome from the Churches of the city, he was stricken down, and carried home by his friends to die. He was buried from the church, on the Sabbath succeeding his death.

"What a glorious death! How fitting for this eminent servant of God to be thus translated from the Church on earth to the Church triumphant in Heaven."

The Baptist Church has multiplied, and divided, and there are, now, two English-speaking Churches, having elegant and commodious places of worship, and one German and one French. The last two are small, and have not yet supplied themselves with commodious churches. There is, also, one Church among the colored people.

There are two Methodist Episcopal Churches among the colored population, each having a house of worship, but they are not under the control and management of the white Church. Still, they are identified with them, and are to be enumerated with Episcopal Methodists. They are doing a good work among their own people.

Having run over the general history, it is well to call attention to some special occasions. The Annual Conference met here, for a second time, in 1845; Bishop Janes presided. This was the longest and most tedious session which has ever occurred in Michigan. It did not adjourn till near midnight on Friday of the second week. There were several causes for this; Bishop Janes was young, and had had little experience in presiding at Conferences, having been elected to the Episcopal office the year before ; and there was an unusual number of trials among the preachers. Bishop Janes preached on the Sabbath, to the great delight of the people. There has never been a greater season of revival in the Methodist Church than in 1856-7, under the labors of F. A. Blades, stationed here then. A very large number were added to the Church.

According to the statistics of the different leading denominations in the city, for the year 1876, they stand as follows, viz:— Methodist Episcopal, 1,900 members—colored 334, total 2,234 ; Protestant Episcopal, 2,397; Presbyterian, 2,022 ; Baptist, 1,179 ; Congregational, 670 ; United Presbyterians, 350.

There is another minister whose relations to the work in Detroit was such as to warrant the introduction of his memoir in this connection. He was stationed in the Woodward Avenue Methodist Episcopal Church, in 1852, and remained for two years, that being the disciplinary limit at that time ; and then was appointed Presiding Elder of that District, and died just a few weeks before his term of four years expired. He was a very strong and healthy-appearing man, and would have been readily selected as one who would be likely to live long and endure much hard labor. But how soon the fairest prospects may be laid low! In the prime of life, and in all the vigor of a noble manhood, he is cut down, What an admonition to be always ready, having our work faithfully and well done, for the night cometh in which no man can work ! The following is the official memoir as found in the Minutes for 1858:

"REV. WELLINGTON H. COLLINS, late Presiding Elder of Detroit District, was born, May, 1816, in Walcott, Wayne County, New York. In 1830 he emigrated to this State with his father, the year before the rest of the family, and settled in Washtenaw County.

"He embraced religion at a Camp Meeting held in Washtenaw County in 1835. Soon after his conversion to God he turned his attention to a preparation for the work of the Christian ministry. Such was his success and his promise of usefulness that, in 1837, he was employed by the Presiding Elder to fill a vacancy in Farmington Circuit. At the close of this year he was recommended by the Quarterly Conference of Farmington Circuit as a proper person to be received into the Michigan Annual Conference on probation.

"The Michigan Conference then embraced the north part of

REV. WELLINGTON H. COLLINS.

the State of Ohio and all of Michigan. His first appointment from the Conference was to the Dearborn Circuit, which at that time embraced what is now known as the Wayne, Trenton and Flat Rock charges. Here he labored with great acceptance and usefulness, as many of the older members of the Church still remain to testify.

"At the close of this year, at the Conference, he was stationed at Defiance, Northern Ohio. The May following, at the General Conference held in Baltimore, the Michigan Conference was divided, and the North Ohio was set off, which left Brother Collins in the North Ohio Conference. But, by arrangement, he was permitted to fall into the Michigan Conference, and at the close of this year he was ordained Deacon by Bishop Hedding, at Marshall, in 1840, and admitted into full connection in the Conference. His next field of labor was Medina, in the south part of this State, where he remained two years. Having now completed his four years' course of Conference study, and approved himself to the Church and his brethren, he was ordained Elder by Bishop Morris, at Adrian, in 1842. He was married in September of this year.

"His next charge was Edwardsburg, thence he removed to Niles. From Niles he was removed to Albion; from Albion he was transferred to Dexter. His next field of labor was Northville. He was removed from this field of labor and placed upon the Ann Arbor District, where he remained three years, greatly to the satisfaction of his brethren upon the District, and the edification of the Church.

"At the Niles Conference he was appointed to the charge of the Woodward Avenue Church, Detroit. At the close of his constitutional term here he was placed upon the Detroit District, where four weeks more would have completed four years of service upon this District, and his seventh year of service as Presiding Elder.

"He has twice represented his brethren in the General Conference; first in Boston, in 1852, and lastly at Indianapolis, in 1856. In all of these several fields of labor, and several positions in the Church, it is not too much to say that he acquitted himself as a minister of Christ.

"His memory is too fresh and too sacred for us not to feel that our loss is no ordinary loss, Hence our grief is no ordinary grief. His was a life that will bear examining, and in his singular devotion to God and His work, imitating. His character is a character to study. It is but truthful to say 'a great man has fallen in Israel.' Possibly, the acquaintance of an hour might not detect that greatness in the retiring mien of the deceased. But as acquaintance lengthened, and afforded opportunity to observe him in the discharge of the duties of his place, and there to mark the maturity of his judgment, the firmness of his purpose, his *indomitable perseverance*, the mind was not long in being impressed with the conviction, this is no ordinary man. The feature of his character, to be ever devloping some new peculiarity, and unfolding some hidden mine of wealth, is probably one thing that so endeared him to his brethren, and made his *friends fast friends*. It required an acquaintance and an intimacy of years to know him well.

"His habit of thought was peculiarly his own, as well as his style of expression. On the introduction of any question involving the relations and obligations of men, while many were occupying themsevles with a few facts that possibly might be distorted or mitigated by circumstances, and were seeking to base action on these, his mind seemed carefully to survey the field around him, and then go back to first principles, and the simple question with him was, '*Is it right?*'

"Probably no man more conscientiously resolved all the questions of life into this simple formula than he. Fixed here, he was immovable. Neither the frowns of power, nor the allurements of gain, or honor, or distinction among men, had any power to move him. It was here that he was liable to be misunderstood by those having only a public or passing acquaintance with him, and this peculiarity of his character be construed into a willful persistence, when it was simply his soul clinging to his conscious conviction of right. The world was comparatively but little in sympathy with him in his habits of thought and processes of reasoning, requiring, as it did, so much mental vigor, patience, and research. At times it was irksome for him to attempt to popularize his views, and to address himself to those who were unwilling to toil in the mine of thought themselves, or patiently listen to the elaboration of thought that it had cost labor to evolve, and would cost labor to digest. But when he sat down with a few friends to discuss any great question, or canvass any new field of thought, it was truly amazing to see the change that came over him. His reserve was thrown off, his eye kindled, his countenance brightened up, the enginery of his mind seemed to work with ease and grace, while his utterance was clear, forcible, and sententious. In debate he was at home, and had his marked peculiarities. Relying on his own convictions of right, his attempt was to overwhelm his opponent with the power of that truth that swayed and governed his own action. At times he reached this climax in the pulpit. At such times his efforts were those of a master. Never ordinary in his pulpit efforts, here he excelled. These rare powers made him always the valuable and reliable counselor. Here was pre-eminently his field; and such were the breadth of his views, the logical correctness of his conclusions, associated with his settled determination for the right, that his counsel and advice seemed clothed with authority.

"In his Church sympathies and prejudices he was decidedly Methodistic—this was not of caprice, but of conviction and judgment. Still, no man was more largely catholic in his feelings. His heart always rejoiced, nor was he slack in expressing his joy at the success of his brethren in other branches of the Christian Church. He had a kind word, and a 'God speed you,' for his brethren in the Christian ministry everywhere. In them he recognized fellow-laborers in the Master's vineyard, and his heart dilated with joy as he saw them gathering sheaves for the Master. He was no bigot. His life was a life of activity, of toil and of usefulness. The ministry was to him no sinecure, or place of ease and indulgence. His life illustrated the motto, 'Work here and rest in Heaven.' He was emphatically a man of *one work*. He earnestly devoted to the work of the Christian ministry all the power with which God had endowed him. He seemed to realize in its fullest sense that

> "'Tis not a cause of small import
> The pastor's care demands,
> But what might fill an angel's heart,
> And fill'd a Saviour's hands.'

"Nor was his labor in vain it the Lord; the world felt his power, and eternity shall reveal the fruits of his labor. Life's labor done, he rests at last.

"Afflictive, indeed are the circumstances that gather around the scene of his last suffering. He had been indisposed for some two weeks, yet persistently, against the advice of friends, he pursued his work with brave fidelity, by his actions saying, 'Wist ye not I must be about my Father's business?' until Tuesday, July 20th, he remained at home. Wednesday he was confined to his bed, where, with varying symptoms of improvement and decline, he continued until Friday morning, August 6th. There seemed a marked improvement, which continued until about 4 o'clock on Monday morning, when he was seized with a chill and paralysis, from which he never recovered. By the paralysis he was deprived of the power of speech. Hence no dying farewell to his loved family, as they stood weeping around him; or message of love to his brethren in the ministry. In this state he lingered until Wednesday, August 11th, when, at a quarter before 12 M., he closed his suffering and life.

"Although there is no dying message to his brethren or stricken family, from the scene of his suffering, yet in the monument of a consistent Christian life, and twenty years' devotion to the work of the Christian ministry, it is true, 'being dead, he yet speaketh.' His life needed not the appendix, in the words of the dying hour, to give his brethren and friends assurance of his happy exit from the scenes of time to the glories of the upper sanctuary. " May his mantle fall upon his brethren, and the Master give them grace to follow him as he followed Christ."

Mr. Collins was a man of settled purposes, and emphatically of one work. Had he lived, he would undoubtedly have been a great power in the councils of the Church. But God's ways are not as our ways, neither are His thoughts as our thoughts, and we must bow to His dispensations.

We here furnish the statistics of the principal denominations of Protestants for the County of Wayne, as gathered from their own reports. We should have been pleased to have given the amount of Church property, and the Sunday School statistics, and should have done so only some of them had made no report of either of these items. We give them in the order in which the Churches were first instituted. Methodist Episcopal, 3,695; Protestant Episcopal, 2,475; Presbyterian, 1,843; Baptist, 1,579; Congregational, 973.

HISTORY OF PROTESTANTISM IN MICHIGAN. 209

CHAPTER X.

MONROE—Methodist Society—Mary Harvey—Raisin River—Presbyterian Church—First Church—Methodist Church reorganized—Kent Asks for a Home—Mrs. Harvey—Baughman—Walker—Garwood Converted—Walker Returned—Dr. Adams Becomes Roman Catholic—Memoir of Walker—Revival—Methodist Society in City—Memoir of Garwood—J. W. Finley—Church Built—Protestant Episcopals—Baptists—German Lutherans—J. F. Davidson—Numbers—ST. CLAIR—Old Class Paper—John K. Smith—Subscription for Church—House not Finished—James T. Donahoo—Reasons for Slow Growth—S. A. Latta—A Night on the Lake—Why Methodist Preachers Sent—Other Churches—Numbers—Growth of Country—ANN ARBOR—First Preaching—Presbyterian Church Organized—First Methodist Society—Circuits—Members—First Methodist Prayer Meeting—Sarah J. Brown—Arrangement of Circuits—Accessions—Name of Circuit—Colclazer and Pilcher—Maria Maynard—No defection—Revival 1837–'38—Church Built—Pilcher—Progress—Presbyterian—Protestant Episcopal—Baptist—Congregational—Statistics—J. D. Collins—University—Dr. Cocker—Dr. Haven—TECUMSEH—First Preachers—Society Formed—Names—Joseph Bangs—Wheeler—Cross—Silliman—Quarterly Meeting—Rev. A. Darwin—Presbyterian Church Organized—Revival—Protestant Episcopal—Baptist—Controversy—Remarkable Conversion—Statistics.

IN the order of appointments, the next on our list, after Detroit is Monroe. MONROE was platted, as a village, April 25th, 1818. Previous to this time the locality was known as French Town. The village was incorporated as a city by the Legislature of the State, March 22d, 1837. But it is not our purpose to write the secular history of the city or county, although we have abundant material for that purpose, gathered with much care, labor and expense. It is its religious history with which we purpose to deal.

As in the case of all the French settlements, the Romish Church was established contemporaneously with the settlement, and it has always held a wide sway. We, however, are only concerned with Bible, or Protestant Christianity; for, whatever charity we may have for individuals of that community, we can but regard it as a system of paganism, having just enough of the Christian element in it to give it a semblance of Christianity—enough so that, if individuals will take the pains to search out the Christian elements, and separate them from the mass of pagan rites and ceremonies and superstitions, they may believe in Christ with a saving faith. This, however, is what we fear the multitudes do not do.

The Gospel, in the form of Protestantism, was first introduced here by Rev. William Mitchell, a minister of the Methodist Episcopal Church, who was on the Detroit Circuit, having received his appointment to that work in the autumn of 1810. He received his appointment to Detroit from the Western Conference, at the same time that Rev. Ninian Holmes was appointed from the Genesee Conference. He extended his labors to the few English settlers scattered along the River Raisin, and, such was the religious influence he had over them, that, early in 1811, he organized a Methodist Episcopal Society, or Church, consisting of about *twenty-three* members. This Society continued to exist, and was supplied by Rev. Ninian Holmes, until the ravages of the War of 1812 scattered them all, and the Church was broken up; but it was reorganized, in the spring of 1821, by Rev. John P. Kent, who was then traveling Detroit Circuit. The reorganized Church consisted of the following persons, viz: *Samuel Choat, Elizabeth Choat, Isaac B. Parker, Mary Parker, Lyman Harvey, Sarah Harvey* (the late Mrs. Rev. John A. Baughman), *Mary Harvey, Seth Choat, Ethel Choat, Abigail Choat,* and *Philura West.* There were eleven in all. Samuel Choat, who was the father of the family of Choats, was appointed the class-leader. Of all these only one now remains at Monroe, Mrs. Mary Harvey, wife of Captain Luther Harvey; she is still a member of the Church in the city. Mrs. Harvey was a daughter of Samuel Choat; was born in Canada, and was baptized by Rev. Mr. Sensiman, a Moravian missionary, who was associated with Heckewelder in his labors and sufferings among the Indians in Ohio and Michigan. In consequence of bitter persecutions in Ohio, the Christian Indians, with their missionaries, Heckewelder and Sensiman, came to Michigan and spent the winter of 1779–80, enduring vast sufferings. After this, Sensiman went to Canada to reside. Mrs. Harvey became a Christian, when she was very young, and joined the Methodist Episcopal Church in Canada. The family subsequently removed to Michigan, and constituted the principal part of the Church here, as reorganized by Mr. Kent.

At the time of which we are now writing, the Society worshiped, for the most part, about two miles out of the village, although the ministers preached in the village. The Church did not secure a permanent footing in the village until February, 1832, when a revival occurred under the labors of Rev. James W. Finley, who was then on the Circuit, and was assisted by Rev. Henry Colclazer, then stationed in Detroit. It will be seen, from these facts, that the Methodists were the pioneers of Protestantism in this part of the country, although, after the war, the Presbyterian Church was instituted before the reorganization of the Methodist Church, by a few months— although this is disputed by some of their own authorities. But the Methodist ministers were here, and doing what they could.

The Society organized before the War of 1812 was entirely scattered by that event, as it was most bloody and ruthless in this locality. But those days of blood and disaster have passed away, we hope never to return again to this locality. *Sturgeon* River was changed in name to the Raisin because of the vast quantities of grapes to be found along its banks, although sturgeon still abound. When the cloud of war had cleared away, the few inhabitants who had escaped from the slaughter began to enter upon their peaceful employments, and emigration was again directed hither. The storm had passed, and the time of the singing of birds had come, and the thoughts of the people were directed towards the services of religion as a source of comfort and elevation.

The Presbyterian Church, it is said, was organized on the 13th day of January, 1820, under the labors of Rev. Moses Hunter, assisted by Rev. John Monteith, who was minister in Detroit. The Society embraced all the Protestant professors of religion belonging in the village and adjacent country. The articles of faith were so constructed as to admit of almost any one subscribing to them. This Church has always, since that day, maintained a strong hold on the public mind, and, by this same liberality of religious faith, have secured to membership many who were Methodists in sentiment. Many of the members have become wealthy. They built the first Protestant house of worship in this city and county, which was done in 1831. It was a small brick building.

The Methodist Church was reorganized, in the early part of 1821, by Rev. John P. Kent, as before stated, who was appointed to Detroit Circuit in 1820. The place of meeting, for the most part, was a little above the city, though Mr. Kent preached in the Court House a part of the time. Although the articles of faith of the sister Church were so liberal as to take in almost any one, they did not care to encourage any other denomination. When Mr. Kent first came to Monroe, and preached in the Court House, at the close of the service he stated that he was a stranger, and was appointed to preach on the Circuit, and he would be glad if some of them would offer him a place of entertainment. The congregation all passed out without any one giving him such invitation. But Mrs. Harvey, a widow lady, living a little out of the village, invited him to go to her house. The invitation was accepted. She was a member of the newly organized Presbyterian Church. The officers of that Church, having a great care for the interests of their widowed sister, appointed a committee, who waited on her, a few days after, and remonstrated with her for affording him shelter, stating that she would be ruined by it, they thought. But she thought otherwise. This was at a time when hay was very scarce, and they urged that his horse would consume her hay to her ruin. But she disregarded the remonstrance, and invited him to make his home at her house whenever he had spare time, which he did, and she was not injured by it; for her hay, like the widow's meal, held out, as she told them it would. The good lady thought, as he was a man of God, and worthy of kind offices, she would continue to make him welcome at her house. She was rewarded in the conversion of a gay and thoughtless daughter. A better feeling now exists.

Monroe was made the head of a Circuit, that is, appears in the minutes of appointments of the ministers, first in 1826, and Rev. John A. Baughman was appointed to it. He was then a young man, full of ardent zeal for his Master's work. The Circuit then embraced all the settlements in Michigan south and west of Detroit, and extended into Ohio. It required strong nerves and warm zeal to travel it. But it was done, and the scattered settlements were visited and supplied with the Word of Life. Mr. Baughman was succeeded, in 1827, by Rev. George W. Walker, who labored for two successive years on this Circuit. Mr. Walker was a convert from Romanism; was a man of a strong and vigorous mind, and had a large and healthy frame. He was well suited to the work, and labored with a good degree of success, but did not organize any Society in the village. This was an error; the country members ought to have come to the village, and kept their organization in the town.

Mr. Joseph C Garwood was converted through Mr. Walker's instrumentality, during the first year of his labor, but united with the Presbyterian Church, stating, at the same time, that he did not believe in their doctrines, and that, if there should be a Methodist Society organized in the village, he would wish to unite with it. At this time, through a mistaken policy, the Methodist Society held their

Society meetings about two miles out of the village, because the principal part of the members resided in that neighborhood, and were well accommodated by that arrangement ; they had not learned the importance of concentrating their forces where the greatest number of people could be congregated.

Mr. Walker was returned to Monroe for a second year, with the full expectation that his labors would be confined to the village ; for, towards the close of the previous year, a Dr. Adams, who was a member of the Methodist Church, had settled at Monroe, and was very desirous to have Mr. Walker returned, and to have it made into a Station, pledging himself for large things towards his support. The arrangements were made for a Station, and Mr. Walker was returned. The Conference then, as it did until 1837, met in Ohio, and Mr. Walker was absent for several weeks, during which time Dr. Adams went over to the Romish Church, so, when he returned, he found the plans had all been deranged. What influenced the Doctor to take that step we will leave the readers to determine for themselves, and content ourself by saying that a very large proportion of the village and the surrounding country were of that faith. Patronage is necessary for a physician's prosperity. In consequence of this change it became necessary for Mr. Walker to take in the Circuit, and postpone the establishment of the Church in the village. He served the Circuit faithfully and well, performing great labor, and enduring much privation, exposure and suffering for the sake of the cause. He was a man of a sound and deep Christian experience— confiding in the atonement—and of much resolute perseverance.

We will take occasion, just here, to incorporate a little fuller notice of the experience and life of Mr. Walker, which we think will be quite acceptable. He was born in Maryland, November 26th, 1804. His father being a Roman Catholic, he was baptized in that Church in his infancy, and was educated in that faith. His parents, with him, emigrated to Ohio in 1810. Here, more out of curiosity than for any other reason, his father purchased a Bible, which was read, at first, in the same spirit of curiosity, and which resulted in the conversion of his father, then of his mother, and, finally, of the whole family. George was converted while young, and attached himself to the Methodist Church, and entered the itinerant ministry in 1826. He died in 1856, having been just thirty years in the active work of the Christian ministry. In relation to his labors in this country, the Official Minutes hold the following language : " Soon after his entrance into the ministry, he was sent by the authorities of the Church to Michigan. Two years he spent in that new and distant Territory, exposed to numberless perils and privations. The West has not, perhaps, opened a harder field of labor for an itinerant than Michigan at that period. But no swollen river, no dismal swamp, or dangerous fen could daunt the lion-heart that beat in the bosom of George W. Walker. He fulfilled his mission, and returned to Ohio." He was a laborious and useful man—a man of more than ordinary talents, and he commanded the respect and esteem of all who knew him; and those who knew him best esteemed him most highly. He was honored by his conference with a seat in the General Conference for several sessions, and he occupied some of the most important Stations in the Ohio and Cincinnati Conferences.

One so devoted to his Master's work, as was Mr. Walker, might be expected to find Divine consolation when he should be called to contend with the rising waters of death; so, in his last sickness, he found religion to be a delightful support. He often adopted this prayer, "Create in me a clean heart, O God!" frequently adding that sweet stanza,

"Take my poor heart, and let it be
Forever closed to all but Thee;
Seal Thou my breast, and let me wear
That pledge of love forever there."

He died, in great peace, in the fifty-second year of his age.

There was a regular succession of ministers, without any special change in the aspect of things in the village—now city—of Monroe, until in February, 1832, when, under the labors of James W. Finley, assisted by Rev. H. Colclazer, then of Detroit, a very precious, though not very extensive revival occurred, and the Society became firmly established in the village. Several persons had settled here during the fall and winter, who were Methodists, and desired to be recognized as members of this Church. Now, Mr. Joseph C. Garwood immediately united with this Church, according to his declared purpose, at the time he united with the Presbyterian Church, about three years before. We add here a brief memoir of him.

Mr. Garwood was a very quiet and unpretentious mechanic, but a man of good sound sense and consistent piety. By industry at the anvil and good economy he acquired a handsome property, and became, pecuniarily, a very important factor in the Church. He was a faithful Christian, attending very constantly on the social meetings of the Church, and contributing of his influence for the advancement of the cause. He died of the cholera, July 12th, 1854, and has gone to receive his rest in Heaven. He was a faithful mechanic and Christian, but has been called by the Great Master from the labors of earth to the refreshments of the Heavenly Home. The accession of Mr. Garwood to the Church at this time, he being a permanent citizen, may be regarded as the real beginning of the permanent establishment of the Methodist Church in the place. Most of the other men, who helped to compose the Church here, were rather migratory, and did not add very much to their ability to maintain the Gospel. They were willing enough to sustain the interests of the Church, but they were poor as well as migratory. They did what they could, but he could do and did more than they. When Mr. Garwood deceased, he left a wife and eight children, three sons and five daughters. One of the daughters has since become the wife of a missionary, and has gone to Peking, China.

At the time James W. Finley was sent to this Circuit—1830—it extended from Defiance, in Ohio, to Tecumseh and Adrian, requiring vast labor and exposure to accomplish the rounds on it, but he persevered, for two years, through all difficulties—though the Circuit was much diminished the second year. He was a man of a thorough Christian experience, and he was fired with an ardent zeal for the salvation of the people. These elements in his character led him to brave the most formidable difficulties, to perform his assigned work. In a Circuit so extensive as his was the first year, one break in the chain of appointments must occasion several, hence, whatever might be the condition of the unbridged streams, he felt he must go. On one occasion, being at Fort Defiance, and having his chain of appointments, extending off into Michigan, to meet, he determined to go, notwithstanding the Auglaze River, which he had to cross, was high and the ice very unsafe to cross on, he set forward on horseback; but, before he reached the opposite shore, the ice gave way, and let them both into the deep water, where they remained for two hours or more, struggling for life, until both nearly perished with cold. When he finally reached the shore, there was no human habitation near, where he could find shelter. Wet and cold, as he was, he had to set out on an Indian trail. After some time he came to a Pottawatamie wigwam, where the squaw afforded him such help and comfort as she could. He and his horse must have perished had it not been for this kind relief. These exposures and labors were too much for his physical condition, and, towards the close of his second year, his health failed. He went into Ohio and then into Kentucky, but never fully recovered from the shock of these years.

REV. JAMES W. FINLEY, nephew of Rev. James B. Finley, was born in Ohio, December 24th, 1800. He was converted to God while young, and, in the twenty-second year of his age, he gave himself up fully to the work of the ministry. He was possessed of very respectable preaching abilities and of such amiability of character as to endear him to all who knew him. His intense and extensive labors prostrated him, and brought him to his grave prematurely. He died in June, 1838. In regard to the closing period of his life, we find the following notes in the Official Minutes: "In the midst of great sufferings, God sustained him; and, when gasping for breath, he would say, 'What peace I feel!' To his weeping mother and family he exclaimed, just as he expired, 'Oh! how precious the Lord is to my soul! Glory! Glory!'" He has gone, but his works follow him.

Mr. Finley was succeeded, in 1832, by Elijah H. Pilcher and Elnathan C. Gavit, and it was still a four-week's Circuit, and they preached in Monroe only every other Sabbath. They occupied the Court House still. The next year, that is, in the autumn of 1833, the extent of the field was diminished, and it was so arranged as to have preaching in Monroe every Sabbath, and E. H. Pilcher and William Sprague were appointed to it. They were both single, and, in order to carry out the plan of supply, they hired a room in the Court House, at their own charges, and lodged there when in the village, there being no place among the members where they could find a home. This plan they carried out for one half of the year. The Lord revived His work to some extent, and a considerable accession of strength to the Church occurred. During this year preliminary steps were taken towards building a church. Trustees were appointed, and a religious incorporation was created, and a lot contracted for, and an interest on the subject created; but the Church was not built, or completed, until 1838, under the ministry of James F. Davidson, who was in the Station, for it had been created a Station, and under his labors a very precious revival of religion occurred, which added considerable strength to the Church. In the meantime, several Methodist families had settled here, as Hon Ira Mayhew, Julius D. Morton, and some other families.

The Protestant Episcopal Church was organized in 1831. Rev. John O'Brien made the following entry in the Parish Register: "I took charge of Trinity Church, Monroe, Michigan, in December, 1831, at which period there were only three persons who could be considered communicants." It was then, and continued to be for several years after, a Mission Station. They erected a small, neat church in 1832. They have increased, and now have a fine stone church.

A small Baptist Church was organized in 1833, but was disbanded in a few years. They, however, have reorganized, but, for some reason, have not become strong. A German Lutheran Church was established for the benefit of the large number of Germans who had settled here, and they have increased so that a second church has been established.

It is proper to introduce a brief notice of one living minister, who was connected with the work in this city, and, though he has supplied many appointments, and has had many revivals, there seems to us to be no place more appropriate to introduce him than this. We refer to Rev. JAMES F. DAVIDSON, than whom there is no man who has been more faithful and true to his work, never having failed to respond to his name at roll-call at Conference since he first entered the itinerancy in 1831, and never having failed to take and supply an appointment since that time; and to-day appears as vigorous and able to work in the ministry as he ever was.

Mr. Davidson was descended from Irish parents, and was born on the ocean, on the passage over, in 1810. His father settled in Ohio, in the vicinity of Cincinnati, where our subject was brought up. He was converted to God in his youth, and joined the Methodist Episcopal Church. Feeling himself called to the work of the ministry, he was admitted to the Ohio Conference, on trial, in 1831, and was appointed to the Oxford Circuit, in the Miami District, in Ohio. The next year, 1832, he was appointed to Tecumseh Circuit, in Michigan. He has remained in Michigan ever since, filling Circuits, Stations, and Districts. He was appointed to Monroe Station in September, 1836, and continued for two years. It was during this time that he had the revival before mentioned. At the end of his term, he reported *one hundred and twelve* members for the city. This was the first report for the city as separated from the Circuit. The next year, that is, 1838, he was appointed to Coldwater Circuit, on which he had a very gracious revival, and many members were added to the Church in the Village of Coldwater. In 1841, he was appointed Presiding Elder of the Kalamazoo District, which he worked efficiently for four years. He has always been a man of industry in his work, and has been the means of bringing great numbers of people into Church. He has served the Church for forty-six consecutive years, without any interruption for any cause, and bids fair to continue so for many years to come.

The Presbyterian Church has become very numerous, having a fine and valuable Church property; and the Methodist Church has built, on the same old lot, a large and very beautiful Church, with all the conveniences and appliances for Sabbath School and other Church work.

The English-speaking denominations are numerically, according to the reports for 1876, as follows: Presbyterians, 262; Protestant Episcopalians, 85; Methodists, 160; Baptists, 98.

ST. CLAIR is the next place to be considered as it appears on our Minutes of the Conferences. It was first placed in the list of appointments in 1824, and was supplied from the Genesee Conference this year. The Canada Conference was created by authority of the General Conference of 1824, and St. Clair was included in that Conference for 1825, but, in 1826, it was included in the Ohio Conference, and was called a Mission. It surely could not have received much support from the Missionary Society. As it was used at this date, the name did not signify any particular locality, but the country watered by that noble river. The principal points in the Circuit was the settlement opposite the upper end of Walpole Island, known then as Point de Chaine, but since known as Algonac. There was a small settlement at Belle River, now known as Marine City, and one, a little farther up, at Pine River, where the City of St. Clair now stands, and another, still farther up, at Black River, now the City of Port Huron.

Although this is the first appearance of the name in our Minutes, it was not the beginning of the work, as it had been visited as early as 1817, and continued to be visited by ministers, occasionally, from that time forward, both from Canada and from the Detroit Circuit, and classes were organized. We have been furnished with an exact copy of a class-paper, which bears date December 20th, 1824, which has the following on one side, and the names of the members on the other: "Class-paper for the 2d class on the St. Clair river. John K. Smith, Leader. Wm. Griffes, Jr., Preacher." This shows the method of keeping our Church records, in most Circuits, in those days. The class-paper, above-referred to, contains the following names, viz: John K. Smith, leader; Charlotte Smith, Charles Phillips, Derutia Phillips, Catherine Harrow, George Harrow, Mary Grummond, Jacob G. Streite, Sarah Robeson, Rachel Ward; and then, near the bottom, separated from the rest, is this, included in brackets, " Colored, Harry Sanders." There are eleven members at that date. How long the Society had existed, prior to this date, we have not been able to ascertain; but it had existed; for on the paper it shows that a class-meeting was held on the 19th of December, and the attendance of the members is marked, and several of the members are marked as absent, which would not have been the case if the

Society, or Church, had been first organized on that day. The Society was located at what is now Algonac.

Mr. Smith was the most prominent man in the community at that time and for many years after. It was our pleasure to make his acquaintance, first, in February, when we attended Quarterly Meeting there in company with Rev. James Gilruth, who was the Presiding Elder. That acquaintance was renewed in 1842, when we were appointed in charge of Detroit District, which still included this part of the country. We found him to be a man of ability and piety, and a decided Methodist. He was a very worthy Christian gentleman. He died in peace, after having served the Church faithfully, for many years, as class-leader and trustee and Circuit steward.

We have also in our possession a copy of a subscription-paper for building a church at this place. The paper and the subscriptions are interesting. The paper runs thus:

"We, the undersigned, do agree to pay to a committee that may be appointed by the Methodist Episcopal Church, the sums by us subscribed, for the purpose of building a Methodist meeting-house at or near Point de Chaine, to be paid when called upon. January 10th, A. D., 1830." The subscription ranges from one dollar up to twenty, except a few items of shingles and lumber, described by the amount and not by the price. We find these two items, which are interesting as showing the spirit of the times, viz: "Laura Graham, $1.25, in sewing. Lucretia Peer, $1.25, in short stockings. Paid." There is one subscription of fifty cents, which is the only one below one dollar.

The house was erected and enclosed, but never finished. They managed the best they could with it for about twelve years, when a new one was built and finished, and was dedicated in 1843. Mr. Smith managed the financial part of the matter in both cases. This last was enlarged, and finally substituted by a larger and more valuable one.

Rev. James T. Donahoo was appointed to St. Clair, in 1826, from the Ohio Conference. He found everything in a disorganized state, as it had been left without a supply the previous year, and there was no return of members, neither was there any plan furnished him. He had to search out the places, and organize everything. He attended to his work faithfully, and, at the next Conference he reported thirty members. How many members he had to begin with we have no means of knowing, and, consequently, we have no means of determining the progress of the work this year. The Circuit, embracing all the coast settlements, continued to be known by this name until 1838, when it was diminished in extent by the creation of the Port Huron Circuit, and the name was changed to Palmer for a few years. It has since been trimmed down, so that the charge of that name is confined to the City of St. Clair.

We here furnish a few facts relating to Rev. James T. Donahoo. He was admitted into the traveling connection by the Ohio Conference in 1821, consequently he had considerable experience at this time. He was a man of respectable talents and good social habits, sprinkled a little with oddity and Irish wit—for he was of Irish descent, and possessed, to some considerable extent, the proverbial loquacity. He labored in Michigan only this one year, and returned to Ohio. He continued in the itinerant work until 1848, when he located.

Although St. Clair appears in the Minutes of appointments from and after 1824, the number of members increased very slowly, so that, in 1840, there were only one hundred and seventy-eight members reported for all this country. There were two reasons for this slow growth ; one was found in the face of the country. Back from the river the land was level, and not well adapted to agriculture, so the settlements progressed slowly. The other reason was in the character and occupation of the people. They were mostly poor, and not disposed to religion, and were occupied in lumbering, fishing, boating and hunting—employments not conducive to piety specially. Societies had been established at Algonac, Newport, now Marine City, at St. Clair, sometimes called Palmer, and at Port Huron, but they were all feeble, and found it very difficult to support ministers.

St. Clair, at the Conference of 1827, was left to be supplied. The supposition is, the Presiding Elder found some local preacher who could do the work that year, or, possibly, no one was found to fill it, as there was no report of members at the next Conference. But the next year, that is, at the Conference of 1828—Elias Pattee, a very zealous pioneer, was appointed to it, and reported forty-nine members at the end of the year. Mr. Pattee was succeeded, in 1829, by Samuel A. Latta, who reported ninety-five membess at the Conference of 1830. This field was so separated from the other settled portions of the country that it was a kind of exile to go to it, and it required men of faith and courage to go to it and work it; but such men were found, still it was too much to ask them to do this kind of work for more than one year at a time.

We will take the liberty to introduce here a brief notice of Mr. Latta and an incident connected with this work. Rev. Samuel A. Latta was a healthy, stout, energetic man, and did his work well

He was a physician by profession, and left that for the ministry, under the impression that he was called of God to this work. He was admitted to the Ohio Conference in 1829, and this was his first appointment. It was a pretty hard experience to begin with. He was a man of talents, and capable of wielding a strong influence for the cause of religion. His labors, after leaving Michigan, having remained here but one year, were mostly in the vicinity of Cincinnati, Ohio. In the division of the Church, and the organization of the Methodist Episcopal Church South, growing out of the question of slavery, he sympathized with the South, and united with that Church in 1846. He has since died.

The following, taken from the *Ladies' Repository* for 1844, written by Rev. Bishop Hamline, from the facts as related to him by Dr. Latta, the young man referred to, will be read with great interest in this connection, as giving a good description of some of the difficulties encountered in preaching the Gospel along the St. Clair River.

A NIGHT ON THE LAKE.

"Perils await thee hour by hour—
Tempt not the deep alone."

In 1829, a young man just then admitted into the Ohio Conference, was appointed to a domestic mission, which embraced the borders of civilization in the northern part of Michigan Territory. In such a climate where deep snow and extreme cold are companions of all the winter months, it was a severe service to travel amongst the few new settlers, whose rude log cabins were thinly scattered over an extensive forest region. These frequent and formidable obstacles interrupted the traveler in his progress. Many creeks and rivers were to be crossed, and at that time bridges were very rare. Our young missionary had a vigorous constitution, great muscular energy, and a purpose of soul in his Master's service which led him to look at the labors and exposures of his appointed field with a good degree of resolute composure.

He accomplished the service assigned him to the satisfaction of all concerned; but, at that early date, his physical condition, strong as it was, suffered a blow from which it never recovered. He continued for several years, under much embarrassment from feeble health, to occupy more pleasant fields of labor, until, at the early age of thirty-five, he was compelled to take his station amongst the superannuated, without the least prospect of being restored to active work.

Amongst the trials of that year, several of which, as we have heard him state them, would compare with the experiences of our venerable fathers in the primitive days of Methodism, we select the following, which is romantic in its features, and threatened a tragic consummation. Its moral purpose is to illustrate, convincingly, the care of Providence over blind, helpless and distressed mortals.

The field of this young man's labors bordered on Lake St. Clair. His rides extended northward, also, on the American shore of the strait which connects that smaller body of water with Lake Huron. Some time during the year he had occasion to sail down the former lake, along its western shore. As he was going aboard the schooner in which he had taken passage, some of his acquaintances asked permission to place under his protection three ladies who were bound for the same point. They set sail. Toward evening the captain of the vessel resolved to "lie to" during the night. He chose to anchor off the mouth of Clinton River, about a mile distant from the shore.

The passengers, of whom there were several, noticed a dark cloud resting on the horizon; and, from all observable portents, they were led to expect a severe thunder-gust. Deeming the position of the vessel unfavorable to endure a heavy blow, they became solicitous to get on shore. A short distance above the mouth of the river, on its banks, was a comfortable inn. It was finally determined to employ one of the schooner's hands to row them into the estuary, and land them near the tavern. The boat was accordingly lowered; but several boorish *gentlemen*, who had no ladies in their company to care for, ungallantly leaped in till it was fully laden, and secured the first trip, leaving the missionary, Mr. L[atta], and the ladies with two strange gentlemen, to take their chance afterward.

Before the return of the boat it began to be quite dark; and Mr. L[atta] became somewhat anxious lest the waterman, a garrulous Frenchman, should not be able to strike the mouth of the river. He was assured, however, with Galic volubility and positiveness, that there was no difficulty. Taking counsel of their fears, as the threatening cloud now spread over the heavens, and the lightning began to play on the surface of the lake, they trusted themselves to his pilotage, and launched forth.

Thick darkness shut in upon them suddenly. The Frenchman rowed with might and main, as was supposed, towards the shore. But when it was certain that he must have run the skiff far enough to have reached the landing place, there were yet no tokens of land. The whole company became uneasy, and hurriedly inquired if he was not wrong ; but he assured and re-assured them that he must be right, and resolutely propelled the boat so much the faster to convince them and himself that they were safe. Mr. L[atta] finally warned him that the water was certainly getting deeper. Upon this, after considering a little, the pilot himself became alarmed, and finally announced that they were lost.

Lost! What a sound was that in the circumstances which surrounded them! At first they could not realize their condition. But the quick-thoughted missionary soon perceived the imminency, or at least the extent of their exposure. He recollected that when they dropped off from the vessel a light shone from the window of the tavern, which he supposed would be the pilot's guide toward the estuary. But now—whether by moving a lamp, or closing a blind, or whether (which was probable enough) by the intervention of a bluff, or a forest—no light could any longer be seen. In considering the probability of missing their course, if they had bethought themselves to secure a stationary light on the deck of the schooner, to guide their return in case of such misadventure, all would have been well. But they had forgotten that, and were forlorn of such comforting resorts.

[So the sinner, in the midst of probationary means, urged by friends, warned by Providence, and drawn by the Holy Spirit, too often declines a preparation for the voyage. While near the cross, and at liberty to apply its cleansing blood, and set up in his soul the light of devotion enkindled there by the ever-blessed Spirit, he disregards the necessity of this wise provision. In the midst of this forgetfulness death overtakes him. Stretched helpless on his uneasy couch, he begins at length to look around. This is to him a new point of observation; and, O how it changes the aspects of surrounding scenes! He is now on the ocean's shore. Its waters are seen to be a boundless waste, and its surface, vexed by the fury of the untempered storm, presents a scene most appalling to the soul. Just launching forth on this sea of terrors, night closes in upon him. The heavens are vailed in gathering clouds, which seem blended with sin-avenging wrath! It is the wrath of dread Omnipotence provoked by years of crucifying scorn poured upon the long-suffering Redeemer of mankind. He feels that it must be *unrelenting* wrath, because it falls on an unrepenting victim. He looks once more towards the cross; but it recedes. No star of hope remains. He exclaims, in husky tones, "*There is no help!*" At length his voice is hushed, and his eyes are fixed in staring ghastliness. While the signals of distress are hung out on every feature, expiring tremors seize his frame—he groans despair, and dies. *All else is hell.*]

Let us fancy now, as nearly as we are able, the condition of the missionary and his charge. The clouds had, by this time, spread over the zenith, and covered the face of the heavens. The wind was tempestuous. The short, broken billows of the lake began to toss themselves angrily into every shape of danger. The livid lightning ever and anon turned the thick darkness into a momentary blaze, which, instead of revealing, as they hoped it might, the ship or the shore, only gave them a glance of the surrounding terrors, and impressed on them more deeply than the boldest imagination could have done, the appalling horror of their state. The rain fell in torrents, and a conflict seemed to transpire, in which the elements above strove fiercely and wildly with the elements beneath. Then, truly, "deep called unto deep at the noise of His water-spouts." One thing only could be added to increase the terror of the scene, and that was not long wanting. The Frenchman proved to be a most profane wretch; and though he might have been, at first, somewhat cowered by the discovery of his novel and sad condition, yet, gathering either courage or despair, as the perils thickened around them, he began to utter horrid oaths and imprecations, and, thenceforward became furious and flagitious in his blasphemies in proportion as the dangers multiplied. This is a picture of the hardening influence of sin. Procrastinators often encourage themselves with the hope of being urged to Christ by the near approach of death. Such an one recently died in this vicinity [Cincinnati], uttering this, among several death-bed imprecations, "*I feel as though I could curse Jesus Christ from His throne.*"

It soon became necessary to point the boat's bow so as to cross, if possible, the fitful waves, and propel her, in some direction, amidst the raging of the storm. The glare of the lightning, therefore, became of great importance; for it enabled the poor Frenchman, whose task was now a serious one, to hold the slender craft to what he judged the safest point. It employed his utmost skill and energy to avoid the troughs of the sea, and to move forward so as to reduce the chances of swamping, in which they were, every moment, in great danger. This wicked man labored incessantly at the oar for four weary hours, more or less, and all that time none could form the least conjecture which way they were sailing, whether parallel with the shore, inclining towards it, or (as they ultimately judged most probable) out into the stormy bosom of the lake. At length, after suffering no little apprehension on his own account, as well as for his fellow-passengers (and, most of all, for those affrighted females who had been committed to his protection, and whom it became his duty to encourage by suggestions which scarcely sustained his own hope of deliverance) Mr. L. insisted that an attempt must be made to change their course. They had sailed far enough, as he believed, to prove that they were not approaching the shore at an inclination which promised them relief; and, although the danger of "coming about" was extreme, he urged it as affording the only chance of escape. After much demurring, the effort was made. By the mercy of Providence it succeeded. They endeavored, on their new tack, not exactly to reverse their former course, but, diverging from it as far as the running waves would permit, they called into requisition all the strength that remained in the now exhausted oarsman, and pushed ahead.

About midnight they perceived, from the tokens of shallow water, that they must be nearing land; and not long afterwards the suffering females, drenched in the rain and spray, almost senseless through fear, were conveyed, in a helpless condition, to the shore, which they reached five miles below the mouth of the river, where the schooner was at anchor. The gentlemen themselves, who in turns engaged in unlading the boat of the water she took from the dashing of the waves, were far enough from suffering no exhaustion, yet, unlike the ladies, they were able to stand and walk.

On calculating, as nearly as they could, the courses they sailed and the time they were lost, the conclusion was, the boat had pushed out seven or eight miles from the shore. Reviewing all the circumstances, it appeared to them a special providence that the skiff had not only been kept adrift, but, (what was still more admirable), that in the tossings and alarms of so dark and stormy a night, none so far lost their presence of mind as to miss their hold, and plunge into the sea.

The next day these sufferers were restored to the comforts and fellowships of life, but were soon separated, to meet, if not before, at the judgment seat of Christ, where the blasphemous Frenchman, the two strangers, the suffering females, and the missionary who strove to cheer and comfort them in danger, all mercifully preserved by an interposing Providence, will appear, to render their last account, and receive their final doom.

We will add that Mr. L. closed this narrative in some such words as the following: "Even to this late hour, as often as memory wanders back to that night of raging tempests, and dwells upon its scenes of unimaginable horror, my heart sinks within me, and my blood seems almost to curdle in my veins."

How significant are the following familiar lines in connection with the narrative:

> "Once on the raging seas I rode,
>   The storm was loud—the night was dark,
> The ocean yawned—and rudely blow'd
>   The wind, that toss'd my found'ring bark;
> Deep horror then my vitals froze.
>   Death-struck, I ceased the tide to stem;
> When suddenly a star arose—
>   It was the star of Bethlehem.
>
> " It was my guide, my light, my all—
>   It bade my dark forbodings cease;
> And through the storm and danger's thrall,
>   It led me to the port of peace.
> Now safely moor'd, my perils o'er,
>   I'll sing, first in night's diadem,
> Forever and forever more,
>   The star—the star of Bethlehem."

We have given the foregoing article in full because it is both interesting and profitable to read.

The circumstances which led to sending a Methodist missionary to the St. Clair country, in 1826, were these: Presbyterian missionaries had been sent there, from time to time, who had had little success among the people, and the appointment having been left by the Canada Conference, some gentlemen on the river having had some information in regard to the influence of Methodism in reforming men, wrote to Rev. William Simmons, stationed at Detroit, and having charge of Detroit District, requesting a Methodist preacher to be sent to them, and pledging fifty dollars towards his support. The gentlemen, whose names Mr. Simmons is not now able to recall, stated that they had received a favorable impression with regard to the influence of Methodist preachers, and stated that their Sabbaths were spent in horse-racing, drinking, gambling, and other demoralizing practices; and that they felt an interest in the religious welfare of the people. The letters were laid before the Bishop at the Conference in 1826; fifty dollars were appropriated from the Missionary Society, and Rev. James T. Donahoo was sent, as before stated, who labored, and gathered a few members. The *people* said to those in authority in the Church that he accomplished more in one year, at a cost of only fifty dollars to the Missionary Society, than the Presbyterian ministers had done in the same region, at an expense of *twelve thousand dollars.* Mr. Simmons states that he was told this on what he considered good authority. This application to Mr. Simmons for a preacher was made in the summer of 1826. It is no wonder that even irreligious men often desire to have religious services in the place where they reside, as a matter of self-protection, for there is such a reforming power in the Gospel of Christ that even those who do not become experimental Christians are elevated and improved by it. The statement of those gentlemen as to the character and practices of the people, furnishes a reason for the slow progress of the Church in this region. But, notwithstanding the difficulties, the Church made progress, and triumphed over many obstacles.

We state with pleasure that other denominations have established Churches at all the chief points along the river, as Presbyterians, Baptists, Congregationalists, though the last, according to a plan of union, were included in Presbyterian Churches, until 1842, and Protestant Episcopalians.

In what was originally St. Clair Circuit, there are now thirteen charges—Methodists—supplied with ministers, embracing 1,600 members, having fine and valuable churches. The Presbyterians, finally, all became Congregationalists, and they number 385 members. The Protestant Episcopalians number 141, exclusive of Port Huron, which was organized in 1840, and probably, numbers about 100 members at the present time. The Baptists number 296 members. These numbers are taken from the statistical reports for 1876.

In the meantime there has been a great change in the country. The forests have been cleared away; roads have been made and improved; railroads have been constructed; farms have been opened and cultivated; the rude log house has given place to frame and brick; school-houses have been erected and occupied, and Christian civilization has been advanced; villages have been created and two flourishing cities have grown up, where, then, there were only the lumberman's rude camps. It is pleasant to contemplate that Christianity has kept pace, at least, with the increase of population. The power of Christianity is felt and acknowledged.

Ann Arbor has assumed such importance that it will justify a brief history or sketch of the place before writing its religious history. ANN ARBOR—what is it, and where is it? It is the county seat of Washtenaw County, situated on the Huron River, about forty miles west from Detroit. It is an incorporated city and the seat of the Michigan University. It is well laid out, and tastefully and beautifully ornamented with trees, shrubs, and gardens. It is a most beautiful, healthful, and inviting town, surrounded by a rich and well cultivated farming country. But it is not purposed now to write any more of its topography and history than is necessary to give a general idea of the place. The first location or purchase of land from the General Government was made in February, 1824, by John Allen, Esq. He associated with him Mr. Walker Rumsey. They brought their families here the same year. They immediately laid out a village, and, in honor of their wives, they named it Ann Arbor —for Mrs. Allen's name was Ann, and Mrs. Rumsey's was Mary Ann. The Arbor part of the name was suggested by the beautiful grove of burr oaks which stood upon the spot. Some of the oaks still remain as ornaments and witnesses of the past. Christianity was early introduced, or, rather, in its services it nearly came with the people, for the first settlers had hardly become established in their new and rude habitations before the minister of the Lord Jesus presented himself, and offered them the Bread of Life.

Rev. John A. Baughman, then in his youth and the vigor of his Christian ministry, was appointed to Detroit Circuit, which embraced all the settlements in Michigan outside of the city, in 1825. Some time in November of that year he visited Ann Arbor, and stopped with Colonel Allen, father of John Allen, Esq., lately come from Virginia, and preached in his house. The family were not Methodists, but they received the messenger of peace with all gladness, and entertained him hospitably. He remained several days, and preached every evening. This was the first introduction of religious services into this place. The Circuit was so extensive that he could not make this place a regular appointmentment, especially as there were no members of the Methodist Church residing here. In the spring of 1826, Rev. William Simmons, who was stationed in Detroit, and had charge of Detroit District, visited Ann Arbor, and preached for them. After the visit of Mr. Baughman, reading meetings were established as a substitute for preaching, until they could secure the services of the living minister, which they did in 1826.

The first Christian Church organized in Ann Arbor was Presbyterian. It was constituted, August 21st, 1826, by Rev. Noah M. Wells acting as Moderator, and Rev. Ira Dunning, acting as Secretary. It consisted, at the time, of seventeen members. Rev. William Page, a Presbyterian minister, who had come here to reside, not intending to devote himself entirely to the ministry, was employed as their first minister, as a stated supply.

In the spring of 1827, a Mr. Brown, who had two daughters— young ladies, who were Methodists, settled here. On their way out from Detroit, these young ladies found a newspaper containing a notice of a Camp Meeting, signed by Z. H. Coston, Presiding Elder, which was to be held in the vicinity of Detroit. They immediately addressed a note to Mr. Coston requesting him to send some one to preach and organize a Methodist Society or Church. In compliance with this request, Mr. Coston directed Mr. Baughman, who was in charge of Monroe Citcuit, to visit Ann Arbor again, and if practicable to organize a Society, and to supply them with preaching. Mr. Baughman came, and on the 29th day of July, 1827, organized a Society consisting of Eber White, Harvey Kinney, Hannah B. Brown, Rebecca G. Brown and Calvin Smith. Mr. Smith was only a transient person, but gave his name to help form the class, and never met with them but once after that day. This was a small beginning, still it was equal to the first Methodist Society formed on this continent, and God was in the movement. This place was made an appointment in the Monroe Circuit for the first half of the next year, beginning in September, 1827, and George W. Walker was the preacher, but for the last half of the year, it was included in Detroit Circuit, John Janes was the preacher. But in 1828 a new Circuit was organized called Huron, which included Ann Arbor, and it so continued for the next year. Not one of these original members now remains here. Eber White was the last one. He resided on a farm just a little west of the village, and occupied the same farm till his death, which occurred but recently. He was a very quiet, good man. Harvey Kinney was a young man in the family of Esquire Brown, and did not remain long. Hannah B. Brown, a young lady of deep and earnest piety, of a strong and well cultivated mind, in a little over a year united her fortunes and labors with Rev. John Janes. Soon after her marriage with Mr. Janes she removed with her husband to Ohio, and shared with him for many years, the privations and responsibilities of an itinerant life. Well was she qualified for the post, and well and faithfully did she perform her part while he lived, and survived him, still to do good and bless the Church for several years.

Mrs. Janes was converted at her home in the State of New York, in 1825, and immediately connected herself with the Methodist Church. She did this at a time when it required some courage to do so. Her father was a professed Universalist, and her mother was a member of the Presbyterian Church, and a very good woman. She was glad to have her daughter pious, and was not very particular as to what Church she should be united with. The young lady herself was very decided in her Methodistic predilections. The Methodist doctrines and usages pleased her; especially the doctrine of entire consecration and holiness. She very beautifully exemplified in her life, "the beauty of holiness," and by her life as well as by her words, commended it to others.

Rebecca G. Brown, a younger sister, was a young lady of much more than ordinary intellectual ability, and had enjoyed good advantages for mental culture, for the times. These cultivated powers she consecrated to God on the altar of religion under the Methodistic form. She was brought to experience the renewing grace of God at a meeting near Middleport, New York, in 1826. She consecrated her whole soul to the work, and shortly after her conversion, she found by happy experience, that "the blood of Jesus Christ cleanseth from all sin," and like her sister, became a strong advocate for Christian purity. Under the influence of such an experience she became a very active and useful member of the Methodist Episcopal Church. She felt herself fully identified with the interests and fortunes of the Church. The class and prayer meetings were her delight, and to labor in the Sabbath School afforded food to her soul. Her activity occasionally provoked the censure of the inactive, because it was a standing reproof to them. When in the congregation her very presence was an inspiration to the minister, because she was such an attentive and interested hearer, and because her soul was so absorbed in fervent prayer for the success of the Word. She had engaged herself to share the fortunes and trials of a young and active itinerant preacher—Rev. L. D. Whitney—but before the nuptials were celebrated, she was stricken down by the hand of death—was called by her Heavenly Father from labor to reward. She died in great peace and holy triumph, May 8th, 1834. Her dust sleeps in the cemetery at Ann Arbor.

The first Methodist prayer meeting here was held very soon after the organization of the Church in 1827 Harvey Kinney, Hannah B. Brown, Rebecca G. Brown, and Lemuel Brown a lad about twelve years of age and a brother of the two sisters, and not then a professor of religion, but since a member and local preacher, were the only persons present. The second was attended by about the same number of persons. But these young persons were decided, though not bigoted Methodists, advocating with calm dignity, the duty of Christians to love God with all their hearts, and so persevered in their work that God gave them success. Sarah J. Brown, another of the same family, was the first person converted here through Methodist labors, and the first person who joined the Church on trial. She joined the Church on trial, in February, 1828, and experienced an evidence of pardon in May, following. She, probably, was the first person converted in the town and the first to join a

Church on profession of faith. She became very active and devoted in the cause. Having a ready flow of language, she generally took an active part in social meetings. She was never possessed of very robust health, but her health so failed that she was for many years confined to her bed, and lingered as a monument of God's abounding grace. She was confined to her room, and mostly to her bed for twenty years, but all this time she rejoiced in God and suffered without a murmur.

The Circuit was so arranged in 1827, as to supply preaching here once in two weeks on the Sabbath; and continued so till 1833, when it was made into what was called a half station. A part of the time it was supplied with only one and a part of the time with two preachers. When it was made a half station it was supplied with two preachers, and it was so arranged that one of them should be in the village every Sabbath, that is, they rotated so as that one of them should be here two successive Sabbaths, and the other for the same length of time. This arrangement continued for two years, when it was made a full station.

The Society received considerable accession of strength in the spring of 1828, by the coming in of Christopher Gee and his family, he himself and six of his family were members of the Church. In the autumn of the same year, Dr. Benjamin H. Packard settled here, he and his wife being active members. Not far from the same time David Page and a daughter, being active workers, united by letter. These were further strengthened soon after by Ezra Maynard and wife, and a few others whose names do not appear. Mr. Maynard and wife had been members of the Presbyterian Church at the East, but chose now to identify themselves with Methodism. Mr. Page was father of Rev. William Page, the Presbyterian minister here at the time, but he was a decided Methodist and was soon appointed class-leader, an office which he had long held in Vermont. He was of great value to the Church at this time. All the individuals named above as having been added to the Church at this period have gone to reap their reward for their works of faith and labors of love. For the year 1828, it was supplied by Benjamin Cooper, a very quiet and sweet-spirited man, who did little else than to organize the Circuit and put it in form. At the Conference in September, 1829, L. B. Gurley, now of the North Ohio Conference, was appointed to Huron Circuit. During the winter of 1829–30, he had a revival in Ann Arbor, which resulted in adding considerable strength to the Society. Mr. Gurley was a man of power both in the pulpit and in his social habits. Among the persons converted at this revival was a lad about fourteen years of age—very interesting, and who was as firm and decided a Christian as anyone of mature years. Great hopes were entertained that he would become a useful laborer in the Church, but the Head of the Church was pleased to take him home early, for William Barr died in great peace in December, 1831. Mr. Gurley remained only one year. A strong effort had been made to secure a man of some age from the Genesee Conference to be transferred, but the effort failed, for, though the man had given some encouragement that he would come, he finally declined and they had to be content with the young men sent from Ohio.

At the Conference in September, 1830, the name was changed and Ann Arbor appears on the list of appointments for the first time. *Henry Colclazer and Elijah H. Pilcher*, the former only twenty-one years of age and the latter much younger, were appointed to it. They felt that they were supplied with boys indeed. But, if they were young, they had zeal, and filled the appointments, and had some revival and accessions to the Church. How well they performed their work is not for us to say, as they are both still living, and in the effective work, the former in the Wilmington Conference, and the latter in the Detroit Conference, having always remained in Michigan. There were some very valuable accessions to the Church this year. Among these was Maria Maynard, a young lady of fine mind and well cultivated, who became very useful in the Church. She experienced very strong convictions for sin at a quarterly meeting held in Ann Arbor, where she resided, in the early part of the year, but did not then obtain salvation from sin. A few days after this the junior preacher called at the residence of a married sister, where she happened to be visiting; and after some conversation with them on the subject of a religious experience, he prayed with them before leaving. During the prayer she was brought into the light and liberty of the Gospel. She united with the Church, January 2d, 1831. She lived happily and usefully, and died in Christian triumph, some years after.

One thing is very agreeable to notice, that is, down to the present period no disastrous circumstance has ever happened to this Church. They have had their perplexities, but no great division or rupture has been occasioned in the process of administering Christian discipline. Its course has been steadily onward—regularly progressive. It is well to observe that, from the time the name appears on our Minutes, there has been a regular circumscribing of the boundaries of the charge, until it came to embrace only the village in 1835. Ann Arbor had acquired so much notoriety and Methodistic importance as to be made the head of a District in 1835, and Henry Colclazer was appointed in charge of it. Until this time it had been included in Detroit District.

Various seasons of revival have been enjoyed, from which much good has resulted. But, perhaps, at no time has there been so extensive a work, in proportion to the population, and productive of so much good, as the one which occurred in 1837–8, beginning in December, 1837, and running on through the year. One hundred and eighteen, in all, united with the Methodist Episcopal Church, and a large number with the Presbyterian Church. The revival was productive of a vast amount of good. The good did not consist, altogether, in the number of persons who were converted, reclaimed, and brought into the Church, though that was great, but partly in the persons converted. Judson D. Collins, a small lad, who afterwards became our first missionary to China, of whom a full sketch will be given below, Isaac F. Collins, late a member of the Kansas Conference, now deceased, were converted at this time. Walter D. Collins, who became an active and successful missionary among the Indians and in Texas, for a number of years, was reclaimed, he having been converted, a few years before, but, trying to live out of the Church, lost his piety. These three brothers united with the Church in Ann Arbor in the month of March, 1838, and have since died in holy triumph. We would not arrogate to ourselves the whole of the credit of this revival; for, though it commenced in the Methodist Church, it was transferred to the Presbyterian Church, and carried on as a union work. They had just completed their church, and, in connection with the dedication, they had engaged a Mr. Parker, an evangelist, to labor for a time. The Methodists cheerfully joined with them in the work, as their place of worship was much the largest. Mr. Pilcher went heartily into the work, and, when the union was closed, he held meetings, for a short time, in his own church, and carried with him a large proportion of the converts. The Presbyterians had a valuable accession. Mr. Parker had one peculiarity in his instructions to seekers, which Mr. Pilcher found it necessary, in a quiet way, to counteract, that was, he required them to say that they were willing to be damned—that they felt so when they submitted themselves to Christ. It seemed absurd that a man who was anxious to be saved should be willing to be damned.

The building of a church was found to be a desideratum for several years, but was not undertaken until in the spring of 1837, under the labors of Rev. Peter Sharp. Some preparations for the work had been previously made. The basement of the church was made ready for use in November, 1837, and its occupancy was followed by the glorious revival before mentioned. The body of this church was not finished until in the summer of 1839, under the labors of Rev. Elijah Crane. This year the Michigan Conference held its session here for the first time. The dedication services were performed on the first day of the session, in the afternoon. The sermon was preached by Jonathan E. Chaplin, since deceased. The majestic and venerable Bishop Soule attended this Conference, and was invited to attend the dedicatory services. As he was on his way to the church, Rev. Henry Colclazer, Presiding Elder of the District, said to him, "Bishop! Perhaps I ought to say to you that the choir have taken great pains to prepare music for the occasion, and will have one or two instruments to assist them." As quick as the Bishop heard that, he whirled on his heel, saying, "Go on, brethren, and dedicate your church. I will have nothing to do with it." This is the same Bishop Soule, who, a few years after, could affiliate with the South on the subject of slavery. and give his influence to a division of the Church. He could strain at this gnat and swallow that camel. This session of the Conference was of great interest to our cause. Bishop Soule preached a most eloquent and powerful sermon on Sabbath morning. *William L. Harris*, now Bishop, was admitted into full connection, and ordained Deacon, at this Conference, and so was Lorenzo Davis, the second Michigan convert who had entered our ministry.

Ann Arbor was made a station in 1835, and Thomas Wiley was appointed to it. His health was not very firm at the time, but soon began to decline and he died on the 4th of April, 1836, in the thirtieth year of his age, beloved in the Church, and respected by all. During his sickness when asked as to his state, his uniform answer was "Peace." He had not been quite five years in the ministry having been admitted into the Ohio Conference in September, 1831. Mr. Wiley having died, Rev. Goodwin Stoddard, a superannuated member of the Oneida Conference was employed by the Presiding Elder to fill the remainder of the year. The number of members returned this year was 136. Hitherto, this place had been connected with country appointments, and this is the first report of members for the village alone.

At the Conference in September, 1836, Peter Sharp was appointed to this charge. Mr. Sharp is still living. He was succeeded in September, 1837, by Elijah H. Pilcher. He remained but one year, having been appointed Presiding Elder of Marshall District, and in September, 1838, Elijah Crane was appointed, and remained two years, and he was succeeded, in 1840, by Jonathan Hudson.

Both of these last were good, pious men, and rendered effective service, and are both dead.

It is not important to follow minutely the fortunes and labors of this Church. Suffice it to say, they have labored much—have had many seasons of revival, have now a very large and beautiful church, corresponding with the growth of the city—for it is now a city— and the demands of the great State University located within the city. The present numbers will be furnished below. There is also a German Methodist Episcopal Church, included in the statistics below at 85.

We have already said that a Presbyterian Church was organized in 1826. They, in a short time, erected a small frame church, being the first Protestant church built west of Wayne County. That gave way to a larger and more elegant one, dedicated January or February, 1838, and that, again, has been superseded by a large, commodious, and beautifully finished one. The Society has advanced in numbers and wealth.

The Protestant Episcopal Parish was organized in 1827, and has worked and grown. They are now occupying the second church, which is a valuable stone structure, and they are commanding a wide influence in the city.

The Baptist Church was organized in 1832, and now have a good, though not elegant house of worship. They have, more recently, organized a second church, which is very small.

The Congregational Church was not organized until March, 1847, the Congretional members, prior to that time, having been absorbed in the Presbyterian Church. But, at this time, there were some difficulties in the administration of Church discipline, which made a favorable opportunity for them to separate, and they availed themselves of it. They are now occupying the second church which they have erected. This is a costly stone structure, beautifully located in front of the University Campus.

The statistics of the different Churches we now furnish from the reports as given in for 1876. We give them in the order of organization: Presbyterians, 342; Methodist Episcopals, 700; Protestant Episcopals, 228; Baptists, 264; Congregationalists, 263; African Methodist Episcopals, 59.

It is right to take into the account that these Churches all have their Sabbath Schools corresponding, somewhat, with their membership, in estimating the amount of Church work which they are accomplishing. What an army of children and youth, for a city of this size, are being trained every Sabbath!

We here insert the official memoir of one who was converted at Ann Arbor, and whose whole religious life was, in fact, connected with this place, although he went to a foreign land. Because of the importance of his work, we shall be justified in transcribing the whole of it, though it is long.

"JUDSON DWIGHT COLLINS, Superintendent of the China Mission, was born in the town of Rose, Wayne County, N. Y., and came to Michigan when eight years of age. He was blessed with an early religious education, which secured his youth from vicious habits, and eventuated in his conversion, under the Gospel ministrations of Rev. E. H. Pilcher, at the age of fourteen, when he united with the Methodist Episcopal Church. Love of learning seemed to be an inherent principle of his nature, and manifested itself in persevering, successful efforts to obtain a sound collegiate education. He entered the Michigan University at its first organization, in 1841, and graduated, with high honors, with its first class, in 1845. In college he maintained his Christian integrity, and, by his uniform piety, his well-governed life, and consistent efforts to promote the interests of religion, commanded the respect and excited the admiration of his friends and associates. He labored efficiently as Bible distributor, Sabbath School superintendent, class-leader, exhorter, and local preacher. On his graduation, he was appointed a teacher in the Wesleyan Seminary, at Albion, for one year. He was received on trial in the Michigan Conference in September, 1846, and at this Conference he was appointed to Tompkins Circuit, with the expectation of receiving an appointment as missionary to China, which he did in the spring of 1847, when he immediately set out for the field of his future labors, where he arrived in August of the same year. During three years and nine months, which comprised the time of his stay in China, he devoted himself to his work with a zeal and earnestness that knew no limits but his ability and strength. But his robust and vigorous constitution yielded to the unfriendly influences of the climate, and a severe attack of disease brought him nigh to the grave, so that, when the state of his health permitted it, in accordance with medical advice, he returned to his native land— to regain his health, as he fondly hoped, for the prosecution of his work in that great empire of idolatry, but, alas! to suffer and die. He reached Michigan in time to visit his brethren of the Conference at the session of 1851, when the entire change wrought in his appearance, the emaciated look, above all the joy and tenderness with which he greeted them, melted them to tears. For eight months he patiently suffered the will of God, though his grief at the thought that he would no more return to China to prosecute his missionary labors, was more painful than the prospect of death, and, in May, 1852, at his father's house in Lyndon, Washtenaw County, Michigan, surrounded by his friends, and amid the sweet associations of home, he quietly passed away from the scenes and toils of earth to the infinite rewards and felicities of Heaven, at the early age of twenty-eight.

"Brother Collins was a man strong both in his bodily and mental constitution. This self-preparation for life's earnest work included physical as well as intellectual training. His understanding was clear, sound, powerful, though not rapid in its action. His reflective faculties were searching and comprehensive, ever reaching after principles, and tracing out their connections. His conversational powers eminently qualified him for imparting knowledge, indicating in their action logical thought and accurate perceptions, rather than descriptive fancies and rhetorical abilities. His speech was instructive rather than amusing, his language argumentative rather than eloquent. The entire structure of his mind was Saxon and philosophic, positive in its qualities, and high-toned in its sentiments. His capacities, in a word, were those of thought, of reason, of energy, of action.

"Brother Collins' religious character was of the highest order, combining the noblest principles with the purest affections. His was a manly, cheerful piety, an unwavering integrity of purpose, a lofty aim and one of action, harmonious attributes of excellence, elevated conceptions of duty, a heart fixed upon the CROSS, and a life radiant with purity. His Christian love was rich in its elements, essentially missionary in its character, intense and regular in its action; and his Christian faith was simple and majestic, allying his existence in blissful fellowship with the infinite existence of JEHOVAH-JESUS. His goodness of heart was truly great, and fruitful of all active virtues. In him was not only a brave, rational *perception*, but, also, a real consciousness of the 'beauty of holiness.'

"As a man, he was manly; as a Christian, he was Christ-like; as a minister, though youthful, he possessed elements of great ability and usefulness, and, as a missionary, he was a model. Having a stout physical frame, a richly endowed, well balanced mind, and a temperament susceptible of warm and high emotions, yet singularly free from rashness and excitement, had he lived to develop his mind and character in the missionary work, he would have been a star of the first magnitude in the dark heavens of China. Years before our Church established her mission there, while prosecuting his collegiate studies, he pursued a course of reading on China, preparatory to a whole life of missionary labor among its benighted millions, and his mind had no rest until it was actually surrounded by their darkness and misery. No temporary impulse led him thither, no transient, fervid feelings urged him to a life of toil in that distant land, but a permanent conviction of duty possessed his mind, one great idea of supreme service to Christ controlled his whole existence, and carried all his thoughts, all his affections, all his impulses to that extensive territory of heathenism, and his martyr-like attachments to his work were only loosened by death—to be transferred from the Cross to a crown of righteousness. In the very embraces of death, when Heaven was opening its glories upon his mind, his heart was with his brethren in the vast field of missions —*he preferred to die where he so earnestly desired to live.* As a missionary, then, we embalm and cherish his memory in our holiest recollections of human character and excellence. While the truth and love of Christ dwell within us, in our heart of hearts we will remember thee, JUDSON DWIGHT COLLINS. Thy name shall not perish, and thy beloved China shall be redeemed! Thanks to the INFINITE for the legacy of thy character and example to the Michigan Conference."

The foregoing tribute, written by T. C. Gardner, D. D., is but just and true, and we will add that our Church had no thought of establishing a mission in China, until, by his persistent applications to the Missionary Secretary, Dr. Dubin, it was thought to be a providential opening. He said that he *must* go, God had called him to it, and, if the Church would not send him, he would go, if he had to work his way as a common sailor. Still, he was willing to wait a proper time for the action of the Church; and his desire was accomplished. China is not forgotten by us, for two members of the Detroit Conference and one of the Michigan are there now.

The blessed and glorious work of Christianization, which is now making such glorious progress in China, is traceable back to that blessed revival in Ann Arbor in the winter of 1837-8. God called that young man, then converted, to go, in His name, and begin that work. It may be regarded as a singular fact that a son of Mr. Collins' spiritual father, in after years, should have felt himself called of God to go to that same empire as a missionary, and Leander W. Pilcher, who received a part of his education, also, at the Michigan University, son of Dr. E. H. Pilcher, is now laboring successfully at Peking, the capital of the empire. It is honor enough and compensation enough for a whole lifetime of ministerial labor to have raised

E. O. HAVEN, D.D., LL.D.

up two such missionaries for the redemption of China. What more grand and sublime in human life than to see a young man, such as Mr. Collins was, forsaking all the dear associations of country and home, to devote himself to the redemption of a fallen, idolatrous nation! What an honor to the Church in Ann Arbor to have furnished such a young man, converted to God and educated among them!

THE UNIVERSITY OF MICHIGAN holds so important a relation to Ann Arbor and the State, that it deserves a little special notice. It was located at Ann Arbor in 1837, and as soon thereafter as practicable was opened for students, and graduated the first class in 1845. There was no regular President or Chancellor elected until in 1852, when Rev. H. P. TAPPAN, D.D., LL.D., a man of very commanding mien, of large and vigorous intellect, of broad culture and profound scholarship, was unanimously elected to that post by the Board of Regents, and entered on the duties of his office. Being a man of large ideas, he at once set himself at work to enlarge the influence of the University, and so far succeeded, that during his term of eleven years, the University of Michigan took rank as the fourth Institution in the United States—a rank it has not lost; as his successors have not only sustained, but increased its reputation. He was succeeded by Dr. E. O. HAVEN in 1863, of whom a sketch is given below—who resigned in 1869. A period followed in which *Prof. H. S. Freeze* was acting President, and then Dr. JAMES B. ANGELL was elected to the office, and who still holds the position. The Department of Medicine was early established, and that was in due time followed by the Department of Law. This Institution possesses as many advantages for a thorough educational training as any in the United States. Dr. B. F. COCKER, one of the most remarkable men, intellectually, of the present age, is in charge of the Department of Philosophy, and is deservedly very popular with the students, and is exerting a very wide influence. He is the author of " Christianity and Greek Philosophy," and some volumes of very valuable and interesting lectures.

REV. E. O. HAVEN, D. D., LL. D., came to the State of Michigan in 1853. Born in Boston, Massachusetts, in 1820, of Methodist parents, and early converted, his precocity in scholarship led to his college education and he graduated at the Wesleyan University in 1842, at the age of twenty-one. He resigned the principalship of Armenia Seminary in 1848, and spent five years in the New York Conference. Even thus early in the ministry he obtained great popularity, and was in constant demand for dedications and anniversary addresses, and other special occasions. It was understood that the Regents of the University of Michigan were desirous of obtaining a Methodist Professor, and many of various denominations, in New York, recommended the election of Mr. Haven. He entered upon a professorship in 1853 and remained only till 1856. During these years, in addition to his faithful work as a Professor, he became known almost all over the State, by his sermons, lectures and writings. Among other things, he attended the State Political Convention in 1854, at Jackson, where the Republican party was named; and being called out, made an eloquent speech against the repeal of the Missouri Compromise, which was widely commented upon. As all the Regents were Democrats at that time, the party press urged that Professor Haven be at once dismissed, but the attempt was not made.

He left Michigan to take the Editorship of *Zion's Herald* in Boston, Massachusetts, which place he held till 1863. During these six years the variety of his duties and honors was remarkable. Besides the charge of the paper, he supplied feeble Churches as pastor, lectured, acted as a member of the State Board of Education, and was twice elected to the State Senate, and was, perhaps, the most widely known representative of his denomination in New England.

In 1863 the University of Michigan passed through its severest trial. Rev. Dr. H. P. Tappan, its first President, having served eleven years in that office, was much admired by many, and was bitterly opposed by others. An irreconcilable contest sprung up between him and the Board of Regents, and his place was declared vacant. At once the Regents, seeking a successor, thought of Dr. Haven, and unanimously elected him, and informed him of the fact by telegraph. Fortunately, as he afterwards said, he knew nothing of the facts, but supposed that Dr. Tappan had resigned, as he had often talked of doing, and that the Regents had, after proper deliberation, called him to this high and difficult post. He accepted by telegraph. Immediately after, meetings of the citizens of Ann Arbor and Detroit, and of the students, and of the Alumni, were called, all of whom protested against the departure of Dr. Tappan, and some of them formally requested Dr. Haven to withdraw his acceptance. He learned from the Regents that, if he withdrew, Dr. Tappan would not be reinstated, and he determined to abide by his first decision. He said he had no regard for the honor, but somebody must hold the office, and he was willing to try it at least six months, till a new Board of Regents entered upon their office. Already four other universities had offered him a presidency, and he was not anxious for himself whether he should succeed or should fail. Besides, a majority of the Faculties—some of them his old associates—anxiously asked him to accept the office.

Those only who were near the scenes could imagine the difficulties of his position for the first year. They will, probably, never be described, unless by himself. But in every struggle he seemed to gain an advantage. The new Board assembled, and, in spite of his offer to resign, and to sustain their action if they should accept it, they, at first, with only one dissenting vote, resolved to re-elect him, and, finally, unanimously resolved to sustain his administration. The very first year the University had more students than ever before, and, before the six years of his administration closed, the University reached nearly double the number of students, and double the income it had when he accepted the Presidency. Previous to that the State had never really aided the institution by money, except in an indirect way, and to a small extent. President Haven spent much time with every successive Legislature, and prevailed upon them to initiate the practice of granting pecuniary assistance to the University.

While in Michigan, Dr. Haven preached much every year, giving, at least, one course of Sunday afternoon lectures to the students, which were always largely attended. One of these courses of lectures constitutes the volume entitled, "The Pillars of Truth, or, Lectures on the Decalogue." His "Young Man Advised, or, Confirmations of the Bible from Philosophy and History," was published, also, while he resided in Michigan. His "Rhetoric, a Text-Book for Schools and Colleges," was founded on lectures given in the University.

He was prevailed upon to leave Ann Arbor to take charge of the Northwestern University, at Evanston, Illinois, by the urgent solicitation of the trustees of that university. During his three years Presidency over that institution he had his accustomed popularity and success. A Medical Department was added, a Woman's College established, and the institution assumed the proportions of a University. In 1872, Dr. Haven represented the Detroit Conference, as he did in 1868, in the General Conference, and he was unanimously elected Corresponding Secretary of the Board of Education of the Methodist Episcopal Church—the first time such an officer was elected by the General Conference. In 1874, he accepted the Chancellorship of Syracuse University, in Syracuse, New York. Though his residence in Michigan, in all, covered only about ten years, he was widely known, and left an impress on the history, especially of the University, that will never be forgotten. His name became familiar in all homes.

He represented the New England Conference in the General Conference of 1860, and the Central New York Conference in the General Conference of 1876. He was chairman of the committee that reported in favor of lay representation, and the adoption of the report carried that measure. He was also chairman of the Committee of Revision in 1872, and of Education in 1876. He was appointed by the Bishop, pursuant to authority given by the General Conference, a representative delegate to the British Wesleyan Conference of 1878, in which relation he will, undoubtedly, do great credit to his country and his Church.

Dr. Haven is a devout and earnest Christian, a genial companion, and a good friend. He possesses excellent executive abilities, as shown in his great success as President of Univerities. As a minister of the Gospel, he is clear in expression, refined in diction, lucid in thought, and eloquent in language and manner. He has shown himself to be worthy of the fullest confidence and the highest esteem of the whole Church.

REV. BENJAMIN F. COCKER, D. D., Ph. D., who was elected to the chair of Philosophy in the University of Michigan, in the autumn of 1869, was born in Yorkshire, England, in 1829. Of pious parentage, he became a Christian in his youth. When but a young man, he went to Australia, and entered into trade and business for a few years. He came to America and to Michigan in the spring of 1857. That autumn he was admitted to the Detroit Conference, on trial, and, in 1859, was admitted to full membership in the Conference. The following are the pastoral charges he has served with distinguished ability, viz.: Palmyra, Adrian for two terms, Ypsilanti, and Ann Arbor for two terms. At the Conference, in 1869, he was appointed to the Central Church, Detroit; but, having been elected to his position in the University immediately after the session of the Conference, a position which he accepted with the consent and advice of his brethren, consequently he did not supply the pastoral charge. Dr. Cocker has shown great ability, not, simply, in his high popularity in the professor's chair and in the pulpit, but in his authorship. His first effort was in the preparation of a chart of the Greek verb. This is one of the most complete and perfect things of the kind ever prepared. This was followed by valuable and able articles in Reviews. His "*Christianity and Greek Philosophy*" is a most valuable and interesting work. His "*Theistic Conception of the World*" is a deeply interesting volume. "The Uni-

versity Lectures on the Truth of the Christian Religion" is a most valuable work for young men.

These writings constitute a noble and enduring monument to his name. All this work has been accomplished, and this distinction attained, in a constant struggle with ill health. His indomitable will has triumphed over disease.

CHAPTER XI.

TECUMSEH—First Preachers—Society Formed—Names—Joseph Bangs—Wheeler—Cross—Silliman—Quarterly Meeting—Rev. A. Darwin—Presbyterian Church Organized—Revival—Protestant Episcopal—Baptist—Controversy—Remarkable Conversion—Statistics—YPSILANTI—First Preacher—First Society—Second Preacher—The Grove—Toils—Early Ministers—Elias Pattee—J. A. Baughman—1830—Two Young Men—Ira M. Weed—Minister raised up—Circuit—Station—First Quarterly Meeting—Present State—Presbyterian Church—Protestant Episcopal—Baptist—Statistics — KALAMAZOO — First Missionaries — Society Organized — Names—Other Churches—Extent of Circuit—First Camp Meeting — Circuit Curtailed —New Societies—Poor —New Members—Walter—Swayzee—Advance—Special Attention—Church Begun—R. R. Richards Retained a Third Year—Station—Entertains Conference 1848—Secret Societies—Bishop Janes' Sermon—No Disaster—Mrs. Davidson—W. C. Comfort—Statistics—J. Ecanbrack--Robe—NILES--Coston Visits-Felton Organizes Society—Appears in the List—Station—Conference Session—Incidents—Work in the Country—Biographical—G. M. Besswick—B. Cooper—Williams—Dissension—Other Denominations—Statistics—ROMEO—Methodist Society—Congregational—Baptist—Original Members—Revival—Additions—Church—Numbers—Name Appears—District—Revival Incidents—Southwell—Abel Warren—R. R. Richards—Others—Mrs. Pilcher—Sabbath School—Statistics—SAGINAW—Missions—Discouragements—Numbers—Conference Sessions—Other Churches—Biographical —B. Frazee—W. II. Brockway—O. F. North—C. Babcock—J. Hudson—Summary—COLDWATER—Statistics—Jas. Fisk — MARSHALL — Population — Rivals — Religious Services— Methodist Society Organized—Sidney Ketchum—Katherine Ketchum—Randall Hobart—First Love Feast and Sacrament—Increase—Revival—B. Sabin—Appears in Minutes—District—Conference—Bishop Hedding's Sermon—Second Conference—Supplies—Review—Presbyterian—Cholera—Other Churches—Spread—A. M. Phelps Incorporated—Educational.

TECUMSEH appears in our list at the Conference in September, 1831, through error, but, having been introduced, it has been continued, and regularly supplied. It is situated in the midst of a beautiful and fertile country, on the north branch of the River Raisin, about thirty miles west of Lake Erie. It is a beautiful and flourishing village. It possesses the advantages of mill power both on the Raisin and Evans' Creek, which form a junction at this point. The creek bears that name in honor of *Musgrove Evans*, the first settler here. This first settlement was made in June, 1824, and for some time it was the most prominent and important village in the county, as it was the first location made in the limits of the County of Lenawee. We have now to deal, principally, with its religious history, and not secular.

Rev. Noah M. Wells, a Presbyterian minister, who was exploring the country in the summer of 1825, came here and spent a Sabbath, and preached one sermon. Rev. John A. Baughman, was the first minister who made this a regular appointment; this he did in 1826. It was included in Monroe Circuit. Mr. Baughman was succeeded on the Monroe Circuit by Rev. George W. Walker, in September, 1827, who continued the appointment at Tecumseh, and organized a Methodist Society, or Church, in January, 1828, consisting of Josiah Wheeler and wife, Margarette Cross, Betsey Silliman, Mary Bangs, Mary Woodard, Isaac Bangs and wife, and three others whose names cannot be recovered. Josiah Wheeler was appointed the class-leader. He was a very good and earnest Christian man. Mr. Walker continued for two years, and was succeeded by Jacob Hill, and he by James W. Finley, in 1830, and at the close of his term, that is, in September, 1831, Tecumseh Circuit was created, taking a part of Monroe and a part of Ann Arbor Circuits, and taking in new territory on the west and north. Elijah H. Pilcher and Ezekiel S. Gavit were assigned to the new Circuit, the geography of which has already been given.

The Methodist Society here, soon after its organization, was greatly favored by the addition of *Rev. Joseph Bangs*, a very useful local preacher and brother of the celebrated Nathan Bangs, D. D. He immigrated to this place in the autumn of 1828. He was a man of a thorough Christian experience, and insisted very strongly on the possession of deep piety of heart. He was born in Bridgeport, Connecticut. He was converted to God through the instrumentality of his brother Nathan, who had been led to the Saviour while teaching school in Canada. Immediately after his conversion, he wrote his brother Joseph an account of his experience, occupying several sheets of paper. While reading this, Joseph was awakened to a sense of his sins and a need of a Saviour, and was soon after converted; whereupon he joined the Methodist Episcopal Church, in which he continued a faithful and honored member and laborer till his death, which occurred January 7th, 1848, aged seventy-two years, and having been a local preacher for forty-five years. He was licensed to preach as a local preacher in the latter part of the year 1802.

He never became connected with the Conference, but continued to work at his trade as a blacksmith and at farming, and preached as the occasion offered, which was quite frequent. Everybody liked to hear "Father Bangs" preach. He was universally esteemed in the community. While he was decided in his views of Methodistic doctrines and discipline, he was friendly with and charitable to all others. The doctrine of Christian purity or sanctification was his great theme in preaching, although he never said much on the subject as connected with his own experience, except in the following modest terms: "I love God with all my heart; the love of God casts out all fear, that has torment; I know the blood of Jesus Christ cleanseth from all sin." These terms express "the fullness of the blessing of the Gospel of Peace." At what precise time he entered into this experience, we have not been able to ascertain, but, probably, it was shortly after his conversion. His last sickness was very brief, and his mind was clear to the last. One says, "He was not as triumphant as some, but he was as peaceful as the close of a summer's day." His physician, who was somewhat skeptical as to experimental religion, and who had often heard him express his confidence of future bliss, when he told him there was no hope of his recovery, asked him how he felt about the future. "Doctor," said he, "I have not neglected that matter till this time. That [a preparation for the future life] was attended to long ago, and I have no fears." As he uttered this, a smile of joy lighted up his countenance, as if he already tasted the joys of heaven.

Mr. Bangs was a good and useful man, possessed of respectable preaching talents and a good share of ready wit. Many interesting anecdotes of this latter feature in his character might be given, but we will content ourself with the following one: The Bishop of the Protestant Episcopal Church, having preached in Tecumseh, and Mr. Bangs being present, was introduced to him as a Methodist preacher, and, having expressed his kindly feelings towards that Church, the Bishop remarked, "You ought to feel well towards *us*, and respect us, as Mr. Wesley was always one of us, and he was your founder." "*Yes*," said Mr. Bangs, "and *you* ought to think much of us, as you are indebted to him, under God, for all the religious life you have in your Church." So the matter ended.

It is proper here to say a few words in regard to the members of the original Society, as they, except one, have now passed away, or, at least, are not members of this Society. Josiah Wheeler was a small and somewhat eccentric man, but very pious and active as a Christian. Margarette Cross was a noble-looking and a noble-spirited woman, a true lady, from Ireland. She had been converted in her youth, and was well acquainted with Rev. John Wesley. She was now a widow. Her husband was a local preacher in Ireland under Mr. Wesley, and they had entertained him at their house. She was a woman of sound and consistent piety, always delighting to converse on religious experience. She was a very intelligent woman, and has gone to join the society of the blest above. Betsey Silliman was a maiden lady, and sister to Mrs. Rev. Joseph Bangs, and was a very active and faithful Christian. She married late in life. Before she died she made a will, from which the Superannuated Preachers' Aid Society of the Detroit Annual Conference realized about twelve hundred dollars. Her married name was Betsey Young. Mary Bangs was the wife of Alanson Bangs, a son of Joseph Bangs, and is, or was recently residing at Tecumseh. Of Mrs. Woodard, as of others, we have not been able to obtain any certain information. Isaac Bangs was another son of Joseph Bangs, and opened his house for services. The Saturday services of a Quarterly Meeting in November, 1830, which we attended, were held in his house. This small Society advanced in numbers both by letter and by conversions, but we cannot say how many members there were in the village at any time before it was made a Station.

The first Quarterly Meeting was held here in the summer of 1829, by Z. H. Coston, Presiding Elder, and the next by Curtis Goddard, Presiding Elder, and James W. Finley, preacher, in November, 1830. The love-feast in connection with the first Quarterly Meeting was not numerously attended, but was one of peculiar interest. Those who had come into the country from the East had expected to be deprived of such privileges for years, but, being supplied with them so soon, their hearts overflowed with gratitude to God for them. This gratitude burst forth in songs and expressions of thanksgiving.

Rev. Alanson Darwin, of the Presbyterian Church, visited Tecumseh in the fall of 1826, and preached, but did not settle here until September, 1827. Under his ministry, a Presbyterian Society, that is, a legal corporation, was formed in October of that year, but the Church was not organized until April 6th, 1828. The Church, at its organization, consisted of *ten* members, as follows: John Huyck and wife, William F. Finch and wife, Milla Ketchum, Euphemia Hillock, Emelia Holbrook, Maria Hixon, Mary Darwin, and Mary Metcalf. Mr. Darwin became their supply, and died here.

Various changes have taken place in this Society and in the pastorate, as in the other Churches. *Rev. Mr. Darwin* the first minister of the Presbyterian Church, died December 15th, 1831, aged 48 years. He was a very good man, and had a sound, genuine religious experience, but was not very popular as a preacher, as he was rather slow of speech. An extensive revival, for the number of the inhabitants, took place here, the season before his death, in which he labored efficiently. Rev. Joseph Bangs, joined with him in the labor, and was the most effiicient instrument in it. Over thirty joined the Presbyterian Church in one day. The Methodists also shared largely in the fruits of the revival.

Rev. Mr. Lyster, of the Protestant Episcopal Church, first represented that Church in this place, and organized a Church in 1832. The corner-stone of their church edifice was laid October 10th, 1833. This was the first church erected in the place. The parish was called St. Peters. They have not made very rapid progress, as they occupy the same church to this day.

The Baptist Church was organized April 10th, 1830, consisting of twenty-seven members, and now they have a good church property. They have been supplied with able ministers.

For the most part a very harmonious feeling has existed between the different denominations in this place, but there was one exception to this. In 1834, Rev. Thomas Wiley, of the Methodist Church, was in charge of this Circuit, and a Rev. Mr. Wells—not Noah M. Wells—supplied the Presbyterian Church. The latter gentleman pushed forward the peculiar dogmas of Calvinism in such a manner as to lead Mr. Wiley to preach against his views, and the matter was carried to such an extent that Mr. Wells gave him a challenge for a public discussion, which was accepted by Mr. Wiley. The day was set; the judges were appointed; the preliminaries were settled; and these theological gladiators entered the arena. The contest lasted for about two days, and excited a good deal of interest. Having occupied their allotted time in their alternate passes, the question was given to the judges to render their decision. The judges very prudently took time to deliberate, and so far as we know are deliberating still, for they have never yet found it practicable to promulgate their decision. However, it was conceded by some of Mr. Wells' own friends, that Mr. Wiley had the weight of the argument on his side, but they remained Calvinists still, for they attributed the failure not to the weakness of the cause, but to the weakness of their advocate. That is about the effect such controversies generally have on the public mind.

One of the most remarkable conversions that ever took place in this vicinity was that of Peter Davidson, now deceased. R. R.

Richards was on this Circuit in 1837-38, and during the winter held a series of meetings in a school house at which there was much interest and many were converted. Mr. Davidson was desired to attend, but he refused. He became so angry at Mr. Richards for holding the meetings that he threatened to flog him; but before he got ready to do this, the Spirit of God got such a deep hold on him that he felt this was his last chance for salvation. He had been a very wicked man. He submitted and was very powerfully converted, and became a very zealous Christian. It seemed as if he could not do too much for Mr. Richards.

The different denominations, according to the reports of 1876, stand as follows:

Methodist Episcopal	260	Protestant Episcopal	104
Presbyterian	375	Baptist	167

They all have pleasant, and some of them elegant churches and are in a condition to do good Church work.

About thirty miles west from Detroit, on the line of the Michigan Central Railroad, and located on both sides of the River Huron, is situated the beautiful City of YPSILANTI. It is the location of the State Normal School, and boasts of one of the best union, or graded schools in the State. Ypsilanti is only the successor of Woodruff's Grove, which was near by, and as the settlement was first called. The settlement of the country west from Detroit was very slow at first, because of the difficulties of passing the belt of low and densely timbered land surrounding the city. Still Mr. Woodruff and a few others had accomplished the feat, clearing a track for their wagons through a dense forest and black-ash swales, and had made a settlement here. They needed the Gospel and ought to be furnished with the ministry of the Word.

When and by whom was the Gospel of the blessed Saviour first preached in Ypsilanti? In the autumn of 1824, Rev. Elias Pattee and B. O. Plympton, then members of the Ohio Conference, were appointed to the Detroit Circuit. This was the only Circuit in the Territory of Michigan at that time. It embraced all the settlements, except on the St. Clair, as far as their time and strength would allow them to visit them. Mr. Pattee, that indefatigable minister, was not content with the plan of the Circuit as he received it —he was on the lookout for new places, and, as fast as he could hear of any new settlement having been begun, he visited it. In pursuance of this policy, as soon as the settlers here had erected their shanties, Elias Pattee extended his Circuit—came to them and preached the Word of Life—the blessed Gospel of Peace. This was in the month of May, 1825. He established a regular appointment, and organized a Methodist Church. This was the first regular religious service established in Washtenaw County. It was our good fortune to have been somewhat acquainted with some of the original members of the first Church organized in Washtenaw County, as the Phillipses, Phineas Silsby, and some others. We were also well acquainted with Elias Pattee, and have had the story of his first visit to Woodruff's Grove, or Ypsilanti, from his own lips. None of these original members now reside here, if any of them are living. Mr. Pattee was succeeded the next year, that is, in the autumn of 1825, by that earnest, active and very effective preacher, John A. Baughman, who extended his visits to Ann Arbor, where a settlement had recently been begun. The services were first held in private houses, then in school-houses, and then they built a small brick church down on the flat, on the northeast side of the river, which, in a few years, gave place to a larger frame one on the other side of the river. In the meantime, the Society had been greatly strengthened by Eleazer Smith and family, Justus Norris, Dr. Town and others.

We now turn back, in thought, to the time of the first sermon, and stand in the midst of the oaks of the grove, and hear them murmur: "What sound is this, so strange and new to us! These words carry in them civilization, progress, the extinction of the red man, the displacement of the natural forests and groves. They presage our dissolution; the woodman's axe will not spare us; we must be made subservient to the interests and pleasures of the white man, as we have furnished the cooling shade for the aborigines. But it is high honor to have heard these words, so full of life and comfort to the human race. The coming generations will forget us and our murmurs of praise to our Maker; but we will not complain, for he is best who best performs the work assigned him—the behests of Heaven." Oaks may have voices, if we know how to interpret them. The old oaks are gone, and those who first settled among them are gone also, and a new generation of men and things has taken their places.

The Methodist Society was organized in the summer of 1825. When we say this, it suggests the fact of great labor, toil, and suffering on the part of the ministers, for they had to find their way by blazed trees through the low lands and swamps. The nearest appointment was on the Rouge, about five miles out from Detroit. So the minister not only had to find his way out here, but he had to travel over the same bad road to return the next day. It is very difficult for those now residing here, and enjoying the privileges of the beautiful City of Ypsilanti, to form any just conception of the difficulties of a time when there was dense forest between it and Detroit; but so it was at the time of which we write. It was a little improved when we first came to Ypsilanti, direct from the mountains of West Virginia, in 1830. These things furnish but a faint idea of what difficulties the minister had to grapple with, in order to supply the Gospel to these few settlers in the wilderness. If he could have settled down and remained, after he once arrived, it would not have been quite so bad, but he was an itinerant, and had to retrace his steps, and come again. He must repeat his visits, and pass through the same difficulties, time after time. It required no little fortitude, as well as grace, to do this work. But men were found, having a sufficient amount of both, to do it.

Among the early ministers, we must not forget to mention Elias Pattee, the first, and John A. Baughman, the second, who visited this place to preach. These were as unlike as two men could well be, except in one thing, that was zeal—a zeal which carried them through all difficulties, and which impelled them to labor with great ardor. Pattee was tall, bony, coarse-featured, and well advanced in years, with very limited scholastic advantages, and without polish in the pulpit or out of it. Baughman was young, handsome, sleek, polished and educated, though not a classic, and refined in character and manners. The desire to save souls was to them both as a consuming fire. Pattee came here from Canada, and Baughman was from southern Ohio. Pattee would travel on a Circuit as long as he could get anything to live on, and then he would stop, and go to work and earn money, and would take the Circuit again. So he labored in the ministry, not for the money but for the salvation of lost sinners.

Mr. Pattee was born in Vermont, September 11th, 1784, and died in Iowa, November 5th, 1860. He experienced converting grace in the State of New York, in 1807, and six months after was licensed to preach, and joined the New York Conference. In company with C. Hulbert, a brother-in-law, and their wives, he went into Canada as a missionary. He was appointed to Bay Quinte Circuit, and Mr. Hulbert to Oswegotchie. The wives rode on horseback, and the men traveled on foot. It was a long and tedious journey, but they reached their destination, and performed their work with good success. After some years of labor in Canada, Mr. Pattee became connected with the Ohio Conference, and was a member of that Conference at the time when he was appointed to Detroit, and during this year visited Ypsilanti. He located in 1838, so that he was not a member of the Conference at the time of his death. He was a very good, Christian man, and always true to the Church. We find the following notice in Connable's "Genesee Conference," and copy it entire. He "commenced his itinerant career in 1807. He was large of stature, commanding in personal appearance, dressing in breeches, stockings and shoe-buckles, which costume, with his graceful, natural attitudes, set off his portly, symmetrical figure to great advantage; strong in lungs and voice, and, although dignified, zealous and emotional. He was regarded by the simple people of those days as a very powerful preacher. An authentic incident will illustrate this matter. An old Dutch brother, being interrogated as to the character of a Camp Meeting from which he had recently returned, said, 'It was a poor, tet, tull time, and no goot was tone till tat pig Petty come; but mit his pig fist he did kill te teivil so tet as a nit, and ten te work proke out.' The Methodists of that day were fond of the demonstrative." This was in his early ministry. His zeal continued, and his voice, even in family devotions, sometimes sounded like a trumpet. He did much good in his day. His great labors and excessive use of his lung power put him on the superannuated list at a comparatively early day. He had sufficient native talent to have made him one of the very first preachers in the denomination, if he had had proper scholastic training.

The next in order—Mr. Baughman—was born in Hereford County, Maryland, but removed to Ohio while quite young, where, at the age of nineteen years, he was converted, and joined the Methodist Episcopal Church. He joined the Ohio Conference in 1823. He labored, in all, twelve years in Ohio and thirty-two years in Michigan. Mr. Baughman was a man of great eloquence and power in the pulpit, and of untiring zeal; somewhat verbose in style, yet convincing in argument, and successful in his work.

The changes which have taken place in Ypsilanti, even since our time, are very wonderful. In the first week in October, 1830, two young men, well dressed, well mounted on horseback, carrying all their wardrobe and library in their saddle-bags, might have been seen, towards evening, riding into the new and scattered village of Ypsilanti, and inquiring for Eleazer Smith, with whom they expected to find entertainment, and from whom, when found, they received a cordial welcome. These young men had come, one from central Ohio and the other from the mountains of West Virginia, having been appointed together to Ann Arbor Circuit, which included Ypsilanti. They came around once in four weeks each, supplying preaching at Ypsilanti once in two weeks regularly. They were

Henry Colclazer and Elijah H. Pilcher, both of whom are still living and in the effective ministry. They were the only ministers who rendered regular services here at the time. There was, and had been occasional Presbyterian preaching, but, as yet, there was no Church organized of that faith. Rev. Ira M. Weed, a young Presbyterian minister, fresh from the Theological Seminary, came a few months after Colclazer and Pilcher, and established himself here, and, shortly after, organized a small Church, which has since become a very strong one. The Methodists, in their zeal to supply all the country, did not concentrate as much effort here as would have been desirable.

It seems like a very strange thing, and yet it is true, that up to this time, 1837, but two ministers had been raised up from converts in Michigan, so the third Methodist minister, who was converted in this State, was from this place. All prior to them were converted elsewhere and sent into Michigan to supply the work. This was Lorenzo Davis, who had been residing in Ypsilanti for some time as a clerk, in the employ of Mr. Mark Norris, merchant. He joined the Conference in 1837, and continued in the ministry for a number of years and then located. He was in the work for seven years, and located in 1844.

Ypsilanti appears in our Minutes as the head of a Circuit in 1831, and in 1837 was made a Station. In 1839, the first year that the members for the village were reported separately, there were 144, which were increased so that in 1840 we had 155 members.

The first Quarterly Meeting of which we have any knowledge as having been held here, was in the spring of 1831, Curtis Goddard, Presiding Elder, and H. Colclazer and E. H. Pilcher, preachers. It was a time of much interest, and people came long distances to attend it.

The Methodists now have a fine church and a most elegant parsonage—a very large and prosperous Sabbath School. The Annual Conference has been well entertained there at different times. The little one, in a half century and a little more, has become a mighty one, developing much vigor and healthful Christian strength.

Mr. Noah M. Wells, of the Presbyterian Church, preached here occassionally, but they had no regular preaching till in the autumn of 1830, when Mr. Weed came. A Presbyterian Church was instituted in July, 1829, informally, without Ruling Elders, by Rev. Wm. Page, of Ann Arbor. In October, 1829, Rev. Wm. Jones was sent out to this country as a missionary and he devoted his attention to the temperance reform, specially, for some time in Ypsilanti. Mr. Weed continued to labor among them as stated supply until in the autumn of 1834, when he was formally installed as pastor. This Church has labored, prospered—succeeded, and have a large membership with an elegant house of worship.

Protestant Episcopal services were occasionally conducted by lay readers and ministers from 1828, but no formal organization was effected until in 1830. They too have a valuable brick church.

The Baptist Church was rather slow in organizing in this village, now city, so they did not organize till in October, 1836. They also have a comfortable house of worship.

The statistics of the Churches, according to the reports for 1876, stand as follows:

Methodist Episcopal............474	Protestant Episcopal...............183
Presbyterian.....................455	Baptist......................... 447

The population of the city, which was chartered in 1858, was in 1874, 5,211.

KALAMAZOO, the county-seat of Kalamazoo County, was first settled in 1829, or, rather, Mr. Titus Bronson located or purchased the land of the General Government that year, and at once built a log cabin. This village is beautifully situated on a burr-oak plain, and is sufficiently elevated to be very pleasant. The beauty of the situation, with the advantages of water-power, for it is on the Kalamazoo River, soon attracted the attention of others, and Mr. Bronson was not long left in his solitary glory, for, in the rush of emigration westward, this location secured attention, and the settlement increased rapidly. It was early selected by the Baptist Church as the location of their denominational college and Theological Institute. The educational advantages have become very excellent, and it is a desirable place for residence. The State Asylum for the Insane is located here, and the Kalamazoo College is an object of interest. But it is not our purpose to do anything more in this direction than simply to furnish an idea of this locality; not to write its history.

The introduction and progress of Methodism—of Protestantism generally—is that with which we have to do specially. In 1830, Kalamazoo was included in the St. Joseph Mission, that being the name of the charge which included all this southwestern quarter of Michigan. But, in 1831, Kalamazoo Mission appears in our Minutes, with Erastus Felton as the missionary. The Circuit was thus named, probably, from the name of the river or the county, as the village of Kalamazoo was, at that time, called Bronson, in honor of the eccentric man who had made the first effort at a settlement. The most of the labors of the missionary were bestowed on the settlements on the prairies situated on the south and west of this. Still, he did what he could for the few people here. No Society was formed at this immediate settlement during this year, but he returned *thirty* members for the Circuit at the next Conference.

At the next session of the Conference, that is, in September, 1832, James T. Robe was appointed to this Circuit. He continued to preach here, but did not organize a Society during this year. He was succeeded by Rev. Richard C. Meek, in 1833, who organized a Society in the fall of that year, or in the spring of 1834, consisting of the following persons, as well as we have been able to ascertain, viz: Harrison Coleman, leader; Elizabeth Coleman, Julia Coleman, E. A. Coleman, Fanny Coleman, George Patterson, Rebecca Patterson, and Hannah Wood. The Society was much increased during the next year. This was the first organization of a Christian Church in this beautiful town. This, in due time, has been followed by the organization of a Baptist, a Presbyterian, a Protestant Episcopal, and a Congregational Church, each of which has a commodious house of worship.

Mr. Robe's Circuit spread all over the country, wherever there was a settlement springing up, and reached as far as Allegan. At the end of his year he returned *one hundred and fifty-six* members for the Circuit. But it is to be remembered, it took in a wide range of country, Niles and Allegan being included in it. This part of Michigan was included in the Indiana Conference from 1832 to 1840. *James Armstrong*, a man of great power in the pulpit, was the first Presiding Elder. The first Camp Meeting held in this part of the country was held under the presidency of James Armstrong and James T. Robe, on Big Prairie Ronde, beginning August 24th, 1833. It was a time of very great religious interest. In the autumn of 1833, Richard C. Meek, a young, unmarried man, was appointed to this charge. He still extended the bounds of the Circuit as new settlements were formed, and that was very frequently, as there was a wonderful tide of immigration, and he had no thought of concentrating labor at any point. He returned *two hundred and fifteen* members, but we have no means of determining what proportion of these belonged to the village Society.

Rev. James T. Robe was appointed to this charge, for the second time, in the autumn of 1834, and one more Circuit had been created in this part of Michigan, so that his labors were curtailed on the southwest, but all the northwest was before him. Kalamazoo, at the end of this year, only shows *one hundred and twenty* members, and yet the cause had advanced. Mr. Robe had formed Societies at the following places in this county during the year, viz: Genesee Prairie, Judge Harrison's, East Prairie, Comstock, Indian Fields, and Climax; but, by the division of the Circuit, the members reported are fewer than last year. Thus, from year to year, this place appears in the Minutes of the appointments, and men are assigned to it; but it is impossible for the present inhabitants to appreciate the privations and sufferings these ministers endured to lay the foundations for the privileges and advantages they now enjoy.

In 1839, we find two men assigned to this charge; but it was a four weeks Circuit, and Kalamazoo was supplied with Methodist preaching only once in two weeks. In the meantime, ministers of other denominations had come in, and were supplying services in their forms, and the people were not so anxious for Methodist preaching as they had been when there was no other. The Society was small and poor, and had to worship in a school-house. They, however, were much strengthened, this year, by the accession of two families by the names of Walter and Swayzee, who had considerable pecuniary ability, and several members of the families were members of the Church. They at once identified themselves with the poor and feeble Society, as they were in duty bound to do, without stopping to inquire how it might affect their respectability. Some of the would-be aristocrats wondered that people of their means and standing would be Methodists in this place. They, however, did not regard this, and went steadily on in their adherence to the Church of their choice, considering that, if it was not respectable, it was their duty to make it so if they could.

Mr. Walter, in his old age, became carried away with Swedenborgianism, and withdrew from the Church, but his wife and children remained firm to the cause. Mr. Swayzee continued steadfast in the faith and in his attachment to the Church as long as he lived, and was a useful man in it. He died, in great peace, in the summer of 1850. He was much lamented when he was removed to the Church above.

No effort was made to concentrate labor in the village until 1840, when R. R. Richards and R. H. Cook were appointed to this work. It was now determined to hold services here every Sabbath. It was constituted a half Station, that is, though the preachers alternated, one of them was to preach in the village every Sabbath. This was a move in the right direction, for no considerable success can attend labors only once in two weeks in a village, especially if there are other denominations existing, as there were in this case. This,

FIRST METHODIST EPISCOPAL CHURCH, KALAMAZOO.

then, is a step in advance—looking to concentration—a step from which there has been no receding.

The next year, that is, in 1841, the appointments stand as follows: James F. Davidson, Presiding Elder; R. R. Richards and E. L. Kellogg, preachers. During the preceding winter, Mr. Richards had bestowed considerable labor on the Church in the village, and held a series of meetings, which were attended with some degree of success, but still the Church did not have any great accession of strength, but they carefully husbanded all they had previously gained. The Presiding Elder of the District, which was now called Kalamazoo, located himself in this village, which added a little to the interest of the Church, as he could give some attention to it—more than if he were residing somewhere else.

Some effort was now begun towards building a church—a thing that was very much needed—indeed, it was essential to the prosperity of the cause. This effort was successful after a little time. But the advantage the Methodists had in being the pioneer Church had been so long neglected that it was found to be very difficult to recover what had been lost. Mr. Richards had done such good service for the two years he had been on this Circuit, that they were very desirous to retain his services in the village for another year, if possible. A little pardonable strategy was resorted to for this purpose. His health was not very good, so that it was doubtful whether he could do full work on a Circuit. Advantage was taken of this to place him on the supernumerary list, and he was attached to the Kalamazoo Circuit as such, with the understanding between the Presiding Elder and the people that he was to supply the village work, which he did to good advantage. The Circuit was now pretty well narrowed down, but still they returned at the Conference for 1843, *three hundred and forty-four* members; probably, however, less than one hundred of these belonged in the village.

In 1844, the charge was narrowed down to what might be called a Station, although the ministerial labor was not confined, entirely, to the village, but yet this was the chief point of his labor. The returns at the end of this year show *one hundred* members. This may be regarded as the strength of the village Society at this time, for the appointments out were in such proximity to the village as that they ought to have formed a part of the village congregation. The Methodist people have been very slow to learn the value of concentration, and so have lost a part of their strength by dividing up into small congregations. The cause advances a little every year.

The Society, in 1847, had become sufficiently numerous to think they could entertain the session of the Annual Conference, and an invitation was extended to that body to hold its next session in this place. Accordingly, the Annual Conference held its session here in 1848, Bishop Janes presiding, and it was magnificently entertained. On some accounts this was a memorable Conference, and deserves a little notice. Early in this session, a committee was appointed on the subject of secret Societies, so called. That committee made a report which prohibited the members of the body from joining or meeting with any secret society. This included Sons of Temperance, Odd Fellows and Free Masons. This report was adopted without discussion, those who were members of such societies choosing, at that time, to let the opponents go as far as they pleased. It had been agreed on, beforehand, among the members of the Conference who belonged to any of these societies, that, if the report should be adopted, one of their number should call a meeting of them all. Accordingly, when the time came for giving out notices, he announced that there would be a meeting of all the members of secret societies at the Odd Fellows' Hall, that afternoon, for consultation. They met, and drew up a protest against the action, denying the right of the Conference to interfere in that way, and declining to submit to such action. This protest was signed by them all, not a very formidable body as to numbers, to be sure. This was put into the hands of the Secretary of the Conference, to be presented to the Conference, and to ask that it might be spread on the journal at the proper time.

When it was understood that this course had been agreed on, some who had been forward in the matter, and had voted with the majority on the adoption of the report, promised that, if it would be withheld, they would move a reconsideration of the vote by which it had been adopted, and have it laid on the table. This was so far satisfactory that the protest was kept back, waiting for this promised action. But the last session had come—an evening session for the purpose of receiving the appointments—and the time was passing on, the business was completed, and no motion of reconsideration was made. The Secretary arose in his place, and announced to the Bishop that he had a paper to present, and proceeded to read the protest, and moved that it might be spread on the journal. This opened the discussion, which lasted till near midnight, and which resulted in the consideration of the former vote, and laying the report on the table. This is the only real discussion that has ever been had on this subject in the Conferences in Michigan. Every minister has his own opinion on this question, and so have the members, and the Conference has made no further effort to control the matter. This session very greatly promoted the cause of Methodism in this place. Bishop Janes preached on the Sabbath with wonderful power and eloquence. He said we should neither wear out nor rust out, but burn out in our work. Bishop Scott was then here, representing the Book Concern at New York, and gave great satisfaction. The visits of such men among us at that time left a very favorable impression on the public mind.

There are no very remarkable incidents to be recorded in connection with this charge; only, it may be well to say that the progress of the Church has not been without the usual trials and interruptions. It has met with its reverses, and yet there have not been any very strongly marked defections, nor any very peculiar ministerial latches or misconduct to bring a reproach on the cause. It is an interesting fact to know that, with all the liabilities of human nature to be drawn away from the right, we do not have to record any special defection in our Church at this place. Few members have been expelled, but several have been peacefully transferred, in triumph, to join the Church of the First-born in Heaven. Among those to be placed in this list is Mrs. Louisa Davidson, wife of Rev. James F. Davidson, who, at the time, was Presiding Elder of the District. She was a woman of a good mind, and possessed a meek and quiet spirit. She bore her sickness with much Christian resignation, and met death in triumph in the spring of 1845. She had buried four children, and left one living, but she, too, has gone to meet her mother above; so that Rev. Mr. Davidson now has a wife and five children who have passed on and are waiting for him in the Paradise of God.

Among the ministers who have labored here and have died, we may name WILLIAM C. COMFORT, a very devout and earnest and intelligent Christian. He joined the itinerant ranks in 1842, and labored very usefully and successfully in this work for many years, and his dust quietly sleeps in the cemetery here, awaiting the resurrection of the just.

We ought not to dismisss this place without furnishing a statement of the denominational numerical condition according to the reports for 1876. They stand thus:

Methodist Episcopal............546		Protestant Episcopal............313
Presbyterian...................325		Congregational............443
	Baptist............456.	

We introduce one other name in this connection, because he

was the Presiding Elder of the Kalamazoo District for one term. He was a short, thick, and venerable-appearing man—a man of very lively temperament and warm sympathy in all his religious exercises. He was very successful in turning sinners to God—seldom failed of having his charge in a blaze of revival. His early ministry was in connection with the Oneida Conference, and it was only in his later years that he served in Michigan. We here introduce the official memoir, as found in the Minutes for the year 1852.

"REV. JOHN ERCANBRACK died at his residence in Bronson, Michigan, March 7th, 1852, aged sixty-one years and eleven months.

"He was converted to God in early life, and joined the Methodist Episcopal Church. He entered the Christian ministry in 1817, and continued in the same until death.

"In his various fields of labor, and in the different stations which he occupied in the Church of God, he acquitted himself honorably and usefully; and his name is as ointment poured forth. Few men in western Michigan have been more beloved than this venerable Father in Israel. He emphatically loved to preach the Gospel. *He died in peace and holy triumph.*"

This is a brief, but a very expressive memoir. His labors were all in the western half of the State. He served one term, of four years, on Kalamazoo District.

We take the liberty of introducing, now, a brief notice of one who was connected with this place in the beginning, and to whom we have been indebted for much information of the early history of religious work in this part of the State, and whose charge once included all the settlements north of the St. Joseph River and west of Battle Creek. He visited the first settlements in Allegan County, and opened the way for the labors of William Todd, deceased, and F. Gage, who still lives to labor. Many will be pleased to find an engraving of this early pioneer, which we have great satisfaction in presenting.

REV. JAMES T. ROBE was born in Woodbridge, New Jersey, April 12th, 1807, but removed with his father's family to Cumberland County, Pennsylvania, in 1809. He was brought to an experience of the renewing power of Divine grace, and joined the Methodist Episcopal Church, when about fourteen years of age. He removed thence to the State of Indiana in 1830. There he was licensed to preach, and joined the Conference, in 1831, and was appointed as junior preacher on Wayne Circuit, Wayne County, Indiana. In the fall of 1832, he was appointed to the Kalamazoo Mission, as before noticed.

Your's truly
James T. Robe

Mr. Robe was the first minister of any denomination who preached in Kalamazoo. It was then called Bronson, after the proprietor, Mr. Titus Bronson, in whose house he preached. In the winter of 1832-3, he had a very blessed revival on Prairie Ronde, and, in the winter of 1834, he had a good work in Kalamazoo, in which several precious souls were converted and added to the Lord.

Mr. Robe has lived to see Kalamazoo grow from a few shanties to be the largest village, it is said, in the world; for, while other places of even less population have taken on city government and city airs, this has been content to be a village. We may say, in passing, that it is one of the most beautiful and thriving places in all the country, and is surrounded by a farming country of unsurpassed beauty and fertility. He has the proud satisfaction of having laid the foundation of its religious prosperity, though now laid aside from the active ministerial work by reason of age and infirmity—infirmity superinduced, no doubt, by his pioneer labors, and he now resides in Kalamazoo. He has lived to see the little Society he organized grow to the number of 560 members, and have a Church worth $50,000, free from all debt. This is only one branch of the Christian Church which has sprung up; for there is no town in the West better supplied with Churches whose courts are better filled with attentive listeners on each Sabbath day. Mr. Robe is a devoted Christian man, and has been an able, efficient and useful minister.

Among the new appointments appearing in our list, in the year 1836, is NILES, a town situated on the St. Joseph River at the point where the Michigan Central Railroad crosses that river, and is the principal town in Berrien County. It is sufficiently varied, with hill and dale—with depressions and elevations—to give it a very pleasing variety to the eye. It has a population of about five thousand. It is but a few years, comparatively, since this was a hunting-ground for the wild Indians. How applicable are the following strains:

> " Art hovering o'er thy once wild home,
>   Poor old man's spirit, now
> Where thy free nature loved to roam
>   Like bird from bough to bough!
> 'Who mourns for Logan?' Oh, not one!
>   Ah! brave and stalwart chief,
> 'Twas phrenzy to thy soul that none
>   O'er thee should bow in grief."

The red men have passed away—they have gone, and the works of art are reared where they roamed so free. We have no laments for the changes which have taken place, only that the aboriginal occupants have been so nearly extinct. It is fitting that the arts and advantages of a Christian civilization should take the place of the savage state. Wrongs may have been perpetrated on them in bringing about this change, because all men are not governed by the law of right, but the change itself is right. It is manifest that Providence never intended these fertile lands to remain mere hunting-grounds for savages.

Niles was laid out as a village, as recorded in the Register's office of Lenawee County in 1829, and settled, mostly, by people from Ohio and Virginia. The first footsteps of the first settlers had scarcely become cold before the ministers of the new and everlasting covenant were found among them, with their messages of love and mercy, warning the ungodly and encouraging the pious. The pedagogue soon followed, to assist in intellectual culture.

In May, 1829, Rev. Zarah H. Coston, who was then Presiding Elder of Detroit District, made a trip into this part of the country, visiting all the settlements, and came as far as Niles. He preached in the house of a Friend Quaker a few times—found a few members of the Methodist Church scattered here and there in the wilderness, but did not organize a Church, because he did not, then, find any one suitable for class-leader. He, however, made arrangements to have a preacher sent into this part of the country, who came on in the autumn, and gathered up the scattered sheep. It was included in the St. Joseph Mission, and Erastus Felton was the preacher. He organized a small Society in the spring of 1830. The beginning was very feeble, and, being visited only once in four weeks, they did not grow very rapidly.

The power of the Gospel has been seen in its renewing influence in this community, and gracious manifestations have been enjoyed—seasons of precious revival. A goodly company have already been gathered home, to sing before the Throne the "song of Moses and the Lamb," while others are left to labor and rejoice below. The few have expanded into a numerous and flourishing Society, and they have a large and beautiful church in which to worship.

Niles appeared, first, in the list of the appointments of the preachers in 1836, with Thomas P. McCool as preacher; it was then in the bounds of the Indiana Conference. The Circuit then, and for several years after, was quite extensive, but, with the growth of the surrounding country and the increase of the town, it was narrowed down, till it came to be a Station in 1843, with Ransom R. Richards as the stationed preacher. At the end of this year they numbered *one hundred and ten* members. This is the first report we have for the village alone. It became the head of the District in 1860, which is now ably filled by James W. Robinson.

The town had become sufficiently large and the Church sufficiently numerous to warrant inviting the Michigan Conference to hold its session here in 1852. It was so held that year. Bishop Scott presided. The session was one of mournful interest, as two of the members had died during the year. Rev. John Ercanbrack and Judson D. Collins had been called from labor to the refreshments on high by the Master of Assemblies, and a funeral sermon was preached for each; for the first by Rev. John A. Baughman, and for the second by Rev. C. T. Hinman. The latter was published. The session of the Conference was profitable for our cause in the town.

The following incident, which occurred here, though in no way connected with Protestantism, will be tolerated by all, and read with interest by some, as showing that no reliance can be placed in clairvoyance. The circumstance, at the time it occurred, created a good deal of stir in the community for some weeks, and was thought to be rather a serious affair. The substance of it was this: A farmer came in from the country, a few miles, with his team, and put up at a hotel; and suddenly disappeared, leaving his team, no one knowing how or why he had disappeared. Suspicions of foul play—murder and robbery—soon became rife, and, on examination of the premises, it was thought signs of violence and of his death were found, but not enough to warrant the arrest of any one. As no satisfactory clew to the whereabouts of the man could be found, resort was had to mesmeric clairvoyance. Now, it was reduced to a certainty that the man had been murdered, and his body thrown into the river. Forthwith, the people gathered at the designated place, and dragged the river, without finding the body, but the clairvoyant persisted in saying that he was there, and at a certain place, but a little deeper than they had reached. A new search was made, with no more success, and the matter was given up—he was lost irrecoverably. Things passed on in this way for about three weeks, when the man appeared among them, as suddenly as he had disappeared, alive and well. He had been East, somehere, visiting some of his friends, and now returned to find himself mourned for as dead. He had gone off, in that way either from a freak of eccentricity or from a fit of insanity. He was entirely reticent on the subject, and gave no explanation of the matter.

There is another incident, having a more intimate connection with

Methodism, which we will narrate as it was related to us, and which will show how some people are influenced in their selection of Church relations. A young man, just from the East, settled himself down in this village, and opened a law office. He was not a professor of religion, but his mother was a Methodist, and he had always attended that Church; so, when he came here, as was right, he did not stop to inquire which was the most popular Church in the place, but commenced at once to attend this Church. After a few weeks, a young man came into his office, and, after some other conversation, inquired of him where he attended Church. He frankly said he attend the Methodist Church. "But," said the young man, "that is not the popular Church here, and it perhaps would be for your interest to attend somewhere else." "Well," said the lawyer, "where do *you* attend?" "Oh! I go to the —— Church, that is the *popular* Church here." "But," said the lawyer, "do you believe the doctrines of that Church?" "I don't know," said he, "for I don't know what they are." The lawyer then gave him a synopsis of the doctrines of that popular Church, and asked him if he believed them. "Oh! no," said the young man, "but that is the popular Church." Then the lawyer gave him a summary of the doctrines of the Methodist Church, and asked him what he thought of them. He said they were right, and he could believe in such doctrines. "Well," said the lawyer "I'll tell you what we'll do, then; you and I will go to the Methodist Church, and make that the popular one, if we can." The lawyer continued to attend as before.

Niles being the principal town in the County of Berrien, it is suitable to furnish a general idea of Protestantism in the county under this head. It is not necessary to tell how the itinerants happened to visit each particular locality. Suffice it to say that their ears and hearts were open to all calls, and they were ready, as far as possible, to attend to them, and Societies were organized by Rev. James T. Robe and others; and there are now several Stations and Circuits. Niles was not known in the Minutes of the appointments earlier than 1836. Prior to that time it was included either in St. Joseph or Cassopolis Circuits. Other Churches, in their order, have been established in all parts of the county.

Niles, of course, has been regularly supplied with ministerial workmen. Many of them are still living, and some of them have departed, and it might be interesting to insert here a biographical sketch of all those who have departed to their reward; but most of them will be mentioned in other connections, so we shall content ourselves with introducing a brief memoir of three of the early pioneer men.

REV. GEORGE M. BESWICK, who was appointed to this Circuit in 1832, and traveled it for one year, was born in the State of Kentucky, October 11th, 1811. His father was a member of the Methodist Episcopal Church, and settled in Indiana in 1815. George was early impressed with the necessity and importance of religion, and was converted in the fourteenth year of his age, and immediately united with the Methodist Episcopal Church. He was licensed to exhort in the sixteenth year of his age, and to preach at eighteen, and was admitted, on trial, in the Indiana Conference in his twentieth year, and appointed to a Circuit. He has filled some of the most important appointments in his Conference, as Circuit and stationed preacher and as Presiding Elder, and was a delegate to the General Conference of 1852. At the time of his death, he was Presiding Elder of one of the most important Districts in his Conference. Having nearly completed his third round on the District, he was attacked with typhoid fever, in a very malignant form. Early in the disease his brain became involved, and he was delirious most of the time. He had his lucid moments, however, and these intervals were improved in rejoicing, exhorting his friends, and comforting his family.

In Mr. Beswick, the virtues which constitute a Christian gentleman were harmoniously blended. He was a talented—a bold and original thinker. His motto, firmly adhered to, was to fear God and do right, no matter what the consequences might be. He had a sound, pure, Christian experience, and was a very useful minister. He fell asleep in Jesus in the spring of 1854. In this sketch we have very closely followed the Minutes.

We have now to introduce to the reader a tall, lank, pleasant-visaged man, who was appointed to this Circuit in 1832; one who belonged to the son-of-consolation class, whom everybody would esteem for his mild goodness, and would respect for his evident sincerity; one who always wore the old-fashioned, round-breasted coat, and who would be taken, at first sight, for a Methodist preacher of the olden time; not that there is any virtue in the cut of a coat, but, for many years after the fashion changed, and other men wore coats cut in another style, the Methodist preachers adhered to this fashion of Continental times, and some of them, with just as much sincerity as that Quarterly Conference in the vicinity of Pittsburgh, who voted that "they would do all they could to put down the ungodly practice of wearing suspenders," would have voted to put down the ungodly practice of wearing coats of any other cut. The ministers of this denomination were distinguished in this way for a long time. The subject of this sketch held on to the faith and practice of the fathers in this respect. The following is the memoir, taken from the Official Minutes of the Ohio Conference, to which he belonged, for the year 1846:

"REV. BENJAMIN COOPER died at his residence, in Hancock County, Indiana, May 13th, 1846. He was born in Perry County, Ohio, June 3d, 1802, to which place his parents had removed a short time before his birth. His parents were pious members of the Methodist Episcopal Church. Amongst all the disadvantages of a new settlement, his father, Joseph Cooper, succeeeded in bestowing upon his children a religious education. Benjamin was a bright example of early piety. Being given to studious habits, he acquired a good English education. When a young man, his sober deportment would have done honor to one of gray hairs. He loved the society of the aged and the upright rather than that of the young and frivolous. In a word, he dared to be singular in order to be wise and good. He had a great amount of retiring modesty, perhaps to a fault; for, when God called him to the work of the ministry, had not his brethren pushed him out, he would, no doubt, have hid his useful talents 'in a napkin.' But the Church, which is as good, and, perhaps, a better judge of a young man's gifts than himself, gave this young man license to preach, and recommended him to the Ohio Annual Conference, to be received on trial as a traveling preacher. In 1827, he was admitted on trial, and appointed to Mansfield; in 1828, Pickaway; 1829, to Huron [Michigan]; 1830, St. Clair; 1831, St. Joseph [which included Niles]; 1832, Brush Creek; 1833, Bainbridge; 1834 and 1835, Rushville; and in 1836 was superannuated.

"He traveled all these Circuits with honor to himself and usefulness to the Church; for, at all times and in all places, he breathed the spirit of the Gospel he preached, and discharged the duties it enjoined. No man, in his proper mind, could spend an hour in his society without being benefitted; for in his life he had a living comment on the Gospel of Christ. But the Being, Whose ways 'are past finding out,' permitted this good man to lose his health in the midst of his usefulness. He, therefore, asked and obtained a superannuated relation to his Conference, in 1836. In this relation he spent the balance of his life; but, judging it best for himself and family, he sold his patrimonial inheritance in this State, and moved to Indiana, where he continued to preach, as his health would permit.

until the Lord and Master came to call him home. When approaching the valley of the shadow of death, he said: 'My confidence is firm. Jesus Christ came into the world to save sinners. He saves me; saves me from all sin; saves me now.' To a young minister he said, 'Go, young man, and preach Jesus to a lost world.' Then, lifting his eyes to Heaven, and his countenance beaming with unearthly grandeur, he said: 'O Death, where is thy sting?' He has, doubtless, joined the General Assembly and Church of the Firstborn.

"Brother Cooper was a man of sound mind, his preaching talents were respectably good, his deportment was sober and dignified, and his spirit was as sweet as a newly blown flower."

There is something grand and beautiful in the experience and course of life of such a man as this. He not only shows himself to be sincere, but, by the sweet serenity of his life, shows that his religion accomplishes what it purposes—it makes him pure and happy. To see a man lay aside the selfishness which adheres so strongly to our natures—sacrifice the pleasures of home and the hope of worldly gain and of worldly honor—devote himself, unceasingly, as long as his physical energies hold out, to the moral reformation and elevation of his fellow-men, is most sublime; it is more—it is noble, God-like. But this was what Mr. Cooper did, and what every faithful minister does when he becomes an itinerant, and devotes himself, perseveringly, to his ministerial duties and work. The same nobility and God-likeness attaches to every faithful Gospel minister of any denomination.

One other case will be introduced here because Niles and Kalamazoo, each for one year, were the only appointments he ever supplied in Michigan. The rest of his itinerant life was spent in Indiana. He was appointed to Niles in the autumn of 1837. The memoir is taken from the Minutes of the Indiana Conference for 1841.

"REV. SANFORD S. WILLIAMS was born of religious parents, in Hamilton County, Ohio, where he was religiously brought up, called to the ministry, and finished his earthly sufferings. The precise date of his birth cannot be ascertained. In the year 1834, he was licensed to preach the Gospel, and admitted, on trial, in the Indiana Conference, at its session in Centerville, the ensuing autumn. His first appointment was to the charge of Versailles Circuit, where he labored with acceptability and usefulness. After this he traveled, successively, the Kalamazoo Mission, Greenville, Niles, and Vevay Circuits, and, lastly, Pipe Creek Mission, where he greatly endeared himself to his people, and left seals to his ministry. Toward the close of the year 1840, while zealously engaged in the labors of his Mission, his health failed him, though he did not retire from the work till the ensuing session of the Conference, at which time he was compelled by affliction to ask for, and obtained a superannuated relation. From Conference he returned to his father's house in Hamilton County, Ohio, where he continued to suffer, under the ravages of pulmonary consumption, until May 1841, at which time he finished his course, and calmly fell asleep in Jesus."

What is more sublime than to see the Christian fall asleep in Jesus! Even Stephen, when the shower of stones was falling on him, fell asleep in Jesus, and furnishes an instance of sublimity not surpassed by any other. The death-bed scenes of Christians and Christian ministers, so calm and so glorious as contrasted with the departure of the sinner conscious of his condition, become occasions of exceeding interest and encouragement to devotion and holiness.

It is but right to remark here that the course of the Church, in this place, in its earlier stages, did not always run smoothly. Some dissensions have existed, especially on the subject of Church music; some wishing to have a choir, and others insisting on "*lining the hymns,*" and having no choir. Sometimes these dissensions ran so high as to alienate brethren, and retard the operations of the Church for good. These dissensions, however, have been long since buried, and at the present time they are enjoying peace and harmony—loving as brethren, and having favor with the people. It is now a wonder that there was ever any dissension in any of our Churches on the subject of choirs, and, even, organs to lead our Church music. It was confidently asserted that, if these things were allowed, we should lose all our spirituality, and that the glory of the Church, as an instrument in the conversion of sinners, and the sanctification of believers, would quickly depart from us. But these predictions have not been realized, for the Methodist Church has never had more power, in these respects, than at the present day.

Other denominations were introduced as the increase of population progressed, and have done their work. There may have been a little rivalry between the different Churches at times, but yet, they have, in the main, worked harmoniously, and have accomplished a glorious work for humanity. It is not specially important to state the precise time when these different Churches were organized, and, yet, it would be a matter of some interest to some, and we would insert these dates only that we have been unable to procure them.

The different denominations gave in their statistics for 1876 as below, viz :

Methodists	390	Baptists	214
Presbyterians	257	Protestant Episcopalians	341

In the same year that Niles appears on our Minutes, another place, in the eastern part of the State, appears for the first time—a place that is worthy of notice here because of several interesting incidents connected with it. The very first establishment of Protestantism in it was an occasion of very great interest. We mean Romeo.

ROMEO, a village of considerable notoriety in the northwest part of the County of Macomb, was settled, in 1823, by Asahel Bailey, Frederick Hoxey, J. C. Hoxey, Albert Finch and Ebenezer Kitridge, with their families. These were soon joined by others, making quite a settlement in a little time. Its growth has not been rapid but steady and healthy. It was made the location of one of the branches of the University of Michigan in 1837, and continued to be such as long as that policy continued, and acquired a considerable literary fame. The branch of the University was succeeded by the Dickinson Institute, which yielded to the union school in 1867.

The Methodist ministers, who are always on the alert to find and supply every new place, were not unmindful of this new town; so that, within one year from its origin, a Church was organized. Rev. Elias Pattee, who was traveling the Detroit Circuit, organized a Methodist Society here, consisting of *Albert Finch and wife, Joseph Freeman and wife, and James Leslie and wife.* Joseph Freeman, then an aged man, was appointed the class-leader. This was the first Christian Church organized in this village. This was done in 1824. No other was formed till in 1829, at which time a Congregational Church was instituted, consisting also of six members, which, on the plan of union, became Presbyterian for a time; and a Baptist Church was organized in 1846, consisting of nine members.

Of the *six* persons composing the first Christian Church in this town, not one remains to the present time. All have passed to their reward on high. Albert Finch and his wife both died in the year 1826 or 1827. They died broken-hearted because their little son had been stolen from them by the Indians, and carried away.

In the year 1826 there was a very powerful and extensive revival—extensive for the population—in this place. Most of the young people were converted, and joined the Church, and became useful members of Society. The work commenced under the labors of Rev. *Abel Warren*, of precious memory, and it was on this wise: He had given out the hymn,

"Plunged in a gulf of dark despair,
We wretched sinners lay," &c.

Two daughters of Captain Gad Chamberlain were standing together, and singing, when they came to the words,

"Oh! for this love, let rocks and hills
Their lasting silence break,"

the two sisters dropped the book out of which they were singing, and fell into each other's arms, and most earnestly supplicated for mercy. The feeling became general. The next evening, at a prayer-meeting, they both experienced pardoning grace. They both became ornaments of the Christian cause. One of these sisters married Rev. William T. Snow, who traveled this Circuit in 1829. The other married a Presbyterian minister, lived an exemplary Christian life, and has gone to her great reward, having died happy in the love of God.

This Church was strengthened, a few years later, by the coming of the Hoveys, of John A. Tinsman and family, and others, and by the conversion, in 1839, of James Starkweather, Martin F. Southwell and others. They erected a small church in 1839, and the basement of it was finished for use in 1842, and the body of the Church at a later period. In 1855, under the labors of Rev. George Taylor, the Church was enlarged and improved, at a considerable cost. Again, in 1867, they expended over a thousand dollars in renewing the basement and in other improvements. In the meantime, a parsonage had been purchased. Under the ministry of Rev. James S. Smart, the corner-stone of a new church was laid on the 30th of July, 1872. Bishop Haven officiated on the occasion. This church was beautifully finished, and dedicated the next year.

The little Society planted in 1824 has grown from *six* to *two hundred and ninety-one* in 1876, besides those who have gone out to strengthen the Church in other places, and those who have gone over to increase the Church triumphant on the other side of the flood. Among the latter may be mentioned the original six, John D. Holland and wife, Martin F. Southwell, Roxana Starkweather, Sarah Ann Tinsman, Angelica Chamberlain, James Starkweather, Mrs. Rev. E. H. Pilcher, and many others of whom time would fail us to speak more particularly, except one.

"Mrs. PHEBE M., wife of Rev. Elijah H. Pilcher, D. D., of Romeo, died at the parsonage, August 23d, 1866, in the forty-eighth year of her age. She was the daughter of James Fisk, Esq., of Coldwater. Sister Pilcher gave herself to the Saviour's service, and united with the Methodist Episcopal Church in Penfield, N. Y., at the age of twelve, and ever maintained her regular standing in the Church. In the winter of 1839 and 1840, she made a perfect consecration of her heart and life to God, and for nearly twenty-seven years consecutively she enjoyed the evidence of that perfect love that casteth out all fear. She learned by blessed experience that Christians may have a perfect trust in God, and that this brings constant peace. For twenty-four years she endured without complaint, even gladly, the privations and trials incident to the itinerant ministry. Many in the respective fields of labor occupied during that time, by her husband, will bear witness to the purity, wisdom and efficiency of her Christian life; her chief care was to secure the present favor of God by the prompt discharge of duty, and all the days of her appointed time to wait until her change should come. During her last illness, which was protracted and very painful, in patience she possessed her soul, never murmuring, calmly saying as she fell asleep, 'Lord Jesus, receive my spirit.' This was her last voluntary expression. So die none but those who first reckon themselves dead indeed unto sin. In the domestic and social relations she was what good natural endowments improved by education and early purified by grace, combine to make a true woman, a good wife, mother and friend. A bereaved family all cherish the hope of meeting her where sin and death are no more."

"JOHN RUSSELL."

She folded her arms across her breast and closed her eyes, just as if she had gone to sleep. The day before her death she was very triumphant, and for a long time shouted the praise of God aloud, so as to be heard all over the house. Her last moments were as a peaceful sleep, with the smile of heaven on her pale face.

Various seasons of revival have been enjoyed, out of which valuable men and women have been raised up, and some men for the work of the ministry. The work has not advanced without its contests and its repulses—repulses from the apathy of friends, and some times from the defection of those who ought to have been firm and reliable; still the church has grown and become strong.

Romeo was included first in Detroit Circuit, then in Oakland, next in Mount Clemens, and in 1836, it appears in the list of appointments with Arthur B. Elliott and Larmon Chatfield as preachers. But the name now represented a large district of country; indeed nearly all that is included in a Presiding Elder's District, at the present time. By the organization of new charges, the work has been so narrowed down that it became a Station proper in 1853, and it had now assumed so much importance, Methodistically, as to give name to a district; and Romeo District appears in our Minutes, in that year, and Jonathan Blanchard was the Presiding Elder, who continued for four years. In the enlargement of Districts in 1876, Romeo was absorbed in Port Huron, and the name dropped.

This church has been favored with many seasons of revival— many have been converted and added to the church. During these seasons some incidents have occurred which may be of some interest to record. On one occasion a man became so much wrought upon as to way-lay the minister to ask him to pray for him, that is, as the church was between his house and the parsonage, he went, at the close of the meeting, towards the parsonage and waited till the minister came along, and hailed him and asked him to pray for him. The minister took him home with him and talked and prayed with him—he was converted and afterwards became a minister.

During the winter of 1838-39, when James Shaw and R. R. Richards were holding a series of meetings in this village, which resulted in much good, after some degree of interest had been created, a few had been forward for prayers, and some had been converted; one evening a Mrs. Southwell was among the seekers of religion. Next morning Mr. Richards heard that Mr. Southwell, her husband, was very much enraged, and had made a declaration that in case he called Mrs. Southwell forward for prayers again, he would horse-whip him. Soon after receiving this information, as he was walking the street, he heard some one walking behind him with a quick step.

In a moment the person came up with him, and he saw that it was Mr. Southwell, when the following conversation occurred:— "Good morning Mr. Southwell." Mr. Southwell, greatly excited, responded, " Good morning," " Fine morning," said Mr. Richards. To which, with increased excitement, Mr. Southwell replied, " Yes," and immediately added, " You must not call my wife forward for prayers again; if you do I will horse-whip you." To this Mr. Richards simply replied, " I did not speak to your wife about coming forward. I gave a general invitation, when she came of her own accord. I shall repeat the invitation to-night, and in case she comes I should not like to tell her to leave." Mr. Southwell then replied " Remember what I say;" and they parted. Mr. Southwell bought his raw-hide, made preparations to execute his threat, and " nursed his wrath to keep it warm."

That evening Mr. Richards gave the invitation as usual, and

Mrs. Southwell was again at the altar, deeply distressed on account of her sins. Next morning, as Mr. Richards was walking the street, he saw Mr. Southwell making his way across the street after him with great rapidity. He was soon by his side. When he came up with him, Mr. Richards said, "Good morning, Mr. Southwell; this is a lovely morning"—looking, at the same time, how he might ward off the blow that he expected would be attempted. Mr. Southwell made no reply to the salutation, but walked on with him for some distance, and, it is said, he had his whip concealed under his coat. At length he said, " Mr. Richards, I should like to have you go with me to my house, and talk with my wife." "I thank you," said Mr. Richards; "it will afford me great pleasure to do so."

They immediately turned about, and went in the direction of his house. "Surely," thought Mr. Richards, "the lion has become changed into the lamb." Mrs. Southwell not being in the parlor when they arrived, they sat down and conversed together until she came in, though Mr. Richards thought it not advisable to say anything to him, just then, about his own soul. Presently Mrs. Southwell came in, whereupon, Mr. Richards, turning to Mr. Southwell, said, "If it be your pleasure that I should converse with Mrs. Southwell, I shall do so, but I do not choose to do so unless it meets with your approbation. To this he replied, " It is my desire that you should talk with her." Mr. Richards then conversed freely with the lady, in his presence, on the subject of salvation, pointing her to the Lamb of God that taketh away the sin of the world, after which they engaged in a season of prayer, when he observed that Mr. Southwell quickly fell upon his knees, doubtless for the first time in the presence of any human being.

After prayer, Mr. Richards bade them good morning, without having said a word to him on the subject of religion. But Mr. Southwell followed him out, when he thought it was time to press the claims of the Gospel upon him, which he did. He found that, like Saul, while "breathing out threatening and slaughter," he had been slain by the Spirit—that he had kept up his opposition to God and His cause, and his determination to flog Mr. Richards, until about one o'clock that morning, at which time he came into his house, having been out till that hour engaged in sawing wood, not from necessity, but from anger and spite; and frankly confessed to his wife that he was a sinner, and must be saved by the mercy of God in Christ Jesus, or be lost forever. He and his wife were soon happily converted, and rejoiced in the knowledge of sins forgiven, and joined the Church.

Mr. Southwell lived for several years an ornament to the Church, filling the offices of trustee, steward, and class-leader with great fidelity and usefulness; and, though called, in the discharge of his duties, to mingle much with the world, having held the office of Sheriff of the county for some time, he always maintained a close walk with God, and sustained the purity of the Christian character, He died, in the full and certain hope of eternal life, in the summer of 1844.

We here introduce a short memorial notice of some of the men who have been identified with the work here. *Abel Warren* is a name ever dear to those who knew him. He was known all through this region of country as "Elder Warren." His was a name that was always pronounced with pleasure, and was a synonym for sympathy and kindness—a name that will live in the hearts of many while they live, and multitudes will come up at the Judgment to call him blessed. He was called on to bury the dead, and marry the living, more frequently than any man in the country during his time.

ABEL WARREN was born in Hampton, Washington County, New York, August 3d, 1789. He was converted to God, and joined the Methodist Episcopal Church in Covington, Genesee County, New York, in March, 1817. He came to Michigan, and settled in the town of Washington or Shelby, in Macomb County, in 1824. He was licensed to preach at a Quarterly Meeting held in Detroit in June, 1825, at which time there were not more than *fifteen* members of the Church present at the love-feast on Sabbath morning. He had visited the Territory of Michigan in 1820, and went up as far as Pontiac, but did not settle here till the date named. He served the Church for several years as class-leader, during which time he often felt impressed with a sense of duty to preach. He received license to exhort four years after his conversion. He was a soldier in the War of 1812, and was at the battle on Queenston Heights, and was wounded and taken prisoner. We will give his religious experience in his own words, as he communicated it to us. He says:

"With regard to my religious experience, I have to say that I lived a life of sin until my twenty-ninth year; but, during that part of my life, I was often the subject of deep and frequent convictions. Sometimes I experienced this when thrown among those who were full of frivolity and wickedness, but more particularly in the hour of imminent danger. Especially can I call to remembrance the anguish of mind that seized me when on one occasion it seemed certain that

I was being doomed to a speedy death by being swept over the Falls of Niagara. The terrible conviction of my sinfulness—my utter inability to stand acquitted before the Almighty, pressed upon me. I was overwhelmed at the thought of the folly and wickedness of the life I had been living.

"Also, on another occasion, in 1812, when on the Heights of Queenston, approaching the enemy, and when the carnage of battle was all around me, my heart was deeply pierced with the arrows of conviction for sin. As I heard the terrible exclamations of the wounded and dying, calling upon God to have mercy upon them, and, for Christ's sake, to save them, and being myself wounded and a prisoner, I knew not but that myself, also, was soon to appear before the judgment seat of Christ, it affected me very deeply.

"I continued to be thus convinced of sin, and, yet, striving against those convictions, until the morning of February 28th, 1817, when the conflict ended, and I found peace with God. For three days previous to this, I had labored under mental agony altogether intolerable, and, on the evening of the 27th, I went to the barn to pour out my anguish of soul in prayer. On returning to my house, like Saul of Tarsus, I fell to the ground, and, for ten or fifteen minutes, lay senseless in the public road. At length I arose, and, on reaching the house, I said to my wife, I am lost forever. But I was not left long in this condition. I fell asleep, and, on waking in the morning, I found myself at peace with God, and with a heart full of love and praise." Thus was he brought into the liberty of the sons of God, which liberty he continued to enjoy for a long life. His religion was of the cheerful, happy type.

Mr. Warren always felt and manifested a very warm attachment to the interests of the Church, and, though no bigot, he always labored to promote the interests of this branch of the Church. He was a man of very respectable talents as a preacher, but it was his warm sympathy which gave him such a strong hold on the affections of the people. He always had a tear for the afflicted and bereaved, as well as a word of hearty good cheer for the joyous. He was very industrious as a preacher, and very useful, having labored so effectively for the revival interests of this village, at one time, that his name deserves to be embalmed in its records. He was the first man ever licensed to preach in Michigan. He was a man of sterling common sense. Being stricken down with paralysis, he was unable to say but a few words, but his reason was unimpaired. A little while before his departure—several Christian friends standing near his bed—he manifested a desire to have singing and prayer. They sung the hymn commencing:

> "O for an overcoming faith,
>   To cheer my dying hours;
> To triumph o'er approaching Death
>   And all his frightful powers."

During the singing, an air of holy triumph, utterly beyond the power of language to describe, sat upon his countenance. He waved his hand in token of the completeness of his victory. Thus, on September 5th, 1863—

> "Out of his late home, dark and cold,
> He passed to a city, whose streets are gold;
> From the silence that falls upon sin and pain
> To the deathless joy of the angel's strain."

Such was the end of one of the noblest and best local preachers we ever had the privilege of associating with. It was, indeed, a privilege to be associated with him; he was so full of love to God and man, and of kindly, good words, that one could hardly be with him without feeling a strong desire to imitate his Christian virtues, and to join with him in his Christian work. His memory is like ointment poured forth.

REV. RANSOM R. RICHARDS, who has already been mentioned in connection with a revival scene, died, on the 13th of July, 1872, at Hudson, in this State, in the faith and peace of the Gospel. He was admitted into the Michigan Conference in September, 1837. He was a very active and useful preacher—was successful in Circuits, Stations, and Districts as Presiding Elder. Many were converted to God, and joined the Church, under his ministry. He did much for the promotion of the interests of the Church in conducting revivals, and building churches and parsonages. He was liberal himself, and succeeded in calling forth the liberality of others for such enterprises. He died at his post, having preached in his charge on the second of June, 1872, for the last time. In a month and a week he died in the midst of his people, mourned and lamented by them all. He was a true and noble-hearted Christian gentleman, and a reliable friend. His last days were cheered by the consolations of that religion which he had so successfully preached to others. Mr. Richards was a man of commanding, noble bearing, of fine preaching abilities, and always true to the interests of the Church, which never suffered in his hands. He left a wife and one small child— a son.

It would be interesting, had we space to so devote, to speak of

Josiah Breakman and others of the noble men who have labored in this charge—who maintained the faith, fought a good fight, and finished their course with peace and joy, and have gone to their heavenly home.

The work of a Church is not always to be determined by the number included within its fold, for these are constantly changing, but by the experience and religious character of those under its care, or, more properly, composing its body, and by the efforts made to instruct and save the young. Apply these tests to this Church. At the time of its organization there was no Sabbath School existing, but, for many years past, this work has been actively prosecuted, with high success.

According to the last report—for 1876—there was one school, having *twenty-seven* officers and teachers and *two hundred* scholars, with all the appliances necessary for the interesting and successful prosecution of their work. But, in the passing years, this school has sent out many to be laborers in other parts of the great field of Christian work, and many have been saved from sin. The Sabbath School work forms a very interesting feature in its work.

The number of members and probationers, according to the report for 1876, was *two hundred and ninety-one*, having a church valued at $45,000, and a parsonage valued at $1,500. These figures show a very successful growth. The other churches have been named, but we here subjoin the statistics for 1876. We place them in the order of organization.

Methodists..........................291 | Congregationalists............... 200
Baptists...............................120.

SAGINAW is a name which represents a large district of country, known as the Saginaw Valley, in which is included the cities of Saginaw City, East Saginaw, and Bay City, with a number of villages. These cities and villages have grown up very rapidly, and have been dependent, mainly, on the manufacture of lumber, and, for a few years past, the manufacture of salt has been added to that of lumber. The prosperity of this whole region will fluctuate according to the state of the lumber and salt market. The agricultural capacities, which are not supposed to be very promising, have not yet been fully developed. Probably, when the lumber material has been used up, which will not be for many years yet, they will give their attention more to agriculture. For a long time after the settlements began in this valley, it was very difficult to reach them, as the country south was flat and swampy for many miles, but yet the ministers did penetrate the swamps, and carry the glad tidings to the few people settled here, at a very early day in the settlement. Many important Indian councils and treaties were held here.

In 1832, Saginaw Mission appears in our Minutes, with Bradford Frazee as preacher. He made some visits to the valley, but his labors did not accomplish much; and the prospect of success was so poor, as compared with the labor and expense, that it was dropped from the list in the Minutes, and does not appear again until the Conference of 1835, when it reappears, with William H. Brockway as the preacher. Mr. Brockway included Flint in his Circuit, and as many other settlements as he could visit once in four weeks. The people were poor, and lived mostly in shanties, and the minister found it very difficult to obtain shelter and entertainment for himself and horse. In 1836, Oscar F. North was the preacher, and, in 1837, Charles Babcock was appointed to this charge. In 1838, Jonathan Hudson was the minister. He attended to the Circuit, which still included Flint, for one year But Flint having assumed more importance than Saginaw, the latter was dropped, and Flint was substituted for it in the Minutes for 1839. Saginaw does not again appear till 1848. It now appears to remain. Societies were organized at Saginaw City, East Saginaw, and at Bay City; and, as these cities have grown, and the Church has acquired sufficient strength, they have been erected into Stations, and the villages into Stations and Circuits. For the two years, 1848 and 1849, Andrew Bell was the preacher in charge, and did good service. William Blades—father of Rev. F. A. Blades, so long and active a member of the Detroit Conference—a most excellent man, and a warm-hearted, sympathetic, good preacher, was appointed in charge in 1850, and served them well for one year. For the next year, 1851, Carmi C. Olds, a scholarly, excellent man, was appointed, and did faithful work for one year. Since then, with the growth and development of the country, the work has regularly expanded, and been divided, so that, in this valley, we now have sixteen Circuits and Stations and 1,497 members, with several fine and valuable churches, and having the necessary appliances for Sabbath Schools and other Church work.

The Detroit Annual Conference has held two sessions in this valley. In 1867, it was magnificently entertained in Saginaw City. In 1872, it was held in East Saginaw, and it was entertained to the entire gratification of the members of the Conference. Bishop Janes presided at the first, and Bishop Ames at the second session. These occasions were of great value to our cause in the valley. This degree of success has been achieved by much hard toil and many

THE COUNCIL AT SAGINAW.

sufferings on the part of the ministers who have been charged with the responsibility of carrying forward the cause.

We must not overlook or ignore the fact that other denominations of Christians are here, and have been from a very early time. They have their organizations and churches, and are doing a good Church work, and are worthy of praise for the efforts they are making to evangelize the people.

It may be expected, doubtless, as it is proper, and may be interesting, that we should say a few things in regard to the pioneer ministers of this valley, although we do not intend any lengthened biographical sketch.

BRADFORD FRAZEE, whose name appears in connection with this appointment when it first appears in our Minutes, was a young man of superior abilities, and he had acquired an excellent education. He was, indeed, an elegant and eloquent preacher. Still, he did not accomplish anything of importance in this charge. He remained but one year. There were some reasons for this want of success. One of these was to be found in the character of the population, that is, they were lumbermen—scattered in the woods, attending the mills, and running logs on the rivers. Men may be good in any morally lawful business; but when we separate men, whether young or old, from the associations and influences of home, they will throw off the usual restraints of society, and become, comparatively, reckless— less inclined to goodness. They become comparatively wild and ungovernable. Mr. Frazee was a man of a good deal of refinement of tastes and manners, and he found it difficult to adapt himself to the circumstances, and so to mingle with the lumbermen in their camps as to secure their confidence and good will. He could not lodge in their shanties, nor eat muskrats or salt pork with them.

Another reason was to be found in the fact that he devoted a good deal of time away from his charge in wooing and marrying a wife. It is lawful for a man to woo and marry, but it may, nevertheless, interfere with his ministerial success for the time being. There was philosophy in the Mosaic provision that a man should be exempt from going to war for one year after his marriage. If the circumstances of his charge had been such that Mr. Frazee could have taken his wife on to it, it would have made a considerable difference, no doubt, but he could not have found any home for her, nor could he get anything for her support; he had, therefore, to leave her with friends in the older settlements, and that divided his time and attention.

Mr. Frazee continued to labor in connection with the Conference until 1845, when he located, and went into Kentucky, where he and his wife both died, near the same time, a few years after. Having located, there is no official memoir from which we can derive any information as to the precise time and circumstances of his death.

WILLIAM H. BROCKWAY, whose name is connected with Saginaw in its next appearance in the Minutes, is still living, and has resided at Albion, under the shadow of the college, for many years, has been agent, and trustee, and President of the Board of Trustees of the college, and labored in various ways for its interests. Mr. Brockway did not confine himself to the Saginaw Valley, but took in the nascent village of Flint, and whatever other settlements there were in Genesee County. He performed the difficult and arduous labor faithfully for one year, and was relieved, and sent to Ypsilanti and Huron Mission. He was sent in 1838, to take charge of and develop the Indian Mission at Sault Ste. Marie and in the Lake Superior country. He was a very laborious and useful missionary for several years. For the last few years his health has been such that he has had to retire from the active ministerial work, and his name stands in the list of superannuates in the Michigan Conference.

Mr. Brockway was licensed to preach in the spring of 1833, and in the autumn of the same year was admitted on trial in the Annual Conference, and appointed to Huron Mission, which embraced the country below Ypsilanti, along the river, and extended out to Dearborn. He included the settlement of Wyandotte Indians near Flat Rock, where he had taught the Mission school the year before. He, in due order, was admitted into full connection, and advanced to the order of Deacon and Elder. He has done much valuable work.

OSCAR F. NORTH succeeded Mr. Brockway. He was a very modest young man, and one who did not seem to be very well adapted to the rough work of a wild, lumbering region. He was a most estimable man, and did very worthy work in the Conference for a number of years. He finally located, in 1847, and settled down at Pontiac, where he occupied a good position in the community, having filled the office of Judge of Probate for some time. He looked well to the interests of the Church in that place while he lived. He died in peace and in holy triumph some years ago.

CHARLES BABCOCK, whose name appears as in charge of Saginaw in the Minutes for 1837, was admitted on trial in the Conference in 1836; consequently he had been in the work only one year,

and was, at the next Conference, appointed to Waterville, on the Maumee River, in the edge of Ohio. We do not purpose to trace his appointments from year to year. He remained in connection with the Michigan Conference till 1844, when he was transferred to the Rock River Conference. He continued in the active ministry in that Conference till 1849, and then located, and disappears from our record. He was a man of fair preaching ability and a good degree of zeal. His piety was undoubted, and he had ordinary success in advancing the cause of true religion.

In 1838, JONATHAN HUDSON, an interesting and promising young man, just recently from Norwalk Seminary, in Ohio, and of two years experience in the ministry, was sent to Saginaw. The Circuit still extended southward, so as to include Flint and the surrounding country. Mr. Hudson had a very pleasing address, was very social and genial in his manners, and, for many years occupied a good position in the Conference, filling some of the first appointments. He located in 1847, settling down at Trenton, where he entered into business. When the War of the Rebellion broke out, he went into the army as chaplain to a regiment of cavalry, and did well. He died in peace, in the spring of 1876, after a long and painful sickness—finally determined to be cancer in the stomach—which he endured with Christian resignation.

It would be a pleasing task to speak of other men who have labored in this valley, but we cannot include all, so we have to content ourself with these few notices.

The summary of the different denominations, taken from their reports for 1876, in this valley, stands thus:

Methodist Episcopal..............1,497
Presbyterian...................... 667
Congregational......................406.
Protestant Episcopal............715
Baptist............ 838

COLDWATER, which appears in the Minutes of the Conference as the name of a Circuit in 1835, called a Mission, began to be settled in the summer of 1831. It was included in Tecumseh Circuit for one year, and in Calhoun Mission till this time. Mr. Allen Tibbits and Joseph Hanchett planted themselves on a small prairie, and laid out a village that summer. The former occupied a rude log house, which had been erected by some squatter, and the latter built for himself a more pretentious one, though of logs, for the logs were larger, and hewed flat, and the house was a story and a half high. The next season they were joined by a few more. A store and a postoffice were established. Shortly after, the county-seat, which had been located at a place called Branch, a few miles southwest and off from the main, or Chicago road, was changed to this place. Mr. Tibbits is living, and still resides in this city, but Mr. Hanchett is dead, and a memorial notice of him has already been given. From such a small beginning, it has grown to have, in 1874, a population of 4,330, and was incorporated as a city in 1861.

The Methodist Society, or Church, was organized in 1832, as before stated. In 1835 it received a great accession of strength by the immigration of James Fisk, with a large family, and several families of Crippens. The place and the Methodist Church had so increased that the Annual Conference was magnificently entertained by them in 1844. Bishop Hamline presided, and preached on the Sabbath with wonderful power and unction. The Church has been favored with many very powerful revival seasons, and they now have a beautiful and valuable brick church. It has also given name to a Presiding Elder's District.

Other Churches have been organized as the population increased and the exigences seemed to demand, and have erected commodious houses of worship. The status of the different denominations in the city is as below, viz:

Methodist Episcopal............476	Baptist.............................366
Presbyterian......................255	Protestant Episcopal............140

There was a time when the Spiritists were quite numerous, and had good hopes of carrying the whole place, nearly, or subverting or supplanting the Churches. But these hopes of theirs and the fears of some timid Christians have not been realized. The cause of true piety is constantly on the advance.

We will regard Coldwater as the representative of the County of Branch, and show what is the strength of the denominations in a population of 25,726, in 1874, premising that the villages and rural districts are well cared for by some or all of these denominations, besides some of the minor ones.

Methodist Episcopal...........1,329	Baptist.........................632
Presbyterian..................... 396	Congregationalist...............238
Protestant Episcopal......................180.	

So much has been said, in other parts of this History, in regard to this beautiful city, that it is not necessary to say more here. We will be allowed a memorial notice of one who did much for the Church in this city at an early day, which we copy from one of the city papers:

"DIED.—On the 11th of August, 1870, in the City of Coldwater, Michigan, at the residence of his son, JAMES FISK, aged eighty-two years.

"The deceased was born in Amherst, New Hampshire, August 4th, 1788, of industrious and pious parents, who, in the strict New England manner, attended to the moral and religious education of their children. Inheriting an excellent physical constitution, which became strengthened by an early life of activity and plain living, he developed into a man of rare physical and moral vigor. While yet a young man, he left his native State, and removed to Ulster County, New York, when in June, 1815, he married Miss Eleanor Ransom, the death of which faithful wife and mother preceded his by about fourteen years. Although always a believer in the doctrines of the Christian religion, he did not yield himself up to the Saviour, and receive pardon and converting grace, until he was about forty years old, but ever after he appeared to live as one who was 'redeeming the time.'

"This short but comprehensive record of his early history, received from members of his family, brings us to the time of his removal to Coldwater, in 1835—a pioneer in the settlement of the country. For thirty-five years he has been a faithful witness for the Master. The name of 'Father Fisk'—by which he was familiarly and widely known—had long since become a synonym for *religion*, with which his whole soul and body seemed to be permeated. Although he was a faithful member and founder of the Wesleyan Church in this city, yet no Church walls or creed could confine his great heart, so full of love for the Saviour and for lost and perishing men ; he was a welcome guest in all the churches. How often have our souls been borne up to the very gates of Heaven as we have bowed with him in prayer! How often have our hearts said, *God certainly hears such prayers!* He lived by *prayer*, and seemed to be a living example of the injunction, 'Pray without ceasing.' He was also a man of great faith; like Abraham, he believed God; like Stephen, he was full of faith and the Holy Ghost. He was also a zealous worker in the vineyard; rarely, if ever, for these many years, has he received and returned the salutations of the day, even, without speaking a word for Christ, kindly but earnestly. He ceased not, night or day, to warn the impenitent, and to entreat them to be reconciled to God. His theology was of a very practical character ; it was reduced to aphorisms and axioms so well stated as to need no argument to defend them. He seemed to enjoy a perpetual revival of religion ; when others were cold and indifferent, he was awake, and full of earnestness and interest.

"But the prayers of Father Fisk, like those of David, the son of Jesse, are ended. But they are the inheritance of his children and of the Church, and have won a revenue of glory for himself, his family, the Church, and for many a soul ready to perish. Verily, a prince and a good man in Israel has fallen. The loss is ours, but to him an abundant entrance has been ministered, with a 'well done, good and faithful servant,' into the kingdom of our Lord and Saviour Jesus Christ."

In the list of new appointments in the Minutes in 1837, MARSHALL is found. This place is the county-seat of Calhoun County, is pleasantly located at the confluence of Rice Creek with Kalamazoo River, about one hundred and five miles west from Detroit, is situated in the midst of a fertile country, and is inhabited by a very intelligent and moral population. The first settlement in Calhoun County was made here in the spring of 1831. Messrs. George and Sidney Ketchum, two brothers, took up the land, and erected a saw-mill that spring, but did not bring their families till in August following. The first settlers were of the first order of society, and gathered around them a similar class of inhabitants, so that this place has always held the first rank for morality and intelligence.

Schools, churches, and other evidences of intellectual and moral advancement are to be found, possessing much healthful vigor. The population now numbers about 4,700. The growth of this town has not been quite so rapid as some other places in the State, not because it does not possess advantages in itself, but because the county affords so many advantages for building up towns that several rival villages—and one has even attained to the dignity of a city—have sprung into active and vigorous life. Still, Marshall possesses several advantages which must give it an ultimate triumph over them all. It is the county-seat, and it is the half-way place of the Michigan Central Railroad, where they have shops for repairs, and a dining-house, where all their trains stop. This house has been the admiration of all travelers, and has been justly regarded as one of the best railway eating establishments in the United States. This railroad, by the way, is one of the best constructed, and one of the very best managed roads in the whole country.

We must now pass from this general outline to the religious history of this city and vicinity. In August, 1831, Rev. Randall Hobart, a local preacher, arrived here, and, on the 14th of this month, preached in the log house of Sidney Ketchum, which, by the way, had neither doors nor windows, and was only partially floored with split plank. This was the first religious service ever held in this county. The first families who settled here were Christian people, and commenced to have religious services as soon as they arrived.

At the session of the Ohio Conference in September, 1831, Elijah H. Pilcher and Ezekiel S. Gavit were appointed to Tecumseh Circuit, the bounds of which have been described in connection with Tecumseh in the general outline, and included this place. About the first of October of this year, the preacher in charge, Elijah H. Pilcher, came here and preached, which was the first visit of an itinerant preacher to the place. He was followed, in two weeks, by his colleague, Mr. Gavit. On the sixth day of November, Mr. Pilcher organized the Methodist Episcopal Church in Marshall, which, at the time, consisted of *Randall Hobart, Ruth Hobart, Sidney Ketchum, Katherine Ketchum, Seth Ketchum* and *Eliza Ketchum;* only *six.* Of these, not one now remains here. Seth Ketchum, at the time, was a very old man—was the father of Sidney and Eliza—and soon after passed to the rest of the Christian. He was not converted till late in life, but became very devoted and pious. He lived with his son Sidney. Although he came in at the eleventh hour, he has gone to receive his reward in Heaven. Sidney Ketchum was a decided and earnest Christian, and very much attached to the Methodist doctrines and discipline, and was a man of large and noble plans for good—for the intellectual and religious elevation of those around him. In consequence of his large plans and undertakings, he became very much embarrassed in the financial crash of 1836–38, and found it best to change his residence to New York City for a time; but the people of Marshall may say of him, "He hath built us a synagogue;" for, in 1837, at his instance, a stone church, forty-five by fifty feet, of Gothic architecture, was commenced, the basement of which was completed for use in 1839. This church cost Mr. Ketchum about six or eight thousand dollars. At a later period the same work might have been done for much less money, but this does not lessen the amount that Mr. Ketchum paid, nor does it diminish the good he intended to do for the Church. It was a noble conception, although a little in advance of the times. Mr. Ketchum was born in Northumberland, New York, January 1797, and died at Marshall, Michigan, September 17th, 1862. He was a very good man, and commanded tne respect of all who knew him.

Katherine Ketchum, wife of Sidney, was a very intelligent, amiable, refined, and deeply pious lady. She was strongly attached to the Church of her choice, and was always delighted with its prosperity. She was always ready to contribute what she could of influence and money for the advancement of the cause of true

Christianity. She died, in great peace, in 1839, respected and lamented by all who knew her. In her death, the Church here lost a firm, valuable, and valued friend. Mrs. Hobart, who was a most estimable Christian lady, died in great triumph, and passed to her heavenly rest in about three or four years after coming here.

Rev. Randall Hobart was a local preacher of more than ordinary ability. He supplied services when the itinerants were not present. After the death of Mrs. Hobart, he married a second time, and removed to California in 1849, where he not only retained his piety, but was respected as a local preacher. But we have now lost sight of him.

Eliza Ketchum, a sister of Sidney, withdrew from the Church in 1832, having lost her spiritual life and enjoyment. Thus this original number has become entirely scattered, but, in the place of these, the Lord has raised up a host of others to praise His name, some of whom have gone up to sing the song of Moses and the Lamb on high, among whom Ambrose M. Phelps may be named, of whose life and experience a sketch will be furnished at the end of this article; but a strong body still remains to labor and succeed.

The first love-feast and communion season ever held in this county, was at a two days meeting held by E. H. Pilcher, preacher in charge, assisted by Rev. William Fowler, of the State of New York, who was an Elder, and consecrated the elements, Mr. Pilcher being only a Deacon. This meeting was held in the new schoolhouse, not yet finished, June 16th–17th, 1832. There were but few to commune, but they partook of the emblems of the broken body and shed blood of the Lord and Saviour with great interest. It was a delightful occasion to these few sheep in the wilderness.

The original six had been strengthened by additions, by letter and on trial, so that, at the time of Conference, in September, 1832, there were *fifteen* members. This was a very large increase considering the circumstances; for the settlement had been almost depopulated by the cholera, which had prevailed so fearfully at this place during the early summer of 1832.

The Church here has been visited with many precious seasons of revival, by which other denominations have been greatly benefited as well as the Methodists. One of the most important of these revivals commenced about the middle of December, 1839. Some interest had been growing up for some time, and, as the Presiding Elder was passing through the city to attend a Quarterly Meeting at Battle Creek, and being strongly solicited to return and preach on Sabbath evening, he consented to do so. At the close of the sermon, being strongly impressed to invite seekers of religion to manifest themselves, he gave an invitation to such as wanted religion to rise. Several did so, and such was the interest that a meeting was appointed for the next evening. So it continued, from evening to evening, for three months, during which time the church was lighted up every night but one. It was estimated that not less than *one hundred and fifty* professed conversion, and over *one hundred* united with the Methodist Church, on trial.

Rev. Benjamin Sabin, a venerable and most excellent man, was in charge of the Station, and was assisted much by the Presiding Elder of the District, E. H. Pilcher, who was induced to adopt the plan of going to his Quarterly Meetings, and then returning here on Monday or Tuesday, and remaining as long as he could, and reach his next appointment. The Church was greatly strengthened by the revival—several valuable and important accessions were made. Some of the converts have been transferred to the Church above, while others are still on their way. Among the active and successful workers at this time may be mentioned Dr. O. C. Comstock and wife, Ambrose M. Phelps, Ira Wood and wife, Miss Cornelia Hopkins—now Mrs. Comfort, of Kalamazoo, and E. G. Squiers.

Marshall appears in the Minutes, for the first time, in 1837. Previous to this time, except for 1831, as before stated, it was embraced in Calhoun Mission, taking the name of the county rather than that of the village. It was made a Station at the Conference in September, 1839, at which time Battle Creek Circuit, taking the balance of the county and some of Eaton County was formed, and was made to appear in our Minutes.

Marshall also gave name to a District in 1838, which name has been substituted, at a later date, by that of Albion, and that, in 1876, was swallowed up in the name of Jackson. This was a District indeed, as it regarded the extent of travel. It included the following counties, viz: Hillsdale, Branch, Jackson, Calhoun, Ingham, Eaton, Barry, Ottawa, Kent, Ionia, Clinton, and Shiawassee, with the western half of Genesee, of Washtenaw, of Lenawee, and the eastern half of Allegan, that is, *twelve* full counties and a part of four others, being equivalent to *fourteen* counties. Such was the newness of the country and the state of the roads, that the Presiding Elder was obliged to travel on horseback altogether, and some portions of the time, to be absent from home for four and five weeks at a time.

The Michigan Annual Conference, having been invited, held its session here in 1840. The venerable Bishop Hedding presided. This was a time of interest to the people of this, then, beautiful village. They had not yet completed the body of their church, but had arranged temporary seats, and the house was very much crowded with interested hearers on the Sabbath. The venerable Bishop preached on Sabbath morning with eloquence and great power, having for his text: Luke, 24th chapter, verses 46, 47 and 48. We shall never forget one remark, which seemed to thrill the whole assembly as with a shock of electricity. He had represented the Saviour as giving his commission to his disciples to go and preach repentance and remission of sins to all nations, beginning at Jerusalem, and then said He, "Go out into the streets and tell them all, I have died for them, and, if you meet my murderers, tell them I died for them; if you meet the soldier who pierced my side, tell him I died for him." This was delivered with his peculiarly dignified pathos; and the effect was overwhelming. The Conference was well entertained, and the session left a fine impression on the public mind.

The Conference met here again in 1846, Bishop Janes presiding. Bishop Waugh was also present on the first day of the session, and dedicated the church on that day. He was on his way to attend a western Conference, and stopped over for one day only. The business of the Conference was transacted with a good degree of dispatch, and it adjourned in good season. The Conference was held here again in 1859, Bishop Janes presiding.

This charge has been supplied from time to time with some of the best talent the Conference afforded, and the Church has grown strong, and is attending to the interest of the children and youth by keeping a Sabbath School running in excellent order—indeed, they commenced a Sabbath School at once, and have always maintained one in a very high state of perfection. They have an excellent stone church, and a parsonage contiguous to the church. So there is no good reason why they should not prosper, and have favor in the eyes of all the people. The only thing for them is to maintain the true spirit of piety and zeal for the salvation of souls.

Let us now take a brief review of our own Church. We began, in 1831, with preaching in a private house once in two weeks, and a membership of only *six*. Now, in 1876—forty-five years—we find a fine church, valued at $16,000, and a parsonage, valued at $2,000; a station, with services twice every Sabbath; a flourishing Sabbath School, and 182 members and probationers. This condition of things has not been attained without much toil and patient waiting.

Rev. John D. Pearce, a Presbyterian minister, settled here with his family in the autumn of 1831. He came not as a minister, but as a man of business, to engage in business, but he commenced preaching and holding religious services in his own house after he arrived, and organized a Presbyterian Church in the summer of 1832, composed of but a few members. But this Church has grown to be a strong and prosperous one, having a membership of 268. A Congregational Church was organized in 1869, and now has 79 members.

Marshall was desolated by the ravages of the cholera in 1832. Mrs. Rev. John D. Pearce, an amiable and valuable lady, was among the victims of its power. The first victim was a Mr. Hurd, a young man who had gone to Ann Arbor at the time it was raging in Detroit, and before it had reached any farther west. At the time Mr. Hurd was at Ann Arbor, there was much excitement in regard to it, and the military had been called out to guard the roads from Detroit to prevent its progress to the village, and many fears were expressed in relation to it. It was a common topic of conversation at the hotel at which Mr. Hurd put up. He, to make it appear that he was free from any apprehensions in regard to it, took a piece of pie in his hand, and went around the house, eating a little of it occasionally, saying, "I've got the cholera! I've got the cholera!" He started for home, and, in less than forty hours he was a corpse, having died of cholera. The scourge passed over Ann Arbor and Jackson, for the time being, and settled down on Marshall. Was this a visitation of God upon Mr. Hurd for his folly? or was it brought on by his fears which he had attempted to keep down by such bravado? Whichsoever it was, the lesson which it suggests is important. This was a sad time for the few settlers of this new village. It has never since been visited by that disease.

It is proper here to say that other denominations have contributed, and are still contributing their efforts for the moral and religious training and elevation of the people. The Presbyterians, Protestant Episcopalians, and Baptists all have large and flourishing Societies, besides several of the smaller denominations, so that, though we were the first in the field, we have not monopolized it.

From Marshall, as a starting-point, the work of religion has more than kept pace with the increasing population, so that, in every new village and neighborhood in the county, a Methodist Society has been planted, and is now doing its work, to the glory of God.

It is time, now, to bring this sketch to a close, and we will do so by giving a memorial notice of Ambrose M. Phelps, as before promised, without which it would be imperfect.

This sainted brother was born at Canandaigua, New York. His father was a member and leader of the first class formed in the State of New York, west of Cayuga Bridge. At the age of *fifteen*, Ambrose Phelps entered the army as a musician, and was honorably discharged after five years' service. When twenty-six years of age, he was converted to God, and joined the Methodist Episcopal Church at Canandaigua. Some eight or nine years of his life were spent in Rochester, N. Y., where he was a class-leader of uncommon labor and usefulness. In 1837 he emigrated from the latter place into Marshall, from which period, to the close of his life, March 8th, 1853, he was, indeed, a pillar in the Church of God. He was either class-leader or exhorter or, both, for more than twenty years. His public performances, replete with clearness and moral power, were always accompanied with the outgushings of a warm and sanctified heart. He never failed to make his mark where duty called him to labor. Eternity alone can disclose the saving results of his faithfulness.

Toward the close of his life he joined the Masonic Lodge in Marshall, and was made at once, and continued until his death, its chaplain. This circumstance is only mentioned that the following fact may be better understood. The evening upon which the Lodge met occurring upon the same evening with a Church meeting, a brother, not a Mason, moved that the Church meeting be held on some other evening of the week for the accommodation of Brother Phelps, who, it was presumed, desired to attend both meetings. For a few moments, Brother Phelps poured upon his brethren such a flood of love for them and religion that no doubt was left, if indeed any ever existed, that Christ and His Church took precedence, with him, of everything else. He insisted that the change should not be made—"though," he added, "I love you more for having offered to do so." The following obituary appeared in the Marshall papers at the time of his decease:

"DIED.—In this village, on the morning of the 8th, Ambrose M. Phelps, in the fifty-seventh year of his age.

"The decease of this estimable citizen has made a wide chasm, not only in his family, but in the Church to which he was attached, and of which he was an honor. He was born in Canandaigua, Ontario County, New York. He emigrated into this State in 1837, resided one or two years in St. Joseph County, and, from the elapse of that period, he has lived in this village. He was an active and exemplary member of the Methodist Episcopal Church, and, for depth of piety and Christian sacrifices and labors, he had no superiors. For months preceding his decease he had led the devotional exercises of the African Church of this village, and, indeed, was suddenly seized with illness, which terminated his life, at that church, one week ago last

Sabbath. He had a clear and discriminating mind, a warm and generous heart, and a benevolent sympathy, which enabled him to look upon and treat every man as his brother, irrespective of color or condition. His loss to his family is irreparable. His brethren rejoice, amid their tears, that their brother's conflicts are ended, and that he is now enjoying, in all its fullness and fruition, 'the rest of of Heaven,' upon which he was wont rapturously to address them."

We are mainly indebted to Dr. O. C. Comstock, of Marshall, for this sketch, although we knew him personally.

Marshall was incorporated as a city in 1859, and, according to the census of 1874, has a population of 4,623, being 302 less than that of 1870. It is a very interesting and important locality. The educational interests are very thoroughly promoted and cared for, although the aspirations and expectations at one time indulged have never been realized. Marshall College was once chartered, and, under the leadership of Rev. John P. Cleveland, a preparatory department was opened, and high expectations were indulged that a college would be established and maintained under the fostering care and patronage of the Presbyterian Church. The enterprise, however, was never fully inaugurated, and all the hopes built upon it have fallen to the ground.

CHAPTER XII.

ADRIAN—First Preacher—First Church—Additions—J. W. Finley—School-house—Preaching on Sabbath—Davidson and Wiley—Revival—Nathan Comstock—Aunt Kitty—Appears in Minutes—Church—Parsonage—F. A. Blades—Revivals—Remarkable Manifestations—Baptism—Addison J. Comstock—Others—Another Revival—Millerism—S. C. Adams—Second Church—Difficulties—Opposition—J. A. Kellam—Minister Flogged—Trap—Ira Bidwell—Milton Foot—Thomas Fox—J. V. Watson—Sabbath Schools—Other Churches—Work in the County—Numbers—Property—Camp Meeting—Devil's Lake—PONTIAC—Infidel Club—Mock Baptism—Death of Administrator—D. LeRoy—First Preacher—Baughman—Small Societies—Station—Churches—Property—McConnell—Revival—Bad Policy—Name—Donation Chapel—Defections—Other Churches—Troy—Summary—Jacokes—Conclusion—Statistics—PORT HURON—Methodist Society Organized—Church Built—Congregational Church—Protestant Episcopal—Bishop Waugh—Revival—Parsonage—District—Statistics—German Society—Fish—GRAND RAPIDS—Appears in Minutes—O. Mitchell—In Ann Arbor District—Marshall District—Frees and Chatfield—Camp Meeting—Lyons—Wants Met—Jacob Dobbins—Danger—Ionia—Defection—Revivals—Immersionists—Singular Incident—L. Chatfield—A. Staples—Incident—Society Organized—Unsuitable Appointment—Frees—Review—Bad Policy—Progress—Change of Policy—Progress of Settlement—Special Attention to the Rapids—Anecdote—Increase—Station—F. A. Blades—Revival—Second Charge—Numbers—Property—Other Denominations—Atwater—FLINT—Schools—First Preacher—First Society—Brockway's Account—First Quarterly Meeting—First Sacrament—Appears in Minutes—Church—W. Blades Licensed—Station—Church Burned—Second Church—Other Churches—Conference Sessions—Statistics—Rev. W. Blades—Lee.

ADRIAN appears in our Minutes of appointments first in 1837, and was then an extensive Circuit. Who has not heard of Adrian? It is a flourishing city, the county-seat of Lenawee County, containing a population of about 10,000. It is well situated, healthy and pleasant; contains an active, enterprising and intelligent population. It was founded by Addison J. Comstock, in 1827, and incorporated as a city in 1853. Mr. Comstock located his land in 1826, and having erected his shanty, removed his family into it in 1827. Though a professed infidel, in the seclusion of the wilderness, the visits of the ministers of the Cross were cheering to him. A few families settled here also in 1827. While Mr. Comstock and his associates were yet living in their rude cabins, *Rev. John Janes*, a minister of the Methodist Episcopal Church, came, and preached in the house of Mr. Noah Norton. This occurred in the autumn of 1827. He was the first minister of any denomination who visited this place. The settlement was then so small, and separated so much from other settlements, that it could not be taken, regularly, into any Circuit.

Mr. Janes was succeeded, at irregular intervals, by others, until in the spring of 1830, when Rev. Jacob Hill, a member of the Ohio Annual Conference, who was supplying Monroe Circuit, made a regular appointment, coming once in four weeks. He organized the first Christian Church—a Methodist Episcopal Church—of the place in the summer of that year, that was, in the summer of 1830. This Church consisted, at the time of its organization, of the following persons, viz: *William Barrus and wife, Americus Smith, and John Walworth and wife*—only *five*. William Barrus was a local preacher of considerable talent, and Americus Smith a licensed exhorter of considerable power. These original five have all passed away. These were reinforced, in September of 1830, by Milton Foot, a local preacher, Lois Foot, Pharez Sutton, Hannah Sutton, Samuel Gregory, Ada Gregory, and Altha Spink, all of whom were active and influential Christians.

At the session of the Ohio Conference in September, 1830, Rev. James W. Finley was appointed to Monroe Circuit, which included Adrian, and he made his visits here regularly, once in four weeks, on a week-day evening. Adrian had not yet assumed much importance. These visits were made at a great expense of time and labor; but these were regarded as nothing when the spiritual interests of the people were involved. Mr. Finley was a noble-spirited man, and ardent in his Christian work, "not counting his life dear unto himself" if he could but win the people to Christ. He finally fell a martyr to his work. (*See Monroe.*)

In September, 1831, Tecumseh Circuit is made to appear in our Minutes, which included Adrian; but as Adrian was then much inferior to Tecumseh in population, Adrian had to be put off with a week-day evening appointment. *Elijah H. Pilcher* and *Ezekiel S. Gavit* were the preachers this year. There being two of them, and each coming around once in four weeks, furnished preaching once in two weeks, but only on a week-day evening. The services continued to be held in private houses until in the winter of 1831-2, when a frame school-house was built and opened. As soon as this house was completed, Mr. Pilcher and his colleague occupied it for preaching. This school-house continued to be occupied for religious worship until the different denominations erected houses for themselves. It has since been perverted to the profane purpose of shoeing horses.

In the autumn of 1832, Tecumseh Circuit was so changed and arranged as to supply preaching at Adrian once in two weeks on the Sabbath. This was an important advance movement. Rev. James F. Davidson was appointed in charge, with Thomas Wiley as his colleague. This was the first appearance of Mr. Davidson in Michigan from Ohio, having been in the ministry one year. Under the labors of these zealous and indefatigable young men, a very gracious revival of religion occured in the spring of 1833. Many in the village and surrounding country were converted, and added to the Church. This was a very valuable work, and added much strength to the cause. This work extended to all the settlements adjacent to the town, and was one of very great interest.

Among those converted at this revival were two persons very opposite in every respect, and are worthy of notice here. *Nathan Comstock* and *Catherine Fay*. Nathan Comstock was a well educated and talented man, who had been brought up a Quaker, and was a birthright member of the Society of Friends. He became deeply and thoroughly convinced of sin, and of his utter ruin without Christ as his Saviour. Under the influence of this conviction, he sought and obtained a clear witness that he was adopted into the Divine family. It was, indeed, an interesting scene to see this noble-looking man bowing as a penitent, and pleading for mercy; and still more interesting to see him rise, with a countenance radiant with joy, to testify to the love of God in Christ Jesus. He immediately united himself to the Methodist Church. He was licensed to exhort, and became a zealous, active and useful member. After a few years, he returned to the State of New York, where, amongst his old friends and associates, he maintained a good profession. A single case like this is a recompense for much labor and toil.

Perhaps the most remarkable case of conversion which occurred at this time, or even since, was that of *Catherine Fay*, a widow, lately from Ireland. She had been educated in the Romish Church, and, withal, was not able to read. She was a strong Roman Catholic, and was born in the County of Limerick. In her early youth she had attended Methodist meetings a few times, and had learned one of their hymns, which begins—

"And let this feeble body fail."

She came to America in 1823, and to Adrian in 1831. During the meeting held by Mr. Davidson, as above, an Irishman went to her house and asked her to attend meeting that evening; to which she replied that she did not know whether she would or not. He said she had better, as an Irishman was to preach—Mr. Davidson is Irish. She went to the meeting, but hid herself behind the door in the school-house. During the evening, Mr. Davidson, who is a fine singer, sung the above hymn. This affected her very deeply. When the invitation was given for persons to come forward to seats provided for seekers of religion, she went, or, at least, she found herself there without knowing how she got there, her feelings had become so intense, so overwhelming. She felt she was alone in this world, and "without God," and without hope. A sense of her guilt came upon her with great force, and pressed her down with agony and grief. In her distress, she cried unto the Lord, and he heard her, and delivered her from all her fears. Before the meeting closed that night, she felt she was a new creature in Christ Jesus, but did not receive a clear witness of it until some time after, while attending a Camp Meeting near Clinton. While there, the evidence became so clear to her that she never afterwards doubted her conversion.

When she went home from that first meeting, in the school-house, she was very strongly assailed by the temptation that she had done wrong, as she was a Catholic, and all her ancestors had been so before her. Under this influence she fell on her knees before the Lord and prayed; which was a very right thing for anyone to do. Her soul became so earnest that she prayed so loud as to wake up her son, a small boy, but she prayed on until she found a satisfactory answer that she had done right. What but the Spirit of God could have led her to this? She had often felt convicted for sin and was often made unhappy by a sense of her guilt. She had not gone to the priest for a long time, feeling he did not afford her the comfort she wanted, but now she found what she had long desired in vain, peace of conscience.

"Aunt Kitty," as she was familiarly called, was in some respects a very remarkable woman. She was entirely without education—could not even read, and yet she would pray in social meetings with very great correctness and propriety; and would sometimes exhort with great power and effect. She was very highly respected by the wealthiest families in the Church. For many years she adorned the doctrine of God our Saviour, and died in peace but a few years since.

Adrian remained in connection with the Tecumseh Circuit until September, 1837, when it was made a Station, and John H. Pitezel was appointed to it. The county-seat had been removed from Tecumseh to Adrian by act of the Legislature, in 1836, making Adrian the more important town. Eleazer Thomas appears in our Minutes as the preacher for 1838, but he did not come to it, having been appointed to a charge in the Genesee Conference at the same time. The Presiding Elder, Henry Colclazer, transferred Oliver Burgess from Dexter to this place, and he filled out the year, with a fair degree of success.

The project of building a church, a thing very much needed, was set on foot in 1838, but the church was not completed, except the basement, until 1840. This church, though considered large and commodious, has given place to a much larger and more imposing structure, beautifully and tastefully finished. This latter was undertaken and carried through by the enterprise of F. A. Blades, who was stationed here in 1862, 1863, 1864—three years—and then was in charge of the District for three years. A comfortable parsonage was built in the summer of 1845, under the administration of E. H. Pilcher, who was the pastor from 1844 to 1846. This, too, in time, was displaced by a much larger one, which has since been disposed of.

There have been several seasons of very great revival in connection with the labors of this Church. Nearly every year of its history has been distinguished with gracious manifestations, but some years have been much more marked than others. Some of these seasons we will notice. One of these occasions was in the winter and spring of 1842, under the pastoral labors of Rev. James V. Watson. This was a remarkable one, because of the manifestations of Divine power among the people. Many were prostrated and would lie for a long time without the power to move, and when they came to be able to speak, uttered the most joyful expressions. It was not simply the most excitable persons that were affected in this way, but all classes irrespective of age or sex. Many were converted and added to the Church.

There were meetings held in the Baptist Church at the same time, attended with considerable success, and the minister of that Church thought it advisable to make the subject of immersion very prominent by dwelling much on it, and insisting strongly that that was the only baptism. The matter assumed so much importance that Mr. Watson concluded to preach a sermon on the subject, and did it in such an effectual way that it put an end to the controversy for the time being. The spiritual baptism was very wonderful and glorious, and such as should have stopped all caviling.

There was one case of conversion which occurred during this revival which is worthy of being recorded with some degree of extension. The subject of it was the original proprietor of the town, who was educated an orthodox Quaker, his father being a preacher in that denomination, but the younger man had first become a Universalist in belief, from which he easily and naturally glided into open infidelity. He had become a ridiculer—a scoffer at religion, though he had often been impressed with a sense of his need of it, but these impressions had as often been thrown off. He was emphatically a man of business and of the world. With the growth of the town and of the county at large his property had increased in value until he was regarded as being worth several hundred thousand dollars. He had at different times held important positions in the affairs of the State. He was a member of the Legislature when it was determined to sell out the railroads to companies, and advocated and sustained that important measure—a measure the wisdom of which has been fully sustained by the results. He was one of the company which projected and built the first *thirty miles* of railroad ever constructed in the West—from Toledo to Adrian—a most valuable enterprise for this town, and indeed of great value to all the West.

He has not always been successful in business, for in two several attempts at banking he suffered much loss of property and of reputation, especially in the last case. He was for some time President of the Erie & Kalamazoo Railroad Bank, in which he suffered himself to be drawn on to an over-issue, and to place so much confidence in one of the principal stockholders, that when the bank was threatened with embarassment, he allowed him to take a large amount of the securities to negotiate in New York, from which the bank never realized anything, and when the bank failed, though he had ceased, some time before, to hold any real relation to it, he had to stand the burden, both pecuniarily and as to reputation. In this last case, he was the victim, and gave up all his property, and was so completely crippled that he never recovered in property, but he had the confidence of the general public as to his integrity and honesty.

During the progress of the revival under the labors of Mr. Watson, in the spring of 1842, this gentleman, although he had studiously avoided attendance at the meetings, became very powerfully awakened to a sense of his sinfulness and danger. So disturbed were his feelings that he determined to leave the place for a time, to seek relief in retirement from the scene of action, hoping that the excitement of the meeting might pass away, and, with that, quiet be restored to his mind. For that purpose, he took his wife into a carriage, and drove, that day, about fifty miles into Calhoun County, under pretense of having business which demanded his attention. He found no relief in this way ; his feelings became more and more disquieted as he advanced, and that first night away an impression came over his soul as if a voice had spoken to his ear, This is the last call. With this impression on his mind, the next morning he started, and hastened home ; went to the church that night, and, as soon as the opportunity was given for penitents to come forward, he went forward for the prayers of the Church. This kind of movement was contrary to all his education and former notions of right and propriety; but he felt that he was a sinner condemned to death, and must find relief, if possible. He had not been at the altar of prayer long before he fell prostrate to the floor, and lay, for some time, insensible to everything around him. When he came to himself, he began to shout aloud the praises of God through Christ Jesus as his Saviour. So clear and powerful was the change in him that all could see it. So clear was the evidence of his pardon and adoption that we have often heard him say, "Whatever may become of me, I *know* that the religion of Christ is true, and that I have been converted to God." For weeks after his conversion, he could scarcely give any attention to business. He became a very earnest and active Christian for many years.

In consequence of his business embarrassments from the failure of the bank last named, he, under erroneous advice, chose to occupy a very retired position in relation to the cause of religion. It certainly is a great mistake, when a man fails in business, especially through the latches of others, to retire from the duties and privileges of that holy religion which they then specially need. He did not, by any means, give up his trust in God, nor his private and family devotions. These he continued to observe as diligently as ever; but he did seclude himself, to a large extent, from the associations and fellowships of the Church. The members of the Church should not have allowed that. They ought to have taken the more pains to sympathize with him, being willing to bear a part of a brother's reproach.

Mr. Addison J. Comstock, of whom we have been speaking, was a small, unpretending man in his personal appearance, but he had a fine intellect and a large, noble heart, and the Lord delivered him out of all his troubles. In his last years, he came again into closer union with the Church of his choice. His death, when it came, was very sudden. On a Sabbath, he had been at church, attended class-meeting, and testified to the power of God to save, and went home, rejoicing in God. He sat down in his easy chair, and his wife stepped out for a moment to look after some refreshments, and when she returned he was dead, sitting in his chair. To him, the step from earth to Heaven was a very short one.

There were other valuable conversions and additions to the Church, some of whom remain steadfast in the faith, while some have gone back to the "beggarly elements of the world," and some have been called from "labor to reward"—have been transferred to the Church above.

The next season of extensive spiritual revival occurred under the labors of Rev. John A. Baughman, who was stationed here in September, 1842. He succeeded Mr. Watson. He entered on his labors with his usual energy and activity. He remained in the Station till October, 1844, and, during the winter of 1842-43, he had the pleasure of seeing many profess religion, and unite with the Church. This revival, though vastly more extensive as to numbers than the former, was not as permanent among those generally who professed to be converted, yet, during this revival, several active young men were converted, who have since entered the ministry. Among these was Andrew Bell, still a member of the Detroit Conference, though he has been on the superannuated list for a number of years. It will be remembered by some that the country was all excited by the calculations of a Mr. Miller, of New England, that the world was to come to an end in 1843. Many, very many, who rejected the notion, felt it might be so, and it was best to prepare for it; and, having no higher view of a Christian's experience and life than simply to get ready to die, when the apprehended danger was past, they forgot their vows. Under this feeling of apprehension, they thought it advisable to seek for the consolations of religion. Multitudes flocked to the Church for refuge at this time. This is a false view of a religious experience and life. A higher view must be in the mind—to become holy—to glorify God—to do good—before a genuine experience can be secured. When, then, the time had passed, and "all things continued as they were before," many relapsed into their old ways, reminding one of what is said of the aborigines of one portion of South America, who, when there was an eclipse of the sun, would bring their offerings, make their vows of devotion and of a good life, if their god would only spare the life of the sun, and then, when the eclipse was over, they would return to their old practices, and say their god must be very foolish to think they had any intention of doing as they promised. This backsliding was not any fault of Christianity, but occurred in spite of its teachings. Notwithstanding these drawbacks on the general permanency of the work, it was still a deep and extensive revival, and resulted in much permanent good.

Another occasion of special and extensive outpouring of sacred influence was in the spring of 1856, mainly in the month of March. The pastor, Rev. A. J. Eldred, had secured the assistance of Rev. S. C. Adams, an eccentric, yet very good and efficient laborer. He was a local preacher from western New York. He labored with great earnestness, laying the truth on the conscience in a very plain way. The excitement was very intense—the church was crowded day and night—the whole city became enlisted for and against his labors. His manner of labor was peculiar, and some people took great exceptions, and set themselves against the work as conducted by him. Had it not been for this kind of opposition, the work would have been much more extensive. As it was, there was over *one hundred* united with the Methodist Church, most of whom remained faithful.

It is proper here to remark that in the summer of 1851 it was considered desirable to organize a second Methodist Church here, which was done with very flattering prospects; but those prospects have never been realized. The town has not grown as rapidly as was anticipated, for one reason, and various others operated to prevent the success of the enterprise. So, in the spring of 1858, this second Church disbanded, a part of the members returning to the old Church, and a part of them remaining outside the fold altogether.

It is not to be supposed that this Church has always moved on without any friction any more than others. Church music has been made the occasion of some unpleasantness; renting, or selling of pews, a steeple and bell, have had their times of calling up the feelings of the heart. But, with all these, there have been no disastrous disturbances and no ruptures.

Neither have they always met with the approval of the world; if they had, they would not have fulfilled their high mission—they have had opposition to meet with from the world. While human nature remains in possession of its present characteristics, "fightings without and fears within" will be the common lot of the Christian

Church. It cannot be expected that the enemy of all good will be inactive while the ministers of the Cross are laboring with zeal and success to spoil his house. Hence opposition, such as dares to be made in this country, has sometimes showed itself in this place, although it has seldom broken out into any considerable degree of violence. There is one incident, however, which ought to be named; the parties to it we will not name, except the minister.

REV. JAMES A. KELLAM, a man of considerable talent and of zeal for the cause of Christ, was stationed here in the autumn of 1839. In the winter, perhaps in January, 1840, he held a series of meetings in the basement of the church, as the main audience-room was not yet finished, which resulted in a good degree of success. These meetings were often disturbed by the rude conduct, developed in various ways, of several young persons, just budding into manhood and womanhood. Reproof had been administered to them, gently and kindly, without any effect. Upon consultation, it was determined to obtain a list of their names, and to publish them before the congregation, if they did not desist after having given them due notice of the design. Names were taken and notice given; but the annoyance continued. So, at the close of a meeting, the minister read off a list of the disturbers. This was too much for them to endure quietly. They must be avenged on the preacher. The next evening, as he was going from his house to the church, which stood very near, just a little before time to begin service, he was attacked by several young women—perhaps some of them were men in women's clothes—with rawhides. They evidently designed to flog him well; but, being fleet of foot, and not having any relish for that kind of sport, he soon left them behind. He did not suffer much violence; but it was all the same as far as their design was concerned. His flight was so precipitate that he was not able, positively, to identify any of them. Some who were believed to be engaged in this affair were arrested, the next day, and brought before a justice of the peace; but, as they went directly to a dancing-party, which had evidently been arranged as a part of the programme, when they were brought before the court, as he could not positively identify any of them, nor swear positively as to the hour at which the whipping occurred, they proved an *alibi*, and so escaped. The community, however, very readily fixed their minds on the perpetrators of the outrage.

In a short time after this occurrence, one of the young women, who was believed to be engaged in this matter, sent a request to the minister, saying she would like to see him alone about this matter; she said she would not state what she knew in relation to it in the presence of any one, but she would state it to him alone. He sent back a message that he would not see her alone, but would see her only in company with some one else. They did not meet. In less than nine months that young woman became a mother without having a husband. Had the minister visited her as she requested, it can easily be imagined what the result would have been—how the minister would have been accursed and ruined. No serious disturbance has occurred since.

There are many interesting cases, both of men and women, who have been connected with this Church, which it would be pleasant, and, perhaps, profitable to introduce ; but, among the laity, we must content ourself with one in addition to those already named. There are many which would show the power of grace to purify, save, and sustain ; however, this additional one must suffice.

IRA BIDWELL, a private member of this Church, has figured so largely in the financial affairs of this city and the Methodist Church in it, that we introduce a short sketch of his life. He was regarded as one of the wealthiest men belonging to the city, and, probably, during his residence here, he had a larger money income than any other citizen. He was a man of respectable abilities, having but a very limited education.

When he was about twenty years of age, his father told him he might shift for himself, if he chose, or, if he would remain with him a few years longer, he would try to help him to a piece of land. His father was poor, and the prospect of help was very unpromising. He decided to shift for himself then, rather than to wait. He taught school, for a short time, and acquired *seven* dollars. His education was too limited to do much in this line. With these *seven* dollars, he determined to build his fortune, which he succeeded in doing most admirably. With this first acquisition, he went to the City of Rochester, where he made a small purchase of goods, getting a little credit, and started out as a hand-peddler through the city. In this he succeeded well. The next winter he spent mostly at school, to increase his limited stock of learning. On the opening of spring, he started out on a rather larger scale of peddling, having purchased a horse and an old wagon. This he continued for a short time, and then commenced business in Bergen, New York. Here he married, and remained one year. From thence he went to Brockport for a short period. Then he went again to Rochester, to open trade, and remained a year or a little more. At one of these business points, no matter which, he took in a partner. They had a good business, but when they came to reckon up, settle and divide the profits, he had gained nothing, though his partner, as poor as he at the beginning, was able to build himself a fine house. He eschewed partnership after that.

While in Rochester, Mr. Bidwell laid the foundation for all his real prosperity; for it was here that he and his wife both consecrated themselves to the service of God, and experienced religion, under the labors of *Rev. Glezen Filmore*, in 1830, and connected themselves with the Methodist Episcopal Church. His conversion was clear, and took place as he was passing from his house to his barn. He had declared his purpose and desire to be a Christian, but was beset with an unwillingness to give himself up to Christ; but now he yielded all, and in a moment was filled with peace. Now, having become a Christian, he determined to do business on Christian principles. He started out with these three words for his motto, to wit, "*Honesty, perseverance, economy.*" He believed that by observing these three things he should succeed. He included liberal contributions for the support of the Gospel and for the benefit of the *deserving* poor, under the head of Honesty.

The first eight years of his business life, that is, after he had married, he gained only $2,200. It was with this sum as a capital that he came to Adrian in the autumn of 1836. He opened business here, at first, by selling at auction. Not having obtained a license as a merchant, as the law then required, the men in trade, being offended at his interference with their business, had him fined for it. This excited the sympathy of the people in his favor, and proved to be a great advantage to him in the end. He had not intended to transfer his whole business here until the next spring, but this affair determined him to bring all his interests here at once. So he flung his flag to the breeze, and set out in trade with a full stock of goods, for the times.

During the first three years he was in business here, he made a clear profit of *twenty-seven thousand dollars*, over and above the support of his family; and, in one of these years, his profit was *eleven thousand dollars*. These are small profits as compared with what he received at a later date. But we are to remember that $2,200 had gained for him, over and above the expense of his family, a clear sum of $27,000 in three years, an enormous profit for the amount invested. His piety has been uniform and constant, and his attendance on the social means of the Church did not diminish in consequence of his having increased in wealth.

Like other men who have succeeded in business, he had to meet with opposition, and by some he was called hard-hearted; but those who knew him intimately, knew that he contributed large amounts for the benefit of the poor. He did not hand it out indiscriminately, but he selected his own objects of charity. It is but just to say that Mrs. Bidwell adopted the same motto with her husband, and well sustained her part in relation to it. They harmonized perfectly in this matter. How many an industrious and faithful man has been rendered bankrupt by the want of economy and perseverance on the part of his wife! Mrs. Bidwell died a very triumphant Christian death, about 1862.

We have introduced this case for two reasons. One is, because with his coming to this place a new aspect was given to business here. Goods were sold cheaper, and produce brought a higher price than before, which gave new life to business, and soon created the reputation of the town for commerce, which was greatly to the advantage of the town. The other is to show the connection between a liberal support of the institutions of Christianity and prosperity in business. We remember very distinctly having heard him make the following remark to a young man who was hesitating about renting a pew in the church. The rent was to apply on a debt on it. "Take care, my boy; there will be a falling off in your business this year. I have always considered what was given for the cause of religion as money at interest." He said he never accumulated money for the sake of the money itself, but as a means of doing good. When property came into his hands, he felt himself bound to take care of it, and not waste it, and to have it at command, as the Lord might make drafts on him for it. This was his own view of the property which came into his possession. He was a faithful steward of what was committed to his care, and, yet, with some there was a doubt as to the correctness of taking as high interest, as he sometimes did, for money loaned.

In the progress of building the church here, which was commenced in 1838, the subscription was exhausted before the basement was finished, and there appeared to be no prospect of ever finishing it. At this juncture he came forward, and advanced the means to finish it, to the amount of *three thousand* dollars, and took a mortgage payable in *fifteen* years. He intended, as he told us once, to have donated the whole amount, after having received the interest for three or four years, but some of the members thought he wished to make a speculation out of the church, and insisted on having the matter closed up, which was done by selling the pews. At the sale, he took about twelve hundred dollars worth of them, so as to extinguish the debt. For these pews, he made no effort to collect rent, but allowed people to occupy them as free seats.

Mr. Bidwell was mortal, and had his defects, still he hoped, through faith, to prove victorious at last, and gain the eternal rest provided for the pious in Heaven. For the last ten years of his life, he resided at St. Paul, Minnesota, to which place he had transferred his business interests. Here he fell asleep in Jesus, as we trust, in 1876.

REV. MILTON FOOT was one of the early members of this Church, having come into the country, and identified himself with this Society, in the fall of 1830. He died in the town of Adams, Hillsdale County, Michigan, November 13th, 1842, aged 53 years. He was brought to experience the pardoning grace of God in Lock, Cayuga County, New York, in 1814. Having been taught that a simply moral life was enough, he was somewhat contented until Mr. Bassett, the class-leader, had a conversation with him on the subject, and set up a prayer-meeting in the neighborhood. Three men came ten miles to attend that prayer-meeting, which was held in a private house.

Soon after this time, they procured preaching, and held class-meetings. Mrs. Foot attended, and was converted in the first class-meeting she had ever attended. She expected her husband would oppose her, as he had said that he would not live with her if she became a Methodist. Still, she made up her mind to be a Christian, and risk the consequences. When she came home, he told her she need not be afraid to speak her feelings, as he would have stayed to class if he could have done so. Next Sabbath he attended prayer-meeting, and was deeply convicted for sin. Towards evening, he went out from his house, and was gone so long that his wife became uneasy about him, and went to look for him. She found him by the roots of a fallen tree, on his face, praying aloud for mercy. She returned to the house without disturbing him. Soon after this, he came into the house, praising God with cheerful voice, having obtained peace through the blood of the Lamb. The next time the Methodist preacher came there, they both joined the Methodist Church, and became firmly attached to it. He never wavered in his attachment to his Church and its institutions. He was conscientiously devoted to God and a pious life.

At one time, he was to be absent from home with his family, for a few months, and a youngerly man wanted to occupy his house during the time, but he would not consent until he agreed to conduct family devotions regularly during his absence. He wanted his very house to be considered as being consecrated to God's service.

Having seen some persons apparently deprived of their strength under religious influence, and not being satisfied that it was from the Spirit of God, he prayed, very earnestly, that, if it was from God, he might feel the same influence. He was brought to feel the same thing, and was satisfied. At an early period in his Christian life, he felt it was his duty to preach, but he refused, or, rather, excused himself until after he had lost all his property, and was obliged to go to a new country. He regarded his loss of property as a great blessing to him, because, if he had continued to prosper, he would have lost his soul by his refusal to preach. When he went to the new country, he was very soon accused of being a "*Jonah*," and the minister gave him license to exhort, contrary to his wishes, about six years after his conversion. About one year and a half after this, they gave him license to preach, which he continued to hold till his death. He also held the office of steward in the Church for many years. When he removed from Adrian to Adams, he went into the wilderness, but he soon gathered the scattered inhabitants at his house for worship; and his house became a preaching-place for the itinerants, and the early Quarterly Meetings were occasionally held at his house and barn.

His last sickness was only about three weeks in duration. He had had the asthma for about six years, but died of typhoid fever. For the first ten days of his sickness he was in a comatose state for most part of the time, but after that he revived and his mind was clear until about two days before he passed away. At the beginning of this lucid period he made his will, after which he seemed to think of nothing earthly, but was constantly talking of the goodness of God and calling on all around him to praise the Lord. He has gone to his glorious rest.

Mr. Foot was a man of very respectable abilities, and if he had given himself up to the work of the ministry at an early period of his life, he would have ranked high as a preacher. He was very particular in his observance of the Sabbath, not doing anything on that day that could be done on another, not even to shave himself. His piety was sincere and uniform, deep yet cheerful, and depending only and always upon Christ Jesus the Lord. His comunion was sweet and glorious.

A sketch of two of the ministers, viz: Thomas Fox and James V. Watson, who labored here, must close our memorial notices in connection with this Church.

REV. THOMAS FOX died of pulmonary consumption, in the village of Northville, at the residence of his father-in-law, Hon. David Rowland, in July, 1847. He was born May 17th, 1817. His parents resided on Allen street, New York City, at the time of his birth. He became the subject of a sound religious experience at eighteen years of age, and soon joined the Methodist Episcopal Church; and subsequently filled the several positions of Sabbath School teacher, superintendent, class-leader, exhorter, local preacher, and itinerant preacher. In 1840 he was employed by the Presiding Elder to fill a charge; and the next year was admitted on trial in the Michigan Annual Conference. In 1842 he was appointed to Pontiac Station, where he labored with great success and usefulness. There was a very extensive revival in connection with his labors in this place, and a large accession was made to the Church. Before this time the Society was very feeble and it was considered quite an experiment to make it a Station and appoint a single man to it. The venture was crowned with success and the Church became well established.

At the end of his fourth year in the ministry, his health having much declined, he retired from the active work for one year; by this means he was so far restored that, in 1846, he was appointed to Adrian Station. The labor and responsibility of this charge were too much for him. He labored for a short time only, but usefully, before his insideous disease, from some slight exposure, came upon him with fearful rapidity. "Though frequently urged to do so, he did not desist from preaching and tear himself away from the people he so much loved, until he was smitten down helpless upon a sick-bed, from which he never arose. During his lengthened illness he was sweetly submissive, patient and triumphant. His soul held unceasing and transporting communion with the Saviour—the Word of God and the voice of prayer became peculiarly sweet and delightful to him." After having been confined to his house for a long time, and having lost all hope of being able to do anything more for his people, he was removed from their midst to the residence of his wife's father, in the summer. Though he had been lingering long and looking for death, almost hourly, that event at last came upon him suddenly, and he only had time to lisp the name of his wife and Saviour, and sunk to rest on the bosom of his Saviour.

"*Thomas Fox* was a young man of deep piety, great frankness, simplicity and winningness of demeanor. His attainments were respectable, and his talents above mediocrity. He was always studious and acceptable, and highly useful wherever he labored. He stood among the first of the growing lights of the junior members of the Conference, who now mourn their loss. But his highest praise is that many souls ready to perish, conducted to God through his instrumentality, rise up to bless his memory."

In person Mr. Fox was small, in manners pleasing, having good natural powers of mind; but his greatest source of power was in the warm sympathy of his heart, which was well regulated by grace. Had he lived, he undoubtedly would have wielded a great influence for good in this country of his adoption. He died in the thirtieth year of his age. He left a wife, but no children, to mourn his absence.

REV. JAMES V. WATSON, D. D., a man of remarkable versatility of talent and extraordinary perseverance, died at Chicago, Illinois, October 17th, 1856, in the forty-second year of his age. His death, though long anticipated, came suddenly at last. He died at a quarter before 3 o'clock P. M. of the above day. In the morning, had dictated an editorial for the *Northwestern Christian Advocate*, of which he was editor, and had appointed for his amanuensis to come to his room at 4 o'clock P. M. to finish it, but before that hour had arrived he had gone to the land of rest, where sorrow and pain are unknown—he had slept the sleep that knows no waking in this world. He spent an hour in the forenoon in cheerful conversation with some friends, and spoke with delight of the bright land beyond the grave—was in a joyous mood, and, at 11 o'clock A. M. he laid down to rest, and fell asleep sweetly—a sleep from which he never awoke in this world.

Dr. Watson was born in London, England, in 1814—the precise day cannot be ascertained without referring to the parish register—he was, therefore, *forty-two* years old. When but a lad, he emigrated with his parents to the United States, and, after a brief stay on the Atlantic coast, he passed on to the West, with which he became fully identified.

He was led to seek for and obtain the consolations of religion in 1828, and joined the Methodist Episcopal Church immediately, under the labors of N. B. Griffith and E. G. Wood, who traveled the Lawrenceburg Circuit, in Indiana, that year. His first Christian experience was bright and clear—a glorious assurance of the Divine favor. Soon after his conversion, he felt an impression of duty to preach, but hope of his success was not very promising; young, green, awkward in appearance, it was thought to be a doubtful experiment to give him authority to preach. He received his first license to exhort, March 24th, 1832, from the hands of Rev. Joseph Oglesby, and was licensed as a local preacher and recommended to the Annual Conference, by the Quarterly Conference of

Union Circuit, Missouri, August 18th, 1832, and in September of the same year he was admitted on trial in the Missouri Conference, and appointed to a Circuit. Thus obscurely he began a race, which terminated in a hale of glory.

Dr. Watson after a time was transferred to the Indiana Conference and fell into the Michigan Conference by the change of boundaries, and was stationed in Adrian in 1841. He was a man of indomitable perseverance. In this particular he was a very extraordinary man. For the last twelve years of his life, he looked more like a walking skeleton than a living man, having suffered incalculably from asthma. No one who had never seen him during a paroxism of this disease can form any adequate conception of the intensity of his sufferings. At these times the struggle for life was really fearful, and a less determined will than his would have yielded long before. But even in the midst of these sufferings his exuberance of spirits would burst forth. An instance—while residing in Adrian he and the minister stationed in the city, were visiting at the house of a mutual friend, soon after he had been suffering from one of these agonizing paroxisms—he was just able to be up, but was constantly gasping for breath. The conversation having turned on the matter of his suffering, he remarked that he expected to die soon; and turning to the minister, he said, he wanted him to preach at his funeral when he died. "Now, Mac.," said he, "you must put in your best licks; I don't want any of your poor, shriveled up things; I want your best."

When he was compelled to desist from the pastoral work, as he was in 1846, he could not think of sinking into obscurity, and ceasing to do good, or to exert a moral power for the reformation of society. Having removed his residence to this city, he commenced the publication of a periodical—a religious periodical, which he continued to edit and publish under many discouragements until, at the General Conference of the Methodist Episcopal Church, held in Boston, in May, 1852, he was appointed to the editorship of a new weekly paper entitled The Northwestern Christian Advocate, to be published at Chicago, Illinois, which came into actual existence on the first of January, 1853. Perhaps it is not exactly accurate to say that he was appointed to that editorial position at that time, but arrangements were made which resulted in his being so appointed.

Here was now opened before him an ample field for the exercise of his fertile imagination, free from any consideration of the financial question, as that was committed to other hands. He at once gave a life and spirit to the paper which secured the favor and good will of the patrons. However some might differ from his rhetoric, his logic or his theology, all admitted that the paper had a spice, which attracted. So well had he succeeded in this work, that at the General Conference held in Indianapolis, May, 1856, he was returned to the same work, in which he continued to the last hour of his life.

Dr. Watson was first a member of the Missouri Conference, then of the Indiana Conference, and in 1840, by the change of Conference boundaries, he became a member of the Michigan Conference, and when the Michigan Conference was divided, and the Detroit Conference was created, in 1856, he became a member of the latter Conference. His last message to the Detroit Conference was that, though he was sick, he was determined they should not have a sickly paper. So it was; for no one who read the paper would have supposed that the editor was holding a vigorous contest with death for the mastery. The editorials were as sprightly—sparkling as much with wit and sound good humor as if he had been in perfect health. This is accounted for in two ways; naturally he was of very boyant spirits, and in the next place, all his strength of will was brought to bear to keep up that natural cheerfulness which was well tempered with grace. Perhaps history does not afford an instance of greater results from the determination of the will than this. At no period of his history was this trait in him more fully developed than during the session of the General Conference of 1856, of which he was a member. Exceedingly few men with his state of health would have supposed that they could have left their beds even, but he went to the seat of the Conference, and nearly every day was in the Conference room. Many will long remember how they were occasionally startled at his shrill "Mr. President," and then at his pale and haggard countenance, as he occasionally enchained them with his bursts of genuine eloquence, when some subject of great interest was under discussion, The question, "What keeps Mr. Watson alive," has been asked a thousand times, perhaps, to receive the one answer, "His will." This exercise of will was not for the sake of life itself, but for the sake of whatever might be accomplished in this life.

His social talent was of the highest order—never at a loss for thoughts, or for words in which to express them. His imagination was so fruitful that if he could not call up incidents in real life to illustrate his thoughts so as to instruct and even amuse, he could manufacture them at will; and sometimes this very characteristic came to his relief in difficult places. To illustrate: when he was stationed at Adrian the Church and congregation were somewhat agitated on the subject of Church music, some being opposed to a choir, and especially to instruments, while others were strongly in favor of both. He had not expressed himself on that question, but had as yet preserved his neutrality. A gentleman who was not a member of the Church, but strongly in favor of the choir and instruments, having met him in the Postoffice, thought to draw out of him an expression, and after various social converse, and finding him in a pleasant and communicative mood, asked him how he liked the choir and instruments. Without seeming to notice the particular question, he said, " I was preaching in a large town, where Mr. Russel, a concert singer, was stopping at the time. When I came to a certain point in the discourse, Mr. Russell, who was sitting in the front of the gallery, struck up and sung a verse exactly applicable to the point. It produced the most thrilling effect I ever saw." He said no more, but the gentleman was so convulsed with the story, that the question was passed over without being answered. He made all about him feel cheerful and pleasant.

His imagination took in a wide range and gave him great power as a public speaker. On one occasion, in preaching on the resurrection, he painted the rising of the dead—the coming of the little infants to the embrace of their mothers—the meeting of friends long separated, in such a vivid manner that the congregation seemed to be mingling with the scenes, and mothers who had buried children were looking as if expecting to embrace them the next moment. For the want of scholastic training, his tropes and figures were not always rhetorically correct, but the defects were overlooked, even by the learned, because of the exuberance of good spirits with which they were accompanied—his impassioned eloquence.

His early advantages for education were only such as could be furnished in the log school houses in Indiana; in his boyhood days, but he applied himself assiduously in after years. While attending the common school in his boyhood he performed a feat, rather for amusement, and to show what he could do, than from any expectation of deriving any advantage from it, which proved to be of immense value to him; that was, to commit the whole of the English Dictionary to memory. He would have some of his school-fellows hear him recite; and to amuse and astonish them he would repeat page after page of the book without missing a word. This was what gave him such a great flow of words. In after years, all he had to do was to wave his wand, and the words would step forth to do his bidding.

In his nature, he was open, frank, and generous, and was fond of such good cheer as was consistent with Christian character. He was a genial companion, and all who associated with him were impressed with his remarkable fertility of mental resources. He received the honorary degree of D. D. from the Indiana Asbury University, in June, 1856, just a few months before his decease. Though not a classical scholar, he was worthy of his doctorate.

Perhaps this sketch cannot be better closed than in the language of the *Methodist Quarterly Review* for January, 1857, edited by Rev. D. D. Whedon, D. D., who knew him quite intimately. "Dr. Watson, in the midst of great infirmities, exhibited rare powers. Without early scholastic advantages, he rose by the native vigor and brilliancy of his own mind to an eminence in the pulpit, upon the platform, and in the editorial chair, which few, with the happiest external aids, have been able to obtain. He excelled not in the process of regular and adamantine logic, but saw things with clear-sighted, intuitive sagacity. He was no thoroughbred metaphysician, and yet he blended a rare subtlety of perception with that of transparency of imagination, in which the nicest discriminations of truth are readily detected. He had never mastered the technical accuracies of language, yet he handled the powers of the English tongue with a mastery, a range, and sometimes a creativeness, which, while it needed the pruning hand of severe criticism, attested the possession of the gifts of genious, and rendered him possessor of a great popular sway. He often failed in a purity of taste, and yet seldom is found a more exquisite tone of esthetic refinement, or a richer exuberance in the production of the varied forms of imaginative beauty. Had it pleased Almighty God to grant him a healthy frame of body, he had, in the measure of human age, years of great service in him. Humanity and religion would have drawn large installments from his ever-willing treasury of powers. Had large physical strength waited to execute the volitions of his ardent soul, he would have excelled in wreaking his powers upon the accomplishment of masses of good. But the living spirit maintained a constant struggle with the corporal wreck, his attenuated frame fully obeying the rapid impulses of his soul. His pale features, singularly lighted by the eye beaming with the intensity of powerful conception, his panting chest heaving for the breath to pour the vocal conductor of electric thoughts, were perpetual reminders to his friends of his brief delay, and momentous to himself to hurry his task before the damp shades were upon him. How did his triumphant spirit, amidst the parting fragments of its tenement, pour forth the last products of its glorious energies! Who that read, for the last few months, the columns of the

Northwestern Christian Advocate, could have imagined that its copious flow of rich thought were the last utterances dictated from the couch of an expiring man? The magnificent strains, ringing through the wide air, of the dying swan! They seemed to flow as long as the heart beat, and stop with its closing collapse. The echoes were yet rolling while the freed spirit was ascending."

In the department of Sabbath Schools, that most difficult part of our work, this Church has generally taken an active interest. They have generally maintained a large and interesting school, and, at the present writing, they are very prosperous in this department of Christian work, and are laboring assiduously to fill their mission to the young.

Although writing a specific history of the Methodist Episcopal Church, it will not be out of place to record that other Christian Churches were organized at an early day in the history of the town. The Churches were organized as follows: Methodist Episcopal, June, 1830; Baptist, December, 1831; Presbyterian, in the fall of 1832; Protestant Episcopal, autumn of 1838; Congregational, in the summer of 1853. Hence it appears that the Methodists have a priority of existence by a little more than one year. The membership in 1876 was 510, including probationers, having a church valued at $50,000, and free from debt. The other denominations have valuable houses of worship.

We have now furnished a pretty good idea of the origin, progress, and present condition of Protestantism in this city; and it is well, from this standpoint, to take a hasty survey of its operations through the county. We cannot go into the minutiæ, but will give a general statement. The first Christian Church in this county was organized in January, 1828. It was a Methodist Society, and consisted, at the time, of only *eleven* members. The ministers of this denomination, in the early settlement of this country, were almost constantly in the saddle, searching out the new settlers, and calling them together in their shanties, as soon as a half dozen or more could be gathered together. They did not wait for them to build villages, erect school-houses or churches, and then call for them to occupy them, but they went after the people to call them to be reconciled to God. This course subjected the men who did so to many inconveniences and hardships—to much toil and suffering.

From the foregoing facts, it would be expected that they should gain an extensive influence among the people at large. This expectation is found to be realized from the statistics below. There is one drawback, that is, while they were extending their labors so far, they did not attend sufficiently to the *important* points which they had gained. The villages just springing into life, and ambitious of a reputation, were not cared for so as to secure permanently the footing which had been gained; so that, in some of them, though we were the first to erect a standard, we have not the strength we ought to have had, and might have had. Others were allowed to reap the fruit of our planting. More of the people, probably, were gathered into the Church upon the whole, for the time being, than would have been had they pursued a different course, but, by neglecting the centers, perhaps, we are not so strong in any one locality as we might have been. By this activity of our itinerant men—they were, emphatically, itinerant—nearly every nook and corner of the county has been supplied with the Gospel.

We now reckon, according to the Minutes for 1876, the following charges in the County of Lenawee, having the number of members and probationers attached, viz:

Adrian	510	Hudson	1C6
Tecumseh	160	Franklin	158
Clinton and Macon	157	Ridgeway	195
Deerfield	140	Clayton	125
Blissfield	151	Fairfield	159
Palmyra	81	Addison	245
Morenci	404		
Medina	77	Total	2,808

These charges have, in the aggregate, a Church property valued at $175,200.

The first Camp Meeting held in this county was held near Clinton, in the summer of 1832, and it was a time of much religious interest. Camp Meetings have been held since then at different points, at various intervals, and with varying success. These gatherings of the people to worship in the groves have generally proved to be of signal benefit to the church. Two were held in the limits of this county during the summer of 1857, the fruits of which were very glorious. There was but little difficulty in preserving good order at either of them. These two meetings were not signalized so much for the number of conversions as for the depth of the work in the hearts of Christians. The Christians, both ministers and people, went out from them so thoroughly imbued with the spirit of holiness that the succeeding winter was characterized by remarkable revivals.

There is one locality—a beautiful place it is—where a Camp Meeting was held for several years in succession, and to which the attention of the people was directed as one of the fixed points of this feast of tabernacles, that is, "The Devil's Lake." This is a singular conjunction of names—"The Devil's Lake" and a Methodist Camp Meeting! It savors a little of attacking Satan in his very seat. But, if the evil genius ever presided here, he has been exorcised; for the meetings have always been seasons of spiritual interest and profit to the Church. There is an Indian tradition in regard to the origin of this name for this beautiful lake, which we will not now record.

Statistics for the City of Adrian should not be overlooked. They are as follows:

Methodist Episcopal..............510 | Baptist........................353
Protestant Episcopal..............194 | Presbyterian..................298
Congregational..........................282.

PONTIAC is one of the oldest settlements in this State, after leaving the lake and river coast. Mr. Orson Allen settled here in 1819. This was the beginning of the place. It is the seat of justice for the County of Oakland, is situated on the Clinton River, twenty-five miles northwest from Detroit, and possesses the advantages of the Detroit & Milwaukee Railroad. The Pontiac Railroad had been known for many years. This was one of the earliest structures of the kind in the West, having been completed from Detroit to Pontiac in the spring of 1843, although it had been commenced as early as 1835. The city is favored with good water-power, and it contains a population of nearly 4,000 souls. It is a very interesting and important town, although it has not fully met the early expectations in regard to its growth.

Christianity, although introduced at an early day—Mr. Allen is said to have been a member of a Christian Church—has had more to contend against in this town than in almost any other in this State. Many of the early settlers were professed infidels, and carried their opposition to Christianity to a very great extent. It has been stated, on what seemed to be good authority, that there was an infidel club, or organization there, yet, the probabilities are that there were, simply, six or eight men of that cast, who were drawn together, at the taverns and stores, on the principles of affinity, and who carried on their opposition as chance or an appetite for strong drink happened to draw them together, without any systematic combination for that purpose. They were the leading spirits of the town, and were led by *spirits*, as they were liberal customers at the bars of the taverns. At some of these times, they would have mock sacraments and baptisms. On one occasion, they caught a lad, and baptized him with whisky, in the name of the

Father, Son, and Holy Ghost. The man who officiated on this occasion retired to bed that night as well as usual, but was found dead in his bed next morning. What an awful thought, that one should go out of the world so suddenly with such a crime on his soul! These men are all dead now; most of them have died a miserable death. There was only one exception to this last remark. He was a lawyer by profession, and first settled in Macomb County in 1817. After some time, he removed to Oakland County, and filled several important offices. He was a man of fine abilities, but, at this early day, he fell into the same spirit with these infidels, and made himself wretched as well as those around him. However, at an advanced age, he became a convert to the Christian faith, and an experimental Christian. "He died at Fentonville in February, 1858, at the advanced age of *eighty-four* years, in the full possession of his vigorous mind, and in the faith of the Christian religion."

The following extracts from a memorandum book kept by him while in Macomb County, will show some of the difficulties with which the early settlers had to contend: "1817—1 ax and helve, $4.00; Oct. 27—Whiskey (a "necessary of life"), $2.50 per gallon. 1818, Nov.—1 lb. tea, $3.00." These are given only as specimens. We refer to D. LeRoy, Esq. It is to be regarded as a very extraordinary manifestation of Divine mercy that any one of that class of infidels should ever have been converted to the experience of pardoning grace. We knew him personally.

Rev. John P. Kent, a Methodist minister, who was appointed to Detroit Circuit in 1820, established an appointment at Pontiac; so that, in June, 1821, when James B. Finley, the Presiding Elder, visited the Circuit, and held a Quarterly Meeting at Detroit, Mr. Kent had an appointment for him at Pontiac, on a week-day, which he filled. Mr. Kent does not appear to have formed any Society at this place. There is no evidence that his successors kept up the appointment— but it is probable they did not—until Rev. John A. Baughman came on, who established a regular appointment here. While he was on the Detroit Circuit, having only to take in all the settlements in Michigan, with a few in northern Ohio, and being full of zeal for the cause of religion, he took in this place, also, in 1825. He, however, did not form any Society in the village that year. The policy of organizing Societies around the village, instead of concentrating in it, was adopted, and followed for several years, because the village was considered a hard place. Indeed, it had a hard name; so that, in speaking of persons who had gone bad, for a number of years it was said that they "had gone to Pontiac." This policy of having preaching within a mile or so on each side, was wrong and unwise, but so it was; and now we are unable to say precisely at what time the Church was concentrated at the village. When we traveled the Circuit, in 1834, we found a very small Society there, and a small one on each side of it, only a short distance off. This small Society had to struggle with embarrassments—indeed, had to struggle for life—until 1843.

In September, 1842, Pontiac was made a Station, and Thomas Fox—a single man and young in the ministry—was appointed in charge of it. Hitherto, for years, they worshiped in the old courthouse—a very inconvenient place; but now they had undertaken to build a small but neat church. This church was completed, and dedicated to the service of Almighty God, by Rev. Elijah H. Pilcher, the Presiding Elder of Detroit District, January 20th, 1843. His text was, 1st Peter, 4th ch., 11th v.—"If any man speak, let him speak as the oracles of God." His effort was to set forth the cardinal doctrines of the Bible, as believed by the Methodists, and assured the people that these were the doctrines they might expect to hear from that pulpit. The occasion was one of great interest, especially to the Methodist people, as they had so long labored under great disadvantages for the want of a convenient place in which to worship. This church, in a few years, became too small, and they have built a large, beautiful, and commodious one, which was dedicated by Bishop Simpson, in 1864. This work was commenced under the ministry of Rev. S. Clements. It is free from debt. They also have a very good parsonage, free from debt. The The whole Church property is valued at $27,000.

The interests of this Society had begun to assume an encouraging aspect in the autumn of 1842—before the dedication of their first church. Mrs. C. B. McConnel, wife of one of the merchants in the village, had attended a Camp Meeting in the summer of that year, and became anxious for salvation, and seemed disposed to identify her interests with the fortunes of this Church, which was very encouraging to the feeble Society. The way now seemed to be opening for them to prosperity. They were soon after greatly encouraged; for, on Christmas day, her husband, a man of a good deal of influence, attended services in the Court House. After preaching by the Presiding Elder, the Society tarried to hold class-meeting, and Mrs. McConnel with them. Mr. McConnel went out, but soon returned, and took his seat for the class-meeting. He had never manifested any desire for religion, but now, when the minister spoke to him, he arose and said, with a good deal of emphasis, "*I am determined to be a Christian.*" His wife had not made any profession of a religious experience, though she was now, and had been for some time, very desirous, and had expressed a desire for religion. It was not long before they both were converted, and united with this Church. Their conversion and union with the Methodist Church produced a profound sensation in the community. This was the state of affairs at the time when the dedication occurred. From this time, the work of revival went forward until a large number were converted and added to the Church. On the 22d of January and on the 29th of March, the Presiding Elder baptized fifty-nine of the converts. These were adults, and some of the most influential people in the town. The preacher, Mr. Fox, was unordained, which was one reason why the Presiding Elder attended to the baptisms. Since then, this Church has been favored with many seasons of very precious revival and refreshings from the presence of the Lord. According to the Minutes for 1876, the Society now numbers 290 members, besides the number who have gone from them to benefit the Church in other places, and have gone to the Church above.

In relation to this place, the same kind of economy had been adopted which had obtained among the Methodists in many other places, that is, they contented themselves with making a feeble effort in the village, because it seemed to be a hard place, and bestowed their labor, and concentrated their energies, or, rather, scattered them, in the country round about. Pontiac, although a considerable and thriving town for a new country, did not even furnish a name for a Circuit or Station earlier than 1838. At this date, it appears in the Minutes for the first time, with Rev. Josiah Brakeman as the preacher; and, yet, there was no special concentration of force. As evidence of this scattering of the forces in the country, we find a church, built of logs, about three miles out of the village, a little to the north of east. It was known as " Donation Chapel." It was built in 1828 or 1829, by a Mr. Hathaway and a Mr. Turner, and presented to the Methodist Episcopal Church by them; hence its name. These men were worthy members of the Church, and have gone to worship in that "house not made with hands, eternal in the heavens." They designed well; but, had they concentrated their force in the village, how much better would it have been for the cause of religion. It is true that a soul in the country is in itself as valuable as in the village, but Churches need to be planted in the midst of the people; besides, all know that the towns and villages have much to do in shaping the character of the country round about them. We do not intend, in these remarks, to censure either the ministers or people, but simply to say that it is a pity that more importance was not attached to labor in the village. We know well, however, how difficult it is to concentrate labor in a place where there were so few members as there were here at an early day. As late as 1835, when we were on this Circuit—called Farmington—we had to be contented with preaching once in the day—on the Sabbath—once in two weeks. But everything is now changed.

The Church here has met with some reverses and drawbacks, as well as having a good deal of opposition from the world. One minister, who was appointed to the Circuit in 1839, about the middle of the year, became disaffected, joined the Baptists, and then lectured against the polity of the Church he had left. His colleague, *Rev. R. Sapp*, then a young man, answered his lecture so effectually and completely that he failed to draw away many disciples. Still, this incident so diverted public attention as to prevent any special advance in the cause for a time. What were the motives which influenced him to this course, we will not now pretend to say. He was a man of promising talents, and, had he remained true to the Church, might have held a good and useful position, but, for some reason, he has not done much for the world since. He quickly sank into obscurity, and no one speaks the name of Miles Sandford with any special interest.

Another one, in 1852, adopted and pursued such a course as that the brethren found it necessary to arrest his character, and to have his case investigated by the Presiding Elder, according to the provisions of discipline in such cases. He was suspended from the ministry until the next Annual Conference, at which time he was expelled from the ministry and Church. After his suspension, he joined the Baptist Church, and became a minister among them, before the final adjudication of his case before the Annual Conference. A third, though he finished the term of his appointment, joined the Protestant Episcopal Church at the end of the year. Although he filled his term, and honorably withdrew, any one may well see that, having determined to leave, he could not labor with any zeal to build up the Church—a Church which, according to his new theory, was not a Church at all, and that he was determined to abandon, and only waited for the time to come when he could do so honorably to himself. Notwithstanding these defections, the Church has kept on its way, and has prospered, showing that the Church is not dependent on one or two or three men. There is a most wonderful recuperative energy in the Methodist Church.

Other Christian Churches, as the Baptists, Presbyterians, Congregationalists, and Protestant Episcopalians, have been established, and have done their work towards the moral and spiritual renovation and elevation of this community.

We may now append to this sketch of Pontiac a notice of our work in this county at large. The township of Troy was the first point at which a Methodist Society was organized, and that township has always maintained a good reputation in this respect. Indeed, some very valuable men have come from revivals in that township, as Joseph Jennings, Riley C. Crawford, Manasseh Hickey, and some others, in the ministry, living and dead.

In 1820, we find the introduction of the Gospel, under the operations of Methodism, into this county, about which time a small Society was organized. The Society was few and scattered, but the country has become thickly populated, and religious instruction is furnished to the people in great abundance.

Among the greatest achievements attained in this county may be named the building of a large and beautiful brick church at Birmingham, which was dedicated in the autumn of 1873. Rev. Robert Bird was stationed there in 1869, with the expectation that he would secure the building of a church. When he first opened the subject, everybody considered it perfectly chimerical and absurd. But he went about it, and persevered until it was done. Our cause has been wonderfully advanced by it. Nobody but Robert Bird would have succeeded in such an enterprise under the circumstances. He was five years about it. He remained in the Station three years, and the state of the work was such that he could not safely leave it. He took a supernumerary relation, and remained at the work. The next year he took the responsibility of not going to his charge to finish this work. He, by the way, is perhaps the greatest church builder in the Conference. This church is a perfect gem, and is, doubtless, the best and most beautiful church edifice on this continent, in a village of the size.

Instead of one or two small Societies, without any Church property, in 1820, we have, according to the reports at the Conference of 1876, the following Churches and Stations, with members and probationers attached, viz:

Pontiac............................	290	Milford.........................	191
Troy................................	143	South Lyon....................	96
Rochester........................	35	Walled Lake...................	110
Oxford............................	187	Commerce......................	84
Orion..............................	77	Farmington...................	103

Clarkston	90	*Southfield	43
Brandon	171	Birmingham	154
*Lakeville	45	Royal Oak	90
Davisburg	131	Highland	113
Holly	187		
Total			2,340

There is an aggregate of Church property valued at $137,400. These items make an encouraging showing, and yet it is not all that should have been done.

We ought not to fail to show that Rev. Isaac Ruggles, a Congregational minister, settled in Pontiac, in 1824, and operated as much as he could, and was successful in organizing a small Church in the town of Farmington, which has always been spoken of as Presbyterian. We cannot say definitely which form of organization it took. They had built a small church as early as 1830. At the time of the specially blessed revival under the labors of Rev. William T. Snow, of the Methodist Church, that Society was supplied by a young man named Bridgman, who had never seen anything of the kind and did not know what to make of it. Mr. Ruggles may, therefore, be regarded as the father of Presbyterianism in Oakland County. He always lived in this county, but removed for the latter part of his life into the township of Farmington.

We conclude this article, remarking that there have been many precious seasons of revival in this city and accessions to the Church, but in the changing population, many of the converts have gone elsewhere, and other communities enjoy the benefit. The Detroit Annual Conference held its session in Pontiac, in 1859, Bishop Janes Presiding. It was well entertained and the session was an occasion of much value to our cause in the city.

The denominations stand, in 1876, as follows:—

	In the City.	In the County.
Methodist Episcopal	290	2,340
Baptist	181	568
Presbyterian	124	504
Protestant Episcopal	164	164
Congregational	233	410

We take great pleasure in presenting a sketch of one who has been stationed in this place.

REV. DANIEL C. JACOKES, D. D., was born in the State of New York, in 1809, and came to Michigan when but a young man. He spent several years in Detroit, and was then a member of the First Presbyterian Church. He studied for the ministry, intending to

---
* Only so much of these charges as lies in Oakland County.

enter that work in the Presbyterian Church; but, becoming more acquainted with the doctrines and discipline of the Methodist Episcopal Church, he found that his mind and heart were more in accord with them. He, therefore, changed his Church relationship, and was duly recommended, and was admitted into the Michigan Conference in 1840, and has continued in the active work until the Conference of 1876, when, in consequence of the feeble health of his wife, he took a supernumerary relation to the Conference. For several years of his early ministry he was a missionary among the Indians, and endured all the hardships and inconveniences incident to such work, which were neither few nor small.

Dr. Jacokes has filled many of the important appointments in the Conference—as Lafayette street, Detroit; Port Huron; Dexter; Pontiac, and Hudson. Hudson was the last charge in which he labored. He always remained in the same charge the full disciplinary term. He was appointed to the Adrian District In 1868, and remained on it for four years, discharging the duties of the office with great activity and fidelity. He was honored by his Conference by being elected a delegate to the General Conference, which met in the City of Baltimore in May, 1876.

Dr. Jacokes has always been a great student and has a very large library of his own, and is justly entitled to all the honors conferred on him by literary institutions, the titles conferred being more of an honor to the institutions than to him. He is a very worthy Christian gentleman, and we are very happy to be able to furnish a portrait of him—of one whose name has become so familiar to the Michigan public, as being an able minister and a scholar of commanding attitude.

PORT HURON, a flourishing young city, situated at the outlet of Lake Huron, or at the head of St. Clair River at the point where the Black River enters the St. Clair, appears in our Minutes as an appointment in 1838. Prior to this time it had been included in St. Clair Circuit. This was made a point of rest and a small settlement, by the French, almost as soon as Mackinaw; but no considerable progress, by way of settlement, was made until a much later date. The village was surveyed and platted in 1836, and it was incorporated as a village in 1849, and chartered a city in 1857, and now contains a population of about 9,000, or nearly that.

The first Society of the Methodist Episcopal Church was organized by Rev. Benjamin Cooper, in 1830; but this became scattered, made up as it was of a floating population, but a permanent organization was made in 1834. Their first house of worship was

completed in 1844, and dedicated by Rev. E. H. Pilcher. This house became too small for the Church and community, and they decided to dispose of this and build a larger one. This first house was sold to the Roman Catholics, and a new and superior one was completed and dedicated to Divine service in December, 1856, by *Rev. Thomas C. Gardner.* This, again, has been superseded by a large and elegant brick structure, under the labors of Rev. James S. Smart, who is noted in Michigan for dedicating churches and raising money—the basement of which was dedicated by Bishop Ames, in May, 1875.

The Congregational Church was first organized as a Presbyterian Church, in 1837, by *Rev. O. C. Thompson,* who served as a temporary supply, but it was changed into the Congregational form a few years after. They have an excellent house of worship, and a lage and flourishing Society. The Protestant Episcopal Church was planted here in 1839. They have a good house of worship, built in 1857.

The Detroit Annual Conference held its session here in September, 1857, and was nobly entertained by the people. The venerable Bishop Waugh presided. He preached and exhorted with the zeal and fire of his youth, giving an example to the members of the Conference which was felt in its influence by them throughout the whole year. No one can fully estimate the value of the active and zealous labors of the venerable and chief men of the Church, who do not seem to think that their position excuses them from the active, direct labor for the salvation of souls. This Conference was a time of great spiritual interest. Some were converted during the session, and a glorious revival followed, extending through the whole year, resulting in the addition of *eighty-six* as a neti increase for the year, under the labors of that zealous and faithful pastor, Rev. Seth Reed, who still lives and is abundant in labors. Another result was the erection of an elegant parsonage for the accommodation of the minister's family.

Port Huron District appears in our Minutes in 1857, and Manasseh Hickey was the Presiding Elder. So this city has come to occupy, deservedly, an important place in the operations of Protestantism in this country. The District, at this time, was no sinecure, for though the charges were so arranged that nearly all of them reached to the river and lake, a Presiding Elder could not visit all his work by steamboat. Oftentimes he had to travel on foot for miles to reach the place of the Quarterly Meeting. He had to endure a great deal of inconvenience for lodging places, and to put up with much coarse living. These labors and discomforts were so great and numerous that Mr. Hickey could not endure them longer than two years; his health so failed that he had to be relieved from it, and E. H. Pilcher succeeded him for one year.

The principal evangelical Churches have a good Church property, and a membership as below, according to the reports for 1876:

Methodist Episcopal..............277 Congregational....................283
Protestant Episcopal..not reported. Baptist.................................228

We have said so much in regard to this whole region, under the head of St. Clair, that it is not necessary to add anything here on the general subject. There is a Methodist Episcopal Society among the Germans, embracing quite a membership, but as it is included in the Marine City Circuit, we are not able to give the exact number and so do not include them in the number of members in the city, which would add considerably to the number of the Methodists as given above.

We will conclude what we have to say about Port Huron by adding that in the winter of 1859–60 there was an extensive work of grace under the pastorate of Rev. S. Clements, who was much assisted by E. H. Pilcher, the Presiding Elder. Rev. James S. Smart was stationed here in 1873–76, and, under his pastorate, they erected their large and valuable church, the basement of which was dedicated, in 1875, by Bishop Ames.

We also take great pleasure in inserting a memorial sketch of a layman who was one of the lay delegates to the General Conference of 1872:

"Mr. Henry Fish died at his residence in this City, at 5:30 o'clock Friday evening, May 26, 1876, after an illness of several weeks, the culmination of a painful disease that had afflicted him for some years.

"Mr. Fish was well known throughout the State of Michigan, and respected by all who knew him. In Port Huron he was known by every one, and although his vigorous advocacy of prohibition made him some enemies, none could say aught against his character, while by all the better class of people he was held in the highest esteem. He was a man of vigorous intellect, of uncompromising honesty, firm in his adherence to the principles he believed to be right, generous in support of his Church and all worthy charitable and educational institutions fostered by it, kind and liberal to the poor, ready with his influence and his purse to forward all deserving public enterprises, and in every way an admirable and valuable

H. FISH.

citizen. His death is a serious loss to the city, and to the Methodist Episcopal Church, of which he had been an almost life-long member, as well as to his family and friends.

"Mr. Fish was born near Montreal, Canada, February 14, 1824, and was, consequently, a little more than 52 years of age at the time of his death. His parents were of New England birth, but removed to Canada at an early day. In the year 1836 the family came to Michigan, and settled in Macomb County. In 1848 Mr. Fish removed to Port Huron, where his brother Allen had located some years before, and the two brothers entered into mercantile and lumbering business, under the firm name of A. & H. Fish, which has been maintained to the present time, or nearly thirty years. He was an excellent business man, and the firm has always been prosperous.

"Mr. Fish's greatest prominence before the public has been as an active member of the Prohibition Party. He was earnest and conscientious in his support of the principle of prohibition, never swerving from it or proposing any compromise in the hope of political preferment. In 1870 he was the candidate of the party for Governor, and again in 1872. He was active in the movement for the formation of the National Prohibition Party, at an early date. During the war he acted with the Republican Party.

"Mr. Fish was a member of the Board of Education of this city for several years, and in that capacity did much to advance the interests of the schools.

"As a member of the Methodist Episcopal Church, Mr. Fish was scarcely less prominent. He always gave liberally for its support, and was a constant attendant at all the meetings, leader of the choir, class leader, and at times, we believe, Superintendent of the Sabbath School. He was a good speaker, and when addresses were in order was nearly always called upon. To Mr. Fish, as much, or perhaps more than any other man, is due the credit of securing the erection of the new Methodist Church in this city.

"Mr. Fish's family consists only of his wife and one daughter, Miss Gertrude, an only child. It was a comfort to him, during his last illness, to know that he would leave them above pecuniary want, and as his business matters had been put in order, free from care regarding them.

"Mr. Fish was one of a family of six children, having had four sisters and one brother. Three sisters had died before him, leaving Mr. Allen Fish and Mrs. Spalding, both of this city, the only survivors of the family. In their great affliction, his family and relatives will have the earnest sympathy of the entire community, who mourn a good man—a great and noble heart lost to the community and to the world."—*Port Huron Times.*

The funeral took place at the family residence on the 28th. Rev. J. M. Arnold, D. D., of Detroit, officiated, the pastor, Rev. J. S. Smart, being absent in attendance at the General Conference at Baltimore. We knew Mr. Fish well, and knew him to be a very devout and consistent Christian.

GRAND RAPIDS.—We have selected this place as a nucleus around which to cluster the Protestant History for a large extent of country, because this is the most important town in what is known as the Grand River Valley, and because this was the point at which this Protestant History begins. Grand Rapids Mission appears in our Minutes for the first time in 1835. Rev. Osband Monnett was the preacher. No itinerant preacher had, as yet, visited the ground, but a few adventurers had located themselves at the Rapids and other points along the river, and among them were a few Methodists. These had desired a preacher to be sent. Mr. Monnett had everything to do, as he had no plan of his work; he had to inquire out the settlements, and find his way to them as best he could. The appointment proved to be a very unsuitable one; for, although he was a pious, good man, he was timid and bashful, and had no push about him, so he made but little headway. A few points were visited, and something of form was given to the work. In some respects, the next appointment, at the beginning, was more promising, because the man had more energy of character; and things began to look well, when, alas! the sun set in darkness. They had now extended their labors up and down the river as far as there were any settlements of sufficient numbers to warrant a visit from a minister of the Gospel.

Rev. Oren Mitchel, one of the most quiet, good and inoffensive men ever thrust out into the wilderness to look after the wandering sheep, was sent to this field in 1837. He found himself so trammeled with what had occurred the year before that he could scarcely hold up his head, and did little more than to furnish the people an example of piety and true devotion to God. The settlements had so increased during the year that it was thought best, at the end of the year, to make two Circuits in the valley. Grand Rapids and all the valley belonged to Ann Arbor District for the first two years, but the Presiding Elder, Rev. H. Colclazer, was not able to visit it. For the year 1837, it was attached to the Flint River District. Rev. S. P. Shaw was the Presiding Elder, and he was able to make a

GRAND RAPIDS, 1830.

partial visitation of the country, going as far down as Grand Rapids. In 1838, Marshall District was created, and Elijah H. Pilcher was appointed to it, and this valley was included in it. In order to reach Grand Rapids, the Presiding Elder had to travel from Marshall without any intervening appointments, and, in order to complete his work in that part, to pass on up the river, to attend to all the appointments on that route without returning home, and then, as was the case sometimes, travel from Fentonville, in Genesee County, to Jackson, without any intervening charges. This kind of labor, however, only came to him once a quarter, or, rather, from four to five weeks in each quarter; but the Circuit preachers, though they had not so extensive a ride, had less time in which to perform it, and had no relief by being a part of the time in the open country.

In 1838, the country was divided into two charges. James H. Frees was appointed to Grand Rapids, about whom we have nothing to say—only, that the cause was not much advanced by him. Larmon Chatfield was appointed to Lyons Circuit. A Congregational minister had settled at Grand Rapids, but his labors were confined to that place. There was here and there a Methodist local preacher who did good service to the people in their destitution of the means of grace. Mr. Chatfield gave shape and order to the work in Ionia County and in the northern part of Eaton. In this work he was greatly assisted by the local preachers and exhorters. The Quarterly Meetings were times of great interest. The people would travel from *twenty* to *thirty* miles, with ox teams, fording streams, and plodding through the mud, to attend them. When there, they received such full and glorious manifestations of love and grace as made them rejoice that they had attended.

The first Camp Meeting ever held in this valley, was in Ionia County—E. H. Pilcher Presiding Elder, and L Chatfield, preacher— in June, 1841. It was a very interesting meeting, though not very numerously attended, because of the sparseness of the population ; but order prevailed without any difficulty, so that those who had the charge of it could retire at night, and rest as quietly as if they were at their own homes. A goodly number of sinners were converted, and it was a time of great refreshing from the Lord. The Church received a great accession of permanent strength from this meeting.

The village of Lyons was made a preaching appointment in 1836. A few men of means had established themselves there, and it was fully expected that it would immediately be a great place. This expectation, like a great many others which sprung up in

1836-7, was destined to be disappointed ; for, though this valley is very fertile, and rich in its minerals and lumber, time was required for the development of these resources. As the country has advanced, the villages have increased in their population, although many of the original settlers, not realizing their fond hopes, abandoned them for other localities. As soon as these people found themselves settled down here, they desired to hear the Gospel, or, possibly, they thought it might be more for their credit, and tend to facilitate the settlement, to have religious services conducted on the Sabbath. Whatever their motives may have been is no matter now. They wanted the services, and our ministers were ready to respond to the call, and the only ones. They were supplied in this way through the country for many years before any other ministers came in to establish themselves in these wilds.

It is an interesting fact that, however extensive were their Circuits, or however laborious the work of our ministers, they have always been ready to respond to such calls, and make arrangements to supply them. No sacrifice has been too much for them to make, or labor too severe to be performed, or exposure too intense to be endured by them to meet the wants of the people. The fact is, there have not been wanting martyrs to the work, or noble heroes to meet and brave labors and dangers, among the men to whom has been assigned the cultivation of this field.

Some of the local preachers were as ready to brave these dangers as the itinerants. Rev. Jacob Dobbins, a local preacher, had settled in the timbered land in the north part of Eaton County, and on the south side of Grand River, not far from the river. In stature he was a small man, but in determination a giant. He had his regular appointments, and attended to them faithfully. On one occasion, his appointment was on the north side of the river, and the water was high, the ice running, and it presented a very discouraging prospect to make a passage across the river even with a good craft. It was at some distance from any house on either side. The canoe, in which he expected to make the transit, to his great disappointment, was on the other side of the flood. A faint heart would have quailed and returned, but not so with him. The few people must not be disappointed. He was not a good swimmer, so that a passage in that way was out of the question. In casting about to decide what to do, he found two small logs so situated that he could roll them into the river, which he did, and lashed them together with some withes, which he had cut with his knife, so making a raft; then stripping off his clothes, fastened them around his shoulders, and, after much labor and suffering from the cold, as it was early spring, he reached the opposite bank, donned his clothes, and so passed on to his appointment. What was the motive for all this? Simply, to preach Jesus and the resurrection to a few people in the wilderness, without any pecuniary compensation. This is a species of heroism more grand than the meeting of armies in battle. Mr. Dobbins afterwards joined the Conference, and labored usefully for many years. He still lives, but is on the superannuated list.

While on this upper, or, rather, middle portion of the valley, we may as well finish what we have to say before we float down the stream. The first settlers at Ionia, the county-seat, were Baptists in sentiment, and, though they preferred Methodist preaching to none at all, they did not give any encouragement to the organization of a Society. The result of this was that, though we ministered to them, they did not make a Church, and it was some time before our people acquired any special footing there. Besides this, there was an instance of defection in a local preacher, living in the vicinity, that operated unfavorably to us. He was a young man of some talent and more assurance—of a sour spirit. He had once applied to the Conference, before he came to this place, to be admitted into the traveling connection, and was not accepted. Having a very good opinion of his own abilities, he never recovered from the bad feeling which this occasioned. He pushed out into this new region, retaining his relation to the Church, but, all the while, grumbling and complaining against the usages and economy of it, till finally he withdrew from us, and joined the Congregational Church. Upon the whole, it was a relief when he withdrew from us, as he was operating to the damage of the body more by his complainings while he retained his membership than out of it. Notwithstanding these difficulties, our cause has finally triumphed, and we now have a strong footing at that point, as hereafter noted.

Several revivals have occurred at Ionia, taking in their way several men of position in the community, some of whom had been avowed infidels. That indefatigable and always successful laborer, *Allen Staples*, was appointed in charge of Lyons Circuit, which included all that portion of country which we may designate as the middle part of the Grand River Valley, in 1840, and, as was customary where he labored, the whole country was in a blaze of revival. Many were converted and added to the Church. Since that time, the work has gone on with growing interest, widening in its extent, and increasing in its power, as the settlements have extended and increased in population. (*See Ionia.*)

Some oppositions and some competitions have been encountered, but this valley has been thoroughly Methodized. In 1840 and 1841, a good deal of effort was made in this region by two or three young preachers of the immersion faith to convert the people to their belief, but without any very considerable success. This effort led one of them to deliver a discourse specially on the subject of baptism, in which he took occasion to comment on the common objection to the immersion of the three thousand on the day of Pentecost, to wit, the want of water. "Why," said he, "that is a very frivolous objection. There was no difficulty at all; for the river Jordan runs right along there by Jerusalem, and furnished plenty of water. There was no difficulty at all." This state of things gave rise to the following incident at a Quarterly Meeting held in the town of Eagle, in May, 1841. On the Sabbath, during his discourse, the Presiding Elder—E. H. Pilcher—took occasion to allude to the subject of baptism, and referred to the very oft-repeated objection to infant baptism, that is, that persons become dissatisfied with it when they come to years of maturity; and made some remarks in answer to it. Just at that point in his discourse, Rev. L. Chatfield, who sat in the desk of the school-house behind him, pulled his coat. The Elder looked around, when Mr. Chatfield arose, remarking as he did so, "If one be prophesying, and anything be revealed to another that sitteth by, let the first hold his peace." Hearing this, the Elder sat down, and he went on, "I want to tell an incident which occurred with me once." Said he: "I was baptizing a few years ago, during which a young lady came to me, and said she wished me to baptize her. But, said I, have you not been baptized? She said she had been immersed *in* water, but she did not consider that baptism, as the Scriptures say we must be baptized *with* water." The application was easy. When he finished this story, he sat down, and the Presiding Elder went on with his discourse, just as if no interruption had occurred.

Before leaving this part of the country, we will take the liberty of providing a brief notice of two men whose names are associated with the work here, Larmon Chatfield and Allen Staples.

REV. LARMON CHATFIELD was born in Windham, Green County, in the State of New York, in 1812. His father was a Deacon in the Presbyterian Church, and the son was thoroughly instructed in the doctrines of that Church. But, while he was yet a boy, his soul revolted against the doctrines of Calvinism, and, when he came to hear the Methodists preach the doctrines of free grace—free salvation for all who would receive it—he joyfully accepted the doctrine, and was converted to God in his early youth; but, not finding the help which he needed, as he expressed it, "he fell from grace." When he was a young man, he came to Michigan, and settled near Tecumseh. There, under the preaching of Rev. Joseph Bangs, at the age of twenty-two years, "he renewed his covenant with God, and joined the Methodist Episcopal Church."

In the Official Minutes of the Michigan Conference for 1876, it is said of him: "Always of a religious turn of mind, he thought out those fundamental doctrines of Christianity for himself, and, 'searching the Word of God for authority, stored his mind with the truths he found therein—truths which, in after years, proved their value in his matchless controversial discourses upon Calvinism, the Doctrine of Decrees, Reprobation, and the Final Perseverance of the Saints. He was, emphatically, a doctrinal preacher, who would, in a sermon of an hour or more, probe to the bottom the fallacies of Calvinism, Unitarianism, and Universalism.

"Immediately after joining the Methodist Episcopal Church, he entered upon the work of the ministry, was licensed as an exhorter, and took his first work, as a subordinate, in the old Ohio Conference of 1835, and was sent to Mount Clemens. In 1836, his name appears in the Mansfield Conference Minutes, [that is, in the Minutes of the Michigan Conference held at Mansfield Ohio], and he was sent to Plymouth, and there he was married to a Miss Lorimer. She left his side, in six or eight months, to join the hosts of the redeemed. In the year 1838, he was sent to Lyons charge, then embracing the territory now covered by the thriving town of Portland. Here he assisted at the funeral of Philo Bogue in 1839, and, two years after, was married to Mrs. Eliza Bogue, by Rev. Allen Staples, of blessed memory. Serving two years upon the Lyons Circuit, he was then appointed Presiding Elder of the Shiawassee District. Four years of District work, traveling from Grand Rapids to Saginaw, proved his efficiency, and, at the expiration of his term here, he was sent, as Presiding Elder, to the Adrian District.

"Here he lived, at Adrian, for three years; poorly paid, but laying upon the hearts of the people such grand truths that, far and near, there remains indelibly fixed in the minds of those who heard him, profound impressions of the preaching of Larmon Chatfield."

Although his early school advantages were very limited, he was very accurate in the use of language, and, though he was ignorant of the technical rules of logic, he understood how to reason logically, and was a man of great power in the pulpit. He died at Portland, Ionia County, where he had resided for many years, in August, 1876, full of days and good fruits.

REV. ALLEN STAPLES was a man of very moderate preaching abilities, if the capacity for analyzing a text and arranging a sermon be taken as the standard; but, if the power to reach the heart and influence the judgment of his hearers be taken as the rule of determination, he was much above mediocrity—he was superior. His educational attainments were limited, but they were used to the best advantage. He was born in Cheshire, Massachusetts, July 15th, 1810, and was converted to God when about fifteen years of age. Notwithstanding he had to meet with opposition, he soon joined the Methodist Episcopal Church. He was licensed to preach in 1836, and the same year was admitted on trial in the Michigan Conference. His second appointment—1837—was to Bean Creek. The whole country was so new and sparsely settled that the Circuit was named after the Creek, and not for any town—but Hudson has become a large and pleasant town in it since then, and has been made a Station, having good churches of the different denominations.

His zeal for the conversion and salvation of sinners was so all-pervading and so all-consuming that he could well adopt the language of the prophet, "For Zion's sake I will not rest, for Jerusalem's sake I will not hold my peace." His zeal was so great that he could not devote his time to reading and study, but he must be looking after sinners, and laboring with them to bring them to Christ. Blessed and extensive revivals of religion uniformly attended his labors. By means of such excessive labors, he soon became worn out, and was for several years on the superannuated list. On his death-bed, he advised his brethren not to follow his example, in the excess of his labors, as he believed he had shortened his days by that means. He seemed always to forget himself, and used his lungs to their utmost capacity. It is a question, which every one must settle for himself, whether he could accomplish as much good in a short life, made short by incessant labors, as in a longer one, prolonged by a moderation of zeal. But, perhaps, after all, the injury to the physical man does not result so much from an earnest zeal as from an undue straining of the lungs by attempting to speak when the lungs have become exhausted of air—from the want of a proper attention to the rules of elocution. If a man will stand erect, and keep his lungs properly filled with air, he will not fail from earnest speaking.

Mr. Staples had fixed his residence at Albion, after he became superannuated, from whence he was called to his heavenly rest.

The following is extracted from the official memoir as found in the Minutes for 1848:

"Of our departed brother much might be said that would be greatly to his praise. He had many qualities that adorn their possessor, and make him the subject of grateful remembrance. He was modest and unassuming, ever esteeming others better than himself. Though kind and warm-hearted, he had, nevertheless, a happy faculty of being familiar with all classes without becoming subject to their disrespect. As a Christian, he was eminent. In his piety, more than in anything else, lay the secret of his usefulness and influence. Wherever he went, he carried the Saviour with him. Sanctification, or perfect love, he enjoyed for many years, and, to the end of his career, it was a prominent item of his conversation as well as his public ministry. In a word, he had plunged deep into the ocean of Immanuel's love, and had grown in grace as life advanced.

"Brother Staples was not what would be styled a great preacher, nor did he aim to be—and, yet, if eminent success in bringing sinners to God entitles a minister to greatness, he was truly great, greater than many of more pretensions. He never labored where there were not more or less revivals of religion during the year, and frequently hundreds were brought to the Saviour. His zeal for the salvation of men was proverbial, and, no doubt, he died a martyr to its excessiveness.

"Brother Staples left this world on the 21st of October, 1847. His disease, which had been his ailment from time to time, when interrupted in the ministry, was pulmonary consumption. During the last six months of his life, he was an extreme, yet a patient, uncomplaining sufferer. His death was triumphant, as his life had been devoted. May we follow him as he followed Christ."

We will add one incident which will develop his characteristic zeal with its success. At a Quarterly Meeting, on his second Circuit, he, with the Presiding Elder, put up at the house of a gentleman who made no profession of religion. After dinner, on the Sabbath, the Presiding Elder, being much fatigued, laid down and took a nap, from which he was aroused by the sound of Mr. Staples' voice. When he awoke, he found Mr. Staples talking to his host with tears in his eyes, and exhorting him to seek religion at once, while the gentleman himself was bathed in tears. Soon after they kneeled for prayers, and the host was happily converted to God. His zeal led him out in much personal effort, and his kindly spirit gave him great success in securing the confidence and affection of those for whom he labored.

It is time, now, to return to Grand Rapids, and see what has been the course of events in the lower part of the valley. It is proper to say that a small class had been organized at the Rapids in the summer of 1837, made up of persons who wanted as much of Church fellowship as they could have. A Baptist man, whose wife and one son were Methodists, had moved into the place, and joined, for the time being, and was made the class-leader. The progress of settlement was retarded by the money panic of 1837, and this, of course, affected the growth of the Church. Still, a few were added to the Church. The circumstances looked discouraging and dark.

We left Rev. James H. Frees in charge, he having been appointed in the fall of 1838. The Circuit then included all the settlements below Flat River. The traveling was attended with great difficulty and almost incredible labor and much suffering, but the missionary persevered, with no earthly prospect other than some expectations of receiving *one hundred* dollars, a part of which only was received.

This appointment was an unsuitable one for the charge. The Rapids, though as yet but a small village, was growing in interest and importance, and contained some very intelligent and well-educated people. They had a good degree of refinement. The preacher had neither the one nor the other. He was good in his intentions, but was very ignorant, and had never mingled in refined society. He could not make any favorable impression for us in the village, and but little in the country.

The Presiding Elder, E. H. Pilcher, felt this most painfully whenever he went there to attend the Quarterly Meetings, which he did every quarter. By the way, his predecessors on the District had not succeeded in getting as far down the river as the Rapids, except once. He felt, however, that he had no responsibility in the case, as he had not had anything to do in making the appointment. This year, as all the preceding ones, was a little worse than a blank, so far as the village, now City of Grand Rapids, was concerned; for, though a small Society had been organized, there was a prejudice against Methodist ministers created, which it was very difficult, afterwards, to wipe out. It will not be out of place to give a fuller delineation of this young man, to whom was entrusted the work of giving shape and character to Protestantism in that important portion of the State. He had very little advantage for education, and had never mingled in refined society. Nevertheless, he was very communicative, and exposed his ignorance on all occasions. He believed that snakes had feet, and said he had made them protrude them by exposing them to a hot fire. On one occasion, he was stopping at the house of an intelligent gentleman, one of whose daughters was a Methodist, and finding a copy of Shakspeare's Works on the table, he took it up, and, turning to his host, addressed him in this way: "Who was *Shakspar?* I never heard tell of Shakspar before." Then, taking the book, and turning it over a few minutes, he observed, "I reckon this would be a good book for me to read, wouldn't it?" We give these items only as specimens. They might be multiplied indefinitely. Yet he was sent here to lay the foundations of religious Society and of Methodism among an intelligent people.

In reviewing these first four years, we are astonished that we have any footing at all in this part of the valley. It can be attributed only to two causes; one is the intrinsic excellency of Methodist doctrines and polity; the other is, the the special blessing of God on the labors of his faithful, trusting servants, who have since occupied the field.

How strangely we have acted, sometimes, in supplying the new fields! The prevailing thought often seems to have been that anybody would do for the new country. It is true that people would put up with services in the destitute places, which would not be tolerated at all when the country became older and more densely populated. But when the foundations are to be laid, and shaping and character are to be given both to society and the Church, it is of the utmost importance that the very best talent, as well as the best experience of grace should be selected. As a Church, we have lost immensely in many portions of this country from such bad policy. This has arisen not altogether from choice, but partly from the necessity of the case. The older towns have demanded, and the greater competitions have suggested, that our most talented and experienced men should be appointed to them; and the inability of the newer places to support men of families has seemed to shut us up to the necessity of appointing young and inexperienced men to them, whatever may be their prospects of importance.

This whole valley only returned *twenty-seven* members in 1836. The next year there was no report, owing to circumstances over which we prefer to draw a veil. But, in 1838, there were *sixty-eight* members returned; and in 1839 we had increased to *one hundred and one;* still included in only two Circuits, and two ministers. This year may be regarded as the beginning of a vigorous religious life for this valley. The two Circuits here had been supported, in part, by the Missionary Society, but it seemed to be time that they should not only support themselves, but begin to make some return to the Society from which they had been deriving a part of their life.

The Presiding Elder, E. H. Pilcher, this year—1839—having fully surveyed the ground by personal visitation to all the Quarterly Meetings on each of the two Circuits, determined, if possible, to obtain a change of policy, and to secure the appointment of some of our most talented, active and successful men to that isolated field. We call this an isolated field because it had so little connection with any other part of the work. The settlement had followed the watercourse almost entirely, and, consequently, there were no good roads coming in from the south. In many directions there were long stretches of woods, with scarcely anything worthy of the name of road. The Presiding Elder regarded this field as a very important one prospectively, and thought it ought to be well supplied and thoroughly occupied. He, therefore, applied to the Bishop, at the next Conference, for four men, where only *two* had been employed the year before, and where only *one hundred and one* members had been reported, Grand Rapids having *fifty-five* and Lyons *forty-six* members. It seemed to be a desperate venture, but he pledged that, if he would give him the men he wanted for the Rapids and a good supply for Lyons, they should be struck off the list of missions at the next Conference, because he believed they would be made self-supporting. His wishes were met entirely in regard to the Rapids; the men he wanted were appointed, and Lyons was well supplied; so that, in the Minutes for 1839, the appointments stand: Grand Rapids. *Ransom R. Richards,* Allen Staples; Lyons, Zebulon C. Brown, Levi Warriner. These were all indefatigable men and successful ministers. They are all deceased.

During the winter of 1839-40, there were blessed revival seasons at several places on each of the charges. They returned 388 members at the Conference in 1840, making an increase of 287 members this year, and no missionary appropriation was asked for the next year. The Presiding Elder had his eye specially on Grand Rapids, and encouraged the brethren to bestow special attention on that locality, which they did. He rejoiced to find the labor was not in vain, for, when he visited the Circuit at the last Quarterly Meeting before Conference, which was held at the Rapids, he found a large and interesting congregation, with a good membership, and all in good heart.

At this Quarterly Meeting the following little incident occurred: On the Sabbath, at the close of the sermon, the Presiding Elder called for the public collection, as usual, and made some remarks to the people to call forth their liberality. There were two young men sitting together, one of whom remarked to the other that if the Elder would tell them a good story he would put in a dollar. Without any knowledge of this remark, the Elder told the following anecdote, or rather, fact, as illustrating the returns which are often made to those who give liberally for the support of the cause of religion: "At the General Conference of 1840, which was held in the City of Baltimore, one of the delegates from the West, and who had never visited the City of Washington, set apart a certain sum of money to defray his expenses in visiting that city, being all that he could spare at that time for such a purpose ; but, before the day arrived which he had fixed upon to make the contemplated visit, information came to the Conference that a hurricane had swept over a certain town, and had destroyed the Methodist church; that the Society was poor and unable to rebuild without assistance ; that a church was essential to their prosperity; and an appeal was made to the members of the Conference for aid. This delegate at once determined to forego the pleasure of making his visit, and contributed that sum for the benefit of the distressed Church. On the evening the Conference adjourned, a letter was put into his hand, which, when it was opened, he found to contain the exact amount he had contributed, and containing the request that he would accept of that sum from one who desired to be holy." This was the story. The young man put in his dollar On his way home from church he picked up a *three-dollar bill*, for which he could find no owner. He said he should always believe what that Elder said.

Mr. Richards, the preacher in charge at the Rapids, was then in the fullness of his strength and in the activity of his labor. While his health endured he was a giant in labor, and Mr. Staples was even then proverbial for success. Both of these men fully sustained their reputation in the success they had this year. At the beginning, they had *fifty-five* members ; at the end, they reported *one hundred and fifty-one*, making a net increase of *ninety-six*. Lyons Circuit was increased from *forty-six* to 237, making an increase of 151. We have an increase for the valley, then, of 247, making 388 in two Circuits.

Mr. Brown, in charge of Lyons, was a very sound-minded man, and could attend well to the business of the Circuit, and Mr. Warriner was an indefatigable laborer for the conversion of sinners. Mr. Warriner, by his warm and earnest exhortations, could lead them penitently to trust in Christ, and Mr. Brown could well and thoroughly indoctrinate them. By this combination of talent the work was both advanced and confirmed. In the light and glorious halo of Christian piety which constantly shone about these *four* men, all former embarrassments were nearly forgotten by the people. Their industry and piety laid a good foundation for Christian society in all this valley.

We have again wandered away from Grand Rapids, and must now return. The Church in this place has met with various vicissitudes and drawbacks, according as the appointments of the preachers happened to be favorable or unfavorable. Sometimes they were full of hope, and sometimes nearly in despair. This town was erected into a Station in 1844, and *Andrew M. Fitch* was appointed to it, and remained two years. He found only about *fifty* members of the Church in the city, but at the end of his term he returned *one hundred and thirty*, having had a net increase of *eighty* members in the two years; but the Society had advanced much in its position and stability, and in its moral influence in the community. This may be regarded as the beginning of a vigorous life to the cause in this city. It has gained a position from which it will never retreat or recede. For the next four years there were various successes, and the Society remained nearly stationary. In 1850 *Rev. F. A. Blades* was appointed to this Station, and supplied it for two years, during which time the Society diminished *three* members, according to the numbers reported. But we cannot always determine precisely the numbers in a village Society from the published statistics, simply because sometimes there are small country classes connected with the village to be visited on a week-day evening, or it may be on Sunday afternoon, which, as soon as it becomes more convenient to visit them from some of the Circuits around, are lopped off from the village or city Station, greatly to the relief of the stationed preacher, but making an apparent decrease in his membership. The facts in this case were that his predecessor had withdrawn from the Church, and had so managed that he had taken nearly the whole Church with him. The first service Mr. Blades held was attended by only about a dozen persons, and before his term expired he had a full congregation, and restored the membership to the former number, nearly. He had a successful term. The Society in this city was now in good heart, having gained much in strength, and were in a fair way to flourish. During the time of Mr. Blades's ministration, they had enlarged and improved their house of worship, and upon the whole had made much permanent advancement.

In 1852 *Rev. Andrew J. Eldred* was assigned to this Station and remained two years. In the winter of his second year of labor there was a very glorious work of revival, in which it was estimated that more than *three hundred* were converted to God, a large portion of whom united with the Methodist Episcopal Church. This was an occasion of immense labor and anxiety, but one of glorious success. The Church interests were greatly advanced by this revival. A second charge was organized in this city—located on the west side of the river—in 1855, which has continued to grow and prosper. According to the Minutes of 1876, we now have four charges, embracing 770 members and probationers, and a Church property valued at $107,200—with all the appurtenances for the work of Sabbath Schools appropriate to such a membership. One of the above charges is among the Germans.

Other denominations are here and in this valley. A Congregational minister settled at Grand Rapids early and gathered a Church around him, which has grown and increased. The Presbyterians, the Baptists, and the Protestant Episcopalians, all have their Churches planted and are doing Church work according to their views of such work. They each have good and valuable Church property, and are well situated in the midst of the city. We present the statistics of the different denominations at one view:

Methodist Episcopals...............770 Congregationals.....................649
Protestant Episcopals..............767 Baptists............................485
          Presbyterians.......................282

LUMAN R. ATWATER was one of the early settlers in the Grand River Valley, and is worthy of a little notice. We here present a small but accurate engraving of him. He was born in Burlington, Vermont, June 23rd, 1810, and was born of the Spirit in Plattsburg, New York, January 1st, 1832, and joined the Methodist Episcopal Church on the 8th of the same month. Soon after his conversion he went South and stopped for some time in Millidgeville, Georgia, and in December, 1833, was appointed class-leader, which office he has filled most of the time since. He came to Michigan in May, 1837, and settled in Lyons, Ionia County. Here he was soon appointed class-leader and steward. He immediately opened what he called a Methodist tavern, that is, he opened his house for the entertainment of the itinerant ministers. In this he was greatly blessed and prospered for seven years.

Mr. Atwater removed to Grand Rapids in May, 1844. Here he

immediately took all the honors the Church was competent to bestow. He has been "Superintendent of the Sabbath School for twenty-five years; class-leader, steward and trustee to the present time—a servant of the Methodist Episcopal Church, but an heir of heaven."

When the plan for incorporating lay delegation into the General Conference was adopted, Mr. Atwater was sent as one of the delegates to the Electoral Conference in 1871, and was urged very strongly to allow his name to be used for delegate to the General Conference, which he firmly declined, but was elected the first Reserve. At the Electoral Conference of 1875, he was elected the President of the body. He is a devoted and consistent Christian, and has the confidence and respect of his brethren. He still resides at Grand Rapids. We shared and enjoyed the hospitalities of Mr. Atwater and his good wife, who has gone to her heavenly rest, from the autumn of 1838 to 1842 while we were on the Marshall District, and we found him to be a true man of God.

FLINT is a flourishing young city, having been incorporated as such in 1855, and contains about 8,000 inhabitants. It is situated on the Flint River, which here furnishes excellent water power. It is the seat of justice for Genesee county, and has the advantages of a good surrounding country. Pine grows in the vicinity in great abundance, so that pine lumber and shingles form a great part ot its commerce. The settlement was begun in 1835, and increased so rapidly as to attract considerable attention in 1836. The State Asylum for the Deaf and Dumb and Blind, which has been in successful operation for a number of years, is located here.

The location is pleasant and healthy, and it will in time be the chief town in this part of the State. From the very beginning, attention has been given to education; for before they had erected good habitations for themselves, the people provided the shantee school-house. They were the first in the State to adopt the union, or graded school system, and have one of the finest public school buildings in the State. The religious history is that with which we are more specially concerned at this time.

A small settlement having sprung up at Saginaw in 1834, Rev. Bradford Frazee was appointed, from the Ohio Conference, as missionary, and on one of his visits there he stopped at Flint and preached once, in the summer of 1835, which was the first religious service in that region, of which we have any account. In the autumn of 1835, Rev. Wm. H. Brockway was appointed to Saginaw Mission, made Flint a regular appointment, and organized a Society in July, 1836, consisting of *Daniel S. Freeman and wife, James McAlister*

and wife, Benjamin F. Robinson *and wife*, Mrs. Miller, the mother of Mrs. McAlister, and *John Martin and wife*. No leader was appointed at this time, and O. F. North, who succeeded Mr. Brockway at the Conference in 1836, appointed Daniel S. Freeman leader. Mr. Brockway states, in regard to the place and work this first year, as follows: "I think at that time there were not more than four or five families on the ground now embraced in the city of Flint. I generally came from Saginaw every third week and preached at Flint, and also five miles north, at Mt. Morris, then called the 'Coldwater Settlement.' At Flint my home was generally at the tavern of Mr. Beach, and my preaching place his little bar-room. During the summer of 1836, a frame store was built by Messrs. Stage & Wright, opposite Beach's tavern. When the floor was laid we got permission to use the upper story, and I preached there once, I think, in July, 1836; and then and there the first class was organized. To the best of my remembrance, it consisted of nine persons; most of them were from the settlements near Flint. The whole of Michigan was in one District, and the Rev. James Gilruth was Presiding Elder; but he never came further north than Pontiac." This small Church was soon after strengthened by the addition, by letter, of Dr. Joel Fairchild and wife, David A. Miller and Margarette Miller.

Rev. Oscar F. North was appointed, at the Conference in 1836, to succeed Mr. Brockway. Mr. North's labors were very successful in the conversion of many, and in additions to the Church. These seemed like great revivals, and so they were in proportion to the number of inhabitants. A Quarterly Meeting was held at Flint on the 14th and 15th of January, 1837. The Presiding Elder not being present, and neither Mr. North, nor Rev. L. D. Whitney, who assisted him, being in Elders' orders, they could not have the sacrament. This was the first Quarterly Meeting held here. Another one occurred on the 30th July, 1837, at which the Presiding Elder, *Rev. Wm. Herr*, was present and officiated. This was the first sacramental season they ever had, and was the first time that Flint was favored by a visit from a Presiding Elder.

In 1837, Flint River Mission appears in the Minutes of the Conference for the first time, with Luther D. Whitney for preacher in charge, who continued for two years, and was quite successful in advancing the Church.

The first movement towards building a church was in the autumn of 1839. It, however, was not till 1841 that they secured the grounds now owned by the Court Street Church, and commenced the erection of a building. Rev. F. B. Bangs was the preacher in charge. He was returned to the charge in 1842. During the summer of 1842 the church building was raised and covered. This building was enlarged, burned down and replaced by a much finer and better one. A Quarterly Conference held in Flint, June 24th, 1843, E. H. Pilcher, Presiding Elder, and F. B. Bangs, preacher, was a very important one, from the business done. The trustees reported a parsonage completed, with a debt remaining unpaid of only $62.47-100. The most important thing was that William Blades and Daniel S. Freeman were licensed to preach. Both these men have done very effective work as local preachers, and considerable good work as itinerants. During Mr. Bangs's term the Sunday Schools received great attention, and the interests of the Church generally were prosperous.

Flint was made a Station separate from the country in 1847. Since then the Station has been nobly supplied and has prospered greatly. There was one dark hour that came to this Church. They had struggled hard and had erected a church at a cost of $4,000, and had enlarged and repaired it at a cost of $3,000, and were feeling that they were now in a condition for work and religious enjoyment, when 'on Tuesday night, the 19th of March, 1861, the church was discovered to be on fire, and in an hour it was reduced to ashes, with all its contents, Sunday School library, musical instruments—in short everything which it contained, as well as the beautiful house, was consumed. There was no insurance. The fire was undoubtedly the work of an incendiary, probably incited to this dastardly act by the liquor men, who considered themselves aggrieved by the activity of the Methodist Church people in the temperance movement.' From this disaster originated a new church located on the north side of the river, called Garland Street Church. So there are now two Stations in the city of Flint. According to the report in the Minutes for 1876, there are 683 members and probationers; two churches and two parsonages, aggregating $42,000 in value, with Sunday Schools correspondingly prosperous, having all necessary apparatus and fixtures for success.

The Methodists were not left alone to minister to this people, but others came in and organized Churches. Rev. Mr. Dudley organized a Presbyterian Church in 1837, consisting of *seven* members. They at first adopted the Congregational form of organization, but subsequently changed it to the Presbyterian form of government. The Protestant Episcopal Church was organized December 25th, 1839; and the Baptist Church was constituted in

1853, consisting at the time of *twelve* members. There is also a Congregational Church organized at a later day. These all have valuable houses of worship.

The Annual Conference has been entertained here at three different times, to wit · In 1855, Bishop Ames presiding; in 1865, Bishop Clark in the chair; and in 1875, Bishop Harris presiding. The session each time was in the month of September. The Conference was grandly entertained, and the sessions were occasions of great interest to the Methodist people.

As usual, we subjoin the statistics of the five denominations:

Methodist Episcopal............683 | Protestant Episcopal............263
Presbyterian............244 | Baptist............329
Congregational............186

REV. WILLIAM BLADES has been referred to in these pages before, and now, as we supposed we had finished what we had to say in regard to Flint, the announcement comes to us that he has been taken to his reward. This event occurred early in May, 1877, at Flint, where he had resided for many years. We avail ourself of the following biographical sketch, which was read at the funeral by Dr. George W. Fish, whose graceful and appreciative words we heartily endorse. The sketch was published in the *Michigan Christian Advocate*, and is as follows:

"I know not why the tearful, though pleasant, task of pronouncing a brief biography of our venerable and beloved friend should have been assigned to me, unless it be that an uninterrupted friendship extending over a period of almost thirty-eight years, and in its nature not unlike that which existed between David and Jonathan in the olden time, may be supposed to fit one for such a duty. Very pleasant hast thou been unto me, my brother; thy love was wonderful, passing the love of ordinary worldly friendship. The earthly life that has so recently closed has been a very plain and simple one. I am inclined to the opinion that the inventory of his realty—bonds and mortgages, stocks and cash in bank—will not cover many pages of 'legal cap;' nor will there be a fierce contest of greedy heirs and unscrupulous lawyers, about the distribution of an estate. And yet, I think, to-day, the possesions of Ward, Vanderbilt, Astor and Stewart combined, shrivel into insignificance beside the dying legacy left by this good man

"Of what the world calls culture, learning and science, he claimed no great share; nevertheless, in the sphere in which God placed him, he has accomplished more than Tyndal, Spencer, or any of their compeers. His has been a beautiful, harmonious, Christian life. What can be more cheering and desirable than such a life with such an ending?

"William Blades was born in Worcester County, Maryland, in 1798. His parents were God-fearing people. His father dying while he was yet a mere child, the road by which his boyish feet found their way up to manhood was a rough and rugged one. At the age of nineteen years he was converted, and joined the Methodist Episcopal Church, of which he remained a "lively member" for sixty-one years, and until the Great Bishop transferred him to the Church triumphant, where he doubtless had a place for him. In his boyhood he learned the hatter's trade, at which he wrought until he came to Michigan, when he became a tiller of the soil.

"About fifty-six years ago, in his native State, he married her who still survives him, and together they have shared the lights and shadows of an eventful and protracted pilgrimage. From Maryland he removed with his family to Newark, New Jersey, thence to Western New York, and still later, in 1834, to Michigan, and settled in the town of Grand Blanc, and has resided in this county ever since. He was elected, and served as magistrate, and also as sheriff of the county, altogether for a term of ten or twelve years. My recollection of his public services is that he was noted as a peacemaker, and, consequently, he was not particularly popular with the court men and lawyers, one of whom declared that 'if the squire went on in that way much longer, he would dry up the courts altogether, as he was always advising litigants to settle their disputes between themselves, and not take them into court,' and that he almost always succeeded in persuading them to do so. In 1848, he was elected to the State Legislature, and served during the first session ever held at the present capital. In all these places of trust and responsibility, he proved himself worthy and well qualified. The few aged men and women who were his associates in the olden times, and who still survive him, will bear me out in saying that as a private citizen and public servant he has acted well the part assigned him. With very pronounced political opinions, he merged the partisan in the patriot, and loved his country with a devotion and constancy that knew no abatement.

"In 1833, before leaving East Avon, New York, Mr. Blades was licensed as an exhorter, and on the 24th of June, 1843, the Quarterly Conference of this Church voted him a local preacher's license. In 1847, he was ordained Deacon by Bishop Morris, at Ypsilanti, and in 1864 he was admitted to Elder's orders, and ordained by Bishop Baker at the Adrian Conference. He was an efficient and successful worker in the itinerant ranks, during which time he traveled Flint, White Lake, Grand Blanc, Flushing, and Genesee Circuits. When the infirmities of age and failing health compelled him to retire from the more active itinerant work, he did effective service in the local ranks, in which capacity he was known as a most efficient worker—he has attended more funerals and officiated at more weddings than most of his ministerial brethren who are in the regular work. And when unable to preach at all, he has served his brethren in the capacity of class-leader, which office he filled till a very recent date. And here allow me to say that, to my mind, Father Blades was one of the best class-leaders I have ever known. Since this couple, Father and Mother Blades, commenced life's journey together, they have given back to the Lord six darling children whom He had lent them for a time, and now the father has gone to join them in the 'house of many mansions.' For about two months, our brother had been waiting patiently and cheerfully for his Master's call. Though a great sufferer at times, he had been wonderfully uplifted and sustained. To those who have visited and conversed with him during those weary weeks of suffering, it is unnecessary for me to say that the sunshine of the dear Saviour's countenance has never been obscured by a single cloud, and we have felt that Father Blades's sick-room was 'privileged beyond the common walks of virtuous life—quite in the verge of Heaven.' In reviewing thus hastily such a life, we come to the conclusion that there is not much over which to mourn. With a brave heart and honest purpose, he settled in this then western wilderness, and has lived to see the rude frontier changed to a prosperous commonwealth. The somewhat heterogenous elements of our rude pioneer civilization, during his lifetime, have crystalized into harmonious beauty, and to this result our departed brother has contributed his full share. His life, extending as it does over a period of more than three-quarters of a century, rich in historic memories, affords a beautiful and instructive example to our young men.

"There is so much to commend, and so little to criticise, that I venture to hold up the example of my dear brother's life as being as near a perfect model as poor humanity ever attains. It seems to me like a beautiful poem, or a bouquet of fragrant summer flowers. As the father and head of his family, his example is worthy of imitation. He honored God, and his children have risen up to call him blessed. As a citizen, he contributed his full share towards the defence of virtue, truth and honesty, and towards the condemnation of vice in every form. As a Christian, and a devoted Churchman, his love of the Bible and its Divine Author, and his absolute faith in its teaching, touched his lips and inspired his heart. It would be a blessing to this world of ours to have a thousand such men added, rather than one taken away.

"I will not attempt to offer a word to this circle of numerous mourners, but leave that duty to be performed by one better qualified to do it justice. In the day when the Lord cometh to make up his jewels, Father Blades will doubtless be there, with a crown and 'everlasting joy upon his head,' and he will bring a multitude of redeemed with him, as sheaves gathered by him for the Master. Such lives are the richest heritage of the Church."

The name of LUTHER LEE, D. D., has long been familiarly known to the world as a minister of the Gospel, of great power as a controversalist, as a writer, and as a friend to the slave. In his early years, he acquired the *sobriquet* of "The Logical Lee," a name to which he was justly entitled, and which he still honors.

Luther Lee was born in the State of New York, on the 30th day of November, 1800. From this it will be seen that he is nearly seventy-eight years old. He was converted, and joined the Methodist Episcopal Church, in 1820. He was early licensed, but did not join the itinerant ranks until 1827. When the slavery question began to agitate the Church, in 1836, Mr. Lee soon took the side of the oppressed. In 1843, he took a prominent part in the organization of a new Methodist Church, which was known as the "True Wesleyan Methodist Connection in America." The great foundation of this new body was anti-slavery. Dr. Lee continued to take a very active and prominent part in this Church, until in 1867, when the cause of his separation from his mother Church being removed by the abolition of slavery in the nation, he, with several others, returned, and were received into the Detroit Conference at the session held in Saginaw City in September, 1867. He has since filled the Stations of Flint and Ypsilanti, but has now, for the last few years, been placed on the superannuated list. He resides at Flint, where he has many friends and admirers, in the enjoyment of the sweet consolations of grace. Dr. Lee is a very able divine and writer, and still wields a vigorous pen. He is a very strong advocate of total abstinence and a prohibitory liquor law.

LUTHER LEE, D. D.

CHAPTER XIII.

JACKSON—Appears 1839—County Organized—Judges—Anecdote—Hard Name—Reading Meetings—First Sermon—Society Organized—Quarterly Meeting—Martin Flint—Vicissitudes—Numbers—Sabbath School—Presbyterian Church—Congregational Church—Baptist Church—Elizabeth Thompson—Difficulties—The County—Camp Meeting—Spring Arbor—Revival—C. M. Pilcher—Maria Fitzgerald—Charles Brown—Terrible Death—Station—Church Built—Struggle for Lots—Spencer—Statistics—BATTLE CREEK—Church Organized—Names—Circuit—Revival Incident—Anecdotes of Bible Distribution—ALBION—College—Preston and Endowment—Revivals—Principals and Presidents—C. F. Stockwell—Dr. Hinman—Organization of Churches—Quarterly Meeting—Episode—Revival Meetings—Dr. Grant—Dr. Jocelyn—Fiske—LANSING—Early Preachers—Society Organized—Population—Right Policy—Appears in Minutes—District—Conference Session—Mrs. Richards—IONIA—Methodist Polity—Monnett—Station—Church First Organized—Z. C. Brown—George Bignell—R. Sapp—Romantic Incident—Other Churches—Conclusion.

JACKSON, the county-seat of Jackson County, is situated on the Grand River, seventy-six miles from Detroit, according to the railroad survey. It is favored with some water-power, but the chief dependence is on steam for manufacturing purposes. It has become a great railroad center, and has the advantages of the following railroads: Michigan Central; Jackson Branch of the Michigan Southern; Jackson, Lansing & Saginaw; Fort Wayne, Jackson & Saginaw; The Air Line, and Grand River Valley. It is centrally located in the county, and can never have any considerable competition from villages springing up around it.

The first location of land or purchase from the General Government was made—and it was the first in the county—by Mr. Lemuel Blackman, in the autumn of 1829, which was quickly followed by entries by Dr. B. H. Packard and Isaiah W. Bennett. In

February, 1830, a few shanties were erected, and in the spring, Mr. Blackman's family, with a few others, came in, and fixed their abode here. In the spring of 1830, a village was laid out by Lemuel Blackman, Dr. Benjamin H. Packard, and Isaiah W. Bennett, proprietors. The county-seat was fixed here by commissioners, and confirmed by Governor Cass in February, 1831. The Fourth of July, 1830, was celebrated, with a great deal of patriotism, in the midst of the forest trees, as many of them were yet standing. It is to be regretted that many more of them had not been left as ornaments to the town. Mr. John Durand, an old gentleman and the only praying man in the new settlement, officiated as chap-

FIRST M. E. CHURCH, JACKSON.

lain. This Mr. Durand was a Methodist, and a very pious, consistent Christian, of a sound mind, but of small capacity for any kind of public speaking. But his services on this occasion were delightedly received. He has since died in the quiet and peaceful hope of the Christian.

The difficulties connected with the first settlement of this place, and the heroism required to accomplish it, can hardly be appreciated at this day. The imagination may do something towards it, when it is remembered that, in 1830, when the first few families settled here, there were but two or three houses on the road west of Ann Arbor, so that they were, in fact, pushing out forty miles into the wilderness. It is true, the route lay mostly through oak openings, but these were traversed by many marshes and marshy brooks, which rendered the passage very difficult. All their provisions, as well as household goods, had to be conveyed on wagons drawn by oxen. To the naturally timid, there was even a worse difficulty than all these in the many Indians who still lingered about these parts. The name of old *Pe-wei-tam*, a savage-looking old fellow, who frequented these parts, was a source of terror to the timid.

But the stakes were driven, the difficulties and dangers were braved, a town was made, which by the Legislature of the State was created a city in 1857, and now rejoicing in that title, numbers about 14,000 inhabitants. The original name was Jacksonburg, which was considered too long, and the *burg* was dropped off.

The County of Jackson was organized in the winter of 1833. The first judges were Dr. Oliver Russ, as presiding judge, and Samuel Wing and William R. DeLand, associates. Only a few terms of court were held by these judges before there was a change in the judicial organization, and Wm. A. Fletcher as Circuit Judge, and Wm. R. DeLand as associate, were appointed by George B. Porter, the Governor. The first term of court for this new county was held on the 3rd day of June, 1834. This is the beginning of the records. Dr. Samson Stoddard was the County Clerk.

There are some amusing anecdotes told of Judge Russ, which indicate that he was better qualified to deal out pills—he was a good doctor—than to preside over a court. All the business of the first term of his court was transacted in a part of a day. When he was called on to charge the Grand Jury, he stood with one foot on a round of the chair before him, and, leaning his elbow down on the back of it, talked to them for a few minutes in relation to their duties. He was very desirous to have a bill of indictment found against a grocer for selling liquor to the Indians, but the Grand Jury found themselves a little troubled about how to make it out, and referred the matter to the Judge, who took up the pen and wrote:

JOHN DOE to Jackson County, Dr.,
To selling liquor to Indians..$20 00

remarking, "that is a good enough bill."

Whether the man was ever convicted on such an indictment tradition saith not.

It must be confessed that Jackson obtained a hard name at an early day of its existence, from which it did not recover for a long time. So when it was determined that the Penitentiary should be located here, it was sneeringly remarked that it was only necessary to wall in the town to furnish it with fit inmates. It is true there were some causes which operated to give it this hard name. Many of the early settlers were poor men, and some of them were men who had failed in business at the East. They were not able to make the necessary appropriations and outlay of means to make the place inviting and healthy. The result was that the stagnant water remaining in the unworked streets produced disease and death, and the habitations were repulsive. Another thing which operated unfavorably was that, in the time of the wildcat banks in 1836-38, there were two banks opened here which ran but a short race. When Commissioner Felch came around to investigate their affairs—their solvency—he found in one of them several boxes containing specie, which, upon examination, were found only to have a layer of specie, beneath which were nails. No very considerable improvement occurred until after the Central Railroad was completed to this point, in 1841. This made some difference in the activities in business. But time was necessary to wipe out the reproach attached to the town, which now has been done, and Jackson is considered one of the very interesting cities of the Peninsular State.

Soon after the first settlers had seated themselves on the soil, Mr. Blackman, though not a professor of religion, thought it too bad that the Sabbath should be spent in idleness without any kind of religious services. It was determined to call the people together and have a sermon read. The first Sabbath the sermon was read without any prayer, as there was not a praying man in the settlement at that time. These reading services were kept up until they could be supplied with preaching. Some religious men came in shortly after, so that they had prayers connected with readings, but it was not till in the fall of 1831 that they could be supplied with preaching on the Sabbath, and then for a year or two more, only once in two weeks.

The first sermon ever preached here was by a Baptist minister, who had come here on business, and preached on a week-day evening—January 26th, 1831. The preachers on Ann Arbor Circuit having been solicited to take this place into their Circuit, E. H. Pilcher, the junior preacher, visited Jackson for the purpose, and preached January 27th, 1831, in the evening. This was the second sermon, but it was the *first by any one who came for that purpose*, the former one having been merely incidental to the preacher's private business. The services were held in a log tavern, kept by Wm. R. Thompson. Mr. Pilcher was followed, in two weeks, by Rev. Henry Colclazer, the preacher in charge; from thenceforward they supplied it regularly once in two weeks, on a week-day, until the Conference. After the Conference in September, 1831, the Circuit was so arranged as to give them preaching on the Sabbath, still only once in two weeks. It was included in Tecumseh Circuit, Elijah H. Pilcher and Ezekiel S. Gavit, preachers.

In July, 1831, Rev. Henry Colclazer, preacher in charge of Ann Arbor Circuit, organized a Methodist Society or Church, consisting, at its first organization, of *John Durand and wife, Ezekiel T. Critchet and wife, Orin Gregory and wife, and Mrs. Judge DeLand.* These were increased shortly after by several others. Even those who were members of other churches united, so as to have church privileges, until a church of their original choice might be organized. The first Quarterly Meeting, including love-feast and sacrament, was held by Rev. E. H. Pilcher, assisted by Rev. Elias Pattee, April 14-15, 1832. The services were held in the sitting-room of the tavern kept by Wm. R. Thompson, who, by the way, had thrown out the liquor from his bar some time before. This was a peculiarly interesting occasion, not because of the numbers, but because of the interest felt by the pious present, some of whom had been deprived of a communion season for about two years, and because of the manifestation of Divine grace. This was the first Communion of the Lord's Table ever held in this county, or even west of Ann Arbor, in this State. At this meeting Martin Flint, a young man, was converted and joined the Church. His was the first case of conversion that had occurred in the county. He came out clear and strong in his experience in the love-feast. He became a very consistent and devoted Christian, and finally fell a martyr to his religion, dying of pulmonary consumption a few years after, developed by blows inflicted by a young man. They were associates, and this young man was so offended at Flint for being a Christian that he would fall upon him and pound him with the fists on his back and chest, which blows were never resisted. If he could ever find him engaged in secret prayer, as he did occasionslly, he would be sure to fall upon and pound him. He finally dealt out to him several severe blows on the breast and stomach with the butt-end of a whip, which developed the disease of which he died. He died in great peace. The Church had quite an accession during this year by letter—two families of Thompsons, in which there was a mother, two sons and their wives, joined in November, 1831.

The Methodist Church here has had to pass through various changes of prosperity and adversity—seasons of great revival and dimunition—and now have a beautiful house of worship, valued at

$75,000, and, according to the report for 1876, 480 members and probationers.

The greatest glory of this Church is the Sabbath School, which has been under the continuous superintendency of J. Henry Pilcher for about eighteen years, with but one year's intermission. It is said to be one of the most enthusiastic and successful schools in the State. As reported in the Minutes of 1876, the school numbered 380 members, which is very large for a town of that size.

As will hereafter be seen, for several years the Methodists had the entire ground, but, as it was called a hard place, and the ministers found very little support, they rather shunned it, and did not even name the Circuit after it while there was any other place which could well be substituted for it. In this way, others stepped in, and furnished the people with a more frequent supply of ministerial labor, and entered into the harvest the Methodists had prepared, who did not wake up to the matter until it was too late to recover all they might have retained.

Rev. John D. Pearce, a Presbyterian minister, who had settled at Marshall, preached here a few times in 1832, which was the first preaching by that denomination; but a Church was not organized or constituted until the 10th of June, 1837, when Rev. Marcus Harrison organized one consisting of *thirteen* members. Mr. Harrison became their pastor, supporting himself, in part, by teaching, and labored with considerable success. He was originally a Congregationalist, and so were a portion of the members; but, as there were no Churches of that order in the State, according to a certain plan of union they all united in making it Presbyterian. They continued such until in 1841, when, some difficulties having arisen in the administration of Church discipline, and finding it very difficult, as they thought, to get rid of some disorderly members, a meeting was called, and, on the 6th day of March, 1841, a Congregational Church was organized, consisting of *fifty-six* members, taking the most of the members of the Presbyterian Church. The few left endeavored to maintain an existence, until 1846, when they merged themselves with the Congregational Church, and have so remained. A very extensive revival occurred in the Church in the spring of 1847, under the labors of Rev. Mr. Avery, an evangelist, who had been engaged to assist the pastor, Rev. G. L. Foster. There were estimated to be, at least, two hundred conversions, most of whom united with that Church, but quite a number joined the Methodist Church, under the pastorate of E. H. Pilcher. Some very hard cases were converted, who have remained steadfast, while some relapsed into their old ways.

The regular, or "Close Communion," Baptist Church, was organized in 1834. The Society was very small, and was supplied then with only occasional preaching. They have grown, and have a good house of worship.

The Protestant Episcopal Church was organized in 1837, by Rev. Mr. Cummings, of Ann Arbor, and Rev. George Fox was the first Rector. They have a large and commodious house of worship.

We will here introduce to notice a venerable lady, who, though she did not reside at Jackson at the time of her decease, was one of the early members in this place, having joined the Church here on November 20th, 1831, by letter. A peculiar interest gathers around her character from the fact that she was one of the earliest converts to Methodism in New England. The following sketch is from the pen of Rev. Henry Colclazer, who knew her well, and was her pastor at the time of her death.

"MRS. ELIZABETH THOMPSON, the subject of the following biographical sketch, was one of the first persons who espoused the cause of Methodism in the New England States; she was one of those who dared to stand in defense of the truth in the days of severe trial and and danger. While her piety recommends her to all the lovers of Christianity. her connection with the rise of Methodism in our own country presents her as an object of esteem and veneration to all those who look with emotions of pleasure upon the prevalence of those principles which she embraced at so early a period.

"She was born in the town of Norwalk, in the State of Connecticut, on the 5th of August, 1770. Her father, Mr. William Raymond, was one of the earliest emigrants to that region. During the Revolutionary War he was a seaman, and commanded a merchant vessel, which was chased by a British ship. After great exertion, he succeeded in saving his life, but had the misfortune to lose his vessel. His mother was the daughter of Mrs. Hoyt—a widow lady at that time—whose house was the only one left standing when the British destroyed the village of Norwalk. Although the subject of this memoir was but eight or ten years old at the time, yet she retained a vivid recollection of those scenes of peril and suffering throughout her life.

"In the year 1788, when our sister was in the eighteenth year of her age, Boston Mills and Daniel Smith were preaching on the Circuit, which included Norwalk, under the superintendence of Jesse

Lee, Presiding Elder. After meeting much opposition, Miss Raymond succeeded in becoming a regular attendant upon the services of these men of God. In a short time, her mind became impressed with the truth, and she resolved to embrace the doctrines of free grace and full salvation, and it was not long before she gave evidence, not only that she had embraced those sentiments theoretically, but that she had become a subject of the work of grace in the deliverance of her soul from sin. Her parents and many of her friends at this time were members of the Presbyterian Church, and, as would be supposed, exercised all their authority to bring her over to the orthodox faith, and threatened her with banishment from their society if she would not renounce her heretical sentiments. But all their efforts proved unavailing; for, the more she was opposed, the stronger she became in the faith; and, in the twentieth year of her age, she became a member of the Methodist Episcopal Church, and remained, for some time, the only member in the town of Norwalk, thus giving evidence of a superiority of intellect and a love for the truth uncommon under such circumstances; she stood like an isolated being upon a rock in the midst of the ocean, while wave after wave dashed in fury around her.

"In 1792, she was united in marriage to Mr. John Thompson, who had taken an active part in the celebrated Battle of Monmouth.

"After several removals, in 1831, she came to this Territory, in order to enjoy, during her last days, the society of her children who are living in and about Ann Arbor. Since her removal to this country, she has been looked upon by the members of our Church as a relic of bygone days; in looking upon her, we insensibly mingled with our feelings some of that enthusiasm which animates a lover of his country when he sees standing before him one of the patriots of the Revolution; he is but a man, but he venerates the man, because his name stands united with the most glorious deeds recorded in the annals of his country. So stood our sister among us, as a monument of the days of trial, when our fathers laid the foundation of that revival of religion which has spread so universally throughout our country.

"On the 17th of November last, while living with her son, Wm. R. Thompson, a disease of a pulmonary character, with which she had been afflicted for some years, came to a crisis, and terminated her earthly existence on the Sabbath following. Her sun went down in splendor and triumph.

"Her funeral sermon was preached to the largest congregation ever assembled in this country, on Sabbath afternoon, the 24th of November, from a text of her own selection, in Revelations, 'Blessed

are the dead which die in the Lord from henceforth; yea, saith the Spirit, that they may rest from their labors, and their works do follow them.' "H. COLCLAZER."
"ANN ARBOR, December 4th, 1833."

Mrs. Thompson was present when Jesse Lee preached his first sermon in Norwalk, and became interested in his cause at once. He was refused the use of the church, and he preached under a tree in the streets. Under this sermon she was convinced of sin, and never had rest after until she found it through faith in Jesus Christ. She was a woman of deep and constant piety. We knew her well.

To carry on the work in this place, as in all new places, persevering labor was required. Some idea of the labor to be performed, and the difficulties to be overcome, by the first ministers, in order to furnish the Word of Life to these people in the wilderness, may be found in the statement of a few facts. When *Mr. Pilcher*, as he was the first minister who ever visited this place for the *purpose* of preaching, first went through from Ann Arbor in January, 1831, there were but four or five houses on the way between the two places. The ground was covered with snow, and the path was but dim; the marshes were frozen over then, but when they thawed out in the spring they were found to be very difficult to cross, and sometimes large circuits had to be made to find a safe crossing place, and then often the horse would mire down. This lonesome and difficult road was to be traveled over twice, every visit, on horseback, making a distance of *eighty miles*, to preach twice to a few people, as Grass Lake was supplied at the same time. Yet these trips were regularly made by Colclazer and Pilcher up to August, 1831. As strange as it may now seem, Mr. Pilcher, having to go from Jackson to Ann Arbor in October of that year, and to cross Grand River on the main street, found the round logs so afloat that his horse got down among them, so that he had to dismount and manage to extricate him from the logs, and to make him swim by the end of the bridge.

We may be permitted to relate another incident of travel connected with the work of supplying Jackson. On the 28th of November, 1831, the weather became suddenly cold, so that in less than twenty-four hours the ground was frozen solid and the streams partially. Mr. Pilcher, preacher in charge, was at Jackson, on his westward tour. On the 29th he set out. When he reached the Sandstone Creek, which was unbridged, he found it partly frozen over. In order to cross it the horseman had to go into the creek, and then pass up its channel about ten rods to reach a place where the marshy bank could be passed. At this time the creek was nearly frozen over. The edges were quite hard, leaving but a narrow space in the middle—not wide enough for a horse to pass. The creek was about two rods wide at this place.

What was to be done? Here now was a difficulty. This creek must be crossed to reach the preaching place, which was a little more than a mile distant. Looking about, he found an old handspike, or small lever, with which he broke the ice next the shore, so as to get his horse started in, then mounting him, he would strike forward and break down the ice. When the middle of the stream was reached, the water was found to be nearly up to the skirts of the saddle, but with feet and handspike he worked a passage up to the point of egress. The wind was blowing fearfully cold at the time. Then a new difficulty met him. The depth of water brought the ice so high that the horse could not be induced to mount it, and he himself had become so cold and weary that he could not well use his club at such disadvantage; but to go back was contrary to his motto. After beating on the ice for a while he managed to get his horse by the side of it, so as to dismount, when he broke it down to better advantage, which having done he brought the horse up by the side again and remounted, and now by much coaxing and some threatening, he induced the animal to lift his fore feet onto the ice which settled down under them. After repeated trials in this way, a passage was made to the shore, and both passed over. It required nearly, or quite, three hours to work this passage. The work was done, and now a mile more had to be traveled, over a rough, hubby road, before finding shelter. Man and beast were pretty well covered with ice, and thoroughly chilled.

As Jackson is the chief locality of interest in the county, we may cluster all the Methodist history around it. As settlements sprang up at different points, as at Grass Lake, Leoni, Napoleon, Sandstone, Spring Arbor, Concord and Parma, they were at once supplied with Methodist preaching, and Societies were organized. The settlement of this part of the country was so rapid that it kept the Itinerants constantly on the alert to find the new places for preaching. They could not wait for roads to be made, but followed any kind of trail they could find to pass from one point to another.

The first Camp Meeting held in this county was held in the edge of the town of Pulaski in the summer of 1837. It was a time of very great interest. The scattered inhabitants gathered together, and dwelt in tents for a week, and the Lord was with them in power —many were converted. From this Camp Meeting a revival of great interest sprung up at Spring Arbor. Here meetings were held for about two weeks, with great profit to the cause of Christ.

Spring Arbor is the name of a township in this county, originating in the fact that there are a great many beautiful springs in it. The first who settled here was a Mr. William Smith, with his wife and son-in-law (Mr. Swain), and his wife. They came here in 1831, and settled where the Indians had formerly had a village. The country was beautiful in its wildness. Mr. Smith, wife, and daughter were professors of religion of the Christian order. Dr. B. H. Packard, a Methodist, settled by the side of Mr. Smith in the spring of 1835. Previous to this time, they had had but occasional preaching, now it was regularly established, and a Society formed. As this was the point settled upon at this time for the establishment of a Methodist Seminary, it attracted a good deal of attention, and high hopes were entertained of building up a village of importance, and the Circuit was named Spring Arbor rather than Jackson. These bright visions of greatness faded away when, in 1837, the project of building a Seminary was found to be impracticable. But this is wandering away from the revival, which occurred in August, 1837, following the Camp Meeting. This was a very valuable revival, and there were some noble accessions to the Church. There were two cases of conversion during this revival worthy of notice.

Mr. —— was a man of a strong and well-educated mind, but greatly averse to religion—rather skeptical in regard to the truth of the Bible. He was a large, well-built man, and very much of a gentleman, except when the subject of religion was introduced to him. In the course of his advancement to manhood, he had acquired a most unreasonable prejudice, and, even, a spirit of rancor against all Churches. This gentleman became deeply and powerfully awakened to a need of a Saviour. The struggle with him was a severe one, but short. The stubbornness of his will and the pride of his heart rose against the convictions of his judgment and his feelings. His better emotions finally triumphed, and, one evening, he declared his desire to become a Christian. Earnest and fervent prayers were offered for him that night. The meeting closed. He returned home, not to sleep, but to pray. That night, his feelings became so intense that he sought solitude for prayer. While alone, pleading, in the agony of his soul for salvation, Jesus appeared to him as his Saviour in power, and spoke peace to him. His whole nature was melted and subdued, and formed in the mould of love. He became, emphatically, as a little child. All was tenderness and love. The next day his very countenance was radiant with the light of his soul. Never was man more clearly converted than he. His

theme was the power of grace. He was a man of such talents and
education, and his conversion so clear and powerful, that great
hopes were entertained of his usefulness in the cause of religion.
These hopes, alas! were destined to be disappointed. He hesitated
to join the Church; he gave place to his old prejudices; he began
to cavil at doctrines and discipline. There was no Church in that
part of the country, at that time, except the Methodist Episcopal, and,
though they had been instrumental in his awakening and conversion,
he set himself to find difficulties and objections in doctrine and discipline, and, finally, he could not satisfy himself with any Church.
He never united with any, but lost his religious life. He became
very disconsolate. Had he united himself at once to the Church,
and entered earnestly on the duties demanded, he would have been
a bright and shining light; but, alas! he turned away, and his light
was lost in the darkness.

We now present a case in contrast with this, occurring at the
same meeting. *Maria Fitzgerald* was a young lady of a strong and
well-cultivated mind, and possessed a very determined will. She
resided about two miles from the place of meeting. Her parents
were good people, and strict Calvinistic Baptists. They had instilled
their Calvinistic views into her mind thoroughly. In her estimation,
any excitement or noise at a religious meeting was very much out
of order, and to shout, when happy, was a shame. One evening,
being at the meeting, she was very powerfully awakened to a sense
of her guilt and need of a Saviour, but resisted all the persuasions
of her friends to manifest a desire for religion. There she sat
during the exercises, exerting all the force of her strong will to
prevent any external manifestations of the emotions of her heart.
The meeting closed for the evening, and she stopped for the night
near by with a cousin, a pious young lady. About day-dawn next
morning, a messenger came for the writer and the family with whom
he stopped, to go over and pray for Maria, as she had not slept any
all night, and was almost in despair. We went as soon as possible.
When we entered the house, we found her sitting, and presenting
as complete a picture of despair as could well be furnished. We
spoke to her, and said, "Maria, do you not think Christ died for
you?" "No, not for me," said she; "he died for others, but not for
me." "But he died for all—'he tasted death for every man,'" said
we. "But there is no mercy for me," said she, with a sigh. We
asked, "Do you not desire to be saved through Christ?" "Yes,"
was her quick and earnest reply. "Then, do you think he would
produce in you that desire if he were not willing to satisfy it?"

"No," said she. "Then He is willing to save *you*," we responded. After referring to a few of the promises, we had a season of prayer. She was encouraged to pray for herself, which she did with much fervor of spirit. We inquired of her, as we were kneeling, if she could not now trust herself to the Saviour. "I can," she said. "Then, do you not find light for your soul?" we asked. "A little," she replied. "Praise Him for that!" we responded. It was but a moment more until she was on her feet, shouting, "Glory to God!" at the top of her voice, so wonderful was the change. In a few days after she united with the Methodist Episcopal Church, in which she continued a faithful and devoted member until she was removed to the Church above, which was done by leading her through a lingering consumption. She was a very useful Christian. Her sufferings were endured with Christian fortitude and triumph, and her departure was in a halo of glory.

Mark the difference in these two cases. The latter did not stop to cavil at what might not be exactly as she might express it, but united with the Church and devoted her heart and life to the promotion of piety, lived happy, and died triumphantly, having done much good. The former began to cavil and object, then to condemn, and refused to join the Church, lost the power of the spirit, and failed to retain his own piety, and did not promote it in others.

During the months of January and February, 1839, there was an extensive revival in the town of Concord, in this county, Many of the young people were converted to God. There was a young man—Charles Brown—who had made a profession of religion before coming to Michigan, but had foolishly and wickedly forsaken God, and had given himself up to the pursuit of vain pleasures. Many of his young associates were converted to God, who exhorted and entreated him to return to the Lord at once. His usual reply to all their kind entreaties was, "I mean to be religious before I die, but not now. I *must* attend the dancing parties of this winter first, and after that I mean to be religious." So the winter passed, and Charles remained away from the Saviour. Some time in the spring his mother, a pious woman, entered into conversation with him on the subject of his salvation, with much sympathy and earnestness. In the warmth and earnestness of her maternal and Christian feelings, she said, "Charles, my son, seek the Lord and become religious now." "Mother," said he, "I mean to become religious; I do not mean to die without religion, but I cannot attend to it now; I am nearly done sowing my wild oats, and then I will attend to religion."

A few days after this conversation, he attended the raising of a mill, and as he was passing around giving some directions, one of the bents fell and struck him on the head, while the profane oath was but half uttered upon his lips; in a moment he was senseless. He lingered a few hours, and expired without hope in Christ. Here is an admonition to all who know their duty and postpone attention to it.

We take the following from the *Ladies' Repository* for January, 1841, which has this foot note: " Obituaries will seldom be admitted into the *Repository*, but the following notice is peculiarly interesting, and will be read with great profit by those who admire the manifestations of Divine grace."

THE CHRISTIAN IN DEATH.

CAROLINE MATILDA, late consort of Rev. Elijah H. Pilcher, of the Michigan Conference, was the daughter of Doctor Benjamin H. Packard, and was born in Middleport, Niagara County, New York, November 21, 1818. She was instructed in the principles of the Christian religion—her parents having been members of the Methodist Episcopal Church for some years before her birth. Caroline evinced a great aptitude to learn, and an ardent desire for knowledge. In the summer of 1828 her parents emigrated to Michigan, and settled in Ann Arbor. Here she had the advantages of schools and society, both of which were diligently improved. Indeed, it was her ardent attention to study that laid the foundation for many of her subsequent afflictions. Her parents moved to Spring Arbor, Jackson County, in February, 1835, [where she died.]

Caroline embraced religion in the thirteenth year of her age, through pastoral labors bestowed on her the day previous to that event. Her repentance was thorough, and her evidence of pardon clear. The following is her own account of this great work:

"It was Monday, July 18, 1831, when, for the first time, the light of God shone into my benighted mind. O, what joy then filled my heart! All was happiness within, and I felt truly like a *new creature*. The consideration that God was reconciled almost overwhelmed my soul. Strange, indeed, did it seem to me, that God should ever observe one so unworthy. I felt, indeed, that I had been ungrateful to Him for the Holy Spirit, which had been so often sent to convince me of my sins—the remembrance of which was grievous to me. Then I *humbly* repented before God—I believed that there was efficacy in the blood of Christ to take my sins away."

On the 15th of August, the same year, she joined the Methodist Episcopal Church, of which she continued a worthy member until taken to the Church above. Her piety was uniform, and her attachment to the Church ardent. She was naturally distrustful of herself. In religion she usually spoke with a good degree of confidence, yet hesitated to express all her feelings, lest it should *appear* beyond the truth.

Her communion with God was deep and clear, as will appear by the following extracts from a diary she kept for a few years:

"February 25, 1834.—I feel that I am in the hands of God. I am toiling to be directed by Him, for He will do all things for my good. It fills my soul with joy when I think that, after I have passed the sorrows of life, I shall see 'those who have come up through great tribulation, and have washed their robes and made them white through the blood of the Lamb.'

"May 24.—I look forward with a pleasing hope that one day I shall gaze on the beatific beauties of my King, and swell the notes of the heavenly choir. Yes, on the other side of Jordan, with the saints of God, I hope to cast my crown at the feet of my Saviour, and cry, '*Holy, holy* is the Lord of hosts!' O, how pleasing is the hope of the Christian! He knows that this world is not his abiding home, but he seeks a city out of sight. He is only a sojourner here, hastening to a land where everlasting spring abides.

> 'No chilling winds nor pois'nous breath
> Can reach that healthful shore;
> Sickness and sorrow, pain and death,
> Are felt and fear'd no more.'"

Her desire for *holiness* is sometimes very strongly expressed. On May 25, 1834, she writes, "I do realize my unworthiness this day in the sight of God, but I *do trust* that he is fashioning me after His own likeness, and humbling me at the foot of the cross. O, that I might there remain, until the all-cleansing blood of the Saviour shall be applied to my heart, and wash away all my sins.'

> ''Tis all my hope and all my plea,
> For me the Saviour died.'

O, for a dedication of my soul and body to the service of God."

In view of a change in her relation in life, she expresses a strong sense of the responsibilities of a minister's wife; but in this, as in other cases, she states that her help is in God, and that if she can but be the means of saving souls, she is willing to sacrifice all. She feels that God will always be with her; and though she may leave the society of friends, He will be her support. In view of this, under date of July 19, 1834, she writes as follows: "I must expect to be separated from the friends I love. Yes, we meet and part here below, but will soon reach heaven. Glory to God, there is a resting place! God will take care of me. I wish to feel a cheerful resignation to His will in all the dispensations of His providence, and then I shall be happy. I *do rejoice* in God."

These extracts are the more valuable as they express her private feelings—not being designed for the eye even of her intimate friends, and, indeed, were not seen until after her death.

She was married to Rev. Elijah H. Pilcher, of the Ohio Conference, June 4th, 1835. It will be remembered that the Ohio Conference included the State of Michigan, until the General Conference of 1836, when the Michigan Conference was created.

For the last three years of her life she enjoyed much of the fullness of love divine. Having been brought just to the borders of the grave several times, she always had strong confidence in God.

On the 25th of August, 1839, she obtained a clear witness of perfect love—at which time her prospect of health had been fairer than it had been for a long time previous. But how soon are our prospects blasted!

On the 5th day of September following, while her husband was absent at Conference, she was brought down to her bed with disease, from which she never recovered, but continued to suffer until the 5th of April, being just seven months.

She had a complication of diseases, but suffered with singular patience. Her father remarked that, though he had practised medicine more than twenty-five years, he had not met with a case of such *continued severe suffering*, and that he had never witnessed such patience. During her protracted sickness, she was never heard to utter the least complaint against the dispensation of Providence.

When her friends remarked, as they frequently did, that her sufferings were great, her usual reply was that she had *great* support, sometimes adding that she would willingly suffer more if it would be for the glory of God. At all times, she spoke of death as calmly as on any other subject. She was anxious to be useful, and to have her husband so; hence, she was unwilling that he should stay from any of his appointments on her account, although the prospect often was that she would not live until his return. On one of these occasions, while he was absent, she called for a small Bible, which had been presented to her by her husband, and, with a pencil, wrote on a blank leaf, as follows:

"February, 1840.—O heavenly treasure, guide of my youth, my solace in the hour of affliction, and blessed beacon, which points my soul to a land where I shall flourish in immortal youth! I return *thee* to the *dear one* who has been the partner of my joys and sorrows, but who will shortly be left to feel that his *little boy* is motherless, and he himself is bereft of the *companion* of his early days. Then, O then, my dear *Elijah*, open this book, and read, for your consolation, of that *glorious morn*, when the *trumpet shall sound*, and we shall be raised incorruptible, to suffer no more.   CAROLINE."

This was about six weeks before her death. Her conversations in reference to her future prospects were interesting. Some of them, noted down by her friends, are as follows:

February 24th.—(To her husband.)—"This is a scene of conflict, but I feel that the Almighty arm on which I lean will carry me safely through."

February 26th.—(To the same.)—"When I pass through the waters, they shall not overflow me. Deep—deep! The waters below appear deep and dark, but the sky above is clear and glorious, and I shall rise above all. Sometimes I fancy I have been a long sea-voyage all alone, tossed and driven by the wind and waves; sometimes almost at the port, then driven away again upon the ocean. Thus I have struggled with wind and tide, but now I feel as if I was near the port, and every wave carries me nearer.'

March 25.—She asked her mother to get her hymn-book, and read to her the hymn on the 487th page, which begins,

"Why should we start and fear to die?"

When she came to the last stanza, which is,

"Jesus can make a dying bed
Feel soft as downy pillows are,
While on his breast I lean my head,
And breathe my life out sweetly there,"

she put her finger on it, and remarked that she realized it all, then took the book, marked the place, and presented it to her mother as a token of her love. About the same time, addressing her father, she said, "God only takes from you what he lent. You have been a kind father, but I ask one favor. When I have done breathing, I wish you would see that this wreck be deposited where some of the family will lie; have no pomp, but mark the spot with a tree, vine or shrub—I was always fond of something green—that my *little son* may be pointed to the spot." Her son, named *Jason Henry*, was then fourteen months old, and was her only child.

April 3.—After many other things, she said: I would willingly *suffer* on my three score years and ten if it would be for the glory of God. I am just ready and waiting. Hallelujah! *hallelujah!* HALlelujah ! I never expected such a halo of glory. What unfading glory awaits for me ! Oh, that ineffable glory! it almost bursts this tenement of clay. My heart is so full! My head rings every moment with hallelujah ! No wonder so many have shouted *glory* when leaving this world. I feel I have no longer to feel suffering, but to praise and dwell in His presence forever. *Oh, glory!* Never was language formed full enough to tell what I feel. Where shall I find words to express it? I expect to walk the golden streets above, and to eat of the Tree of Life. My palsied tongue almost fails me to speak of that which my heart can hardly contain."

During the day of Saturday, the 4th, she said but little, yet was occasionally heard—amidst the greatest pain—to say, " Hallelujah!"

These are but a few of the expressions of joy which she uttered during her protracted sufferings. No one who has not been present, near the closing hour of a Christian's life, can form any idea of such a scene. Her death was triumphant, as will appear from what follows: About 3 o'clock A. M., when she felt her life was fast ebbing, she said she was going, and requested her friends to be called into her room. As they entered, she said, "It is all raptures untold." At sunrise her door was opened—there was bright sunshine. Being told that it was Sabbath morning, she exclaimed, " It is the sweetest Sabbath morning I ever saw." Awhile after, all being still, she asked why they were so. On being told that they did not wish to disturb her, she said, "I want to be *shouting*. Oh! if I had strength, I would shout!" When mention was made, again, of the Sabbath, she added,

"Sweet Sabbath of eternal rest,
No mortal care shall seize my breast."

In this frame of mind she remained until the spirit returned to God who gave it. She expired on Sabbath, April 5th, 1840, at one o'clock P. M., in the twenty-second year of her age. E.

But we must not go into all the details of each town and the incidents connected therewith. This county has been very fruitful in revivals. There are now twelve Circuits and Stations, including 1,939 members, and an aggregate of Church property valued at $164,600, according to the Minutes for 1876.

Jackson appears in the Minutes of the Conference as a distinct appointment first in 1839, and in 1843 it was made a Station. Prior to this time it was included in a Circuit with two preachers, though for several years, it had been so arranged that one of them preached in Jackson every Sabbath. The importance of the place and the value of concentrated labor seems not to have been properly appreciated, until others had very nearly crowded the Methodists out. When they did finally wake up to the fact, alas! it was only to toil and struggle with great difficulties, for when Mr. Pilcher was appointed to the Station in, 1846, the membership had been reduced to only *fifty* nominally, and to many less really, and they had bought a little house, about 20 by 30 feet only, which had belonged to the Presbyterians. The prospect was very discouraging. But there were a few men who were personally acquainted with Mr. Pilcher, and who had asked for him to be stationed there, to which he consented. During his term of two years the Society was increased to 116 and the erection of a Church was commenced.

The first Methodist Church here was commenced in 1848, and finished and dedicated in 1850, by Bishop Hamline, after great labor and exertion, for, at the time, the Society was very feeble, having but few persons of any pecuniary ability connected with it. The exertion succeeded, however, and they had a very respectable Church. It was dedicated with a crushing debt on it, which was extinguished by the indefatigable labors of Rev. S Clements. This Church has been superseded by one of the most beautiful churches in the State. They also erected a very nice parsonage on lots which were set apart for the Church by the original proprietor of this part of the town, when it was first platted. "And thereby hangs a tale." These lots once nearly slipped from the hands of the Society. When it was determined to build a church on another lot, a Mr. Foot set up a claim to these lots; on what grounds it is not necessary now to explain, only that by building elsewhere they had forfeited their right to them. The Church had had possession of them for some time; and now gave directions to the stationed minister to exercise acts of ownership over them, to show that they had not abandoned them. This he did. But Mr. F. being intent on getting the possession of them, employed a man to fence them in. The minister had forbidden the workmen going on, and various delays had occurred in the accomplishment of this end. Some weeks had passed without anything being done, or the minister giving any particular attention to it. One Sabbath, as he came out of the house, occupied as a church, he happened to cast his eye in that direction, and observed there was a fence about two-thirds of the way around the lots. He said to himself, not to any one else, not even to his wife: "My ax will find employment in the morning." He concluded a little "muscular Christianity" might be of service just now. On Monday morning, immediately after breakfast, he took his ax, went to this fence, knocked off the boards as carefully as he could, and laid them out into the street; then he cut down a part of the posts and laid them away. The ground was frozen so that he could not take them up. While he was doing this work, which he was not willing to trust to anyone else, the gentleman who had been employed to build the fence came near enough to recognize who it was that was engaged in this work of demolition, and then went away without saying a word. The next morning the constable waited on the minister with a warrant in an action of trespass. When the return day came, the minister, who was himself an attorney, was obliged to be absent, but appeared by attorney, pleaded the general issue, and obtained an adjournment for three months. In the meantime he continued to improve the lots, and to clear them of all property belonging to Mr. F. Some two days before the day to which the hearing stood adjourned, he got a man to plow a part of it, as the most ostensible improvement that could be made, excepting to build a house. While this plowing was going on, as he was walking the street in full view of the lots, Mr. Foot met him, and, laughing, reached out his hand to shake hands, saying as he did so, "Mr. Pilcher, you got up too soon for me this time. I will withdraw that suit." "Very well," said Mr. P., "that is what I intended to do, and you may do as you please about the suit; I shall beat you if you go on with it." Ever after this when they met, Mr. Foot was sure to laugh, doubtless thinking of that action for trespass. Thus by this bold maneuver were these valuable lots saved to the Church, for there was so much shadow on the title that if the other claimant had gotten the possession the Church would never have recovered them. They finally gave two hundred dollars to quiet the title. The lots were eight rods square, and on a corner. They sold the corner lot for a good price and built a parsonage on the other—the most complete house in all its fixtures then to be found in the State as a parsonage. This parsonage was finally sold, and its avails applied on the new church.

We here present the statistics of the Churches, having before given the date of their organizations:

Methodist Episcopal.................480 | Baptist............................478
Congregational........................464 | Protestant Episcopal............312

BATTLE CREEK—*Wa-po-kis-ku*—is situated at the confluence of the Kalamazoo and the Battle Creek rivers, in Calhoun County, about *fourteen* miles west from Marshall. The Battle Creek is so much lower than the Kalamazoo, or rather there is so much fall in the Kalamazoo at this point, that the latter is turned into the former, by a race about a mile in length passing through the city, so as to afford an immense amount of water power. This water power is well utilized. It is a very active business place, and is a formidable rival to Marshall. Operations were not begun here as soon as at Marshall, but they have been prosecuted with more vigor.

Nothing of any importance was done here earlier than 1836. Hon. Sands McCamley was one of the earliest settlers. The Merritts and Harts, of the Society of Friends, or Quakers, were very early settlers and active men. They quickly looked after the educational interests, and have always maintained a school of high order.

What gave rise to the name of the Creek is all left to conjecture. We have taken some pains to ascertain from the Indians the origin of it, but they, at least those last residing in the county, had no tradition on the subject. Imagination may supply this lack of information. We can well conceive of the meeting of hostile tribes or bands at this locality, far back even in the youth of the peninsula, when foe stood to foe, hand to hand in bloody conflict, in a long and desperate struggle for the mastery; the waters are made red with the mingling of the crimson life-tide—many noble braves float on its surface—the forests along its banks were made to resound with the fearful war-whoop, and finally with the triumphant, savage shout of victory, by the conquerers. After such a conflict, and such destruction, they might well exclaim "*Wa-po-kis-ka*," or "Battle Creek." Some thing of this kind was, probably, the origin of the name of the Creek, from which the city has taken its name. But now we may very appropriately adopt the beautiful lines of Mrs. Hemans and say:

> "Come to the land of peace,
> Come where the tempest hath no longer sway,
> The shadow passes from the soul away—
> The sounds of weeping cease.
>
> "Fear hath no dwelling there,
> Come to the mingling of repose and love,
> Breathed by the silent spirit of the dove,
> Through the celestial air."

Although there are a good many of the followers of William Penn, both orthodox and Hicksite, residing here and hereabouts, and though the inhabitants are generally very moral and orderly, and though the panting, trembling fugitive from slavery always found here a safe retreat, an asylum from his tormenters, the pugnacious spirit was not always wanting, and some instances of violence and bloodshed have occurred.

The City of Battle Creek, for it was incorporated a City in 1859, according to the census of 1874, contained a population of

5,323, which is a little less than that of 1870. It has the advantage of two railroads.

As soon as there were a few scattered settlers in this vicinity, the ministers of Christ sought them out, ministered to them the Word of Life, and joined in Church fellowship such as desired to be recognized as Church members. The Methodist Church, which was the first organized, was formed, in 1835, by *Rev. James F. Davidson.* The names of the original members we have not been able to ascertain; but, in 1836, the members were as follows, viz: *Festus Hall, Thomas Hickman, Sally Jane Hickman, Isaac Hickman, Maria Hickman, Daniel Clark, Clarinda Clark, Roger Francis, Norman Rugg, Julia Rugg, Asa Phelps, Ada Gregory, David Howell, Julia Howell, Delight Clark,* and *Altha Spink.* This was a small beginning, but God does not despise the day of small things, neither should we. This number has been increased, from time to time, till, according to the Minutes of Battle Creek Station for 1876, they numbered 164 members and probationers, and have Church property valued at $27,800. Battle Creek first appeared in the Minutes as a Circuit in 1839. The Church has grown with the growth of the community, and has maintained its work in all departments.

Many precious seasons of revival have been enjoyed by this Church, and much good work has been accomplished for God's cause. One incident connected with one of these revival seasons is worthy to be recorded. There was residing here, at the time referred to, an aged man, who had fought in the battles of his country for freedom, and, as was often the case with that class of men, he had contracted a fondness for intoxicating liquors. A part of his family had already made a profession of religion. This old gentleman was awakened—finally he was converted, and lived a consistent Christian life. While he was laboring under the burden of an awakened conscience, one of his sons, who, by the way, was not a professor of religion, became very anxious for his conversion, and, though he could do nothing for him himself, he visited his brother, who was a class-leader, every day, to ascertain how his father was getting along, and, in the earnestness of his heart, he said, "James, do not give father up until he is converted—hold on to him." God heard the prayer, and the old man was converted and saved from drunkenness.

As strange as it may seem, that son lived for several years without seeking religion for himself; but he, too, afterwards sought the Lord, found favor, and since has died in great triumph. The

Lord is good to them that seek His face—forgives and adopts them into His family.

One of the ministers, who was appointed to this charge, took up the work of visiting every family in three towns, and distributing Bibles. He met with several interesting incidents, two of which are here given. Having called at a house a little out of the city, he found the family to consist of a young man and his wife, just commencing in the world. He asked him if he would like to buy a Bible. "A Bible?" said the young man, with apparent surprise, "I don't believe there is a Bible on this street. Indeed, a Bible would be as much out of place here as a pirate in a prayer-meeting." "Yes, there is a Bible at the next house back," said the colporteur, in the meantime taking out and showing his Bibles. "It can't be possible," said he; "if they have one, they certainly don't read it." "There is a very neat Bible for only twenty-five cents," said the Bible man. He replied, "I can't read a Bible that does not cost more than that." Having learned, in this way, that he had no Bible, he urged him to buy, but he said he had no money. The colporteur offered to trust him, but he said he could not be trusted for a Bible. After a little further colloquy, the wife, in the meantime, having become interested in the matter, took a fancy to one of them, so she proposed to use a little money, which he had given her, for that purpose, if he did not object. He did not. The bargain was effected, and the Bible left with them.

In order to get the full interest of the following incident, the reader must conceive himself as having been traveling through the woods, in which stands a small log cabin, on the side of a slope, and fronting up the hill; that between the road and the house stands a hovel for cattle, nearly in front of the house, so that the drainage from the hovel flows directly towards the cabin, saluting the olfactories with its peculiar odor. Having made this external survey, let us enter. Everything is of a similar character, and we find an old lady, just from the Green Isle, saluting us with the peculiar brogue of her country; then follows the conversation:

"Would you like to buy a Bible," said the man of the satchel. "A Bible!" said she, looking with surprise; "and what kind of a Bible is it?" "Oh, it is a common Bible, such as is commonly read," said he. "And is it a Catholic Bible?" To this he replied, "It is such a Bible as Catholics sometimes read, and may read with safety." Not satisfied with this answer, with increased energy she demanded, "And is it a Protestant Bible?" "It is such as Protestants sometimes read, and may read with safety," he replied.

Becoming a little more erect, she exclaimed, with warmth, "Indade, and I jist think, *sir*, that the Bible is a very bad book for ignorant people to read; they can't understand it." "Oh! yes, the Bible is a very good book, and easy to be understood, and will teach you the way to Heaven," said the minister. "Indade, and I jist think, sir, I *larnt* that a great while ago," she replied. "Oh! well, then, it will assist you in it, and it is a very good book, and easy to be understood," said the colporteur. To this she replied, with great energy, "There is one Lord, one faith, one baptism, and one THROUGH CHURCH, out of which nobody can be saved." "It is true," said he, "The Bible says 'there is one Lord, one faith, and one baptism,' and it is a very good book." "Why are there so many religions in the world, then, if the Bible is so easy to be understood?" she asked. "There are various reasons: people fix their notions without the Bible, and then go to the Bible to try to prove them; but the Bible is a very good book, and can be understood without difficulty in all that is necessary to our salvation." When he had said this, she raised herself to her full height, and, pointing her finger at him, exclaimed, with very great energy, and prolonging the words in capitals to a very great length: "Indade, and I jist think, sir, that neither Y-E, nor A-L-L the likes of ye, have got intellects enough to understand the Bible." "Oh, yes!" said the man of the Bible, "It is a plain, good book, and easy to be understood." To this she answered, in full warmth, "Oh! but there are so many of ye! There are the Methodists, there are the Swaddlers, and the Divil and all knows how many there are of ye!"

This ended the conversation, excepting that he asked her if she would read a Bible if he would leave one, and received for an answer that she would not, but would put it in the fire and burn it up. This incident shows the true bigotry of Popery, and what would become of our Bibles if it had the power.

We conclude what we have to say in regard to this city, by introducing a pen-portrait of one whose face ever appears pleasant, and whose manner carries a sweet aroma with it; one who lives in the memory of many, although several years have elapsed since he was stationed in the city of Jackson.

REV. HENRY F. SPENCER was born in Leyden, Lewis County, New York, March 21st, 1834. He yielded to the claims of the religion of the Lord and Saviour, experienced renewing grace, and united with the Methodist Episcopal Church in Lowville, New York, in 1834, where he received his first license to exhort. He prepared for college at Fairfield Academy, and entered the M. G. B. Institute at Concord, New Hampshire, in 1859, graduating in 1862.

HISTORY OF PROTESTANTISM IN MICHIGAN. 383

During the latter part of his senior year in the Biblical Institute, he served as supply in the State Street Methodist Episcopal Church in Watertown, New York, and in the spring joined the Black River Conference. He was returned to the State Street Church, Watertown. In 1863, he was appointed to Clayton, New York, where he remained three years. In the spring of 1866, he was transferred to the Michigan Conference, and stationed at Lansing. He has filled the following appointments, viz: Lansing; Jackson; Division Street, Grand Rapids; Kalamazoo;—and is now in his third year in the last-named place, having remained the full term of three years at each field.

Mr. Spencer is a preacher of much more than ordinary power, and a man of great industry. He has been successful in every place. The beautiful church at Jackson was erected during his pastorate, and a heavy debt has been removed from the church at Kalamazoo since he has been their pastor. The spiritual interests have been greatly promoted, and many converted and added to the Church under his ministration.

The Churches of Battle Creek stand as follows, viz:

Methodist Episcopal...............364 | Baptists..................... 306
Presbyterian.. .. ..220 | Protestant Episcopal............ 71

ALBION is near the east edge of Calhoun County, and is located at the junction of the two principal branches of the Kalamazoo River. These two streams furnish excellent and abundant water-power, which is well utilized. This is now a flourishing and interesting village. Mr. Tenny Peabody made the first purchase of land at this point. Marvin Hannah, Jesse Crowell, and W. Warner soon followed. The village was laid out, or platted, in 1837, by a company known as the "Albion Land Company," of which Messrs. Crowell and Warner were members, and the former the principal agent. This village is very near the center of the State, from east to west, on the line from Detroit to Lake Michigan. It is on the line of the Michigan Central Railroad, which is also crossed at this point by a railroad from Lansing to Jonesville. It possesses many natural advantages, such as a clear and beautiful stream, furnishing excellent hydraulic power; it is in the midst of a healthy country, and one that is very productive of everything of interest that can be produced in this climate.

The artificial advantages are by no means indifferent, such as the railroads, common schools, churches, and last, though not least, ALBION COLLEGE, under the fostering care of the Methodist Episcopal Church in Michigan. This institution is the great object of attraction to the visitor, as its relative position to the village is such as to give it a commanding appearance. There are three buildings, separated from each other by a few rods, standing on an eminence, at the eastern edge of the village and fronting to the west. The center building is forty by one hundred feet, four stories high, presenting a side front, and is surmounted by a small observatory, from which is presented a splendid view of a wide extent of beautiful, fertile country. At either end of this is another building, standing distant as before named, forty by eighty feet, three stories high, presenting the end to the west. These buildings are of brick, and stuccoed to resemble granite. They stand on an oblong square, sixteen by twenty rods, having a lawn in front, twenty by thirty-eight rods, extending down the side of the eminence towards the village—a lawn which, when graded and arranged according to design, will present a most charming and lovely appearance, and furnish a most desirable retreat. In the rear is a triangular lawn, extending eastward, having its base on the College square and its apex about thirty rods away. This lawn is now covered with a beautiful grove of native forest trees, and may be called " *Quercan Lawn*," as the trees are oak.

The origin of *Albion College* is traceable back to 1833. In the spring of this year *Rev. Henry Colclazer, Dr. B. H. Packard*, then residing at Ann Arbor, and *Rev. Elijah H. Pilcher*, in consultation determined to make an effort to secure the establishment of an institution of learning of a high order in this peninsula. Notice of that purpose was circulated through the country, and in the summer of 1834 propositions were made by the inhabitants of several localities, offering as a bonus for its location large and liberal subscriptions in land and money. These propositions were presented to the Ohio Annual Conference which then had ecclesiastical jurisdiction over this country. A committee was appointed by that body to determine the location, and to apply to the Legislative branch of the Territory for an act of incorporation. The proposition coming from Spring Arbor, in the County of Jackson, was accepted and a charter obtained in March, 1835, fixing the location at an old Indian village in that town. As it proved, the location was not well selected. Various obstacles were thrown in the way of commencing operations by some who professed to be its friends, until its real friends became disheartened, and were ready to abandon the enterprise. In the meantime the village of Albion had sprung into life, at least so far as being laid out on paper could give it life, so that in 1838 a proposition was made, accompanied by a large subscription—large for the population—asking that the location might be changed to that place.

ALBION COLLEGE.

All hope of succeeding at the former location having failed, this proposition was accepted by the Michigan Annual Conference, and accordingly a successful application was made to the Legislature in 1839, for an amendment to the charter changing the location to Albion, and reconstructing the Board of Trustees. This new board was duly organized and prepared to fulfill the trust committed to them. In the autumn of 1839, *Rev. Loring Grant*, a superannuated preacher of the Genesee Conference, having removed to this place, was employed as agent by the Board of Trustees, to solicit subscriptions and raise funds to erect suitable buildings, in which work he served actively for some time. A system of scholarships was adopted at this time, which, though it was the means of raising funds so as to build the center building, came near ruining the institution afterwards. The system was to give a certificate of free tuition for the term of four years to every subscriber of one hundred dollars, the subscription payable in four equal annual payments; the said certificate was not available until the whole amount of the individual subscription was paid. The plan appeared very plausible and fair, but there was one very important item overlooked at the time, which was that if the funds raised were used up in building, there would be no means left to pay instructors, and the institution could not be carried on.

This system was found afterwards to embarrass the institution very much, because so many students came on these certificates that the tuition received did not nearly meet the annual expenses of the teachers. This plan was thought, subsequently, to have been a great blunder; perhaps it was. It was an experiment; but this is to be considered as an extenuation of the guilt of those concerned in the project, that it appeared to them to be the only means of raising funds to build, and there appeared to them to be no alternative but to adopt this plan or have no institution. The plan was adopted, and, under it the first—the center building—was erected, and the school opened.

Having raised funds so that it was thought safe to proceed, the corner stone of the center building was laid in June, 1841, with appropriate ceremonies. After the stone, containing various appropriate articles sealed up in a copper box imbedded in the stone, was put in its place, by the trustees under the direction of the Master Mason, the Hon. Henry W. Taylor, then of Marshall, standing on the stone, delivered a very able and appropriate address. This stone was placed in the southwest corner of the building. The Marshall brass band discoursed soul stirring music for the entertainment of the large concourse of people gathered for the occasion. This was considered a high day for Albion.

The Seminary was made ready, and opened for the reception of students in November, 1843. Rev. Charles F. Stockwell was employed as the Principal, assisted by a full corps of teachers. The first exhibition, which was held in March, 1844, was a grand affair, an exciting occasion. The decorations of the hall, the music, the speaking—everything seemed under the influence of enchantment. It might, possibly, have been regarded as an indifferent affair in an old country and a long-established institution, but it was, indeed, a "high day" for this country, which had but so recently been the home of savage beasts and wild Indians.

A new system of scholarships was inaugurated in 1849, for the purpose of raising a permanent endowment, and an enlargement of powers secured, making it a Female College in addition to the Seminary, and, again, in 1861, another amendment to the charter was obtained, giving it simply the name of "Albion College," Wesleyan Seminary and Female College being dropped out.

The second, or north building, was completed in 1853, but, unfortunately, it was consumed by fire within one year after its completion and occupancy. It was rebuilt in about one year after. The third, or south building, was erected in 1857.

This institution has had to struggle with much financial embarrassment, and the friends of the enterprise have trembled, sometimes, lest it should fail for want of financial support. Errors may have been committed in the management of its affairs, but this is no more than has occurred with every institution in the land, whether State or private.

Notwithstanding these financial struggles, this institution has gone on steadily, blessing the land by sending out, annually, a large number of young ladies and gentlemen, well educated and well instructed in moral principles, who have gone into every part of the State. Men of wealth could not do a nobler act, for the good of the State, than to appropriate a portion of that wealth to complete the endowment of this college—to place it beyond financial want or fluctuation.

It will be specially interesting to the Christian to know that this institution has been blessed with many seasons of precious revival of religion, and many of the students have been happily converted to God and gone out to bless the Church. A good many young men who have been educated here have entered the ministry, and have done and are doing good work for the cause of Christ.

Since the first organization of the Faculty, there have been eight Principals and Presidents, viz: Rev. Charles F. Stockwell, Rev. Clark T. Hinman, Hon. Ira Mayhew, Rev. Thomas H. Sinex, Rev. George B. Jocelyn, Rev. J. L. G. McKeown, Rev. Dr. William B. Silber, Rev. Dr. L. R. Fiske. The first of these men entered upon his duties at the opening of the institution in 1843, continued in charge for two years, when he resigned, and gave his attention to the study and practice of law. He has since died, and it is proper to insert a short memorial notice of him.

Rev. Charles F. Stockwell was a graduate of the Wesleyan University at Middletown, Connecticut. He was a local preacher—never connected with the Conference. He was a man of good abilities, well developed, and capable of doing much good. He acquitted himself well as a teacher and Principal, and maintained the dignity of a Christian. He married a lady in Albion, and, after he left the Seminary, addressed himself to the study of law, and was admitted to the practice. When the tide of emigration set in so strongly for California, in 1850, he started for that far-famed land of gold, not from a desire for gold so much as from a desire to do good. He died on the ocean, before he reached that land, and was buried in the deep. A monument to his memory, with others, stands in the college grounds.

Rev. Clark T. Hinman was elected to the charge of this institution in September, 1846, and continued until he was elected President of the Northwestern University at Evanston, Illinois, in 1853, having held his relation to the institution for seven years. It was during his time that the higher position of Female College was taken, and the new system of scholarships was adopted, which proved to be no more satisfactory than the former system. It is proper here to give a full sketch of his life and character, as he has gone to his long rest. We will make a liberal use of the memoir published in the Minutes of the Conference for 1855.

REV. CLARK T. HINMAN, D. D., died in Troy, New York, October 21st, 1854, aged thirty-five years. He was born in Courtland County, New York, August 3d, 1819, and was distinguished, in early life, for intelligence above his years. He was converted to God at ten years of age, and never after doubted his salvation from the power and guilt of sin, through faith in Jesus Christ. He prepared for college at Cazenovia Seminary, New York, and graduated at the Wesleyan University at Middletown, Connecticut, in 1839, at twenty years of age. He spent a portion of his' college life under the Presidency of the lamented and sainted Dr. Wilbur Fisk. For seven years he served as a teacher in the Newberry Seminary, Vermont, and, subsequently, as Principal, from which position, in 1846, he was called to the charge of the Wesleyan Seminary at Albion. He now devoted all his active energies to give elevation and stability to this institution. His ever-active mind was constantly on the alert for some means of increasing the importance of the school with which he felt himself so intimately connected. In 1853, he was elected President of the *Northwestern University*, an institution yet to be, and requiring active labor to bring it into real life. He saw there, as he thought, an opening to lay the foundation and rear up an institution of learning to accomplish immense good. Having accepted the appointment there, he resigned his position here, and devoted all his mental and physical energies to this new work. On this noble and extensive enterprise, Dr. Hinman set his whole heart, and it is not at all unlikely that his consuming zeal, ceaseless and untiring labors in its behalf, by inducing a jaded and over-worked condition of constitution, though naturally healthy, and even vigorous, may have hastened his lamented death. Even while laboring under the disease—the choleric dysentery—which terminated his existence, despite the remonstrances of friends, he was found pleading the cause of his favorite interest, and refused to stop while his engagements remained unfulfilled, until to proceed farther became, literally, a physical impossibility. Returning East, where he was to meet his family, he found himself, or, rather, was found at an inn in Troy, by Rev. H. W. Ransom, who took him to his own house, where, despite all that kindness and skill could do for him, in a few days he was before the Throne.

He received license to preach in 1838, the year before he closed his college course, and was admitted into the traveling connection, by the Vermont Conference, shortly after he entered upon the administration of the Newberry Seminary. In 1846, he was transferred to the Michigan Conference, with which he remained connected until his death. He received the honorary degree of D. D. from the Ohio Wesleyan University in 1851. Sadness was wide-spread through his country when it was announced that he was dead.

That he possessed talents of a high and commanding order, the high positions he was called to occupy abundantly testify. His great success in those positions presents him as a rare example of having diligently improved the talents committed to his trust. In no position was he placed in which he did not more than equal the hopes of his friends, and disappoint the wishes of his opponents. He was a ripe scholar, and emphatically "apt to teach." His sermons were always earnest and instructive, and often eloquent. He was truly a Christian gentleman. His presence brought light into every circle, and he could adorn any society. Envy of the position and reputation of another never seemed to have any place in his mind.

"Doctor Hinman lived the life of the righteous, and his end was peace. Though the last hours of his life were 'dark on this side,' as reason had failed him, yet were there scintillations through the darkness that showed how bright they were on the other side. When evidently deaf and unconscious to the interrogations of surviving friends and dear ones, amid his murmurings, ejaculative utterances were often heard, 'face to face,' 'all glorious!' But in the early part of his short but fatal illness, in anticipation of its probable termination, he said, 'I should love to live for my little family, and to do a little more good, but the Lord's will be done, for me to die is gain.' Yes, doubtless, death has been to our dear brother gain; but no one who knew him, or who reads this brief notice of him, can fail to feel that the Church had sustained such a loss as she but rarely suffers in the death of a single son—a son whose life was short in years, but long in noble deeds."

His light was brilliant, and burned with an intensity that soon consumed itself. Whoever visits the grounds of Albion College will be attracted at once by a beautiful monument, on three sides of which are the following inscriptions—on the south side: "In memory of Rev. Charles F. Stockwell, First Principal of the Wesleyan Seminary at Albion. Died, June 30th, 1850, Æ. 33. 'And the sea shall give up her dead.'—*Rev.*" On the west side: "In memory of Rev. Clark T. Hinman, D. D., First President of the Wesleyan Seminary and Albion Female Collegiate Institute. Died, October 21st, 1854, Æ. 35. 'Behold the Lord doth take away from Jerusalem the eloquent orator.'—*Isaiah.*" On the north side: "In memory of Rev. Judson D. Collins, A. M., First Missionary of the Methodist Episcopal Church to the Empire of China. Died, May 25th, 1852. 'Go ye into the world and preach the Gospel to every creature.'—*Christ.*"

The blank side of this monument will doubtless be filled with the name of Rev. George B. Jocelyn, who was the fifth elected President. After several years he resigned, but after an intermission of about three years, was re-elected, and was in service when he died, February 27th, 1877.

To say that this institution is a model of perfection would be saying too much, but to say that it has wielded, and is destined to wield, a powerful moulding influence on the educational development of the Peninsular State, would only be to say what is already felt and acknowledged to be true; more even than this may be said —if this institution were now to be blotted out of existence its power would be felt for years to come; the thousands of students —for thousands have been in attendance at different times—who have received educational training within its walls, will make their impress on society for years to come. In this view, it must be a source of great pleasure to those who have toiled and contributed of their money for its establishment, to review the past and to contemplate the future of this institution. It is much to be regretted that this College has not yet been fully endowed, so as to be above all embarrassment. May we not say it will live for many long years as a memorial to the praise of the men who projected the scheme, and of the enterprise and zeal of the denomination of Christians, through whose energy and perseverance it has been erected and maintained? Their sons and daughters will rise up to call them blessed.

In December, 1870, at a Methodist Convention held at the College, the question of a more complete and permanent endowment was discussed. At this time David Preston, Esq., of Detroit, proposed that if a certain specified number of men would subscribe the sum of $50,000 within two years, he would pledge himself to raise $60,000 more from the people. This money was to go into the hands of a committee outside of the Board of Trustees, to be funded, and the interest only to be applied for the support of the faculty. Both parts of the proposition have been met within the specified time. Mr. Preston devoted almost his entire time to this work for one year, and attained the end just a few weeks before the expiration of the specified limit. It would seem to have been very providential that the time for raising this money was limited as it was.

The fifty thousand dollars having been subscribed according to the terms of the proposition, Mr. Preston addressed himself to the fulfillment of his part of the engagement. He issued a circular, to be sent to all the Methodist ministers in the State, dated September 4th, 1872, in which he detailed the circumstances which gave rise to the proposition, and then adds:

"While this resolution was being discussed, one of the ministers of the Detroit Conference said if we took *fifty* of our best men to raise the $50,000 from, it would be impossible to raise $50,000 more from the people. He contended that the $50,000 should be raised from *twenty-five* or a less number of persons. Up to that moment I had never thought of making the proposition I did make. I then arose and said: 'You may have ten, you may have twenty, you may have *fifty* persons to raise $50,000 from, and I will stand with the people, and not only raise $50,000, but will raise $60,000 from them.' I had faith in the people then, I have faith in the people now. If I cannot, with the aid of 400 ministers, with the aid of the press, and with the aid of the quickening influence of the Holy Spirit, inspire confidence enough, and interest and enthusiasm enough in the hearts and heads of 48,000 or 50,000 men, women and children who have been washed and redeemed by the blood of Christ, to raise from them the average of one dollar each for sustaining and enlarging the influence of a Methodist College in Michigan, THEN, and not till then, will my confidence in the ability and willingness of the Methodist people of Michigan to give liberally and to give cheerfully, be abated.

"More than twenty months have elapsed since I made this pledge. I have not forgotten it. *It has been in my mind and in my heart every day since.* I don't want to forget it. I don't expect to forget it, or to evade it. If God spares my life until the first day of September, 1873, I expect to see it FULFILLED, I do." On October 8th, he issued a second circular. In these two he detailed his plan, and asked the co-operation of all the ministers. But he found it necessary to devote the most of his time to it, and to take the field and visit most of the important towns and cities in the State. Wherever he went he inspired the people with a part of his confidence and enthusiasm, and in that way large sums were raised. He had the sympathy and co-operation of most of the ministers, but still his presence and enthusiasm were necessary to call forth the money. He succeeded so that at the time limited it was done. It was accomplished in the right time—just before the terrible financial crash of 1873 came. Had it been delayed another year, it could not have been effected. By this $110,000, in addition to what endowment they before had, the College is put on a living basis, and yet it is not the amount it ought to be, nor is it the sum that the Methodists of Michigan are able to give to it.

Mr. Preston's success in this enterprise illustrates what a man of faith in God and faith in the people and prayer may do. Both of these elements are essential to success where the people are concerned.

Mr. Preston deserves the warmest gratitude of the Protestant public for his zeal and success in the accomplishment of this grand work. This was an addition to a partial endowment, which had before been made, but yet further endowment is all important to put the institution in the financial position it ought to occupy.

In connection with this endowment fund, we must present a brief notice of the life of the author of it. He is a layman, residing in Detroit, and his name has become a synonym for benevolence. Though unpretending in appearance, he has exerted an extensive influence in the benevolent operations of the Church in this State. He is the son of a Methodist preacher, and became a Christian in early life.

DAVID PRESTON arrived in Detroit on November 4th, 1848. He was converted, and united with the Methodists in the old church on the corner of Woodward Avenue and Congress Street, in December, 1848, under the pastorate of Rev. Samuel D. Simonds, now of California. He commenced business for himself in May, 1852, by opening a banking-office on a small scale. He confined himself to a legitimate exchange and banking business, and prospered greatly. It is a pleasing fact that, though Mr. Preston's business has become very extensive, he is almost invariably found at the prayer and class meetings, and is a teacher in the Sunday School. He has also served as Superintendent. In the beginning of his business life, he adopted the principle of contributing liberally for the support of the Church and Christian charity generally. He is a successful hand at raising money for Church purposes, partly because he is known to give liberally himself, and his success in raising the *sixty thousand dollars*, as above, has made the name of David Preston a household word in many families. He was very active and liberal in the erection of the Central Church, and after that work was completed, he took hold of the enterprise of building the Simpson Church, in Detroit. He has a heart in the work of the Lord, and delights to see that work prosper.

We have, incidentally, stated that President Jocelyn had been called to his reward, and we shall, hereafter, insert a memorial notice of his life and death. It was to be expected that the vacancy would be filled. We take pleasure in inserting a brief sketch of Dr. Jocelyn's successor—REV. LEWIS R. FISKE, D. D.

At a Camp Meeting on the Coldwater Circuit, held near Union City, in June, 1842, a young lad, of an excellent and religious family, was converted to God, and joined the Methodist Episcopal Church. His conversion seemed to create in him a strong desire for a thorough education, and to inspire him with a higher ambition for noble work. Very soon after this, he began to make preparations for entering the University of Michigan, and graduated in the class of

1850. When he had graduated, he thought to stifle the convictions he had had of a duty to preach the Gospel, and commenced the study of law; but he was elected Professor of Natural Sciences in the Wesleyan Seminary at Albion, where he had been a student in his preparatory course, which he accepted, and which dispelled all ideas of the law, for his convictions of duty to preach were revived. After remaining at Albion for some time, he was elected to a chair in the State Normal School at Ypsilanti. While in this latter institution, he received license to preach, and was admitted into the Annual Conference on trial. From this place he was transferred to the State Agricultural College. In this institution he not only sustained the reputation he had acquired as an educator, but increased it. Here he remained for several years, and was, for some time, the acting President, but he resigned his connection with the college, and entered into the pastoral work. In 1863, he was stationed in Jackson, as his first charge. He remained three years and was then appointed to the Central Church, Detroit. He fulfilled his relation here for three years, to the great satisfaction of the people. From this Church he was transferred to Ann Arbor, remained here, also, the full term of three years, and then was appointed to Ann Arbor District. At the end of his first year on the District, the Central Church at Detroit being vacant, his return to that was asked for, and he was, accordingly, appointed to it for a second time. At the close of his term here, he was asked for, and stationed at Tabernacle Church, Detroit. He continued here but one year; for, in June, 1877, there being a vacancy in the Presidency of Albion College, he was unanimously elected to that position, which he accepted. In the meantime, the degree of Doctor of Divinity had been conferred upon him. He was honored by his brethren by being elected as a delegate to the General Conference of 1872, and also of 1876. Such is a brief running sketch of the life and labors of REV. L. R. FISKE, D. D. He has been, and still is, a man of studious habits, having a pleasant manner, of fine mind, and is every way worthy of the honors placed upon him, and the confidence reposed in him. He is emphatically a Michigan man, having come here when but a small boy.

Some one probably has been asking what connection this sketch thus far has with the history of Protestantism in this place. The answer is found in this, that the foundation of Albion College was a scheme projected and carried into effect by the Methodist Episcopal Church—it is a Methodist institution—denominational, but not sectarian—religious, without bigotry—a Protestant College.

There is nothing peculiar in the introduction and progress of Protestantism in this place. As soon as there was a sufficient number of people to constitute anything of a congregation, they were supplied with the ministry of the Word. Rev. Henry Ercanbrack, a superannuated member of the Oneida Conference, was the first minister who took up an appointment here. He had settled down in the neighborhood with the intention of remaining, but after a year or two he returned east. Rev. John Kinnear, who was traveling the Spring Arbor Circuit, was the first to make this a regular appointment for preaching, and organized a Methodist Society or Church in the fall of 1836, consisting of *Almon Herrick, Lorenzo Herrick, Thomas W. Pray, Polly Pray, Betsy Montcalm, Noah Phelps*, and *Mary Ercanbrack*. These *seven* constituted the first Christian Church organized at Albion. Mr. Herrick was appointed the class-leader. The first addition to this number was that of *Charles Cobb* and *Armeda Cobb*. This was a small beginning, but they were to increase.

Rev. Mr. Taylor, a Baptist minister, settled on a farm near the town, and organized a Baptist Church at an early day in its history. This Church did not prosper as much as some of the others, although the beginning was as promising as with any. They now have a good Church, and are doing well, with a membership of 160.

The Presbyterian Church was constituted shortly after these two, and was the first to erect a commodious house of worship. They have advanced, and hold a very good position in the community, and own a fine church which, singularly enough, stands on the ground on which the Methodists built their first chapel, they having changed location when they came to build a good church.

The Protestant Episcopal Church was a little more tardy in its beginning, although a Church was constituted at an early day. They were organized in 1840, and now have a house of worship, and a membership of 66.

The Methodist ministers supplied this appointment with preaching as often as they could consistently with their other labors and the right of other denominations, for they all had to occupy the same school-house, after one was built. Nothing occurred to excite any special interest until the time of holding the first Quarterly Meeting ever held here. This first Quarterly Meeting occurred January 19th and 20th, 1839, George W. Breckenridge and Thomas S. Jackway, preachers, and E. H. Pilcher, Presiding Elder. This meeting, from some circumstances connected with it, excited considerable attention. At the time when the meeting was appointed to be held at this place, the brethren, who requested that it be done, stated that the different denominations occupied the school-house, and the appointments were so arranged as not to interfere with each other; but they added, that if the meeting should occur at a time when the Methodists were not entitled to the use of the house, such was the feeling of friendship among the several sects that the matter would be arranged satisfactorily, they had no doubt.

Some four or five weeks prior to the time of the meeting, one of the stewards called on the pastor of the Baptist Church, Rev. Mr. Jones, and observed that they were to have a Quarterly Meeting there some time hence, he did not know exactly the time—perhaps it might fall on a day when he was entitled to occupy the house, and, if so, he wished to know if any arrangements could be made by which the Methodists could occupy it on that day. "O, yes, certainly," said he. Here the matter rested until the time of the meeting was announced, which was two or three weeks in advance of the time of its occurrence. It was now ascertained that the Methodists had the occupancy of the house in the forenoon, and Rev. Mr. Jones at one o'clock P. M. The brother now called on him and asked if the accommodation could be made, offering him the advantage of the next Methodist time for morning service, if he desired. "*No*," said he,. "no such arrangement can be made," and then added, very crustily, "the Methodists are always trying to crowd us out." Here the matter dropped, for the brother did not know what more to do.

When the Presiding Elder arrived on Saturday morning, the steward informed him of the circumstances, and seemed to be much distressed that matters stood as they did. The Presiding Elder simply said, very coolly: " O, well, we'll try and get along with it, somehow." He, however, determined if there was anything to be made out of it to turn it to the best account. His plans were soon laid, but as he was not a talkative man, he said nothing about them. How far he was justified in what he did is left for each one to judge. He kept his plans to himself, thinking that secrecy in such a case was very essential to prompt and effectual execution.

The people gathered at the house for Saturday service, and at the close the Presiding Elder announced the services for the Sabbath, making the love-feast to begin half an hour earlier than usual, and urged the people to be very prompt, "as we shall be straitened for time, since the Baptist brethren would not arrange the appointment even for a Quarterly Meeting." He intended, by getting the people together early, to close the services before the time for the other brother to have the use of the house. At night the same thing was repeated. It is but right to observe that the body of the Baptist

Church had not been consulted—that they had a Church meeting that afternoon, and sent word in the evening to the Presiding Elder that if he could not get along without it, they would give up the appointment at one o'clock P. M. To this he replied that he *could* get along without it. The people were on hand in good time, so that the preaching began a little before the hour appointed, as the house was crowded to its utmost capacity, and even Rev. Mr. Jones was present.

The Presiding Elder preached, and, as he waxed warm on a particular part of his theme, he remarked that he would like to say more on it, but he was "*straitened for time*," and he passed on. At the close of the sermon, he had to attend to baptism, before the sacrament, so he said the candidates for the ordinance should come forward, without delay and without singing, as he was "straitened for time." The interest in the audience had become intense. At this point, the Rev. Mr. Jones called out, " How much time do you want, sir?" The Presiding Elder replied that he could not tell exactly, as these services were of such a nature that they could not be abridged. Everything was done with the greatest promptitude. As the Presiding Elder was about to dismiss the congregation before the sacrament, he requested those who intended to retire, to do so with as much promptitude as they could—it would be received as a great kindness, as he was "straitened for time." At that, the Rev. Mr. Jones arose, and said he would recall his appointment for ten cents. "You need not do so; you shall have the house before that time," said the Presiding Elder. He then gave a full explanation of the whole matter. Everything conspired to effect promptness, and, in this way, the services of the Quarterly Meeting closed before the time for his meeting; for, although he had recalled his appointment, the Presiding Elder preferred not to encroach on his time. This incident created a considerable stir for some time, and the sympathies of the people were generally on the side of the Methodists in the matter, so that the Rev. Mr. Jones gave up the pastoral care of that flock in about three months after. This circumstance seemed to operate unfavorably to him and the Church, and turning the tide of feeling more towards the Methodists, proved to be to their advantage.

In the month of April, 1839, there was a very blessed revival of religion in this place, from which the Methodist Church derived great strength. The Presiding Elder took time to devote several days to pastoral visiting, and preaching every evening, as the Circuit was so large that the preacher could not give much attention to this par-

Yours very Truly,
L. R. Fiske.

ticular kind of work. Other Churches were benefited by this work also. Indeed, there was a revival spirit all through this region of country, and multitudes were converted and added to the Churches.

As is very often the case in revivals, the subject of baptism became a topic of considerable conversation and some controversy. By special request, the Presiding Elder made an appointment on the 9th day of June, 1839, to preach on that particular topic. It was Sabbath and a lovely day. In anticipation of a large concourse of people, the friends had prepared seats in a grove, and well it was they did so, for the school-house would not have held one-quarter of the people. He preached, traversing the whole controverted field. At the close of the sermon, he administered the ordinance of baptism to *forty-six* persons, and only *two* of them by immersion. Several had come with their changes of raiment, prepared for immersion, but took them away without being used, having been baptized by affusion. This ended the controversy on that subject in that part of the country for the time being and for a long time after.

In the spring of 1840, the Society here erected a small house of worship, which they designated as their Sabbath School room. It was located on the east side of the river, a little out of the town, as it was then built up, but between that and the location of the Seminary. This little house they occupied just ten years; for, in 1850, they had erected a large brick church on the other side of the river, which was dedicated to the worship of God by Bishop Morris, in September of that year. This church was greatly changed and beautified, in 1876, under the pastoral labors of Dr. W. H. Perrine. They have, in 1876, 390 members and a Church property valued at $11,500.

The village of Albion and the Church had so much increased that, by invitation, the Michigan Conference held its session, in September, 1850, in it. The College Chapel was used for the daily business session. The Conference was well entertained, although the session was a brief one for those days, having adjourned on Tuesday morning. Bishop Morris presided.

This Church has passed through the usual vicissitudes of human society, having had its times of trial and of prosperity, but still it has held on its way. The Lord has blessed them with good pastors, and many precious seasons of revival. Albion was made a separate Station in 1846, and William Mothersill was appointed to it. The existence of the Seminary and College here has been of very great service, both to the village and Church.

There have been several very interesting Camp Meetings

held in this vicinity, which resulted in much good; and the grounds owned by the District here are very pleasant—even beautiful. One held in June, 1841, on a ground a little east of the village, was a time of special manifestation of the Divine power. Many were converted, and the Church was specially edified. The communion season, on Monday night, was an occasion of a wonderful display of Divine glory. There was no sermon, but, after the first altar-full had communed, as they turned away, so many were prostrated and helpless, that the service had to be closed. That night, probably there were *one hundred* persons who were deprived of their strength, some of them remaining so for a short time only, and some continuing helpless for the whole night. It was a time of very great joy and gladness.

It will not be displeasing to the student of Protestant History to introduce, in this place, the memoir of one private member who belonged to this Church at the time of his demise, though he was not converted here.

DR. ISAAC GRANT was a venerable man, and, in some respects, a remarkable one. He was born on April 6th, 1759, in the town of Litchfield, Connecticut. From the circumstances of his early education, he was a Calvinist in sentiment in his youth. He had been taught this dogma, and, in his early days, had never heard it called in question. After coming to maturity, he studied the profession of medicine, and gave no particular thought to religious devotions, although he acknowledged and felt the importance of a religious life. When he married, although he made no open profession of religion, nor had attached himself to the Church, for a long time he read the Scriptures and prayed in his family. His children never knew the time when he did not attend family devotions, if the frequent duties of his profession allowed him to be at home at the proper time. All this was attended to without having any experience of grace as yet. He had settled at a place called Whitney Farm, in Vermont. Here the Methodist preachers visited him, and put into his hands some of the standard works against Calvinism. These he read with care, was thoroughly changed in his sentiments, and embraced the truth as it is in the Bible and expressed in the Methodist articles of faith.

In 1798, Rev. Asher Smith, who was in the second year of his itinerancy, having been appointed to Queen Ann's Circuit, and his health having failed, came to the town where Dr. Grant resided, and called on him for professional advice, by which means an acquaintance was formed and a friendship grew up. Mr. Smith gave out an appointment to preach, and, although his health was feeble, he continued to preach every Sabbath with marked success. Many were awakened and converted, and the minister was greatly beloved. When he was about to return to his field of labor—much to the regret of the people, who were to be left as sheep without a shepherd —he suggested the propriety of banding themselves together, that they might mutually help each other's faith. He said one might be appointed to act as a leader or kind of teacher, while they were without a preacher. The people looked at each other, and finally looked at the doctor, who soon remarked that he did not think of being a Methodist, and that to do as the preacher, Mr. Smith, had proposed would not make them Methodists; he thought, therefore, the plan to be a good one. Eighteen or twenty gave in their names; whereupon Mr. Smith made out a class-book and gave it to Dr. Grant, whom he appointed leader, telling him what would be his duty as a class-leader. When Mr. Smith was about to leave he gave Dr. Grant a Discipline and a few other Methodist books. As the doctor never charged a minister anything for professional services, perhaps Mr. Smith thought he ought to do something in that way for him, but more probably, however, he wished to show the converts, through their leader, the real marrow of the Gospel, and that they were gathered into the Gospel fold under the Methodist banner. The leader soon saw that they were in the Church, and, as he was always peculiar for frankness and honesty, he told the class that he had read and re-read the Discipline, and that there was no use to try to evade the truth—they were all Methodists according to the rules of the Church, and, on the whole, he did not regret it.

Soon it was noised all through the country that Dr. Grant had become a Methodist. It was considered a wonderful piece of condescension on his part, and it was indeed a remarkable occurrence at that day and in that country, that a professional man should become a Methodist. Methodism was such a new and strange thing that a man was regarded as losing caste if he became connected with it. But Dr. Grant had really become a Methodist. Now, having embraced the truth, he had to set himself to its defense, and this brought him at once into collision with "*the standing order.*" Many a hard contest had he to engage in, but such was his success in them that it really seemed as if God had raised him up, in that day of Calvinistic theology, to battle for the truth every day and almost everywhere. This contest he sustained most nobly.

The precise time of Dr. Grant's conversion to God he could never determine, but through a period of about *forty-three years* he enjoyed an evidence of acceptance with God and witnessed a good confession before the world. At the urgent request of the Quarterly Conference he took license as a local preacher, which he continued to hold between twenty and thirty years. For most of this period he held also the offices of class-leader and steward. He was a man of vigorous and well cultivated mind, and carried a great weight of influence where he lived. His Christian character was uniform and consistent. He had two sons, who became itinerant Methodist preachers, and who accomplished much for the cause of God in the Methodist Church during the time of their active service—Rev. Isaac Grant, in the Oneida Conference, now deceased, and Rev. Loring Grant, of the Genesee Conference, also deceased. The latter of these was a very prominent actor in the history of Methodism in Western New York for many years. He lived to a good old age, and died in peace, having spent a number of years in Michigan, and was active in building up the College while residing in Albion.

Dr. Grant was living with his son, Rev. Loring Grant, at Albion, at the time of his death, and had been for some time before. It was here that we became acquainted with him, and esteemed him highly. It became our mournful duty to preach his funeral sermon when he died. He had been a soldier in the War of the Revolution; he was a warm-hearted and excellent preacher when in his prime; he died in Christian hope and peace, November 9th, 1841, in the eighty-third year of his age. Few live so long, and fewer still fill up their lives with so much uniform usefulness. But he has gone to receive the reward of the faithful in heaven.

We cannot better close this sketch than by inserting the following memorial notice of REV. GEORGE B. JOCELYN, D. D.:

"Died at his residence in Albion, Michigan, early in the morning of the 27th of February, 1877, of inflammation of the lungs, George Bemis Jocelyn, D. D., the distinguished President of Albion College, aged fifty-three years and twenty-four days. Born in New Haven, Connecticut, in 1824, he was early removed by his parents to Cincinnati, Ohio, in 1826, and from thence to New Albany, Indiana, in 1830. Here, at the age of fourteen years, he was converted to God, and joined the Methodist Episcopal Church. License to preach was given him in the fall of 1843, soon after which he was received on trial in the Indiana Annual Conference, and appointed, under Peter Guthrie, to Paoli Circuit. In 1844 he was appointed to Rockport, under George Walker. His health failing here, and yielding to the advice of his physicians, he was at the ensuing Conference discontinued at his own request. In June, 1844, he opened a select school in Vincennes, Indiana, and in September of the same year was placed in charge of the Preparatory Department of Vincennes University, which position he held until September, 1849, when he returned to New Albany and opened the Methodist College, now De Pauw College—using the basement of the Centenary Church. In 1853 he was elected Professor of Mathematics and Natural Sciences in Whitewater College, and in 1855 to the Presidency of the same institution.

"In 1856, his health again failing, he found outdoor employment in traveling as a general agent for a Western railway company and the Northwestern University. In June, 1857, he was appointed to Fifth Street Church, Des Moines, Iowa, and in 1859 to Old Zion Church, Burlington. In 1861 he was elected President of the Iowa Wesleyan University, Mt. Pleasant, Iowa, serving meanwhile as pastor of the University and Asbury Chapels.

"In 1864 he was elected President of Albion College, and was transferred from Iowa to the Detroit Conference. Resigning the Presidency in 1869, he was transferred to the Michigan Conference, and stationed at Division Street, Grand Rapids. In 1871 he was re-elected as President of the College, which position he continued to fill until the time of his death. In personal appearance President Jocelyn bore the impress which nature loves to set upon her favorite sons, the patent of their nobility. Possessed of large natural endowments of brain and heart, and cultured by long-continued literary and educational pursuits, he stood among the abler and more efficient educators of the Church.

"As a preacher, in power of thought, perspicuity of style, and impressiveness of manner, he had but few superiors. The ringing clearness of his voice, and the ease and naturalness of gesture, together with his commanding logical vigor and lively play of imagination, gave to him as an orator, at all times, unusual strength, and, when the conditions were most favorable, an almost resistless power.

"As Professor of Mental and Moral Philosophy, his rostrum was a "hill not to be commanded." His lectures upon "The Evidences" will never be forgotten by those who heard them. It was, however, as President of the College that he performed his most invaluable service, and achieved his most enduring fame. When he came to its Presidency, the college was out of money, out of credit, out of friends, and out of character. Debts, doubts, and dilapidation were evidently approaching; dissolution and death were the strong points in the case. Our endowment of seventy-five thousand dollars having been squandered, his very first measure was the creation of an "Endowment Trust Fund Committee"—distinct from the Board of

Trustees—to be charged with the duty of holding or investing all endowment funds, and of paying over to the Board of Trustees only the semi-annual interest accruing thereon—a measure which instantly restored confidence, and has ever since constituted the very mainspring of the successive efforts to create and enlarge the endowment of the College.

"As a monument of this provident sagacity and of his general executive efficiency, Albion College to-day stands before the world the best endowed College in Michigan—the best endowed College in Methodism.

"President Jocelyn was three times elected to the General Conference—once from the Detroit and twice from the Michigan Annual Conferences. At his last election he stood at the head of his delegation. He was also President of the recent National Temperance Convention held at Saratoga, New York.

"His last illness, an acute attack of inflammation of the lungs, in combination with several chronic ailments, was painful in the extreme, and yet he bore all with the same fortitude which had ever characterized him in the season of trial. Calmly debating at times with his physician or friends the doubtful symptoms of his case, at others in cheerful Christian converse, or in commending his loved ones to God, steadily, yet fearlessly, he went down to the margin of the clouded stream, and, wishing all who stood about him 'Good night,' he quietly passed away.

"His funeral obsequies were largely attended by members of both the Detroit and Michigan Conferences, by distinguished friends of the family from abroad, and by an immense concourse of citizens. Rev. H. M. Joy, a former pastor, Rev. I. Taylor, Presiding Elder of the District, Dr. Edwards, of the *Northwestern*, assisted in the services. Dr. Perrine, long associated with the lamented President in the College, preaching the memorial discourse from II. Samuel, 3: 38.   W. H. P."

LANSING, although a city, was not always so, for, as late as 1847, the ground on which it stands was a dense forest. The town had no existence, even in name, prior to the spring of 1847, and then came into existence only in consequence of the location there of the seat of government for the State by the Legislature. It is true, there were a few scattered inhabitants in the country, preaching had been established among them by the indefatigable Methodist itinerants, and a small Society had been formed in that part of the town which for a long time was known as Lower Town, before the State Capital was located there. As soon as the location was settled for the State Capital, Rev. O. Whitmore, who was then on Mapleton Circuit, made this an appointment, thus being the first minister of any denomination to establish services here. A Congregational minister, by the name of Brown, came here and spent a Sabbath about the time the commissioners surveyed and platted the town. He preached, but he did not establish services.

In the summer of 1847, Rev. William C. Comfort, who was then on Lyons Circuit, went up there and organized a Methodist Church at that point, although one had been previously formed down the river a short distance, which has since been concentrated in the north part of the city. At the session of the Conference in September, 1847, Lansing was included in Mapleton Circuit, with Rev. F. A. Blades as preacher in charge, and Rev. James Shaw as Presiding Elder. The District was named Grand River, and Mr. Shaw, the Presiding Elder, fixed his residence at Lansing.

It seemed like a very strange thing when the Legislature fixed on so wild a place for the Capital of the State. It was said to have been designed by some, who voted for it in the first place, as a joke, in order to ridicule the idea of removing it from Detroit. But, when they wished to undo what they had done, they found it to be a "fixed fact" and no joke. We have nothing to do with the political management to secure this location—whether any men were bribed by grants of land, as was charged by some disappointed ones, is not for us to say. It is enough for us to know that the State Capital was so located; that a town was laid out, and has been built up so that, according to the census of 1874, there was a population of 7,445, having Churches of different denominations, and schools of a high order; and everything is flourishing.

At the session of the Conference in September, 1848, Lansing appears in the Minutes of the appointments, having been made a Station—a wise act, a right policy—and Rev. Ransom R. Richards was placed in charge of it. Mr. Richards suffered much in his own health, and still more in the sickness and death of his wife, a most estimable lady, of whom more will be said hereafter. The next year, 1849, Rev. R. Sapp was appointed to this very important field. Mr. Sapp was regarded as a very able minister. It was the right kind of policy to appoint this class of ministers to such a place as this, not that the village amounted to much at the time, but because it was destined to become a central point of influence for the State, and was prospectively great. Let the foundations of the Church be well laid at the beginning, and then it will be comparatively easy to maintain the cause. It was wise, too, to concentrate labor here instead of making it only an appointment in a Circuit, as so many other places were in earlier years. For the next two years, that is, from September, 1850, to September, 1852, Rev. Oren Whitmore was appointed in charge, and did most excellent service. It is not necessary to follow out the annual appointments any further, but we may simply say that it has been most ably supplied.

Lansing appears in the Minutes first in September, 1848, and the first report of members was in September, 1849, when there were *seventy* reported. Now—in 1876—according to the Minutes of Conference, there are two English and one German Stations, having 451 English and 133 German members, making a total of 584 members, and a property valued at $37,500.

Lansing was included in the Grand River District from 1847 to 1856, but at this latter date the Lansing District was created. By invitation of the people, the Michigan Conference held its session here in 1857, and was well entertained. The Church has had the ordinary conflicts to contend with, but its progress has been steadily forward.

We have before stated that while Mr. Richards was stationed at Lansing, his wife, a most amiable, excellent and pious lady, died, after a long and painful illness, which she endured with most cheerful Christian fortitude. It is well, in this place, to give a short sketch of her life and Christian experience. She had been converted to God in early life, and had a deep and sound Christian experience— she knew the "fullness of her Saviour's love." For a good many years she had given herself up to become subject to the privations and labors of an itinerant minister's wife. Faithfully and well had she performed her work, and has gone to receive her crown, which is doubtless studded with many gems.

MRS. HARRIET RICHARDS was born in Warsaw, New York, November 4th, 1816; she died in Macomb, Michigan, February 8th, 1849, in the thirty-third year of her age. She sought and found salvation through faith in Jesus Christ at the age of fourteen years, and immediately united with the Methodist Episcopal Church. Shortly after her conversion her father emigrated to Michigan, and settled in Macomb County, where she adorned her Christian profession by a pious and devoted life.

On the 29th day of March, 1839, she was united in marriage to Rev. R. R. Richards, but a few rods from the spot where, ten years afterwards, she triumphantly departed this life. She did not possess a very marked degree of intelligence which would have singled her out from among her associates, but she possessed a sweetness of disposition, and a dignity in all her movements which commanded at once the love and respect of all who knew her. She had exceedingly few enemies, and was peculiarly fitted to be a minister's wife. She endured all the trials incident to her situation as the wife of an itinerant preacher, without a murmur, regarding it not only her duty to do, but to suffer the will of God. She was a Christian in the highest sense of the word; ever ready to do her duty at home and abroad; yet she had very humble views of her own attainments in religion, often remarking, "It will be a wonder of wonders if one so unworthy as I am ever gets to heaven." While she seldom failed to speak or pray in the prayer meeting, it was in her closet in private communion with God that she found her happiest moments. Her husband had to be absent at his work much of the time, but often on returning home he had the happy privilege of finding her praising God aloud, with tears of joy flowing from her eyes, and her face shining with a divine radiance, like that of Moses when he talked with God. As she lived, so she died, at peace with God and all His children.

When she went to Lansing she little expected to survive through the year, as she saw that death was approaching, but to her he was robbed of his sting. The only occasion on which she was known to manifest any unwillingness to depart was when she and her husband were riding past the graveyard at Lansing, and observing two or three newly-made graves among some old logs and brush, she said, "It hardly seems to me that I can be buried here." When it became manifest that she could survive but a short time, she was removed by her husband to the residence of a sister in Macomb County, that she might be with her relatives in her last moments, and be buried among her kindred. Soon after her arrival she requested her friends to procure the materials for her grave clothes, that she might make them with her own hands. After providing for her among her relatives, her husband returned to his pastoral charge, expecting to be informed if there should be any change for the worse. For some time she seemed to improve, but suddenly growing worse, the message was sent for her husband. He hastened to her bedside. On reaching the place, he found her evidently near the close of life, but perfectly composed, and looking up to him with a sweet smile, she said: "I did not believe the Lord would let me die till you came," and inquired how he got along in his work. When she drew near to her end, and it seemed as if she could breathe but a few times more, on reviving, her husband said, "You seemed almost gone." She replied, "I thought I could breathe but a few times more, but I did not see the chariot." After remaining for some time with her eyes closed, she opened them, looked all around, and then upwards, exclaiming, " A light—*a light.* You did not see that light. It was most beautiful." So she came to her end in peace, with the light of God on her path.

IONIA.—Although we have made a general survey of the Grand River Valley, under the head of Grand Rapids, we cannot repress the desire to speak of this place specifically. Ionia is near the Grand River, about fifty miles above the Rapids, and is the seat of justice for Ionia County. The settlement, though begun a little earlier, did not attract much attention until the Land Office for the northwestern part of Michigan was located there in 1835.

The first settlers, among whom were the Yeomanses and the Dexters, were of the Baptist persuasion, but yet they were not supplied with preaching of their own faith for some time after the Methodist itinerants had visited and preached Christ to the people. When Osband Monnett, a modest, retiring, but very pious young man, was sent as a missionary to Grand River, he followed the water course in each direction from the Rapids, searching out the few settlers scattered through the woods, and came to this place in 1835.

It may not be out of place to indulge in a few reflections just here on that part of the Methodist economy which enabled that Church to supply the Gospel so soon and so faithfully to the settlers in the new country. The itinerant system of the Methodist Episcopal Church is peculiarly adapted to the wants of a new country, and to maintaining religious services in sparsely populated districts. It is equally adapted to older settlements, even though they can later supply themselves with the services of a minister. The itinerant, with a salary fixed by rules, but yet entirely dependent on the people whom he serves, and at the disposal of the superior officers of his Church, without a voice in regard to the particular appointment he is to serve, or in regard to his pay, receives his orders from his Bishop at the Conference, and takes possession of the field of labor assigned him with a zeal and devotion worthy of the great cause in which he is engaged. Like the famous Mississippi postmaster, who kept the office in his hat and delivered the mail along the shore, the itinerant, whose waterproof portmanteau contains his wardrobe and library, is ready for any call, and can draw on that portmanteau in any emergency. Mounted upon a stout horse, and with heavy riding whip, Bible and hymn-book in hand, with a single change of clothing perhaps, and less than a dollar in change in his pocket, he seeks his field of operations half a thousand miles distant—it may be savage or civilized, prairie or wilderness, Indian trail or turnpike, it makes no difference, the chalk-mark of the Bishop is before him; the success of his enterprise and a good report at Conference now occupy his attention. His sermons are studied in the saddle, and brought into consistency by a prior delivery to an audience of trees, imagined to be people.

This system of training may not produce a very learned ministry, or often secure the affix of D. D. to the name, but it frequently produces strong original thinkers and very fine natural orators. The policy of Conference usually assigns the frontier Districts and Circuits to the young men, not as a penance exactly, but, perhaps, on the authority of the New Testament, where two principal characters commenced their ministerial teaching in the wilderness, or upon the example of an eminent French missionary, who returned from his barbarian audiences to astonish all Paris with his eloquence.

This system of an *itinerant* Gospel ministry prevented many of our Southern States from relapsing into barbarism; and to it our own State is indebted for many, indeed for most of its early religious privileges, and for its subsequent advantages.

The Territory of Michigan was included in the Ohio Conference from 1820 until the autumn of 1836, and the Michigan woods became the dreaded field of the Ohio itinerant, not so much on account of the woods, to which he was accustomed, as on account of the necessity of contact with the Yankee settlers, who, accustomed to the ways of the world, the Church and the school-house, could frequently instruct the young parson, in the science of civilization, at least. The Ohio preachers were, however, usually well received in Michigan, and they occasionally deemed themselves well repaid for enduring Yankee jokes and witticisms by being able to report at Conference the capture and possession of a rosy-cheeked Yankee maiden, transformed into a wife.

In the year 1835, the Grand River Valley becoming known on the maps of the Territory, excited attention, and settlers rushed into it by scores. The Conference wishing to extend its jurisdiction over it, and to supply the new settlers with the Gospel, despatched young Monnett, as before mentioned, to gather into the fold the scattered sheep in this northern wilderness. He was young and modest, was mounted on a fine Ohio horse, and appeared on his field of labor in the height of the land excitement, which filled the woods with speculators. That fine horse of his, among the Indian ponies, became the horse of the woods, and was deemed too good an animal for a preacher to own. The result was, the horse disappeared in the night-time. Some one, not having the fear of the preacher before his eyes, appropriated him to his own use without his owner's consent, and Monnett was obliged to travel on foot. In his report at the Conference, in which the lost horse occupied a conspicuous place, he consoled himself by saying that, if the horse had not been stolen, he certainly would have starved to death during the winter, and it was safer for him to run the risk of possible over-driving in the hands of a Yankee than certain starvation in the Grand River woods. If this was not a case of the philosophy of religion, it was certainly a specimen of religious philosophy. This was a time to try what kind of stuff the man was made of, and to test his fidelity to the work to which he had been appointed. He continued faithfully in the field until his allotted term of service expired.

Methodistically considered, at that time Ionia did not have as much importance attached to it as Lyons, some six or eight miles further up the river, because at the latter place a Methodist Society was formed in the spring of 1836, and, though the itinerants preached at Ionia, they could not organize a Society, so, when the Grand River Mission was divided, the upper part of it was called Lyons instead of Ionia. The latter place does not appear in the list of appointments until the autumn of 1853. Rev. George Bignell was appointed to it, and, at the end of the year he returned *one hundred and sixty* members. From this time forward it has been continued a station. The Presiding Elder's District is now called Ionia.

The Methodist Episcopal Church was first organized in Ionia in 1839 by Rev. Zebulon C. Brown, who at the time was in charge of Lyons Circuit. The Society consisted of only *five* members. Mr. Brown, who organized this Church, was a man of a very strong intellect, and cultivated, but rather slow and moderate in speaking, and consequently was not very popular among the people generally, but among men of thought he ranked high, as he well deserved to do. We once heard him preach on this passage, "God is a spirit." It was a most close and masterly sermon, showing the spirituality of God and the necessity of spiritual worship. He possessed a sound Christian experience, and was truly devoted to God, but his health was rather feeble, which prevented him from putting forth that active, energetic labor which the people demanded. He located in 1843, and settled at Saline, where he adorned the Christian profession by a consistent and devoted life. He has since died as such a man would be expected to die—in great peace, giving glory to God through Jesus Christ our Lord.

The minister whose name stands connected with Ionia, when it first appears in the list of appointments, after having filled several other Stations, returned to die among this people, to whom he was very much attached, and who were very much attached to him.

"REV. GEORGE BIGNELL was born in Carlton, New York, January 28th, 1823, and died at Ionia, Michigan, December 31st, 1858, of consumption. At the age of *ten years* he was powerfully converted to God, and offered himself to the Church to unite on probation, but was refused admission on the ground of his being too young. This refusal had a discouraging influence on his mind, and resulted in his backsliding. Under the ministry of Rev. D. C. Jacokes, he was reclaimed, in Oakland County, Michigan, in the eighteenth year of his age. He soon felt it to be his duty to preach the Gospel, but, instead of making preparation for that work, he, through timidity of character, fled from duty, and took refuge in one of the great pine forests in the northwestern part of Ionia County, hoping to escape the call of God. An incident occurred here which closed up all vacillation, and determined his course. While felling trees, in company with his brother and another man, he looked up, and saw a large pine tree within ten or fifteen feet of him, coming with a mighty crash. With a scream to his brother, he sprang aside, barely escaping being crushed into the earth. With a soul already deeply agitated, the effect of this incident may be imagined. He, on the spot, pledged himself to his Maker to do his duty, and, in a short time, he left the forest, returned to his home in Oakland County, and commenced the preparation necessary to enter upon the work of an itinerant minister.

"In May, 1846, he was licensed as an exhorter; in 1847, he was licensed as a local preacher, and employed by the Presiding Elder to travel on Farmington Circuit. He was admitted on trial into the Michigan Conference, at Kalamazoo, in 1848, and appointed to Talmage Circuit; 1849, to Paris; 1850, he was admitted to full connection, ordained Deacon by Bishop Morris, and appointed to Niagara; 1851-2, to Hastings; 1853-4, to Ionia; 1855, to Greenville, Montcalm County; 1856-7, to Edwardsburg, Cass County, where, early in the second year, he ceased to work, and went to Ionia.

"He was pleasing in his address and successful as a minister; perhaps *five hundred* were converted under his labors. He was a man of untiring, quiet zeal, of marked integrity, of one work. His sickness was long-continued, but through all of it he was graciously, wonderfully supported. In 1858 he was placed on the superannuated list, and he returned to this place. His death was one of the most blissful and triumphant. Just before he died, some friends commenced singing:

"Could we but climb where Moses stood,
And view the landscape o'er;

"'Stop! Stop!' said he, 'I am done climbing. I am up there. Sing:

"The promised land from Pisgah's top
I now exult to see;
My hope is full, O, glorious hope!
Of immortality.'"

And so he fell asleep in the arms of Jesus. We acknowledge ourself indebted mainly to the pen of Rev. R. Sapp, who was stationed at Ionia at the time, for this sketch.

REV. R. SAPP, who was stationed here in 1858, was one of the ablest ministers in the Michigan Conference, having occupied some of the most important positions as stationed minister and as Presiding Elder. He was honored by his brethren by being elected as delegate to the General Conference several times. He made a good record during a ministry of many years, and when he came to pass the Jordan of death he found himself ready, and passed triumphantly over. He had suffered much and long, but endured all trustingly, "as seeing Him that is invisible." He was Presiding Elder of Grand Rapids District at the time of his death, which occurred in the spring of 1872. He was a man truly devoted to the interests of the Church, and rejoiced in its prosperity. He has left an enduring name, for he had filled charges in most all parts of the State of Michigan—though all of his latter years were in the west half of the State.

We will now return to the first introduction of the Gospel into Ionia. There is a romantic incident connected with it worth recording, to which we now invite attention. We are indebted to one of the parties concerned for the facts.

Late one afternoon, in 1835, a young man might have been seen running out from the little village along the Indian trail, eastward, to meet another who was seen coming on an Indian pony, with a camp-kettle and other accoutrements dangling by his side. As he drew near the horseman, he made demonstrations to have him stop, and when the rider drew up the other cried out, "Are you a Methodist?" "Certainly," said the man on the horse. "Then I want you to come to Deacon Yeomans's to preaching to-night. They are good people there, but they won't pray for me. Will you come?" "Certainly," answered the horseman, "and you go to all those crowds of men and tell them there is to be meeting there, and invite them to come, and they will do it." "But will you be there and help me?" asked the footman. "Yes, certainly," was the reply. This was young Monnett, the missionary, and the man on horseback was Joseph Brown, then of Ann Arbor. The occasion of all this was that there were five or six hundred men here waiting the opening of the United States Land Office, and not being able to find accommodations in the few log houses while they were waiting for the opening of the office, which had been delayed a few days for the want of suitable buildings, they had camped around log heaps. Monnett had passed around among them inquiring after a Methodist. One group had sent him to another, until they began to feel a little mischievous over it, when one, seeing Brown coming at a distance, directed his attention towards him, and remarked to the preacher that "that boy yonder, coming over the bluff upon an Indian pony, with his camp-kettle dangling at his saddle, is a real live Methodist." Away he started, with a countenance betokening the last stages of the "blues." That which was intended for a joke proved to be true in this instance. He was a Methodist, and when the young preacher learned the fact, he said, "I am glad of it; you must come down and take holt." "Very well," said Brown, "are there no professors about here?" "Yes," said the preacher, "there are a few Baptists, but they won't pray." "Never mind," said Brown, "we will hold the meeting." Brown found they had criticised the Ohio preacher in his homespun pretty thoroughly, which he, having endured well, they engaged as a body to go and hear him preach. As Brown was about leaving for tea some two miles distant, Monnett reassured himself by privately saying to Brown: "You will surely be there?" "Of course," said he.

At dusk, on arriving at the Deacon's, Brown found the house crowded, and many in the yard. "Look here," said the preacher, "I will sing and open the meeting, and you must exhort and close." "Very well," said Brown, "but you just open, read a long hymn, and line it, as we have no books; then read a long chapter, and make some remarks upon it; pay it on to these land sharks, it will do them good." The meeting proceeded according to programme. The hymn was lined, and the Grand River woods rang with the chorus from six hundred voices. After listening to a very fine exhortation of half an hour, the services were appropriately closed. Brown's part consisted simply in reading the closing hymn.

What a change has come over this country, and over the people.

This was the beginning. The progress has been glorious, and the end will be triumphant. The present population of the city, according to the census of 1874, is 3,251, having all the appliances of a growing and prosperous town.

The different religious denominations established themselves in due order, and having had their successes, are engaged in the work of evangelization according to their peculiar views and modes of work.

According to the Minutes of the Michigan Conference for 1876, the Methodist Society has a church building valued at $10,000. They have also given due attention to the Sunday School work, and in this department they are successful and prosperous. The Annual Conference held its session here in September, 1873, and was satisfactorily entertained. Thirty-seven years have now elapsed since the *five* were organized into a Church, and that Church has grown to number *three hundred and fifty-eight*, besides those who have gone over the river to their glorious reward. Verily, God has been with this people, and has crowned their labors with success.

ALLEGAN has been mentioned before, but it is desirable to say a few words more in relation to it. We have already said that Mr. Robe extended his Circuit into this county in 1832, while he was traveling the Kalamazoo Circuit. This was considered as one of the desirable portions of country on account of its advantages for lumbering. Hon. Flavius Littlejohn and other important personages, settled at the village bearing the name of the county, laid out a town, and gathered around them civilizing and elevating influences, such as religious services and schools. The names of William Todd, now deceased, and Franklin Gage, still living, are very familiarly associated with the early history of this country as pioneer ministers. As the country has developed, and the inhabitants have increased, Churches of the different denominations have been established, and have exerted their preserving and elevating influence. We are pleased to record that the early settlers of the town of Allegan were religious people, and availed themselves of such ministerial services as they could obtain. How rapidly the country has been settled may be inferred from the fact that in 1874 the population of this county was 32,381. This is one of the interesting and valuable portions of the State. Being one of the Lake counties, it must always be one of the finest growing ones, and will attract attention.

We take pleasure in presenting, in this connection, a brief notice of one who feels a deep interest in this region of country, and who, having recently become office editor of the *Michigan Christian*

Advocate, expects to do much valuable work for God and humanity in that connection.

REV. JAMES H. POTTS was born in Canada, June 12th, 1848. With his father's family, he moved to Kalamazoo County, Michigan, and having, by hard study, qualified himself for teaching, he engaged his first school at the age of sixteen. At the close of the war, having served as a soldier, he graduated from Mayhew's Business College, intending to devote his life to mercantile pursuits. While visiting his early home, however, the memories of his childhood and the counsels of his deceased mother, so operated upon his mind that, in January, 1857, he experienced religion, and united with the Church. Yielding to a long-resisted conviction that he should preach the Gospel, he was duly licensed, and, while prosecuting his theological studies, served as a local preacher. In the fall of 1869, he was married to Miss Alonsa C. Cole, of West Le Roy, Michigan, and united with the Michigan Conference at its session held at Grand Rapids in that year. While serving as pastor, he wrote considerably for the press. In consequence of the loss of hearing, to a large extent, he found it difficult to do the work of the pastorate, so in September, 1877, he accepted an editorial position on the *Michigan Christian Advocate*, and moved to the City of Detroit.

While in the pastoral work, Mr. Potts did very valuable service, and retired from it for editorial work, greatly to the regret of the people with whom he had served, and with much reluctance on his own part. He now is in a position to speak to thousands of persons every week without the embarrassment of an ear-trumpet. His trumpet will give no uncertain sound. The pen is now to take the place of the voice. He has a clear mind and a warm, Christian heart.

CHAPTER XIV.

Task Nearly Finished—German Work—Wesleyans—Other Protestant Churches—Time Elapsed—Statistics—Comparative Progress—Church Property—Congregational Church—Indian Work—M. Hickey—Unitarian Notice—Book Depository—J. M. Arnold—"Michigan Christian Advocate"—"Northwestern Christian Advocate"—Dr. Edwards—Bay View.

E have now nearly completed our allotted task, and presented an outline history of the progress of Protestantism in this Peninsular State, and yet there are a few items which we could not very well introduce into any place in the body of the work, which we may present in this concluding chapter.

A very important work of evangelization among the German immigrants settled in the City of Detroit, was begun in 1845, by Rev. John M. Hartman, a Methodist preacher, which has been carried forward till there are now in the city two German Methodist Episcopal Churches doing a good work. The work has extended to all the towns and cities where there is any considerable German population, so that there are now in this State 1,608 members and *fifteen* ministers connected with the Methodist Episcopal Church.

In 1841, there was a small defection from the Methodist Episcopal Church on account of slavery. The controversy had been going on for several years, but now the defection took shape, and resulted in the organization of a branch of "The American Wesleyan Church" in Michigan. This took a few members and local preachers, among whom, Marcus Swift, Samuel Bibbins, and Guy Beckley were the most prominent—all deceased; but the principal cause of the separation having been removed by the abolition of slavery in the nation, a large proportion of the ministers and people have returned to the Methodist Episcopal Church. The prime movers of the movement in this State, Marcus Swift and Samuel

Bibbins, were very good and conscientious men. Mr. Swift died early after entering on the work of building up this new denomination. Mr. Bibbins, a very devoted Christian man, lived to return to the Church in 1867, and died in great peace, a member of the Detroit Conference. He died in May, 1877. Dr. Luther Lee, who was active in this movement in the East, came to Michigan, and in 1867 returned to the Methodist Episcopal Church, as did Dr. McEldowney.

There are small bodies of Protestant Christians in this State which have not been mentioned particularly, such as the Free Will Baptists, who were very early in the field, and who are maintaining a college at Hillsdale; the Methodists, or, as they are more familiarly known, Protestant Methodists; the United Brethren, United Presbyterian, the Dutch Reformed, the Free Methodist, the Wesleyan Methodist, and, among the colored people, the African Methodist Episcopal Church, the Zion Methodist Episcopal Church, and, perhaps, there may be one or two others. We have omitted these because they are so few in any given place that to give sketches of them would have required too much minuteness of detail, and it has been impracticable for us to obtain their statistics.

It is now sixty-six years, for which we take account of statistics, since the first Protestant Church was organized in Michigan, consisting, at the time, of only seven members—three men and and four women. This first Church has always maintained its existence, notwithstanding the disasters of war and other difficulties. Other Churches were organized in due time and entered on their spiritual work. We are able to present a summary of the numerical strength of the principal denominations, giving the date of their first organization, with this remark, that the Congregational Church does not appear before 1842, although some of the early Churches were organized on that plan; yet, by a plan of union with the Presbyterians, they lost their identity till the date given. The ministers are included in the membership. We show, at the same time, the value of Church property—that is of Churches and parsonages, and not including Sabbath School libraries and furnishings:

	Date.	Members.	Value of Property.
Methodist Episcopal	1810	56,100	$3,000,000
Presbyterian	1820	13,348	No report.
Protestant Episcopal	1824	8,969	No report.
Baptist	1827	24,508	No report.
Congregational	1842	13,935	1,076,233
		116,860	

It is well now to compare this progress of Protestant communicants with the progress of population. In 1810 the population of the Territory was 4,762, and only *seven* Church members or communicants, or one in 680 of the population. According to the census of 1874, the population had increased to 1,334,300, and the Church members or communicants have grown to 116,860, which would make about one communicant for every *eleven and one-third* of the population. The increase of the population for the last two years will be fully met by the number of communicants in the minor denominations not enumerated. We find, then, great reason for hope for the future of our State in a religious aspect. We have not made any general statement as to the number of children and youth, who are every Sabbath engaged in Bible study in the various Church Sabbath Schools. And there are very many such.

The Roman Catholics, according to their last Ordo Book, claim to be numerically and influentially, as follows, in the State of Michigan, viz.:

Churches, 192; priests, 114; hospitals, 4; orphan asylums, 5; religious institutions, 15; schools, 54; population, 175,000. The population includes all their adherents of all classes, children as well as adults, which is about one-eighth of the population of the State.

We certainly have nothing to fear from Romanism if Protestants are only faithful to themselves, because there is a constant advance in true Christian power over the increase of population. After all the croakings and boastings of skeptics of various classes, Christianity is on the advance. The figures given in relation to the Protestant Churches show only the actual membership, which is to be multiplied by 3 for adherents, making 350,250, or one in about three-eighths of the whole population.

We here present a synoptical history of the Congregational Church in Michigan, furnished us by the author. We should have been glad to have done the same thing for other Churches if such had been furnished us.

"*An historical sketch of the Congregational Churches of the State of Michigan during the century preceding A. D. 1876. Prepared at the request of the authorities of the State for the Centennial Exhibition at Philadelphia. By Rev. P. R. Hurd, D. D., Secretary of the General Association.*"

Congregationalism, as a system of Church order, is well understood. And yet it may not be amiss to state that it consists in allowing no man, or body of men, "to lord it over God's heritage," but in asserting the essential independence of the local Church, in connection with a substantial fellowship with all the Churches.

Congregationalism in the State of Michigan, as in most of the other States west of the Hudson River, was at first largely merged into Presbyterianism. Under the famous "Plan of Union" the government of the Churches was mixed, members belonging to each denomination being allowed to enjoy their own preacher from within the particular Church. And although many of these Churches were organized under the name and title of Congregational, yet, since they were subjected to the care of the Presbytery within whose bounds they happened to be, and since their ministers, though for the most part from Congregational New England, were also members of this body, it very naturally turned out that by far the large majority of them became at length distinctively Presbyterian. Nearly all the older and stronger Churches of the State, irrespective of their original organization, are now to be found in that communion. Traces of the origin of some of them appear in the corporate name of the ecclesiastical Society with which they are connected. That name remains to this day Congregational. As might have been anticipated, some Churches were formed at that early day in the settlements which failed to become centers of population or business, and which, therefore, were either disbanded, or merged in others which, afterwards formed, promised a greater permanency.

The first Congregational minister that ever visited the new State of Michigan, and, indeed, it is to be believed, the first minister of any evangelical denomination, was Rev. David Bacon, of Connecticut, the father of the present Rev. Leonard Bacon, D. D., of New Haven, Connecticut. Mr. Bacon arrived at Detroit on the 11th day of September, 1800, on an exploring expedition for the establishment of a Mission among the Indians. After spending a few months in that vicinity, he returned to Connecticut, where he was ordained and married. Returning the following spring, and not meeting with the success in the Mission that was anticipated, he soon retired, and became the founder of the town and Church of Talmadge, Ohio.

In July, 1824, Rev. Isaac Ruggles came from Connecticut, and established himself in Pontiac, then an Indian trading-post; from which place he radiated in every direction, traveling on foot, preaching the Gospel and founding Churches as he found opportunity. At that time there were very few Church organizations of the affiliated denominations outside of Detroit, and, so far as can be ascertained, no Congregational or Presbyterian minister, except the Rev.

Mr. Ferry, a Presbyterian—the father of the present Senator Ferry —who was then a missionary to the Indians at Mackinaw.

Previous to 1830, several Churches had been organized, some by the name of Congregational, and some Presbyterian, the representatives of which, together with the six ministers then in the Territory, composed the Detroit Presbytery. Up to this date, Presbyterianism, therefore, had everything its own way.

In June, 1831, John D. Pierce arrived in the Territory, under commission from the American Home Missionary Society. On consulting with the Missionary Committee of the Presbytery of Detroit, as to his future operations, as he was advised to do by the Secretary of the Society, Mr. Pierce was gravely informed that he would be expected to connect himself with the Presbytery; and that it would be neither desirable nor wise for him to organize distinctively Congregational Churches. The reason given for this was the assertion that, while Congregationalism was well enough for New England, it was not at all adapted to the new settlements of the West, an assertion which was so often and so emphatically repeated in those days, that it came to be believed even in New England itself, and had much to do in repressing the growth of Congregationalism on the entire Western field. This advice of the Committee he did not see fit to take, very logically considering that if this young Church order had proved itself sufficiently strong for the infant settlements of New England, it could not be wanting in adaptation to those of any other region. Mr. Pierce finally settled in Marshall, and took an active part, subsequently, not only in shaping the polity of the Churches of the State, but also in giving form to that excellent system of public instruction, with the University at its head, which is the glory of the Peninsular State.

Previous to 1835, eight Churches were organized, which never relinquished the Congregational polity, nor lost the Congregational name, viz: The Church in Rochester was formed in July 1st, 1827; in Romeo, August 16th, 1829; in Lima (now extinct), January 17th, 1830; in Pontiac, February 6th, 1831; in Clinton, January 19th, 1833; in Bruce, July 31st, 1833; in Barry (now extinct), January, 1834.

These Churches, however, either stood alone or were connected with a Presbytery; and therefore were not reckoned as belonging to the denomination, until after 1840, when the first Association and Conference were formed in the eastern part of the State. In addition to these, the Churches of Marshall, Homer, Richland and Ypsilanti (1829), were organized Congregational, and remained so until, through the pressure of outside influence, they became distinctively Presbyterian. The Church of Battle Creek (1836) was also organized on the "Plan of Union," and retained that status, reporting alike to Synod and Association, until, in 1874, by the compact of Union adopted by the General Assemblies of the Presbyterian Church, it was obliged to relinquish its mixed character, when it elected to be numbered with the Presbyterians.

From 1835 to 1840, nineteen other Churches were formed, which still retain their connection with the denomination. But these Churches, like those already on the field, were of a limited membership, and widely scattered over a vast extent of country; thus rendering fellowship, if not absolutely impossible, yet extremely difficult. But they were firm in their adherence to the simple polity of the Pilgrims, and manfully resisted any attempt to wrest from them the liberty which we have in Christ Jesus our Lord.

About this time the inquiry began to be agitated, "What can be done to draw the scattered Churches closer together in sympathy and fellowship?" and thus to establish them all the more firmly in the ways and practices of the Fathers. As the result of this inquiry, the Eastern Association was formed May 12th, 1840, and the Jackson Association May 17th, 1842. In the eastern part of the State, an organization called the Consociation, which afterwards took the name of the Eastern Conference of the Churches, was also formed.

In the meantime several young men, among whom was Rev. L. Smith Hobart, Rev. Harvey Hyde, Rev. Henry L. Hammond, and Rev. Thomas Jones, had come into the State, by whom this inquiry was taken up, and zealously agitated, until finally, at a meeting of the Jackson Association, held on the 6th of July, 1842, a call was issued inviting the Congregational ministers and Churches of Michigan to convene at Jackson, on Tuesday, the 11th of October, at six o'clock P. M., for the purpose of organizing a General Association of the State. In response to this call, at the time and place appointed, there were assembled the following ministers and delegates of the Churches:

Ministers. — Rev. Sylvester Cochrane, Vermontville; Rev. Hiram S. Hamilton, Mt. Clemens; Rev. Marcus Harrison, Jackson; Rev. L. Smith Hobart, Union City; Rev. Harvey Hyde, Saginaw; Rev. Thomas Jones, Grass Lake; Rev. Jason Park, Sandstone; Rev. Ebenezer McDonald, Royal Oak; Rev. Joseph W. Smith, Grand Blanc; Rev. John D. Pierce, Marshall.

Delegates from Churches.—A. S. Ames, Milford; Chester Yale, Jackson; E. C. Clapp, Litchfield; Jacob Hayward, Leoni; Drusus

Hodges, Leoni; Jesse Adams, Grass Lake; L. H. Jones, Grass Lake; Stephen Watkins, Grass Lake; Alpheus Saunders, Union City; John N. Stickney, Union City.

After mature deliberation and prayer, these ministers and messengers of the Churches adopted a Confession of Faith, Constitution, and Rules of Procedure, and thus the General Association of Michigan was fairly ushered into being. From that time to the present, the denomination has had a recognized existence among the forces which have been at work in moulding the moral and religious condition of the State, with a history growing brighter and still brighter as the years have rolled on.

Just how many Churches of this order there were in the State at this time, and how many members they contained, it is now impossible to ascertain. Some attempts at the gathering of statistics were at once made by the indefatigable Secretary, Rev. L. Smith Hobart, but they were not very successful. In 1845 there were reported in connection with the General Association, five (5) Conferences, consisting of fifty-three (53) Churches, with a membership of two thousand one hundred and fourteen (2,114). But seven of these Churches, it should be observed, furnished no report.

In 1855, the number of Conferences had increased to seven (7), with a total of one hundred and six (106) Churches, seventy-two (72) ministers, and four thousand nine hundred and eighty-seven (4,987) members.

In 1860 the number of Conferences remained the same, but the number of the Churches increased to one hundred and thirty (130), of the ministers to one hundred and one (101), and of the members to seven thousand two hundred and fifty-five (7,255).

In 1865 there were nine (9) Conferences with one hundred and forty-one (141) Churches, one hundred and thirty-one (131) ministers, and eight thousand three hundred and seventy-two (8,372) members.

In 1870 there were still nine (9) Conferences, one hundred and seventy-four (174) Churches, one hundred and fifty-one (151) ministers, and eleven thousand five hundred and forty-one (11,541) members.

In 1875 the Conferences had increased to ten (10), the ministers to one hundred and seventy-four (174), the Churches to one hundred and ninety-nine (199), and the members to thirteen thousand two hundred and nine (13,209).

It is but quite recently that attempts have been made to ascertain the amount of annual offerings made by these Churches to the various causes of benevolence, and the reports are as yet very imperfect. But imperfect as they are, the reports of 1875 present an array of figures which, considering the infancy and weakness of most of these Churches, evinces that the spirit of benevolence is by no means wanting within them. These figures aggregate the sum of twenty-four thousand four hundred and ten dollars, and ninety-three cents ($24,410.93), while the amount expended for parish purposes during the same year was two hundred and twenty-three thousand two hundred and ninety-one dollars and eighty-seven cents ($223,291.87).

The estimated value of property held by them is:

1. Houses of worship—Nine hundred and ninety-four thousand, seven hundred and thirty-three dollars ($994,733).*

2. Parsonages—Sixty-one thousand dollars ($61,000).

3. Salaries and funds—Fifteen thousand one hundred and ninety dollars ($15,190).

The Sunday School work has been prosecuted by them, during their entire history, with unabated vigor. Without attempting to trace the progress of this work from one period to another, it will be sufficient to state that, according to the report of 1875, the schools connected with the denomination aggregated sixteen thousand eight hundred and sixty (16,860) members.

Congregationalism has ever been but a synonym of education. In its history, the church and the school-house have always stood side by side, the one esteemed quite as necessary as the other. With it the old monkish dogma, that ignorance is the mother of devotion, has found no favor. Its piety has rather been wont to be measured by the intelligence of its faith. An educated ministry in the pulpit, and an enlightened people in the pews, are the two great pillars on which it has been built, and on which alone it can hope to stand. As a consequence, wherever it has obtained a footing, it has become the advocate and promoter of all sorts of learning. In this State, it has been by no means false to its traditional character. From its ministry the first Superintendent of Public Instruction was furnished. And in the successful establishment of a Christian College at Olivet, and the endowment of a Professorship in the Theological Seminary at Chicago, it has fully vindicated its ancient promise.

These plain facts have been placed on record, in this Centennial year of our National existence, that it may be known to those who come after us, from what small beginning, and through what earnest struggles, this glorious inheritance of a simple, Scriptural Church

*Since the above was written, $20,500 have been reported, making the whole value of Church property reported, $1,015,233.

polity, received from the Pilgrim Fathers, has been handed down to them.

We have already noticed the work among the Indians of the Lake Superior country, but it is well now to bestow a little attention on that work in the Lower Peninsula, as the circumstances of its introduction were peculiarly interesting. It commenced among a band, residing at the time in Oakland County, which was known as the Lakeville band. They had become as degraded as it is possible for human beings to become, it would seem. They were the terror of the country around them—drunken, thieving and quarrelsome to the last degree. In the spring of 1840 or '41, they held a solemn council to decide on their fate. They felt their degradation most keenly, but they saw no light for themselves. In this solemn conclave, they discussed their condition; that they were in a very low condition, they could not deny. But what was to be done? After spending some time over the question, there appeared to be no hope for them, and the conclusion at which they arrived was that there was nothing better for them than to procure whisky enough, and drink themselves to death. In accordance with this resolution, they procured a quantity of whisky, and commenced the debauch. Just at this juncture, Rev. Mr. Scott, a missionary among the Indians in Canada, near Sarnia, appeared on the scene, and proposed to the Chief to preach the Gospel to them. But the men were too drunk to hear him then. The Chief begged of the missionary to remain, and he would try to get his men and women sober enough, in the course of a day or two, to hear him. He remained. The Chief did as he proposed; they came to hear the missionary, and the Gospel took such effect upon them that every man and woman, except one man, in a few days, professed to be converted, and the remaining one, after a time, was converted, and joined the Church. This was a very sudden transformation of a drunken, savage band into a Christian people. They adhered firmly and faithfully to their faith in Christ, and became a sober and orderly people. They required attention and instruction, so a missionary was sent among them, and the work extended to other bands in the Lower Peninsula. Rev. D. C. Jacokes was, for some time, a very laborious and successful worker among them. He was succeeded in that work by Rev. Manasseh Hickey, who visited most of the bands; so the work has been cared for, and there are now several of these Mission charges in the Lower Peninsula. Who can doubt the power of Divine grace to change and save man when such a revolution as this has been produced? No merely civilizing agency has ever accomplished such a work as this. There has been but very little backsliding among them.

These Indians, after their conversion, having declined to go west of the Mississippi, and thus failed to obtain annuities which would have amounted to several hundred dollars, they were very poor. We once asked the Chief why he did not go, and take his band with him. He replied that he was afraid to go, lest, getting off there among the wicked pagans, and away from the means of grace, his men would be led away—would backslide, and be lost; and they would rather be without the money than to run the risk. We thought that was a noble sacrifice. How very few, even among enlightened people, are willing to make such a sacrifice for the sake of being preserved from sin.

We take great pleasure in adding a few words in regard to one of the two missionaries mentioned above. As he is still living, the notice will be but brief.

Rev. Manasseh Hickey was converted to God in his early youth in the town of Troy, in Oakland County, Michigan, and, from the time of his conversion, has been a very earnest and zealous Christian. Soon after his conversion, he felt himself called to the work of the Christian ministry. He felt, also, the need of a higher education, and spent several years at Albion Seminary in study, acquiring a considerable knowledge of the classics and of Hebrew. While a student at Albion, his zeal did not abate, and he was very useful among the students, as well as in the neghborhoods around about. He joined the Conference in 1848, and was for several years in the Indian mission work. He has been very useful in the ministry, and many have been turned to righteousness by him, who will appear as stars in the crown of his rejoicing. He has filled Circuits, Stations and Districts greatly to the advantage and edification of the Church. In the winter of 1872, while Presiding Elder of Flint District, he was thrown from a carriage, striking on his head on the frozen ground, and was senseless for twenty-four hours. Though he has partially recovered, he has been a great sufferer ever since, and unable to do effective labor. His heart is still in the work, and, if his physical condition would allow, he would still glory in active itinerant labor.

We will be pardoned for quoting the following from an article from the pen of Rev. C. H. Brigham, a Unitarian minister, formerly at Ann Arbor, contributed to an Eastern paper in 1866:

"The Methodists are the only denomination in Michigan whose increase is very marked and rapid. The Presbyterians rather lose than gain ground. The Baptists barely hold their own. The Congregationalists do not grow so fast as the population. The Episcopal Church is suffering just now from an unfortunate quarrel in its largest congregation, in which the Bishop is implicated, and which makes ridiculous the boasted unity of that peaceful communion. But the Methodists are zealous, united, hopeful and prosperous, to a degree which amazes even their own preachers and leaders. They rival, even surpass the Episcopal body in the size and cost of their churches, in the richness of their decorations, and in the completeness of their appointments. In a short time they will have, in all the cities of Michigan, not only the largest number of worshipers, but the finest show in worship, and, perhaps, the most real influence. Church extension, more than Church discipline or dogma, is their care in this Centenary year. And it is a great help to their cause that one of their preachers is at the head of the University."

At the General Conference of 1864, which was held in Philadelphia, provisions were made by which the agents of the Western Book Concern could establish a Depository in Detroit, so that our ministers and people could be supplied with Methodist and other religious books at the same rate as in New York or Chicago.

REV. JOHN M. ARNOLD, D. D., who had been stationed in the Woodward Avenue and other Churches in the city, was appointed in charge of it. The establishment has been greatly enlarged, and the business greatly extended, and though it is not *now* an official Depository of the Church, the same advantages are to be obtained from Arnold & Willyoung, as the firm is now styled. This having been found a great convenience to Sabbath Schools and others who wished to replenish their libraries, Mr. Arnold enlarged the idea, and extended the plan so as to take in religious and Sunday School books for all denominations of Protestants. He has now added to this a general assortment of school, literary, historical and scientific books.

Mr. Arnold is a minister of long standing, having joined the Conference in 1849, and served as Circuit preacher, been in Stations and fulfilled the work of a Presiding Elder. Though charged with many duties, he does a large amount of preaching. He is emphatically a Michigan man, having been brought up, educated, converted to the experience of Divine love, and entered the Christian ministry here. His is one of the cases, where men break away from their parental religious or rather denominational training, for his parents were "Close Communion" Baptists. Mr. Arnold takes special interest in the Sunday School department of Christian work, and

has been very successful in that field. Mr. Arnold is a man of extensive reading and good literary acquirements, and is often called on to fill the pulpits of other denominations. For the last two years he has been the associate and managing editor of the *Michigan Christian Advocate*. Indeed, he has had the principal part of the work of that paper on his hands, as the editor-in-chief was a pastor, and had a heavy charge to serve, which demanded his time and attention.

THE MICHIGAN CHRISTIAN ADVOCATE.

The importance of a religious newspaper under the fostering care of the Methodist Church, in this State, which, while it should be Methodistic in its management, and devoted to the interests of that denomination, would not be offensively sectarian, had long been felt. But no one was prepared to undertake its establishment. Some efforts had been made from time to time to organize a company for that purpose, without success. But in the autumn of 1874, Rev. Oren Whitmore who was Presiding Elder of Adrian District, commenced the publication of a small monthly sheet, for the special benefit of his own District, the idea of which was enlarged by the co-operation of other Districts, and it assumed the name of the *Michigan Christian Advocate*. This was not entirely new, for Rev. J. V. Watson, many years before, had edited and published a paper by the same name, for a short time, at Adrian. As the small sheet originated by Mr. Whitmore did not seem to meet the felt want, the matter was brought before the Annual Conference, which, by a decided vote recommended the publication of a weekly paper. This, however, did not meet the difficulty in the case, for, who shall do it, was the ever recurring question. After many conferences of ministers and laymen, a stock company was organized according to the following articles of association:

THE METHODIST PUBLISHING COMPANY.

We, the undersigned, do certify that we do hereby associate together as a body corporate, under and by virtue of the laws of the State of Michigan, in the manner and for purposes as follows, that is to say:

1st. The name of this Association is The Methodist Publishing Company, and the purpose for which it is organized is to print and publish a religious newspaper entitled the *Michigan Christian Advocate*, and to carry on the business of book and job printing, in connection therewith, and the publication of such other matter as may be decided upon by said corporation.

2nd. The location and place of business of said Company is at the City of Detroit.

3rd. The amount of Capital Stock of this Company is ten thousand dollars, divided into one hundred shares of one hundred dollars each.

4th. The amount of property, real and personal, which said Company may hold, shall not exceed fifty thousand dollars.

5th. The first meeting of this Corporation, for the purpose of completing the organization of the same, the election of officers and the transaction of any other business, shall be held on the twenty-third day of December, A. D. 1874, at 2 o'clock P. M., at the office of Robinson & Flinn, in the City of Detroit.

6th. The names of the Stockholders, with their respective residences, and the number of shares held by each, are as follows, viz:

Names.	Residences.	No. of Shares.
Oren Whitmore	Adrian	5
Alfred F. Bournes	"	5
Oren Whitmore	"	5
John M. Arnold	Detroit	11
George O. Robinson	"	5
Mark S. Smith	"	5
Christopher R. Mabley	"	5
Lewis R. Fiske	"	3
Francis A. Blades	"	2
Thomas Stalker	"	2
W. H. Pearce	"	1
Dr. James Stimson	"	1
Lewis P. Davis	"	1
Elijah H. Pilcher	"	2
John W. Kermott	"	2
Erasmus D. Allen	Morenci	30
George W. Robinson	Detroit	1
Charles Ten Winkel	"	5
William H. Benton	Royal Oak	1
William H. Shier	Ann Arbor	1
O. J. Perrin	Saginaw City	1
Isaac N. Ellwood	Morenci	1
J. B. Atchinson	Detroit	1
J. T. R. Brown	"	2
J. Owen	"	2
Wm. J. McCune	"	3
H. Hitchcock	"	1
Charles H. Gaston	"	1

7th. The term of the existence of this Corporation is thirty years.

In testimony whereof, we have hereunto set our hands and seals, this twenty-second day of December, A. D. 1874.

(Signed) OREN WHITMORE,   [Seal.]
  "   J. M. ARNOLD,   [Seal.]
  "   ALFRED F. BOURNES,   [Seal.]
  "   GEO. O. ROBINSON,   [Seal.]
  "   CHARLES TEN WINKEL,   [Seal.]
  "   H. HITCHCOCK,   [Seal.]
  "   W. J. MCCUNE,   [Seal.]
  "   LEWIS R. FISKE,   [Seal.]
  "   C. R. MABLEY,   [Seal.]
  "   WEBSTER H. PEARCE,   [Seal.]
  "   ELIJAH H. PILCHER,   [Seal.]
  "   J. W. KERMOTT,   [Seal.]
  "   ERASMUS D. ALLEN,   [Seal.]
  "   M. S. SMITH,   [Seal.]
  "   W. H. BENTON,   [Seal.]
  "   J. B. ATCHINSON,   [Seal.]
  "   J. T. R. BROWN,   [Seal.]
  "   J. OWEN,   [Seal.]
  "   F. A. BLADES,   [Seal.]

STATE OF MICHIGAN, } ss.
COUNTY OF WAYNE,   }

On the twenty-second day of December A. D. 1874, personally appeared before me, a Notary Public in and for said county, the above named: Oren Whitmore, John M. Arnold, Alfred F. Bournes, George O. Robinson, Charles Ten Winkel, Lewis R. Fiske, C. R. Mabley, Webster H. Pearce, Elijah H. Pilcher, J. W. Kermott, Erasmus D. Allen, and M. S. Smith, personally known to me as the persons executing the foregoing instrument, and severally acknowledged that they executed the same freely, for the purposes therein named.

[SEAL]   E. H. FLINN,
                          Notary Public, Wayne Co., Mich.

The following officers were immediately elected: Elijah H. Pilcher, D. D., President; John M. Arnold, D. D., Vice President; George O. Robinson Esq., Secretary and Treasurer. Rev. O. Whitmore, was appointed Editor, and Rev. L. R. Fiske, D. D., was shortly after added to the editorial staff. The first number of the new paper with the old name was issued the first week in January, 1875. Since its first organization a number of changes, both in the Publishing Company and in the management of the paper, have been made. The job printing department has been given up entirely, the whole attention being devoted to the extension and the improvement of the paper. Dr. Pilcher having resigned, Dr. Fiske was elected President and also Editor-in-Chief, with Dr. J. M. Arnold as

Associate and Business Manager. The editorial staff was made still more effective by the appointment of a number of corresponding editors, from various parts of the State, and the creation of an office-editorship, of which the Rev. J. H. Potts is the present incumbent. This new enterprise, which was looked upon by many as a doubtful experiment, has so well succeeded that it has already attained a circulation of *over five thousand* copies, and the last year yielded a handsome dividend on its paid up stock, and paid *twenty-five dollars* to each of the annual Conferences in the State, for the benefit of the superannuated preachers. This success is unparalleled in the history of such enterprises. This patronage has been secured without interfering materially with the circulation of other religious periodicals. Very nearly that number of families have a religious paper, who would have had none without it. If the future management shall be equal to the past, there remains a brilliant career for this young member of the *Advocate* family.

The *Northwestern Christian Advocate*, although not located in Michigan, is, nevertheless, the product of Michigan brains. Rev. J. V. Watson, an eloquent and successful preacher, laid aside by physical infirmity, from the active work of the ministry, was not content to be idle. He, therefore, applied himself to religious journalism, on a small scale, in the City of Adrian. But, being a man of a large heart and sagacity of intellect, he decided that this was not the locality at which a journal should exist to wield the proper influence. In casting about, he concluded Chicago was the eye of the Northwest, and that, in order to control that vast territory, the key to it must be in that city. He, therefore, proposed that the General Conference of 1852, which was to meet in Boston, should provide for the establishment of a member of the *Advocate* family at that place. He was in attendance at the seat of the Conference, but, being a reserve, he took a seat before the close, and urged the matter in private conversation with delegates, being actively seconded by E. H. Pilcher, who was a delegate. Provision was then made for the establishment at Chicago of a depository for books, and for the publication of such a paper under the control of the Western Book Concern. Mr. Watson was appointed Editor of the paper, and the publication was commenced on the 1st of January, 1853. This paper has been very largely patronized in Michigan, though not so much so as its merits have deserved. For the last thirteen years, a member of the Detroit Conference has been connected with the editorial department of the paper, and that justifies its introduction into this History; besides, it has always been outspoken on all questions affecting the interests of Protestantism, and has been a powerful agent for its promotion in this Peninsula.

ARTHUR EDWARDS, D. D., the present able and deservedly popular Editor of the *Northwestern Christian Advocate*, was born in Ohio, in 1834, but is, decidedly, a Michigan man. He was brought up here, though he received his collegiate education at the Ohio Wesleyan University, under the care of the sainted Bishop Edward Thompson. While pursuing his college studies, he was converted to God, and joined the Church. Soon after graduation, he entered the ministry, and joined the Detroit Conference in 1858. When the War of the Rebellion broke out, his patriotism led him to enter the service as chaplain, in which he continued for about three years, and in 1864 he was appointed Associate Editor of this paper, in which relation he continued for eight years, doing excellent service. In 1872, he was elected Editor by a large majority, and in 1876 was re-elected by acclamation. Dr. Edwards is an incisive, facile writer, and thoroughly adapted to editorial work—a man of untiring industry, possessing iron-like endurance. He makes a superior paper, and one well worthy of a more extended patronage than it now has. He has served for a number of years with great acceptability as Secretary of the Detroit Conference, and has been sent as a delegate to the General Conference several times.

BAY VIEW.

With the growth of the country and the increase of wealth among the people, there is an increasing desire for some place of resort for the heated term, and yet it is desirable to have such places as free as possible from the allurements to vice and folly usually found at watering-places. At the suggestion of Mr. S. O. Knapp, seconded by Rev. J. H. McCarty, D. D., the Annual Conferences of the Methodist Episcopal Church in Michigan, at their session in 1875, appointed a committee, consisting of the following persons: Rev. E. H. Pilcher, D. D., Rev. Seth Reed, Rev. Robert Bird, and David Preston, for the Detroit Conference; Rev. J. H. McCarty, D. D., Rev. W. H. Brockway, Rev. A. P. Moors, and S. O. Knapp for the Michigan Conference; with full powers to investigate and settle the question in regard to such a place of resort within the State. This committee organized, and examined the various localities suggested. After such examination, they became satisfied that the project was feasible, and, on the ninth day of November of that year, effected an incorporation, under the statutes of the State, by adopting the following articles:

Articles of Association of the Michigan Camp-Ground Association of the Methodist Episcopal Church:

STATE OF MICHIGAN, } ss.
COUNTY OF JACKSON,

We, the undersigned, do hereby certify that we desire and agree to form an incorporated Association, pursuant to an act of the Legislature of the State of Michigan, entitled, "An Act to provide for the incorporation of Associations, Conventions, Conferences of religious bodies for literary, religious, or other benevolent purposes. Approved March 27th, A. D. 1867," and amended by "An Act, approved February 2d, 1875," under the name of "The Michigan Camp-Ground Association of the Methodist Episcopal Church," and do adopt the following articles of Association:

First. The purposes for which this Association is formed are the securing, developing, establishing and maintaining, within the State of Michigan, grounds for an annual Camp Meeting and summer residences; for holding Camp Meetings and religious services in connection with summer residences, and for the transaction of all business in connection therewith.

Second. The principal office for the transaction of business, and at which the annual meetings shall be held, shall be on the camp ground, unless otherwise directed, or at such other place or places as the Association or the Board of Trustees may from time to time direct, except as to the annual meeting, which shall be on the camp grounds.

Third. The business of this Association, in the intervals of the meetings of the Association, shall be conducted by a Board of nine Trustees, and Joseph H. McCarty, of Jackson, Elijah H. Pilcher, of Detroit, William H. Brockway, of Albion, Seth Reed, of Ann Arbor, Aaron P. Moors, of Traverse City, Robert Bird, of Rochester, Samuel O. Knapp, of Jackson, David Preston, of Detroit, and D. Burnham Tracy, of Detroit, shall constitute the first Board of Trustees, and are divided into three classes, in the order in which their names appear above; the first class to continue in office for three years, the second class for two years, the the third class for one year, or until their successors are elected and accept their trust, so that one-third will go out of office each year. The full term of office shall be for three years; and the election shall be by ballot at the annual meeting, as fixed by the By-Laws: Provided, always, that said Trustees shall be members of the Methodist Episcopal Church, and a cessation of membership shall vacate the office.

In testimony whereof, we have hereunto set our hands, this ninth day of November, A. D. 1875.

JOSEPH H. MCCARTY,
ELIJAH H. PILCHER,
W. H. BROCKWAY,
SETH REED,
AARON P. MOORS,
SAMUEL O. KNAPP,
DAVID PRESTON,
D. BURNHAM TRACY,
JOHN WESLEY KERMOTT,
JOHN M. ARNOLD,
SILAS HEYSER,
JAMES GOULD,
J. HENRY PILCHER,
GEO. O. ROBINSON.

{L. S.}

Petoskey, at the head of Little Traverse Bay, was selected as the place. Over three hundred acres of land, about one mile from the village, were donated, and the first Camp Meeting was held in the first week in August, 1866. The place has been named Bay View. We here present the latest circular of the Association, which will furnish a clear view of the objects and conditions of the Association.

"BAY VIEW CAMP GROUND.

"*Officers of the Association.*—Rev. W. H. Brockway, President; Rev. J. M. Arnold, First Vice President; William Phelps, Second Vice President; Rev. R. N. McKaig, Third Vice President; Rev. Seth Reed, Secretary; David Preston, Treasurer.

"*Trustees.*—D. F. Barnes, Grand Rapids; E. H. Pilcher, Detroit; William H. Brockway, Albion; S. Reed, Ann Arbor; A. P. Moors, Traverse City; R. Bird, Petoskey; S. O. Knapp, Jackson; David Preston, Detroit; D. B. Tracy, Detroit.

"The Trustees of the Michigan Camp Ground Association of the Methodist Episcopal Church are now ready to offer to the public a resort which, it is believed, cannot be surpassed for healthfulness, accessibility, picturesqueness of scenery and inexpensiveness, anywhere in our country. They ask attention to the following points:

"*Location.*—Bay View Camp Ground is situated at the head of Little Traverse Bay, and one mile north of the growing village of Petoskey. Being alike accessable to the Upper and Lower Peninsula, it is in all respects a most desirable point for a summer city. The land owned by the Association lies on the southeast side of the Bay. It rises in natural terraces, thus affording any number of most desirable building sites. From these sites a delightful view is had of the lovely Bay as well as of the great Lake Michigan, upon whose waters the vessels of commerce can be seen plying between Chicago and the great Eastern cities. The ground has about one mile of Bay front, along which runs a gravelly beach, admirably adapted for drives and walks.

"Bay View is in the Mackinaw region of country, being about twenty-five miles from the Straits and Island of Mackinaw. A steamer usually plies daily between the Island and Petoskey, and hence it is in a region which must ever be an attractive summer resort for the great Northwest.

"*Health.*—The Little Traverse region is known to be a *Sanitarium* for hay fever, asthma and catarrhal affections. Bilious diseases and fever and ague are positively unknown here. The climate is remarkably invigorating, just such as thousands of enfeebled constitutions and other thousands of strong but over-worked men and women need during the hot months of summer. The air is free from all malaria, as it comes sweeping across a hundred miles or more of fresh water from the west and northwest. The water is remarkably clear, and pure as can be found anywhere in the world. The Traverse region is not mountainous, yet somewhat broken and varied, and the scenery is very attractive. In short, the acknowledged *healthfulness* of this point was one of the strong reasons, in addition to its other natural attractions, for its selection as a place of summer residence and religious convocations. Indeed, we are highly pleased that we can now invite the people of the Northwest to a Sanitarium equal, if not superior, to those sought at much greater expense along the Atlantic coast.

"*Recreation.*—Bay View Camp Ground is surrounded by facilities for recreation which are simply endless. In its vicinity are several large inland lakes, some of them from twelve to fifteen miles in length and from five to seven in width, and which abound in a great variety of fish, such as rock bass, black bass, pickerel, perch and white fish. The streams flowing into the lakes abound with the much coveted speckled trout and grayling. That Little Traverse Bay, from which the views are so enchanting, whether seen in the morning or evening sun, will always invite the lovers of the sail and the oar. Those large, almost unbroken forests, that stretch away for many miles, abounding in game, both of the foot and wing, will afford ample enjoyment to gentlemen who love the rifle.

"Tourists, too, will here find satisfaction. A great variety of attractive routes will invite them from this point. At Petoskey they can take a steamer north for Mackinaw, Marquette, and the Lake Superior ports; or east for Cheboygan, Saginaw and Detroit; or south and west for Traverse City, Ludington, Grand Rapids, Chicago and intermediate ports. At Bay View Station they can take train on the Grand Rapids & Indiana Road southwest to the Grand Traverse country, which abounds in attractive features; or south to Reed City, where they may take the Flint and Pere Marquette Road either east or west; or still south to Howard City, where they can take the Detroit, Lansing & Northern Road to Lansing and Detroit; or still further south to Grand Rapids, where so many lines center tending to all parts of the country.

"A more enjoyable trip, however, will doubtless be to leave the Camp Ground by stage, four miles to Crooked Lake, thence by steamer through Crooked Lake, Burt Lake, Indian River, Mullet Lake, Cheboygan River to Cheboygan, a distance of about forty miles from Bay View. This route has been opened through since the location of the ground. At no distant day it will probably be intersected by the Jackson, Lansing & Saginaw Road, whose northern terminus is now at Gaylord, but whose ultimate destination is Mackinaw. Thus it will be seen that Bay View has a liberal list of attractions to the pleasure-seeking tourist.

"*Arrangements.*—The Association has a warranty deed of 330 acres of land, covered with a thrifty growth of hard timber, both great and small, and on which is a fine stream of beautiful water, which can be brought into use for drinking and other purposes. A portion only of this land has as yet been platted, but the platting has been done in the line of a general plan which shall ultimately embrace the entire grove. The streets and avenues will be wide and the lots ample, averaging about one hundred by fifty feet. The lots will be leased to parties for the purpose of erecting cottages thereon, the lease to run fifteen years with privilege of renewal, and subject to an annual rental, at prices varying according to location, for the first five years from two to ten dollars. Every person leasing a lot with the view of erecting a cottage will be required to join the Association, the fee for life membership in which is ten dollars. Those who do not wish a voice in the Association, but wish simply a lot for the year, can be accommodated upon their paying the assessment of from two to ten dollars, according to location. A committee will also designate places for those who wish merely a spot for the year on which to erect a cloth tent, where the price will be merely nominal.

"*Cottages and Tents.*—Bay View has the advantages of being in a country where timber is plentiful and cheap. Manufacturing companies in that vicinity have advised the Association that they will furnish lumber of all kinds, both rough and dressed, for Camp Meeting purposes, at the lowest possible figures. Their mills have facilities for all kinds of work, and it is surprising to many how cheap cottages may be built. Information upon the subject of building will be furnished by Rev. R. Bird, of Petoskey, or S. O. Knapp, Esq., of Jackson, Michigan. Those who wish to rent tents for the season will confer with Colonel William Phelps, of Detroit.

"*Entertainment.*—The Association contracted for a boarding-house to be built upon the ground, and which was finished in the month of July, 1877. It was first made two stories high and 25 by 75 feet on the ground, but constructed with reference to additions, as the demands should increase, some of which have recently been made. Its site commands one of the finest views of the water to be had upon the entire ground. In this hall, good day board is furnished at the following rates: $5.00 per week; $1.00 per day; 50 cents for single meals.

"Good hotel accommodations will also be found in the village of Petoskey, at reasonable rates.

"Lodgings will also be furnished for those who do not occupy cottages. But the lodgings provided by the Association for the present year will consist simply of bunks and straw. Persons expecting to lodge on the ground, should bring blankets and pillows with them.

"*Limits.*—The Bay View Camp Meeting for 1877 will commence Tuesday, July 31st, and will continue one week. It will be in charge of the Committee on Worship, viz: Rev. D. F. Barnes, Rev. A. P. Moors, Rev. W. H. Shier.

"*A Sunday School Congress* will be held on the Bay View Camp Ground, commencing July 24th, and continuing one week. To this all Sunday School workers are cordially invited, irrespective of denominations. It is in charge of the following general committee: Rev. I. N. Elwood, Port Huron ; Rev. J. B. Atchinson, Detroit; Rev. W. W. Washburn, Detroit; Hon. C. R. Brown, Port Huron; Mr. H. Hitchcock, Detroit; Rev. H. M. Joy, Niles ; Rev. W. J. Aldrich, Jackson ; Rev. Levi Tarr, Big Rapids ; Mr. J. S. Tuttle, Niles ; Mr. J. H. Pilcher, Jackson.

"*Transportation.*—All persons desirous of attending the Sunday School Congress and State Camp Meeting at Bay View can do so at one fare for the round trip by going over any of the following lines of railway, viz: Grand Rapids & Indiana; Cincinnati, Hamilton & Dayton; Wabash (all points between Toledo and Lafayette); Indianapolis, Pennsylvania & Chicago, (from Indianapolis); Pittsburgh, Fort Wayne & Chicago (from local points in Indiana); Michigan Central and all its branches (from all points east of and including Niles, also from Chicago); Detroit, Lansing & Northern; Detroit & Milwaukee; Flint & Pere Marquette; Chicago & Lake Huron.

"Tickets will be on sale at their respective offices from July 22d to August 5th, inclusive. Return limit, August 15th.

"The Grand Rapids & Indiana, Detroit, Lansing & Northern, Detroit & Milwaukee, Flint & Pere Marquette, (and probably other connecting lines), will also give the following reduced rates, viz: *two cents* per mile each way, from June 15th to August 30th, with return limit, August 31st. This class of tickets may be extended a few days if necessary.

"Close connections will be made at Richmond, Fort Wayne, Kendallville, Sturgis, Kalamazoo, Grand Rapids, Howard City and Reed City.

"Two trains daily (except Sunday) will run between Cincinnati and Petoskey (Bay View Station). Sleeping coaches on night trains."

ERRATA.—On page 398, line 18 from the top, the word "not" should be left out. Also on same page, line 18 from bottom, in place of the words "ten cents" should be "one o'clock."

—On page 413, line 9 from bottom, "Niagara" should be "Allegan."

—On page 416, line 4 from bottom should read "finest fruit growing ones," etc.

ALPHABETICAL AND CHRONOLOGICAL LIST

OF THE

ITINERANT PREACHERS

Who have ever been entrusted with work in Michigan; beginning with 1809, when Detroit first appears in the List, and ending with 1877.

EXPLANATION.

The figures on the left hand of the name show the date when he became connected with the Itinerant work in Michigan, and the figures on the right hand show the time when the connection ceased; the letter "*l*" means that he located or retired from the work; "*d*" that he died; "*tr*" that he was transferred to some other field; "*w*" that he withdrew from the ministry and Church. A short location is not regarded, nor a short absence from the State; "*ex*" means expelled from the connection. We have taken great pains to have this list accurate, and yet there will probably be some errors in it. The date begins with admittance on trial, and we have made no distinction between discontinuance and location.

1827	Armstrong, James............*tr.*	1828	1822	Baker, Samuel.................*d.*	1823
1831	Allen, Benjamin..............*tr.*	1832	"	Brunson, Alfred..............*tr.*	1823
1832	Armstrong, James, P. E.....*d.*	1834	1825	Baughman, John A..........*d.*	1868
1838	Arnold, E.........................*l.*	1839	1828	Brown, Arza....................*tr.*	1831
1843	Abbott, Isaac C................*l.*	1872	1830	Billings, Alvan.....................	
"	Allen, Alfred......................		1832	Beswick, George M..........*tr.*	1833
1846	Abbott, Norman...............*l.*	1861	1833	Brockway, William H.........	
1849	Arnold, John M................		1835	Buckles, A........................*l.*	1836
1854	Anderson, Charles M..........		1836	Babcock, Charles.............*tr.*	1844
1856	Ayres, Aden T..................*l.*	1859	"	Beers, Hawley B..............*tr.*	1837
1859	Armstrong, James.............*l.*	1867	"	Burns, David.....................*l.*	1877
1864	Austin, Charles W...............		1837	Bennett, Isaac....................	
1865	Armstrong, John...............*l.*	1872	"	Breckenridge, George W...*tr.*	1841
"	Aldrich, William J...............		"	Britain, Flavel..................*l.*	1875
1868	Allen, Charles T.................		"	Brown, Zebulon C.............*l.*	1844
1869	Austin, Lyman C..............*d.*	1874	1838	Blowers, Rufus L..............*l.*	1840
1872	Aiken, James M................		"	Brakeman, Josiah.............*l.*	1849
"	Allington, William...............		"	Burgess, Oliver.................*tr.*	1839
1873	Ashford, Joseph................*l.*	1876	"	Byron, Joseph..................*l.*	1841
"	Atchinson, Jonathan B.........		1839	Barnes, Dan.....................*d.*	1840
1874	Andree, William..................		"	Blanchard, Jonathan.........*d.*	1864
1876	Aust, A...............................		"	Bradley, George...............*d.*	1871
1877	Allman, William H..............		"	Brown, George W.............*tr.*	1854
"	Armstrong, Edmund V.........		1840	Bangs, Francis B................	

HISTORY OF PROTESTANTISM IN MICHIGAN.

Year	Name	Year
1840	Bush, Daniel............l.	1849
1841	Bigelow, William E............	......
"	Briar, James............l.	1843
1843	Berry, Ezra............l.	1845
"	Bruce, Caleb A............w.	1852
"	Bushy, Joseph (Indian)......l.	1847
1844	Barnum, Nelson............d.	1852
"	Bell, Andrew............	......
"	Bessey, Samuel............	......
"	Bird, Robert............	......
"	Blades, Francis A............	......
"	Boynton, Valmore G............	......
1846	Benson, William............	......
"	Brown, Henry N............	......
"	Buchanan, Philander G.....tr.	1852
1847	Borden, Edmund W............l.	1858
1848	Belnap, Giles N............d.	1866
"	Bignell, George............d.	1858
"	Blades, William............l.	1851
1850	Boynton, Jeremy............	......
"	Burnham, John H............w.	1871
1851	Bartlett, Alanson R............	......
"	Bignell, Thomas H............	......
1852	Barker, Sewel P............l.	1856
1853	Bancroft, John O............	......
"	Bennett, Loren M............	......
1854	Baur, Emil............tr.	1857
1854	Bench, Asahel C............	......
"	Brockway, Nelson L............	......
"	Brockway, Edwin H............	......
1855	Bertrams, Gustavus......tr.	1868
"	Bigelow, Andrew J............	......
"	Birdsall, William............	
"	Braggins, John............l.	1861
1856	Barker, Henry P............l.	1867
"	Burth, Sebastian............tr.	1868
"	Black, Andrew J............ex.	1861
"	Bliss, W. C. H............l.	1862
"	Buel, James I............	
"	Burch, Lawrence D............w.	1861
"	Burnett, William Q............	......
1858	Beard, Edgar............d.	1873
"	Bement, Horace H............l.	1870
1859	Barr, Lewis............l.	1861
"	Betts, George I............l.	1870
"	Bird, Samuel............	
1860	Benson, Amos............d.	1863
"	Billing, James............l.	1865
"	Braun, Jacob............tr.	1876
1861	Benton, William H............	......
"	Bourns, Alfred F............	......
1862	Ball, I............tr.	1863
"	Berry, Francis W............l.	1865
"	Boeurs, William A............	1865
"	Blowers, Washington I......d.	1865
1863	Bacon, Elisha D............	......
"	Bigelow, Samuel............l.	1864
"	Buckley, James M............tr.	1866
1864	Berry, Joseph R............tr.	1870
1865	Barnes, D. F............	......
"	Blanchard, B. W............l.	1869
1866	Ball, David O............	......
"	Bacon, D. S............l.	1874

Year	Name	Year
1866	Balls, James............	......
"	Barnes, Leeman............	......
"	Blaker, George L............ex.	1869
"	Brown, Samuel J............	......
"	Buddenbaum, Henry.........tr.	1872
1867	Beckwith, D. T............l.	1869
"	Bibbins, Samuel............d.	1877
"	Bibbins, Elisha............d.	1875
1868	Baldwin, W. W............tr.	1873
"	Ball, William M............	......
"	Barry, Edward............	......
"	Barrett, Wight............	......
"	Blanchard, Samuel G............	......
"	Boggs, Andrew R............	......
"	Borcherding, W............tr.	1870
1869	Bathrick, Linus............	......
"	Bell, Francis I............	......
"	Bronson, W. A............	......
"	Browning, Mark............	......
1870	Bennett, Isaac jr............l.	1872
"	Brass, Newman W............l.	1871
"	Bray, Nicholas............	......
1871	Barnhart, C. L............	......
"	Baskerville, Thomas H............	......
"	Bodmer, J. R............tr.	1874
1872	Bettis, Samuel G............l.	1874
"	Bradley, Franklin............	......
1874	Berry, Joseph F............	......
1875	Bayliss, James H............d.	1876
"	Blood, Alvah G............	......
"	Bready, Robert H............	......
1876	Barnes, Joseph A............	......
"	Bready, John A............	......
1877	Bancroft, Edward B............	......
"	Berry, James............	......
"	Buel, George A............	......
1809	Case, William............tr.	1816
1826	Coston, Zarah H............tr.	1829
1828	Cooper, Benjamin............	1832
1830	Colclazer, Henry............tr.	1846
1832	Cheney, Robert............l.	1833
1833	Crane, Elijah............d.	1868
1835	Chatfield, Larmon............d.	1876
1837	Chandler, Daniel M............d.	1838
"	Colclazer, Jacob............tr.	1838
1838	Chaplin, Jonathan E............d.	1846
"	Collins, Wellington H........d.	1858
"	Cosart, John............l.	1844
1840	Crippen, Elliott M............l.	1847
"	Cook, Remus H............ex.	1845
1841	Comfort, William C............d.	1862
"	Crawford, Riley C............	......
1843	Cogshall, Israel............	......
"	Cowles, William F............tr.	1850
1844	Camburn, Myron B............l.	1872
"	Campbell, Alexander............l.	1853
"	Champion, Thomas J............ex.	1849
"	Chapman, Henry............l.	1845
"	Curtis, David A............	......
1846	Collins, Judson D............d.	1852
1847	Collins, Isaac F............tr.	1853
1848	Calkins, Sylvester............	......
1849	Clements, Samuel............	......

1849	Crane, Rufus C.............................	......	1874	Coates, Frederick....................	......
1850	Card, Ira B........................*l.*	1851	"	Copp, Richard......................	......
1851	Carter, Thomas................*tr.*	1856	"	Chalis, Dewit C....................	......
"	Chamberlain, James B.........*l.*	1352	1875	Cope, Robert L.....................	......
1852	Cawthorn, John W................	......	1876	Callen, Marshall M...............	......
"	Clayson, William..................*l.*	1853	"	Christian, L........................	......
1854	Crittenden, Alvin H...............	......	1877	Crane, Alfonzo.....................	......
"	Calender, Nicholas............*tr.*	1857	1812	Densmore, George W.......*tr.*	1813
"	Camburn, Ira H...................	......	1818	Davis, Alpheus...................*tr.*	1819
"	Chambers, Edmund C.........	......	1819	Dixon, Truman................*tr.*	1820
"	Chase, Benjamin P............*l.*	1855	1826	Donahoo, James T.............*tr.*	1827
1855	Carpenter, M. L.................*l.*	1856	1832	Dixon, Andrew..................*l.*	1833
"	Caster, James H....................	......	1834	Davis, Lorenzo...................*l.*	1844
"	Chipman, George A...........*l.*	1856	1836	Delaney, Mark...................*l.*	1837
"	Clark, Thomas.......................	......	1844	Day, Eri H..........................	......
"	Clubine, John.......................	......	"	Dubois, Robert.................*d.*	1860
"	Congdon, Thomas J..............	......	"	Donelson, Ira W..................	......
1856	Carlton, Henry....................*l.*	1862	1847	Doughty, Benjamin F...........	......
"	Corey, Milo.......................*l.*	1859	1851	Davis, H. G.......................*l.*	1852
"	Crawford, Isaac..................*l.*	1869	"	Donelson, Park S..............*tr.*	1856
"	Crum, W. W......................*l.*	1857	"	Dunton, Alfred A................	......
1857	Caster, Elisha E.....................	......	1852	Dobbins, Jacob.....................	......
"	Cocker, Benjamin F..............	......	1855	Dougherty, Myron A.......*tr.*	1875
"	Coplin, Alanson................*tr.*	1866	"	Dean, Lyman H...................	......
"	Crane, Rufus H.................*tr.*	1872	"	Deshetler, Basil L...............*l.*	1861
"	Crippen, John W..................	......	"	Donnelly, William................	......
"	Cross, Charles...................*l.*	1858	1856	Doust, William.....................	......
"	Chapin, George A.............*l.*	1858	1857	Dwelle, Jedediah................*l.*	1859
1858	Caldwell, Hugh................*tr.*	1870	1859	Dayton, James N..................	......
"	Colby, Harrison.................*l.*	1859	"	Dunning, William...............*l.*	1861
"	Cordon, James R...............*d.*	1876	1861	Darling, A. A.....................	1873
"	Cramer, Densmore.............*d.*	1859	1862	Dorey, James F..................*d.*	1869
1859	Chick, Charles.......................	......	1866	Deitz, Frederick M................	......
"	Cleveland, Newell...............*d.*	1862	1867	Draper, Gilbert C..................	......
"	Child, James L....................*d.*	1874	1869	Davis, George R..................	......
1860	Campbell, William J............	......	"	Dunlap, James A..................	......
"	Chase, Oscar F..................*d.*	1863	1870	Dunning, W. Edson.............	......
"	Clark, William J..................	......	1871	Downs, Henry C................*l.*	1872
"	Curnalia, James H................	......	"	Deacon, George.................*l.*	1874
1861	Church, Charles I..................	......	1873	Draper, James.....................	......
"	Clark, Benjamin M..........*ex.*	1865	"	Davis, Lewis P....................	......
"	Cochran, Isaac C................*d.*	1868	"	Dawe, William.....................	......
"	Colby, William M................	......	1874	Dodds, Lafayette.................	......
"	Calkins, Levi W....................	......	"	Dawe, Edwin......................	......
"	Clough, Albert B..................	......	"	Diverty, James E..................	......
1866	Coe, Hiram.......................*d.*	1867	"	Donaldson, George...............	......
"	Cooley, Elias.........................	......	"	Dunker, Louis..................*tr.*	1875
"	Crosby, Chauncy R............*l.*	1870	1875	Daniels, Eugene D................	......
1867	Cowan, John......................*l.*	1872	1876	Darling, Marcellus W...........	......
1868	Clemo, William C...............*l.*	1869	"	Downs, Allison O...............*l.*	1877
1869	Cadwell, Jason R..................	......	1832	Elliott, Arthur B.................*l.*	1839
"	Casler, David........................	......	1838	Ercanbrack, John...............*d.*	1852
"	Cole, George L.....................	......	1842	Emery, Reuben..................*l.*	1846
"	Coplin, W. M........................	......	1846	Eldred, Andrew J.................	......
1870	Carlisle, J. W. H...................	......	"	Ercanbrack, Caleb K.........*l.*	1849
"	Cleghorn, Thomas................	......	1851	Earl, Lewis W.....................	......
1871	Cogshall, Wilber I.................	......	"	Etheridge, N. C..................*l.*	1855
1872	Carroll, Morton D.................	......	1853	Elliott, Joseph (Indian).......*l.*	1857
"	Clark, Nathan N...................	......	1857	Edmonds, Lewis M..............	......
1873	Campbell, John W................	......	1858	Edwards, Arthur..................	......
"	Campbell, William M...........	......	1859	Engle, David........................	......
"	Craven, Edwin......................	......	1864	Edwards, Timothy.............*l.*	1871
1874	Campbell, William R...........*l.*	1875	1867	Eglers, John C..................*tr.*	1870

HISTORY OF PROTESTANTISM IN MICHIGAN.

Year	Name	Year
1867	Ellis, C. H.	
"	Elwood, Isaac N.	
1868	Elliott, G. C.	
1874	Evans, Henry F.............*l.*	1876
1877	Eland, Albert N.	
1820	Finley, James B. (P. E.)....*tr.*	1824
1829	Felton, Erastus................*tr.*	1831
1830	Finley, James W.............*tr.*	1832
1831	Frazee, Bradford..............*l.*	1845
1837	Flemming, Alanson..........*l.*	1846
1838	Frees, James H..................*tr.*	1839
1839	Fitch, Andrew M.	
1841	Fox, Thomas....................*d.*	1847
1847	Fassett, Noah	
1848	Farnsworth, R. L.............*l.*	1850
1853	Finch, Isaac S..................*l.*	1859
"	Finch, Seth B...................*d.*	1857
1854	Finch, Edwin...................*l.*	1855
"	Fox, William	
1855	Fisk, Lewis R.	
"	Freeman, Daniel S............*l.*	1858
1857	Fowler, Josiah J................*l.*	1874
1858	Freeman, Frederick J	
1860	Fisher, Charles H	
1862	Fox, Daniel O..................*l.*	1866
1865	Fair, Alexander	
"	Ferguson, Larmon Pilcher	
1867	Frey, Theodore S..............*l.*	1874
1868	Force, L. P.	
1868	Frazer, Joseph	
"	Frazee, Elias W.	
"	Friend, William ....*l.*	1871
"	Fuller, James M.	
1860	Fox, C. S.	
1871	Ford, William..................*d.*	1873
"	Foster, George H	
1872	Feidler, Gustav H	
"	Field, George H	
"	Freyhofer, Solomon W......*tr.*	1875
1873	Fawcett, John...................*l.*	1874
1876	Floyd, John E.	
1829	Goddard, Curtis................*tr.*	1832
"	Gurley, Leonard B............*tr.*	1831
1831	Gavit, Ezekiel S.	1833
1832	Gilruth, James.................*tr.*	1836
"	Gavit, Elnathan C..............*tr.*	1833
1834	Gerring, Hiram................*tr.*	1837
1839	Goodale, Osee M...............*l.*	1846
"	Gillet, John K..................*d.*	1860
"	Gray, John	
"	Gage Franklin	
1841	Grant, Loring...................*tr.*	1854
1843	Gardner, Thomas C	
"	Granger, Thomas B.........*d.*	1866
1844	Greensky, Peter (Indian)...*d.*	1846
1846	Glass, Francis	
1848	Glass, William.................*l.*	1852
"	Grimm, C. F.....................*l.*	1849
1849	Goodell Ransom..............*d.*	1855
1853	Gillett, Daniel D................*l.*	
1855	Greenlaw, John B............*l.*	1858
1856	Gee, Alexander	
"	Glass, John	1857

Year	Name	Year
1856	Griffin, Lewis J	
"	Gore, Almon....................*l.*	1863
1857	Gridley, John J................*w.*	1862
"	Gee, Luman....................*l.*	1859
1859	George Thomas T	
"	Green, Oliver H. P.............*l.*	1862
1860	Garlick, Latham M...........*l.*	1869
1861	Graham, Adam Y............*l.*	1870
1862	Gulick, Jehiel	
1863	Gordon, John M	
"	Gray, Wilson....................*d.*	1875
"	Greensky, Isaac (Indian)...*d.*	1876
1866	Gage, Rodney	
1867	Gosling, George M	
"	Gray, A. T.	
1868	Gilbert, George L............*d.*	1874
"	Goss, Joel B	
"	Green, Nelson	
"	Grundy, Thomas C...........*l.*	1870
1869	Graham, John	
1871	Gillett, Agustus H	
1874	Gibbs, Calvin	
"	Giberson, Daniel W	
"	Gould, Amos M	
"	Griffith, S. N....................*tr.*	1875
1876	Glover, John T	
"	Golden, C.	
1877	Gardiner, Washington	
"	George, William	
"	Greensted Joseph	
1810	Holmes, Ninian................*tr.*	1812
1811	Hopkins, Silas..................*tr.*	1812
1815	Hickox, Joseph................*tr.*	1817
1824	Hunter, Isaac C................*tr.*	1825
1829	Hill, Jacob........................*l.*	1830
1831	Hill, Leonard	1834
1834	Hargrave, Richard (P. E.) *tr.*	1835
1835	Herr, William..................*tr.*	1838
1838	Hudson, Jonathan.............*l.*	1847
1839	Hoyt, Urius	1841
1840	Harrison, James S.............*l.*	1847
1841	Hemmingway, George F....*l.*	1848
1842	Hall, Horrace	
"	Haze, William H..............*l.*	1847
1845	Hickey, Manasseh	
"	Hartman, John M............*tr.*	1847
1846	Hinman, Clark T..............*d.*	1854
"	Holt, Joseph W	
1847	Harris, Lovel F................*d.*	1849
"	Hoag, George W	
1848	Helwig Charles.................*tr.*	1850
1849	Hendrickson, Samuel........*l.*	1860
1851	Harder, Jacob S.	
1852	Hascall, Erastus R	
1853	Harrison, Ferris B	1854
"	Haven Erastus O...............*tr.*	1873
1854	Hevener, William M........*d.*	1867
"	House, Samuel N..............*l.*	1856
"	Hanes, Henry...................*l.*	1855
"	Holdstock, Enoch.............*tr.*	1865
1855	Hill, T. S..........................*l.*	2862
"	Hutchins, H. C.................*l.*	1856
1856	Hertzer, Hermon	

Year	Name	Year	Name	Year
1856	Hogoboam, James J...............	1857	Johnston, Peter O...................	......
"	Hollenbeck, Isaac L.................	1857	Johnston, John....................l.	1849
1857	Hazzard, Agustus C............tr.	1865	1850	Johnston, Welcome W............	......
"	Hemmenway, Francis D......	......	"	Jackson, Henry, (Indian)....l.	1858
"	Hicks, Thomas Jr..................	1858	1852	Joslin, Thomas J....................	......
1857	Higgins, Theron C...................	......	1854	Johnston, Robert..................l.	1862
"	Holbrook, Colburn D...............	......	"	Johnston, Charles.................l.	1855
"	Hoyt, John............................	......	1857	Jahrans, John V..................tr.	1866
1858	Haviland, Daniel S..................	......	1859	Joy, Henry M.......................	......
"	Hammond, Daniel W..............	......	"	Jekins, William F..................	......
"	House John......................tr.	......	1860	Joslin, Harvey......................	1861
1859	Hood, Hiram........................	......	"	Johnston, William J..........l.	1869
1860	Hankinson, Joseph T.............	......	1861	Jones, Joseph.....................d.	1877
"	Helmker, Adolph..................tr.	1865	1864	Joslin, John S.......................	......
1861	Hagadorn, Wesley.................	......	1866	Jocelyn, George B...............d.	1877
1862	Hoag, Alva L.......................d.	1870	1867	Johnston, Isaac....................	......
1863	Horton, Jacob.......................	......	"	Jordan, Henry D...................	......
"	Hollister, George E.................	......	1870	Jacokes, Charles A................	......
1864	Heitmyer, Clamer F...............	1877	"	Johns, J. M.......................l.	1873
1866	Haanel, Hugo......................l.	1862	1871	Johnston, J. Milton...............	......
"	Hott, William......................l.	1871	1873	Janes, Frederick N................	......
1867	Harding, Abel W..................d.	1876	1875	Jacklin, James E...................	......
1869	Hamilton, John.....................	......	1820	Kent, John P....................tr.	1822
"	Hickey, George S................tr.	1873	1833	Kinnear, John....................tr.	1839
"	Hicks, George S....................	......	1835	Kellogg, Erastus...................	1841
"	Hunsberger, Aaron.................	......	1838	King, George.....................d.	1851
1870	Haanel, Eugene...................l.	1873	"	Kellam, James A................tr.	1841
"	Hall, Horatio N.....................	......	1840	Kahbeege, John (Indian)...l.	1854
"	Hamilton, S. L......................	......	"	Knox, David.....................l.	1844
"	Heysett, William..................l.	1873	1841	Kellogg, Edward L................	......
"	Hollowell, John W.................	......	1844	Kelly, William...................w.	1854
"	Hopkins, James H.................	......	1845	Kingsley, Calvin.................tr.	1847
"	Hunt, Albert N...................l.	1871	1846	Kellogg, D. R....................l.	1849
1871	Hall, Daniel.......................l.	1874	1850	Klein, John A....................tr.	1852
"	Hildreth, T. F.......................	......	1851	Krehbiel, Jacob.................tr.	......
"	Hills, John..........................	......	1854	Klumph, Erastus..................	......
"	Hudson, Richard...................	......	1856	Kellogg, Jason W...............l.	1867
"	Hulbert, Albert..................l.	1873	"	Krill, Henry......................tr.	1876
1872	Henry, John M....................l.	1873	1857	Kapphaker, Frederick........tr.	1860
"	Holt, William B..................tr.	1874	"	Kern, Joseph G..................l.	1869
1873	Hale, Osmer B.....................	......	"	Kilpatrick, Jesse...................	......
"	Hard, Elijah W....................l.	1874	1858	Klepper, John W...............l.	1860
"	Hollowell, John W.................	......	1862	Kelley, John........................	......
"	Holmes, Alexander J..............	......	"	Kirby, Reuben...................l.	1863
1874	Hodge, John J......................	......	1866	Kitzmiller, Samuel.................	......
"	Hoyt, Almon F.....................	......	1868	Knappen, Ashburn A............	......
"	Hudson, James L..................	......	1869	Kimmel, Samuel B...............	......
"	Hunsberger, Wesley A...........	......	"	Ketchum, Abijah E...............	......
1875	Hulin, James.......................d.	1877	1870	Kilpatrick, James H..............	......
1876	Harper, William..................l.	1877	1872	Kerr, Richard....................l.	1876
"	Holm, Ephraim S..................	......	"	Kratz, Reuben N................l.	1873
1877	Hathaway, William J.............	......	1873	Kellerman, Charles R...........	......
"	Higgins, James C..................	......	1874	Kerr, Joseph.......................	......
1869	Idding, J. T.........................	......	"	Krier, Henry....................tr.	1876
1826	Janes, John.......................tr.	1828	1875	Koch, Charles.....................	......
1835	Jackson, Washington............	1845	1877	Kerredge, J. Mileson............	......
1838	Jackway, Thomas S...........ex.	1844	"	Knapp, Martin W................	......
"	Johnston, Dewitt C.............l.	1839	1817	Laning, Gideon.................tr.	1818
1839	Jones, Janathan.................l.	1844	1829	Latta, Samuel A................tr.	1830
1840	Jacokes, D. C......................	......	1833	Lawrence, Richard............l.	1840
1842	Jennings, Joseph.................d.	1867	1840	Lapham, Samuel...............l.	1843
"	Judd, William P.................l.	1857	1842	Law, Hiram......................d.	1866
1845	Jacokes, Thomas H...............	......	1849	Lee, Samuel P.....................	......

HISTORY OF PROTESTANTISM IN MICHIGAN. 451

1850	Levington, John............*l.*	1874	1865	Morgan, Josiah G...............		
1852	Littlefield, Solomon S........*d.*	1872	1866	Mead, A. P..................*tr.*	1868
1854	Lyon, Thomas....................	......	"	Melitzer, Charles.................	......
1855	Laas, Gustavus................*tr.*	1861	"	Mueler, Wilhelm............*tr.*	1868
1858	Lowe, George W................	......	1867	McEldowney, John...........*tr.*	1876
"	Latham, David R...............	......	"	Maywood, William P........*d.*	1877
1859	Lee, George D.....................	......	1868	McIntosh John H................	......
"	Loet, Menzo S...................*l.*	1865	"	Mash, Norman D................	......
1863	Laing, Aaron R...................	......	"	Maywood, John................*l.*	1876
1867	Lee, Luther.......................	......	"	Mills, Burton S....................	......
1868	La Du, Stullum W.............*l.*	1870	"	Mathias, W........................	......
"	Lanning, Robert C..............	......	1869	McKown, J. L. G.............*tr.*	1870
"	Lich, H. G.........................*tr.*	1870	1870	Masters, Levi......................	......
"	Lyon, George M..................	......	1871	Merrill, S. M......................	......
1869	Leach, William H..............*l.*	1871	"	Millar, David B...................	......
1870	Lee, Charles C...................*w.*	1873	"	Mount, Geo. L....................	......
1871	Locke, Charles...................*l.*	1873	1873	McAlister, John J................	......
1874	Lyons, Nelson G..................	......	"	Mathew, D.......................*w.*	1875
"	Lawrence, Henry S..............	......	1874	McChesney, Edward............	......
1877	Lenox, Lambert E................	......	"	Mathews Scott..................*l.*	1875
1821	Morey, Platt B..................*d.*	1821	"	Misner, Dustin W................	......
1825	Minear, Solomon...............*tr.*	1826	"	Moon, Lewis N..................	......
1833	Meek, Richard C...............*l.*	1850	1875	Morton, James H................	......
"	McGregor, Duncan.............*l.*	1835	"	Mayzolf, J........................*l.*	1877
1835	McCool, Thomas P.............*l.*	1837	1877	McCoy, Frank M................	......
"	Mitchell, Oren..................*tr.*	1838	"	McFawn, David..................	......
"	Monnett, Osband...............*tr.*	1839	1836	North, Oscar F..................*l.*	1847
1838	McIntyre, Ira....................*l.*	1837	1845	Noble, John C...................*l.*	1847
"	Minnis, Adam....................*l.*	1863	1851	Nuhfer, Nicholas...............*tr.*	1854
1840	Marksman, Peter (Indian)....	......	1854	Neier, Daniel....................*tr.*	1859
"	Mothersill, William...........*d.*	1863	1857	Noble, James R..................	......
1842	Mount, Nathan..................*d.*	1876	1860	Nichols, Thomas.................	......
1844	McConnel, Richard.............	......	1861	Nachrieb, George...............*tr.*	1864
"	Morgan, Harrison................	......	"	Noyes, Selah W..................*w.*	1872
1846	McClure, Edward...............*l.*	1855	1868	Newton, Newel...................	......
1848	Mosher, Curtis....................	......	1870	Ninde, William X...............	......
1849	Mason, Octavus..................*d.*	1850	1871	Nagler, F. L....................*tr.*	1872
1850	Mahon, William..................	......	"	Newton, Albert D...............	"
1851	May, Franklin W...............*w.*	1876	1873	Northrup, Henry C.............	......
"	McAlister, Jesse E.............*d.*	1873	1874	Nankervis, Henry................	......
"	McQuig, Lee.....................*d.*	1853	"	Nixon, George....................	......
"	Measures, James.................*l.*	1854	1875	Newton, William E............*tr.*	1876
1854	McKnight, William............*d.*	1872	1845	Osborn, Samuel A.............*d.*	1862
"	Mitchell, Lewis...................	......	1851	Olds, Carmi C....................	......
"	Murray, Charles W............*l.*	1857	1855	Otis, N. L.........................	......
1856	McEwing, Albert...............*l.*	......	1857	Odell, Jeremiah.................*w.*	1861
"	Mosher, Jonathan...............*l.*	1858	1858	Owen, George W................	......
1857	Madison, Granville.............*l.*	......	1845	Owen, T. G.....................*tr.*	1866
"	McArthy, Robert D...........*w.*	1862	1870	Odin, J, R........................	......
1858	McKibbee, William............*l.*	1860	"	Omans, Thomas G...............	......
"	Mills, E. D........................*l.*	1859	1871	Odell, Daniel J..................	......
1859	Marble, Elisha.....................	......	1873	Osborn, Wm. H..................	......
"	Mason, Wm.......................	......	1877	Orwich, J. F......................	......
1860	McCollister, Charles E.......*l.*	1861	1823	Pattee, Elias.....................*l.*	1838
"	Messmore, J. H.................*tr.*	1860	"	Plympton, Billings O.........*tr.*	1824
"	Miller, John W..................	......	1830	Pilcher, Elijah H................*tr.*	1877
"	Mayer, Andreas..................	......	1835	Perkzer, Micah G..............*tr.*	1837
"	Meritz, Henry..................*tr.*	1874	1836	Petczeld, John H................	......
1862	Moore, Aron P...................	......	1839	Parker, Roswell.................*w.*	1846
1863	McClure, John H..............*l.*	1873	1842	Price, Lorenzo D...............*tr.*	1859
"	McIllwain, Jonn A..............	......	"	Pengelly, Richard	......
1865	McCarty, Joseph H...........*tr.*	1876	1843	Parker, Jacob E..................	......
"	Moffat, Wm. C..................*tr.*	......	"	Penfield, Henry.................*d.*	1875

HISTORY OF PROTESTANTISM IN MICHIGAN.

Year	Name	Year	Name	Year
1848	Perry, James I............l.	1851	1863 Reuter, George G............tr.	1866
"	Phelitzer John............tr.	1849	" Roberts, James............	......
"	Pritchard, Benjamin F............	......	" Rolf, Alvin A............	......
1850	Parsons, W. S............l.	1851	" Russell, Andrew J............	......
1851	Perrine, William H............	......	1864 Richards, Andrew J............	......
"	Pierce, D. H............l.	1852	1865 Richards, John H............	......
1853	Palmer, George D............l.	1857	1866 Rice, William............ex.	1874
"	Prindle, Elias B............	......	1867 Riley, James............	1874
1854	Parker, Henry O............	......	1868 Reid, John M............	......
1856	Penland, William............l.	1857	" Reid, James W............	......
"	Pratt, John M............l.	1862	" Ross, J. H............	......
1858	Pardington, Raynor S............	......	1869 Riley, William............	......
1859	Pattison, Holmes A............l.	1868	1870 Rogers, Alonzo............w.	1877
"	Potter, Thomas G............	......	" Robinson, Charles T............l.	......
1860	Perrin, Oliver J............	......	1872 Rork, Martin V............ex.	1877
"	Peck, Henry C............	......	1873 Robinson, James M............	......
"	Pugh, John............	......	1874 Richards, Jonathan E............	1876
1862	Pratt, Byron S............l.	......	1876 Riehl, Daniel C............	......
1864	Pierce, Nathan W............	......	1877 Riddick, Isaac H............	......
1866	Paddock, William M............	......	1821 Strange, John (P. E.)............tr.	1824
"	Pearce, Liston H............	......	1825 Simmons, William............tr.	1836
"	Pickard, Richard F............	1868	1828 Snow, William T............tr.	1840
"	Plumb, Edward M............	1869	1830 Sprague, William............l.	1839
1867	Parker, Horace H............	......	1832 Swift, Marcus............l.	1835
1868	Phillips, Gilbert A............	......	" Sullivan, William M............l.	1837
"	Pullman, Henry............	......	1833 Smith, Newell F............l.	1834
"	Prouty, William............	......	1834 Seaborn, Frederick A............ex.	1837
1869	Pearce, Webster H............	......	" Southard, S. F............l.	1835
"	Potts, James H............	......	1835 Smith, Lewis............	1837
1870	Palmer, Horace............	......	1836 Sabin, Peter............l.	1849
"	Pilcher, Leander W............	......	" Sandford, James D............l.	1837
"	Powers, Charles............	1872	" Sharp, Peter............l.	1853
1871	Parsons, Daniel W............	......	" Staples, Allen............d.	1848
1872	Patterson, George W............tr.	1873	1837 Scotford, John............l.	1844
"	Pearce, Francis E............	......	" Shaw, James............	1857
"	Porter, Frederick W............	1876	" Shaw, Samuel P. (P. E.)............tr.	1838
"	Priestly, John S............	......	1838 Sampson, William H............tr.	1842
1873	Paull, John S............	......	" Sandford, Miles W............w.	1840
1874	Peirce, Edwin P............	......	" Smith, George............d.	1868
1876	Preston, Walter............	......	" Stanley, George............l.	1839
"	Parish, Aza G............	1877	1839 Sabin, Benjamin............d.	1875
"	Pierson, Charles W............	1877	" Sapp, Rezin............d.	1873
"	Pope, Russel B............	......	" Sayre, John............ex.	1840
1810	Ryan, Henry (P. E.)............tr.	1820	" Sheldon, R. P............l.	1840
1827	Runnels, William............tr.	1828	" Steel, Ebenezer............	......
1832	Robinson, R. S............tr.	1834	" Steel, Salmon............	......
"	Robe, James T............	......	1840 Shurtliffe, Gideon J............d.	1849
1837	Richards, Ransom R............d.	1872	" Stringham, Stephen C............w,	1863
"	Ridgway, Robert............r.	1838	1844 Seeley, Thomas............	......
1839	Ransom, Halsey W............	1845	" Simonds, Samuel D............tr.	1850
"	Reese Joseph............tr.	1840	" Shaw, Addison C............d.	1876
1840	Roberts, Hiram M............w.	1850	" Spates, Samuel............	1852
1842	Reynolds, Reuben............w.	1849	" Stockwell, Charles F............l.	1845
1843	Russell, John............	......	1846 Stambaugh, Martin W............ex.	1852
1844	Rhodes, William............	1846	" Sutton, Joseph............	......
"	Reed, Seth............	......	1847 Seddlemeyer John H............tr.	1848
1848	Root, Frederick S............	1850	1848 Smart, James S............	......
1851	Robinson, James W............	......	1849 Sommerville, James............l.	1860
1852	Rothweiler, Jacob............tr.	1854	1851 Stonex, William G............w.	1865
1857	Ramsdell, Stephen L............	......	1852 Schweinfert, John............tr.	1860
"	Russell, Jesse B............	......	1853 Sanborn, Orlando............	......
1861	Rork, William W............tr.	1867	" Seaman, Charles W............l.	1857
1862	Rose, William F............l.	1863	" Sheldon, Barber N............l.	1855

HISTORY OF PROTESTANTISM IN MICHIGAN. 453

1854	Schneider, Peter F..............tr.	1860	1837	Todd, William.................d.	1869
"	Smith, Ira E......................l.	1855	1840	Thomas, David...............d.	1870
1855	Smith, John J....................l.	1858	1841	Taylor, William................	
1856	Savage, John R..................l.	1857	1843	Tooker, Theron C...........l.	1845
"	Shank, Joseph..................d.	1867	1844	Tyler, E. S.....................ex.	1847
"	Sinex, Thomas H..............tr.	1864	1846	Taylor, George................	
"	Sly, William.......................l.	1857	1847	Tappin, Edwin................l.	1849
"	Sumner, Daniel D..............l.	1857	1849	Taylor, Isaac....................	
1857	Seeley, Samuel F...............l.	1858	1850	Taylor, Barton S................	
"	Smith, Moses J..................		1852	Todd, Henry H...............l.	1853
1858	Stillman, David M.............l	1859	1853	Tracy, D. Burnham...........	
"	Searls, Braddock................l.	1860	"	Thoms, Isaac N..............tr.	1873
"	Steel, N. Maffett.................		1855	Tuttle, William..................	
1859	Stafford, William................l.	1863	1857	Torrey, Augustus W.......ex.	1875
"	Stalker, Thomas................		1858	Triggs, William M............	
"	Sherman, George W..........		1859	Tedman, Lucius S.............	
"	Sprague, Jonathan A.........		"	Tuthill, George W.............	
1860	Shaw, William C...............tr.	1861	1862	Tanner, James H..............	
1861	Shier, William H...............		1864	Turner, Pinckney L..........l.	1871
"	Stowe, George...................		1866	Tarr, Levi........................	
"	Swift, William J................		1869	Treadgold, Elight.............tr.	1875
1864	Scott, James W..................l.	1875	1870	Thomas, Charles G...........	
"	Spencer, Thomas J............		"	Truscott, John M..............	
"	Springsteen, Archibald H...l.	1874	1872	Tanner, Edward A............	
1865	Shepherd, Albert...............l.	1876	"	Thompson, Henry W.........	
"	Squiers, A. C.....................	1866	1873	Tallman, I. B....................	
"	Smith, Elijah A..................l.	1867	1874	Templeton, John G..........l.	1875
1866	Schneider, John S.............tr.	1868	"	Thomas, James H.............	
"	Sensabaugh, Andrew J......l.	1875	"	Tilden, William L.............	
"	Shelling, Charles................l.	1869	"	Treftz, Gottlob.................	
"	Simpson, Charles...............		1864	Ulrich, John J..................l.	1871
"	Skinner, Irving H..............		1839	Van Order, Harvey...........l.	1846
"	Smith, B. W.....................		1855	Varnum, Joseph B............	
"	Sparling, H. W................w.	1876	1857	Vandoozer, Samel P.........l.	1863
"	Spencer, Henry F..............		"	Van Horn, George A.........	
1867	Schwimm, George.............tr.	1870	"	Van Wyck, Abram J.........l.	1868
"	Sherman, Jonathan...........l.	1869	1860	Van Antwerp, Charles S.....	
1868	Sargent, Francis D............l.	1869	1864	Venning, James................	
"	Schunk, Frederick............tr.	1870	1867	Van Norman, Ephraim.......	
"	Scott, Marvin J.................		1868	Valentine, Julius S............	
1869	Smith, Henry H................		1869	Vanfleet, James A.............	
"	Sparling, John G...............		1872	Van Every, John M...........	
"	Sparling, W. H................w.	1876	1875	Van Auken, Chauncy........	
"	Springsteen, H..................l.	1870	1827	Walker, George W...........tr.	4829
"	Stark, John K...................		1831	Wiley, Thomas................d.	1836
"	Steer, Edward...................		1832	Whitney, Luther D..........l.	1850
1870	Shier, Dan R.....................		1835	Williams, Sandford S......tr.	1836
"	Silber, William B..............l.	1874	1836	Wareham, Philip.............tr.	1837
1871	Saunders, Nelson...............		1837	Wells, Wesley J...............l.	1838
1872	Sherman, Manly H...........l.	1871	1838	Warriner, Levi................l.	1844
"	Snyder, Sanford.................l.	1875	"	Wood, Aaron (P. E.).......tr.	1840
"	Stinchcomb, William.........		"	Worthington, Henry.........	
1873	Stedman, Ulysses S..........tr.	1874	1839	Watson, James V.............d.	1856
"	Storrer, John....................l.	1876	"	Wells, O. S.....................l.	1840
"	Strong, Frederick..............		"	Whitwom, Samuel...........l.	"
1874	Sweet, John......................		1841	Woodard, Stephen C........	
1875	Sparrow, Peter L...............		"	Warner, George W...........l.	1842
1876	Schneider, J.....................		1842	Whitlock, David..............d.	1844
1877	Schweinfurth, George J......		1843	Wakelin, Thomas.............	
"	Springsteen, James W.......		1844	Warren, Frederick W........	
"	Strickland, S. C................		1845	Whedon, Daniel D...........tr.	1853
1835	Triggs, Robert..................		1846	Whitmore, Orin...............	
1836	Thomson, Edward............tr.	1838	"	Westlake, Eli...................	

1849	Wakefield, Amos................	......	1868	Williams, Henry C............l.	1874
"	Westerfelt, John H..........tr.	1851	"	Williams, William T...........l.	1872
1850	White, Orin D W... ....l.	1857	1869	Welsh, W. W.................tr.	1872
1851	Warner, Silas P................	......	"	Whitman, Barney H.............	......
1852	Whitmore, John J..........d.	1855	"	Wilkinson, Thomas R........l.	1872
1854	Whitcomb, John G............	......	"	Wilson, Samuel S...............	......
"	Williams, Porter..............l.	1857	"	Wilson, Andrew W.............	......
"	Wilber, Albert D............tr.	1856	"	Wood, Alvah B.................	......
1855	Ward, Rowland.............l.	"	"	Wright, Philip S.................	......
"	Webster, James.................	......	"	Wright, B. F...................l.	1872
"	Wells, H. C.....................l.	1856	1870	Walker, John L.................	......
"	Wightman, B. H................	......	"	Warns, Anthony............tr.	1872
"	Wilkinson, Samuel............l.	1861	"	Washburn, W. Wallace.........	......
1857	Watson, Charles P............l.	1858	"	Welch, Rollin C.................	......
"	Way, William C.................	......	"	Wheeler, Arthur J.............	......
"	Wesley, John.....................	......	"	Wilkinson, Thomas.............	......
"	Wright, Elisha................l.	1860	"	Wunderlich, E..............tr.	1874
1859	Warren, Squire E..............	......	1871	Ward, Duncan M...............	......
"	Wheeler, Amos C...........l.	1861	"	Weiler, Gustav.................	......
1860	Wilkinson, Edward.........tr.	1873	"	Whalen, James E...............	......
1861	West, Francis L...............d.	1865	1872	Weber, Adam...............tr.	1873
1862	Wilson, George..................	......	"	Whiteley, Duke.................	......
"	Withey, Jerome B...........l.	1868	"	Woodhams, Ronald.............	......
"	Woodard, David C.............	......	1873	Whalen, Edward............l.	1874
1863	Watkins, Aaron A..........d.	1867	"	Whitwam, Edward A...........	......
"	Wightman, Ira R. A...........	......	"	Wheaton, W. W.............tr.	1874
"	Wright, Dean C.............l.	1865	"	Wightman, Oramel E...........	......
1865	Wehness, Conrad................	......	1874	White, John W..................	......
"	White, Henry S.................	......	"	Whitney, Jonathan M...........	......
1866	Ware, Wm. H...................	......	"	Whitmore, Orin B...............	......
"	Wigle, Eli.......................	......	"	Wilcox, Isaac...................	......
"	Withey, James E................	......	"	Williams, John P..............l.	1876
1867	White, Joshua...................	......	1876	Wilson, Isaiah...................	......
"	Whitcomb, Alonzo..............	......	1877	Weeks, George A...............	......
"	Whitcomb, Lewis J.............	......	"	Willetts, Oscar F...............	......
"	Whitney, George C..........ex.	1868	"	Wright, Henry W...............	......
"	Wilsey, Marcenus B............	......	1841	Young, Ruggles B............l.	1847
"	Wood, James R.................	1869	1849	Young, Erasmus D.............	......
"	Wood, Charles D.............l.	1870	1856	York, Lodowick C..............	......
1868	Wallace, John F.................	......	1863	Yemans, Charles C..........l.	1872
"	Warburton, Charles S........w.	1873	1867	York, Frederick E.............	......
"	White, James E.................	......			

A LIST OF ALL THE

In making up the alphabetical list, a number of names were accidentally omitted, much to the regret of the author. These names are contained in the following list. We have also added to the list those who came into the conferences in 1878.

1878	Atkinson, John....................	....	1868	Hodskiss, Harvey................	......
1866	Barnes, G. S.......................	......	"	Howe, Charles H.................	......
1872	Bradley, Franklin..................		"	Hulbert, Henry H...............l.	1875
1878	Blake, Henry P....................	......	1869	Hazen, Albert R.	......
1832	Davidson, James F.	......	1871	Hopkins, James H.	......
1878	Daniels, Grosvenor...............	......	1873	Hollenbach, J. W...............	......
"	Desjardin, Paul...................	......	1878	Holding, C. B...................	......
"	Elder, W. W.		"	Holmes, Alexander J.	......
1856	Hertzer, C. G.		"	Maveety, Patrick J	......
1858	Horst, John....................tr.	1860	"	Mooney, Warren................	
1859	Hood, Hiram........................		"	Newcomb, George T...........	......
1867	Hayes, Ezra.................tr.	1876	1870	Pearman, Elias E.	......
"	Hicks, Henry W...................	......	1878	Paddock, Orresta A.............	......
"	Houghton, Levi L...............	......	"	Perrin, Donald A.................	......
1868	Haight, George L.	......	1873	Sparling, Ellis H................	......
"	Hall, Henry H.....................	......	1878	Sly, W. S.........................,	......
"	Hamilton, James	......	"	Talmage, Charles H.	......
"	Henderson, Horatio P..........	......	"	Terwilleger, Michael D.	......
"	Hewitt, Shubael P...............	......	1861	Wortley, Jacob Cap.............	
"	Hill, Henry J.	......			

May 1, 1879.

1844. James V. Watson.
1845-6. John A. Baughman.
1847. *Supplied by O. Mason, and E. Crane, P. E.*
1848-9. Samuel D. Simonds.
1850-1. Elijah H. Pilcher.
1852-3. Wellington H. Collins.
1854-5. Albert D. Wilbor.
1856-7. Francis A. Blades.
1858. Samuel Clements.
1859-60. Seth Reed.
1861-2. John M. Arhold.
1863. James M. Buckley.

1864. *It was amalgamated with Woodward Avenue, making the Central Church.*
LAFAYETTE STREET—TABERNACLE.
1849. Joseph J. Perry.
1850. Lorenzo D. Pierce.
1851. George Taylor.
1852-3. Manasseh Hickey.
1854-5. William H. Perrine.
1856-7. James F. Davidson.
1858. Robert Bird.
1859-60. Daniel C. Jacokes.
1861. Seth Reed.

1849	Wakefield, Amos...............	......	1868	Williams, Henry C..............*l.*	1874
"	Westerfelt, John H...........*tr.*	1851	"	Williams, William T............*l.*	1872
1850	White, Orin D W... ....*l.*	1857	1869	Welsh, W. W...................*tr.*	1872
1851	Warner, Silas P................	......	"	Whitman, Barney H..............	......
1852	Whitmore, John J............*d.*	1855	"	Wilkinson, Thomas R........*l.*	1872
1854	Whitcomb, John G...............	......	"	Wilson, Samuel S................	......
"	Williams, Porter................*l.*	1857	"	Wilson, Andrew W.............	......
"	Wilber, Albert D.............*tr.*	1856	"	Wood, Alvah B..................	......
1855	Ward, Rowland..............*l.*	"	"	Wright, Philip S.................	......
"	Webster, James.................	......	"	Wright, R. F.	1872

A LIST OF ALL THE
EPISCOPAL METHODIST MINISTERS

Who have been appointed to Detroit, with the date of appointment. These appointments were all made in the summer or autumn of the year named.

1809. William Case.
1810. Ninian Holmes, Wm. Mitchell.
1811. Ninian Holmes, Silas Hopkins.
1812. George W. Densmore.
1813-14. The War.
1815-16. Joseph Hickox.
1817. Gideon Laning.
1818. Alpheus Davis.
1819. Truman Dixon.
1820. John P. Kent.
1821. Platt B. Morey, *who died, and it was supplied by John P. Kent.*
1822. Alfred Brunson, Samuel Baker.
1823. Elias Pattee, Billings O. Plympton.
1824. Elias Pattee, Isaac C. Hunter.
1825. William Simmons.
1826-7. Zarah H. Coston.
1828-9. Arza Brown.
1830. Alvan Billings.
1831-2. Henry Colclazer.
1833-4. Elijah Crane.
1835. William Herr.
1836-7. Edward Thomson.
1838. Jonathan E. Chaplin.
1839-40. Henry Colclazer.
1841. Andrew M. Fitch.
1842. James S. Harrison.
1843. James S. Harrison, Jonathan Blanchard.

WOODWARD AVENUE.

1844. James V. Watson.
1845-6. John A. Baughman.
1847. *Supplied by O. Mason, and E. Crane, P. E.*
1848-9. Samuel D. Simonds.
1850-1. Elijah H. Pilcher.
1852-3. Wellington H. Collins.
1854-5. Albert D. Wilbor.
1856-7. Francis A. Blades.
1858. Samuel Clements.
1859-60. Seth Reed.
1861-2. John M. Arnold.
1863. James M. Buckley.

Union of Woodward Avenue and Congress Street, making

CENTRAL CHURCH.

1864. James M. Buckley.
1865. James M. Buckley, Joseph H. McCarty.
1866. Joseph H. McCarty, Lewis R. Fiske.
1867-8. Lewis R. Fiske.
1869. Benjamin F. Cocker, *but was supplied by D. D. Buck and G. C. Lyon.*
1870-1-2. William X. Ninde.
1870. Charles C. Yemans, *Assistant.*
1873-4-5. Lewis R. Fiske; 1873-4, J. B. Atchinson, *Assistant.*
1876-7. Wm. X. Ninde.

CONGRESS STREET.

1844-5. Ransom R. Richards.
1846. James F. Davidson.
1847. Harrison Morgan.
1848-50. George Taylor.
1851. John Russell.
1852. Carmi C. Olds.
1853. William Mahon.
1854-5. Manasseh Hickey.
1856-7. Andrew J. Eldred.
1858-9. Francis A. Blades.
1860. Franklin W. May.
1861-2. Orlando Sanborn.
1863. James S. Smart.
1864. *It was amalgamated with Woodward Avenue, making the Central Church.*

LAFAYETTE STREET—TABERNACLE.

1849. Joseph J. Perry.
1850. Lorenzo D. Pierce.
1851. George Taylor.
1852-3. Manasseh Hickey.
1854-5. William H. Perrine.
1856-7. James F. Davidson.
1858. Robert Bird.
1859-60. Daniel C. Jacokes.
1861. Seth Reed.

1862-3-4. Jacob C. Wortley.
1865-6. Orin Whitmore.
1867-8-9. Elisha E. Caster.
1870-1-2. John McEldowny.
1873-4-5. Webster H. Pearce.
1876. Lewis R. Fiske.
1877. Charles T. Allen.

FRENCH MISSION. (*discontinued.*)
1851-6. Thomas Carter.

CITY MISSION—6th st. SIMPSON.
1852. Riley C. Crawford.
1853. Richard McConnell.
1854. Joseph W. Holt.
1855. John A. Baughman.
1856. Manasseh Hickey.
1857. John Levington.
1858. John A. Baughman.
1859. Arthur Edwards.
1860. John Levington.
1861-2. Jason W. Kellogg.
1863. John M. Arnold.
1864. Henry N. Brown.
1865. Silas P. Warner.
1866. Manasseh Hickey.
1867. Squire E. Warren.
1868. William J. Campbell.
1869-70. Thomas J. Joslin.
1871. William H. Shier.
1872-3-4. Thomas Stalker.
1875-6-7. W. W. Washburn.

BEAUBIEN STREET. (*German*).
1846. Charles Helwig.
1847. John M. Hartman.
1848. Chaales Helwig, Charles Grimm.
1849. Charles Helwig.
1850-51. John A. Kleine.
1852-3. Jacob Rothweiler.
1854-5. Peter Schneider.
1856. Emil Baur.
1857-8. Nicholas Nuhfer.
1859-60. John Schweinfurt.
1861-2. George Nachtreib.
1863-4-5. George Reuter.
1866. Charles Melitzer.
1857-8-9. George Schweinn.
1870-1. Anton Warns.
1872-3-4. Henry Pullman.
1875-6-7. Charles G. Hertzer.

LASALLE AVENUE—SIXTEENTH STREET.
(*German.*)
1856. Gustavus Laas.
1857-8. Gustavus Bertrams.
1859-60. William A. Boerns.
1861. Jacob Braun.
1862-3-4. Charles G. Hertzer.
1865. Henry Maentz.
1866-7. John S. Schneider.
1868-9. William Borcherding.
1870. A. Meyer.
1871-2-3. Jacob Braun.
1874-5. Henry Krill.

1876-7. George A. Reuter.

JEFFERSON AVENUE.
1866. Manasseh Hickey.
1867-8-9. Alfred F. Bourns.
1870-1-2. Elisha E. Caster.
1873-4. Alanson R. Bartlett.
1875. James M. Fuller.
1876. Elijah H. Pilcher.
1877. Raynor S. Pardington.

SIXTEENTH STREET.
1872. Henry N. Brown.
1873-4. Lewis P. Davis.
1875. Squire E. Warren.
1876-7. John Russell.

FORT STREET.
1874-5-6. Raynor S. Pardington.
1877. William Q. Burnett.

PRESIDING ELDERS.
Genesee Conference—Upper Canada District
1810-11-12. Henry Ryan.
1815. William Case.
1816-17-18-19. Henry Ryan.

Ohio Conference—Lebanon District.
1820. James B. Finley.
1821. John Strange.
1822. James B. Finley.

Miami District.
1823. John Strange.

Ohio Conference.
1824. James B. Finley. *Sandusky District.*
1825. William Simmons. *Detroit District,*
1826-7-8. Zarah H. Coston.
1829-30-31. Curtis Goddard.
1832-3-4-5. James Gilruth.

Michigan Conference,
1836-7. William Herr.
1838-41. George Smith.
1842-3. Elijah H. Pilcher.
1844-7. Elijah Crane.
1848-51. James Shaw.
1852-3. John A. Baughman.
1854-5. Wellington H. Collins.

Detroit Conference.
1856-7. Wellingtou H. Coollins.
1858-9. James F. Davidson.
1860-63. Manasseh Hickey.
1864-7. Samuel Clements.
1868-71. Francis A. Blades.
1872-75. Elijah Pilcher.
1876-7. James M. Fuller.

GERMAN. (*Mich. District*).
1854-5. N. Callender.
1856-9. Peter F. Schneider.
1860-3. Nicholas Nuhfer.
1864-7. Clamor F. Heitmeyer.
1868-9. H. G. Lich.
1870-3. E. Wunderlich.
1874-7. Gottlob Treftz.

NOTE.—The City of Detroit was made a Station in 1825, that is, the minister was to confine his work to the city; hence only one name appears until 1843. At this time it was determined to create a new Society, and a second man was appointed. The new organization took the name of Congress Street. In 1844 the first Society took the name of Woodward Avenue, and these two worked separately until 1864. when they were united and took the name of Central Church. In 1849 a third Church was organized called Lafayette Street, which is nowknown as Tabernacle. A fourth charge was organized in 1852, called City Mission, then Walnut Street, afterwards Seventh Street, and finally Simpson Church, when they erected their present beautiful house.

The German charges were also uncertain in their names for some time, and finally settled down on the names now appearing in the Minutes.

The other charges were created in the years named with the names now attached to them, to wit: Sixteenth Street in September, 1872, and Fort Street in February, 1874.

INDEX.

	PAGE
Abbott, Robert	40
Abbott, Betsey	46
Adams, S. C.	304
Adams, Dr., becomes Romanist	213

ADRIAN—
Historical..................................296
Appears in Minutes....................296
First Preachers..........................297
Church Organized......................297
Additions..................................297
School-house.............................298
Preaching on Sabbath................298
Revival—Davidson and Wiley....298
Station......................................300
Church Erected.........................300
Parsonage.................................300
Revival—Watson.......................300
Baptism Discussed....................301
Revival—Baughman..................303
Second Church.........................304
Difficulties................................304
Opposition................................305
Sabbath Schools.......................317
Other Churches........................317
Work in the County..................317
Statistics for County.................318
Property...................................318
Statistics for City......................319

ALBION—
Location...................................383
History.....................................383
College.....................................383
Endowment..............................390
Preston....................................386
Revivals...................................387
Principals and Presidents..........387
Churches Organized.................396
Quarterly Meeting....................396
Revival Meetings......................398
Baptism...................................401

ALLEGAN....................................416

ANN ARBOR—
District Created........................113
Sketch.....................................227
Its Name..................................228
First Preaching........................228
Presbyterian Church................228
Methodist Church....................228
Circuits...................................229
Members.................................229
First Methodist Prayer Meeting..230
Arrangement of Circuits...........231
Accessions...............................231
Name of Circuit.......................232

	PAGE
Church Built	233
Bishop Soule	234
Revival	233
Station	234
No Defection	232
Appointments	234
Progress	235
Presbyterian	235
Protestant Episcopal	235
Baptist	235
Congregational	235
German Methodist	235
Statistics	235

Anecdotes—
Mr. Richard.............................. 15
William Case............................ 33
Henry Ryan.............................. 37
Bible Distribution....................379
Collection................................345
Judge Russ..............................359
Armstrong, James....................255
Arnold, Dr. John M..................431
Atwater, Luman R...................347
"Aunt Kitty"—Fay....................298
Babcock, Charles.....................284
Bacon, David............................ 12

Baker, Samuel—
On Detroit Circuit.................... 93
Marries and Dies..................... 93
Memoir of................................136

Bangs, Dr. Nathan—
Journey to Detroit.................... 18
Second Visit to Detroit............. 13
Third Visit—Leaves.................. 13
Memorial of............................. 25
Bangs, Joseph..........................245
Bangs, Francis B......................352

BATTLE CREEK—
History....................................376
Name.......................................377
Incident of revival...................378
Church Organized...................378
Names of Members.................378
Statistics.................................383
Circuit.....................................380
Baughman, John A...........185, 252
Baughman, Mrs. John A..........148
BAY VIEW.................................437
Bell, Andrew............................303
Beswick, George M..................265
Bidwell, Ira..............................306
Bignell, George.......................413
Billings, Alvan........................115
Bird, Robert............................324

HISTORY OF PROTESTANTISM IN MICHIGAN. 459

	PAGE.
Birmingham Church	324
Black Hawk War	125
Blades, William	353
Blades, Francis A	204, 300, 346
Brick Church—	
How Walls put up	98
Never Finished	99
What Became of it	100
Book Depository	430
Brockway, William H	178, 284
Brown, Arza—	
In Detroit	190
Oakland Circuit	192
Memorial of	190
Brown, Hannah B	229
Brown, Rebecca G	230
Brown, Sarah J	230
Brown, Charles, Sudden Death of	369
Brown, Z. C	345, 412
Brunson, Dr. Alfred—	
Detroit Circuit	93
Visits Mount Clemens	136
A Catholic Wants Sins Pardoned	136
Memorial of	134
Camp Meetings—	
In Canada, 1810	21
On the Rouge	91
In Superior, 1831	117
In Bloomfield, 1831	194
" 1832	120
Near Adrian	318
In Grand River Valley	335
In Jackson County	366
Near Albion	401
Central Church, Detroit	199
Charges—	
1828	111
1829-30	115
1831	132
1832	126
1834	128
Chatfield, Larmon…"	338
Cholera	126
Churches in Detroit Organized—	
Methodist	16, 17
Protestant Episcopal	168
Presbyterian	68, 168
Baptist	168
Congregational	168
Church Property	421
Circuits—	
Extent of	94
Geography of	112
Names of	112
Enlargement of	116
Clark, Calvin	132
Clements, Samuel	321
Close of War	56
Cocker, Dr. B. F	242
Colclazer, Henry	115, 232, 300

	PAGE.
COLDWATER—	
Appears	285
Growth	286
Statistics	286
Church Organized	87
Names	87
Collins, W. H	204
Collins, J. D	236
Comfort, William C	259
Comstock, Nathan	298
Comstock, Hon. A. J	301
Comstock, Dr. O. C	291
Conferences—	
Michigan Created	175
Detroit Created	175
Comparative Progress	422
Conclusion—A Summary	70
Congregational Church	422
Congress St. Church	198
Controversy	248
Conversions—	
R. Abbott	21
Catholic Woman	91
French Woman	192
A. J. Comstock	301
P. Davidson	243
Eli Hubbard	117
Cooper, Benjamin	257
Corporation, Detroit—	
Organization	95
Articles of	95
Corporators	97
Coston, Z. H.—	
In Detroit	110
Visits Southwestern Michigan	113
Crane, Elijah	234
Cross, Margarette	246
Darwin, Alanson	217
Davidson, James F.—	
In Adrian	298
Presiding Elder	257
Memorial of	217
Davidson, Mrs. Jas. F	259
Davis, Alpheus—	
On Detroit Circuit	69
Memorial of	81
Davis, Lorenzo	127, 253
Dean, Jerry	138
DETROIT—	
Circuit	13
Circuit in 1822	135
District	108
City—Origin of	11, 156
Growth	157
Attacked by Ottogamies	161
Burned	14
Efforts to Save	14, 15
Casualties	161
New City	15
Savoyard River	159
Pontiac's Siege	162

HISTORY OF PROTESTANTISM IN MICHIGAN.

Periodicals..166
Religious Statistics.....................................204
Educational..168
Religious Societies......................................167
Young Men's Christian Association............168
Diocese—Protestant Episcopal.....................176
Dixon, Truman... 83
Dobbins, Jacob—
  A Local Preacher.......................................336
  Crosses Grand River on Raft......................336
Donahoo, James T..220
Duffield, Dr. George.....................................202
Edwards, Dr. Arthur....................................435
Eldred, Andrew J...347
Episode..397
Ercanbrack, John...259
Evangelistic Society...................................... 68
Farnsworth, L. L..198
FARMINGTON—
  Revival at..116
Finley, Dr. James B.—
  First Visit to Detroit Circuit......................181
  Visits Detroit City.....................................181
  Petitioned for..184
  Memorial of..180
Finley, James W.—
  Monroe Circuit..215
  Revival..214
  Crosses River on Ice..................................215
  Memorial of..215
Fish, Hon. Henry..330
Fiske, Dr. L. R..394
Fisk, James..286
Fitch, A. M..346
Fitzgerald, Maria...368
Flint, Martin—
  Converted...361
  A Martyr..361
FLINT, City of—
  Origin...348
  Shools..348
  Church Organized....................................348
  Brockway's Account.................................348
  Quarterly Meeting....................................349
  Sacrament..349
  Appears in Minutes..................................349
  Church Built..350
  Station...352
  Church Burned..352
  Second Church..352
  Other Denominations...............................352
  Conference Sessions.................................353
  Statistics..353
Foot, Milton...309
Fox, Thomas...310
Frazee, Bradford—
  Saginaw Mission......................................281
  Marries...281
Freeman, Daniel.. 16
Freeman, Daniel S.......................................352

Frees, James—
  On Grand River Circuit............................342
  Capacities for the Work............................342
Friendship Broken.. 64
Gardner, Dr. Thomas C................................329
Garwood, Joseph C.—
  Converted...112
  Joins Methodist Episcopal Church............214
  Memorial of..214
Geography of Circuits..................................112
German Work..418
Gilruth, James—
  Presiding Elder...126
  Memorial of..187
Goddard, Curtis..187
GRAND RAPIDS—
  Grand River Valley..................................334
  Appears in Minutes..................................334
  In Ann Arbor District...............................334
  In Marshall District..................................335
  Wants Met..335
  Defection, Instance of...............................337
  Revivals..337
  Unsuitable Appointment..........................342
  Review...343
  Bad Policy..343
  Progres...344
  Change of Policy......................................344
  Settlement Progresses...............................344
  Special Attention to Rapids......................344
  Increase..345
  Station..346
  Revivals..346
  Second Charge...347
  Statistics..347
  Property...347
  Other Denomitations................................347
Grant, Dr. Isaac—
  Became a Methodist.................................402
  Class-leader...402
  Memorial of..402
Grant, Loring..383, 404
Gurley, L. B...231
Hanchett, Joseph.. 87
Harmon, Thomas.. 69
Harvey, Widow—
  Invites Kent to a Home............................212
  Labored with for it...................................212
Harvey, Mary...210
Hastings, E. P...171
Haven, Dr. E. O..230
Heroism.. 17
Hickey, Manasseh..429
Hickox, Joseph—
  Appointed to Detroit................................ 56
  Desdription of Detroit.............................. 56
  Success in Canada.................................... 62
  Extent of Circuit....................................... 50
  Journey to Detroit.................................... 77
  Col James' Order...................................... 63
  Labors on Circuit..................................... 63

HISTORY OF PROTESTANTISM IN MICHIGAN.

	PAGE.
Interviews with Richard	102
Memorial of	71
Hinman, Dr. C. T.—	
At Albion	384
At Northwestern University	388
Memorial of	387
Hobart, Randall	292
Holmes, Ninian—	
Appointed to Detroit	22
Memorial of	35
Honness, Wyandotte	127
Hopkins, Silas	36
Hudson, Jonathan	285
Hunter, Isaac C.—	
Horse abused	101
Appointed to Detroit	101
Memorial of	147
Immersionists	338
Incidents—	
Romantic	414
Rowdyism	118
"The Power"—Baptist Brother	194
Scotchman and Hell	193
Revivals at Romeo	272
Clairvoyance	265
Church Attndance	265
Singular	118
Interrupting a Preacher	338
Increase—	
Of Settlement	90
Of Work	91
Introductory	99
IONIA—	
Church Organized	410
Station	410
Other Churches	411
Conclusion	411
JACKSON—	
Settlement	357
County Organized	359
Judges	359
Hard Name	359
Reading Meetings	360
First Sermon	360
Church Organized	361
First Quarterly Meeting	361
Vicissitudes	361
Sabbath School	362
Numbers	362
Presbyterian	362
Congregational	362
Revival in City	362
Baptist	363
Protestant Episcopal	363
Difficulties of Travel	365
The County	366
Revival in County	366
Appears in Minutes	374
Station	375
Church Built	375
Statistics	376

	PAGE.
Jacokes, Dr. D. C.—	
Admitted	326
Memorial of	325
Janes, John—	
On Detroit Circuit	110
Visits Adrian	297
Is Married	111
Jesuits—Course Accounted for	9
Jocelyn, Dr. George B.—	
President Albion College	401
Memorial of	404
KALAMAZOO—	
History	254
Appears in Minutes	122
Missionaries to	254
Church Organized	255
Names	255
Other Churches	255
Extent of Circuit	255
Circuit Curtailed	255
New Societies	256
New Members	256
Advance	256
Special Attention	257
Minister for a Third Year	257
Church Begun	257
Station	257
Conference 1848	258
Bishop Janes's Sermon	259
No Disaster	259
Statistics	259
Still a Village	263
Keeler, Mary	116
Kellam, James A	305
Kent, John P.—	
Sent to Detroit	89
Holds Camp-meeting	91
Memorial of	133
Ketchum, Sidney	289
Ketchum, Katherine	289
Lakes—	
Superior	178
Devil's	318
Saint Clair, night on	221
Laning, Gideon—	
Sent to Detroit	69
Revisits the Country	80
Memorial of	79
LANSING—	
Sketch of	406
Early Preachers	406
Church Organized	407
Population	407
Right Policy	408
Appears in Minutes	408
District	408
Conference Session	409
Statistics	410
Latta, Dr. Samuel A.—	
Sent to Saint Clair	220
Memorial of	220

HISTORY OF PROTESTANTISM IN MICHIGAN.

Lee, Dr. Luther..................................356
LeRoy, D..320
Limbocker, Rev. Mr.........................132
Literary Institutions..........................230
Log Churches—
  On the Rouge................................ 83
  History of...................................... 84
  "Donation Chapel".......................131
  History of.....................................322
Lyons..335
Macomb, Sarah............................... 50
McCarty, William............................ 44
McCarty, Maria C........................... 47
McCarty, Dr. J. H...........................435
McConnell, Willard M....................321
McCoskry, R't. Rev. Dr. S. A..........176
MARSHALL—
  Location......................................288
  Population..................................295
  Rivals...288
  Religious Services.......................288
  Church Organized.......................289
  Names..289
  Love-feast and Sacrament..........290
  Increase.....................................290
  Revival......................................288
  Appears in Minutes....................291
  District......................................291
  Conference at............................291
  Bishop Hedding's Sermon..........292
  Second Conference....................292
  Presbyterian Church..................292
  Cholera.....................................293
  Other Churches.........................293
  Incorporated a City....................295
  Educational...............................295
Maxwell, Major Thompson—
  Throws Tea in Boston Harbor....120
  Soldier of the Revolution............120
  Soldier 1812................................120
  Memorial of.................................120
Maynard, Maria.............................232
Methodist Polity............................410
Methodist Publishing Company—
  Articles of Association..............431
  First Officers.............................431
Michigan Christian Advocate........431
Millerism.....................................303
Minister Flogged..........................305
Ministers Raised up.....................127
Missions—
  St. Joseph.................................114
  On Lake Superior (Indian).........178
  In Lower Peninsula (Indian)......128
  Flat Rock (Indian).....................127
  In Detroit (French)....................199
Mitchell, William—
  Appointed to Detroit................. 22
  Organizes a Church.................. 16
  Memorial of............................. 39

Mitchell, Joseph—
  In Detroit 1817........................... 66
  Anecdote of Sermon.................. 67
  Conversation with Monteith...... 67
Mitchell, Oren..............................334
Monnett, Osband—
  Sent to Grand Rapids................411
  Horse Stolen.............................412
MONROE—
  History of..................................209
  Methodist Church.....................210
  Methodist Before the War........211
  Presbyterian Church.........211, 217
  First Church Erected................211
  Methodist re-organized............211
  Revival....................................214
  Pilcher and Sprague.................216
  Station....................................216
  Church Built............................216
  Protestant Episcopal................216
  Baptist....................................219
  German Lutheran....................217
  Statistics.................................218
Monteith, John—
  Comes to Detroit................60, 64
  Organizes a Society.................. 64
Morey, Platt B............................. 90
Neglecter, End of a....................117
New Church........................100, 199
NILES—
  Sketch of................................263
  Coston visits...........................264
  Church Organized..................264
  Appears in Minutes................263
  Station..................................264
  Conference Session...............265
  Statistics...............................271
  Dissensions...........................270
  The Work Around.................266
  Other Churches....................270
Noble, Sally.............................143
North, O. F.............................284
Northwestern C. Advocate......434
Note...87
Offer of Help........................... 99
Other Protestant Churches.....421
Owen, Hon. John...................139
Palmer, Mrs. Mary A..............145
Parke, Dr. Ezra.......................193
Pattee, Elias—
  Sent to Detroit..................... 99
  Goes East to Collect Money.. 99
  Memorial of..........................251
Pearce, John D......................292
Phelps, Ambrose M...............293
Phelps, Hon. Col. William.....198
Pilcher, Dr. E. H.—
  On Ann Arbor Circuit....115, 232
  On Tecumseh........................123
  Extent of Circuit..................123
  First round on.....................123

HISTORY OF PROTESTANTISM IN MICHIGAN.   463

	PAGE.
Extracts from Journal	123
Going through Woods	124
Return to Ann Arbor	124
Blazes the Way	125
Pilcher, Caroline M.	372
Pilcher, J. Henry	362
Pilcher, Phebe M.	272
Plympton, Billings O.	93

PONTIAC—
Sketch of..................................319
Infidel Club...............................319
Mock Baptism...........................320
Death of Administrator..............320
First Preacher............................320
Small Societies..........................321
Station......................................321
Churches Built...........................321
Property...................................321
Revival.....................................322
Bad Policy................................322
Defections................................323
Other Churches.........................324
Summary..................................324
Statistics..................................325

PORT HURON—
Sketch of..................................326
Methodist Society.....................326
Church Built.............................326
Congregational........................329
Protestant Episcopal.................329
Conference Session..................329
Bishop Waugh.........................329
Revival....................................329
District....................................329
Statistics.................................330
German Society.......................330
Potts, James H.........................416
Preliminary......................133, 175
Presbyterian Minister, the first...... 60
Preston, Hon. David..................394
Progress of Churches................200
Prospect.................................... 16

Protestant Ministers—
Different from Jesuits............... 10
Sacrifices to be made............... 10
Quarterly Meeting, the first....... 17

Records, Church—
Loosely kept............................ 56
Loss of Class-books................. 56
Reed, Seth................................329
Reflections................................ 58

Remarkable Manifestations—
At Bloomfield...........................120
At Adrian.................................300
Retrospect.........................23, 130
Review..................................... 94
Richard, Gabriel......................104
Richards, Ransom R................178
Richards, Mrs. R. R.................408
River Raisin.............................211
Roads and Accommodations..... 20

	PAGE.
Robe, James T.	260
Roman Catholics	422

ROMEO—
Settlement..............................271
Methodist Society....................271
Congregational.......................271
Baptist....................................271
Original Members...................271
Revival...................................271
Additions................................272
Church Built............................272
Numbers.................................272
Name Appears........................273
District....................................274
Sabbath School.......................279
Statistics.................................279
Ruggles, Rev. Isaac.................325

Ryan, Henry—
Presiding Elder....................... 17
Memorial of............................ 36
Sabbath Schools.....................128
Sabin, Benjamin......................291
Sacrament, the first................. 17

SAINT CLAIR—
Outline of................................218
Old Class Paper......................218
John K. Smith.........................218
Subscription for Church..........219
House not Finished.................219
New Churches........................219
Slow Growth..........................220
Methodist Preacher sent........226
Other Churches......................227
Numbers................................227
Growth of Country..................227

SAGINAW—
Historical................................279
Missions.................................280
Discouragements....................280
Numbers.................................280
Conference Sessions..............280
Other Churches......................281
Summary................................281
Statistics................................285

Sapp, R.—
At Pontiac..............................323
Memorial of............................414
Sawyer, Joseph...................... 36
Secret Societies......................258
Settlement, difficulties of........107
Sheeley, Hon. Alanson...........129
Silliman, Betsey......................247
Simmons, William.................... 98
Simpson Church......................457
Smart, James S......................270
Smith, George........................154
Southwell, Martin F................276
Spencer, Henry F...................382
Spring Arbor...........................367
Stacy, William......................... 49
Stacy, Betsey......................... 49

	PAGE.
Staples, Allen	340
Statistics, General Summary	421
Strange, John	93, 137
Struggle for Lots	375
Swayzee, Mr.	256
Tabernacle Church	199
Tappan, Dr. Henry P.	239
Tecumseh—	
Geography of Circuit	123
History	244
First Preachers	245
Church Organized	245
Names	245
Quarterly Meetings	247
Presbyterian	247
Protestant Episcopal	248
Baptist	249
Temperance	129, 131
Territory Organized	14
Thompson, Elizabeth	363
Thomson, Dr. Bishop Edward	189
Tibbitts, Allen	87, 285
Time Elapsed	421
Trap, a	305
Trying case, a	117
Troy	324
Two Ministers Appointed	92
Unitarian notice	429
University of Michigan	168, 239
Visit, a	121
Walker, George W.—	
Converted Romanist	213
Appointed to Monroe	212
Returned	213
Memorial of	213
Walter, Mr.	256
Warren, Philip	144

	PAGE.
Warren, Abel—	
Soldier in 1812	277
Wounded at Queenston Heights	277
Memorial of	276
Watson, Dr. J. V.	208
Weed, Ira M.	253
Wells, Noah M.—	
First Presbyterian Pastor at Detroit	200
Memorial of	200
Wesleyans	418
Whitmore, Oren	408
Williams, Sandford S.	269
Witherell, Mrs. Amy	51
Witherell, Hon. Dr. James	173
Witherell, Hon. B. F. II.	172
Work Extending	128
Woodbridge, Hon. William	172
Woodward, Hon. A. B.	170
Wyandottes	127
YPSILANTI—	
Sketch of Settlement	249
First Preacher	249
First Church	250
Second Preacher	250
The Grove	250
Toils	250
Two Young Men	252
Circuit	253
Station	253
Quarterly Meeting	253
Present State	253
Presbyterian	253
Protestant Episcopal	254
Baptist	254
Statistics	254
Population	254

www.ingramcontent.com/pod-product-compliance
Lightning Source LLC
Chambersburg PA
CBHW021419300426
44114CB00010B/557